FOURTH EDITION

Parameters of Power

Canada's Political Institutions

Heather MacIvor
University of Windsor

THOMSON
™
NELSON

Australia   Canada   Mexico   Singapore   Spain   United Kingdom   United States

THOMSON

NELSON

Parameters of Power:
Canada's Political Institutions
Fourth Edition

by Heather MacIvor

Associate Vice President, Editorial Director:
Evelyn Veitch

Publisher:
Chris Carson

Senior Executive Marketing Manager:
Don Thompson

Senior Developmental Editor:
Katherine Goodes

Photo Researcher:
Nicola Winstanley

Permissions Coordinator:
Nicola Winstanley

Production Editor:
Carrie McGregor

Copy Editor:
June Trusty

Proofreader:
June Trusty

Indexer:
Andrew Little

Senior Production Coordinator:
Helen Locsin

Design Director:
Ken Phipps

Interior Design:
Suzanne Peden

Cover Design:
Liz Harasymczuk

Cover Image:
© J. David Andrews/ Masterfile

Compositor:
Interactive Composition Corporation

Printer:
Webcom

Library and Archives Canada Cataloguing in Publication Data

MacIvor, Heather, 1964–
Parameters of power: Canada's political institutions/Heather MacIvor.—4th ed.

Previous eds. written by Keith Archer . . . [et al.]

Includes bibliographical references and index.

ISBN 0-17-641675-7

1. Canada—Politics and government—Textbooks.
I. Title.

JL65.P37 2005   320.971
C2005-900156-9

BRIEF CONTENTS

CONTENTS

CHAPTER 3: POLITICAL PARTIES AND THE CANADIAN PARTY SYSTEM   73

CHAPTER 6: THE POLITICAL EXECUTIVE AND THE PERMANENT EXECUTIVE   269

CHAPTER 7: NONGOVERNMENTAL ACTORS IN THE CANADIAN POLICY PROCESS   329

CHAPTER 8: *CONSTITUTION* I: FEDERALISM   377

CHAPTER 9: *CONSTITUTION* II: FROM "MEGACONSTITUTIONAL POLITICS" TO "NONCONSTITUTIONAL RENEWAL"   439

CHAPTER 10: *CONSTITUTION III: THE CANADIAN CHARTER OF RIGHTS AND FREEDOMS*   485

CHAPTER 11: ASSEMBLING THE PUZZLE PIECES   541

APPENDIX: *THE CONSTITUTION ACTS, 1867 TO 1982*   547

PREFACE
Heather MacIvor

What is the purpose of a first-year textbook? For instructors, one purpose is to provide more extensive information than even the most comprehensive lectures can convey. Another is to generate student discussion, whether in the class as a whole or in weekly tutorial groups. A third is to excite the students' interest in the subject matter by presenting up-to-date information and ideas in a clear and easily accessible way. A fourth is to expose students to some of the primary source documents in the discipline; in Canadian politics, which is the topic of this book, the most important of these are the *Constitution Acts* of 1867 and 1982. Finally, a first-year textbook should organize a mass of complex information within a coherent framework of analysis, to assist the instructor in presenting the material to students who may lack any background in the subject matter of the course.

This fourth edition of *Parameters of Power,* like its predecessor, has been crafted with these purposes in mind. Much of the third edition has been retained, but much new material has been added. The framework of analysis grounds political institutions in their social and cultural context, highlighting the reciprocal relationship between the political system and the society that it serves. This book explains the ways in which political institutions shape the behaviour of political actors, by setting incentives and embodying social norms. It also shows how changing political values in the electorate, and conflicts between new and established subcultures (for example, Quebec nationalists versus Western populists), can create strong pressures for institutional reform.

CHANGES TO THIS EDITION

In response to instructors' requests, the framework of analysis in the fourth edition has been broadened somewhat. It now incorporates some of the external factors that affect Canada's domestic government and politics. In particular, the fourth edition considers the impact of the 9/11 terrorist attacks in the United States on Canada's relations with the United States—which, in turn, have affected our criminal law, the judicial interpretation of the *Canadian Charter of Rights and Freedoms,* the relationship between the legislative and executive branches of government, and the balance of power between the national and provincial governments. It also takes into account the growing influence of globalization and internationalization on Canadian policy-making. While the extent of that influence should not be overstated, there is no question that Canadian governments are increasingly constrained (and, in some respects, empowered) by their legal agreements with other countries. There are important implications for both the content of public policy and the ways in which that policy is created.

The structure of this fourth edition is somewhat different from that of the third edition:

- The ordering of the chapters has been altered. Chapters 8 and 9, which dealt with political parties and elections, respectively, are now Chapters 3 and 4. The *Charter,* which was covered in Chapter 4 of the previous edition, is now the subject of Chapter 10.
- Chapter 3 in the third edition covered federalism and megaconstitutional politics. This unwieldy chapter has now been broken up: federalism is discussed in Chapter 8 of this edition, and megaconstitutional politics in Chapter 9.
- A new concluding chapter, Chapter 11, "Assembling the Puzzle Pieces," sums up the key themes of the book and presents possible future trends, suggesting that students can play a role in this future.

The content of this edition has been updated to reflect recent developments in Canadian politics, including the following topics:

- the June 2004 federal election and the minority government that it produced;
- the replacement of Prime Minister Jean Chrétien by Paul Martin and the resulting changes to the structure of the federal government;
- the merger of the Progressive Conservative Party of Canada and the Canadian Reform/Conservative Alliance to form the new Conservative Party of Canada;
- the creation of the Council of the Federation; and
- 2001 *Anti-Terrorism Act.*

Students will also benefit from other features of this fourth edition, which include:

- at least one updated feature report in each chapter, called a "Dossier," which discusses a current Canadian political issue in some depth;
- a clear and accessible writing style that uses everyday language and examples to clarify otherwise abstract and challenging concepts;
- "Learning Objectives" at the beginning of each chapter, which flag the most important themes in that chapter and help you to read more efficiently;
- "Discussion Questions" at the end of each chapter, to focus your studying and generate debate;
- a "Glossary of Key Terms" at the end of each chapter, which defines the words presented in **boldface** throughout that chapter;
- a "Suggested Readings" section, featuring both print and website information sources, to start you off on any research projects that you may be required to submit.

THIS TEXTBOOK AS A LEARNING TOOL

Students who approach the study of Canadian politics for the first time are sometimes overwhelmed by the unexpected complexity of our laws and institutions. If you are a first-year student or a more advanced student with little previous background in the subject matter of this book, don't panic! The structure of each chapter is designed to guide you through the material as painlessly as possible. Here are a few pointers about the best way to use this book:

- Before you begin to read each chapter, take a few minutes to orient yourself to the material. Read the chapter title, the headings in the table of contents, and the "Learning Objectives."
- Think about how the material in that chapter fits with what you already know about the course content.
- If your instructor has provided you with a lecture outline or some other kind of guide to the key themes in the chapter, refer to those; otherwise, turn to the "Discussion Questions" near the end of the chapter. **To read effectively and efficiently, you must begin by knowing where you're headed and what you need to look for along the way.**
- As you read, remember two key rules:
    - Do *not* highlight whole pages, or even whole paragraphs; use a highlighter to emphasize only key words or phrases, not to turn the entire book into a fluorescent rainbow.
    - *Always* take notes of what you've read; if you write or word-process a brief summary of each chapter, in your own words, you will understand and retain the material far more effectively, and you will find it much faster and easier to study for tests.

- Try to distinguish between the really important points in each chapter, as identified by your instructor, and those that require less time and effort to understand. Do *not* read a textbook like a novel, in which every word must be given equal attention. If you try to do this with all of your first-year textbooks, you will never get your reading done. Instead, practise reading critically and analytically. Use the pedagogical tools in this book to guide you through the chapters, picking out what you need and mastering those elements.
- *Never* fall behind in your reading. If the instructor tells you to read Chapter 4 before a certain class, you must discipline yourself to do so. You can't make the best use of your class time unless you have read—and understood—the assigned chapter(s) before you show up. And don't try to skim a chapter right before the class—you will only confuse yourself and start to panic. Take the time you need to really understand each chapter, or at least those parts that you need to know.
- When you finish reading each chapter, test yourself by jotting down answers to the "Discussion Questions." Then turn back to the "Learning Objectives" to see how many of them you have already met. If you find that you are stuck on a particular point, go back and reread that section of the chapter. By the time you

finish this process, you should be well prepared for classroom discussion and testing.

Above all, I hope that this book will accomplish two things. First, I hope that it will inspire students to learn as much as they can about Canadian politics. This does not necessarily mean majoring in political science (although that would, of course, be an excellent idea!), but it does mean reading a good daily newspaper and staying informed about current political developments. Second, and flowing from the first, I hope that this book will help readers to become active, engaged citizens. The future of our democracy depends on the commitment and energy of young people, as much as it does on the experience and wisdom of older Canadians. Get involved, and use the information in this book as a tool to achieve your goals. Only by understanding our existing political institutions, and evaluating the various arguments for and against their reform, can we make a positive difference for the entire community.

SUPPLEMENTS TO THE BOOK

TEXT WEBSITE. This website is intended to enhance the teaching and learning experience for instructors and students. Browse our extensive and helpful resources at www.parametersofpower4e.nelson.com.

INSTRUCTOR'S MANUAL. This comprehensive guide is organized to provide chapter outlines, overviews, and instructional tips. Available only as a downloadable supplement on the text website.

TEST BANK. This resource includes a variety of questions (multiple choice, short-answer, and essay questions) from which to construct tests and exams. Available only from your Nelson sales representative.

ACKNOWLEDGMENTS

I wish to thank the team at Thomson Nelson, particularly Chris Carson and Katherine Goodes. I am also grateful to the anonymous reviewers for their comments on the third edition and their very helpful suggestions for improvement. The students in my first-year Canadian Politics course at the University of Windsor have been a constant source of inspiration and advice, although they may not know it; their questions and comments have helped me to refine the book and to make it as "user-friendly" as possible.

My deepest gratitude goes to Kendal McKinney. From time to time, every author needs encouragement, practical assistance, and a sympathetic ear. I am particularly fortunate to live with someone who provides all of these on a daily basis, along with a keen insight into Canadian politics and a wicked sense of humour. To my husband, in small recompense for his love and patience, I dedicate this edition.

INSTITUTIONS AND POLITICS

LEARNING OBJECTIVES

- *identify* Canada's national political institutions;
- *explain* how institutions shape individual behaviour;
- *explain* the role of myths and symbols in politics, with examples.

INTRODUCTION: INSTITUTIONS AND SOCIETY

Institutions in Daily Life

Imagine yourself walking into one of your classes. You enter a large room with fixed rows of desks, all facing the blackboard, desk, and lectern at the front. You choose a seat and pull your notebook and pen (or your laptop) from your bag. As you wait for the professor to enter, you exchange information and opinions about the course with the friend who always sits next to you. When the professor arrives, she places her briefcase on the desk and takes out some papers. She arranges them on the lectern, and then writes the outline of the day's lecture on the board. You and your classmates write down the outline and then prepare to listen to the rest of the lecture. You know that this professor has strict rules against talking in class, so you try to resist the temptation to share your comments with your friend (although you sometimes give in). You also know that the prof hates it when students walk in late and disrupt the class, so you always make sure to be there on time. When the lecture ends, you put your stuff back in your bag—while the professor does the same—and you go to your next class with your friend. Although you may not know it, you have just participated in an institution. Like all institutions, the university classroom has its own authority structure, rules, rituals, **myths,** and **symbols.**

An institution shapes the behaviour of everyone inside it, although in different ways depending on each person's position in the authority structure. In other words, everyone in that classroom is playing a role that is preordained by the rules of the institution and by the architecture of the room itself. The professor plays the role of teacher, dispensing knowledge to the students, who either receive that knowledge passively or become active participants in their own learning. While the blackboard, lectern, and front desk are practical tools for teaching, they also symbolize the professor's authority. So do the rows of student desks, which face the source of knowledge (the professor). Everyone has his or her own set of rituals in the classroom, most of which serve the official purpose of the institution (the sharing of knowledge). Everyone understands the myths being re-enacted during the lecture: the wisdom and authority of the professor, the students' eagerness to learn. (Please note: The word "myths" does not mean "lies" or "illusions." The point is that the behaviour of the participants in this situation is structured by a set of common assumptions, not that these assumptions are inaccurate.) And everyone understands the rules and expectations of classroom behaviour—quiet attentiveness, punctuality, preparation—even though they may not always follow them. Students know that if they refuse to obey certain rules, such as the due dates for assignments, the professor can punish them with a poor grade. Myth, symbol, ritual, rules, authority structures, and preordained behaviour patterns are the hallmarks of an institution, even one as small as a university classroom.

Like any institution, the degree to which the university classroom fulfills its assigned functions depends on a number of factors. If the professor disregards the rules, rituals, and symbols by persistently arriving late or unprepared, or abuses her authority by favouring some students over others, the class will become alienated and the myths will lose their power. When a professor is incompetent or careless, the **legitimacy** of the institution diminishes and its outcomes—particularly the grades awarded to the students—may be rejected. If the professor's authority is undermined by outside forces, such as the university administration or a government agency, the effectiveness of her teaching may suffer. If the students are unable or unwilling to follow the rules of the institution, they will not play their roles properly and the professor's performance will suffer. And if the institution itself is out of step with the needs and expectations of the students, its myths and symbols will lose their legitimating power, and no amount of hard work on the professor's part can restore it.

The Approach of This Book

This book is about Canada's **political institutions** and their relationship to the society that they govern. Like the classroom just described, the institutions that make up the Canadian **state** embody unique sets of rules, roles, authority structures, myths, symbols, and rituals. Most of the time, we obey the rules because it is appropriate to do so, and because we believe that the state has the legitimacy to set and enforce them. When the most important rules are broken, the state has the power to punish the offenders. The ways in which we perceive government authority are shaped by the ways in which that authority is exercised. When political leaders fail to deliver the outcomes we expect, or they abuse their authority by violating the myths and rituals of governance, the institutions within which they operate lose some of their legitimacy. Even when our institutions work properly, they may be constrained by outside forces or challenged by a shift in public perceptions and expectations of government; in such instances, their legitimacy will suffer. If a loss of legitimacy is great enough, and it persists for long enough, the entire institutional structure may be weakened.

The differences between political and nonpolitical institutions are not always easy to define. Table 1.1 lists examples of Canada's key political institutions, and contrasts them to social structures that are often considered as "nonpolitical."

On closer inspection, however, the division between the two lists begins to blur. The definition of "the family" has been a hotly contested political issue in many Western countries since the 1970s, as rising rates of marriage breakdown and the increasing participation of mothers in the workplace forced governments to re-examine their assumptions about the relationship between the state and the home. Public policies may encourage or permit the formation of certain family structures while discouraging others (e.g., same-sex marriages). As the feminist slogan has it, "the personal is political." Church congregations may be encouraged by their pastors to engage in political activity, or the clergy themselves may decide to issue public statements on social issues. Minor hockey leagues are directly affected by laws concerning insurance liability, equipment standards, and gender discrimination. Many labour unions are directly affiliated with the New Democratic Party; even those that are not formally tied to the NDP may participate in public demonstrations against particular government actions, or seek to persuade their members to vote in a certain way. In practice, therefore, the distinction between political and nonpolitical institutions is less clear than it initially appears.

Nonetheless, no single book can provide an adequate discussion of every important institution in Canadian society. Therefore, we must draw a line between the institutions that form the subject matter of this book and those that will be mentioned infrequently, if at all. One way to settle the issue is to focus on the main purpose or

TABLE 1.1 POLITICAL AND NONPOLITICAL INSTITUTIONS

POLITICAL INSTITUTIONS	NONPOLITICAL INSTITUTIONS
The House of Commons	Families
The Senate	Churches
The Supreme Court of Canada	Minor Hockey Leagues
The Cabinet	Labour Unions
The Federal Public Service	
The Liberal Party of Canada	
Greenpeace	

function of each institution. Politics may be defined as the process of making and enforcing public rules and decisions that affect all or part of a given population. While those rules or decisions may have a direct impact on private life—for example, a change to the tax laws that allows middle-income couples to claim larger deductions for child-care expenses—they apply generally and are designed to serve a broader public purpose. Therefore, an institution whose main function is to make or to enforce rules and decisions that must be followed by all or part of the population may be considered to be a political institution. The House of Commons and the Senate enact the laws proposed by the political executive and drafted by the permanent executive. Once enacted, those laws are applied and enforced by the permanent executive (and by the police and judges, in the case of criminal laws), and they may be interpreted authoritatively by the courts. In order to perform their assigned functions effectively, the authority exercised by political institutions on behalf of the population must be legitimate. In other words, their structures and operations must conform to a reasonably widespread set of myths, rituals, and symbols.

At the beginning of the twenty-first century, national political institutions in Canada and elsewhere confront a host of challenges:

- Their perceived legitimacy is declining, a decline reflected in public-opinion surveys and falling voter turnout.[1]
- Some of their power to make and enforce decisions for their populations is shifting to local and regional governments, international organizations (such as the World Trade Organization), and nonstate agencies.[2]
- Ethnic and linguistic minorities within their borders are demanding greater rights and more autonomy from their central governments, demands that may lead to the breakup of existing states.[3]
- New communication technologies are blurring national borders and creating new, nonterritorial forms of community over which national governments have no authority.[4]
- The political values and expectations of their populations are changing in ways that conflict with existing political institutions and threaten the legitimating power of the old political myths and symbols that those institutions embody.[5]

Although these are potentially serious problems, national governments are not an endangered species. Institutions can and do adapt to changing environments. The history of Canada's political institutions is a story of continuous adaptations, mostly successful, to changing conditions: the expansion of the federation from four to ten provinces, participation in two World Wars, the management of recurring economic crises, and the evolution of one of the most diverse populations in the world. There is no reason to suppose that the Canadian state will disappear any time soon.

Democratic governments have considerable resources to meet their current challenges. They are not hostages to social conditions nor are they passive victims of external forces. Political institutions have the power to shape public perceptions of politics, create or adapt myths and symbols to legitimate their own authority, and impose new rules and rituals on those whom they govern. Note, however, that the effectiveness of an institutional response to challenge depends on the degree to which it meshes with the attitudes and values of the electorate, and with the values embodied in the rest of the political system. A poorly judged response to external challenges undermines the legitimacy of the entire political system, while a reasonable response may enhance it.

The premise of this book is that political institutions and the societies that they serve constantly redefine themselves and each other. Neither exists in a vacuum. As the political attitudes and values of citizens change, partly in response to the performance of their governing institutions, so do the criteria by which they judge that performance. Chapter 2 examines the changes in Canada's political culture since the end of World War II: the growing emphasis on individual and group rights, rising demands for provincial autonomy, Quebec separatism, the redefinition of "**democracy,**" declining deference to political authority, and a pervasive cynicism toward our political institutions and leaders. The ability of our political institutions to respond to these shifts in political attitudes has been diminished by fiscal constraints, the difficulty of amending the *Constitution*, and the mobilizing capacity created by new communication technologies. Canadians disagree about the ends toward which our political institutions should strive and the means by which those ends are to be achieved. The recurring bouts of "**megaconstitutional politics**" in the 1980s and 1990s (described in Chapter 9) revealed the depth of those disagreements and the difficulty of reforming our political institutions through formal constitutional amendment. We will discuss these disagreements in more detail in Chapters 2, 8, and 9.

CANADA'S POLITICAL INSTITUTIONS

The Three Branches of Government: Parliament, the Executive, and the Judiciary

Each of Canada's political institutions performs a unique set of functions within the state. Political scientists often distinguish among three primary types of function: legislative (making laws), executive (implementing laws), and judicial (enforcing and interpreting laws).

In the Canadian state, the legislative power is exercised by the two Houses of Parliament: the lower house (the House of Commons) and the upper house (the Senate). The executive power is divided among three separate institutions: the Crown (represented by the governor general), the political executive (the prime minister and Cabinet), and the permanent executive (the federal public service). The judicial power is allocated to a hierarchical set of courts, most of them at the provincial level. At the top of the judicial hierarchy is the Supreme Court of Canada, which is both the final court of appeal and the ultimate authority on constitutional issues.

In the classical liberal tradition, as summarized in Dossier 1.1, the legislative and executive powers must be vested in different bodies. To unite the power of making laws with the power to implement them is to invite tyranny. This tradition is epitomized in

In *The Spirit of the Laws* (1748), the French writer Montesquieu (1689–1755) identified "three sorts of powers" in every government: "the *legislative;* the *executive,* in regard to those matters determined by the laws of nations; and the executive, in regard to those matters determined by the civil law" (emphasis added). Montesquieu also called the last of the three the *judicial* power. The legislative power grants the right to make laws "either temporarily, or for all time, as well as correcting or abrogating those already in existence." Using its executive power, the government "makes war or peace, sends or receives ambassadors, ensures security, and makes provision against invasion."

Finally, the judicial power is applied to "punish crimes, or pass judgment upon disputes arising among individuals."[6] By 1787–88, when the United States *Constitution* was being drafted and debated, this division of powers had assumed near-holy status among American liberals. In Federalist Paper No. 47, James Madison relied on Montesquieu's authority to defend the proposed constitution against charges that it united the three powers in a manner that threatened the liberties of Americans. He wrote: "The accumulation of all powers, legislative, executive, and judiciary, in the same hands, whether of one, a few, or many, and whether hereditary, self-appointed, or elective, may justly be pronounced the very definition of tyranny."[7] This formulation has remained influential for more than two centuries.

---

the American *Constitution,* which vests the legislative power in the two Houses of Congress and the executive power in the president. Neither the president nor his Cabinet Secretaries may sit in Congress, and their tenure of office does not depend on their ability to secure and maintain the confidence of either House.

In contrast, the British model of Cabinet–parliamentary government unites the legislative and executive powers in the Cabinet. The prime minister occupies the position at the top of the political executive because he leads the party with the most seats in the House of Commons. His Cabinet ministers must be drawn from the governing caucus (the parliamentary wing of the party in power) in the House of Commons and, to a lesser extent, the Senate. A Cabinet that loses the confidence of the Commons must resign immediately. In effect, the governor general delegates the powers of the Crown to the prime minister, and those powers must be relinquished when the legislative branch withdraws its support. Theoretically, the Commons uses its power to remove the Cabinet to keep the political executive accountable to the electorate. In practice, a majority government—a party that holds more than half the seats in the Commons—need not fear a loss of legislative support. Strong norms of party discipline protect a majority Cabinet against fluctuations in political support and the attacks of the Opposition parties. As a result, the House of Commons cannot hold the executive to account unless the governing party holds less than a majority of the seats. Under a minority government—such as the Liberal government of 1972–74

FIGURE 1.1 DIAGRAM OF CANADA'S POLITICAL INSTITUTIONS

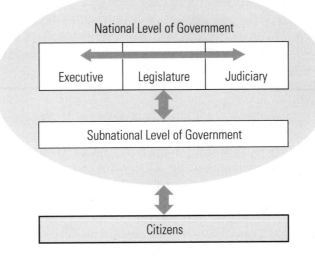

or the Martin government elected in June 2004—the Cabinet is more vulnerable to defections by its members and must make policy concessions to one or more of the Opposition parties in order to remain in power. (See, for example, the discussion of the 1974 *Election Expenses Act* in Chapter 4; this legislation was part of the price exacted by the NDP for supporting the Liberal minority.) The implications of the current minority Parliament are discussed in Chapters 5 and 6.

Both Houses of the federal Parliament have changed substantially over the years. The Senate, which is appointed by the prime minister, has almost as much formal power in the legislative process as the elected House of Commons. But senators rarely exercise that power to its fullest extent by vetoing laws that have been approved by the Commons, because they are aware that they lack democratic legitimacy as nonelected legislators. Down at the other end of the Centre Block, the Commons conducts its legislative business in much the same way as Westminster (i.e., British-style) parliaments have done for centuries. But it, too, has adapted to changing times. Party discipline, which was relatively weak at Confederation, has become the dominant ethos of the institution. While the membership of the Commons resembles the Canadian electorate more accurately than ever before—the numbers of women, visible minorities, and Aboriginal peoples rose in the 1980s and 1990s, although that increase seems to be slowing—the distribution of seats among the four official parties does not reflect the voting behaviour of Canadians. For this reason, among others, the legitimacy of Canada's Parliament has diminished in recent decades. There have been persistent calls for reform of the Commons and the Senate, which have been all but ignored by successive Liberal and Progressive Conservative governments. (See Chapters 2, 5, and 9.)

The third branch of Canada's government, the judiciary, operates independently of the legislature and executive. But, like the other two branches, it both affects and is affected by a changing political environment. The political influence of the Supreme Court of Canada grew significantly after 1982, when the *Canadian Charter of Rights and Freedoms* was proclaimed into law. (The implementation of section 15, the equality rights clause, was delayed for three years; see Chapter 10.) Unlike Parliament and the Cabinet, the Supreme Court is not a characteristically British institution. Since its establishment in 1875, its task as a court of appeal in criminal and civil cases has been overshadowed by its responsibility for **judicial review.**

The evolution of Canadian federalism has been shaped by judicial review. Until 1949, the Judicial Committee of the Privy Council in London (JCPC) was the final court of appeal for Canada. The Law Lords on the JCPC objected to the centralizing elements in the *Constitution Act, 1867,* on the ground that they violated the principle of federalism. They usually decided appeals concerning the division of powers in favour of the provinces, to the frustration of Canadians who preferred a strong central government.[8] The evolution of judicial review under the *Charter* has provoked new controversies about the legitimacy of the court's interventions into politics and policy-making. We will examine those controversies in Chapter 10.

Federalism

Canada is a federation, as are the United States, Germany, Switzerland, and many other democratic states. Britain and France, the first European powers to colonize North America, are unitary states.

One of the most contentious issues at Confederation was whether the new country would have a unitary or a federal structure. The advocates of federalism prevailed, although they had to accept some quasi-federal elements. The national government was given the power to veto or delay provincial laws, which placed the provinces in a subordinate position and weakened their autonomy within their own areas of jurisdiction. Although these powers fell into disuse in the twentieth century, Ottawa has found other methods—in particular, the transfer of huge sums of money to the provinces—to intervene in provincial policy-making. We will discuss the struggles between the two senior levels of government in Chapter 8.

Federalism illustrates the mutual influence of political institutions and the societies that they serve. Canadian federalism exists, in large measure, because the four founding provinces contained ethnically and geographically diverse populations. Neither Quebec francophones nor the distant Maritime colonies would accept a unitary state. They demanded a significant degree of self-government within the larger Dominion. Over time, the provincial governments themselves began to shape the political attitudes of their populations. As they struggled with Ottawa over scarce resources—principally tax revenues and policy-making powers—they created

In a federal state—also called a "federation"—the power to make binding decisions for the population is divided between two levels of government. The national (or federal) government is responsible for matters of national concern, such as defence, foreign affairs, and currency. The regional (state or provincial) governments take care of local or regional needs. Each level of government has its own sources of tax revenue, and neither can invade the jurisdiction of the other without express consent. The regional governments are not subordinate to the national government; their separate existence and powers are guaranteed by a written constitution that cannot be amended without their agreement. Conflicts between the two levels are resolved by the courts.

In contrast, unitary states have only one senior government. The national government may establish local or regional agencies to assist in the delivery of services and the implementation of laws, but these agencies have no independent status and may be abolished at any time. They exist solely to carry out the orders of the central government in the national capital. (Canada's municipalities have a similar relationship to their respective provincial governments.)

In addition to these two ideal types, there is a third category of state: the quasi-federation. In quasi-federal states, the regional governments are both separate from and subordinate to the national government. Their independence is incomplete, and their powers may be curtailed by the national government if they exercise those powers in a way that conflicts with national priorities.

---

new political symbols to increase their legitimacy vis-à-vis the federal government. Even though the electorates of the English-speaking provinces are relatively similar in sociological terms, their provincial governments have redefined them as distinct political communities that can best be served by autonomous provincial states.[9]

> [T]he political language of federalism, and the federal political system with which it is intertwined, have encouraged a politics in which provincial particularisms have been accorded special prominence. Provincial governments, as the claimants for and recipients of federal bounty, have acted as surrogates for the communities they govern . . . The political incentives for the federal government to couch its claims in the language of individual citizen rights and obligations engender a direct conflict with provincial claims on behalf of territorially based communities, the reconciliation of which is worked out in the federal process.[10]

Even as the division of powers between the federal and provincial governments shapes Canadian political attitudes, external forces—including fiscal deficits (and now surpluses), demands for a more democratic political system, and the growing importance of international and subnational organizations—place new strains on the institutions that make up the federal system. We will examine those forces in Chapter 8.

The Constitution

As we will see in Chapter 8, Canada's **Constitution** is a great deal more than the written laws contained in the Appendix to this book. We must also understand the unwritten conventions by which our political leaders operate, and the interpretations of the *Constitution* by the courts, if we are to grasp the full meaning of our "master institution." Although it is the supreme law of Canada, the *Constitution* cannot be enforced in the same way as other laws. Its power to constrain political actors depends largely on its legitimacy. Where the text of the *Constitution* conflicts with deeply held political values, it may cease to operate. For example, the British Crown is technically the source of all executive power and legitimacy in the Canadian state. The Crown's chief representative in Canada, the governor general, could fire the prime minister and seize dictatorial power tomorrow. Such a coup would be perfectly legal under the *Constitution Act, 1867*. It would also be a gross violation of the democratic principles that sustain Canada's representative institutions.

These principles underpin the convention that executive power may be exercised legitimately only by a prime minister and Cabinet that enjoy the confidence of the House of Commons. So direct rule by the governor general would be unconstitutional, despite its formal legality. The *Constitution* evolves in response to changing political values, usually without formal amendment to the legal text; new constitutional conventions develop, gradually acquiring the moral force to restrain the exercise of power by political leaders, and judges interpret the *Constitution* in new ways that recognize and confirm the shifting standards of political legitimacy.

However, it would be a mistake to assume that the *Constitution* is constantly in flux. Certain core principles remain intact, although their meaning and their relative influence change as the political culture evolves.

While a constitution is intended to last for decades, even centuries, its meaning must evolve to keep pace with changing political attitudes. At the same time, constitutional law has a powerful influence on the ways in which citizens perceive themselves and their relationship to the state. For example, Cairns argues that the *Charter of Rights and Freedoms* has transformed our political culture by redefining particular groups—women, Aboriginal Canadians, ethnic and racial minorities—as state-protected "Charter Canadians" with special rights.[11] Many of these "Charter Canadians" take a dim view of political processes that exclude their representatives, particularly closed-door constitutional negotiations among the federal and provincial governments. By redefining individual Canadians as "bearers of rights"[12] and endowing certain groups (but not others) with unique constitutional recognition, the *Charter* has eroded the legitimacy of territory-based politics (i.e., the federal system) and made future amendments

DOSSIER 1.3 The Principles That Shape Canada's Political Institutions

In 1998, the Supreme Court of Canada identified four central principles that underpin our political institutions: "federalism; democracy; constitutionalism and the rule of law; and respect for minorities" [para. 32]. While these principles are not always explicit in our constitutional texts, they are the "lifeblood" [para. 51] that sustains our system of government. None of the four operates in isolation. Each principle modifies the others, and each must be interpreted according to the historical development of the Canadian *Constitution*.

The justices defined "federalism" as the sharing of power between two sovereign levels of government: the national government and the ten provinces. The federalism principle "recognizes the diversity of the component parts of Confederation," "facilitates democratic participation" by assigning specific powers to the appropriate level of government, and "facilitates the pursuit of collective goals by cultural and linguistic minorities which form the majority within a particular province" [paras. 58–59].

The principle of "democracy," as reflected in Canadian law, refers to "the representative and democratic nature of our political institutions" [para. 62]. In other words, Canadian democracy entails the right of the people to choose their legislators through free and fair elections. While the justices defined democracy as "a political system of majority rule" [para. 63], they rejected the argument that "the sovereign will of a people" [para. 61] outweighs the other three principles. Canadian democracy is modified by federalism, which creates "different and equally legitimate majorities in different provinces and territories and at the federal level" [para. 66]. At the same time, "democracy in any real sense of the word cannot exist without the rule of law" [para. 67]. According to the Court, "It would be a grave mistake to equate legitimacy with the 'sovereign will' or majority rule alone, to the exclusion of other constitutional values" [para. 67].

The "rule of law" gives all Canadians "a stable, predictable, and ordered society in which to conduct their affairs" [para. 70]. It imposes the supremacy of law over "the acts of both government and private persons," and requires that "the exercise of all public power must find its ultimate source in a legal rule" [para. 71]. "Constitutionalism" refers to the more specific requirement that "all government action comply with the Constitution" [para. 72]. Political institutions are strictly limited in their actions by constitutional law: ". . . indeed, their sole claim to exercise lawful authority rests in the powers allocated to them under the Constitution, and can come from no other source" [para. 72]. The importance of this principle is reflected in the special procedures for creating and amending a constitution "beyond the reach of simple majority rule" [para. 73]. In other words, the will of the majority cannot override the principle of federalism or the protection of minority rights. While this might appear to be undemocratic, the justices argued that constitutionalism and the rule of law make democratic government possible by "creating an orderly framework within which people may make political decisions" [para. 78].

Finally, "the protection of minorities" is inherent in both our federal system and the *Charter of Rights and Freedoms*. Since 1867,

(cont'd)

the Canadian *Constitution* has guaranteed the rights of linguistic and religious minorities—especially, but not exclusively, French-speaking Catholics in Quebec. While past Canadian governments, both federal and provincial, have sometimes ignored the rights of particular minority groups—such as Aboriginal peoples and Japanese Canadians—the *Charter* makes future violations of minority rights illegal.

Source: *Reference re Secession of Quebec* [1998], 2 S.C.R. 217.

to the division of powers even more difficult than they would otherwise have been. We will examine Canada's changing political culture in Chapter 2 and recent constitutional controversies in Chapters 8–10.

HOW INSTITUTIONS SHAPE POLITICAL BEHAVIOUR

One of the enduring questions in political science, dating back to the very beginnings of political organization, is about the relationship between the state and the citizens. What sort of state is best suited to a particular population? This question goes beyond the immediate issue of designing political institutions that fit the existing political capacities of a given *demos* (group of citizens), although this issue is clearly important. In the fourth century B.C.E., Aristotle argued that each of the different types of state—kingship, aristocracy, and democracy—was naturally suited to different kinds of people. Therefore, it was impossible to favour one type over the others absolutely, because each was the best under particular political and social conditions.[13] In 1762, Jean-Jacques Rousseau advised those who would design political institutions to "investigate the fitness of the people, for which they are destined, to receive them."[14] A century later, John Stuart Mill identified three conditions for the success of any political institution:

(1) That the people should be willing to receive it. (2) That they should be willing and able to do what is necessary for its preservation. (3) That they should be willing and able to fulfil the duties and discharge the functions which it imposes on them.[15]

The twentieth century bore melancholy witness to the truth of these classic insights. In Europe, Asia, Africa, and Latin America, democratic constitutions were imposed on populations that, at that time, lacked the willingness and the capacity to operate and sustain them. In many cases, they quickly degenerated into one-party tyrannies or military dictatorships. Such was the experience of the Weimar Republic, the democratic state established in defeated Germany after World War I. The *Constitution* designed by the victorious Western powers was a model of abstract democratic perfection: a proportional electoral system, opportunities for the electorate to make its own laws through plebiscites and referenda, protection for individual rights, a political executive dependent on the support of Parliament. But 14 years later, the Weimar Republic collapsed. Adolf Hitler brought his National Socialist (Nazi) Party to power, dissolved the representative institutions in Weimar, and effectively threw out the democratic *Constitution*. The failure of the Weimar *Constitution* led to the deaths of millions of innocent people, inside and outside Germany. That failure can be attributed not to any particular flaw in the *Constitution* itself, but to the mismatch between institutions and political culture. In 1919, not enough Germans were ready to accept the compromises and self-restraint that democracy demands.

While there is little doubt that political institutions must be suited to the political culture of the population, political scientists have not always been content with the status quo. They have asked a further question: How can we create political institutions that will not only reflect, but actually enhance, the political virtues of the people? For Aristotle, man[16] is born with the potential to acquire moral and intellectual virtue. He cannot realize that potential unless he receives a good education and lives under good laws. Education, in Aristotle's conception, goes well beyond the acquisition of facts; it knits disparate individuals into a community, and instills in them the principles of justice that promote the good life.[17] Following good laws creates the habit of performing virtuous acts, a habit that eventually makes men virtuous.[18] Aristotle defined happiness as the highest human good, and pointed to virtue as the greatest guarantee of a happy life. Therefore, because the moral training of the people is the chief business of those who design political institutions, political science is the "master" science and gives men the tools to achieve a happy life for themselves and their fellow citizens.[19]

In a similar vein, Mill argued that the chief criterion for evaluating a political institution must be its influence on the moral and political character of the people whom it governs:

> *The first element of good government, therefore, being the virtue and intelligence of the human beings composing the community, the most important point of excellence which any form of government can possess is to promote the virtue and intelligence of the people themselves. The first question in respect to any political institutions is, how far they tend to foster in the members of the community the various desirable qualities, moral and intellectual . . .*[20]

The Federal Republic of Germany, founded by the American, British, and French Allies in the Western zones of occupation after World War II, was carefully designed to avoid the failures of Weimar. (Eastern Germany was occupied by the Soviet Union; it became the Communist state of East Germany, which lasted until the two states finally reunited in 1990.) The institutions established in the Western zones in 1949 were crafted by pro-democratic German politicians, in concert with the occupying powers, to strike a balance between the existing political culture and the requirements of liberal democracy. By the 1990s, survey research revealed that West Germans had adopted the same political values as other Europeans. While this transformation cannot be attributed solely to the political institutions of the Federal Republic—the *Wirtschaftswunder,* or "economic miracle," of the 1950s and 1960s was at least as important—their influence was powerfully beneficial.

The traditional institutionalist perspectives on politics were eclipsed after World War II by the behaviouralist approach. Political scientists sought to understand political life as the result of millions of individual choices, based either on deep-seated psychological characteristics or on a "rational utility" model borrowed from economics.[21] Political institutions were either ignored or reduced to mere "arenas" where the competition among social and individual interests played itself out.[22] In the 1980s, some political scientists rediscovered the independent influence of institutions on political life. They recognized that political behaviour does not exist independently of institutions; rather, "political institutions define the framework within which politics takes place."[23] These "new institutionalists" define politics as an interaction between state and society, not as the exclusive preserve of one or the other.

> *Without denying the importance of both the social context of politics and the motives of individual actors, therefore, institutional analysis posits a more independent role for political institutions. The state is not only affected by society but also affects it. Political democracy depends not only on economic and social conditions but also on the design of political institutions. Bureaucratic agencies, legislative committees, and appellate courts are arenas for contending social forces, but they are also collections of standard operating procedures and structures that define and defend values, norms, interests, identities and beliefs.*[24]

Within the "neoinstitutionalist" school, some political scientists have revived the ideas of Aristotle and Mill. "New constitutionalist" thinkers seek to design political institutions that will "develop and strengthen civic virtue and competence."[25] As we saw at the beginning of this chapter in the discussion of the classroom example, institutions do shape individual behaviour and attitudes. They do this in at least three ways:

1. Setting incentives for those who operate within them.
2. Exploiting symbols to legitimize the authority structures on which they are based.
3. Imposing structured roles and rituals on actors inside and outside them.

We will examine separately each of these aspects of institutional influence on individual and group behaviour.

▪ Incentives

Institutions create incentives for political actors: they require or encourage particular types of behaviour, and discourage or punish others. The effectiveness of these incentives depends on two factors: their congruence with the preexisting beliefs and motivations of the participants, and the clarity with which they are expressed. A student who intends to earn an A in a particular course has a stronger incentive to follow the rules laid down by the professor than the student's friend who aspires only to pass. But if those rules are arbitrary, incomprehensible, or imperfectly enforced, the A student may become frustrated and cease to follow them.

DOSSIER 1.4 The Incentive Theory of Political Institutions

One of the most important criteria for evaluating a political institution is its success in channelling the ambition of individual politicians to serve the public good. Failure to do so can result in corruption, self-seeking behaviour, and the disregard of the public good. Personal ambition is the product of individual psychology. While often condemned by those who fear its effects in political life, personal ambition is more properly regarded as a crucial resource for democracy. An effective institution "transforms private goals into public morality"[26] by creating incentives for ambitious politicians to serve the common good. If an aspiring party leader, for example, can win a leadership contest by deceit and manipulation, he may well be motivated to engage in campaign tactics that undermine the health of his party. But if such behaviour is likely to be exposed and condemned, with fatal consequences for his campaign, the risks of dishonesty may be too great. "Properly channelled, ambition can be used to curb its own natural excesses."[27]

Every institution provides a structure of opportunities for those who are motivated to succeed within it. An ideal opportunity structure in a university course involves deadlines for submitting assignments, clear rules for classroom conduct and academic work, and the chance to solicit help from the instructor when required. Similarly, political institutions set incentives—both formal and informal—for ambitious politicians.

When a political institution channels ambition in ways that conflict with the political values of some citizens, the result can be a loss of legitimacy. For example, the authority of the Canadian Cabinet (i.e., the political executive) rests on the continued support of a majority of the members of the House of Commons. Consequently, the prime minister—as the leader of the largest party in the Commons—has a powerful incentive to ensure that his or her MPs remain loyal. That loyalty is secured through party discipline, a system of rewards, threats, and punishments that reinforces the team spirit already present among parliamentarians elected to represent the same party. A government MP who votes against a budget, or some other key piece of legislation, knows that he or she will provoke the displeasure of the prime minister and jeopardize that MP's own future political career. This is particularly true in a minority government, where every vote can make the difference between survival and collapse. So the incentive structure for ambitious backbench MPs (i.e., those who are not members of the Cabinet) within the government caucus is very clear: if you hope to rise to a Cabinet position, you must vote in favour of your party's proposed legislation. As we will see in Chapter 5, party discipline is increasingly perceived by Canadian voters as a barrier to genuine political representation.[28] Nonetheless, as long as the relationship between our executive and legislative institutions remains unchanged, party discipline will continue to shape the behaviour of our members of Parliament.

Political institutions structure the behaviour of all citizens, not just politicians. For example, it is sometimes argued that institutions that encourage rational, deliberative debate among citizens promote the development of civic virtues.[29] By allowing nonpoliticians to acquire the "habits" of justice and community participation, as Aristotle might put it, these institutions strengthen the commitment to democracy among the electorate. Institutions that create disincentives for public participation, on the other hand, may weaken citizenship and erode the foundations of democratic legitimacy. Critics of Canadian representative democracy often argue that the political parties, Parliament, and Cabinet government exclude "the people" from the decision-making process. These critics believe that the introduction of more direct-democracy provisions, particularly initiatives, referenda, and recall, would give citizens an incentive to become better informed about politics and strengthen their faith in our national institutions. We will return to this debate in Chapter 2.

Symbolism

As we have seen, political institutions both embody and create legitimating symbols. They simplify a world of overwhelming complexity, reducing it to predictable routines and a set of shared meanings.[30]

> *By providing a structure of routines, roles, forms, and rules, political institutions organize a potentially disorderly political process. By shaping meaning, political institutions create an interpretive order within which political behaviour can be understood . . .*[31]

That "interpretive order" includes the primary myths, symbols, and rituals that underpin the political system of a given state. (For examples, please see the glossary near the end of this chapter.)

There are at least three important points to make about political myths and symbols. First, "myth" is not synonymous with "lie" or "deception." To be effective, any myth—political or otherwise—must have some basis in fact. Otherwise, the gap between myth and reality eventually becomes too great, and the myth loses its power to inspire political action or to legitimize political authority. For example, we may call Quebec nationalism a "myth," because it is a powerful narrative of oppression and resentment against the anglophone (i.e., English-speaking) majority in Canada (not to mention the anglophone minority in Quebec, which held a disproportionate share of economic power until fairly recently). Nonetheless, it is indisputably true that the francophone (French-speaking) percentage of Canada's population is shrinking and that there are cultural differences between francophone Quebeckers and other Canadians, which might lead one to conclude that they cannot coexist within the same country. Similarly, Albertan alienation from Central Canada is a powerful myth that affects the ways in which residents of the four westernmost provinces interpret political events. When former Prime Minister Chrétien made a speech in Edmonton in August 2001, in which he called upon Albertans to share the wealth from their oil and gas revenues with the rest of Canada, he inadvertently triggered an explosion of anger and fear about the federal government's intentions toward the province. That intense regional sensitivity and antagonism toward the federal government can be puzzling to non-Westerners, who may not be aware of the historical reasons for it (such as a perceived lack of concern for Western interests by governments based in the larger provinces of Ontario and Quebec).

Second, political myths and symbols are not static. They evolve over time, as social and economic circumstances change:

> In a fully developed civic culture and polity, politics will in part be a process of forming, choosing between, adapting and revising myths and symbols. It is in the nature of myths that they are selective and only deal with some facts and issues, and ignore others. They are intensely ideological, and each major ideology, including nationalism, Marxism, socialism, liberalism, or conservatism, has a system of myths and symbols associated with it.[32]

Third, each political institution embodies its own set of myths and symbols, which are not always compatible with those of other institutions. The decisions of the House of Commons are legitimated, in part, by the symbols of the national political community: the Crown, the prime minister, the general election in which all Canadian citizens may participate. On the other hand, decisions taken collectively by the First Ministers can be legitimated only by the symbols of federalism and provincial rights, which conflict with the idea of a single national interest. As we have seen, federalism necessarily creates a set of conflicting myths and symbols. These undermine the sense of a unified political community, which Aristotle considered to be an essential part of a good constitution.

Finally, we should bear in mind that political myths and symbols rarely carry the same meaning for all members of the community. There are always competing myths and symbols, as Dossier 1.5 illustrates.

Even a universal myth, such as the value of voting in a representative democracy, means different things to different people: "membership in a national political community, an instrumental attempt to attain state benefits, a routine obligation of citizenship, a belief in a particular ideology or worldview."[33] Perhaps we should say "a *formerly* universal myth," given the disturbing decline in voter turnout over the past four Canadian general elections. If the link between political symbolism and political behaviour is as strong as we have suggested in this chapter, the drop in turnout can be attributed (in part) to a loss of faith in the national political community, in the value of citizenship, or in the meaning of political ideology. There are, of course, other reasons why fewer Canadians vote; we will explore some of them in Chapter 4.

Structured Roles for Political Actors

The rules, rituals, and norms embodied in institutions tell us how to behave in varying situations. Without them, most human interactions would be chaotic and meaningless. When you register for a particular course, you know what sort of

As previously mentioned, "megaconstitutional politics" involves a clash between competing myths and symbols of the political community. As the battle rages, the symbolism becomes increasingly crude and polarizing. During the debate over the Meech Lake Accord (see Chapter 9), the struggle to redefine Canadian federalism revolved around two conflicting mythologies: the Quebec myth of "Canada as a duality, a partnership of two founding peoples, with Quebec representing one of the partners" versus an English Canadian myth of "Canada as a partnership of ten equal provinces."[34] The death of the Accord in June 1990 was portrayed in Quebec as a rejection by English Canada of the province and its legitimate constitutional demands, despite the ratification of the Accord by nine provinces (one of which later withdrew its approval) and the federal Parliament.[35] Prime Minister Brian Mulroney became the symbol of support for the Accord and a lightning rod for those in English Canada who believed that Quebec was "getting too much." On the other side, former Prime Minister Pierre Trudeau and Newfoundland Premier Clyde Wells came to symbolize the opposition to the Accord, and they were vilified in Quebec after its demise.

Other symbols that characterized the Meech Lake debate included the West's demand for a Triple-E Senate (Elected, Equal, and Effective);[36] the *Charter of Rights,* which some "Charter Canadians" sought to defend against the "threat" of the Accord;[37] and the secretive process by which the Accord was negotiated in April 1987, encapsulated in the phrase "eleven white men in suits." As one of the participants in the process later acknowledged, "The Accord generated such fierce opposition outside of Quebec because it was seen as an attempt to change the delicate balance in the 'symbolic order of Canada . . . Changes to the symbolic order will be fiercely resisted."[38] Perhaps, but only by those in whom the new symbols inspire no positive emotions. Gradual change in the symbolic order happens all the time, without a public uproar; only the attempt to impose symbols that conflict with deeply held political values provokes resistance. Such is the quandary of those who would reform Canada's political institutions through formal constitutional amendment.

behaviour is expected of you in your role as "student." You probably behave quite differently in your roles as "friend," "sibling," "parent," or "child." Each role imposes particular constraints on your actions, and each entails a set of rules—some of which are imposed without your consent and others negotiated with the people to whom you relate—that make your behaviour fairly predictable. The same is true for your professor, who (in all likelihood) behaves rather differently with his or her friends and family than with students. Without being aware of it, you expect the professor to behave in a certain way—in effect, to "act like a professor"—and you would be shocked and uncomfortable if he or she suddenly started to behave inappropriately (e.g., sexually harassing students).

Political institutions provide scripts for the actors who work within them. They define appropriate and inappropriate conduct for political actors and establish sanctions for inappropriate behaviour. Each political role is defined differently. For example, we expect the leader of a political party to defend his or her partisan position fiercely and to attack the ideas put forward by the other parties. But we would be appalled if the chief justice of the Supreme Court—whose role requires her to be as objective as possible—did the same. We expect the minister of Finance to announce the details of the annual federal budget in the House of Commons, not in a bar in downtown Ottawa. Some of these roles are defined in the written *Constitution;* others are informal and unwritten, and breaches are enforceable only in the political realm (see the discussion of constitutional conventions in Chapter 8). As noted earlier, for example, the governor general has the right under the 1867 *Constitution* to remove the prime minister and exercise executive authority directly. She does not take advantage of this right, because the role of the Crown's representative has been greatly restricted by the growth of democratic norms in Canadian society.

EXTERNAL PRESSURES ON CANADA'S POLITICAL INSTITUTIONS: GLOBALIZATION AND 9/11

Before we conclude this introduction to the Canadian political system, it is important to understand that our political institutions are affected by external as well as internal forces. As we have seen, Canada—like all sovereign states—is affected by external forces that its national government cannot fully control. These forces are often lumped together under the heading of "globalization." For the purpose of policy analysis, it is useful to distinguish between globalization and internationalization: **globalization** describes "a technological and economic process" that is

> *driven by the revolution in telecommunications and computers, massive increases in the movement of capital around the world, greatly expanded capacities for flexible world-wide production sourcing by firms, especially multinational corporations, and environmental spillovers.*[39]

Therefore, the term "globalization" does not refer to public policy; it describes a set of forces originating outside the scope of direct government control. However, the policy decisions of national governments can either strengthen or attempt to resist the impact of globalization within their territories; for example, a government can impose tariffs on imported goods in an effort to protect domestic producers from foreign competition. Most national governments have taken a different approach: they have participated in global negotiations within the framework of the World Trade Organization (formerly the General Agreement on Tariffs and Trade) to lower tariff barriers, and amended their own fiscal and social policies to try to take advantage of emerging global markets (e.g., by lowering taxes in order to lure foreign companies).

The term **internationalization** is more specific, referring to "a process by which various aspects of policy or policy-making are influenced by factors outside national territorial boundaries."[40] This phenomenon is nothing new for Canada, whose economy has been based on the export of commodities to foreign markets since the colonial era. What is new is the burgeoning number of **supranational** organizations and agreements, which place formal constraints on Canadian governments. Examples include the border security arrangements between Canada and the United States; the North American Free Trade Agreement (NAFTA) among Canada, the United States, and Mexico; the United Nations, most of whose Conventions Canada is bound to enforce; and the World Trade Organization (WTO). When a national government signs and/or ratifies a treaty with another government (or several), it undertakes to amend its domestic policies in order to implement that treaty. In the process, it may be forced to change its own priorities or to alter the direction of particular programs. In this sense, internationalization narrows the freedom of choice that a nation–state would otherwise enjoy.

Although the constraints imposed on nation–states by globalization and internationalization are real, these constraints are not all-encompassing. Contrary to a widely held belief that certain types of policy—particularly tax levels and social programs—are completely determined by world capital markets and multinational corporate interests,[41] the evidence shows that nation–states retain a wide discretion over their fiscal policies.[42] The principal exception is corporate taxation, which has fallen in most Western states in response to the increasing mobility of multinational companies (and the jobs that they provide).

The growing internationalization of public policy-making affects some policy fields, such as climate change, more than others. Globalization also affects different areas of social policy in varying ways. When, in 1995, the federal government cut transfer payments to the provinces (Chapter 8), it was driven by the need to cut the **deficit** and avert the possibility of a severe fiscal crisis. The cuts forced provincial governments to slash their spending on health care, education, and social assistance. However, programs directed toward the labour market—training and retraining, job creation, and enhanced productivity—received increased funding, as the federal and provincial governments tried to ensure that Canadian workers would not be left behind in a more competitive global environment.[43]

In general, the external forces discussed here seem to have affected the policy-making process more than the actual substance of laws and programs. As we will see in Chapter 8, globalization does more than transfer power from nation–states to supranational organizations like the WTO and NAFTA. It may also shift power from the national government to subnational governments (provinces and cities)—hence the buzzword "glocalization," which captures both the upward and downward transfers of policy-making authority. However, any reduction in Ottawa's power may be offset by two other developments. First, the national government may be able to use its supranational commitments (e.g., the Kyoto Protocol) as a tool to invade the policy fields of the provinces (Chapter 8). Second, globalization appears to undermine local attachments to particular geographic regions. If this is the case, then we might expect the political force of regionalism—a contributing factor in the intergovernmental conflicts of recent decades—to shrink.

Internationalization also changes the balance among the three branches of the federal government. Specifically, it reinforces the dominance of the executive branch over Parliament. To the extent that Canadian policy is shaped by supranational agreements among prime ministers, presidents, and Cabinet ministers, Parliament's ability to hold the executive accountable is weakened. The levers of economic policy are still largely controlled by the federal Department of Finance, but they must be operated under some global constraints. Therefore, Parliament's "power of the purse" becomes less effective, and the political parties in the Commons exert even less influence on events than they would otherwise have done (Chapter 5).

Globalization and internationalization have been relatively long-term and gradual processes. A more immediate, and perhaps more potent, constraint on nation–states emerged in the aftermath of the 9/11 terrorist attacks. The global "war on terror" and the new American emphasis on border security have forced Canada (and other countries) to adopt new laws and policy measures to protect their citizens and placate the American government.[44] Once again, both the process and products of policy-making have changed in response to external events, although the substance of policy seems to have been more strongly affected by 9/11 than by the other external trends discussed in this section. In the first place, the "war on terror" likely strengthens the national government vis-à-vis the provinces by raising the salience of national security (a federal responsibility). Another result might be revival of the "POGG (peace, order, and good government) clause"—the section of the *Constitution Act, 1867* that assigns the residual power to Ottawa—as a source of "emergency powers" to be exercised at the discretion of the federal Cabinet (Chapter 8). Moreover, the heightened emphasis on national security strengthens the national executive in relation to both Parliament (which has no formal power over foreign and defence policy) and the judicial branch. As discussed in Chapter 10, the Supreme Court of Canada has already signalled that it will defer to the Cabinet in cases involving security policies—even where such policies may violate the rights and freedoms protected in the *Charter*.

As our political institutions adapt to these external forces, they may diverge even further from the political values and attitudes of some Canadian citizens. The "antiglobalization" movement, which is discussed in Chapter 2, reflects a growing unease with the economic consequences of world markets—even as the new communication technologies at the heart of globalization make it easier to organize protests in far-flung cities. The expansion of executive power, at the expense of Parliament and the judicial enforcement of rights, seems to conflict with calls for greater citizen participation in decision-making and the generally positive orientation toward the *Charter*. If the incentives to cooperate with the American government in sensitive policy fields like national security, immigration, and criminal law are believed to outweigh domestic political opinion, Canada's politicians could pay a heavy price. Worse, the legitimacy of the institutions within which they operate could suffer over the long term.

CONCLUSION

The central theme of this book is that institutions shape human behaviour and values, and vice versa. As institutions evolve in response to changing social and cultural conditions, so do the incentives that these institutions create for the people involved with them. The challenge is to ensure that our political system adapts in positive ways, and that it continues to impose incentives that produce constructive behaviour among our politicians.

In formal terms, Canada's political institutions have changed relatively little since Confederation. The three branches of government are much as they were in the late nineteenth century, with the notable exception of the executive branch; its size and activities have expanded beyond anything that the Fathers of Confederation could have imagined. The constitutional division of powers between the federal and provincial governments, which was reasonably well suited to the conditions of 1867, is also intact. In practice, however, the division of policy-making duties between the two levels has mutated considerably over the decades. With the notable exception of the *Constitution Act, 1982,* Canadians have usually relied on nonconstitutional ways to change the rules of the political game.

Such ad hoc adaptations may no longer be adequate. The environment in which our political institutions operate has been transformed since 1867, and our institutions have not always kept pace. The population of Canada is larger and more diverse than ever. Its political attitudes and expectations—shaped by historical events, the rapid diffusion of ideas and information across national boundaries, and the mobilization of regional subcultures—are no longer compatible with many of the myths and symbols embodied in our institutions. Canadians face a choice: to try to restore the legitimacy of our political system by reforming our institutions (either through constitutional or nonconstitutional means) or to make our existing politics and government work better. In either case, we will need a better-informed and more engaged public. It is hoped that this book will contribute to reaching that goal.

GLOSSARY OF KEY TERMS

Constitution: The supreme law that defines the scope of state power and divides it among the various institutions that make up the state. More broadly, a constitution incorporates both the unwritten principles that guide the execution of public activities (see Dossier 1.3) and the sources of political legitimacy in a particular territory (i.e., myths, symbols, and rituals).

Deficit: An excess of spending over revenues in a given fiscal year. For example, Canada's federal government spent $42 billion more than it took in during the 1993–94 fiscal year. In the 2003–04 fiscal year, the federal government spent $9.1 billion *less* than it received in revenues; this is referred to as a "surplus."

Democracy: Literally, "rule by the people." In practice, "we the people" cannot govern ourselves directly on a daily basis. We elect political leaders to make decisions on our behalf and delegate the power to make binding decisions to them. We have the opportunity to reject those leaders at election time if they use that power in ways of which we do not approve. The problem with this system of representative democracy, according to its critics, is that the people who run our political institutions cannot be held accountable between elections. If they exercise the powers of their offices for their own benefit, instead of the benefit of the electorate, we have no legal recourse.

Globalization: A technological and economic process driven by the revolution in telecommunications and computers, massive increases in the movement of capital around the world, greatly expanded capacities for flexible worldwide production sourcing by firms, especially multinational corporations, and growing ecological interdependence and environmental spillovers.[45] The effects of globalization tend to reduce the social, political, and economic importance of nation–state borders and territorial divisions (e.g., provinces).

Internationalization: A process by which various aspects of policy or policy-making are influenced by factors outside national territorial boundaries.[46]

Judicial review: The authoritative interpretation of constitutional law by the Supreme Court. The court's rulings are binding on the other two branches of government. The doctrine of judicial review is an American invention, which conflicts in Canada with the British tradition of parliamentary supremacy. Before 1982, Canadian judicial review focused on the division of powers between the two senior levels of government. Since 1982, the court's powers of judicial review have expanded to include the conformity of federal and provincial statutes to the *Charter of Rights and Freedoms*. Critics of the *Charter* question "the use of judicial power to review and to nullify or modify the policies enacted by democratically accountable decision-makers";[47] some of its defenders argue that the court is too willing to endorse legislation that infringes *Charter* rights.

Legitimacy: The broad base of support within the electorate for the political system as a whole, which translates into acceptance of its outputs (i.e., binding rules and decisions). The exercise of constitutional authority in conformity with prevailing political values (e.g., democracy, federalism, the rule of law, and the rights of minorities) is legitimate; the brutal exercise of naked power by state authorities is not. In liberal democratic theory, legitimacy is founded on the consent of the governed.[48] While citizens need not necessarily give formal consent to each individual law (a practical impossibility, however desirable it might be in practice), they must implicitly accept the political norms and values embodied in the existing political institutions. Legitimacy is also based on the existence of a shared sense of identity—or, in other words, a political community. If no such community exists, because the electorate is divided into competing subcultures with divergent political values, the legitimacy of the political system is questioned. As its legitimacy weakens, its authority diminishes.

"Megaconstitutional politics": A process of reconsidering not just the technical details of a constitution, but also "the very nature of the political community on which the constitution is based."[49] As the debate widens beyond the political elite—i.e., the First Ministers of the 11 senior governments, their advisers, and academic experts—the emotional temperature rises. Powerful, and often incompatible, myths and symbols are evoked to justify conflicting definitions of the political community. (For an example of this process, see Dossier 1.5.)

Myth: A story we tell ourselves to make sense of a confusing and complicated world. It presents a partial account of the past, justifies certain actions in the present, and lays out a particular path for the future. Political myths usually incorporate one or more symbols into a blend of fact and fiction, which is used to evoke an emotional response for or against a particular institution. Example: The Québécois myth of "la survivance" following the English "conquest" of 1759 has become a powerful source of legitimacy for the provincial government in Quebec.

Political institution: An organization, usually grounded in constitutional law (either written or unwritten), that makes and/or enforces binding rules for the population of a particular territory. Its authority rests on its legitimacy in the eyes of the governed—based in some measure on its exploitation of myths and symbols— and ultimately on its monopoly of coercive force (i.e., the police and the armed forces). Canadian examples: the House of Commons, the Senate, the Supreme Court, the federal public service.

The state: The collective term for the political institutions in a particular country: the legislature, the executive, the courts, the armed forces, and the police. The state is responsible for "creating and maintaining internal order," for "protecting its own territorial integrity in the international system," and for making and implementing binding decisions for society "in those areas where private actors are incapable of responding successfully."[50]

Supranational: Literally, "above the nation–state." The term is often used to describe global or regional institutions and agreements like the World Trade Organization (WTO) or the North American Free Trade Agreement (NAFTA). When a national government enters into a supranational institution or agreement, it gives up some of its sovereignty. It accepts the power of the other member states to set policy priorities and directions for its citizens. In exchange, the national government receives an opportunity to participate in the supranational policy process.

Symbol: Any object or procedure—such as an image, a word or phrase, a sound, a person, a historical event, or a set of rules for making decisions—that conveys a particular meaning (either rational or emotional) to those who see or hear it. Often used as a shorthand way to refer to a complex reality. Canadian political symbols include the Maple Leaf flag, *O Canada,* the Peace Tower in Ottawa, the battles at Vimy Ridge and Dieppe, and the *Canadian Charter of Rights and Freedoms.*

DISCUSSION QUESTIONS

1. What is a "political institution"? List some of its defining characteristics. How might it differ from some other type of institution, such as a family or a private corporation?

2. How do institutions shape the behaviour and attitudes of the individuals who participate in them? Give at least two original examples.

3. Name the three branches of government identified in classical liberal theory. Explain the major differences among them. How do Canada's political institutions differ from the classical model?

4. How do myths and symbols affect political life? How do institutions redefine political myths and symbols?

5. What is a "state"? What are the foundations of its power?

6. List and briefly describe some of the challenges facing nation–states in the twenty-first century. If you were prime minister of Canada, how would you try to respond to those challenges?

7. Do you agree with the argument that political institutions shape the character of the people they govern? Why or why not?

SUGGESTED READINGS

Aristotle, *The Politics* and *The Nicomachean Ethics,* various editions and translations.

Harold D. Clarke, Allan Kornberg, and Peter Wearing, *A Polity on the Edge: Canada and the Politics of Fragmentation* (Peterborough, ON: Broadview Press, 2000).

C.E.S Franks, *The Myths and Symbols of the Constitutional Debate in Canada* (Kingston, ON: Queen's University Institute of Intergovernmental Relations, 1993).

Paul Howe and David Northrup, *Strengthening Canadian Democracy: The Views of Canadians* (Montreal: Institute for Research on Public Policy, 2000).

James G. March and Johan P. Olsen, *Rediscovering Institutions: The Organizational Basis of Politics* (New York: Free Press, 1989).

John Stuart Mill, *On Liberty and Other Essays,* edited by John Gray (Oxford: Oxford University Press, 1991).

Pippa Norris, ed., *Critical Citizens: Global Support for Democratic Governance* (Oxford: Oxford University Press, 1999).

Susan J. Pharr and Robert D. Putnam, eds., *Disaffected Democracies: What's Troubling the Trilateral Countries?* (Princeton: Princeton University Press, 2000).

Jean-Jacques Rousseau, *The Social Contract*, various editions and translations.

Peter H. Russell, *Constitutional Odyssey: Can Canadians Become a Sovereign People?*, 2nd edition (Toronto: University of Toronto Press, 1993).

NOTES

1. See Pippa Norris, ed., *Critical Citizens: Global Support for Democratic Governance* (Oxford: Oxford University Press, 1999); Susan J. Pharr and Robert D. Putnam, eds., *Disaffected Democracies: What's Troubling the Trilateral Countries?* (Princeton: Princeton University Press, 2000).

2. See Matthew Horsman and Andrew Marshall, *After the Nation-State: Citizens, Tribalism and the New World Disorder* (London: HarperCollins, 1994); Susan Strange, *The Retreat of the State: The Diffusion of Power in the World Economy* (Cambridge: Cambridge University Press, 1996).

3. Horsman and Marshall, 171–99; Harold D. Clarke, Allan Kornberg, and Peter Wearing, *A Polity on the Edge: Canada and the Politics of Fragmentation* (Peterborough, ON: Broadview Press, 2000).

4. Cynthia J. Alexander and Leslie A. Pal, eds., *Digital Democracy: Policy and Politics in the Wired World* (Toronto: Oxford University Press, 1998); Strange, *The Retreat of the State,* 7–8; Benjamin R. Barber, *Jihad vs. McWorld: How Globalism and Tribalism Are Reshaping the World* (New York: Ballantine, 1996), Chapter 19.

5. Ronald Inglehart, *Modernization and Postmodernization: Cultural, Economic and Political Change in 43 Societies* (Princeton: Princeton University Press, 1997); Ronald Inglehart, "Postmodernization Erodes Respect for Authority, But Increases Support for Democracy," in Norris, ed., *Critical Citizens,* 236–56; Russell J. Dalton, "Value Change and Democracy," in Pharr and Putnam, eds., *Disaffected Democracies,* 252–69; Neil Nevitte, *The Decline of Deference: Canadian Value Change in Cross-National Perspective* (Peterborough, ON: Broadview Press, 1996).

6. Charles de Secondat, Baron de la Brède et de Montesquieu, "The Spirit of the Laws," in Montesquieu, *Selected Political Writings,* edited and translated by Melvin Richter (Indianapolis: Hackett, 1990 [1748]), 182.

7. James Madison, "Federalist Paper No. 47," in Alexander Hamilton, James Madison, and John Jay, *The Federalist Papers,* edited by Clinton Rossiter (New York: New American Library, 1961 [1788]), 301.

8. See, for example, Frank R. Scott, *Essays on the Constitution: Aspects of Canadian Law and Politics* (Toronto: University of Toronto Press, 1977). For a defence of the JCPC, see Alan C. Cairns, "The Judicial Committee and Its Critics," in Douglas E. Williams, ed., *Constitution, Government, and Society in Canada: Selected Essays by Alan C. Cairns* (Toronto: McClelland and Stewart, 1988 [1971]).

9. Alan C. Cairns, "The Governments and Societies of Canadian Federalism" [1977], in Williams, ed., *Constitution, Government, and Society in Canada,* 145.

10. Ibid., 163.

11. Alan C. Cairns, "Citizens (Outsiders) and Governments (Insiders) in Constitution-Making: The Case of the Meech Lake Accord," in Douglas E. Williams, ed., *Disruptions: Constitutional Struggles, from the Charter to Meech Lake* (Toronto: McClelland and Stewart, 1991).

12. Ibid., 117.

13. Aristotle, *The Politics,* translated by Benjamin Jowett and edited by Stephen Everson (Cambridge: Cambridge University Press, 1996), 90.

14. Jean-Jacques Rousseau, "The Social Contract," in *The Social Contract and Discourses,* translated and edited by G.D.H. Cole (London: Everyman, 1993), 217.

15. John Stuart Mill, "Considerations on Representative Government," in *On Liberty and Other Essays,* edited by John Gray (Oxford: Oxford University Press, 1991 [1861]), 257.

16. Aristotle did not believe that women—or, for that matter, male slaves—were fully human. Only free men possessed the full faculty of reason, which was the distinguishing human characteristic. While we would now use gender-neutral language to describe human nature, male-specific language is used in this paragraph in order to reflect the exclusion of women from political science until relatively recently. See Heather MacIvor, *Women and Politics in Canada: An Introductory Text* (Peterborough, ON: Broadview Press, 1996), pp. 20–27.

17. Aristotle, *The Politics,* 37 and 74–75.

18. Aristotle, *The Nicomachean Ethics,* translated and edited by David Ross (Oxford: Oxford University Press, 1980), 28–29.

19. Ibid., 18 and 24–25.

20. Mill, "Considerations on Representative Government," 226–27.

21. James W. Ceaser, "Reconstructing Political Science," in Stephen L. Elkin and Karol Edward Soltan, eds., *A New Constitutionalism: Designing Political Institutions for a Good Society* (Chicago: University of Chicago Press, 1993).

22. James G. March and Johan P. Olsen, *Rediscovering Institutions: The Organizational Basis of Politics* (New York: Free Press, 1989), Chapter 1.

23. Ibid., 8.

24. Ibid., 17.

25. Karol Edward Soltan, "Introduction: Imagination, Political Competence, and Institutions," in Karol Edward Soltan and Stephen L. Elkin, eds., *The Constitution of Good Societies* (University Park, PA: Pennsylvania State University Press, 1996), 2.

26. Joseph A. Schlesinger, *Ambition and Politics: Political Careers in the United States* (Chicago: Rand McNally, 1966), 3.

27. James W. Ceaser, *Presidential Selection: Theory and Development* (Princeton: Princeton University Press, 1979), 14.

28. Paul Howe and David Northrup, *Strengthening Canadian Democracy: The Views of Canadians* (Montreal: Institute for Research on Public Policy, 2000), 78.

29. Benjamin R. Barber, *Strong Democracy* (Berkeley: University of California Press, 1984); James S. Fishkin, *The Voice of the People: Public Opinion and Democracy,* expanded edition (New Haven: Yale University Press, 1997); Stephen L. Elkin and Karol Edward Soltan, eds., *Citizen Competence and Democratic Institutions* (University Park, PA: Pennsylvania State University Press, 1999).

30. March and Olsen, 47–49.

31. Ibid., 52.

32. C.E.S Franks, *The Myths and Symbols of the Constitutional Debate in Canada* (Kingston, ON: Queen's University Institute of Intergovernmental Relations, 1993), 7.

33. Roger Friedland and Robert R. Alford, "Bringing Society Back In: Symbols, Practices, and Institutional Contradictions," in Walter W. Powell and Paul J. DiMaggio, eds., *The New Institutionalism in Organizational Analysis* (Chicago: University of Chicago Press, 1991), 255.

34. Franks, 8.

35. Ibid., 7.

36. Ibid., 21.

37. Peter H. Russell, *Constitutional Odyssey: Can Canadians Become a Sovereign People?* 2nd edition (Toronto: University of Toronto Press, 1993), 143.

38. Patrick J. Monahan, *Meech Lake: The Inside Story* (Toronto: University of Toronto Press, 1991), 258.

39. G. Bruce Doern, Leslie A. Pal, and Brian W. Tomlin, "The Internationalization of Canadian Public Policy," in G. Bruce Doern, Leslie A. Pal, and Brian W. Tomlin, eds., *Border Crossings: The Internationalization of Canadian Public Policy* (Toronto: Oxford University Press, 1996), 3.

40. Ibid., 3.

41. Ibid., 8.

42. Christian Lammert, *Modern Welfare States under Pressure: Determinants of Tax Policy in a Globalizing World* (Montreal: Institute for Research on Public Policy, 2004), 5 and 7; available online at www.irpp.org.

43. Keith G. Banting, "Social Policy," in Doern, Pal, and Tomlin, eds., 27–54.

44. Dirk Haubrich, "September 11, Anti-Terror Laws and Civil Liberties: Britain, France and Germany Compared," *Government and Opposition,* 38:1 (January 2003), 3–28; Canada, Privy Council Office, *Securing an Open Society: Canada's National Security Policy* (Ottawa: Her Majesty the Queen in Right of Canada, April 2004), available online at www.pco-bcp.gc.ca.

45. Doern, Pal, and Tomlin, "The Internationalization of Canadian Public Policy," 2–3.

46. Ibid., 3.

47. Christopher P. Manfredi, *Judicial Power and the Charter: Canada and the Paradox of Liberal Constitutionalism* (Toronto: McClelland and Stewart, 1993), 9.

48. David Held, "Democracy, the Nation–State and the Global System," in David Held, ed., *Political Theory Today* (Stanford, CA: Stanford University Press, 1991), 203.

49. Peter. H. Russell, 75.

50. Alan C. Cairns, "The Embedded State: State–Society Relations in Canada," in Keith Banting, ed., *State and Society: Canada in Comparative Perspective,* volume 31 of the collected research studies for the Royal Commission on the Economic Union and Development Prospects for Canada (Toronto and Ottawa: University of Toronto Press and the Minister of Supply and Services Canada, 1986), 54.

2

CHANGING POLITICAL CULTURE AND CANADA'S POLITICAL INSTITUTIONS

LEARNING OBJECTIVES

- *identify* the five levels of political support, and provide an example to illustrate each one;
- *identify* the unique characteristics of Canada's political culture, and explain how they evolved;
- *identify* three important changes in Canada's political culture in recent years, and *explain* each one;
- *explain* how changes in political culture affect political institutions;
- *identify* and *describe* two key debates about the nature and reform of Canada's national political institutions.

INTRODUCTION

As we saw in Chapter 1, democratic states face a host of challenges to their legitimacy and authority. Among them is an apparent transformation of Western political cultures. National electorates are more diverse than they were 50 years ago, both demographically and ideologically. Long-standing **subcultures,** such as **francophone** Quebec, have been **mobilized** into new forms of political activity (i.e., the sovereignty movement), while new ideologies (e.g., **postmaterialism**) have emerged to challenge the existing political culture. Consensus about the form and functions of political institutions appears to be shrinking. As national institutions confront multiplying and often contradictory demands for reform, public debate about the future of governance becomes increasingly polarized and difficult to resolve.

This chapter examines recent changes in Canada's **political culture.** It argues that while most Canadians are fairly satisfied with the political system, their attitudes toward certain elements of it have lately become more negative. The decline in legitimacy, which can be traced in large measure to a failure to adapt to changing political values, raises questions about the continued viability of the institutions established in 1867. Moreover, particular subcultures within the Canadian electorate—notably Québécois nationalists—are sufficiently well mobilized to press their demands for institutional change. Those demands have sparked debate about the future of our political system, while straining its capacity to respond to present challenges. The chapter begins with a general discussion of political culture and ideology and explains the origins of Canada's primary subcultures. Then it turns to the sources of change in political culture, and considers the implications for our political institutions.

▨ Political Culture

In Chapter 1, we distinguished between the general category of institutions and the more specific set of political institutions. A similar distinction can be made between the broader culture of a specific society and its particular political culture. The culture of a given population is made up of a unique mix of values, attitudes, and rituals. It is shaped by history, economy, geography, **demography,** and religion. Different customs evolve in different societies, in response to both universal human needs (e.g., gathering or growing food, rearing and socializing children) and the challenges posed by local conditions (climate, soil quality, access to fresh water). Within that broad culture, certain values, attitudes, and rituals are explicitly political; others are indirectly related to politics.

At the risk of oversimplifying, the *political* aspects of a given culture relate to power, authority, and the making and enforcement of rules for the entire community. Every human community needs to establish some legitimate authority, however informal or dispersed, to settle disputes and make collective decisions that bind all of its members. Examples range from the agora of ancient Athens, in which the citizens gathered to pass the laws by which they were governed, to tribal warlords and European kings, who exercised absolute power over their subjects. However, the distinction between political and nonpolitical values and attitudes must not be taken too far. To fully understand the political culture of a society, we must interpret it in the context of the broader culture: basic attitudes about human nature, the exercise of legitimate authority, the "natural" **hierarchies** that divide the powerful (e.g., freeborn Athenian men) from the powerless (e.g., Athenian women and slaves), and the major religious doctrines that sanctify authority.

As we saw in Chapter 1, the themes just listed dominated Western political theory from the time of Socrates (circa 400 B.C.E.) until the early twentieth century. The study of political culture enjoyed a revival in the 1950s and 1960s, as political scientists tried to explain why democracy had failed in Germany and Italy before World War II. Why did democratic political institutions work well in some states and not in others? And what, if anything, could be done to prevent future calamities like the fascist regimes that plunged the world into war in 1939?

In their 1963 classic *The Civic Culture*, Gabriel Almond and Sidney Verba argued, "A democratic form of participatory political system requires as well a political culture consistent with it."[1] (Recall the discussion of congruence between political capacities and political institutions in Chapter 1.) The authors defined the political culture of a particular country as the pattern of individual **orientations** toward "the political system and its various parts, and attitudes toward the role of the self in the system"[2] among its citizens. We acquire our political orientations through a lifelong process of **political socialization.** Political orientations fall into three categories:

1. *Cognitive (intellectual):* How much the citizens know about "the political system, its roles and the incumbents of these roles, its inputs, and its outputs."
2. *Affective (emotional):* How the citizens feel about the various aspects of their political system.
3. *Evaluative (opinion):* How the citizens judge the different elements of their political system, and the criteria to which they compare those elements.[3]

To fully understand these orientations and their effects on the political system, we need to distinguish among five component parts of that system.[4] Beginning with the most general, these are:

1. *The political community:* "A basic attachment to the nation beyond the present institutions of government and a general willingness to co-operate together politically"[5] and acceptance of the boundaries of the state.
2. *Regime principles:* Acceptance of the core ideas that underpin the political system (e.g., democracy, minority rights, and the rule of law) and, implicitly, the degree of congruence between the values embodied in existing institutions and those espoused by the citizens.
3. *Regime performance:* Evaluations of how a particular political system works in practice. These can be either procedural (e.g., "the system generally treats people fairly") or substantive (how you perceive particular laws or benefits produced by your government).
4. *Regime institutions:* Perceptions of the individual institutions that make up the state (e.g., Parliament, political parties, and the police).
5. *Political actors:* Feelings toward the individual politicians who hold public office at a particular time.

Whereas earlier theorists had idealized a particular "type" of democratic citizen—fully informed and engaged, rational, and devoted to the community—Almond and Verba argued that an entire population of such people would make stable government impossible. For democratic institutions to work properly, most citizens had to be passive and deferential. A disengaged but supportive majority was needed to "limit the individual's commitment to politics and to make that commitment milder"—to "'manage' or keep in place" the activist minority, which might otherwise destabilize the political system.[6]

Advocates of **direct democracy** reject the claim that passivity is more conducive to political stability than mass public engagement (see Dossier 2.4). Almond and Verba have also been criticized for their pro-American bias and their implicit assumption

CHANGING POLITICAL CULTURE AND CANADA'S POLITICAL INSTITUTIONS that political orientations are distributed evenly among the members of a given population (ignoring the clear differences between classes, genders, and ethnic groups).[7] But Almond and Verba must be given credit for drawing attention to a frequently overlooked issue: the relationship between political culture and political institutions.

> *Political cultures may or may not be congruent with the structures of the political system. A congruent political structure would be one appropriate to the culture: in other words, where political cognition in the population would tend to be accurate and where affect and evaluation would tend to be favourable . . . Political systems change, and we are justified in assuming that culture and structure are often incongruent with each other. Particularly in these decades of rapid cultural change, the most numerous political systems may be those that have failed to attain congruence, or are moving from one form of polity to another.*[8]

More recent theories of political culture—such as Ronald Inglehart's "postmaterialist" approach and Robert Putnam's theory of declining social capital, which we will discuss in "Social Capital" on page 55—recognize that there is no single "political culture" in any modern democracy. Instead, national electorates are divided into political subcultures of varying sizes, which hold distinctive patterns of political orientations. Together, these subcultures account for the overall distribution of political values in a given population.

> *[E]lites typically have distinctive values and norms (and, invariably, more information about the system), and they often lead the way in large-scale value change. Different ethnic and regional groups within a single country often have different value systems and worldviews. In addition, different types of beliefs and norms may prevail in different institutional settings, such as the military, the bureaucracy, and the university. It may even be argued that the differences in basic cultural biases are often greater within nations than between them . . . For these reasons, it is at least somewhat misleading to talk of the political culture of a nation, except as a distinctive mixture or balance of orientations.*[9]

Canada's population is unusually diverse, comprising dozens of ethnic groups, two official language groups, distinct socioeconomic classes, and several distinct regions. This does not mean, however, that our electorate is divided into an infinite number of politically salient (i.e., influential) subcultures. As we will see in Chapter 4, a social **cleavage** does not automatically shape political behaviour. Before a distinct group within the electorate can become an influential subculture, it must be mobilized by one or more leaders. (See the definition of "mobilization" in the glossary near the end of this chapter.) In Canada, the two most salient subcultures are Quebec nationalists and Western populists. Each has a distinct political perspective, which inspires discontent with the current political system and demands for reform:

- Quebec nationalists range from hard-core sovereigntists, whose primary goal is to separate from Canada and establish an independent Quebec state, to "soft" nationalists who want to remain in Canada under certain conditions. Those conditions include greater autonomy for the provincial government and the constitutional recognition of Quebec as a "distinct society." Most Quebec nationalists perceive Canada as a compact between two "founding nations," one English and one French. (Recall the discussion of the "Quebec myth" in Dossier 1.5.) The province of Quebec, as the homeland of the French "nation" in North America, merits special status within Confederation. The political impact of Quebec nationalism has been felt most acutely in debates over institutional and constitutional reform, as we will see in Chapter 9. By and large, Quebec nationalists support the Bloc Québécois in national politics (to the extent that they participate in national politics at all).

- The term "Western populists" is something of a misnomer, insofar as the attitudes and values associated with it are more characteristic of Alberta and British Columbia than of either Manitoba or Saskatchewan.[10] Nonetheless, it will serve as a convenient shorthand to describe this subculture, which combines regional alienation, faith in direct democracy and "the people" (as opposed to traditional political parties funded and led by business elites from central Canada), and a preference for strong and equal provincial governments. In the late 1980s and 1990s, Western populists supported the Reform Party (see Chapter 3). Previously, their votes were divided between regional protest parties—including the Progressives, the United Farmers, and Social Credit—and two of the three major parties (the Progressive Conservatives and New Democrats). Chapter 9 analyzes some of the ways in which Western populists have sought to change Canada's national institutions.

Francophone Quebeckers have constituted a distinct group within Canada, with a common sense of political and social purpose, since at least 1759. In that sense, the Quebec nationalist subculture is nothing new. But it acquired a new form in the 1960s, as a new generation of political leaders strove to modernize the provincial economy and to promote the status of francophones within their own "homeland" (hence the slogan of the Quiet Revolution, "maîtres chez nous," which means "masters in our own house"). As successive Quebec governments battled Ottawa to secure the necessary resources, some nationalists concluded that the only way to ensure the survival of the "distinct society" was to separate from Canada altogether. The Western populist subculture has only rarely acquired a separatist tinge; its primary concern has been the decentralization of power within the federation, coupled with reforms to national institutions that would give the four westernmost provinces—not to mention "the common sense of the common people"—greater influence in the central government. One final point deserves mention: the mobilization of these subcultures has been greatly assisted by the very institutions that they seek to change. Quebec nationalists have used the resources of the provincial government to promote sovereignty (see Dossier 2.3), while Western populists have repeatedly used the electoral system and the House of Commons as a forum for expressing their grievances. Both subcultures have taken advantage of executive federalism to press their demands for reform, as we will see in Chapter 9.

It should be noted, in passing, that the emphasis on these two subcultures does not imply that other groups within the electorate (such as women, postmaterialists, Aboriginal Canadians, or those living in Ontario and the Atlantic region) are unimportant. The point is that these other groups have not been mobilized effectively, or—in the case of Aboriginal Canadians—that their relatively recent mobilization has not yet had a major impact on our national institutions. Nonetheless, as we will see in Chapters 8 and 9, Aboriginal groups have made up for lost time in recent years, and their demands for institutional change (specifically, self-government) are just beginning to bear fruit.

Ideology

Canadian politics is often portrayed as an ideology-free zone. Many critics of our national parties, in particular, bemoan the apparent lack of rigorous intellectual discourse in our political life. In recent years, neoconservatism has gained prominence in the news media (particularly, but not exclusively, the *National Post*) and in Parliament (through the Reform Party/Canadian Alliance, now part of the new Conservative Party of Canada). It is true that by most conventional measures, Canadians appear to be unconcerned with abstract political principles. Nonetheless, it is important to identify the major political ideologies in Canada, if only to set the stage for the discussion of party politics in Chapter 3.

Political ideologies are concerned with power, human nature, and the proper relationship between the citizen and the state. Ideology differs from political culture in at least two ways.[11] First, an ideology is narrower and more distinct. "Political culture" refers to the overall distribution of political values within a population, whereas an ideology may be confined to a particular group. Note, however, that there are no purely ideological subcultures in Canada, as there are in other democracies (e.g., the working-class subcultures of Western Europe); political mobilization in this country appears to require a degree of regional concentration, which explains why we refer to "*Quebec* nationalists" and "*Western* populists." (**Populism** has also been influential in Ontario politics for decades, but without an overlay of regional grievance it has not translated to the national stage.)

Second, an ideology is an explicit and often abstract system of ideas, whereas political culture is less well defined. For example, a self-identified socialist may be fully conscious of his or her political beliefs, and may perceive them as a coherent outlook on the world. But most Canadians devote little attention to their political ideas, and do not seem to be troubled by contradictions among them. Ideology is to political culture what opera is to popular music: it attracts a relatively small subculture of (mostly) well-educated people with the information to understand abstractions and the willingness to differentiate themselves from most of their acquaintances.

Dossier 2.1 briefly describes the most influential **ideologies** in Canadian politics.[12] While these descriptions are necessarily incomplete, they are intended to provide a thumbnail sketch of the contending "world-views" that animate our political debate.

- *Conservatism:* The needs of the organic community take priority over those of the individual, where the two conflict. Community, hierarchy, order, and tradition are at least as important as freedom, equality, and individual rights. Conservatives believe that power should rest with those who are best able to exercise it wisely—that hierarchy and inequality are natural and inevitable. Because human nature is flawed, conservatives advocate a strong government to maintain law and order. Often called "right wing"; also known as "toryism." "Neoconservatism," which advocates traditional moral values, smaller government, and freer markets, is best understood as a synthesis of toryism and liberalism (see the discussion of the "fragment theory" on page 37).

- *Liberalism:* Individual rights and freedoms, based on the capacity for reason inherent in every human being, must be respected by those in power. Liberals defend private property and free markets. They prefer a small government with restricted powers, in order to maximize individual liberty. They emphasize equality of opportunity, not equality of condition. Today, liberals are divided over the role of the state: "business liberals" retain the traditional preference for small government and free markets, while "welfare liberals" believe that the state should provide income security and intervene in the market to promote economic justice.[13] Sometimes called "middle of the road."

- *Socialism and social democracy:* As in conservatism, the public good must take priority over individual liberties, where

the two conflict. Socialists seek equality of condition, not just equal opportunity to compete in a free market. Social democrats are reformist, not revolutionary; they seek power through elections. They advocate extensive state involvement in the ownership and management of the economy to ensure that everyone benefits from the wealth of society. Usually called "left wing."

- *Nationalism:* The belief that "a people"—a group distinguished from its neighbours by language, ethnicity, religion, history, or some other criterion—has the right to govern itself directly. Alternatively, a sense of pride in one's political community (recall the discussion of the political community in the "Political Culture" section). As noted earlier, Quebec nationalism ranges from separatism to demands for a rebalancing of the federal system.

- *Populism:* "The people" are best qualified to make decisions for themselves, instead of trusting political and economic elites. Often hostile toward existing authorities, who are perceived as unaccountable and corrupt. Populists demand direct democracy and smaller government. Some populists inject explicit moral or religious elements into their political programs. Can be either "left wing" or "right wing." At present, the political salience of populism appears to be waning; the apparent abandonment of populist rhetoric by the Canadian Alliance when it merged with the Progressive Conservatives may have deprived populists of the political vehicle they need in order to stay mobilized.[14]

(cont'd)

- *Feminism:* The belief that men and women should have equal opportunities in all spheres of life. Feminists seek to identify and change power structures that oppress women, such as gender stereotyping in the media, the "old boys' network" in party politics, and the "pink-collar ghetto" in the legislative and executive branches of government. Feminism is not a single unified body of ideas; for example, there are liberal, radical, and socialist feminists. Because of their shared emphasis on equal rights and social justice, feminists sometimes cooperate with socialists and postmaterialists in their quest for political influence.

- *Postmaterialism:* "Quality of life" issues—such as the environment; equal rights for women, gays and lesbians, and other marginalized groups; and assistance to developing countries—are at least as important as the more traditional concerns about the creation and distribution of material wealth. Postmaterialists are generally well informed about politics, and they often participate in unconventional political activities (e.g., protest marches). Many reject hierarchical power structures, including political parties and traditional pressure groups; they seek political influence through new social movements.

Each of these ideologies plays a role in Canadian politics. The clash between neoconservatives and traditional conservatives explains the difficulty of "uniting the right" (see the discussion of the United Alternative and the new Conservative Party in Chapter 3). Meanwhile, Canada's political institutions embody the liberal and conservative traditions of Britain and France—which helps to explain why people who reject the older ideologies are more likely to clamour for institutional reform. Indeed, ideologues of varying stripes often find themselves on the same side in "megaconstitutional" debates. For example, both populists and postmaterialists are highly critical of traditional political elites, while neoconservatives and socialists have often criticized the *Charter of Rights and Freedoms.*

Although this book is more concerned with political culture than with formal ideologies, we cannot overlook the connection between ideologies and institutions. An institution that takes shape during a period when a particular ideology—say, conservatism—dominates the political process will reflect that ideology in its structure and operations. A conservative institution is strictly hierarchical, with a small group of leaders who make and enforce rules for their subordinates to follow. By contrast, a postmaterialist institution (such as the German Green Party in its early years) is egalitarian, without rigid power structures; every member has a chance to participate in making decisions that bind the whole group. The conservative cast of our legislative institutions, especially the Senate, helps to alienate Canadians who do not share the political values of their framers. This is not to say that there are no liberal elements in our political system—as we will see in Chapters 8 and 10, federalism and the judicial review function of our Supreme Court were inspired in part by the liberal elements in the American *Constitution*—but rather to highlight the connection between institutions and ideology. Although ideologies may not play as obvious a role in Canadian politics as they do in other Western democracies, it would be foolish to discount them completely in an analysis of our political institutions.

SOURCES OF CANADIAN POLITICAL CULTURE

Canada has never had a single political culture. Long before Confederation, French and British communities coexisted on Canadian soil with the traditions of the various Aboriginal peoples. The legitimacy of the political institutions established in 1867 varied among the distinct linguistic and regional groups in the population, whose numbers multiplied with the European settlement of the West. As we saw in Chapter 1, provincial governments deliberately mobilized regional political cultures as resources in their struggles with the central government. Finally, the developing Canadian economy produced its own social cleavages, both between socioeconomic classes and among the various regions of the country. We will explore the sources of this diverse pattern of political orientations in this section.

History

The pattern of political orientations within a given country is decisively shaped by its history. The most influential accounts of the impact of Canadian history on our political culture are Hartz's "fragment theory" and Seymour Martin Lipset's "formative events" approach. We also need to explore a third factor: the cultural and institutional heritage of British colonial rule.

The "Fragment Theory"

For proponents of the fragment theory approach, the political cultures of the "new nations"—Canada, the United States, Australia, New Zealand, and South Africa—were determined by their unique patterns of European settlement.[15] The colonists who left Britain, Ireland, and France brought their political attitudes with them. These European "fragments" preserved their distinct political cultures in their new homelands. The *habitants* of New France were intensely conservative. They accepted the quasi-feudal structure of the colonial economy, and looked to the Catholic Church for instruction and assistance.[16] The English, Scottish, and Irish settlers, like those in the Thirteen Colonies to the south, were more liberal in their outlook. After France ceded its colony to Britain in 1763, the two cultures—French conservatives and English-speaking liberals—clashed repeatedly. The *habitants* turned inward, determined to survive as a French Catholic community under the British Crown.

After almost 250 years, Canada's political culture is still shaped by the original European "fragments." Fragment theorists claim that Quebeckers are more collectivist and state-oriented than **anglophones;** they are more deferential to their leaders, and more averse to risk. Conversely, English Canadians are more concerned with individual freedom and less tolerant of state interference in their lives. The fragment theory does not seek to explain every nuance of political culture. Instead, it portrays the culture of the first European settlers as "a kind of *genetic code* that does not determine but sets limits to later cultural developments."[17]

In an influential analysis of the differences between Canadian and American socialist movements, Gad Horowitz argued that the political cultures of English Canada and its southern neighbour are less similar than they appear.[18] Although both cultures are essentially liberal, Canadian liberalism is less "pure." It is influenced by both conservatism (which Horowitz calls "toryism") and socialism, two collectivist ideologies that moderate the radical individualism of the classical liberal world-view. The "tory touch," which was present well before Confederation, opened the door to the socialist ideas introduced by British immigrants in the twentieth century. Because Canada's political culture is not monopolized by a single ideology, unlike American political culture, there is more room for legitimate opposing viewpoints. Although Horowitz's analysis overlooks the important differences between ideology and political culture, which we discussed above, it has made a substantial contribution to the historical analysis of Canadian politics.

Critics of the Horowitz thesis have argued that the "tory touch" is a figment of the imagination.[19] They claim that the most important rival to liberalism in English Canada was not toryism, with its emphasis on hierarchy and deference, but American-inspired republicanism. The latter enshrined the values of popular (i.e., elected) government, rooted in the will of the people. In an analysis of the cultural values associated with the Reform Party, Telford proposed a revision of Horowitz to reflect both the "tory touch" and the republican tradition—currently manifested as populism. He argued that a fourth "pole" had been added to Horowitz's threefold model of Canadian ideology: liberalism, toryism, and socialism had been joined by neoconservative populism. Reformers combined "a traditionally conservative view of society" (moral traditionalism plus law and order) with "the liberal principles of equality, individual priority, and market-based competition."[20] Their policy goals were to be achieved, not through the "tory" institutions of representative government, but via new populist mechanisms of direct democracy.

While Telford makes a persuasive case for the existence of an indigenous populist "fragment" rooted in American republicanism (see "The Colonial Heritage" on page 40), he does not fully explain the origins of the neoconservative strand in Canadian culture. How did this synthesis of the social conservative aspects of toryism and the free-market element of liberalism come about? The answer may lie in two recent trends in Canadian political culture. Surveys have shown that Canadians, in the aggregate, are more favourable to market liberalism today than they were in the 1960s and 1970s.[21] At the same time, certain aspects of social conservatism— specifically, support for traditional conceptions of right and wrong, and endorsement of authority—have also gained influence.[22] To the extent that these attitudinal trends overlap, they imply greater potential for the political mobilization of neoconservatism. It is important to note, however, that other aspects of social conservatism are losing ground among Canadians; in particular, popular support for the rights of same-sex couples and ethnic minorities (but not Aboriginal Canadians) has grown in recent years.[23] Nonetheless, the overall picture presented in the survey data suggests that Telford's analysis is probably correct. The liberal, conservative, and republican/populist "fragments" in Canadian society have merged, at certain points, to create a new ideology, which became politically salient when it was mobilized by the Reform Party in the late 1980s and 1990s.

The fragment theory may also help to explain the presence of regional subcultures outside Quebec. Bell notes that each region was disproportionately populated by different European "fragments": English, Scottish, and Irish in the Atlantic region, Ontario, and British Columbia; French in Quebec; and central and Eastern Europeans on the Prairies.[24] Newer subcultures have developed over the past 50 years, as immigration patterns have changed. In effect, Canada's political culture is absorbing new "fragments," mainly from Asia, Latin America, the Caribbean, and the United States. The long-term effect on our politics is not yet clear.

Allophones share most of the key political values of anglophones, which suggests that they have little difficulty adapting to the political culture of their adopted country.[25] But many new Canadians are intensely interested in politics and impatient for entry into our political institutions. Efforts by particular ethnic communities to enter political parties have provoked a backlash against "bussing in" large numbers of Sikhs, Chinese, Italians, and others to vote for "their" candidates in constituency nomination battles. (As we will see in Chapter 3, however, the scope of this practice seems to be more restricted than the conventional wisdom implies.)

Formative Events

According to Lipset, national political cultures are shaped by shared historical experiences. He attributes the "conservative" and "deferential" culture of English Canada to a single cataclysmic event: the American Revolution of 1776–83. More specifically, Lipset argues that because Canadians refused to participate in the uprising against the British Crown, and because English Canada absorbed thousands of Loyalist refugees from the new American republic, our political culture is indelibly marked with the conservative and elitist values of eighteenth-century Britain.[26] These values were embodied in Canadian political institutions, which not only preserved but also reinforced them.[27] Subsequent "formative events," particularly the orderly development of the West (in contrast to the lawlessness of the American frontier), reinforced the relatively meek Canadian attitude toward authority figures (in this case, the Mounties).[28]

Lipset's argument is based on shaky evidence, much of which is contradicted by empirical research. It also rests on the erroneous assumption that "formative events" affect every person and every group in the same way. In reality, most of Canada's "formative events" are perceived quite differently by various subcultures. Take the Battle of the Plains of Abraham in 1759, and the subsequent Treaty of Paris, which transferred control of New France to the British Crown. In English Canada, the British victory is called "the Conquest," whereas Quebeckers bitterly refer to it as "*la cession*" (in other words, "France sold us down the river and abandoned us here with *les anglais*").[29] By ignoring French Canada altogether, Lipset avoids acknowledging the fact that differing interpretations of the same "formative event" produce conflicting myths and symbols.

Subsequent milestones in Canadian history—such as Confederation, the National Policy of 1879, and the death of the Meech Lake Accord in 1990—further divided Canada's subcultures and created new myths and symbols of power, domination, and rejection. The National Policy was designed to counter the flow of trade across the Canada–U.S. border by creating a national market for the products manufactured in Ontario and Quebec; its effect was to turn Atlantic and Western Canada into "a captive hinterland for central Canadian industrial development,"[30] permanently stunting the economies of the peripheral regions and fuelling regional resentments. The divisive mythologies arising from the Meech Lake Accord have already been discussed (see Dossier 1.5). Whereas American history has usually been interpreted in a unifying way (with obvious exceptions, such as slavery and the Civil War), Canadian history has left a legacy of division and mistrust that repeatedly flares up into public debate about the very legitimacy of our political system.[31]

However, the core of Lipset's argument is correct: "formative events"—especially those that shape a nation's political institutions—do leave indelible imprints on its political culture. Such events can further unite populations that already share basic political values, but they can also drive wedges between existing subcultures and create new ones.

The Colonial Heritage

Until fairly recently, the impact of British colonialism has been overlooked by students of Canada's political culture. There are two key aspects of this legacy. The first is the deliberate imposition of British institutions on colonists with French and American political ideas. After the "Conquest," and particularly after the American colonies revolted in 1776, the British government was determined to snuff out "dangerous" radical ideas in its remaining possessions. The *Constitutional Act* of 1791 imposed virtually complete executive dominance over the elected assemblies.[32] Despite Lipset's claim that Loyalist refugees uncritically supported the Crown, the evidence suggests that their political orientations were largely American. They chafed under the autocratic rule of the governors and their hand-picked advisers, and demanded responsible government—the accountability of the executive branch to the legislature. The British government refused until the 1840s. "Had the early nineteenth-century political institutions of British North America been allowed to evolve without British intervention . . . Canadian political institutions undoubtedly would have ended up more American than British."[33] By the 1860s, when the institutions of a sovereign Canada were designed, the pattern of executive dominance under the Crown was firmly set:

> *The Tory-inspired constitution of Confederation emphasized strong national and executive leadership to diminish provincial factionalism and facilitate economic development. By contrast, the Americans distrusted concentrated sovereignty, and devised many checks and balances to limit executive authority . . . A different procedural consensus was preserved in the constitutions of each country. This had significant implications for subsequent evolution, given the importance of institutions as determinants of social conditions, ideological beliefs, and political forces.*[34]

The Confederation debates of the 1860s revealed a deep difference of opinion between the advocates of an American-style "republican" constitution and adherents to the British model. Among the latter, many feared that, whatever form the new Dominion took, the "strong material influences" of the United States would eventually absorb Canada and destroy its "connection with monarchical and aristocratic institutions."[35]

Second, the British Crown remains—contrary to popular belief—a central feature of Canadian government. Three points deserve mention here:

1. The **prerogative powers** of the Crown are now exercised only at the request of the head of government (the prime minister or a provincial premier). Ever since 1763, Canadian politicians have used **patronage** to control their supporters and build political organizations.[36] In so doing, they fostered at least two distinctive characteristics of our political culture: reliance on the state for economic benefits, and exaggerated deference to party leaders (especially prime ministers, with their monopoly over patronage).[37]

2. The executive powers of the Crown are divided evenly between the federal and provincial governments. Sir John A. Macdonald believed that the lieutenant governors—the Crown's representatives in the provinces—would be subordinate to the governor general (representing the Crown at the national level).[38] The lieutenant governors, as appointees of the federal government, would ensure that the provincial governments obeyed the instructions of their superiors in Ottawa. Disobedience would result in the disallowance (veto) or reservation (delay) of provincial legislation. Macdonald's intention was thwarted by the Judicial Committee of the Privy Council, which ruled in 1892 that a lieutenant governor was "as much the representative of Her Majesty for all purposes of provincial government as the governor general himself is for all purposes of Dominion government."[39] This meant that the executive branches of both levels of government possessed the full powers of the Crown, with predictable results for Canadian federalism:

> *The Crown endowed the provinces with unlimited potential for action, a reservoir of power which, when exercised in the absence of a common national denominator, heightened the distinctive characteristics of each province evident since its founding. In turn, the contrasting development that ensued further exaggerated provincial distinctions.*[40]

CHANGING POLITICAL CULTURE AND CANADA'S POLITICAL INSTITUTIONS   **41**

3. The Crown's special relationship with Canada's Aboriginal peoples continues to shape the debate over the future political status of the First Nations. When Britain assumed control over Canada in 1763, King George III issued a Royal Proclamation to his new subjects:

> *And whereas it is just and reasonable, and essential to our Interest, and the Security of our Colonies, that the several Nations or Tribes of Indians with whom We are connected, and who live under our Protection, should not be molested or disturbed in the Possession of such Parts of Our Dominions and Territories as, not having been ceded to or purchased by Us, are reserved to them, or any of them, as their Hunting Grounds. . . . And We do further declare it to be Our Royal Will and Pleasure, for the present as aforesaid, to reserve under our Sovereignty, Protection, and Dominion, for the use of the said Indians, all the Lands and Territories not included within the Limits of Our said Three new Governments, or within the Limits of the Territory granted to the Hudson's Bay Company . . .*[41]

Any British subject who tried to cheat the Indians, to occupy their land, or to purchase Crown land for his or her own use would be punished. The Crown would protect the Indians, in return for peace and loyalty. The Royal Proclamation established

Inuit artist Inuk Charlie, one of a group of artists that crafted the new ceremonial mace for the Nunavut legislature in Iqaluit. Nunavut officially became a territory on April 1, 1999. (© CP/Kevin Frayer)

"a special relationship between the Crown and Canada's aboriginal peoples,"[42] which remains a part of Canadian law and politics. Section 25 of the *Canadian Charter of Rights and Freedoms* explicitly protects the Aboriginal rights arising from the Royal Proclamation, including the requirement that all transfers of land from Indians to the Crown be conducted by treaties (as opposed to ordinary contracts of sale).[43] After considerable debate over the meaning of the document—specifically, whether it guarantees Aboriginal land title and self-government, and if so, whether those guarantees extend beyond the original British colonies[44]—the Supreme Court of Canada settled the issue in the 1997 *Delgamuukw* ruling. The Royal Proclamation is the legal source of Aboriginal land rights in Canada, and it imposes on the Crown a special duty to protect those rights. Consequently, it still helps to define the Aboriginal subcultures within the broader Canadian community.

Geography

Much has been written about the impact of the land on Canadians' perceptions of ourselves. We are, according to Margaret Atwood and others, a nation fatalistically obsessed with "survival" in a harsh land of rock and snow. The contemporary relevance of such claims is questionable, at least to the majority of Canadians who live in modern cities a stone's throw from the American border. Apart from Progressive Conservative leader John Diefenbaker's successful campaign theme in 1958—"a vision of the North"—it is difficult to detect political echoes of Canada's climate and geology. One possible exception is the relative strength of environmental concerns among Canadians, which suggests that our connection to the landscape may be unusually profound.[45] Another exception is the centrality of Quebec's landmass in the rhetoric of Quebec nationalism, which is reflected in Dossier 2.3.

Whether or not our geography has shaped a national political culture, it does help to explain the existence of regional political cultures. The sheer size and diversity of Canada clearly contributes to the sense of "difference" across the regions. As each province developed, from the first European settlement to the present day, "Different environments combined with different technologies and opportunities to produce distinct regional economies."[46] These, in turn, created distinct patterns of political values across the regions. This is not to suggest that geography determines culture; such one-sided explanations rarely offer any genuine insight. It means, instead, that the unique terrain and climate in each part of the country shape the social and political values of those who live there, creating the conditions for mobilization into a formal subculture.[47]

Demography

The most obvious demographic influence on Canadian politics is the presence of a large francophone minority. Almost one-quarter (22.7 percent) of the population claim French as their mother tongue. Anglophones account for 59 percent, and allophones make up 17.6 percent.[48] A majority of francophones live in Quebec, although there

While objective factors such as immigration patterns and geography help to explain the strength of Canadian regionalism, they do not tell the whole story. **Regionalism** is a subjective phenomenon, a social and psychological attachment to a particular place. It has three components: the importance of region in an individual's sense of identity, the degree to which she identifies with her region, and the strength of her commitment to that region.[49] Someone with a strong sense of regional identification and commitment is more likely to vote on the basis of regional interests and to resent perceived mistreatment of her region by the national or provincial government than someone who is more concerned with other aspects of her identity (e.g., gender, class, or language).

Despite recent changes in political culture—including the rise of nonterritorial cleavages fostered by postmaterialism, discussed later in this chapter—regionalism remains unusually influential in Canada's national politics. Cross-national comparisons between Canada and other industrialized democracies reveal the relative weakness of social class and church attendance as determinants of voting choice. Canadians are significantly more influenced by territorial cleavages—the rural–urban divide and region of residence—than are Western Europeans.[50] This may be due, in part, to the incentives set by our national institutions; in particular, the electoral system reflects the view that MPs represent territory, not ideology, and exaggerates regional differences among the various party caucuses in the House of Commons. (See Chapter 4.) As for the rural–urban split, recent evidence suggests that it may be an illusion. There are differences between the attitudes of Canadians in rural areas and small towns and those of Canadians in mid-sized and large cities, but much of the discrepancy appears attributable to varying levels of education, rather than the influence of geography per se. Nonetheless, the differences in political beliefs are real, particularly those relating to traditional moral values.[51]

are significant francophone populations in New Brunswick and Ontario as well. While the language cleavage has always been a central issue in Canadian politics, its implications have become more serious since the Quiet Revolution remobilized Quebec nationalism into the sovereignty movement. Fears about the future of French in Canada help to fuel the campaign for a separate Quebec. Otherwise, the language cleavage appears to have little impact on political values; francophone and anglophone Canadians hold similar views on most political and social issues, although the former are slightly more permissive on moral issues.[52]

Aboriginal Canadians, who accounted for 3.3 percent of the population in the 2001 census,[53] also seek to reform Canada's political institutions. The distribution of the Aboriginal population varies widely among the provinces and territories, from around 1 percent in Prince Edward Island and Quebec to more than 13 percent in Manitoba and Saskatchewan and 82 percent in Nunavut.[54] The intensity of Aboriginal demands for institutional and economic also varies, explaining to some extent why Canadians in some provinces—notably British Columbia and Quebec, which have witnessed divisive and occasionally violent disputes between First Nations and their neighbours—are less supportive of Aboriginal rights claims than those in other provinces.[55] Status Indians, Métis, and Inuit have become important players in debates over Canada's political future. Recent demands for enhanced political and legal status—ranging from an Aboriginal chamber of Parliament to the constitutional recognition of Aboriginal communities as "a third order of government" with significant sovereignty over their own affairs—pose significant challenges to our existing institutions.

Economics

Marxist thinkers dismiss traditional analyses of political culture as biased, deceptive, and even oppressive. Karl Marx (1818–83) argued that the central dynamic of human history was the struggle between two classes: a small upper class, which owned the means of production (e.g., land, factories), and a much larger working class, which owned nothing except its labour. Over time, as the dominant technology of production evolved from agriculture to industrial manufacturing, European economies shifted from feudalism to capitalism. Their political systems changed dramatically, from absolutist monarchs surrounded by fawning aristocrats to Cabinet governments dependent on elected legislatures. Conservatism gave way to liberalism, and Catholicism (in much of northern Europe) to Protestantism. But the underlying power structure remained intact: the tiny economic elite, through its control of the economy and politics, continued to oppress the workers.[56]

For Marxists, what liberals call "political culture" is an ideological smokescreen. It blinds the working class to its own oppression, by either glorifying "natural" hierarchies (as in conservatism) or celebrating individual "freedom" (liberalism). This "false consciousness" must be overcome, and the workers made aware of their exploitation, before the class struggle can reach its climax. At some point, according to Marx, the workers will rise up against the elite, seize control of the means of production, and distribute the proceeds among themselves. This final stage of human history is communism: the abolition of private property, or at least the private ownership of the means of production, and the "withering away" of the state.

Whether or not one agrees with Marx, there is little doubt that the material facts of life shape our view of the world. We have already seen that distinct regional economies can produce variations in political culture. But how can we explain the apparent weakness of class as a determinant of Canadian political values and behaviour?[57] Elsewhere in the Western world, the class cleavage has exerted a powerful influence on voter choice (although that influence has diminished in recent years); Canadians are more likely to vote on the basis of region, partisanship, or short-term factors such as party leaders and campaign issues (Chapter 4). From a left-wing viewpoint, we are victims of "false consciousness," duped by our political leaders into believing that class is less important than region or language.[58] Despite the unfortunate tinge of conspiracy theory in this argument, Marx's central insight remains valid: that despite the growing influence of "postmaterialism," our political orientations are inevitably shaped (though not necessarily determined) by our social and economic status.[59]

RECENT TRENDS IN CANADIAN POLITICAL CULTURE

Before we turn to recent developments, it may be useful to summarize the conventional wisdom about Canadian political culture.[60] Canadians, it is alleged, are more dependent than Americans on the state. We are more deferential to authority, whether that authority is based on democratic processes or on inherited privilege (e.g., the British monarch). We are timid, conservative, and relatively passive in our orientations toward politics. Whatever merit this stereotype may once have possessed, survey data suggest that it no longer applies.[61] Like their counterparts in other Western democracies, Canadians are increasingly apt to challenge authority, demand direct participation in political decision-making, and criticize the status quo. Indeed, we are becoming less deferential to authority than our American neighbors, especially among the youngest cohorts.[62] The old conventional wisdom must be modified, or abandoned altogether, in light of the current evidence.

Measuring Change in the Political Orientations of Canadians

The new conventional wisdom is that Canadians, like the citizens of other Western democracies, are increasingly disenchanted with politics. To make sense of this claim, we return to the five elements of the political system identified at the beginning of the chapter:

1. *The political community:* While support remains high in most democratic states, Canada is a partial exception. Quebec nationalists feel less attachment than other Canadians to "Canada as a whole."[63] At least as worrisome is the relatively low level of attachment among younger Canadians,[64] although it is not clear whether this is the result of disaffection with Canada or an emerging sense of "transnational" or "cosmopolitan" citizenship.[65] Whatever its origin, weaker adherence to the political community is related to lower levels of support for particular national institutions (notably Parliament), for political parties, and for politicians.[66] Generally speaking, however, Canadians' attitudes toward the political community are more positive than their evaluations of the specific elements of the political system.[67]

2. *Regime principles:* Canadians, like most people, approve of democracy as an abstract concept.[68] This does not mean, however, that they are entirely satisfied with the actual performance of our democratic institutions, as the analysis of the next three elements reveals. Support for federalism, minority rights, and the rule of law is more difficult to gauge, because the data are either ambiguous or nonexistent. It should also be noted that support for "democracy" does not necessarily imply

support for the particular conception of democracy embodied in existing institutions. In other words, to the extent that Canadians wish to see a greater degree of direct democracy in public decision-making, they are likely to become disenchanted with representative institutions.[69] (See "Postmaterialism" on page 52.)

3. *Regime performance:* Evaluations of the overall performance of Canada's national political institutions have fluctuated in recent years. Citizens' assessments of regime performance are affected by economic conditions,[70] by the perceived fairness of their treatment by the state,[71] and by the overall competence with which governments handle common problems. While a slim majority of Canadians perceive the federal government as both fair and efficient,[72] a perception that sustains overall confidence in regime performance, poor economic conditions in the 1980s and early 1990s produced temporary dips in confidence.[73] In 1992, in the depths of a recession, 24 percent of Canadians were satisfied with the performance of the federal government, down from 51 percent in 1986.[74] Note, too, that changing cultural values can create new and more stringent evaluative criteria. In other words, better-informed and less deferential citizens may hold governments to higher standards of performance than their parents or grandparents did.[75] Over the past few decades, Canadians' sense of personal political efficacy—their confidence in their own ability to evaluate information and make political decisions—has risen, while their belief that politicians listen to their opinions has fallen. This "efficacy gap" has likely increased Canadians' frustration with, and alienation from, their political institutions.[76]

4. *Regime institutions:* While overall evaluations of the Canadian political system are fairly positive, the same cannot be said for individual institutions. Public satisfaction with Parliament and political parties has dropped sharply over the past 30 years. Between 1979 and 1999 the percentage of Canadians who expressed "a great deal of confidence" in political parties fell from 30 percent to 11 percent.[77] From 1965 to 1993, evaluations of the major federal parties declined steadily, while partisan attachments weakened apace.[78] In 1981, 61 percent of Canadians had either "a great deal of confidence" or "some confidence" in national political institutions; by 1991, that figure had fallen to 46 percent, 7 points below the average reported by the Organisation for Economic Co-operation and Development (OECD). While confidence in other institutions, including the police and the military, also declined, public disaffection with Parliament and the political parties accounted for most of the overall drop in public esteem. Given the argument in Chapter 1, that a loss of public confidence threatens the legitimacy of democratic institutions, this "relative lack of popular confidence in [our] democratic institutions"[79] should be cause for concern. But the news is not all bad. First, evaluations of Canada's political institutions—including Parliament and the parties—have improved since the early 1990s.[80] Second, Canadians appear to have transferred their confidence to other political institutions, instead of giving up on the political system completely. A substantial majority believes that the courts, not Parliament, should have the final word on issues arising from the *Charter of Rights*.[81] We will return to the relationship between the courts and Parliament in Chapter 10.

5. *Political actors:* By 1992, Brian Mulroney had become the least popular prime minister in Canadian history. Two rounds of constitutional bargaining had divided the country and failed to produce results. (See Chapter 9.) The 1989 Free Trade Agreement with the United States provoked equally intense controversy. At the time, some observers feared that the public's anger with the Mulroney government would inflict severe and permanent damage on support for national political institutions. Instead, the relative popularity of Jean Chrétien and his Liberal government seemed to reverse the decline in public confidence. Note, however, that citizens appear to distinguish between the five elements listed here; the popularity of a particular government does not necessarily affect the public's evaluation of the broader elements of the political system.[82] It is more likely that long-term trends in political support are also affected by cultural change and evaluations of regime performance, instead of being determined entirely by short-term attitudes toward particular politicians.

As in most Western states, overall evaluations decline with each element on the list. In other words, Canadians have the most positive feelings toward the broadest level—the political community—and the most negative feelings toward specific institutions and political actors. Table 2.1 reflects this downward trend from the general to the particular elements of the political system.

■ Explaining the Changes in Canadian Political Culture

Quebec Nationalism and the Quiet Revolution

As we saw in the earlier discussion of the "fragment theory," French Quebeckers have had a strong attachment to their political community since the eighteenth century. The passive, inward-looking nationalism that emerged after "*la cession*" was mobilized

TABLE 2.1   CANADIANS' SATISFACTION WITH DEMOCRACY, GOVERNMENT, AND POLITICS, 2000[83]

	DEMOCRACY (%)	GOVERNMENT (%)	POLITICS (%)
Very or fairly satisfied	71	58	53
Not very or not at all satisfied	26	38	43
Not sure/refused	4	4	5
Total	100	100	100
Number of respondents	1278	1278	1278

Note: Columns may not add to 100 due to rounding.

Source: Paul Howe and David Northrup, *Strengthening Canadian Democracy: The Views of Canadians* (Montreal: Institute for Research on Public Policy, 2000), Table 2, p. 7. Reprinted with permission.

by the Quiet Revolution of the 1960s into an aggressive campaign for greater provincial powers and revenues. The myths and symbols of Quebec nationalism have been used effectively to strengthen the attachment of francophones to the sovereigntist project, as the example in Dossier 2.3 illustrates.

DOSSIER 2.3 Quebec Nationalism

In 1995, shortly before the sovereignty referendum that October, the Parti Québécois (PQ) government of Quebec introduced Bill 1, *The Sovereignty Bill*. The preamble contained a strong and lyrical statement of Quebec nationalism, excerpts of which are reproduced here.

At the dawn of the seventeenth century, the pioneers of what would become a nation and then a people rooted themselves in the soil of Québec. Having come from a great civilization, they were enriched by that of the First Nations, they forged new alliances, and maintained the heritage of France. The conquest of 1760 did not break the determination of their descendants to remain faithful to a destiny unique in North America. Already in 1774, through the Québec Act, the conqueror recognized the distinct nature of their institutions. Neither attempts at assimilation nor the Act of Union of 1840 could break their endurance. The English community that grew up at their side, the immigrants who have joined them, all have contributed to forming this people which became in 1867 one of the two founders of the Canadian federation.

We, the men and women of this place,

Because we inhabit the territories delimited by our ancestors, from Abitibi to the Îles-de-la-Madeleine, from Ungava to the American border, because for four hundred years we have cleared, ploughed, paced, surveyed, dug, fished, built, started anew, discussed, protected, and loved this land that is cut across and watered by the St. Lawrence River;

Because the heart of this land beats in French and because that heartbeat is as meaningful as the seasons that hold sway over it, as the winds that bend it, as the men and women who shape it;

Because we have created here a way of being, of believing, of working that is unique;

Because as long ago as 1791 we established here one of the first parliamentary democracies in the world, one we have never ceased to improve;

Because the legacy of the struggles and courage of the past compels us irrevocably to take charge of our own destiny;

Because it is this land alone that represents our pride and the source of our strength, our sole opportunity to express ourselves in the entirety of our individual natures and of our collective heart;

Because this land will be all those men and women who inhabit it, who defend it and define it, and because we are all those people;

We, the people of Québec, declare that we are free to choose our future.

We entered the federation on the faith of a promise of equality in a shared undertaking

(cont'd)

CHANGING POLITICAL CULTURE AND CANADA'S POLITICAL INSTITUTIONS *and of respect for our authority in certain matters that to us are vital. But what was to follow did not live up to those early hopes. The Canadian State contravened the federative pact, by invading in a thousand ways areas in which we are autonomous, and by serving notice that our secular belief in the equality of the partners was an illusion. We were hoodwinked in 1982 when the governments of Canada and the English-speaking provinces made changes to the Constitution, in depth and to our detriment, in defiance of the categorical opposition of our National Assembly. Twice since then attempts were made to right that wrong. The failure of the Meech Lake Accord in 1990 confirmed a refusal to recognize even our distinct character. And in 1992 the rejection of the Charlottetown Accord by both Canadians and Quebecers confirmed the conclusion that no redress was possible.*

Because we have persisted despite the haggling of which we have been the object;

Because Canada, far from taking pride in and proclaiming to the world the alliance between its two founding peoples, has instead consistently trivialized it and decreed the spurious principle of equality between the provinces;

Because we have the deep-seated conviction that continuing within Canada would be tantamount to condemning ourselves to languish and to debasing our very identity;

We, the people of Québec, declare it is our will to be in full possession of all the powers of a State: to vote all our laws, to levy all our taxes, to sign all our treaties and to exercise the highest power of all, conceiving, and controlling, by ourselves, our fundamental law.

We, the people of Québec, through our National Assembly, proclaim: Québec is a sovereign country.

The full text of Bill 1 can be found on the Nelson website for this book at www.parametersofpower4e.nelson.com. Click on "Canadian Politics on the Web," then on "Quebec & National Unity," and then on "The Sovereignty Bill."

Dossier 2.3 reflects at least three central themes in the mythology of Quebec nationalism:

1. The province of Quebec is the homeland of the French people and culture in North America. It is a "distinct society" within Canada. Consequently, the provincial government has a special responsibility to protect and promote that "distinct society," and it requires special powers to carry out that responsibility. If it cannot achieve and exercise those powers within the framework of Canadian federalism, it must become an independent state.

2. Confederation is the product of a compact between two "founding nations": the French and the English. (There is little room in this mythology for the Aboriginal peoples of Canada.) It follows that Quebec is not, and never will be, "*une province comme les autres.*" It has the right to negotiate constitutional change directly with

the federal government, on a nation-to-nation basis. It also claims a veto over any proposed amendment to the Confederation compact that does not meet the needs of Quebec. In other words, even if the federal government and the other nine provinces agreed to a change in the *Constitution,* Quebec should have the right to block that change.

3. National political institutions cannot thwart the democratic will of Quebeckers. That will is sovereign, and it trumps all other constitutional values (e.g., federalism or the rights of minorities within Quebec).

As we will see in Chapter 9, the Supreme Court and the federal government reject the last of these claims, while the other provinces refuse to accept the idea that Quebec deserves "special status." The clash between the "two-nations" and "equal-provinces" visions of Canada is yet to be resolved, despite repeated efforts by political leaders.

The decisive event in generating demands for major constitutional revision was the Quiet Revolution, which transformed Quebec politics in the early 1960s. The decade opened with the defeat of the Union Nationale government of Quebec by the provincial Liberals under the leadership of Jean Lesage. The Lesage Liberals ushered Quebec into the modern era of activist states. Before 1960, the Union Nationale espoused a minimalist, laissez-faire approach to the economy and allowed the church to dominate the realms of education and social welfare. In this deeply conservative vision, Quebec francophones were a Catholic, agrarian people for whom modern commercial capitalism was a foreign activity better left to English-speaking Protestants.[84] By 1960, this ideology was no longer an accurate description of reality: since the beginning of the century, Quebeckers had been leaving their farms in droves and integrating into modern urban, industrial society. The problem was that they had been integrated as workers into enterprises largely controlled and managed by the English community and using English as the language of work, a development that threatened the long-term persistence of French as the primary language in Quebec.

Responding to this reality, the Lesage Liberals abandoned the antistatism of their predecessors. If the French language and culture were to survive in Quebec, the government had to intervene in the economy in order to ensure that it was controlled and operated to a much greater extent by francophones. Commerce was no longer to be disdained as a foreign activity but to be embraced as a form of secular salvation and, wherever possible, was to be conducted in French. By the same token, education and other social services had to be wrested from the church and directed more explicitly to giving French Quebeckers the skills they needed to take control of economic enterprises rather than just supply their labour. In its newfound interventionism, especially in economic matters, Quebec often wanted to go further than the other provinces and occupy realms of activity that had been filled by the federal government. Ottawa, from this perspective, could not be trusted to exercise its powers in a manner congenial to Quebec. Parliamentary institutions are highly responsive to the majority, which implied that Ottawa would follow the wishes of the English majority outside Quebec. The Quiet Revolution, in short, led to the demand for a transfer of powers from Ottawa to Quebec City, a demand that has dominated Quebec politics and shaped the national constitutional landscape ever since.

Postmaterialism

The postmaterialist hypothesis offers a second explanation for changing political orientations in Canada and elsewhere.[85] Since 1945, Western publics have enjoyed unprecedented levels of material affluence, physical security, educational opportunity, and access to information. Children who grew up in this environment have different priorities from those espoused by their parents and grandparents. They are more concerned with "quality of life" issues—equal rights, the environment, the developing world—and they have the political and intellectual skills to put their issues on the public agenda. Postmaterialists are more likely to employ unconventional political tactics, such as protests, largely because they are less attracted to traditional political institutions: "Publics . . . have more information about politics, they are more attentive, and they are more interested in politics, but this does not mean that they are satisfied with the status quo."[86]

This heightened political interest translates into growing political activism, which is clearly a positive trend. The problem, according to Neil Nevitte, is that existing political institutions have not responded appropriately:

> The emergence of increasingly interested, informed, and even critical publics is a healthy sign; it indicates the potential for a more vital and more broadly participatory version of democracy. From this vantage point, democracy is not so much "in crisis" as in a state of transition. All that is in crisis is "old politics"—the traditional notion that democracies work best when publics are passive, disengaged, and relatively uninformed.[87]

TABLE 2.2   MATERIALIST/POSTMATERIALIST ORIENTATIONS IN CANADA, 1981–90[88]

	YEAR	MATERIALIST (%)	MIXED (%)	POSTMATERIALIST (%)
English Canada	1981	17	66	17
	1990	9	68	26
	Change	−8	+2	+6
French Canada	1981	35	52	13
	1990	21	50	29
	Change	−14	−2	+16

Source: Neil Nevitte, "Table 2-2: Materialist/Postmaterialist Orientations within Canada." Copyright © 1996 by Neil Nevitte. Reprinted from *The Decline of Deference: Canadian Value Change in Cross-National Perspective,* by Neil Nevitte (Ontario: Broadview Press, 1996), p. 31. Reprinted by permission of Broadview Press.

It is often argued, by Nevitte and others, that postmaterialist values are becoming increasingly influential in all Western democracies, including Canada. More recent survey data raise a few doubts about this claim: one major study found that the proportion of respondents who considered it very important to "strengthen respect and obedience for authority" rose significantly between 1987 and 1999, a result that directly contradicts the postmaterialist hypothesis.[89]

Even if we assume that some elements of Inglehart's hypothesis are open to question, other values associated with postmaterialism—equality, direct participation in politics, personal freedom—are more prevalent among Canadians born since 1945 than in earlier generations. The implications for Canada's political culture are significant. The cognitive aspect of political culture changes as people become better informed about political issues and processes, while the emergence of new and harsher criteria for evaluating political institutions alters the evaluative and, ultimately, the affective aspects. Nevitte argues that "conventional vehicles for citizen participation, such as traditional political parties, are losing their appeal because they operate from principles that satisfy a shrinking proportion of the public."[90] The principles in question are those that we have identified as conservative: hierarchy, authority, and indifference (if not hostility) to "meaningful citizen participation."[91] If Nevitte's analysis is correct, representative political institutions in Canada and elsewhere may face escalating protests and a continuing loss of legitimacy. Moreover, it may be necessary for politicians to resort more frequently to direct democracy measures such as initiatives and referenda (see Dossier 2.4), or risk escalating social and political protest (see Dossier 2.5).

Quantitative analyses support the link between postmaterialist values and declining public confidence in political institutions.[92] These analyses also substantiate the claim that postmaterialist priorities pose a growing challenge to the political system. Demands for equal rights and environmental protection are difficult to reconcile with the traditional priorities of governments and political parties, as are demands for more direct citizen participation and the reduction of hierarchical control in representative institutions.

Regime Performance

A third explanation for changing political values suggests that citizens are simply disappointed with the way their existing institutions work. In other words, if citizens are less satisfied with their political institutions than they used to be, perhaps the institutions themselves are to blame. There are two dimensions to this argument: procedural and substantive. The procedural approach argues that when political institutions persistently violate social norms of competence, integrity, or democracy—when they just don't work the way people think they should—their legitimacy erodes.[93] Substantive evaluations of regime performance are determined by three factors: "the information to which citizens are exposed, the criteria by which the public evaluates government and politics, and the actual performance of those institutions."[94] Comparative evidence suggests that the first two factors have changed significantly in recent years: political corruption and incompetence may not have increased, but citizens are more aware of politicians' missteps and judge them more harshly than in the past. One reason for this increased awareness may be the sometimes cynical tone of news coverage; we will return to this issue in Chapter 7.

The link between procedural evaluations and political attitudes is clearest in countries like Japan and Italy, where political scandals erupt on a regular basis.[95] The Canadian evidence is mixed. On the one hand, Canadians are relatively satisfied with the fairness and efficiency of our political institutions, and this satisfaction appears to foster support for the political system. On the other hand, negative evaluations of government responsiveness have a weaker effect on overall satisfaction with political institutions.[96] Perhaps the most important aspect of the procedural analysis is the question of evaluative criteria. If the postmaterialist hypothesis is correct, more of us expect to be directly involved in political decision-making; the failure of political institutions to respond appropriately to these new expectations may prove costly in the long run.

The substantive approach focuses on the outputs of the political system: specific outputs, such as laws, public policies, and tangible benefits (e.g., Employment Insurance), as well as generalized outputs (e.g., overall economic performance). When the political system does not provide what the citizens need or expect, its reputation suffers. Once again, the evidence is mixed. Comparative analyses find a very weak relationship between economic conditions and regime support.[97] Citizens will blame—and often punish—a particular government for poor economic performance,[98] but they do not reject the political system as a whole.

The Rights Revolution

Alan Cairns attributes recent changes in Canadian political culture to the effects of the *Canadian Charter of Rights and Freedoms*.[99] He argues that the groups that received particular recognition and protection in the *Constitution Act, 1982*—the so-called "Charter Canadians"—have mobilized to defend "their" rights against perceived threats. Women's groups, Aboriginal groups, multicultural groups, and a host of others helped to defeat the Meech Lake and Charlottetown Accords. One implication is that growing citizen activism, fostered by the *Charter*, is reflected in less deferential political values. Another is that the territorial social cleavages that inspired Canada's federal system, and that in turn have been encouraged by provincial governments, are losing their power to shape political values. In their place are "new cleavages or reinvigorated old cleavages related to sex, ethnicity, the aboriginal communities, the disabled, and others."[100]

Our national political institutions, which are designed to reflect territorial cleavages, are increasingly unsuited to a political culture shaped by *Charter* recognition of groups that are spread across the regions. This does not mean that regionalism is no longer relevant; as we have seen, the presence of provincial governments ensures the survival and continual remobilization of regional subcultures. But it does mean that regionalism is no longer the primary basis for political mobilization. As we will see in Chapters 7 and 10, the role of the Supreme Court in interpreting and applying the *Charter* provides an institutional focus for mobilizing "Charter groups"—which may, in time, produce nonregional subcultures powerful and well organized enough to force significant changes in our national political system.

In a related vein, Morton and Knopff allege that "Charter groups" have successfully used the courts to impose their policy preferences on a reluctant majority. By couching their demands in the non-negotiable language of "rights," they have enhanced the power of a nonaccountable judiciary to override the choices of the democratically elected House of Commons. The growing prevalence of "rights talk" in Canada's political discourse fuels popular discontent with the system and erodes the legitimacy of traditional political decision-making processes based on compromise and negotiation.[101]

While Cairns' narrower argument about the impact of the *Charter* on constitutional politics is plausible, survey evidence contradicts the broader argument that the "decline of deference" was provoked by the *Charter*. The value changes identified by Cairns are rooted in postmaterialism and not in the "citizens' constitution." While Cairns' argument likely helps to explain elite-level changes in political behaviour and attitudes, it does not appear to account for the overall shift in our political culture.[102] There is one possible exception to this claim: a recent study attributes high levels of support for equality rights and civil liberties among Canadians born since 1970, in part, to the effects of growing up with the *Charter*.[103] If this is correct, then the real "Charter Canadians" are those who have no memory of a Canada without entrenched rights and freedoms; unaware of the controversies surrounding the creation of the *Charter*, many take it for granted that gays and lesbians should receive equal treatment under the law or that unpopular minorities should have the right to express their views.

Morton and Knopff are also incorrect, at least insofar as they perceive "Charter groups" to be out of touch with other Canadians. Between 1987 and 2000, twice as many Canadians thought that the courts should have the final word on the constitutionality of legislation compared to those who wanted to give the House of Commons the final word.[104] "The repeated charge that judicial activism is undermining the quality of Canadian democracy has not resonated with the Canadian public at large."[105]

Even if we reject the "Charter Canadians" hypothesis as the *cause* of value change, it is clear that the *Charter* provides an institutional framework for the *expression* and mobilization of postmaterialist values. We will discuss the *Charter*'s impact on Canadian politics in Chapter 10.

Social Capital

Robert Putnam's theory of social capital provides a fifth explanation of change in political values.[106] In a nutshell, Putnam argues that democratic political institutions work most effectively in societies with high levels of social engagement. Volunteer work, attending public meetings on community issues, membership in social clubs, even bowling in a league—all these activities contribute to the stock of "social capital" in the community. Where social capital is high, people tend to trust their neighbours and to support their political institutions. They work together effectively to resolve common problems, care about the well-being of other people in their communities, and have more respect and tolerance for differing viewpoints.[107] As we observed in Chapter 1, a cohesive political community is a prerequisite for legitimate political institutions; as that community weakens, legitimacy is undermined.

Where social capital is low—where people are more isolated from each other, either by personal choice or because of a lack of opportunities for positive interaction—levels of social trust are correspondingly low and support for political institutions drops. A lack of civic engagement on the part of the "silent majority" effectively abandons political involvement to extremists, and reduces public understanding of social issues to dangerously low levels.[108] The performance of government suffers, both because of passive noncompliance with the law (e.g., a lack of reciprocal social trust makes people less likely to pay their taxes) and because political elites know that they will not be held accountable for poor decisions by an uninformed and apathetic electorate.[109]

Putnam concludes that "the health of our public institutions depends, at least in part, on widespread participation in private voluntary groups—those networks of civic engagement that embody social capital."[110] While "the absence of social capital does not eliminate politics,"[111] it reduces public life to a babble of disconnected voices in a social landscape of isolation and mutual distrust.

Putnam's work on social capital has attracted a number of critics. Some argue that Putnam has put the cart before the horse: we are less likely to participate in collective voluntary activities *because* we have less concern for our neighbours, not vice versa.[112] Others accuse Putnam of overemphasizing local sources of social capital and underestimating the impact of regional and national political structures on citizen engagement.[113] Finally, empirical research on individual attitudes finds a very weak correlation between voluntary activity and social trust.[114] Furthermore, there is no direct statistical relationship between social trust and evaluations of government institutions.[115] If individual citizens are becoming increasingly disenchanted with **representative democracy,** the primary reason appears to be discontent with the performance of political institutions themselves and not the decline of social capital.[116] When we look at entire populations, however, we find a strong relationship between social trust and government legitimacy: "Social trust can help build effective social and political institutions, which can help governments perform effectively, and this in turn encourages confidence in civic institutions."[117] So while the link between social capital and support for political institutions is not as direct as Putnam suggests, and while shrinking social capital is not the sole reason for declining public confidence in governments, there is little doubt that democracy is nourished by a strong sense of community and mutual concern.

The Mass Media

The sixth and final explanation for the changes in Canadian political culture is the effect of the mass media—in particular, television. There are two dimensions to consider. First, Putnam argues that television weakens social capital, by isolating us in our living rooms: "A major commitment to television viewing—such as most of us have come to have—is incompatible with a major commitment to community life."[118] Second, critics of the news media argue that shallow and negative coverage of politics makes voters cynical and undermines their faith in the political system.[119] It may also diminish the capacity of citizens to make informed decisions about candidates and issues,[120] a subject to which we will return in Chapter 7.

Empirical evidence reveals a clear statistical connection between heavy television watching and lack of involvement in the community,[121] although it is not clear which is the cause and which is the effect. In other words, we don't know whether television makes people apathetic, or whether people who have no interest in their community are more likely to watch a lot of television. Nor is it clear that television news undermines support for the political system. One study found that regular viewers of news programs display "higher than average levels of political interest, efficacy, knowledge, and social trust."[122] If this finding applies to Canada, it implies that the media have been unjustly blamed for negative attitudes toward politics: "too often we are 'blaming the messenger' for more deep-rooted ills of the body politic."[123] It is possible that cynical news coverage sours our perceptions of individual politicians, but these perceptions do not appear to contaminate the political institutions in which they operate. One possible exception is the House of Commons, which, as we have seen, inspires less confidence among Canadians than other parts of the political system. Is it purely coincidental that the loss of public confidence in Parliament followed the introduction of television cameras into the Commons? (See Chapter 5.)

CURRENT DEBATES ABOUT CANADA'S POLITICAL INSTITUTIONS

The existence of multiple subcultures with varying levels of political satisfaction inevitably creates political tensions. These tensions flare into open conflict during public debates over institutional reform. During the 1980s and early 1990s, repeated rounds of "megaconstitutional politics" (see Chapter 1) revealed the depth of subcultural disagreements over the nature and purpose of Canada's political institutions. Although the rejection of the Charlottetown Accord in 1992 marked a suspension of megaconstitutional politics, debates over institutional reform persist. We will conclude by discussing two of these debates.

Representative Democracy versus Direct Democracy

Critics of representative democracy blame declining public confidence on the lack of direct citizen involvement in policy-making. They want to reform, or even bypass, Canada's existing political institutions by resorting to direct-democracy devices: referenda (the plural of "referendum"), initiatives, and recall. In referenda and initiatives, voters determine the outcome of a particular policy debate by voting "yes" or "no" on a ballot question. Referenda are sponsored by governments, whereas initiatives are triggered by the citizens. A "recall" is an organized campaign to remove a legislator from office between elections. In both initiative and recall campaigns, the organizers must collect and submit signatures on a petition. If they collect enough verified signatures, the government is required to hold a vote—on a particular policy question, in the former case, or on the legislator's right to remain in office in the latter instance. A successful recall vote will normally trigger a special election to choose a replacement for the ousted official.

Referenda and initiatives can be categorized in at least three different ways: binding–advisory, direct–indirect, and positive–negative:

1. The results of binding referenda and initiatives must be enacted into law by the appropriate government. Advisory results may legally be disregarded by political elites, although this strategy carries obvious political risks. (Advisory votes are often called "plebiscites.")

2. Direct votes bypass representative political institutions altogether, and have the force of law as soon as the results are announced; in indirect votes, the question must be approved by the legislature before it goes to the people.

3. Positive votes create new legislation or determine the direction of future legislation, whereas negative or "abrogative" votes strike down existing legislation.[124]

There has been considerable debate in recent years over the introduction of direct-democracy devices into Canadian politics. For populists, direct democracy is the only way to ensure that "the voice of the people" is reflected in public decision-making. Postmaterialists also welcome direct democracy, because it bypasses traditional hierarchies and gives every citizen an equal right to participate. For those who do not share this enthusiasm for individualist, egalitarian politics, direct democracy represents a threat to Canada's system of representative democracy. The controversy is briefly summarized in Dossier 2.4.

DOSSIER 2.4 The Case for and against Referenda, Initiatives, and Recall

The case for referenda and initiatives is straightforward: they allow citizens to govern themselves directly, at least in particular policy areas. As a result, citizens will take a more active interest in, and become more informed about, politics and policy-making.[125] The arguments against referenda and initiatives are more numerous. First, they allow governments to avoid making decisions on difficult issues.[126] Second, they artificially reduce complex issues to "yes" and "no" opposites, and in so doing they divide the electorate without hope of compromise or healing.[127] Third, instead of giving "the people" control over policy-making, they provide an opportunity for wealthy interest groups to "buy" favourable legislation—or, more commonly,

to defeat unfavourable legislation.[128] An entire "initiative industry" has sprung up in the United States: "law firms that draft legislation, petition management firms that guarantee ballot access, direct-mail firms, and campaign consultants who specialize in initiative contests across several states."[129]

Fourth, skeptics argue that "the people are not informed or caring enough to vote on complicated public policy issues."[130] Those who do vote may be motivated by irrational prejudices—either against unpopular minorities or against the government leaders sponsoring a given referendum—or they may simply be too confused to understand what's best for them. Although this argument may be somewhat overstated, there is some evidence to substantiate it.

The "no" side won the 1992 Charlottetown Accord referendum partly for reasons unrelated to its actual content: the personal unpopularity of Prime Minister Mulroney,[131] and the widespread perception among English Canadians that Quebec would never be satisfied, no matter how much the rest of the country tried to accommodate its demands.[132] These findings are typical of most referenda and initiatives.

Finally, critics allege that referenda and initiatives inflame hostility against minority groups and that initiatives provide bigots with a golden opportunity to persecute their targets. These critics point to several recent American initiatives that asked voters in particular states or municipalities to restrict the rights of gays and lesbians, illegal immigrants, and anyone whose first language was not English.[133] Defenders of direct democracy point out that the success rate of municipal anti-minority initiatives was higher than that of state-wide initiatives,[134] and that policies that violated constitutional rights were subsequently overturned by the courts. Opponents of direct democracy counter that the public debate surrounding a discriminatory initiative question deepens the stigmas attached to the targeted groups and permanently reduces the majority's tolerance for "difference."[135]

Advocates of recall argue that voters should not be forced to "wait until the next election to rid themselves of an incompetent, dishonest, unresponsive, or irresponsible public official."[136] Critics argue that recall campaigns are "divisive, disruptive, polarizing, and subject to a myriad of abuses and unintended consequences."[137] They point to the United States, where some recall petitions have been motivated by opposing political parties, resentful interest groups, or "sore losers" in the previous election. The 2003 election of Arnold Schwarzenegger as governor of California is a case in point.[138] A Republican state legislator spearheaded a recall drive to remove Democratic Governor Gray Davis from office, to capitalize on public anger against tax increases to deal with the state's massive budget deficit. Under California law, a recall vote must be accompanied by a special election to fill the post that would be vacated if the recall succeeded. Unlike a regular gubernatorial election, the candidates are not selected in party primaries; anyone can run against the challenged incumbent. Schwarzenegger, a relatively moderate Republican on social issues, would not have been chosen by his party's strongly conservative primary voters. For better or worse, California voters ejected an experienced governor and replaced him, not with the lieutenant governor or a seasoned legislator, but with a wealthy political amateur whose movie-star persona and populist rhetoric promised few sustainable solutions to the problems facing California.

Canada's Royal Commission on Electoral Reform and Party Financing rejected recall for three primary reasons: the recall is inconsistent with a parliamentary system, especially one in which voters are more influenced by partisanship than by individual candidates; it makes little sense to require an MP elected by less than a majority of her constituents to win a majority in a subsequent recall vote; and government would be disrupted if a Cabinet minister or the prime minister were targeted by political opponents.[139]

▉ "Old Politics" versus "New Politics"

Whereas the debate over representative versus direct democracy revolves around the need to reform existing political institutions, the conflict between "old" and "new" politics concerns the legitimacy of political institutions themselves. "Old" politics is about resolving common problems through hierarchical structures such as political parties and Parliaments. The key issue is the production and distribution of material wealth. "New" politics rejects traditional institutions in favour of unconventional political activities, challenges established authorities, and emphasizes quality of life issues: equal rights, reproductive freedom, the environment, assistance to developing countries, and global peace. It is the political manifestation of postmaterialism.[140]

In one respect, the phrase "new politics" is inaccurate. Dissatisfied citizens have always resorted to unconventional protest activities. What is new about "new politics" is the growing readiness to resort to such tactics, especially among postmaterialists. Between 1981 and 1990, the proportion of Canadian respondents to the World Values Survey who reported prior engagement in protest activity rose from 23.6 percent to 32.5 percent. Those who expressed unwillingness to protest dwindled from 67.9 to 56.9 percent of respondents.[141] Contrary to the old stereotype of the passive, deferential Canadian, the World Values Survey found that Canadians were more protest-oriented than Europeans or Americans. If the influence of postmaterialism continues to grow, our political institutions may be confronted with ever more frequent public expressions of dissent.

The recent emergence of the antiglobalization movement provides a dramatic illustration of the conflict between "old" and "new" political values. Political leaders and police have reacted to protests in Vancouver, Windsor, and Quebec City with escalating violence and a disturbing disregard for *Charter* rights (particularly freedom of expression and peaceful assembly). When students at the University of British Columbia expressed their opposition to the human-rights record of former Indonesian President Suharto at the 1997 Asia–Pacific Economic Conference (APEC) summit in Vancouver, some were pepper-sprayed; others were arrested without due process.[142] The April 2001 Summit of the Americas in Quebec City attracted thousands of demonstrators. While a small minority engaged in unjustifiable violence against people and property, most were attracted by the chance to peacefully express their opposition to trade deals that did not ensure protection for the environment and the rights of workers. Police used plastic bullets and tear gas to keep them away from the Summit site and arrested hundreds of protesters without laying criminal charges (a clear violation of the *Charter*). These are not isolated incidents, as the less publicized events in Windsor demonstrate (see Dossier 2.5). While violence in the pursuit of political ends is rarely, if ever, justified, the failure of police and other authorities to differentiate between the peaceful majority and the handful of troublemakers is disturbing.

Until our governments, police, and courts find more positive and measured ways to respond to "new" politics, the legitimacy of "old" politics may well continue to decline. Postmaterialist critiques of the political system go well beyond the current prime minister and Cabinet; they challenge the core values that underlie the authority structures inherent in our political institutions.

In June 2000 the Organization of American States (OAS) held its annual General Assembly in Windsor, Ontario. Local unions, artists, and social activists organized public protests and teach-ins to express their concerns about globalization. While a few protesters engaged in unjustifiably violent activities, most tried to make their point peacefully. Some demonstrators were pepper-sprayed; some were arrested and taken to a "secret jail." The following chronology describes the "new politics" tactics used by the protesters, and the police response.[143]

June 3

Morning	Legal training, civil disobedience training, street medic training
3:00 p.m.	Teach-in sponsored by the Canadian Labour Congress

June 4

10:00 a.m.	Forum on Human Rights and Democracy
12:00 p.m.	Rally at City Hall Square
1:00 p.m.	March to waterfront, speeches
2:30 p.m.	Students attempt to hang banner on fence and are pepper-sprayed

June 5

3:00 a.m.	42 people arrested the previous day are released in a mall parking lot

11:00 a.m.	March to site of OAS luncheon, which is filled with Ontario Provincial Police (OPP) and RCMP tactical squads and riot police
12:00 p.m.	March around the park, hold teach-in surrounded by plain-clothes and undercover police

June 6

11:25 a.m.	Meet at Walkerville High School for rally
12:00 p.m.	Approximately 20 to 25 OPP and Windsor police arrive and target six activists peacefully assembled on sidewalk for arbitrary arrest
3:00 p.m.	Teach-in at City Hall, surrounded by police
4:00 p.m.	Information received that the police plan to move arrested protesters to jails around province
5:30 p.m.	Protest march in front of "secret jail" carrying signs "Political Views Are Not a Crime"
5:45 p.m.	Police order protesters to disperse
7:00 p.m.	OPP riot police arrive
7:15 p.m.	Riot police physically force protesters to move
7:30 p.m.	Protesters continue marching
8:00 p.m.	Riot police surround and arrest eight people, using extreme force

CONCLUSION

The changing political values discussed in this chapter are at the core of Canadian politics. The aggressive Quebec nationalism mobilized by the Quiet Revolution provoked several rounds of constitutional negotiations in the past 40 years. Those negotiations revealed both the depth of Western alienation and the incompatibility of Quebec's "two-nations" perspective with the "equal-provinces" vision cherished by English Canadians. While some of our national institutions, notably the federal system, are flexible enough to adapt to changing values without formal constitutional amendment, others are more difficult to reform.

The process for resolving those territorial conflicts is complicated by growing postmaterialist values and populist demands for direct democracy. The *Canadian Charter of Rights and Freedoms* has become the institutional focus for postmaterialists, who have sought to use its provisions to change public policy even while mobilizing to defend it against territorial political elites. The apparent impossibility of formal constitutional amendment has forced governments to fall back on other methods of institutional adaptation, such as constitutional conventions and nonentrenched agreements between governments. The very meaning of the *Charter* itself is hotly disputed between the ideological left and right, and only partially resolved by the Supreme Court's powers to strike down and amend legislation. As we will see in Chapters 3 and 4, it is impossible to understand Canadian politics without an awareness of our evolving—and often conflicting—political values and ideologies.

GLOSSARY OF KEY TERMS

Allophone: A person whose mother tongue is neither English nor French. The largest allophone populations in Canada speak either Chinese or Italian.

Anglophone: English-speaking. For statistical purposes, the term "anglophone" normally refers to those Canadians who claim English as their mother tongue.

Cleavage: A politically significant distinction among identifiable groups in a given population. Examples: Catholic versus Protestant, religious versus nonobservant, French versus English, working class versus middle class, centre versus periphery, materialist versus postmaterialist. A distinction among groups becomes politically significant when it affects voting behaviour and/or attitudes toward political institutions. Cleavage structures change over time, as new cleavages emerge (e.g., materialism versus postmaterialism) and as older cleavages either acquire new political significance (e.g., the French–English cleavage) or lose their historic significance (e.g., the Catholic–Protestant cleavage).

Demography: The distribution of certain personal characteristics among a particular population. Key demographic indicators include race, ethnicity, language, religion, age, and gender.

Direct democracy: The citizens govern themselves directly, at least in part, by making decisions about policies or the structure of government through the ballot box.

Francophone: French-speaking. For statistical purposes, the term "francophone" normally refers to those Canadians who claim French as their mother tongue.

Hierarchy: A social system arranged like a pyramid, in which those at the top control a disproportionate share of power (political, social, economic, or religious), while those at the bottom are virtually powerless. The criteria by which the members of the various ranks are chosen vary from culture to culture. In a monarchical society, birth determines one's place in the hierarchy: the king or queen is born to rule, (male) aristocrats are born to wealth and privilege, and the majority of the population are born to serve and to be ruled by their "betters." Other hierarchies are based on money, gender (generally speaking, men are more politically powerful than women), race (e.g., the former apartheid system in South Africa), or military prowess.

Ideology: A partial picture of the world, comprising stories about the past, explanations of the present, and a blueprint for the future. Because each ideology is only a partial picture, it must compete with other ideologies for political influence. It is both *empirical* (a description of the way things are) and *normative* (a prescription for how things should be).

Mobilization: The process by which a distinct group within an electorate is transformed into a politically influential subculture. Typically, a political leader from within the group begins to organize members into a cohesive entity with shared goals and values. In the absence of mobilization, a subculture remains latent; its members do not recognize their potential for collective action, and their common goals (if any) remain unexpressed within the political system. Examples of salient subcultures include Quebec nationalists and Western (especially Alberta) populists; postmaterialists may be a latent subculture, because they have not formed a unified organization with a clear political agenda.

Orientation: The psychological response of a particular individual toward a social object. In political terms, the degree to which a citizen internalizes or adopts prevailing social attitudes toward the political system as a whole, its individual parts, the elites who run it, and the laws that it creates and implements.

Patronage: The appointment of party supporters to public office, resting on the exercise of the Crown prerogative by the head of government.

Political culture: "The politically relevant values, attitudes, beliefs, and symbols that exert an unseen but crucial influence on the political life of a society. Political culture helps shape the outlook and discourse of both ordinary citizens and political leaders. It affects the way they react and talk to one another, the problems they consider politically significant, the kinds of solutions and government policies deemed legitimate."[144]

Political socialization: The absorption of political knowledge and values by individual citizens. Socialization begins in childhood, with exposure to the political orientations of the parents. It continues in school, peer groups, and adult life. The process is not linear; many adolescents reject their parents' political values, only to return to them later. Orientations often change over time, as the citizen learns more about politics and acquires different life experiences (raising a family, losing a job, retiring). Orientations can also change in response to major political events.

Populism: See Dossier 2.1, page 35.

Postmaterialism: See Dossier 2.1, page 36.

Prerogative powers: "The residue of discretionary or arbitrary authority which at any given time is legally left in the hands of the Crown."[145] Over the past millennium, the virtually unlimited power enjoyed by British monarchs has been reduced to a tiny sphere of "reserve powers," to be employed only in emergencies. Most of the executive, legislative, and judicial powers of the Crown are now exercised by the Cabinet, Parliament, and the courts, respectively. The prerogative remains an important source of executive authority, especially over appointments—e.g., senators, ambassadors, and federal judges—and is, therefore, the ultimate source of political patronage.

Regionalism: A feeling of attachment to a particular part of the country. That part can be a province (e.g., Alberta), a group of provinces (the Atlantic region), or an area within a province (Northern Ontario). Regionalism has both positive and negative aspects. On the positive side, it provides a sense of belonging and community. The negative aspect of regionalism is a sense of grievance against the central government and other regions—a belief that Ottawa discriminates against your region, or that other regions are reaping greater benefits from Confederation. Gibbins defines regionalism as "the intrusion of territorial cleavages into national politics."[146]

Representative democracy: A division of labour between rulers and the ruled. The citizens elect MPs to legislate on their behalf; if they are not satisfied with the results, they can defeat their MP at the next general election.

Subculture: A distinct and relatively stable group within the broader electorate. It may be distinguished by language (e.g., Canadian francophones), by ethnicity, by religion, by ideology (e.g., postmaterialists), or by region (e.g., Manitoba or Newfoundland). To be politically influential, a subculture must be cohesive and mobilized. In other words, its members must share some basic political principles that they are prepared to work hard to defend. Subcultures affect Canadian politics in various ways: they can form pressure groups to influence public policy (see Chapter 7), they can express their views through a political party (see Chapter 3), or they can simply withdraw from political activity altogether if they become alienated from a political system that appears to be unresponsive to their demands.

DISCUSSION QUESTIONS

1. What are the principal features of Canada's political culture? How did they evolve?

2. What are the primary differences among the ideologies described in Dossier 2.1?

3. How and why has Canada's political culture changed in recent years? How, if at all, should our national institutions change in response to shifting political values?

4. Explain the concept of mobilization. Why is it crucial to the political influence of a distinct group within the electorate? How does it relate to the structure of our existing political institutions?

SUGGESTED READINGS

David V.J. Bell, *The Roots of Disunity: A Study of Canadian Political Culture,* rev. edition (Toronto: Oxford University Press, 1992).

Robert Bothwell, *Canada and Quebec: One Country, Two Histories,* rev. edition (Vancouver: UBC Press, 1998).

Alan C. Cairns, *Charter versus Federalism: The Dilemmas of Constitutional Reform* (Montreal and Kingston: McGill–Queen's University Press, 1992).

Harold D. Clarke, Allan Kornberg, and Peter Wearing, *A Polity on the Edge: Canada and the Politics of Fragmentation* (Peterborough, ON: Broadview Press, 2000).

Paul Howe and David Northrup, *Strengthening Canadian Democracy: The Views of Canadians* (Montreal: Institute for Research on Public Policy, 2000).

John Meisel, Guy Rocher, and Arthur Silver, eds., *As I Recall/Si je me souviens bien: Historical Perspectives* (Montreal: Institute for Research on Public Policy, 1999).

Pippa Norris, ed., *Critical Citizens: Global Support for Democratic Governance* (Oxford: Oxford University Press, 1999).

Susan J. Pharr and Robert D. Putnam, eds., *Disaffected Democracies: What's Troubling the Trilateral Countries?* (Princeton: Princeton University Press, 2000).

Robert D. Putnam, *Bowling Alone: The Collapse and Revival of American Community* (New York: Simon and Schuster, 2000).

David E. Smith, *The Invisible Crown: The First Principle of Canadian Government* (Toronto: University of Toronto Press, 1995).

Lisa Young and Keith Archer, eds., *Regionalism and Party Politics in Canada* (Toronto: Oxford University Press, 2002).

NOTES

1. Gabriel A. Almond and Sidney Verba, *The Civic Culture: Political Attitudes and Democracy in Five Nations* (Princeton: Princeton University Press, 1963), 5.

2. Ibid., 13.

3. Ibid., 15.

4. Pippa Norris, "Introduction: The Growth of Critical Citizens?" in Pippa Norris, ed., *Critical Citizens: Global Support for Democratic Governance* (Oxford: Oxford University Press, 1999), 10–12.

5. Ibid., 10.

6. Almond and Verba, 32.

7. See, for example, Carole Pateman, "The Civic Culture: A Philosophic Critique," in Gabriel A. Almond and Sidney Verba, eds., *The Civic Culture Revisited* (Newbury Park, CA: Sage, 1989 [1980]).

8. Almond and Verba, *The Civic Culture,* 21.

9. Larry Diamond, "Introduction: Political Culture and Democracy," in Larry Diamond, ed., *Political Culture and Democracy in Developing Countries* (Boulder, CO: Lynne Rienner, 1993), 8.

10. Shawn Henry, "Revisiting Western Alienation: Towards a Better Understanding of Political Alienation and Political Behaviour in Western Canada," in Lisa Young and Keith Archer, eds., *Regionalism and Party Politics in Canada* (Toronto: Oxford University Press, 2002), 85.

11. David V.J. Bell, *The Roots of Disunity: A Study of Canadian Political Culture,* rev. edition (Toronto: Oxford University Press, 1992), 11.

12. Although Canada has a Liberal Party and a Conservative Party, these names do not necessarily describe the parties' respective ideologies. The Liberals are a broad political coalition, within which differing ideas are brokered into compromise positions. The Liberal Party has many members who might be described as right wing, and others who are clearly somewhat to the left. We will return to the subject of party ideologies in Chapter 3.

13. Colin Campbell and William Christian, *Parties, Leaders, and Ideologies in Canada* (Toronto: McGraw-Hill Ryerson, 1996), 12–13.

14. Roger Gibbins, "Shifting Sands: Exploring the Political Foundations of SUFA," in Sarah Fortin, Alain Noël, and France St-Hilaire, eds., *Forging the Canadian Social Union: SUFA and Beyond* (Montreal: Institute for Research on Public Policy, 2003), 43.

15. Louis Hartz, "The Fragmentation of European Culture and Ideology," in Louis Hartz, ed., *The Founding of New Societies* (New York: Harcourt Brace, 1964).

16. Hartz, "Fragmentation Patterns: Feudal, Liberal, and Radical" in Hartz, ed., *The Founding of New Societies,* 27; see also Kenneth D. McRae, "The Structure of Canadian History," in the same volume.

17. Bell, 19.

18. Gad Horowitz, "Conservatism, Liberalism, and Socialism in Canada: An Interpretation," in *Canadian Labour in Politics* (Toronto: University of Toronto Press, 1968).

19. Janet Ajzenstat and Peter J. Smith, "Liberal–Republicanism: The Revisionist Picture of Canada's Founding," in Janet Ajzenstat and Peter J. Smoth, eds., *Canada's Origins: Liberal, Tory, or Republican?* (Ottawa: Carleton University Press, 1995), 1–18.

20. Hamish Telford, "The Reform Party/Canadian Alliance and Canada's Flirtation with Republicanism," in Hamish Telford and Harvey Lazar, eds., *The State of the Federation 2001: Canadian Political Culture(s) in Transition* (Montreal and Kingston: McGill–Queen's University Press/Institute of Intergovernmental Relations, 2002), 119.

21. Hamish Telford and Harvey Lazar, "Canadian Political Culture(s) in Transition and the State of the Federation," in Telford and Lazar, eds., *Canadian Political Culture(s) in Transition,* 4.

22. Paul Howe and Joseph F. Fletcher, "The Evolution of Charter Values," in Telford and Lazar, eds., *Canadian Political Culture(s) in Transition,* Table 1, 269.

23. Ibid., Table 1, 269.

24. Bell, 131.

25. Neil Nevitte, *The Decline of Deference: Canadian Value Change in Cross-National Perspective* (Peterborough, ON: Broadview Press, 1996), Tables 9-3 and 9-5, 296 and 308, respectively.

26. See, for example, S.M. Lipset, *Revolution and Counterrevolution: Change and Persistence in Social Structures,* rev. edition (New Brunswick, NJ: Transaction Books, 1988 [1970]), Chapter 2.

27. Bell, 23.

28. Lipset, 67–71.

29. McRae, "The Structure of Canadian History," 231.

30. Harry H. Hiller, "Region as a Social Construction," in Young and Archer, eds., *Regionalism and Party Politics in Canada,* 26.

31. See, for example, John Meisel, Guy Rocher, and Arthur Silver, eds., *As I Recall/Si je me souviens bien: Historical Perspectives* (Montreal: Institute for Research on Public Policy, 1999); Robert Bothwell, *Canada and Quebec: One Country, Two Histories,* rev. edition (Vancouver: UBC Press, 1998).

32. Gordon T. Stewart, *The Origins of Canadian Politics: A Comparative Approach* (Vancouver: UBC Press, 1986), 3; Elizabeth Mancke, "Early Modern Imperial Governance and the Origins of Canadian Political Culture," *Canadian Journal of Political Science,* XXXII: 1 (March 1999), 7–8.

33. Bell, 50; see also Stewart, 3–4.

34. Robert Finbow, "Ideology and Institutions in North America," *Canadian Journal of Political Science,* XXVI:4 (December 1993), 679–80.

35. James Johnston, attorney general of Nova Scotia; speech to the Nova Scotia House of Assembly, March 28, 1864. Reproduced in Janet Ajzenstat, Paul Romney, Ian Gentles, and William D. Gairdner, eds., *Canada's Founding Debates* (Toronto: University of Toronto Press, 2003), 169.

36. Stewart, 30–31.

37. Ibid., 95.

38. Sir John A. Macdonald in *Parliamentary Debates on the Subject of Confederation of the British North American Provinces* (1865), p. 42; J.M. Beck, *The Shaping of Canadian Federalism: Central Authority or Provincial Right?* (Toronto: Copp Clark, 1971), 60.

39. *Liquidators of the Maritime Bank of Canada v. Receiver-General of New Brunswick* [1892] J.C., in Richard A. Olmsted, ed., *Decisions of the Judicial Committee of the Privy Council,* volume 1 (Ottawa: Queen's Printer, 1954), 270.

40. David E. Smith, *The Invisible Crown: The First Principle of Canadian Government* (Toronto: University of Toronto Press, 1995), 23.

41. Source: Nelson website (www.parametersofpower4e.nelson.com); click on "Canadian Politics on the Web," then on "Aboriginal Issues," and then on "The Royal Proclamation, 1763."

42. Smith, 177.

43. Bernard W. Funston and Eugene Meehan, *Canada's Constitutional Law in a Nutshell*, 2nd edition (Toronto: Carswell, 1998), 147.

44. See Christopher McKee, *Treaty Talks in British Columbia: Negotiating a Mutually Beneficial Future*, 2nd edition (Vancouver: UBC Press, 2000), 6; Ken Coates, *The Marshall Decision and Native Rights* (Montreal and Kingston: McGill–Queen's University Press, 2000), 81.

45. Nevitte, 86.

46. Bell, 123.

47. Munroe Eagles, "Political Geography and the Study of Regionalism," in Young and Archer, eds., *Regionalism and Party Politics in Canada,* 13–14.

48. Statistics Canada, 2001 census data; accessed at www.statcan.gc.ca.

49. Ralph Matthews, *The Creation of Regional Dependency* (Toronto: University of Toronto Press, 1983), 22.

50. Russell J. Dalton, "Political Cleavages, Issues, and Electoral Change," in Lawrence LeDuc, Richard G. Niemi, and Pippa Norris, eds., *Comparing Democracies: Elections and Voting in Global Perspective* (Thousand Oaks, CA: Sage, 1996), Table 3.1, 325.

51. Fred Cutler and Richard W. Jenkins, "Where One Lives and What One Thinks: Implications of Rural–Urban Opinion Cleavages for Canadian Federalism," in Telford and Lazar, eds., *Canadian Political Culture(s) in Transition,* 367–90.

52. Nevitte, Tables 7-3 and 9-5, 220 and 308, respectively. See also Michael Adams, *Fire and Ice: The United States, Canada and the Myth of Converging Values* (Toronto: Penguin Canada, 2003), 82–83.

53. The number of respondents who claimed Aboriginal status was 976 305. However, the difficulties of administering the census on some reserves may have artificially lowered the true number. Source: Statistics Canada (www.statcan.gc.ca).

54. Statistics Canada, "Aboriginal Identity Population, 2001 Counts, for Canada, Provinces and Territories," accessed at www.statcan.gc.ca.

55. Howe and Fletcher, 277–78.

56. For a relatively accessible introduction to Marxist theory, see Karl Marx and Friedrich Engels, *The Communist Manifesto* (Harmondsworth: Penguin, 1967 [1848]), Chapters 1 and 2.

57. See, for example, Dalton, "Political Cleavages, Issues, and Electoral Change," 325.

58. Janine Brodie and Jane Jenson, *Crisis, Challenge and Change: Party and Class in Canada Revisited* (Ottawa: Carleton University Press, 1988).

59. It should be pointed out that the theory of postmaterialism, despite the name, is actually grounded in a materialist analysis of history. According to Ronald Inglehart, who first formulated the theory, postmaterialist values flourish in a thriving economy and in the absence of direct threats to physical security. Therefore, to argue that Canadians are increasingly attracted to postmaterialist values does not imply that we are no longer influenced by materialism; rather, it means that material scarcity is no longer the only driving force in political conflict. See Ronald Inglehart, *The Silent Revolution: Changing Values and Political Styles* (Princeton: Princeton University Press, 1977); *Culture Shift in Advanced Industrial Society* (Princeton: Princeton University Press, 1990); *Modernization*

and Postmodernization: Cultural, Economic, and Political Change in 43 Societies (Princeton: Princeton University Press, 1997).

60. See also Nevitte, 32–33, and Bell, Chapter One.

61. Nevitte, 311.

62. Adams, 52 and 95.

63. Harold D. Clarke, Allan Kornberg, and Peter Wearing, *A Polity on the Edge: Canada and the Politics of Fragmentation* (Peterborough, ON: Broadview Press, 2000), 47 and 163.

64. Neil Nevitte, "Introduction: Value Change and Reorientation in Citizen–State Relations," in Neil Nevitte, ed., *Value Change and Governance in Canada* (Toronto: University of Toronto Press, 2002), 20.

65. On the possible emergence of "transnational" notions of citizenship, especially among immigrants and their children, see Will Kymlicka, "New Forms of Citizenship," in Thomas J. Courchene and Donald J. Savoie, eds., *The Art of the State: Governance in a World Without Frontiers* (Montreal: Institute for Research on Public Policy, 2003), 265–309.

66. Nevitte, "Introduction," 20. See also Richard Nadeau, "Satisfaction with Democracy: The Canadian Paradox," in Nevitte, ed., *Value Change and Governance in Canada*, 37–70.

67. Clarke, Kornberg, and Wearing, 47.

68. Paul Howe and David Northrup, *Strengthening Canadian Democracy: The Views of Canadians* (Montreal: Institute for Research on Public Policy, 2000), 6.

69. Russell J. Dalton, "Political Support in Advanced Industrial Democracies," in Pippa Norris, ed., *Critical Citizens*, 75.

70. Arthur Miller and Ola Listhaug, "Political Performance and Institutional Trust," in Pippa Norris, ed., *Critical Citizens*, 210.

71. Norris, "Institutional Explanations for Political Support," *Critical Citizens*.

72. Howe and Northrup, 64–65.

73. Miller and Listhaug, 209; Clarke, Kornberg, and Wearing, 74–75.

74. Robert D. Putnam, Susan J. Pharr, and Russell J. Dalton, "Introduction: What's Troubling the Trilateral Democracies?" in Susan J. Pharr and Robert D. Putnam, eds., *Disaffected Democracies: What's Troubling the Trilateral Countries?* (Princeton: Princeton University Press, 2000), 10.

75. Ibid., 23.

76. Nevitte, "Introduction," 21–23.

77. Ibid., 10.

78. Clarke, Kornberg, and Wearing, 127–29.

79. Ian McAllister, "The Economic Performance of Governments," in Pippa Norris, ed., *Critical Citizens*, 195.

80. Howe and Northrup, 9; Mebs Kanji, "Political Discontent, Human Capital, and Representative Governance in Canada," in Neil Nevitte, ed., *Value Change and Governance in Canada*, 79.

81. Howe and Northrup, 100.

82. Norris, "The Growth of Critical Citizens?," *Critical Citizens*, 13.

83. Howe and Northrup, Table 2, 7.

84. Kenneth McRoberts, *Quebec: Social Change and Political Crisis*, 3rd edition (Toronto: McClelland and Stewart, 1988), Chapter 4.

85. Ronald Inglehart, *The Silent Revolution: Changing Values and Political Styles* (Princeton: Princeton University Press, 1977); *Culture Shift in Advanced Industrial Society* (Princeton: Princeton University Press, 1990); *Modernization and Postmodernization: Cultural, Economic, and Political Change in 43 Societies* (Princeton: Princeton University Press, 1997).

86. Nevitte, *The Decline of Deference*, 54.

87. Ibid., 75.

88. Ibid., Table 2-2, 31.

89. Howe and Fletcher, 280.

90. Nevitte, *The Decline of Deference*, 54.

91. Ibid., 62.

92. Ian Brodie and Neil Nevitte, "Evaluating the Citizens' Constitution Theory," *Canadian Journal of Political Science*, XXVI:2 (June 1993), 235–59.

93. Russell J. Dalton, "Political Support in Advanced Industrial Democracies," in Norris, ed., *Critical Citizens*, 75; Miller and Listhaug, 216; Putnam, Pharr, and Dalton.

94. Putnam, Pharr and Dalton, 23.

95. Susan J. Pharr, "Officials' Misconduct and Public Distrust: Japan and the Trilateral Democracies," and Donatella della Porta, "Social Capital, Beliefs in Government, and Political Corruption," both in Pharr and Putnam.

96. Howe and Northrup, Figures 1 and 2 and Table 25, 9, 10, and 43, respectively.

97. McAllister, 201; Miller and Listhaug, 207.

98. Richard Johnston, "Business Cycles, Political Cycles and the Popularity of Canadian Governments, 1974–1998," *Canadian Journal of Political Science*, XXXII:3 (September 1999), 499–520. Note, however, the contrary findings in Calum M. Carmichael, "Economic Conditions and the Popularity of the Incumbent Party in Canada," *Canadian Journal of Political Science*, XXIII:4 (December 1990), 713–26.

99. Alan C. Cairns, *Disruptions: Constitutional Struggles, from the Charter to Meech Lake,* edited by Douglas E. Williams (Toronto: McClelland and Stewart, 1991).

100. Alan C. Cairns, *Charter versus Federalism: The Dilemmas of Constitutional Reform* (Montreal and Kingston: McGill–Queen's University Press, 1992), 3.

101. F.L. Morton and Rainer Knopff, *The Charter Revolution and the Court Party* (Peterborough, ON: Broadview Press, 2000).

102. Brodie and Nevitte, 258.

103. Howe and Fletcher, 274.

104. Howe and Northrup, Table 24, 42.

105. Ibid., 49.

106. See, for example, Robert D. Putnam, "Bowling Alone: America's Declining Social Capital," in Larry Diamond and Marc F. Plattner, eds., *The Global Resurgence of Democracy*, 2nd edition (Baltimore, MD: Johns Hopkins University Press, 1996); Putnam, *The Decline of Civil Society: How Come? So What?* (Ottawa: Canadian Centre for Management Development, 1996); Putnam, *Bowling Alone: The Collapse and Revival of American Community* (New York: Simon and Schuster, 2000).

107. Putnam, *Bowling Alone*, 288–89.

108. Ibid., 342–43.

109. Ibid., 347.

110. Ibid., 336.

111. Ibid., 341.

112. See, for example, Eric M. Uslaner, "Democracy and Social Capital," in Mark E. Warren, ed., *Democracy and Trust* (Cambridge: Cambridge University Press, 1999).

113. Richard A. Couto with Catherine S. Guthrie, *Making Democracy Work Better: Mediating Structures, Social Capital, and the Democratic Prospect* (Chapel Hill: University of North Carolina Press, 1999), 68.

114. Kenneth Newton, "Social and Political Trust in Established Democracies," in Pippa Norris, ed., *Critical Citizens,* 172–73.

115. Ibid., 180.

116. Ibid., 181–86 passim.

117. Kenneth Newton and Pippa Norris, "Confidence in Public Institutions: Faith, Culture, or Performance?" in Pharr and Putnam, eds., *Disaffected Democracies,* 72.

118. Putnam, *Bowling Alone,* 229.

119. Thomas E. Patterson, *Out of Order* (New York: Vintage, 1994); David Taras, *The Newsmakers: The Media's Influence on Canadian Politics* (Toronto: Nelson, 1990).

120. Neil Postman, *Amusing Ourselves to Death: Public Discourse in the Age of Show Business* (Harmondsworth: Penguin, 1985); Benjamin I. Page, *Who Deliberates? Mass Media in Modern Democracy* (Chicago: University of Chicago Press, 1996).

121. Pippa Norris, "The Impact of Television on Civic Malaise," in Pharr and Putnam, eds., *Disaffected Democracies,* Table 10.4, 238.

122. Ibid., 246.

123. Pippa Norris, *A Virtuous Circle: Political Communications in Postindustrial Societies* (Cambridge: Cambridge University Press, 2000), 20.

124. Ian Budge, *The New Challenge of Direct Democracy* (Cambridge: Polity Press, 1996), 101.

125. Todd Donovan and Shaun Bowler, "An Overview of Direct Democracy in the American States," in Shaun Bowler, Todd Donovan, and Caroline J. Tolbert, eds., *Citizens as Legislators: Direct Democracy in the United States* (Columbus: Ohio State University Press, 1998), 2; Thomas E. Cronin, *Direct Democracy: The Politics of Initiative, Referendum, and Recall* (Cambridge, MA: Harvard University Press, 1989), 182–83.

126. Canada, *Royal Commission on Electoral Reform and Party Financing, Reforming Electoral Democracy,* volume 2 (Ottawa: Minister of Supply and Services Canada, 1991), 238.

127. *Reforming Electoral Democracy,* volume 2, 238.

128. Cronin, 109.

129. Donovan and Bowler, 12.

130. Cronin, 61.

131. Lawrence LeDuc and Jon H. Pammett, "Referendum Voting: Attitudes and Behaviour in the 1992 Constitutional Referendum," *Canadian Journal of Political Science,* XXVIII:1 (March 1995), 31.

132. Richard Johnston, André Blais, Elisabeth Gidengil, and Neil Nevitte, *The Challenge of Direct Democracy: The 1992 Canadian Referendum* (Montreal and Kingston: McGill–Queen's University Press, 1996), 177 and 189.

133. Caroline J. Tolbert and Rodney E. Hero, "Race/Ethnicity and Direct Democracy: The Contextual Basis of Support for Anti-Immigrant and Official English Measures," in Bowler, Donovan, and Tolbert, eds., 209–27; Cronin, 94–96.

134. Todd Donovan and Shaun Bowler, "Responsive or Responsible Government?" in Bowler, Donovan, and Tolbert, eds., 270.

135. James Wenzel, Todd Donovan, and Shaun Bowler, "Direct Democracy and Minorities: Changing Attitudes about Minorities Targeted by Initiatives," in Bowler, Donovan, and Tolbert, eds., 245.

136. Cronin, 133.

137. Ibid., 137.

138. See Samuel Issacharoff, "Collateral Damage: The Endangered Center in American Politics," *William and Mary Law Review*, 2005 (downloaded at http://ssrn.com/abstract=508384 on October 15, 2004); Elizabeth Garrett, "Democracy in the Wake of the California Recall," *University of Pennsylvania Law Review*, volume 152, 2004 (downloaded at http://ssrn.com/abstract=487623 on October 15, 2004).

139. *Reforming Electoral Democracy*, volume 2, 245–47.

140. Inglehart, *Modernization and Postmodernization*, Chapter 8; Brodie and Nevitte, 239–40.

141. Nevitte, *The Decline of Deference*, Figure 4-2, 80.

142. W. Wesley Pue, ed., *Pepper in Our Eyes: The APEC Affair* (Vancouver: UBC Press, 2000).

143. Windsor Peace Committee, *Windsor OAS Days of Action: The Criminalization of Dissent* (Windsor, 2001).

144. Bell, 19.

145. Smith, 32.

146. Roger Gibbins, *Regionalism: Territorial Politics in Canada and the United States* (Toronto: Butterworths, 1982), 5.

3

POLITICAL PARTIES AND THE CANADIAN PARTY SYSTEM

LEARNING OBJECTIVES

- *explain* the difference between a cadre or brokerage party and a missionary/ideological party;
- *identify* and *describe* the three "faces" of party organizations and their principal component parts;
- *identify* and *describe* the institutional incentives set for party activists by the political system and by their own party structures;
- *identify* and *explain* the distinctions among the four national party systems in Canada since Confederation.

INTRODUCTION

Political parties are at the heart of Canadian politics. The job of prime minister, the key figure in the legislative and executive branches, goes to the leader of the party with the most seats in the House of Commons. In a practical sense, the power of the prime minister depends to a significant degree on whether his or her party elected a majority or a minority of the MPs. When the House is sitting, the leaders of the various official parties are the stars of the daily Question Period drama. At election time, most of the candidates on the ballot are nominated by party members in our local constituencies. Without political parties, Canadian politics as we know it would cease to function.

The most visible elements of our parties are the **caucuses** in Parliament, made up of MPs and (in the case of the Liberals and Conservatives) senators. But political parties are also **extraparliamentary** organizations, which (in theory) help to bridge the gap between legislators and citizens. Local party members do more than select and recruit candidates for elective office; they also participate in the choice of political leaders, and—together with the national party structures—organize the election campaigns that give voters a choice of governments.[1] The oldest parties have also played a key role in the politics of federalism. They established provincial organizations across the country, which helped to knit together the various regions of Canada into a national political community.

In the past decade or so, Canada's major national parties have experienced numerous changes:

- The number of official parties in the House of Commons rose from three in the 1980s to five in the 1990s; there are now four parties, since the Progressive Conservatives (PCs) and the Canadian Alliance merged in 2003 to form the new Conservative Party of Canada.

- Although the Liberals have won four consecutive elections (1993, 1997, 2000, and 2004), the respective positions of the Opposition parties in Parliament have fluctuated widely. The national Progressive Conservatives lost the support of Quebec nationalists and Western populists in the 1993 election, and spent the next decade struggling to survive. The federal New Democratic Party (NDP) also flirted with extinction in the 1990s. Both parties were sustained by their provincial wings and by financial support from loyal donors (corporations and labour unions, respectively). The Bloc Québécois (BQ), the Quebec nationalist party founded in 1990, surged in the 1993 election and formed the official Opposition with 54 seats. Another new party, the Reform Party of Canada, enjoyed a similar breakthrough in 1993; it placed second with 52 seats. After it failed to expand beyond its Western populist base in 1997, Reform tried to merge with the federal PCs; it failed, but it managed to attract a considerable number of provincial PCs (especially in Ontario and Alberta). It was renamed the Canadian Alliance in 2000. The Alliance did not live up to expectations in the 2000 election, particularly in Ontario. The merger between the Alliance and the federal PCs finally took place in 2003.

- The formal rules of the political game, as set out in the *Canada Elections Act,* have been amended several times. The amendments affect the rules for party registration, financing, constituency nominations, and leadership contests.

- The structures of Canada's national parties have remained more or less intact. They have three "faces": (1) the extraparliamentary party (the volunteer grassroots members); (2) the party in public office (the parliamentary caucus and its paid staff); and (3) the central office, which is occupied by a cadre of professional organizers and technical experts in various fields (e.g., polling and advertising).[2] However, as we will see in this chapter, the relationships among these three faces are changing.

- Perhaps most important, Canada's political parties have lost much of their legitimacy with the public. According to public opinion surveys, a majority of Canadians believe that parties are essential to our democratic system, but this does not translate into trust for elected parliamentarians or party leaders.[3] Fewer and fewer Canadians are voting in elections, in large measure because they do not find the available party options appealing (see Chapter 4).

Despite their recent loss of legitimacy, Canada's major national parties are an indispensable ingredient in our democratic politics. The future health of our democracy will depend in large measure on the capacity of our individual parties, and the national party system as a whole, to adapt to change. If some or all of the institutional reforms discussed elsewhere in this book (e.g., a new electoral system, or a reduction in Cabinet control of the House of Commons) should take place, the parties would also be forced to adapt to the new institutional incentives that would result. Individual parties may fail to adapt, and disappear (as the federal PCs arguably did in 2003[4]), but the party system as a whole must survive if Canada is to remain a democratic state.

In the nineteenth and twentieth centuries, Canadian parties responded to a host of challenges: war, economic crises, the addition of new provinces, rapid economic and social change, and the emergence of new policy issues (e.g., free trade in the 1980s). But now, in the twenty-first century, there is no guarantee that our major parties, individually or collectively, can adapt successfully to the challenges of the new century—in particular, rising populism and declining faith in representative institutions. These developments appear to have reduced Canadians' trust in their political parties, making it more difficult for them to recruit new members and mobilize voters. The broader cultural changes are also evident within parties, where grassroots party members have demanded (and often secured) a more active role in internal decision-making. This trend toward "plebiscitary democracy" within Canadian parties has helped to erode the old hierarchical structures, although the degree of this erosion is open to debate.[5]

The cultural trends have been reinforced by the evolution of communication and computer technologies. There was a time, roughly a century ago, when most Canadians received their political information and opinions from the parties themselves or from newspapers sympathetic to particular parties. Today, we can choose from hundreds of news sources—print, broadcast, online—few of which seem to present political parties or their activities in a positive way. At the same time, the new technologies have altered the balance of power within the party organizations themselves. Whereas constituency MPs and organizers were once the experts on public opinion in their areas, the introduction of sophisticated and relatively inexpensive computers made it possible to survey voters and analyze the results. The new techniques of opinion research produced a new professional cadre of pollsters and **"spin doctors,"** whose position at the upper reaches of party organization is now fully entrenched.

So despite the growing demands of party members for greater influence in party affairs, the important decisions are increasingly delegated to expert technocrats in party headquarters. The party elites become, or appear to become, further distanced from the grassroots. Over time, the party loses its capacity to link the citizens to the state, both during and between elections. Communication breaks down; the accountability of rulers to the ruled becomes less direct. In the end, the health of our democracy will suffer unless our national political parties can find a way to recapture public confidence.

WHAT IS A POLITICAL PARTY?

The way in which we choose to define the phrase "political party" reveals much about our attitudes toward politics. For the framers of the American *Constitution,* "party" was synonymous with "faction"—a divisive and self-seeking body of men whose pursuit of power threatened the unity of the emerging state.[6] This is clearly a negative view of partisanship. More recent definitions of parties generally reflect a more positive attitude, emphasizing the centrality of political parties to representative democracy. According to one leading Canadian scholar:

> *Parties are, first and foremost, organizations which hinge a society to its institutions of government. In democracies they are the channels which structure and deliver the ideas and leaders thrown up by the social order, and the vehicles which organize the political face of the government. National party systems inevitably reflect the society that has spawned them and the institutions within which they live and work.[7]*

The problem with most such definitions is their incompleteness. They focus on one or two aspects of parties—in the above quotation, their crucial intermediary role between the electorate and the state—while omitting others. Parties are not just creatures of their political systems; they are also organizations in their own right, whose leaders and members are motivated by considerations other than "reflecting their society." The following definition emphasizes these motivations, linking them to the incentives set by the institutions of the political system: *A* **political party** *is an organization of members who work together to achieve one or more common goals.* If we break down this definition into its component parts, we can gain a clearer understanding of what parties are, what they do, and why they do it:

- *An organization:* Parties are more or less stable institutions with their own formal constitutions and bylaws, and their own informal rules of behaviour. While there is no hierarchy in practice, it is customary to identify two distinct levels: national (the parliamentary party, central office, and the party executive) and local (the constituency associations). Although we refer to the local constituency parties as the "bottom" level in the party hierarchy, this should not be taken to mean that they are unimportant. In reality, "the constituency association remains at the core of Canadian parties."[8]

- *of members:* In general, party members do not reflect the demographic composition of the electorate. They are considerably more likely to be white, male, middle-aged, prosperous, and highly educated than the average Canadian voter.[9] Party members are unusual in other ways. They make up a tiny proportion of Canadian voters, roughly 2 percent of whom belong to a party at any given time;[10] approximately 16 percent have held a party membership at some point in their lives.[11] Of those who have never belonged to a political party, 89 percent claim that they have never considered doing so.[12] Those few Canadians who do buy party memberships are generally better informed about and more interested in politics than most people, and they hold stronger views about public policies and political principles.

Despite their interest, a recent survey of party members suggests that most are relatively inactive. The large majority of respondents (almost 80 percent) reported that they had spent three hours or less on party activity in the preceding month, while more than a third had not attended a single party meeting or function in the previous year.[13] (Note, however, that the survey was conducted at a time when there was no federal election, and no leadership contest in any of the parties surveyed; both the number of members and their level of activity are generally low during these periods.) To survive and prosper, each party organization must provide incentives to attract and retain members, and to engage them actively in its operations. We will discuss those incentives in "Party Membership in Canada: Incentives and Networks" later in this chapter.

- *who work together:* Despite the relative autonomy of their component elements, parties are social organizations that bring people together in pursuit of common goals. The necessary chores of party maintenance and campaign organization are divided within and between the different levels of the extraparliamentary organization (see Table 3.1).

- *to achieve one or more common goals:* All political parties pursue two overriding goals: to win votes and to maintain their organizational health. Beyond this generalization, the goals of parties vary widely.[14] For **brokerage or cadre parties,** such as the Liberals, the primary goal is to exercise power—in other words, to form a government. This goal is achieved by electing more MPs than any other party. Others, whose chances of forming a government are more remote, may focus instead on promoting their distinct principles and policy priorities. We will refer to these as **missionary** or **ideological parties.** The Reform Party was originally a voice for Western protest and populism; the New Democratic Party (like its predecessor, the Co-operative Commonwealth Federation or CCF) promotes a social-democratic approach to government. The NDP has never had enough support in the electorate to form a national government, although it has held power in four provinces at various times. The process of transforming a missionary party into a brokerage party is extremely difficult, as the Reform–Alliance–Conservative saga illustrates (see Dossiers 3.3 and 3.4). While the primary goals of parties may differ, these distinctions no longer appear to create varying structures and activities. In theory, the brokerage/cadre and missionary/ideological categories are distinguished by their structures, memberships, funding, and goals:
  - Brokerage/cadre parties tend to be dominated by their leaders and caucuses; their memberships are small, especially between elections, and they rely on corporations for much of their revenue.
  - Missionary/ideological parties are more internally democratic, placing the ultimate authority over policy in the hands of their members. Those members are more numerous and more continuously active than those in brokerage/cadre parties, and they provide a larger share of party revenue.

In practice, the financing provisions in Bill C-24 have largely eliminated the differences in funding sources among Canada's parties, as we will see in the "Party Financing" section of this chapter. One survey of Canadian party members suggests that the members of missionary parties are no more active than their counterparts in brokerage parties, at least between elections; indeed, the respondents from the NDP and the former Canadian Alliance were less active in party affairs than either the Liberals or the former Progressive Conservatives.[15]

PARTY STRUCTURES IN CANADA

The structural elements of Canada's major national parties are broadly similar. They are summarized in Table 3.1.

TABLE 3.1 **THE STRUCTURAL ELEMENTS OF CANADIAN PARTIES**

PARTY ORGANIZATION "FACES"	ELEMENTS	DESCRIPTION	PRIMARY TASKS
Extraparliamentary party	Biennial national convention	Officially the highest authority in the party organization	Meets every two years to pass policy resolutions and elect the national executive
	Leader	Elected by party members either directly (OMOV)* or via delegates to a leadership convention	Fundraises, spearheads election campaigns, maintains volunteer morale
	National executive	Elected by delegates to the national convention; includes representatives from the various sections of the party (e.g., provincial wings, women's and youth clubs, caucus)	Meets at least once a year to manage the business of the party between conventions; delegates most decision-making to committees, party headquarters, and other small groups
	Constituency associations	Operate in every constituency where the party wishes to run a candidate for the House of Commons; run by an executive elected by the membership	Recruit and nominate candidates for the House of Commons, raise funds, organize campaigns (in some cases)
Parliamentary party	Leader	Elected by the party members, either directly (OMOV) or via delegates to a leadership convention	In government, defends the ruling party in Question Period as prime minister; in Opposition, leads the charge against the government

*OMOV: One member, one vote

PARTY ORGANIZATION "FACES"	ELEMENTS	DESCRIPTION	PRIMARY TASKS
	Caucus leaders	House leaders (Commons and Senate), whips, caucus chair	Maintain cohesion and discipline within the caucus, keep the leader informed about the mood of the MPs and senators
	Leader's office and parliamentary staff	Usually party members, often recruited from the youth wing or campus clubs	Communicate with the constituency, organize events, coordinate political activities within the caucus
Central office	National headquarters	Run by a national director, usually appointed by and accountable to the leader; normally a small permanent staff that expands before and during general elections	Clerical staff keeps track of party memberships and other paperwork; organizers prepare for conventions and other major events; technical experts in communications, polling, and political strategy plan and execute national election campaigns
	Official agency	A volunteer board of directors with a small permanent staff; usually located at national headquarters	Records all financial transactions of the national party and discloses them to Elections Canada, submits an annual report for each fiscal year and a separate report after a general election, ensures compliance with the *Canada Elections Act*

While the three "faces" of party organization (the far left column of Table 3.1) exist in every democratic state, the specific forms of the various elements and the relationships among them vary with the unique constitutional and political arrangements in each country. In effect, party structures evolve in response to the incentives set by the institutions within which they operate. In Canada, the primary incentives are:

- Canada's parliamentary institutions reward parties that can elect large numbers of MPs and organize them into stable, cohesive caucuses. The party with the most seats forms the government and its leader becomes prime minister, but only as long as its MPs are prepared to support the party's policies and obey the leader. The incentive to stay in power, or to gain power, usually produces a powerful sense of unity and "team spirit" within a parliamentary party.

- Within the government caucus, the Cabinet system concentrates power in the hands of the prime minister. Although leader dominance is less pronounced in the Opposition parties, other factors—including the regulatory requirements of the *Canada Elections Act,* the news media's focus on individual personalities, and the influence of party leaders on voting behaviour—combine to reinforce the authority of Opposition leaders within their respective parties.

- The structures of our extraparliamentary parties reflect our federal system—the division of powers between the national and provincial governments. The Liberals and New Democrats—and, until 2003, the PCs[16]—operate separately at both levels of government. In other words, there are Liberal and NDP organizations in most provinces, which compete to form provincial governments at the same time that their national organizations compete for power in Ottawa. Each province has a unique party system that has been shaped by its distinct political culture and history. Conflicts between particular provinces and the federal government can strain national party structures to the breaking point. At the national level, the task of coordinating a political organization across a huge country is beyond the scope of the leader, caucus or part-time volunteers (e.g., the national executive); hence the evolution of the national headquarters with its full-time, paid staff.

- Canada's **electoral system** determines the structure of our extraparliamentary parties, and affects the size of the parliamentary wings. It divides the country into 308 separate constituencies, each of which elects one MP to the House of Commons. Consequently, our extraparliamentary parties are divided into as many as 308 local organizations, one for each constituency where they wish to run candidates. The strong tradition of localism, which predated Confederation, is thus preserved by the structure imposed by the electoral system—and perhaps reinforced by the "franchise" structure discussed below, which allows Canadian parties to manage the conflict between the demands of national cohesion and the realities of local decentralization.[17] Our electoral system also creates artificial majority governments, although not in all cases (e.g., the minority Liberal government elected in 2004). It usually gives a party with 38 to 49 percent of the national vote a majority of seats in the House of Commons. Because it is usually possible for one party to govern without the support of other parties in the House, Canadian politics is more adversarial than it might otherwise be; there are fewer incentives to work with other parties than to work against them. (Other problematic aspects of our electoral system are discussed in Chapter 4.)

- Finally, the relationships among the various elements of party organization are affected by the *Canada Elections Act.* The Act regulates party financing, including the flows of money between the national and local parties; it also sets out the requirements for parties who wish to obtain the benefits flowing from registration with Elections Canada. Most recently, relations between the national party office and the local associations have been affected by Bill C-24, *An Act to Amend the*

Canada Elections Act *and the* Income Tax Act (*Political Financing*). The Bill, which took effect at the beginning of 2004, brought the most significant changes in the legal regime for national political parties since 1974. The details are discussed later in this chapter in the "Party Financing" section. Among other things, Bill C-24 recognizes and regulates constituency associations, alters the financial balance between the national and local elements of party organization, and subjects nomination and leadership contests to formal scrutiny. While the full effects of the new law are not yet clear, there is every reason to expect that they will be substantial. Constituency associations will lose some of their autonomy and much of their funding; national headquarters will collect and spend generous new annual allowances from the state. These changes will likely occur in all of our major national parties.

For the most part, the elements of party organization shown in Table 3.1 are similar in all of the major parties. However, there are a few differences worth noting, most of which relate to the parties' national conventions. First, the NDP permits leadership votes at its biennial gatherings. If a candidate steps forward to challenge the incumbent, the meeting is transformed into a leadership convention. To date, no national NDP leader has faced a serious challenge in this manner. Second, the composition of the conventions varies widely. The NDP sets aside 20 to 25 percent of delegate positions for representatives of its affiliated trade union locals. It also awards delegate spots to constituency associations on a sliding scale relative to the size of the local membership, as does the BQ (and the former Canadian Alliance). In the Liberal Party, each constituency association sends the same number of delegates, regardless of membership. Third, the Liberals, BQ, and New Democrats (like the former PCs) made special efforts to increase the number of women and youth (under age 30) delegates at their conventions. As a result, delegates to those national conventions were, on average, younger and less overwhelmingly male than those at Reform and Alliance conventions, where no such accommodations were made. With these exceptions, the different structural elements of Canadian parties are more similar than their divergent ideologies might lead one to expect.

The working relationships among the various elements in Table 3.1 are quite different from the formal arrangements reflected in flow charts. In theory, political parties are hierarchical structures: there is a clear chain of command, with the leader and his or her inner circle at the top and the grassroots members somewhere near the bottom. This simplistic model of party structure, often called the "Iron Law of Oligarchy,"[18] is no longer accurate (if it ever was). Instead, the various elements of party structure enjoy considerable autonomy; the power to make binding decisions is shared among groups and individuals operating at all levels of the organization.[19] The leader remains at the top of the pecking order, but the various components of the party structure operate more and more independently of each other. In Canada, this means that the elements at the centre of the party—the leader, the party caucus, and the national headquarters—make decisions for the party as a whole, while the local party clubs implement those decisions with some degree of flexibility.

This "franchise"[20] model of party organization combines a national "brand name," advertising strategy, and "product line" (policy and leadership) with local "product delivery" (candidate nomination and campaigning) attuned to the regional "market."[21] In practice, this means that constituency associations choose the party's candidates for the House of Commons and provide the necessary services to secure their election. All candidates are expected to use the party logo on their campaign signs and literature, and to "sell" the party **platform** (with some limited leeway to appeal to purely local sentiment); in return, they benefit from the expertise of the headquarters staff, well-researched policies, and—ideally—a popular national leader.

The "franchise" model has always characterized Canadian party structures. Since before Confederation, local constituency associations have enjoyed considerable autonomy from the centre, particularly in the nomination of candidates. However, the model is not a perfect fit, because some leaders are trying to reassert their authority in local party affairs. The clearest example is the power of the Liberal leader to appoint candidates, over the heads (and sometimes the objections) of the activists in those particular ridings (see "Selection of Candidates" on page 90). Nonetheless, the portrayal of Canadian parties as "franchise systems" offers several advantages over competing models. First, it captures the relationships among the three key elements of party organization: the parliamentary caucus, the permanent staff in the leader's office and national headquarters, and the "grassroots." Second, it reflects the need to appeal to diverse electorates in various regions of the country, without losing sight of the national message. Third, the model is flexible enough to cover the variations in Canadian party structures—for example, the degree of cooperation between the national and provincial wings of a party, or the extent of participation by party members in policy development. The point is not that each party affords the same degree of independence to its local activists or its parliamentary caucus, but that each recognizes a similar division of responsibilities among its component parts.

One final point should be made about the informal relationships among the various elements of party organizations: they differ depending on whether the party is in government or in opposition. When the party leader is prime minister, he or she has several tools to impose and enforce discipline, at least within the parliamentary party: a large staff, the option to dissolve Parliament for a "snap" election, and the power to make or break political careers. (See also the discussion of prime ministerial power in Chapter 6.) However, this power comes at a price. The Cabinet is responsible, not to the party membership, but to the population as a whole; in consequence, the policy preferences of the grassroots membership are, at best, a minor consideration. The resulting "disconnect" between the grassroots and the party elite often produces conflict. That conflict became unusually public and visible in the Liberal leadership battle between former Prime Minister Jean Chrétien and his successor, Paul Martin. The leader does not automatically control the extraparliamentary party, either national or local; nor can he or she always count on the loyalty of party staff (see Dossier 3.1).

PARTY MEMBERSHIP IN CANADA: INCENTIVES AND NETWORKS

We have argued that political parties, as organizations, are shaped by the incentives set by Canada's political institutions. In turn, party organizations themselves create incentives for their members. Political parties are volunteer organizations. They cannot force their members to behave in particular ways, by firing them or charging them with violating the party rules. Party elites must find ways to reward their activists for their hard work and devotion, while discouraging them from damaging the party through divisive or self-seeking actions. The shifting relationships between leaders and followers are a constant source of tension within Canada's political parties.

The organizational health of a party depends on the willingness of talented individuals to donate their time and money over a period of years or decades, without any realistic hope of a tangible reward. What sort of people are these, and what motivates them?

Four Categories of Incentives for Party Members

The incentives for party members fall into four categories:[22]

1. **Material incentives:** tangible rewards for loyal service (e.g., a seat in the Senate);
2. **Specific solidary incentives:** intangible benefits that are awarded to a few select individuals (e.g., status, a nomination for Parliament, or a high-ranking office in the party);
3. **Collective solidary/social incentives:** intangible rewards available to all party members (the joy of victory, the satisfaction of working together for a shared goal, and the social value of meeting like-minded people), combined with the motivation to impress friends or family members who support the party; and
4. **Purposive/altruistic incentives:** the sense that one is contributing to the greater good by working to elect one's party of choice.

In Canada, the material incentives for party membership—which are usually lumped together, with a sneer, as **"patronage"**—are less important than many people realize. In the first place, they are available only to members of the governing party. Many Canadians join parties that have little hope of ever forming a government, either national or provincial. In the second place, the early twentieth century brought sweeping reforms to the public service, which shrank the pool of patronage positions to a relative handful. While Order-in-Council appointments (discussed in Chapter 6) are awarded at the discretion of the prime minister, not all of them can be filled purely on the basis of party patronage. Whereas material incentives were once the glue that held our national parties together,[23] they are now relatively unimportant for most partisans. A recent survey of Canadian party members found that material incentives were all but irrelevant for most long-time partisans, although they are "vastly more important in attracting members to the Liberal Party than to any of the others."[24] This is clearly a reflection of Liberal dominance at the federal level.

Specific solidary incentives exist in every party. As we saw in Dossier 1.4, political institutions are most effective when they can channel the ambition of individuals into constructive activity. Political parties harness ambition by creating opportunities for prestige and influence. At the local level, a party member can aspire to—or, in less active organizations, be forced to accept—the presidency of his or her constituency association or a nomination for public office. At the higher reaches of the party organization, a member can pursue a place on the national executive or a seat on the board of the fundraising agency. Informal selective incentives, such as the attention of the leader, are also important. When the leader comes to town for a fundraising reception and greets a local member warmly, that member feels important and valued. Wise party leaders, especially those who can offer few other incentives, try to visit as many constituency associations as possible to strengthen the links between the "franchise holders" and the centre; those who neglect the local activists may become especially vulnerable to hostile factions.

Collective solidary incentives are particularly important for many new recruits. Local constituency associations try to organize as many social events as they can,[25] partly to keep their existing members involved and partly to attract newcomers (the "bring a friend" approach). Most new members are recruited during leadership contests and local nomination battles, although it appears that few of these **"instant" members** become committed party activists.[26] Personal ties are an important draw for some new members; aspiring nominees for Parliament often sell memberships to friends and relatives from outside the party in an effort to boost their share of the vote.[27] It has long been assumed that local party associations depend on local candidates and would-be candidates, along with local organizers for national leadership campaigns, to recruit potential party members. But a majority (59 percent) of the partisans surveyed by Young and Cross reported that they joined on their own initiative, and only 20 percent said that they were recruited by friends or family members.[28] Members of the BQ and the Canadian Alliance were the most likely to join for ideological reasons, and without being asked. Conversely, more Liberals and PCs were recruited by friends and family; members of those parties were less motivated by ideology than their counterparts in the newer parties or the NDP. Most of those who remained in their chosen party for more than a year or two were attracted by its aims and policies, and were not recruited by friends or driven by self-interest. In other words, some people take out a membership card because a friend or relative asks them to do so, but unless they are also drawn to the party for purposive/altruistic reasons, that membership is unlikely to be renewed.

Categories of Party Members

In broad terms, party members can be divided into the inactive majority and the active minority. Within the latter category, there are two primary groups: **"believers" and "careerists."**[29] Believers are motivated primarily by unselfish goals: commitment to the party's principles and policies, emotional identification with the party as an organization, or admiration for its leader. They are likely to respond to the collective solidary/social and purposive/altruistic incentives just described. Careerists are somewhat more self-seeking. Their chief motivations are material (patronage positions) and specific solidary (status within the party hierarchy, business contacts, and the respect of their fellow partisans). In practice, most party members pursue a mix of these goals. Members may be attracted to the party at first by its policies and ideology, and later come to enjoy the personal rewards of status or networking. Nonetheless, it is possible to distinguish the two types by observing parties at work. Some members devote endless hours to "the cause" without seeking recognition for their efforts, while others are driven by personal ambition and unconcerned with policy or ideology.

A successful party must attract and retain both types of members, and give each the rewards they seek. Unfortunately for party leaders, conflict between believers and careerists is endemic to political organizations. Preston Manning's attempt to transform the Reform Party into a real alternative to the Liberals is a classic example (see the discussion of the United Alternative in Dossier 3.3). Reform "believers" feared that Manning was selling out the party's principles in the pursuit of power, whereas the "careerists" blamed him for Reform's failure to establish itself as a credible government-in-waiting. The "believers" tried to derail the United Alternative, while the "careerists" promoted it. The conflict persisted through the founding of the Canadian Alliance, and flared up again after the party's disappointing performance in the 2000 election. However, tensions between the two groups were surprisingly muted when the Alliance merged with the PCs in 2003, which implies that the "careerists" had gained the upper hand within the Alliance organization.[30]

The NDP is also divided between the "believers" who want to take the party further to the left, and the "careerists" (many of them veterans of NDP provincial governments, who have tasted the rewards of power) who want the party to follow the example of Britain's popular Labour government by moving to the political centre. While these particular conflicts were provoked by major transformations in party structure and ideology, less dramatic conflicts between the two groups occur daily in every political party.

A related problem arises when the balance between believers and careerists is too heavily weighted in favour of one or the other. The Liberals dominated Canada's federal politics in the twentieth century, as Table 3.8 on page 118 reveals. Their main rivals, the Progressive Conservatives, were usually relegated to the Opposition benches. Over time, ambitious people who were motivated primarily by power and patronage gravitated to the Liberals. (Recall that the Liberals in the party membership survey were more susceptible than other partisans to material incentives.) The PCs tended to attract members who adhered to particular principles, or who simply felt more comfortable criticizing the government for its failings than building constructive alternatives. By the early 1980s, this **"minority party syndrome"** had seriously weakened the internal unity of the Progressive Conservative Party and diminished the pool of talented people willing to serve as candidates and party officers.[31]

On the Liberal side, the embarrassment of riches proved to be a blessing when the party was in power and a curse when it was defeated. Careerists are more likely to desert their party when the rewards of power are unavailable, taking their talents elsewhere. Shortly after the 1984 election, in which the Liberals were humiliated by the Progressive Conservatives, the Ontario Liberal Party formed a minority government with the support of the provincial NDP. Senior Liberal advisers, fundraisers, and organizers left Ottawa for Toronto en masse, as the national party struggled to rebuild its organization and flirted with bankruptcy. Meanwhile, the proportion of careerists in the PC party grew during the party's nine years in power.[32]

A successful party needs a "critical mass" of both believers and careerists—the former to sustain the party during the lean times and preserve its ideals, and the latter to inject a note of pragmatism and discipline—and it needs to harness the conflicting motivations of the two groups. Therefore, parties need to offer different incentives to different types of members. Managing the contradictions between these incompatible incentives is a constant challenge for party elites.

Party Networks

In Chapter 7 we distinguish between a policy community—a collection of decision-makers with a particular interest in one public issue—and a policy network. We define a "network" as a subgroup within the policy community, whose members share a similar approach to the issue. Within a given policy community, there are usually two or more networks that compete to set its agenda and influence its collective decisions.

The same is true for political parties. As we saw in Table 3.1, responsibilities are divided among several distinct elements of party structure. Some of these divisions—those arising from federalism, the electoral system, and parliamentary government—are formalized in party constitutions. Others, such as the split between active and inactive members, are informal. These informal divisions often produce distinct **party networks**[33] or cliques within each party, with each centred around a particular leader, region, interest, or ideology. Some examples:

- Every national party is divided into regional networks, some more hostile to central control than others. The presence of a federal system led the three "old-line" parties (the Liberals, NDP, and PCs) to establish provincial wings in addition to their national organizations. Tensions between Ottawa and the provinces can strain relations between a party's national organization and one or more of its provincial organizations. Even in the absence of such external influences, regional or provincial networks within parties often disagree on questions of policy and party structure. These differences arise from the varying political cultures of Canada's provincial electorates, as well as the differences in economic structure and resources.
- Leadership contests create new networks and reinvigorate old ones. When a candidate loses, his or her network can survive for years, waiting hopefully for a second chance. The patience of the candidate and his or her supporters eventually

runs out, causing the leaders of the network to undermine the unity of the party as a whole; these disruptive networks are often called "factions."[34] The recent history of the Liberal Party of Canada provides three excellent examples. John Turner placed third at the 1968 Liberal leadership convention with 195 votes on the final ballot. For the next eight years, as he awaited the opportunity to succeed Pierre Trudeau, Turner kept in close touch with his "195 Club," maintaining the loyalty of the core network that would win him the leadership. But Turner left politics in 1976, disillusioned and frustrated. He devoted himself to law and business, and neglected the 195 Club.[35] Although he still managed to win the leadership in June 1984—beating Jean Chrétien in a bitter campaign—the election defeat that followed shortly thereafter left him with little support in the party and few loyal soldiers. Chrétien tended his network even after he left politics in early 1986. That network mobilized in November 1986, hoping to defeat Turner in a leadership review vote; when they failed to unseat him, they continued to undermine the leader in subtle ways. Chrétien easily won the leadership in June 1990, after Turner's retirement from politics. The third example, the Paul Martin "juggernaut" that effectively deposed Chrétien from the prime ministership in 2003, is discussed in Dossier 3.1.

In general, a defeated leadership candidate with future aspirations tries hard to keep his network intact after the defeat. With or without the active encouragement of the leader-in-waiting, his network can destabilize a party organization. John Diefenbaker lost the PC leadership to Robert Stanfield in 1967; he and his supporters in the caucus made Stanfield's life difficult whenever they could. Brian Mulroney placed third to Joe Clark at the 1976 Progressive Conservative leadership convention and spent the next seven years publicly supporting Clark while his network undermined the leader behind the scenes. Clark resigned in early 1983 after a disappointing leadership-review vote, and lost to Mulroney at the subsequent leadership convention.

- The caucus constitutes a distinct network within the party, as does the paid staff at party headquarters and the various consultants who work for the party on contract. While they do not agree on everything, they do have their own shared interests arising from their respective positions vis-à-vis the leader, and they work hard to defend those interests. The leader's entourage is yet another network, although its membership usually overlaps with other groups (e.g., MPs, party staff, and strategists).[36] Collaboration across the distinct elements of the party structure is essential if the party is to remain united in the long term.

- Networks based on a shared ideology are best described as "sects."[37] The members of a sect believe that "the party should redefine its basic objectives, perhaps by revising an existing doctrine or reviving a neglected tradition or even by adopting new ideas more suited to the party's circumstances."[38] The Waffle Movement within the federal NDP is perhaps the best-known Canadian example. Between 1969 and 1971, it challenged the NDP to adopt a more radical approach to policy, including a strong commitment to economic nationalism.[39] After David Lewis became party leader in 1971, he "purged" the Waffle from the NDP, leaving behind "a memory of division and a vigilant core of mainstream party regulars ready to weed out dissent."[40] Nonetheless, sectarian conflict is a fact of life within the NDP, as it is in all social-democratic and socialist parties.

The most recent "ginger group" (a group adding spice to the parliamentary debate) pushing the party to the left is the New Politics Initiative (NPI), launched in June 2001 with the purpose of convincing the party to ally itself with New Social Movement activists who disdain conventional politics. Moderate NDPers claim that left-wing sects frighten away potential voters;[41] the sectarians, in self-defence, portray themselves as the keepers of the party's conscience. At the NDP's national conference in November 2001, the NPI was rejected by a majority of the delegates, but the public clash between the NPI and the moderates (NDProgress) demonstrated both the potentially destructive power of sectarianism, and the difficulty of reconciling "believers" and "careerists" within the same organization. It also illustrates a basic organizational problem for political parties: the incentives that appeal to some members inspire indifference, or even outright hostility, in others.

An individual party member may belong to two or more networks at the same time. For example, a Conservative from Newfoundland may have a distinct regional perspective on policy and party organization, which would not prevent her from joining the national network in support of former leadership candidate Belinda Stronach. As long as the various networks cut across each other, factional strife is generally manageable. Indeed, Carty argues that party networks can actually strengthen the organization, because they often bring people together from different elements

DOSSIER 3.1 The Martin "Juggernaut"

Paul Martin Jr., the son of a long-serving Liberal Cabinet minister, took his first run at the party leadership in 1990. He had been an MP only since 1988, but his prominence in the business community (as owner of Canada Steamship Lines) and his Liberal pedigree gave him a higher profile than most rookie MPs. He placed second to Jean Chrétien on the first ballot at the Liberal leadership convention. Many of the senior strategists from the 1990 leadership race continued to work for Martin, both inside and outside government. For example, David Herle and Mike Robinson were hired by the Earnscliffe Strategy Group, a lobbying and research company in Ottawa.

Terrie O'Leary worked in Martin's parliamentary office; she became his most trusted assistant when he was appointed minister of Finance after the 1993 election. Other Martin supporters worked for the party itself, either as paid staff or volunteers. This tight-knit group was nicknamed "the Board" by Martin's secretary.[42]

After the 2000 election, "the Board" decided that Chrétien had been prime minister long enough; if he stayed on for another full term, Martin might be too old to succeed him. They had already laid plans for a takeover of the party organization in the ridings, in anticipation of a leadership review vote at a future national convention.

Since the 1960s, party members have had the power to pass judgment on their leader's performance, usually at a national meeting. They are asked to vote on a motion that directs the national executive to hold a leadership vote; if a majority votes "yes," the leader is effectively fired. Beginning in 1999, Martin supporters sought and won high-ranking positions in their constituency associations and filled several seats on the national executive. This plan had three aims: to ensure that the next convention would be held early in the government's term; to secure a victory in a leadership review, by giving the Martin forces control over the selection of delegates; and to obtain access to membership forms. The party rationed the distribution of forms for new members to sign up, as a way to restrict the entry of single-issue groups during leadership and nomination contests. Unless Martin's people controlled the constituency associations, they would have difficulty obtaining enough forms to sign up new members in the battle against Chrétien.[43]

Two parts of this strategy worked well. The Martin forces locked up the constituency associations, particularly in Ontario. When rival aspirants started to organize their own leadership campaigns in 2002, they found it impossible to obtain more than a handful of membership forms at a time.[44] By then, a majority of the Liberal caucus supported Martin; some had publicly called on Chrétien to step down. However, "the Board" lost the battle for an early convention. The next national gathering, at which the prime minister would be subjected to a review vote, was delayed until February 2003. If Chrétien survived the review, he could try to lead the party to a fourth majority government; by then, Martin would be in his mid-sixties and his time might have passed. The rising tension between the Chrétien loyalists and the Martin insurgents culminated in early June 2002, when the prime minister reversed his earlier decision to allow his Cabinet ministers to organize leadership campaigns. After a series of damaging leaks and allegations from both sides, Martin quit as Finance minister. He was free to campaign full-time, without being constrained by Cabinet solidarity or the party's disclosure rules for ministers seeking the leadership.

By the late summer, it was clear to senior party officials that Chrétien could not win a review vote. He announced in August 2002 that he would step down in February 2004, after completing an ambitious "legacy agenda." (Bill C-24 was part of that agenda.) The leadership review was cancelled, although squabbling over the date of the convention (now a leadership convention) continued. It was finally held in November 2003, three months before Chrétien's planned retirement date (he later agreed to step down in early December). By the time the delegates gathered in Toronto, there were only two candidates in the race: Paul Martin and Sheila Copps. The other hopefuls—Allan Rock, Brian Tobin, and John Manley—had dropped out one by one after concluding that they had no hope of winning. As expected, Martin won an overwhelming first-ballot victory, with roughly 90 percent of the vote. Copps may have paid a high price for her stubborn refusal to permit a Martin coronation: she lost her Cabinet post and then her Liberal nomination (see "Selection of Candidates" on the next page).

of the party structure.[45] The Martin "juggernaut" began with a few parliamentary staffers, Young Liberals, and a handful of MPs; it eventually grew to encompass members of the national executive, consultants, riding association presidents, and a majority of the caucus. The bitter contest between the Martin and Chrétien forces divided the party in some respects, while uniting each camp internally. But had the split between the two networks reinforced the structural division between two distinct elements of the party structure—e.g., pitting the entire caucus against constituency activists—it could have posed a serious threat to the long-term integrity of the party organization.

Conflict among the various networks within a party is usually managed internally by the leader and other key personnel; it rarely bursts into the open. When it does, the impact on voter perceptions is invariably negative. Between April and July 2001, the Canadian Alliance caucus ruptured. The exodus began with the resignations of the House leader and deputy leader/caucus chair from their caucus positions, in protest against the leadership of Stockwell Day. Over the next three months, 13 MPs left the Alliance caucus to sit as independents. In late July, after Day had promised to resign at some unspecified future date, one of the dissidents returned to the Alliance; the other twelve decided to form a separate parliamentary group, the Democratic Representative (DR) Caucus. Although four of the dissidents soon returned to the Canadian Alliance, the remaining eight agreed to a coalition arrangement with the Progressive Conservatives. The resulting "PC–DR Coalition" did not receive official party status from the Speaker of the House, but its 20 members were allowed to sit together and to carry out their parliamentary tasks as a single unit. During this period of turmoil, Alliance support in the polls plunged into the single digits. A party that appears unable to govern itself will have difficulty persuading voters to trust it to govern them. Public disunity also makes potential donors reluctant to open their wallets and drives away the local activists on whose volunteer labour the party depends.

In general, parties try to keep their internal conflicts "in the family." Canadian parties rarely split into smaller political units, as their counterparts in Western Europe often do. Because our electoral system strongly discourages the formation of splinter parties, unlike the proportional representation systems used in most democratic states,[46] Canada's major parties usually resolve their internal differences as best they can—another example of the effect of institutional incentives on Canadian party politics.

FUNCTIONS OF CANADIAN PARTIES

◼ Selection of Candidates

Parties monopolize the selection of candidates for Canadian public office. It is rare for a candidate to be elected to the House of Commons without first gaining the nomination of a political party. In the 2004 federal election, a total of 1620 candidates representing 12 parties, together with 54 independents and 11 candidates with no party affiliation,[47] contested the 308 seats in the House of Commons. More than four-fifths (81 percent) of the party candidates, and all but one of the independent and unaffiliated candidates, were defeated. So while winning a party's nomination is no guarantee of victory, candidates who lack the endorsement of a major party have almost no chance of winning.[48]

As noted earlier, Bill C-24 subjected nomination contests to state regulation for the first time. The involvement of Elections Canada in the process reflects the importance of candidate nomination within the national electoral process. But traditionally, Canada's major political parties have given their constituency associations a good deal of autonomy in selecting candidates. Although a number of controversial candidate nomination meetings have been held during recent election periods, the general trend is for nomination meetings to be attended by relatively few voters. A recent study of candidate nominations revealed that the typical constituency association has slightly more than 500 members. Only about one-third of the association's membership typically attends a nomination meeting, making these meetings particularly susceptible to takeover by "instant" members.[49]

While such takeovers attract considerable media attention, they are relatively rare. Most nominations are, quite literally, no contest. The majority of party nominations—approximately two-thirds—have only one candidate and are won by acclamation.[50] Sitting MPs enjoy an especially easy road to renomination; almost 90 percent of them are unopposed. The rare exceptions tend to attract a great deal of attention from the media. In the run-up to the 2004 election, constituency boundaries were redrawn to reflect the results of the 2001 census. The new constituency of Hamilton East–Stoney Creek overlapped two old ridings, both held by Liberal MPs. The two sitting members, Sheila Copps and Tony Valeri, squared off in a pitched battle for the new riding. Copps, who had been an MP since 1984 and a Cabinet minister since 1993, had recently lost the Liberal leadership to Prime Minister Paul Martin by a wide margin. Although her defeat was clearly inevitable, Copps insisted that the November 2003 leadership convention should not be turned into a coronation. Her persistence apparently earned her the enmity of the Martin forces; she was fired from Cabinet in December 2003, on the same day that Valeri—a prominent Martin loyalist—received his first ministerial portfolio. Even though Copps controlled the new riding association executive and canvassed hard for the nomination, Valeri won the battle. Copps claimed that the vote was rigged, and appealed to the national executive.[51] They rejected her appeal. Eventually, after flirting with the possibility of running either for the NDP or as an independent, Copps left politics. Another bitter battle between Liberal incumbents took place in a new Mississauga riding; similarly divisive contests plagued new constituencies in Alberta and British Columbia.

Although the constituency association has the right to select the candidate, the nomination cannot become official without the endorsement of the party leader. Under the *Canada Elections Act,* the leader can veto the candidate chosen by a local party organization. The leader's veto has been used in several celebrated cases. It was first used by Conservative leader Robert Stanfield in 1974, when he refused to certify the candidacy of an anti-bilingualism candidate in New Brunswick, and later by Brian Mulroney, who vetoed the candidacy of Sinclair Stevens, a former minister found to have breached conflict-of-interest guidelines. Leading up to the 1993 election, the leader's veto was used by Reform leader Preston Manning and PC leader Kim Campbell. Liberal leader Jean Chrétien increased the number of female Liberal Party candidates, and to ensure the nomination of "star" candidates, by threatening to veto nominations in constituencies that defied his wishes. Since 1992, the Liberal leader has had the power to appoint candidates where such action is necessary to increase the number of women or to ensure the nomination of a high-profile aspirant. In both 1993 and 1997, Chrétien appointed several such candidates; while this practice provoked considerable controversy, most of his hand-picked standard-bearers went on to win seats in the Commons. Paul Martin revived this practice in the 2004 election, appointing "star" candidates in several Ontario and British Columbia ridings. His choice of hockey legend Ken Dryden in York Centre was widely applauded,[52] but the "parachute" candidates in British Columbia were greeted with dismay by local Liberals. One aspiring candidate in Burnaby–Douglas held a tearful news conference, begging Martin for a fair and open nomination meeting. His pleas did not deter the leader from appointing the president of the provincial wing of the party—Martin organizer Bill Cunningham— who lost the election after the entire Liberal riding association executive quit in protest.

◼ Leadership Selection

For the first half-century following Confederation, party leaders were chosen by the caucus. Leaders headed the parliamentary wing of the party; it seemed natural that they would be chosen from among the MPs who supported their policies. The shift to **leadership conventions** began early in the twentieth century, partly because the major parties wished to appear more "democratic." A leadership convention is a gathering of delegates, chosen in the same way as delegates to regular national conventions (recall the discussion of delegate categories in "Party Structures in Canada"). The delegates meet the candidates, listen to speeches, and finally mark their ballots. Only those with delegate status may vote; other party members have no role in the process, apart from electing their representatives to the convention.

The first national convention was held by the Liberals in 1919, shortly after the death of Sir Wilfrid Laurier, while the party was still recovering from the disastrous French–English split over conscription.[53] Had the choice of a leader to replace Laurier been left to the Liberal caucus, most of whose members were francophone Quebeckers, the party's efforts to reconstruct its electoral alliance between French and English would have been seriously jeopardized. So the Liberals held the first national leadership convention, which was won by Mackenzie King. The Conservative Party followed suit and at its 1927 convention selected R.B. Bennett as leader. The CCF–NDP has held leadership conventions since its founding in 1933.[54]

Early conventions (1919–58) were small, elite-dominated, and rarely competitive. Beginning in 1967, leadership conventions were transformed into huge events with as many as a dozen candidates. As the number of constituency delegates mushroomed, the means by which they were chosen became increasingly controversial. Organizers for the various leadership candidates would invade each constituency, sign up as many "instant members" as they could, and bus them to the delegate selection meeting to vote for their candidate's "slate" of delegates. The outcome of a convention was decided long before the delegates arrived at the meeting hall, in the bitterly divisive "trench warfare" at the constituency level.[55] The news media focused on abuses of the process, including the mass recruitment of recent immigrants and allegations of beer parties for minors.

Since 1985, Canadian parties have gradually abandoned the leadership convention in favour of **one member, one vote (OMOV).** In an OMOV system, every party member can vote directly for the leadership candidate of his or her choice. There are at least four reasons for this trend:[56]

1. Giving every member of the party the right to vote for the leader appears to be more "democratic" than a delegated convention. Given the growing appeal of populism (see Chapter 2), anything that gives the parties a chance to shed their elitist image has considerable appeal.[57] Among party members themselves, support for OMOV varies somewhat. Liberals are evenly divided between OMOV and the convention model, while members of the former Canadian Alliance strongly supported direct election.[58] This may help to explain why, of the five major parties surveyed in 2002, only the Liberals continue to choose their leaders in convention.

2. Advances in communication technology—e.g., telephone systems linked to computer databases—have made it possible for party members to vote from their homes, instead of travelling long distances to cast ballots at a convention.

3. The cost of attending a leadership convention—delegate registration, travel, accommodation, meals, and other expenses—have risen sharply in recent years. Under OMOV, a party member can vote inexpensively at home or in a local polling place.

4. The scandals surrounding "trench warfare" forced parties to find a less damaging way to choose their leaders. Most OMOV systems do not require delegate-selection meetings.

In 1998, the federal PCs held a leadership contest in which all party members cast paper ballots in their constituencies. Instead of awarding the leadership to the candidate with the largest number of votes across the country, the party assigned 100 points to each constituency. These points were distributed among the leadership candidates in proportion to their share of the vote in that riding. Thus, a leadership candidate receiving 40 percent of the vote in a constituency would receive 40 points, a candidate receiving 30 percent of the vote would receive 30 points, and so on. The points from all 301 constituencies were totalled to determine the winner.[59] Strictly speaking, the PC system deviated from the strict OMOV principle; the relative weight of an individual vote depended on the number of ballots cast in each riding.

The Canadian Alliance, which elected its first leader in 2000, took the OMOV rule more literally. The party used a mix of two voting systems: party members in urban ridings, and those with large Canadian Alliance organizations, cast paper ballots in their constituencies, while those in sparsely populated or poorly organized ridings voted by telephone. Unlike the federal PCs, the Alliance did not weight the constituency votes equally; whichever candidate received the majority of the votes, wherever those votes were cast, would become leader of the party. Because the first ballot was inconclusive, a run-off vote was held two weeks later. Stockwell Day won convincingly over former Reform leader Preston Manning, although he did not last long in the job (see Dossier 3.3). Partly because of technical problems with the 2000 vote, the party's March 2002 leadership contest was conducted by mail-in ballot; it went smoothly.

When the two parties merged in 2003 (Dossier 3.4), they opted for the PC method of leadership selection. The method used to select the new Conservative Party's first leader was a sticking point in the negotiations between leaders Stephen Harper and Peter MacKay; the logjam was finally broken at the last minute when Harper agreed to the 1998 PC process.[60] The constituency weighting was important to the PCs, who feared that a straight OMOV vote would swamp their smaller membership. The details were left to the Interim Joint Committee of the new party, which decided to use different voting methods in different parts of the country. Party members in well-populated areas would vote at polling stations in their ridings; those in 64 rural constituencies were required to fax their ballots, with copies of three pieces of personal identification, to national party headquarters. Many complained that they did not receive their voting packages before the deadline, because the computerized national membership list apparently could not cope with the large volume of new members.[61] The leadership vote in the constituencies—which was also plagued by organizational problems[62]—was held on March 20. Former Alliance leader Stephen Harper beat his two opponents (political neophyte Belinda Stronach and former Ontario PC Cabinet Minister Tony Clement) on the first ballot, with 55.5 percent of the points (16 149 out of 30 800).[63] Only 37 percent of more than 250 000 party members cast ballots, raising questions about the new party's ability to mount a strong campaign in an impending federal election.[64]

The BQ also uses OMOV to elect its leaders, as does the NDP. The latter was more reluctant to abandon conventions altogether, largely because OMOV conflicted with the institutional arrangement between the party and its affiliated unions. It is impossible to guarantee a specific percentage of the vote to a particular group when all members are empowered to cast ballots. Consequently, the NDP used a "hybrid" system in 1995. All party members were allowed to vote in "primaries" for the leader of their choice; the last-place finisher was dropped from the convention ballot, and the delegates were expected to reflect the primary results in their own decision-making. In the event, they ignored the membership at large. Former MP Lorne Nystrom, who had won the primaries, placed third (and last) on the first ballot at the convention; former Nova Scotia NDP leader Alexa McDonough, who had run a fairly distant third in the primaries, ended up winning the leadership after second-place finisher Svend Robinson pulled out before a second ballot could be held. The federal NDP subsequently decided to follow several of its provincial wings, adopting a straight OMOV system for its next leadership contest. Toronto municipal councillor Jack Layton won the 2003 contest by a convincing margin over longtime MP Bill Blaikie.

Unlike the NDP, the federal Liberals continue to use a hybrid system. When members gather to elect delegates to a leadership convention, they cast a separate ballot for the leadership candidate of their choice. The delegate spots from each riding are allocated among the candidates in rough proportion to their shares of the local vote. The PCs, who were disappointed with the lacklustre media coverage of their 1998 contest, adopted the same system for their June 2003 leadership vote. The Liberals' refusal to abandon the leadership convention altogether reminds us that the old "undemocratic" system of party leadership selection provides important benefits. Delegate positions have long been the most important specific solidary incentives for local party members. Conventions provide an opportunity for activists from across the country to network with one another and rub elbows with party leaders and notables. By bringing activists together from across the country, conventions strengthen the national party organization[65] and help to bridge the gap between partisans in different regions. Perhaps most important, leadership conventions attract the attention of the media and the public. At several past conventions, the suspense built through each successive round of voting, as the last-place candidates were dropped from the ballot and the front-runner approached a majority. There was high drama as the eliminated candidates announced whom they would support, and the convention waited to see how many of their voters would make the move with them.

Unfortunately for the Liberals, their 2003 convention was anything but dramatic. Paul Martin's overwhelming first-ballot victory was such a foregone conclusion that the party seriously considered cancelling the vote altogether.[66] To generate excitement and media coverage—and to entice more delegates to show up in Toronto for a dull weekend[67]—the Liberals invited Bono (leader of the Irish rock band U2) to address the convention. On the other hand, the PC convention of June 2003 provided all the drama and suspense that one could wish. To secure a victory over Calgary lawyer Jim Prentice on the fourth ballot, Peter MacKay signed a hastily written deal with party maverick David Orchard in which he promised never to merge the party with the Alliance. His subsequent decision to renege on that pledge severely damaged MacKay's political career (Dossier 3.4).

The 2004 Conservative leadership race was more interesting than the Liberal contest, especially after the entry of glamorous neophyte Belinda Stronach, but the coverage of the results was just as dull as in previous OMOV contests. While it may be more "democratic" to allow all party members to vote in their separate ridings, the media find it difficult to cover such events. The old post-convention "bounce" in the polls, which is still a feature of American presidential politics, can no longer be taken for granted.

At the time of writing, the new leadership-selection provisions in Bill C-24 had not yet been put into practice. The 2004 Conservative contest was exempted from the law, because it officially began in late 2003. However, it is interesting to speculate on the future impact of these provisions. In the past, some leadership candidates were tarnished by their refusal to disclose the sources of their campaign funds. There was widespread speculation after the 1976 PC contest that third-place finisher Brian Mulroney had been supported by big business interests; there is no evidence to prove or disprove these suspicions, because Mulroney never filed the financial report required by the party. Similarly, there were allegations that Paul Martin's 2003 leadership bid was generously funded by some of the same businesses with whom he had worked closely as Finance minister. Unlike leadership rivals John Manley, Allan Rock, and Sheila Copps, Martin was not a Cabinet minister during the last several months of the race; only members of the government were required by the party to publicly disclose their campaign donors. Martin has never provided a full list of his supporters or the amounts donated by each one.[68] Now, under the recent amendments to the *Canada Elections Act,* anyone who seeks the leadership of a registered party will be required to make his campaign finances public. By requiring weekly disclosure during the last month of a leadership contest, the law will give party members or delegates some insight into possible conflicts of interest and other potential problems before they make their final choice.

■ Party Financing

The relationship between parties and the state is complex. On the one hand, parties are voluntary, private organizations of citizens. This implies that they should be subject to little, if any, state regulation. On the other hand, because parties perform functions that are essential to the health of the political system, they are also public institutions. This latter perspective suggests that parties should be both funded and regulated by the state. The tension between the public and private characters of parties—like the conflict between their national and local characteristics—has grown more acute in recent years, as the public has grown increasingly suspicious of political ethics. Until recently, Canadian parties were subject to relatively little regulation, compared to those in other Western democracies. The trend was clear, however: since 1970, their internal operations have been subject to increasing legal scrutiny.[69] The growing recognition of parties as "public utilities"[70] has expanded both their regulatory burden and their financial support from the state.

With Bill C-24, the era of parties as "private clubs" is over. For the first time, the internal operations of our national parties—as distinct from their purely electoral activities—are subject to state regulation and sanctions for misbehaviour. In this context, the key provisions of the new law are as follows:

- Constituency associations (called "electoral district associations," or EDAs, in the Bill) are now required to register with Elections Canada (section 403). Failure to register prohibits an association from receiving or spending funds.
- Nomination contests, which were formerly governed by the parties themselves, are now governed by the *Canada Elections Act* (section 478). Anyone who wishes to seek the nomination of a registered party for election to the House of Commons must appoint a financial agent; those who raise or spend $1000 or

more are required to file a report with Elections Canada after the nomination meeting. No nomination contestant may spend more than 20 percent of the maximum spending limit for that particular constituency in the previous federal election. In most ridings, that means a cap of roughly $16 000.[71] While few aspiring candidates can afford to spend that much, the limits are intended to ensure that the wealthy do not squeeze out women and members of visible minority groups. In the past, many such aspirants have been hampered by lack of funds, especially in constituencies where their party is expected to win.[72]

- Leadership contests are also subject to state regulation. A registered political party (see below for a discussion of registration) must inform Elections Canada as soon as a leadership race begins. All leadership candidates must register with the agency, and each must begin to report any campaign donations and expenditures as soon as his or her registration has been certified by the Chief Electoral Officer and the party leader. The candidate (more precisely, his or her official agent) is required to file a financial report in each of the four weeks immediately preceding the leadership vote, and submit a complete report within six months after the race ends. Note, however, that the law does not impose spending limits on leadership contests; the establishment and enforcement of such limits is still left to the discretion of the party itself.

Money is the "mother's milk of politics." Election campaigns in the television age are hugely expensive, running into millions of dollars for the major national parties. Maintaining a national organization between elections is also a costly undertaking. In order to survive, major national parties must raise substantial amounts every year. Until the *Election Expenses Act* took effect in 1974, reliable information on parties' financial affairs was difficult to find. The law required every registered party to disclose its annual revenues and expenditures, and to file a separate report after each election campaign. It also imposed limits on campaign spending and guaranteed public subsidies for party activity.

The amendments in Bill C-24 have radically altered the finance regime established in 1974. For the first time, contributions to political parties and candidates are limited by law. Corporations and unions, once the most significant sources of funding for particular parties (see Tables 3.3 and 3.4), are now severely restricted in their capacity to support political activity. Both monetary donations and gifts "in kind"— e.g., skilled volunteer labour—are now subject to stringent rules. Contribution limits also apply to individual donors, although these are higher than the caps imposed on associations. To make up the shortfall in donations, Bill C-24 introduced a new system of annual allowances for registered parties and raised the reimbursements for election spending by both parties and candidates. Electoral activity is now primarily funded by the public sector, not private interests and individual voters.

Another recent, and potentially significant, change to the *Canada Elections Act* concerns the registration scheme for political parties. Since 1970, the Chief Electoral Officer has maintained a *Registry of Parties* for the purpose of administering the Act. Only registered parties were eligible for the monetary benefits introduced in 1974;

in return, they were required by law to submit annual and post-election financial reports. To qualify for registration, a party had to run at least 50 candidates in a federal general election. In June 2003, the Supreme Court of Canada struck down the 50-candidate rule as a violation of the *Charter of Rights* (see the discussion of the *Figueroa* case in Dossier 10.5).[73] The federal government responded in May 2004 by passing Bill C-3, which redefined the criteria for party registration. Instead of nominating 50 candidates, a party wishing to become or remain registered must nominate at least one candidate and present written proof that it is a serious political organization. The safeguards in the Bill are intended to prevent the formation of fraudulent "parties" for the purpose of abusing the political tax credits. Those credits, which were established in 1974 and revised in 2000 and 2004, allow a contributor to deduct a percentage of each political donation from his or her income tax for that year. Their purpose is to encourage individuals to donate money to political parties, thus reducing the latter's dependence on corporate funding. Shortly after the new party-registration rules took effect, the number of registered parties rose from 9 to 12;[74] none of the new parties took more than a handful of votes.

The full effect of the amendments to the *Canada Elections Act* will not become apparent for some time. In principle, they should ensure a more level playing field among the parties—at least the major parties. Tables 3.2 and 3.3 present the financial returns for the five major federal parties in 2003. Total revenues for registered federal parties ranged from a low of $54 821 for the Marxist–Leninist Party[75] to $24 million for the Liberals and over $10 million for the NDP. (Total revenue for the NDP is not directly comparable to that for the other parties, however, because the NDP total includes funds receipted by the party's provincial sections; the other national parties report only the financial transactions of their national organizations.) For the PCs, their 2003 revenues reflected a considerable decline from past financial glories— which probably helps to explain their decision to merge with the Canadian Alliance. In 1992, for example, while they still formed a majority government, the PCs raised $11.5 million, more than any other federal party that year. Conversely, the Liberals, who raised the most funds in 1999, when they formed the government, raised only $7.6 million in 1992, when they were on the Opposition benches. There are obvious

TABLE 3.2 **INCOME AND EXPENSES OF CANADA'S MAJOR NATIONAL PARTIES, 2003 FISCAL YEAR, $**

PARTY	TOTAL INCOME	TOTAL EXPENSES	NET GAIN (LOSS)
BQ	1 251 770	1 609 608	(357 838)
Canadian Alliance	6 589 285	7 443 329	(854 044)
Liberal	28 922 028	28 112 392	809 636
NDP	11 856 751	8 012 667	3 844 084
Progressive Conservative	5 442 315	5 188 053	254 262

Source: Data compiled and used to create the above chart was taken from the website of Elections Canada: www.elections.ca. It is used with the permission of the Chief Electoral Officer but extrapolations and analysis rest with the author.

TABLE 3.3 SOURCES OF PARTY FUNDS, CANADA'S MAJOR NATIONAL PARTIES, 2003 FISCAL YEAR, $ AND (%)

PARTY	INDIVIDUALS	BUSINESS	UNIONS	OTHER	TOTAL
BQ	444 537 (44)	67 209 (7)	20 300 (2)	481 235 (47)	1 013 281
Canadian Alliance	5 356 912 (65)	1 319 144 (16)	—	1 627 481 (20)	8 303 537
Liberal	6 194 925 (26)	10 816 396 (45)	111 938 (<1)	7 037 190 (29)	24 160 449
NDP	4 782 777 (47)	109 958 (1)	5 198 171 (51)	5 596 (<1)	10 096 502
PC	3 152 867 (73)	1 155 746 (27)	—	15 734 (<1)	4 324 347

Source: Data compiled and used to create the above chart was taken from the website of Elections Canada: www.elections.ca. It is used with the permission of the Chief Electoral Officer but extrapolations and analysis rest with the author.

financial benefits to being the party in government. With the exception of the Green Party, which raised almost $235 000, none of the registered parties outside Parliament raised as much as $100 000 in 2003; most received considerably less.

Table 3.3 reveals substantial differences in the parties' sources of funding. The Bloc Québécois received most of its money from individuals. Until 2000, its internal rules prohibited the party from accepting donations from corporations and unions. Among the other parties represented in the Commons in 2003, all but the Liberals relied heavily on donations from individual Canadians. The Liberals received the lion's share of donations from corporations, whereas the NDP received much of its funding from trade unions, as Table 3.4 reveals.

The parties' fiscal reports for the 2004 fiscal year will be substantially different from those filed in 2003, in at least three ways:

1. The business and union donations will be gone. Bill C-24 prohibits any contributions to national parties from corporations, trade unions, and other associations, although it does permit small annual donations (up to an annual total of $1000) to local constituencies, candidates, and nomination contestants.

2. The few individual donations over $5000 will disappear; the Act forbids any individual to give more than that amount to a party and/or its constituency associations, candidates, and nomination contestants in any given year. (This does not apply to a deceased individual who leaves a bequest to a particular party in his or her will, or to a nomination or leadership contestant who funds his or her own campaign.)

3. A substantial proportion of the 2004 revenues for each of the major parties will come from the new annual allowances in Bill C-24. Beginning on January 1, 2004, any registered party that received at least 2 percent of the national vote (or 5 percent of the vote in the constituencies where it ran candidates) in the previous general election will be entitled to an annual payment of $1.75 per valid vote. (The original figure was $1.50; it was increased at Report Stage in the House of Commons,[76] largely in response to concerns among Liberal MPs that the lower

Liberal Party of Canada—Average donation: $298; average size of donation: $1107 ($809 more than the average for all registered parties)

NAME OF DONOR	CATEGORY	AMOUNT
55555 Inc.	Business	2 974 341
Bombardier Inc.	Business	139 795
CN Railway Co.	Business	119 580
Grant Forest Products Inc.	Business	105 889
EnCana Corp.	Business	103 474
Kruger Inc.	Business	103 000
Donald Meehan	Individual	100 000
SNC–Lavalin Inc.	Business	84 665
Bell Canada	Business	78 470
Power Corp. of Canada	Business	70 000

Canadian Reform/Canadian Alliance—Average size of donation: $101 ($197 less than the average for all registered parties)

NAME OF DONOR	CATEGORY	AMOUNT
Magna International Inc.	Business	39 700
Scotiabank	Business	37 140
Bank of Montreal	Business	25 400
CanWest Global Communications	Business	25 000
Telus Corp.	Business	24 800
Lethbridge Constituency	Other	22 820
Edmonton Southeast Constituency	Other	20 000
George Weston Ltd.	Business	20 000
Kelowna Constituency	Other	15 000
Canadian Sable Fish Association	Business	15 000

Bloc Québécois—Average size of donation: $192 ($106 less than the average for all registered parties)

NAME OF DONOR	CATEGORY	AMOUNT
Dessau–Soprin Inc.	Business	5200
Banque Nationale du Canada	Business	5000
Groupe CGI, Inc.	Business	5000
Benson & Hedges	Business	5000

NAME OF DONOR	CATEGORY	AMOUNT
Socodec Inc.	Business	5000
UFCW Canada National Council	Union	5000
UFCW Canada National Office	Union	5000
Sécuriplex Inc.	Business	4750
Babillard Synapse	Business	4500
Imperial Tobacco	Business	4400

New Democratic Party—Average size of donation: $303 ($5 more than the average for all registered parties)

NAME OF DONOR	CATEGORY	AMOUNT
CEP National Office	Union	761910
UFCW Canada	Union	740600
CAW National Headquarters	Union	736733
CUPE National Office	Union	334710
USWA National Headquarters	Union	316090
USWA District 6	Union	259823
OPSEU–SEFPO	Union	252620
Canadian Labour Congress	Union	219440
IAM & AW National Headquarters	Union	202500
SEIU National Headquarters	Union	131650

Progressive Conservative Party—Average size of donation: $241 ($57 less than the average for all registered parties)

NAME OF DONOR	CATEGORY	AMOUNT
Power Corporation of Canada	Business	45000
Scotiabank	Business	43674
BCE Inc.	Business	25000
McCarthy Tétrault LLP	Business	23060
Bell Canada	Business	18096
Middlefield Bancorp Ltd.	Business	16560
Jetport Inc.	Business	15000
Bombardier Inc.	Business	13245
Rogers Group	Business	13060
Bennett Jones LLP	Business	12664

Source: Data compiled and used to create the above chart was taken from the website of Elections Canada: www.elections.ca. It is used with the permission of the Chief Electoral Officer but extrapolations and analysis rest with the author.

figure would not adequately compensate their party for the lost corporate donations.) Starting in 2005, the allowances will be paid in quarterly installments (i.e., four times a year). However, the 2004 allowances were paid in one lump sum at the start of January, as part of the transitional arrangements to bring the Act into effect. The Liberals received $9.2 million; the Conservatives, $8.5 million (based on the combined vote of the PCs and Alliance in 2000); the BQ, $2.4 million; and the NDP, $1.9 million.[77] The latter party found itself awash in funds, partly because of the new allowance and partly because unions rushed to donate to the party before contributions were banned.[78] The Green Party, which won less than 2 percent of the vote in 2000, campaigned hard to qualify for the allowances in the 2004 election. It told voters that every ballot cast for the Greens would mean $1.75 in public funding in each year until the next election, as long as the party reached the vote threshold to qualify.[79] It succeeded: the Greens won 4.3 percent of the national vote, which entitles the party to an annual allowance of over $1 million beginning in 2005.

The results of the 2004 election were less lucrative for the Liberals, whose vote total was lower than in the previous election. Their annual allowance will fall by roughly half a million dollars a year. The Conservatives did even worse: the seven-point drop from the combined 2000 vote of the Alliance and PCs produced an annual loss of $1.5 million. For the BQ and the NDP, the news is much better: the former will see an annual increase of more than half a million dollars, while the latter almost doubled its allowance to $3.7 million a year. One feature of the new financial arrangements is particularly noteworthy: while the contribution limits may pose problems for constituency fundraisers, the allowances are paid directly to the national headquarters. This means that the fiscal balance between the centre and the local associations will likely shift, in favour of the former.

The spending limits shown in column 3 of Table 3.5 are calculated according to a formula in the *Canada Elections Act*. Each party can spend up to 70 cents per elector in every riding where the party has nominated a candidate. Between 2000 and 2004,

TABLE 3.5 ELECTION EXPENDITURES REPORTED BY CANADA'S MAJOR NATIONAL PARTIES, 2004, $

PARTY	NO. OF CANDIDATES	OFFICIAL SPENDING LIMIT	REPORTED EXPENDITURES
BQ	75	4 591 747	4 511 087
CP*	308	17 593 925	17 284 257
Liberal	308	17 593 925	16 640 947
NDP	308	17 593 925	12 041 249

* "CP" stands for "Conservative Party of Canada."

Source: Data compiled and used to create the above chart was taken from the website of Elections Canada: www.elections.ca. It is used with the permission of the Chief Electoral Officer but extrapolations and analysis rest with the author. Retrieved January 2005.

TABLE 3.6 SELECTED CATEGORIES OF ELECTION EXPENDITURE, CANADA'S MAJOR NATIONAL PARTIES, 2004 GENERAL ELECTION, $

PARTY	ADVERTISING (BROADCAST)	ADVERTISING (OTHER)	POLLING	LEADER'S TOUR	OTHER
BQ	1 443 407	977 687	56 761	389 041	497 353
CP	5 875 764	1 402 240	341 260	3 780 432	909 033
Liberal	7 578 406	2 589 017	641 515	2 836 782	883 494
NDP	4 388 233	1 044 464	1 361 146	2 453 019	210 646

Source: Data compiled and used to create the above chart was taken from the website of Elections Canada: www.elections.ca. It is used with the permission of the Chief Electoral Officer but extrapolations and analysis rest with the author. Retrieved January 2005.

the limit for a party with candidates in every constituency rose from around $12 million to over $17 million. This is partly the result of the increase in the number of ridings (from 301 to 308) and the increase in the voting population as measured by the 2001 census. However, it also reflects the wider definition of "election expenses" in Bill C-24 (see Table 3.6 for examples of these election expenses). For the first time, polling costs—a substantial proportion of campaign costs for a major party—are included in the total. In consequence, the per-voter limit rose from 62 cents in the 2000 Act to 70 cents in the new Act.

WHAT IS A PARTY SYSTEM?

There are almost as many definitions of **"party system"** as there are of "political party." Some experts include every official party, while others restrict their focus to the parties in Parliament. For the sake of brevity, this chapter takes the latter approach; for the most part, we have restricted the discussion of Canada's party system to the five parties currently represented in the House of Commons. This does not mean that the smaller parties are irrelevant. As Table 3.7 reveals, there were 12 parties were on the Official Register in June 2004. Collectively, the seven smallest parties received 5.47 percent of the vote in the 2004 federal election; none was able to win a seat. (However, as noted earlier, most of that vote went to the Greens, who succeeded in qualifying for the new annual allowance.)

To some extent, Elections Canada treats all registered parties equally. Each must meet the same criteria for registration. As we saw in the previous section, these criteria were amended in May 2004 in response to a ruling by the Supreme Court of Canada. They currently include

- nomination of at least one candidate before the nomination deadline at each general election, or in a by-election;

TABLE 3.7   NATIONAL REGISTER OF PARTIES, JUNE 2004

NAME OF PARTY	PARTY LEADER	LOCATION OF NATIONAL HEADQUARTERS
Bloc Québécois	Gilles Duceppe	Montreal
Canadian Action Party	Constance Fogal	Toronto
Christian Heritage Party	Ronald Gray	Ottawa
Communist Party of Canada	Miguel Figueroa	Toronto
Conservative Party of Canada	Stephen Harper	Ottawa
Green Party of Canada	Jim Harris	Ottawa
Liberal Party of Canada	Paul Martin	Ottawa
Libertarian Party of Canada	Jean-Serge Brisson	Embrun, ON
Marijuana Party	Marc-Boris St-Maurice	Montreal
Marxist–Leninist Party of Canada	Sandra Smith	Montreal
New Democratic Party	Jack Layton	Ottawa
Progressive Canadian Party	Ernie Schreiber	Ottawa

Source: Data compiled and used to create the above chart was taken from the website of Elections Canada: www.elections.ca. It is used with the permission of the Chief Electoral Officer but extrapolations and analysis rest with the author. Retrieved June 2004.

- submission of an annual fiscal report by the party's designated official agent, as approved by its official auditor; and
- filing an application for registration with the Chief Electoral Officer, including the endorsement by signature of 250 party members (with full names and addresses), an official party name and logo, and the names of the party's leader and three other officers; all party members and officers must be listed in the *Permanent Register of Electors* (discussed in Chapter 4).

In addition to the financial provisions discussed under "Party Financing" later in this chapter, each registered party also has the right to list its party affiliation on the ballot. In addition, all registered parties belong to the Elections Canada Advisory Committee, which meets regularly with the Chief Electoral Officer to discuss regulatory issues and suggest improvements to the election regime. So our exclusion of 7 of the 12 registered parties may strike readers as arbitrary or unfair, especially the exclusion of the Green Party. Nonetheless, given the impossibility of discussing each of these parties in a brief chapter, we define the Canadian party system as follows: *The sum total of the parties represented in the House of Commons at a given time.* In other words, we will restrict our discussion to the five parties that won seats in the House of Commons in the 1993, 1997, and 2000 federal elections, and the four that won seats in 2004. Two of the parties that contested the 2000 election, the Canadian Alliance and the Progressive Conservatives, merged in late 2003—hence the reduction from five to four.

Although much of the literature on party systems focuses on the number of parties, some authors have taken other variables into consideration, such as the relative size of the parties or their ideological "distance" from each other. The conventional wisdom is that Canada has a two-and-a-half-party system at the national level. The "half" was the NDP, which won enough seats to play a role in Parliament (especially during Liberal minority governments) but never had a real chance to form a government. The other two parties were the Liberals and the PCs, which alternated in power (albeit fairly infrequently) from 1867 until 1993. The PC collapse in the early 1990s left the Liberals as the only national party capable of winning an election; therefore, according to one recent study, "Canada is now a one-party predominant system."[80]

Numerical categories, even those that incorporate other variables, provide relatively little information. They do not explain the number of parties in a given party system, nor do they tell us much about the relationships between the party system and the political system as a whole—or, indeed, about the relationships among the various networks within each party. Carty and his co-authors[81] provide a broader and more satisfactory account of party systems, which incorporates the following variables:

- relationships among the various networks within each party (the caucus, the leader and his or her entourage, and the local members in the constituencies);
- impact of changes in other national institutions upon the party system (e.g., the shift of power from the legislative to the executive branch, decentralized federalism, changes in electoral laws, and the introduction of the *Charter*);
- number of parties inside and outside Parliament;
- methods of choosing party leaders;
- relationships between national parties and particular subcultures (regional, linguistic, economic, and ideological);
- sources and regulation of party finance; and
- technologies of mass communication.

As these variables change over time, so does the party system. By situating the party system within its broader political context, Carty's approach allows us to develop a richer and more useful understanding of party systems. We will return to Carty's theory of party-system development in "The History of the Canadian Party System" on page 117.

However we define a party system, one core idea remains constant: in democratic states with two or more parties, no party operates in isolation. Each affects, and is affected by, the other members of the system. Parties compete with each other for money, votes, and other scarce resources. When one party in a system adapts to a change in the competitive environment—e.g., responding to public demands for greater "democracy" by adopting an OMOV system for choosing its leaders—the others feel pressured to follow suit or risk electoral disadvantage. In the electoral context, a strategic choice by one party often provokes a response from rival parties and may even inspire the creation of one or more new parties—as we will see when we discuss Brian Mulroney's inadvertent role in the establishment of the Reform and BQ parties. On the other hand, if one party is too dominant, two or more smaller parties may merge in order to provide a more effective challenge (Dossier 3.4).

Where Do Political Parties Come From?

Political parties do not simply appear, as if from nowhere, on the political scene. They arise at particular points in time in response to a variety of opportunities and constraints, with the purpose of achieving particular representational or governing objectives. The three major theories of party development emphasize social, mobilizational, and institutional explanations, respectively.[82]

Social Cleavages: Political Culture and Class

Societal approaches to the development of the party system emphasize the role played by changes in the economy, social relations, or political culture of a society. From this perspective, a party system is largely determined by and reflective of social relations and/or attitudes of individuals. To understand the development of a particular party system, one must examine the evolution of the underlying social relations. By implication, a party system would change only if the underlying social forces also changed. Although there are many variants of the social approach to party development, two have been particularly popular in Canada: the political culture model and the class politics model. As we saw in Chapter 2, the "political culture" of a given country is the overall pattern of political orientations within its population. Canada does not have a single political culture, but rather a set of subcultures, including Quebec nationalism and Western populism. The political culture model suggests that the number and ideological diversity of parties in a given party system reflect the different subcultures in the electorate. When we talk about the effect of social divisions on voting behaviour, we refer to them as **cleavages** (see the discussion of Canadian voting behaviour in Chapter 4). In general, social cleavages are based on long-term demographic characteristics such as religion and class. However, ideological cleavages are becoming increasingly important in Western societies, as environmentalism and populism grow in influence; purely partisan cleavages also play a role, especially for the Liberal Party (see the discussion of party identification in Chapter 4).

As we will see in Chapter 4, the mere presence of a particular cleavage does not automatically affect the party system. To understand why some subcultures shape the national party system and others do not, we need to consider two factors: the institutional incentives and constraints that affect the creation of political parties, and the organization and strategies that are required to transform a societal cleavage into a political party. Political parties cannot survive unless they attract substantial support—both electoral and financial—from the subculture(s) that they purport to represent. The missing link between political culture and the party system is **mobilization.**

Mobilization

Politics is about more than passively responding to inputs and channelling them into governmental or policy outputs; it is also about establishing priorities, setting goals, and implementing strategies that enable one to pursue objectives. Political actors are strategic actors. As previously noted, parties are not passive victims of their environments. They are active agents with the power to define the issues of importance in political conflict and to mobilize voters behind their issue positions. That power has its limits, however. A **political entrepreneur**—an individual who identifies an unmet need in the political marketplace and establishes a new party to fill that need—does not start from scratch. He identifies an existing or latent subculture and mobilizes its members by appealing to their unexpressed political values. To create a new party, therefore, the entrepreneur requires at least three things:

1. a preexisting base in the electorate, among one or more groups of voters whose political needs are not met by existing parties;
2. the opportunity to exploit that dissatisfaction with the existing party system; and
3. the resources—money, volunteers, media attention—to establish and market a new alternative.

The mobilization of targeted groups of voters is not solely the responsibility of entrepreneurs seeking to create new parties. The leaders of existing parties also make strategic choices when they decide which subcultures in the electorate they wish to attract. In so doing, they can reshape voting patterns that might otherwise remain intact.[83] The most basic choice is whether to retain and reinforce the party's existing base—its "heartland" within the electorate—or to risk alienating that base by reaching out to subcultures that have not previously been included in the party's electoral coalition. Either option carries risks and opportunities.

Maintaining the traditional base is the safest strategy in the short term. But if that base shrinks, or its ties to the party weaken, the party may fade away over the long term. The troubled relationship between the NDP and organized labour illustrates the point. The private-sector unions that provide the lion's share of NDP resources are losing members, as plants close and manufacturers contract out to nonunionized suppliers. While public-sector unions have grown rapidly since World War II (at least until the recent era of downsizing), they may be constrained in their ability to support a particular party by laws and norms that require public servants to remain politically neutral. They are also affected by the new contribution rules in Bill C-24, which limit the amount of money and volunteer labour that unions can donate. Even in the heyday of the union movement, the NDP failed to capture even a plurality of the labour vote. Relations between the party and its key labour supporters—both private-sector unions such as the Canadian Auto Workers and public-sector unions such as the Canadian Union of Public Employees—became tense and sometimes antagonistic in the 1990s. Partly in response, leader Jack Layton deliberately targeted environmentalist voters in the 2004 election campaign; it is not yet clear whether those appeals had much effect, especially given the rise in the Green Party's vote, although the NDP vote also increased substantially over its 2000 performance.

Trying to bring new subcultures into the existing electoral coalition is often risky. It can pay off handsomely in the short term, but it can erode a party's traditional base in the long term. As Bickerton, Gagnon, and Smith have argued, "party manoeuvring in search of strategic advantage and the support of the weakly committed median voter [erodes] the commitment of core supporters and therefore the stability of historic party vote shares."[84] The collapse of the federal Progressive Conservative Party in 1993 provides a classic example. When he became party leader in 1983, Brian Mulroney promised to win power by appealing to voters in Quebec. In order to do so, he had to find a way to bridge the ideological and regional chasm between Western populists— a core element of the party since the days of John Diefenbaker—and Quebec nationalists. The PCs won a smashing victory in 1984, taking every seat in Alberta as well as a majority of Quebec's francophone ridings. The party believed that it had engineered a historic realignment of the Quebec electorate. In reality, and despite its increased seat share in Quebec in 1988, the PC's "connection with Québécois voters was tenuous at best."[85] In 1993, Quebec Tory voters shifted en masse to the Bloc Québécois. In exchange for the dubious prize of temporary Quebec nationalist support, the Tories ended up sacrificing their Western base and the conservative principles that had sustained their members in Ontario and the Atlantic region:

> [T]heir Quebec caucus, membership, and voter base was distinctly to the left of the rest of the party on social policy and had a starkly different understanding of the character of the national identity and Quebec's place within Confederation. In the end, the effort to bridge these yawning differences created the agents of the Conservative Party's demise (in the guise of Reform and the Bloc).[86]

Many PC members believed that their party leadership had deserted them, and they reacted in kind.

Compared to the leaders of established parties, political entrepreneurs have more freedom to concentrate on one particular subculture and to mobilize it in the most effective way: by refusing to compromise the needs and goals of that specific group of voters. Dossier 3.2 identifies five long-term subcultures in the Canadian electorate, the last two of which have repeatedly shifted between parties in response to the strategic decisions of party leaders.

From this perspective, the five-party system that emerged in 1993 represents not a transformation of Canadian politics, but simply the latest reflection of a stable pattern of subcultures within the electorate. The subcultures themselves are not new; the novelty lies in their successful mobilization into separate party organizations by entrepreneurial political leaders. Preston Manning seized the opportunity to create a separate party based on the Western populist subculture (Reform/Alliance) (see Dossier 3.3), while Lucien Bouchard exploited the unfilled political market for a Quebec nationalist party (the Bloc Québécois) (see Dossier 3.5). A different type of political entrepreneurship is evident in the decision by Canadian Alliance leader Stephen Harper and PC leader Peter MacKay to merge their two parties in late 2003 (Dossier 3.4). Their intent was to bring two of the subcultures in the Mulroney coalition—conservatives and Western populists—back together. These subcultures are not entirely compatible, as the decline in the 2004 Conservative vote (relative to the combined 2000 vote shares of the two parties) suggests. For the foreseeable future, the Quebec nationalist subculture will remain separate; its party, the BQ,

DOSSIER 3.2 Five Long-Term Subcultures in the Canadian Electorate

Ever since 1921, Canada has had a **multi-party system.** Parties have come and gone, but not these five components of the system:

1. A Liberal party with a national coalition capable of governing. At times in the 1970s and 1980s, the Liberals were virtually shut out of the West, as they are today in francophone Quebec, but they have usually maintained appreciable strength in all parts of the country . . .

2. A Conservative or Progressive Conservative party claiming a national base, but in fact coming to power only in exceptional circumstances and then governing only for short periods of time . . .

3. A social-democratic party claiming to be national but with real strength only in Western Canada and Ontario. This element became visible as early as the mid-1920s, when a group of left-wing MPs emerged amid the wreckage of the disintegrating Progressive party. These MPs went on to help found the Co-operative Commonwealth Federation in 1932. The CCF regrouped in 1961 as the New Democratic Party . . .

4. A right-wing populist party based in Western Canada. Social Credit, the first modern example, entered the House of Commons in 1935. Despite a long history of ups and downs, it continued to elect western members through 1965. Provincial Social Credit parties governed Alberta until 1971 and British Columbia until 1992. The Reform party inherits the conservative populist tradition. Its first leader was Preston Manning, himself a federal Socred candidate in 1965 and the son of Ernest Manning, the long-serving Social Credit premier of Alberta.

5. A francophone nationalist party in Quebec, such as the Bloc Populaire in 1945, the Union des Électeurs in 1949, the Ralliement Créditiste in 1962 through 1979, and the Bloc Québécois in 1993. Plus nationalist parties that ran for office at the provincial level—Maurice Duplessis's Union Nationale, which replaced the Conservatives and dominated provincial politics from the 1930s until 1960; the Parti Québécois, which has governed on and off since 1976; and, most recently, Mario Dumont's Action Démocratique. Interestingly, these nationalist parties have spanned almost the entire ideological spectrum, from socialist left to monetary-reform right.

Source: Reprinted from Stephen Harper and Tom Flanagan, "Our Benign Dictatorship," *The Next City,* Winter 1996–97, 38.

made a remarkable comeback from near-oblivion in 2004. As Dossiers 3.3, 3.4, and 3.5 point out, the histories of the Reform/Alliance, the new Conservative Party, and the BQ illustrate both the risks and the rewards of entrepreneurial political leadership.

DOSSIER 3.3 The Reform Party of Canada and the Canadian Alliance

The key to understanding Reform's emergence appears to be in its mobilizational success. Precisely because Westerners placed such high expectations on the Conservatives after the 1984 election (and despite the high profile of Westerners in the Conservative caucus and cabinet) it proved impossible for the party to fulfill those expectations, particularly given the regional underpinnings of the Westerners' support for the Conservatives. As a result, a space opened within the matrix of party competition for a new party to fill.[87]

By 1987, when Preston Manning founded the Reform Party, Albertans and British Columbians were disillusioned with both major national parties. After years of Liberal governments, which many Westerners perceived as either unsympathetic or downright hostile to their region, the PCs had become the dominant federal party in Alberta and competed strongly with the NDP in British Columbia. The election of the Mulroney Conservatives in 1984 brought the region back into a national government, sparking hopes that Canadian politics would now focus less on the demands of Quebec and more on the needs of the peripheral regions. In the fall of 1986, those hopes were shattered when the federal government awarded a maintenance contract for CF-18 fighter aircraft to a Montreal firm, despite the superiority of a Winnipeg bid. Western fury at this evidence of continued Central Canadian dominance, reinforced by resent-

ment of the "two-nations" vision embodied in the 1987 Meech Lake Accord (see Chapter 8), led to several fringe separatist movements. Manning sought to counter the appeal of Western separatism by creating a regional party in national politics: the Reform Party's original slogan was "The West Wants In."

Reform appealed to voters concerned about the federal debt and deficit, and those alienated from unresponsive political institutions, as well as voters who believed in "traditional values" and objected to what they perceived as "special treatment" for Quebec. It also capitalized on the growing appeal of populist values in the electorate, particularly the demand for direct democracy. While it enjoyed its greatest electoral success in the two westernmost provinces—winning 22 of 26 Alberta seats and 24 of 32 British Columbia seats in 1993—its mobilization strategy was less successful elsewhere in Canada. Although Reform had begun to organize intensively in Ontario after 1991, it took only one seat in that province in 1993 and none in 1997. The perception of Reform as a "regional party" was perhaps its strongest appeal in the West, but it hurt the party in Ontario.[88]

After the 1997 election, Manning launched the United Alternative project to boost Reform's popularity in Eastern Canada. He asked his membership to approve a plan to found a new party, a coalition of groups that might include former Conservatives, Quebec nationalists, and others opposed to the Liberal government. In essence, Manning wanted to realign Canadian politics—to re-create the two-party system that had characterized Canadian politics in the nineteenth century. The two parties would be the Liberals and his proposed United Alternative. At the 1998 Reform Assembly, 91.3 percent of delegates voted to hold a United Alternative convention to formally initiate the process.[89] By the time the first UA convention opened in February 1999 in Ottawa, opposition was growing within Reform ranks. No one was entirely sure what Manning intended to do: merge with (or take over) the PCs, absorb new subcultures into the Reform Party, seek joint nomination of candidates to avoid vote-splitting, or something else altogether.

At the February 1999 UA Conference, participants were given four options: launch an entirely new party; pursue local initiatives with other parties, such as joint nomination meetings; unite behind an existing party (which, given that 80 percent of those in attendance were Reform members, presumably meant a Reform takeover); or merge two or more parties.[90] Creating a new party was the most popular of the four options at the convention, but when it was submitted to the Reform membership in a May 1999 referendum, it was supported by only 60.5 percent of those who voted (less than half of those eligible). Despite Manning's sales pitch and his efforts to persuade Reformers that the status quo was not an option, there was little enthusiasm for change among the "believers" in his party. The UA appears to have had its greatest appeal to the "careerists" who wanted to displace the Liberals as the party of government.

Nor was there much excitement among the prospective partners in the UA enterprise. Members of the Progressive Conservative party voted against participating in the UA, by the overwhelming margin of 95 percent.[91] While this was a heavy blow for advocates of a Reform–PC merger, it did not derail the UA process. In January 2000 a new party, the Canadian Reform Conservative Alliance, was formally launched. Two months later, Reform was officially absorbed into the Canadian Alliance by an overwhelming vote (92 percent) in a second party referendum.

Although Manning succeeded in creating the Canadian Alliance, the rest of his plan went awry. He lost the leadership of the new party to Alberta PC Treasurer Stockwell Day, after a bitter and divisive contest. Day became a controversial figure almost immediately, despite his easy victory in a British Columbia by-election in September 2000. When Prime Minister Chrétien called an early election in October, the Alliance had not had time to jell as a party organization.[92] The scars from the UA debate and the leadership contest were still fresh. To make matters worse, Day did not live up to the expectations of his supporters. Not only did he fail to lead the Alliance to a breakthrough in Ontario—the party won only two seats, largely because of local factors—but his poor performance in the campaign damaged his reputation and that of his fledgling party.[93] By the summer of 2001, 13 MPs had quit the Alliance caucus in protest against Day's leadership. Five later returned, while the remaining eight dissidents formed the Democratic Representative Caucus and announced that they would work with the Progressive

(cont'd)

Conservatives in Parliament. Although Day announced in July 2001 that he would resign and ask the executive council to hold a leadership contest, he neither set a date for his departure nor announced whether he would run. After several weeks of uncertainty, the national council announced that it would hold a leadership vote in March 2002; under the party's constitution, this meant that Day would have to relinquish the leadership in December 2001. He duly did so, and announced his candidacy for his former job in January 2002. He lost the leadership to former Reform MP Stephen Harper a few months later.

The lessons for future political entrepreneurs are not encouraging. In a country as divided as Canada, the successful mobilization of one subculture—alienated Westerners, for example—may preclude the mobilization of others (Atlantic Canadians, francophones, and/or Ontarians). The dilemma for a new party is this: in order to survive and grow, it must define its political base and appeal strongly to those targeted group(s). But if it defines that base too narrowly and espouses political values that are shared—albeit strongly—by only a minority of Canadian voters in the hope of a short-term political payoff, its long-term prospects for building a broad electoral coalition and winning power are seriously compromised.

DOSSIER 3.4 The Merger of the Federal Progressive Conservatives and the Canadian Alliance, October 2003–March 2004

After the failure of the United Alternative in Ontario, there was only one promising option for the Alliance: a formal coalition or merger with the Progressive Conservatives. Stephen Harper seemed to be open to negotiating with the PCs; Joe Clark, whose second stint as PC leader began in 1998, was hostile to the idea. Merger talks had to wait until Clark stepped down. As noted earlier, Nova Scotia MP Peter MacKay won the PC leadership in June 2003 by promising rival David Orchard that he would not merge the party with the Alliance. Shortly thereafter, MacKay entered secret negotiations with Harper. Each leader appointed three "emissaries" to hammer out a deal that members of both parties could accept. The talks appeared stalled by late summer, although the two leaders promised that their caucuses would cooperate in the House of Commons when Parliament resumed in September.[94]

By the fall of 2003, the popularity of aspiring Prime Minister Paul Martin seemed certain to produce a smashing Liberal victory in an anticipated spring 2004 election. Many senior figures in both parties regarded a merger as the only way to survive the onslaught.[95] If such a merger were to happen, it would have to be accomplished quickly: little time remained for a new party to prepare for an election campaign, and the ban on corporate donations in Bill C-24 was set to take effect at the end of the year. For years, Canada's business elite had been calling on the two parties to "unite the right." Advocates of a PC–Alliance deal wanted to take full advantage of corporate generosity, which meant that a merger had to happen no later than mid-October.[96]

News of the merger talks leaked to the public in late September, forcing Harper and MacKay—especially the latter—to quell dissent within their respective parties. The deal was finalized shortly after Thanksgiving, and announced on October 15. To counter fears of an Alliance takeover, Harper had made significant concessions on policy and organization. In addition to adopting the 1998 PC leadership-selection system, the Alliance agreed to endorse several PC principles, including:

- "A balance between fiscal accountability, progressive social policy, and individual rights and responsibilities";
- "the supremacy of democratic parliamentary institutions and the rule of law";
- "a belief in the equality of all Canadians"; and
- "a belief that all Canadians should have reasonable access to quality health care regardless of their ability to pay."[97]

There was no reference to direct democracy, social conservatism, or private medical clinics. Indeed, the references to "the rule of law" and "equality" seemed to contradict the deeply held view of many Alliance members that the *Charter of Rights* should be weakened, judges put on a political leash, and same-sex marriage outlawed (see Chapter 10).

The backlash began immediately. While there were some dissenters in Alliance ranks, the loudest opponents were PCs. David Orchard charged MacKay with breaking the written agreement the two men had signed at the June 2003 PC leadership convention, and later filed a lawsuit

in an unsuccessful attempt to prevent the merger.[98] Joe Clark left the party, along with other prominent PC MPs. The deal required the members of both parties to ratify the merger by December 12. This was an easier proposition for the Alliance, whose constitution could be amended by a simple majority vote of the members, than for the PCs. Their constitution stipulated amendment by a two-thirds vote at a national convention. Because of the tight time frame, the PC Management Committee decided to hold a "virtual" convention on December 6. Party members in the constituencies would elect delegates to regional meetings, which would be linked electronically;[99] if two-thirds of the delegates voted in favour of the merger, the party would disappear. The cutoff for new members to join the PC Party was set for November, infuriating merger opponents who argued that this would allow Alliance members to flood into the party in order to vote for the deal. There were some anecdotal reports of "crossover" members,[100] although it is not clear whether they made much difference to the outcome.

In early December, after a sustained selling campaign by Harper and MacKay, both parties ratified the October 15 agreement. Almost 96 percent of the Alliance members who voted in their party's referendum—60 percent of the total membership—opted to merge with the PCs.[101] The day after this result was announced, 90 percent of the 2500 delegates to the "virtual" PC convention did the same.[102] Two days later, on December 8, the new Conservative Party of Canada was officially registered with Elections Canada. In the meantime, the unofficial merger had produced the desired financial result: whereas

(cont'd)

the two founding parties had been mired in debt, the prospect of a united Conservative Party inspired an outburst of corporate generosity.[103] As it turned out, the new party did not manage to capture as many votes in the 2004 election as its two founding parties had won in 2000 (see Chapter 4). Nonetheless, it ran a surprisingly strong and well-organized campaign for a party that had come into being six months before the election call.

Peter MacKay and Stephen Harper announce the merger of their two parties, October 15, 2003. (© CP/Tom Hanson)

DOSSIER 3.5 The Bloc Québécois

As we will see in Chapter 9, Quebeckers reacted angrily to the death of the Meech Lake Accord in June 1990. Even before the Accord officially expired on June 23, that anger prompted the formation of a separate Quebec nationalist party. The Bloc Québécois began as a group of eight Quebec MPs—six former Progressive Conservatives and two ex-Liberals—who broke with their parties in the spring of 1990.[104] They soon decided to form a new party, led by charismatic former Cabinet minister Lucien Bouchard. With the assistance of the provincial Parti Québécois, the BQ quickly acquired an extraparliamentary organization. In August 1990, BQ candidate Gilles Duceppe won a by-election in Montreal, becoming the first openly sovereigntist candidate elected to the House of Commons.[105] The BQ's membership grew rapidly, despite its lack of official party status in Parliament (it did not have the 12 MPs required for recognition by the Speaker). It gained a national profile during the 1992 referendum on the Charlottetown Accord, the defeat of which further alienated Quebec nationalists from the Progressive Conservatives and boosted support for sovereignty in the province. The BQ under Bouchard won 54 seats in the 1993 federal election, becoming the official Opposition to the new Liberal government.

The purpose of the BQ was twofold: to represent Quebec nationalists in the federal Parliament and to assist the PQ in a future sovereignty referendum. This narrow focus, and the ineffectiveness of many caucus members in speaking English, weakened the BQ's performance as official Opposition. After the PQ returned to power in 1994, most BQ MPs divided their time between Ottawa and Quebec. They promised to return home for good if the referendum passed, to help build the new Quebec state. Little thought appears to have been given to the long-term future of the party if the referendum failed.[106]

Shortly after the 1995 sovereignty referendum (see Chapter 9), Bouchard left federal politics to become the premier of Quebec. His successor, Michel Gauthier, lacked Bouchard's fiery oratory and electoral appeal. After less than a year, he

stepped down and was replaced by Duceppe. Despite a poor campaign in 1997, which may have cost it official Opposition status, the BQ managed to hold most of its seats. Although Duceppe redeemed himself with an energetic campaign in 2000, thousands of BQ voters stayed home on election day. For the first time in its history, the party placed second to the Liberals in its home province. Despite this evidence that Quebec nationalist voters appeared to be turning away from federal politics once again, 68 percent of Quebec respondents to the 2000 *Canadian Election Study* identified the BQ as "the party most able to defend Quebec's interests."[107] Only 21 percent named the Liberals.

Former Prime Minister Chrétien was deeply unpopular in his native Quebec. His leading role in the 1980–82 constitutional negotiations and his public opposition to the Meech Lake Accord made him reviled by sovereigntists. Chrétien's presence as leader of the federal Liberals kept the BQ on life support after the 2000 election. Many BQ supporters feared that his replacement by Paul Martin would spell the end of their party, especially after the election of a federalist Liberal government in the province in 2003. By the end of that year, the BQ caucus was in disarray and the party was low in the polls. There were widespread predictions that the Liberals would win a majority of Quebec seats in the next federal election, reducing the BQ to an irrelevant rump.[108]

The party's fortunes began to revive as soon as the sponsorship scandal made the headlines in February 2004 (see Dossier 6.2). Many Quebec voters were infuriated by national media portrayals of their province as money-grubbing and corrupt; they were

(cont'd)

also incensed by the government's apparent assumption that their loyalty to Canada could be bought for the price of a few Maple Leaf flags. They took out their anger on the federal Liberals, who were also damaged by a growing backlash against the cost-cutting policies of their provincial cousins. The BQ soared in the polls. Liberals who had confidently expected to win up to 50 of the 75 Quebec seats suddenly had to hope that they could hold on to the seats they already had.[109] In his third campaign as BQ leader, Gilles Duceppe ran on the slogan "Un parti propre au Québec." The French word "propre" carries a double meaning: "Quebec's own party"—a shrewd appeal to the party's greatest political strength—and "a clean party," unlike the scandal-tainted Liberal machine. Prime Minister Martin had tried to reach out to soft nationalists by appointing former Liberal Cabinet minister, and founding BQ MP, Jean Lapierre as his Quebec lieutenant. The move backfired: Lapierre's perceived arrogance and his ill-judged public statements weakened the Liberal organization in the province. In the end, the Liberals lost over a dozen seats to the BQ in 2004.

Technological Change

As the channels of mass communication evolve, so do the parties that rely on them to persuade voters. Before the widespread use of radio in the 1930s, political communication was restricted to newspapers, magazines, books, and pamphlets. The spread of television in the 1950s transformed Canadian politics, allowing voters to see their aspiring prime ministers, close up, in their living rooms. It also created new advertising techniques based on emotions and images instead of reason and information. As we will see in Chapter 7, television tends to "personalize" abstract issues; consequently, party leaders became even more prominent in election campaigns. The cost of campaigning soared as parties turned to professional advertisers and "spin doctors."

At the same time, the rapid evolution of computer and telephone technologies created a new breed of political professional: the pollster. Public-opinion data, gathered and interpreted at great expense, were turned into integrated campaign strategies by teams of experts. In the process, the role of the backbench MP was reduced; she was no longer the primary source of political intelligence from the far-flung regions of the country. Her constituency association also found itself enmeshed in a newly centralized campaign organization, using the same "talking points" and images featured in the national campaign.

In recent election campaigns, the major parties have struggled to exploit the potential of the Internet. They have tried to use their websites as campaign tools, with limited success. When they employ sophisticated applications such as video streaming and interactivity, they risk alienating users with incompatible hardware or software.[110] Some parties lack the resources required to maintain and update an information-rich site during the chaos of a 36-day campaign.[111] The 2000 federal election was the first in which all the major parties explored the full potential of the Internet; its effectiveness as a campaign tool will likely increase in the future. Between elections, the major parties use their websites to keep in touch with their members and provide links to important documents, including the party constitution and policy platform. While they may not win over potential members or voters, they are a valuable source of information for students and researchers. However, their impact on party structures is not yet clear.

Most recently, wireless hand-held devices (the BlackBerry, cellphones with text messaging) have reshaped communication within parties and between parties and the media. Instant messaging allows political strategists to keep in close touch, no matter where they happen to be. It also makes it easier for the "war room" staff—those responsible for "rapid response" during an election campaign—to "spin" a particular story to reporters within minutes. The BlackBerry has become the latest "must-have" accessory for Canadian politicos, at least those who are comfortable with the technology. Paul Martin's supporters gave their BlackBerrys a workout during their fight to depose former Prime Minister Chrétien, messaging each other frequently to report new developments in the party's civil war.[112] There are also anecdotal reports of Cabinet ministers thumb-typing memos to their staffers during meetings.[113] A cellphone conversation in the midst of a Cabinet meeting would doubtless attract the ire of the prime minister, and its contents would be anything but confidential; text messaging is both quieter and more secure. It would be an overstatement to say that instant text messaging will transform Canadian parties, but it appears that this new tool has made communication even faster and easier than previously.

In summary, party systems are shaped by several long-term factors, among which social cleavages and political institutions are the most important. They continue to evolve over time, as short-term variables—such as communication technology and mobilization strategies—change. To understand the patterns of continuity and change in Canada's national party system, we must consider all these variables.

THE HISTORY OF THE CANADIAN PARTY SYSTEM

Table 3.8 presents the results of national elections from 1867 to 2004.

According to R. Kenneth Carty and his co-authors, Canada has had four distinct party systems since Confederation:
1. patronage politics and caucus parties (1867–1911);
2. brokerage politics and ministerialist parties (1921–57);
3. electronic politics and personal parties (1963–84); and
4. postmaterialist politics and targeted parties (1993–).[114]

There have also been three periods of transition between party systems: 1911–21, 1957–63, and 1984–93. In every case, the beginning and end of each system are marked by general elections. While we can observe changes in Canadian politics between elections, the extent of those changes is measurable only when the votes are

TABLE 3.8   PARTY SEATS AND VOTES IN FEDERAL ELECTIONS, 1867–2004

In this table, the seat total of the party that formed the government is shown in boldface. In each cell, the first number is the percentage of the national vote received by that party; the percentage of seats is shown in parentheses.

YEAR	LPC	CONS.	CCF/NDP	SC	BQ	PROG./RPC/CA/CP	OTHER
1867	49 (40)	**50 (60)**	—	—	—	—	1 (0)
1872	49 (48)	**50 (52)**	—	—	—	—	1 (0)
1874	**54 (67)**	45 (33)	—	—	—	—	1 (0.5)
1878	46 (31)	**53 (69)**	—	—	—	—	1.2 (0)
1882	47 (34)	**50 (66)**	—	—	—	—	2.5 (0.5)
1887	49 (41)	**50 (59)**	—	—	—	—	1 (0)
1891	47 (44)	**51 (56)**	—	—	—	—	2 (0)
1896	**45 (55)**	46 (41)	—	—	—	—	9 (3)
1900	**51 (62)**	47 (38)	—	—	—	—	1 (0)
1904	**52 (65)**	46 (35)	—	—	—	—	1.5 (0.5)
1908	**50 (61)**	47 (39)	—	—	—	—	2.7 (0.4)
1911	48 (39)	**51 (61)**	—	—	—	—	1.4 (0)
1917*	40 (35)	**57 (65)**	—	—	—	—	3 (0)
1921	**41 (49)**	30 (21)	—	—	—	23 (27)	6 (2)
1925†	**40 (40)**	47 (47)	—	—	—	9 (10)	5 (2)
1926	**46 (52)**	45 (37)	—	—	—	5 (8)	3 (2)
1930	45 (37)	**49 (56)**	—	—	—	3 (5)	3 (2)
1935	**45 (71)**	30 (16)	9 (3)	4 (7)	—	—	13 (3)
1940	**52 (74)**	31 (16)	9 (4)	3 (4)	—	—	7 (2)
1945	**41 (51)**	27 (27)	16 (11)	4 (5)	—	—	12 (5)
1949	**50 (74)**	30 (16)	13 (5)	2 (4)	—	—	5 (2)
1953	**49 (65)**	31 (19)	22 (9)	5 (6)	—	—	4 (2)
1957	41 (40)	**39 (42)**	11 (9)	7 (7)	—	—	3 (1.5)
1958	**34 (19)**	54 (79)	10 (3)	3 (0)	—	—	1 (0)
1962	37 (38)	**37 (44)**	14 (7)	12 (11)	—	—	0.4 (0)
1963	**42 (49)**	33 (36)	13 (6)	12 (9)	—	—	0.4 (0)
1965	**40 (49)**	32 (37)	18 (8)	8 (5)	—	—	1 (1)
1968	**49 (59)**	31 (27)	17 (8)	5 (5)	—	—	1 (0.4)
1972	**39 (41)**	35 (41)	18 (12)	8 (6)	—	—	1 (1)
1974	**43 (53)**	35 (36)	15 (6)`	5 (4)	—	—	2 (0.4)
1979	40 (40)	**36 (48)**	18 (9)	5 (2)	—	—	1 (0)

YEAR	LPC	CONS.	CCF/NDP	SC	BQ	PROG./RPC/CA/CP	OTHER
1980	**44 (52)**	33 (37)	20 (11)	2 (0)	—	—	1 (0)
1984	28 (14)	**50 (75)**	18 (11)	1 (0)	—	—	3 (1)
1988	32 (28)	**43 (57)**	20 (15)	—	—	2 (0)	3 (0)
1993	**41 (60)**	16 (1)	7 (3)	—	14 (18)	19 (18)	4 (1)
1997	**38 (52)**	19 (7)	11 (7)	—	11 (5)	19 (20)	2 (0.3)
2000	**41 (57)**	12 (4)	9 (4)	—	11 (13)	26 (22)	2 (0)
2004	**37 (44)**	30 (32)	16 (6)	—	12 (18)	—	6 (1)‡

Key to Party Names:

LPC = Liberal Party of Canada

Cons. = Progressive Conservative Party of Canada (1942–2003)

CCF/NDP = Co-operative Commonwealth Federation (1933–61) and New Democratic Party of Canada (1961–)

SC = Social Credit (includes the Ralliement des Créditistes)

BQ = Bloc Québécois (1993–)

Prog./RPC/CA/CP = Progressives (1921–35); Reform Party of Canada (1987–2000); Canadian Alliance (2000–03); Conservative Party of Canada (2003–)

*As explained in the text of this chapter, the 1917 election was highly unusual. Instead of a contest between the Liberals and the Conservatives, it pitted the Union Government of Sir Robert Borden—Conservatives and English-speaking Liberals—against the francophone Liberals opposed to conscription.

†After the 1925 election, in which the Conservatives won the plurality of seats, Liberal Prime Minister Mackenzie King refused either to resign or to call Parliament. He was afraid that the Commons would pass a vote of nonconfidence and push him out of office. After several months, he was finally forced to call Parliament; his government was indeed defeated, and the governor general refused King's request to dissolve Parliament and call a new election. Instead, Lord Byng called on Conservative leader Arthur Meighen to form a government. Meighen's government was also short-lived, and after he lost the confidence of the Commons, Lord Byng granted a dissolution. The conflict between the Liberal prime minister and the governor general has gone down in Canadian history as the "King-Byng Affair."

‡The one seat assigned to "Other" in 2004 belonged to Chuck Cadman, an independent candidate and former Canadian Alliance MP. None of the smaller parties won a seat in that election.

counted. The transitional periods are marked by flux, uncertainty, and electoral volatility. We cannot be certain whether a new party system has taken shape until it has remained essentially intact for at least two electoral cycles. An election that appears to herald a new alignment of subcultures, such as the 1984 PC breakthrough, may turn out to have been the beginning of a transitional period—not the start of a new and stable party system.

While most Canadian scholars agree with Carty's analysis of the first three party systems, there is considerable debate about the fourth party system. For example, Clarkson argues that the distinction between the third and fourth systems is exaggerated: "there is much less evidence of change than [Carty, Cross, and Young] maintain—whether this be change in the party system, change in the nature of the parties themselves, or change in the manner in which they wage their campaigns."[115] In defence of the fourth party system, we might argue that the contours of the system are not yet entirely clear. In addition, it is difficult to assess the long-term importance of current political events, or the ways in which today's trends— for example, the use of the Internet as a campaign tool—will develop in the future.

For the moment, let us assume that the third party system ended in 1984, and that the fourth system took shape in 1993. On that basis, we will briefly describe Canada's four party systems.

First Period: 1867–1917

As we saw in Chapter 2, Canadian politics at the time of Confederation were the product of British colonial rule. Although legislatures had existed in Upper and Lower Canada since 1791, there was no incentive for their members to form disciplined caucuses until after responsible government had been granted in the 1840s. In the Legislature of the United Province of Canada (now Quebec and Ontario), building a legislative majority meant bridging the linguistic, cultural, and religious divide that separated French-speaking Catholics in Canada East from English-speaking Protestants in Canada West. In the pre-Confederation period, relatively weak coalitions of conservative English-speaking representatives joined with their conservative French-speaking counterparts under the Liberal–Conservative label. They were opposed by an equally fragile alliance of Liberal anglophones and francophones. The divisions among the various subcultures often brought down governments over linguistic, cultural, and religious issues.

Confederation established a federal system and relegated language and cultural issues to the provinces. But the French–English cleavage remained a powerful force in national politics. To form a majority government, a party had to win seats inside and outside Quebec. At the same time, the prime minister had to unite MPs from both language groups into an increasingly disciplined caucus. Before 1878, the incentives for party discipline imposed by "a Constitution similar in Principle to that of the United Kingdom" were undermined by the persistent localism of Canada's political culture and party organization. In the 1880s and 1890s, parliamentary caucuses became increasingly cohesive and leader-dominated. A national leader had enough trouble bridging the gaps among MPs from the various regional, religious, and linguistic subcultures; he could not afford to create even more divisions by staking out clear ideological positions on the issues of the day. Both the Liberal and Conservative parties hugged the centre of the political spectrum during the first party system.[116] The Conservatives were considerably more successful than the Liberals during the first three decades after Confederation; the latter remained a loosely knit group of parliamentary factions until well into the 1870s.

Both parties also minimized the divisive influence of their electoral subcultures by keeping power in the hands of their parliamentary caucuses. As classic examples of cadre parties,[117] the Liberals and Conservatives were slow to develop extraparliamentary organizations. In the first 50 years after Confederation, the Liberal Party held only one national convention, and the Conservatives none. Both parties limited political debate to the parliamentary forum and wooed supporters through the widespread use of patronage.

The first party system was also characterized by dominant leaders, secretive and sometimes corrupt party finance, and a partisan press. Because the two parties were so similar in ideological terms, the personalities and rhetoric of their leaders became the main focus of electoral competition. As the French writer André Siegfried wrote of Canadian parties in 1906:

> It is of the first importance to the success of a party that it should be led by someone who inspires confidence, and whose mere name is a programme in itself. As long as the Conservatives had Macdonald for their leader, they voted for him rather than for the party. So it is with Laurier and the Liberals of today. If Laurier disappeared, the Liberals would perhaps find that they had lost the real secret of their victories . . . They vote as much for the man who symbolizes the policy as for the policy itself.[118]

The leader was not just the living symbol of his party; he was also its chief fundraiser. The burden of soliciting donations added considerably to Sir John A. Macdonald's workload as prime minister. He was forced to seek party funds from industrialists and financiers who worked with the government—an apparent, if not actual, conflict of interest.[119] Macdonald's begging letters to the head of the Grand Trunk Railroad provoked the 1873 Pacific Scandal, which brought down the Conservative government. While there were some tentative efforts to clean up party patronage and fundraising in the 1870s, these had little effect until after World War I.

As if raising money, creating a disciplined caucus, and symbolizing the party were not enough, party leaders also spent considerable time managing the press. This task was made somewhat easier by the open partisanship of most newspapers. Macdonald knew that he could count on sympathetic treatment from Conservative papers, while his Liberal opponents expected the same from the Liberal press.

> A great majority of the weekly and daily newspapers, which existed in far greater numbers than they do today, were little more than partisan instruments. Even as late as 1900, the circulation of the party papers exceeded that of the growing independent press. Politicians wanted and expected subservience, not objectivity, from the media.[120]

Second Period: 1921–57

During the first two decades of the twentieth century, Canadian society underwent important changes that placed considerable strain on the party system. The continual movement toward urbanization and industrialization (especially in Ontario and Quebec), the rapid agrarian settlement of the Prairie provinces, and the continued support by both political parties of the National Policy—which was perceived (correctly) as favouring the industrializing centre at the expense of the agrarian periphery—led many in the outlying regions to question the degree to which their interests were, or could be, adequately represented in either existing party.[121] While the settlement of the Prairies was facilitated by the Liberal government of Sir Wilfrid Laurier (1896–1911), neither the Liberals nor the Conservatives fully mobilized this expanding pool of voters. The stage was set for an expansion of the party system, and for the emergence of a new subculture: Western populism.

As we have seen, the tensions within the party system were heightened during the conscription crisis of World War I (1914–18). The conscription issue blurred the distinction between the two political parties and confused political allegiances by forcing the creation of the Union government. It also inflamed French–English tensions, and reinforced the attachment of the Quebec nationalist subculture to the Liberal Party.[122] In 1917 the Liberals won 62 of the 65 seats in Quebec; in 1921, they won all 65.

A significant institutional change also affected party development during this era. The *Civil Service Commission Act, 1918,* placed the authority for recruitment into the civil service squarely in the hands of a nonpartisan agency, thus eliminating the lion's share of party patronage. This institutional change drastically reduced the material incentives for party activity and could have seriously weakened the party system. But because disciplined national parties were (and are) essential ingredients in a system of responsible Cabinet government, the parties survived and adapted to the changing political system. As the number of cleavages in the electorate multiplied—with the addition and growth of new provinces, immigration, the enfranchisement of women, and rising nationalism in Quebec—the parties in the second party system had to knit the diverse groups into a national political community. From local patronage machines, they became regional brokers.[123]

The brokerage strategy of the Liberals and Conservatives was based on the premise that conflict could best be mediated within the extraparliamentary parties, rather than between parties inside Parliament. One key element in that strategy was the development of **ministerialism:** individual Cabinet ministers represented particular regional, cultural, or economic groups within the party decision-making process. At the same time, the ministers were required to explain and communicate those decisions to the members of their designated interest group.

If one measures the success of the brokerage strategy by the level of electoral support obtained by the parties, the Liberal Party was without question the better broker of competing interests. It won eight of the nine elections held from 1921 to 1957 and governed for 31 of those 36 years. Its only defeat during this period occurred shortly after the onset of the Great Depression, when the Conservative Party under R.B. Bennett captured 137 of 245 Commons seats, only to plummet to 40 seats five years later. The Liberals were led throughout this period by William Lyon Mackenzie King and Louis St. Laurent, both of whom were noted conciliators.

However, the electoral record also illustrates the limitations inherent in the brokerage model. Groups that perceived the Liberal and Conservative parties as either unwilling or unable to effectively represent their interests had an incentive to establish "third" parties to speak on their behalf. Highly mobilized subcultures that were concentrated in a particular region—notably, Western populists—were more successful in electoral terms than latent subcultures and those scattered across the country (the working-class voters courted by left-wing parties). Nonetheless, the electoral data presented in Table 3.8 indicate that both types of parties emerged during the second party system, although neither was able to rise to a governing position. The two-party system was shattered in the 1921 election, in which the Progressives elected 65 MPs—14 more than the Conservatives. The Progressives won all but a handful of Prairie seats and almost one-third of the Ontario seats (most in northern or rural Ontario). As the second-place party, the Progressives were entitled to form the official Opposition in the House of Commons. However, the Progressive caucus was dominated by populist members who were hostile to the existing system of disciplined party combat in the legislature, which they saw as placing inordinate power in the hands of party leaders. (For a definition of "populism," see Dossier 2.1.) Thus, instead of using their Western regional base as a platform from which to challenge the Central Canadian orientation of the major parties, the Progressives refused the mantle of official Opposition and supported the minority Liberal government instead. Progressive leader T.A. Crerar was even co-opted into the government ministry. This cooperation with the governing party cost the Progressives much of their populist support over the next decade, and the party had disappeared as a national force by the 1935 federal election.[124]

The Progressives inaugurated a new era of regionally based third parties, including a new party of the left. The 1921 election witnessed the election not only of 65 Progressives but also of 2 independent labour candidates, J.S. Woodsworth and William Irvine. By the late 1920s, there had emerged in Parliament a loose association of labour MPs and some of the more radical Progressive MPs; they were known as the Ginger Group, for the spice they added to parliamentary debate. At the instigation of the Ginger Group and the League for Social Reconstruction (LSR)—a university-based group of socialists modelled on the British Fabian Society—a meeting of the Western Labour Conference in 1932 voted to create a new socialist political party.[125] The party held its founding convention in Regina the next year, calling itself the "Co-operative Commonwealth Federation—Farmer, Labour, Socialist." As its subtitle suggested, the CCF tried to appeal to regionally (Western) based farmers, the working class, and intellectual socialists.

The farmer–labour alliance within the CCF was an uneasy one. The tendency of farmer votes to be tightly clustered geographically (particularly in the Prairies) and of labour votes to be more dispersed resulted in the CCF's winning more contests in rural Western constituencies than in urban constituencies. Thus the parliamentary wing of the CCF had a distinctly Western-farmer character, which made it more difficult for the party to appeal to the urban working class. That difficulty was compounded by divisions within the union movement, regarding both its organizational structure and its approach to political action. For most of the period of brokerage parties, the major central union organization, the Trades and Labour Congress (TLC), was dominated by American-based multinational unions that chose to remain politically independent. In the mid-1930s, a more militant and politically active group of industrial unions was expelled from the TLC and formed the Canadian Congress of Labour (CCL). Beginning in 1942, the CCL declared at each convention that the CCF was the "political arm of labour" and (unsuccessfully) urged its member unions to affiliate with the party.[126] Organized labour was not able to take a more unified and politically active position until the merger of the TLC and CCL into the Canadian Labour Congress (CLC) in 1956. As we shall see, that merger provided the impetus for the transformation of the CCF into the NDP in the early 1960s. Along with the Liberal and Conservative parties, the CCF–NDP is one of the five relatively stable components of the party system identified in Dossier 3.2.

In addition to contributing members to the Ginger Group and thus influencing the creation of the CCF–NDP, the Progressive Party also demonstrated the tendency of the electoral system to generate regional third parties. Whereas some forms of regional discontent found voice in the leftist CCF, others were more at home in a populist party of the ideological right: Social Credit. Following the political ideas developed by British engineer Major Clifford Douglas and articulated in the Canadian West by fundamentalist minister and radio preacher William ("Bible Bill") Aberhart, the Social Credit Party emerged during the 1935 election, in the middle of the Great Depression, as an important voice for Western farmers.[127]

Social Credit's support (measured by the party's seats rather than votes) came almost exclusively from Alberta during this third period of party development, and from 1935 to 1957 it captured all but a handful of the Commons seats from that province. The party collapsed in 1958 when the Western populist and Quebec nationalist subcultures switched to the Conservative party, led by the fiery Westerner John Diefenbaker, contributing to a landslide Conservative victory.

By the beginning of the second party system in 1921, leadership conventions had already become the preferred method for choosing party leaders. This development reflected another important change: the establishment of extraparliamentary wings by all the major parties. National party offices, staffed by permanent employees, began to appear.[128] As the caucus lost the power to choose the leader, and the representational functions of government backbenchers shifted to regional ministers, power within party structures became more decentralized. Successive fundraising scandals, particularly the Liberal Beauharnois scandal of 1930, convinced party leaders to delegate their fundraising chores to party "bagmen." These individuals, many of them senators, met privately with corporate and individual donors to solicit funds for the new party organization and the special demands of national campaigns. Meanwhile, the partisan press had disappeared, a victim of advertising, public demand for independent papers, and the new medium of radio.[129] Broadcasters were regulated by the federal government, which required them to present balanced news coverage as a condition of licence renewal.

The second party system came to an end with the election of 1957, which brought the Conservatives to power for the first time since 1935. Although Conservative leader John Diefenbaker managed to win only a minority, the period of unchallenged Liberal dominance appeared to be over. The 1958 election gave Diefenbaker a massive majority, nearly wiping out the CCF and prompting the formation of the NDP. The New Party (its original name) was launched in 1961, the product of a marriage between the Canadian Labour Congress and the remnants of the CCF. At the same time, the Liberals spent their time in opposition rebuilding their organization from the ground up. By the time the second transitional period ended in 1963, Canada's national party system and the environment in which it operated had changed dramatically.

◼ Third Period: 1963–84

The electoral realignment brought about by Diefenbaker's Conservatives integrated Westerners once again into one of the two major parties and temporarily ended the Liberals' stranglehold under the brokerage model. Thereafter, the representation of third parties in Parliament gradually declined until only the NDP was left.

By 1963, most Canadians had access to television news. The new medium focused on the party leaders, relegating the once-powerful regional ministers to the background. All three parties sought to appeal to voters across the country, using "pan-Canadian"[130] rhetoric and symbolism to overcome subcultural divisions. Instead of brokering among competing interests, the parties used television and other new technologies— public-opinion polling and sophisticated advertising techniques—in an attempt to overcome them. The availability of public-opinion polling enabled the party leadership to bypass traditional sources of information and measure the attitudes and preferences of Canadians directly. No longer was it necessary to have a regional spokesperson represent the views of a section of the country. Such information could now be obtained more directly, and perhaps more accurately, through public-opinion polling.

The CCF–NDP provides a good example of the nationalized or "pan-Canadian"[131] approach that characterized the third party system. Whereas the CCF had attempted to unite the disparate groups that were opposed to the economic powers of Central Canada—namely, farmers, industrial workers, and socialists—the NDP was created to advance the interests of the predominantly urban working class. The strategy was for the NDP to form stronger ties with organized labour and for unions and their members to play a more active role by supporting the party directly.[132] Despite the electoral system's tendency to reward regional voting strength, the NDP adopted an explicitly national approach to political competition and downplayed the regional character of its appeal.[133]

Although the NDP survived this period of declining third parties, the regionally based Social Credit/Ralliement des créditistes party did not. In his landslide election of 1958, Diefenbaker won a majority of seats in each region of the country, not only capturing the traditional Liberal bastion of Quebec but also displacing third parties from the Prairies. Although the Conservatives were unable to hold Quebec, which briefly drifted to the Créditistes before throwing its support behind the Trudeau Liberals in 1968, they were able to retain the West. The Social Credit caucus, an uneasy mix of Western populists and Quebec nationalists, held the balance of power in the Commons after the 1962 and 1963 elections. It split into separate Western and Quebec caucuses in 1963 and gradually faded away.

Party development in this third system was influenced by profound social and cultural changes. Canadian society was far more urbanized and industrialized in the 1960s and 1970s than it had been at the end of World War II. Thus, Canada's regions became less socially and economically differentiated. Similarly, there was a shift of economic power westward. The economic centre of the country moved from Montreal to Toronto and there was substantial growth in the economic clout of Vancouver and Calgary.

Parties that thrived in the 1960s, 1970s, and 1980s—the Liberals and Conservatives, and, to a lesser extent, the New Democrats—were forced to adapt themselves to electronic politics. Perhaps the most profound consequence of the third party system was the increased importance of political leadership. With the personalization of electoral politics, a premium was placed on choosing a party leader who could appeal to a broad spectrum of the electorate. The party leader had to sell the party's platform and principles in both official languages, a requirement that met with considerable resistance in the Conservative Party. When the PCs finally chose a telegenic, fluently bilingual leader from Quebec—Brian Mulroney—in 1983, they were rewarded with a huge majority surpassing even the Diefenbaker landslide of 1958. Once again, the temporary end of Liberal dominance signalled the end of a party system. And once again, the Conservatives paid a heavy price for this victory; as we saw earlier, Mulroney's failure to keep the Western populists and Quebec nationalists together in his electoral coalition led to the collapse of his party in 1993. The creation of two new regional parties initiated the fourth party system, in which explicitly regional politics has once again taken the place of nationalizing political appeals (though not, as Clarkson points out, for the Liberals).[134]

The institutional environment for political parties changed in important ways between 1963 and 1984. The shift from cooperative to executive federalism (see Chapter 8) increased the prominence of provincial premiers in national politics, which further reduced the brokerage role of the national parties and effectively ended the ministerialist approach to regional representation in the federal government. But regionalism remained a central theme of public discussion, and no amount of nationalistic rhetoric could change the regional reality of partisan politics. Despite their attempts to appeal to the national electorate, the three major parties were often regionally fragmented in the House of Commons. For most of this period, the electoral system gave the Liberal Party a disproportionate share of Quebec seats and shut out both the Conservatives and the NDP in the province. Likewise, the Conservatives (and to a lesser extent the NDP) were strong in the West, while the Liberals were also-rans in the region. Even the Liberal majority produced by the so-called Trudeaumania election in 1968—the biggest Liberal majority of this period—was based largely in Ontario and Quebec (120 of the Liberals' 155 seats came from those two provinces); Trudeau at his most popular was unable to improve his party's performance much in the Prairie West or Atlantic Canada.

A second major institutional change was the fundamental shift in the registration and financing of political parties brought about by the 1974 *Election Expenses Act*. As noted earlier in this chapter, the Act established public financing of parties through a system of tax credits for political donations, as well as partial reimbursement of campaign expenses from the public purse. It created a more open and accountable funding system in which parties were required to publicly declare their revenue and expenditures. Finally, it set limits on the amount of money parties and candidates could spend in election campaigns and on the amount of television exposure parties could purchase. The net effect of these changes was a substantial improvement in the financial stability of each of the major parties (albeit with significant fluctuations, depending on the party's electoral performance) and a consequent expansion in their national headquarters. Parties responded to the new institutional environment by developing direct-mail campaigns and appealing for funds beyond their small memberships.

As party organizations became stronger, more stable, and more financially secure, they were increasingly dominated by the party leader and his entourage. As we have seen, parties relied increasingly on professional consultants to craft their campaigns. The costs of campaigning soared. (As we will see in Chapter 4, this was one of the main reasons for the 1974 election finance law.) As campaigning became more "capital-intensive,"[135] local party members in the constituencies felt increasingly neglected. Parties tried to create new incentives for their members, including a vast increase in constituency-delegate positions at leadership conventions. But throughout the third party system, Canadians who wanted to participate in politics began to drift away from the parties toward pressure groups. Changing political values and intractable economic problems undermined the credibility of party politics, and opened the door for "anti-party" appeals. The "content-free" political rhetoric of the major parties eroded their ties to the electorate,[136] while alienating potential party members who sought more meaningful politics. By 1984, the stage was set for a fourth party system.

▇ Fourth Period: 1993–?

As we have seen, Brian Mulroney's strategic decision to draw the Quebec nationalist subculture into the Conservative electoral coalition ultimately led to the collapse of the party. The Western populist subculture defected to the Reform Party after 1987, while the establishment of the Bloc Québécois in 1990 provided a political home for the Quebec nationalists. Although the 1988 election produced little overall change, the results of the 1992 Charlottetown Accord (see Chapter 9) revealed deep voter frustration with the three "old-line" parties. Two unsuccessful rounds of constitutional negotiation, together with the divisive trade policy of the Mulroney government, alienated voters from the PCs. The Spicer Commission found a deep sense of betrayal and alienation among Canadians, as well as a belief that political parties were unresponsive to and unconcerned about their needs. The cultural changes described in Chapter 2 were about to make themselves felt in the national party system.

According to Carty, Cross, and Young, "there are substantial continuities between the third party system and the system that is currently taking shape."[137] Nevertheless, they have identified five distinct characteristics of the fourth party system:
1. "the entry of two new parties [the BQ and Reform/Alliance], which have eclipsed both the Conservatives and NDP in Parliament";
2. a regionally fragmented pattern of party competition;
3. the increasing tendency of party strategists to target particular groups of voters, instead of appealing to a national electorate;
4. greater ideological diversity among the major parties; and
5. more internal party democracy, as the parties respond to "the participatory demands of an assertive citizenry."[138]

We have already discussed the reasons for the breakthrough of Reform and the BQ in 1993: disenchantment with the "old-line" parties (except, perhaps, the Liberals); the entrepreneurial leadership of Preston Manning and Lucien Bouchard; and the strategic errors of the PCs. The sheer number of official parties in the Commons is the clearest indicator of a new and distinct party system. The rising number of parties on the Elections Canada register is also a response to Bill C-3 (see Table 3.7).

The four-party system in the Commons as of 2004 does reflect the regional fragmentation of the vote, although the extent of that fragmentation is exaggerated by our electoral system (see Chapter 4). The Liberal majorities elected in 1993, 1997, and 2000 were heavily skewed toward Ontario, where the party won almost every seat with a bare majority of the vote. The Opposition benches are filled with MPs from the West, most of them in the Conservative (previously the Reform/Alliance) caucus. The regional skew was somewhat less pronounced following the 2004 election; the Conservatives enjoyed considerably more success in Ontario, winning 24 of the 106 seats. However, the Liberals remain weak in the West and they lost ground in Quebec. Paul Martin's minority government is even more dependent on Ontario and, to a lesser extent, Atlantic Canada.

Table 3.9 displays the regional bases of three parliamentary parties in the fourth party system (the BQ, which runs candidates only in Quebec, is excluded). The number in each cell is the percentage of each party's caucus elected from a particular region. While there is some fluctuation over the four elections—particularly in the Atlantic region—the trends are clear. Ontario dominates the Liberal caucus, at least numerically. The Reform/Alliance caucus was almost exclusively Western, with particular strength in Alberta and British Columbia; the new Conservative caucus is more balanced. Despite its unprecedented 1997 success in the Atlantic region, and recent gains in Ontario, the NDP remains a primarily Western party. Quebec, which deserted the national parties for the BQ in 1993, was gradually returning to the Liberal fold in 1997 and 2000; as explained earlier, the sponsorship scandal reversed that trend in dramatic fashion.

While some elements of the fourth party system are not yet as well established as Carty et al. suggest, the regionalization of party competition is clearly evident. It is also cause for concern. As long as Canada had only one major national party, the Liberals were guaranteed to remain in government for years. Both the United Alternative (Dossier 3.3) and the creation of the new Conservative Party (Dossier 3.4) were attempts to create a second national party that could challenge the Liberals and ultimately form a government. The Canadian Alliance failed in 2000; the Conservatives did considerably better in 2004, although their success probably owed more to a desire for change after three straight Liberal majorities and anger over the sponsorship scandal than to the party itself. In some ways, the fourth party system may be a throwback to the second system, in which the Liberals took full advantage of a weak opposition. They governed from 1935 until 1957, 22 years, without interruption. As noted earlier, the appearance of a multiparty system after 1993 is misleading. Instead, Canada has returned to one-party dominance, with all of the attendant risks of corruption, stagnation, and voter apathy.

1993

PARTY	ONTARIO	WEST*	QUEBEC	ATLANTIC
Liberal	55.4 (98/177)	16.4 (29/177)	10.7 (19/177)	17.5 (31/177)
Reform	1.9 (1/52)	98.1 (51/52)	—	—
PC	0.0	0.0	50.0 (1/2)	50.0 (1/2)
NDP	0.0	100.0 (9/9)	0.0	0.0

1997

PARTY	ONTARIO	WEST*	QUEBEC	ATLANTIC
Liberal	65.2 (101/155)	11.0 (17/155)	16.8 (26/155)	7.1 (11/155)
Reform	0.0	100.0 (60/60)	0.0	0.0
PC	5.0 (1/20)	5.0 (1/20)	25.0 (5/20)	65.0 (13/20)
NDP	0.0	61.9 (13/21)	0.0	38.1 (8/21)

2000

PARTY	ONTARIO	WEST*	QUEBEC	ATLANTIC
Liberal	58.1 (100/172)	9.9 (17/172)	20.9 (36/172)	11.0 (19/172)
Canadian Alliance	3.0 (2/66)	97.0 (64/66)	0.0	0.0
PC	0.0	16.7 (2/12)	8.3 (1/12)	75.0 (9/12)
NDP	7.7 (1/13)	61.5 (8/13)	0.0	30.8 (4/13)

2004

PARTY	ONTARIO	WEST*	QUEBEC	ATLANTIC
Liberal	55.6 (75/135)	12.6 (17/135)	15.6 (21/135)	16.3 (22/135)
Conservative	24.2 (24/99)	68.7 (68/99)	0.0	7.1 (7/99)
NDP	36.8 (7/19)	47.4 (9/19)	0.0	15.8 (3/19)

*"West" includes Manitoba, Saskatchewan, Alberta, British Columbia, and the Territories.

CONCLUSION: THE FUTURE OF THE CANADIAN PARTY SYSTEM

As more and more voters turn away from electoral politics, Canada's traditional parties may be losing their capacity to link the electorate to our national political institutions. When that linkage function erodes, two consequences generally follow: political entrepreneurs create new parties (often, new types of parties) to fill the void, and nonparty organizations (e.g., the antiglobalization movement) emerge.[139] Both developments have occurred in Canada and both pose important challenges to our national party system. It is possible, though difficult, for existing parties to adopt new structures and activities. But reaching out beyond the party's base to build new coalitions with subcultures in the electorate is fraught with difficulty. Moreover, the low voter turnout among young Canadians (Chapter 4) is mirrored in the small and aging memberships of our parties. The new financing measures in Bill C-24 have lessened the parties' dependence on individual donors (and perhaps individual volunteers); nonetheless, they cannot perform their crucial political tasks without active and motivated members. It is worth asking whether our parties can offer any incentive to membership that can overcome the apathy and disaffection of young Canadians.

The ability of our national parties to respond to their internal and external challenges, as the fourth party system takes shape, will help to determine the health and legitimacy of our national institutions in the twenty-first century. The quality of candidates and leaders, the substance of public policy, and the responsiveness of our elected legislators depend on vibrant and diverse party organizations. As Chapter 4 ("Voting and Nonvoting") explains, voters who are personally contacted by party volunteers are more likely to cast ballots in elections. This direct connection between the local party "franchises," and the health of our electoral democracy, highlights the need to revitalize Canadian political parties.

GLOSSARY OF KEY TERMS

"Believers" and "careerists": Two categories of party members, distinguished on the basis of their primary motivations for party activity. "Believers" are motivated by their faith in the party's principles or its leader; "careerists" are more interested in their own status within the party hierarchy.

Brokerage or cadre party: A political party whose primary goal is to win a majority of seats in Parliament and form a government. Because it seeks to appeal to as many voters as possible, it tends to downplay potentially divisive ideologies and principles. Usually a small membership, dominated by the leader and the caucus.

Caucus: The parliamentary wing of a political party. Includes all the MPs (and senators, if any) who represent that party in Parliament.

Cleavage: A stable and long-term division between groups of voters. Examples include religion (Catholic versus Protestant, observant versus nonobservant), language (English versus French), region (West versus East, Quebec versus Alberta), gender, and class.

Collective solidary/social incentives: Intangible rewards for party effort, available to all party members (the joy of victory, the satisfaction of working together for a shared goal, and the social value of meeting like-minded people).

Electoral system: The rules and procedures by which legislators are elected in a given country. Canada's electoral system is called single-member plurality (SMP), because each constituency elects one MP and the candidate with more votes than any other wins the seat.

Extraparliamentary: The party organization outside Parliament. Includes the national headquarters, the national executive, and the local constituency associations.

"Instant" party members: Individuals and groups recruited to join a local constituency association en masse, for the purpose of electing a slate of convention delegates committed to a particular leadership candidate (or, under OMOV, to vote directly for the candidate). Also used by organizers for aspiring constituency candidates to "swamp" the nomination meeting. While leadership contests and nomination battles are important opportunities to attract new members to the party, "instant" members rarely stick around for the long term. Increasingly controversial, especially the wholesale importation of people who are not eligible to vote in Canadian elections (e.g., recent immigrants, minors). All parties except the Conservative Party allow ineligible voters to participate, in the name of openness and for recruitment of future citizens.

Leadership convention: A gathering of party delegates to choose a new leader. Thousands of delegates—most elected by constituency associations, campus clubs, women's and youth organizations, and other party branches—cast ballots in successive rounds of voting, until one candidate receives a majority of the valid votes.

Material incentives: Tangible rewards for loyal party service (e.g., a seat in the Senate).

Ministerialism: The practice of treating Cabinet ministers as representatives from their regions. During the second party system (1921–57), the federal Liberals used regional ministers as both conduits of political intelligence and dispensers of patronage. Ministerialism was a key ingredient in the Liberals' successful strategy of regional brokering.

Minority party syndrome: An imbalance between "believers" and "careerists" within a party's membership, caused by prolonged periods of electoral defeat. The internal culture of the party becomes adversarial (instead of constructive), fractious (rather than united), and oriented to criticism instead of governing.

Missionary or ideological party: A party whose primary goal is to promote a particular ideology or policy; while it would welcome the chance to implement its proposals in government, it is less focused on electoral victory than a brokerage/cadre party. More internally democratic, less leader-dominated, and places a greater emphasis on attracting a large membership.

Mobilization: The process of organizing a particular subculture to support a new or existing political party. Examples include Brian Mulroney's attempt to bring Quebec nationalists into the Progressive Conservative Party of Canada in 1984 and Preston Manning's appeal to Western populists to join his fledgling Reform Party in the late 1980s.

Multiparty system: A party system in which three or more parties compete for inclusion in a governing coalition. Usually associated with proportional representation electoral systems.

One member, one vote (OMOV): A system of party leadership selection in which every party member can vote directly for the candidate of her choice, instead of electing delegates to vote on her behalf.

Party networks: Distinct groups within a party organization. Include factions (formed around leadership aspirants), regional networks, the caucus, the leader's entourage, and ideological sects.

Party system: The sum total of the parties represented in the House of Commons at a given time, reflecting the social cleavages and subcultures in the electorate and the structure of party competition.

Patronage: The practice of appointing party supporters to fill public offices, such as the Order-in-Council appointments awarded at the discretion of the prime minister. Less common today than in the nineteenth century. Often regarded as corrupt and harmful, but this perception is not always correct; material incentives for party members may help to attract and retain the volunteers needed for a vibrant representative democracy.

Platform: The statement of policies and principles issued by a party during an election campaign (e.g., the Liberal *Red Book* of 1993, 1997, and 2000). In theory, a platform provides the foundation for both the party's electoral appeal and its activities if elected to government; in practice, as we will see in Chapter 4, platforms do not necessarily bind parties in office.

Political entrepreneur: An individual who perceives an unmet need in the political marketplace and creates a new political party to fill that need. Examples include Preston Manning's establishment of the Reform Party of Canada to express the views of the Western populist subculture in federal politics and Lucien Bouchard's creation of the Bloc Québécois to give Quebec nationalists a distinct voice in Parliament.

Political party: An organization of members who work together to achieve one or more common goals.

Purposive/altruistic incentives: The sense that one is contributing to the greater good by campaigning for a candidate or advocating a particular policy or ideology.

Specific solidary incentives: Intangible benefits that are awarded to a few select individuals (e.g., status, a nomination for Parliament, or a high-ranking office in the party).

"Spin doctors": Professional consultants who advise political parties about using the news media effectively. May also include party staffers and volunteers who make themselves available to reporters seeking the party's "spin" on a particular issue or event.

DISCUSSION QUESTIONS

1. Do you support a particular political party? If so, why?

2. In your opinion, are Canada's major parties still relevant? Give reasons for your answer.

3. Why has the Liberal Party been so successful over the past century? What are the major reasons for its continued political dominance?

4. Should political parties be prohibited from taking donations from unions and corporations? Why or why not?

5. Voter turnout has declined significantly over the past five federal elections. Young people are particularly reluctant to cast ballots. In your opinion, are the major parties to blame for this trend? Explain your answer.

6. How, if at all, can one or more of the current Opposition parties mount a serious challenge to the Liberals?

SUGGESTED READINGS

Books and Articles

Keith Archer and Alan Whitehorn, *Political Activists: The NDP in Convention* (Toronto: Oxford University Press, 1997).

Herman Bakvis, ed., *Canadian Political Parties: Leaders, Candidates, and Organization,* volume 13 of the collected research studies for the Royal Commission on Electoral Reform and Party Financing (Toronto: Dundurn, 1991).

James Bickerton, Alain-G. Gagnon, and Patrick J. Smith, *Ties that Bind: Parties and Voters in Canada* (Toronto: Oxford University Press, 1999).

André Blais, Elisabeth Gidengil, Richard Nadeau, and Neil Nevitte, *Anatomy of a Liberal Victory: Making Sense of the Vote in the 2000 Canadian Election* (Peterborough, ON: Broadview Press, 2002).

Canada, Royal Commission on Electoral Reform and Party Financing, *Reforming Electoral Democracy,* volume 1 (Canada: Minister of Supply and Services, 1991), 207.

R. Kenneth Carty, *Canadian Political Parties in the Constituencies,* volume 23 of the collected research studies for the Royal Commission on Electoral Reform and Party Financing (Toronto: Dundurn, 1991).

R. Kenneth Carty, "Parties as Franchise Systems: The Stratarchical Organizational Imperative," *Party Politics,* 10:1 (2004).

R. Kenneth Carty, William Cross, and Lisa Young, *Rebuilding Canadian Party Politics* (Vancouver: UBC Press, 2000).

R. Kenneth Carty, Lynda Erickson, and Donald E. Blake, eds., *Leaders and Parties in Canadian Politics: Experiences of the Provinces* (Toronto: HBJ Canada, 1992).

John C. Courtney, *Do Conventions Matter? Choosing National Party Leaders in Canada* (Montreal and Kingston: McGill–Queen's University Press, 1995).

William Cross, ed., *Political Parties, Representation, and Electoral Democracy in Canada* (Toronto: Oxford University Press, 2002).

William Cross and Lisa Young, "The Contours of Political Party Membership in Canada," *Party Politics,* 10:4 (2004).

Maurice Duverger, *Political Parties: Their Organization and Activity in the Modern State,* translated by Barbara and Robert North (London: Methuen, 1964 [1954]).

Lawrence LeDuc, Richard G. Niemi, and Pippa Norris, eds., *Comparing Democracies 2: New Challenges in the Study of Elections and Voting* (Thousand Oaks, CA: Sage, 2002).

Jon H. Pammett and Christopher Dornan, eds., *The Canadian General Election of 2000* (Ottawa: Carleton University Press, 2001).

Lisa Young and William Cross, "Incentives to Membership in Canadian Political Parties," *Political Research Quarterly,* 55:3 (September 2002).

Lisa Young and William Cross, "The Rise of Plebiscitary Democracy in Canadian Political Parties," *Party Politics,* 8:6 (2002).

Websites

Most of the registered parties in national politics have their own websites. Go to the Nelson website for this book (www.parametersofpower4e.nelson.com), click on "Canadian Politics on the Web," and scroll down to "Political Parties."

Alternatively, go to the Elections Canada website (www.elections.ca) and click on "Political Parties, Candidates and Third Parties," where you will find a complete list of registered parties, with links to their Web pages. Elections Canada also provides Acrobat files containing the *Canada Elections Act* and other documents relating to the regulation of national parties (go to "Election Law and Policy" and "Election Financing").

NOTES

1. Canada, Royal Commission on Electoral Reform and Party Financing, *Reforming Electoral Democracy,* volume 1 (Canada: Minister of Supply and Services, 1991), 207.

2. This categorization is based on Peter Mair's "three faces" of party organization: the party on the ground, the party in public office, and the party in central office. Peter Mair, "Party Organizations: From Civil Society to the State," in Richard S. Katz and Peter Mair, eds., *How Parties Organize: Change and Adaptation in Party Organizations in Western Democracies* (Thousand Oaks, CA: Sage, 1994), 4.

3. Paul Howe and David Northrup, *Strengthening Canadian Democracy: The Views of Canadians* (Montreal: Institute for Research on Public Policy, July 2000); available online at www.irp.org.

4. Some scholars would argue that the national PC Party did not disappear when it merged with the Canadian Alliance, inasmuch as it left an organizational legacy in Parliament and in the constituencies. Rose and Mackie, for example, would categorize the PCs as a party that persists, albeit in a radically different form, and not as a failed party. See Richard Rose and Thomas T. Mackie, "Do Parties Persist or Fail? The Big Trade-off Facing Organizations," in Kay Lawson and Peter H. Merkl, eds., *When Parties Fail: Emerging Alternative Organizations* (Princeton: Princeton University Press, 1988).

5. Lisa Young and William Cross, "The Rise of Plebiscitary Democracy in Canadian Political Parties," *Party Politics,* 8:6 (2002), 673–99.

6. James Madison, "Federalist No. 10," in Alexander Hamilton, James Madison, and John Jay, *The Federalist Papers,* edited by Clinton Rossiter (New York: New American Library, 1961 [1788]).

7. R. Kenneth Carty, "For the Third Asking: Is There a Future for National Political Parties in Canada?," in Tom Kent, ed., *In Pursuit of the Public Good: Essays in Honour of Allan J. MacEachen* (Montreal and Kingston: McGill–Queen's University Press, 1997), 147.

8. Carty, *Canadian Political Parties in the Constituencies,* volume 23 of the collected research studies for the Royal Commission on Electoral Reform and Party Financing (Toronto: Dundurn, 1991), 12.

9. William Cross and Lisa Young, "The Contours of Political Party Membership in Canada," *Party Politics,* 10:4 (2004), 430–38.

10. Carty, *Canadian Political Parties in the Constituencies,* 28–29; Cross and Young, "The Contours of Political Party Membership," 430.

11. Howe and Northrup, 89.

12. Howe and Northrup, 91.

13. Cross and Young, "The Contours of Political Party Membership," Tables 10 and 11, 439.

14. For a sophisticated analysis of party goals, see Robert Harmel and Kenneth Janda, "An Integrated Theory of Party Goals and Party Change," *Journal of Theoretical Politics,* VI:3 (July 1994), 259–87.

15. Cross and Young, "The Contours of Political Party Membership," Tables 10 and 11, 439.

16. Although the national PC Party no longer exists as an independent entity, there are still provincial PC parties in seven provinces (excepting Quebec, British Columbia, and Saskatchewan).

17. Carty, "For the Third Asking: Is There a Future for National Political Parties in Canada?," 148–49.

18. The phrase was coined by Robert Michels in his book *Political Parties: A Sociological Study of the Oligarchical Tendencies of Modern Democracy* (New York: Free Press, 1962 [1911]).

19. R. Kenneth Carty, "Parties as Franchise Systems: The Stratarchical Organizational Imperative," *Party Politics,* 10:1 (2004), 7–9.

20. In this context, the word "franchise" denotes a structural similarity to companies like McDonald's, in which local businesspeople purchase the right to use the company name, menu, and graphic design in their home markets. It should not be confused with the political meaning of "franchise," which refers to the right to vote in elections.

21. Carty, "Parties as Franchise Systems," 11.

22. The first two categories are taken from James Q. Wilson, *Political Organizations* (Princeton: Princeton University Press, 1995 [1974]), 33–34. The third and fourth combine categories used by Wilson ("collective solidary" and "purposive") with two from Lisa Young and William Cross, "Incentives to Membership in Canadian Political Parties," *Political Research Quarterly*, 55:3 (September 2002), 550 ("social norms" and "altruistic").

23. See Gordon T. Stewart, *The Origins of Canadian Politics: A Comparative Approach* (Vancouver: UBC Press, 1986), Chapters 3 and 4.

24. Young and Cross, "Incentives to Membership in Canadian Political Parties," 558.

25. Carty, *Canadian Political Parties in the Constituencies*, Table 3.17, 60.

26. Cross and Young ("The Contours of Political Party Membership," 436) found that the major parties (except the governing Liberals) had attracted few new members in the decade prior to their survey. They speculate, with good reason, that many (if not most) "instant" members allow their new memberships to lapse shortly after the nomination or leadership contest ends.

27. Carty, *Canadian Political Parties in the Constituencies*, 173–76.

28. Young and Cross, "Incentives to Membership in Canadian Political Parties," Table 1, 556.

29. These terms are taken from Angelo Panebianco, *Political Parties: Organization and Power* (Cambridge: Cambridge University Press, 1988), 26.

30. This conclusion may be supported by a finding from the 2000 survey of party members. People who joined the Reform Party in the 1990s placed somewhat less emphasis on policy and ideology than those who had signed up in the 1980s. See Young and Cross, "Incentives to Membership in Canadian Political Parties," 565.

31. George C. Perlin, *The Tory Syndrome: Leadership Politics in the Progressive Conservative Party* (Montreal and Kingston: McGill–Queen's University Press, 1980), 198–200.

32. This conclusion is supported by Young and Cross, "Incentives to Membership in Canadian Political Parties." Figure 2 (564) shows that for PCs who joined the party in the 1980s and 1990s, material and other self-seeking incentives were considerably more important than for those who joined during the party's "wilderness years" of the 1960s and 1970s.

33. S.J.R. Noel, "Patronage and Entourages, Action-Sets, Networks," in A. Brian Tanguay and Alain-G. Gagnon, eds., *Canadian Parties in Transition*, second ed. (Scarborough: Nelson Canada, 1996), 247–48; Mildred A. Schwartz, *The Party Network: The Robust Organization of Illinois Republicans* (Madison: University of Wisconsin Press, 1990).

34. B.D. Graham, *Representation and Party Politics: A Comparative Perspective* (Oxford: Blackwell, 1993), 156.

35. Ron Graham, *One-Eyed Kings: Promise and Illusion in Canadian Politics* (Toronto: Collins, 1986), 191.

36. See Noel for a discussion of the leader's entourage.

37. B.D. Graham, 154.

38. B.D. Graham, 154.

39. Alan Whitehorn, *Canadian Socialism: Essays on the CCF–NDP* (Toronto: Oxford University Press, 1992), 190.

40. Ian McLeod, *Under Siege: The Federal NDP in the Nineties* (Toronto: Lorimer, 1994), 11.

41. Whitehorn, 119.

42. Susan Delacourt, *Juggernaut: Paul Martin's Campaign for Chrétien's Crown* (Toronto: McClelland and Stewart, 2003), 256–57.

43. Ibid., 137–38.

44. Ibid., 214 and 224.

45. Carty, "Parties as Franchise Systems," 15.

46. Maurice Duverger, *Political Parties: Their Organization and Activity in the Modern State*, translated by Barbara and Robert North (London: Methuen, 1964 [1954]), 230.

47. Independent candidates are those who have not been nominated by a political party. Candidates with no party affiliation were nominated by a party, but the party failed to fulfill the requirements for registered party status, one of which is to nominate candidates in at least 50 constituencies before the deadline. If the party fails to fulfill the registration requirements, candidates nominated by that party are listed as having no affiliation.

48. Former Alliance MP Chuck Cadman is a notable exception. Shortly before the 2004 election, Cadman lost the Conservative nomination in his riding of Surrey North. He decided to run as an unaffiliated candidate, and won. He was the only independent candidate to win a seat in the election.

49. R. Kenneth Carty and Lynda Erickson, "Candidate Nomination in Canada's National Political Parties," in Bakvis, ed., *Canadian Political Parties*, 114.

50. Carty and Erickson, 120.

51. Oliver Moore, "Copps wants nomination battle restaged," *The Globe and Mail*, March 10, 2004; Jane Taber, "Copps alleges tampering by Valeri campaign," *The Globe and Mail*, March 10, 2004 (both accessed at www.globeandmail.com).

52. Gloria Galloway, "Dryden makes his candidacy official," *The Globe and Mail*, May 18, 2004; accessed at www.globeandmail.com.

53. In 1917, the British government asked Canada to send more troops to Europe to support the Allies. Because the pool of willing volunteers was more or less exhausted, the Canadian government had to consider imposing conscription—mandatory military duty. The idea was bitterly opposed by French Canadians, who saw no reason to send their sons to die for the British cause. The Liberal caucus split, with the anglophones joining the ruling Conservative caucus (thus creating the Union government) under Prime Minister Sir Robert Borden; the Union government won a federal election in 1917, and promptly imposed conscription. Francophone Liberals were left as a rump caucus in Opposition.

54. For a comprehensive history of national leadership conventions in Canada, see John C. Courtney, *The Selection of National Party Leaders in Canada* (Toronto: Macmillan, 1973) and *Do Conventions Matter? Choosing National Party Leaders in Canada* (Montreal and Kingston: McGill–Queen's University Press, 1995).

55. See R. Kenneth Carty, "Campaigning in the Trenches: The Transformation of Constituency Politics," in George C. Perlin, ed., *Party Democracy in Canada: The Politics of National Party Conventions* (Scarborough: Prentice-Hall Canada, 1988), 84–96.

56. See Heather MacIvor, "From Emergence to Electronics: Explaining the Changes in Canadian Party Leadership Selection, 1919–1995," *National History*, I:2 (Spring 1997).

57. Young and Cross, "The Rise of Plebiscitary Democracy," 678.

58. Young and Cross, "The Rise of Plebiscitary Democracy," 687.

59. David K. Stewart and R. Kenneth Carty, "Leadership Politics as Party Building: The Conservatives in 1998," in William Cross, ed., *Political Parties, Representation, and Electoral Democracy in Canada* (Toronto: Oxford University Press, 2002), 55–67.

60. Brian Laghi, "Last-minute offer aims to unite right," *The Globe and Mail*, October 7, 2003; accessed at www.globeandmail.com.

61. Brian Laghi, "Stronach team calls for delay of leadership vote," *The Globe and Mail*, March 11, 2004 (accessed at www.globeandmail.com); Michael Tutton, "In 'remote' ridings, some Conservatives find voting confusing," Canadian Press, March 14, 2004 (accessed at www.canada.com). The number of names on the party roster jumped from 142 000 (most of them former Alliance members) to 251 700 during the leadership contest; another 25 000 reportedly joined after the deadline to vote had passed. John Ward, "Tories sign up members in droves after deadline passes," Canadian Press, March 17, 2004 (accessed at www.canada.com).

62. Canadian Press, "Reports suggest widespread voting problems," March 20, 2004; accessed at www.canada.com.

63. Official results obtained from the Conservative Party's website (www.conservative.ca). The party used an ordinal ballot (see Chapter 4), which required the members to rank the three candidates in order of precedence. If none had received a majority on the first ballot, the third-place finisher (in this case, Clement) would have been dropped and his second preferences allocated to Harper and Stronach. Because Clement finished a distant third, with less than 10 percent of the vote, his second preferences would not have put Stronach ahead of Harper.

64. Steven Chase, "Voters in West and Ontario delivered win to Harper," *The Globe and Mail*, March 22, 2004; accessed at www.globeandmail.com.

65. Daniel Latouche, "Universal Democracy and Effective Leadership: Lessons from the Parti Québécois Experience," in R. Kenneth Carty, Lynda Erickson, and Donald E. Blake, eds., *Leaders and Parties in Canadian Politics: Experiences of the Provinces* (Toronto: HBJ Canada, 1992), 174–202.

66. Allison Dunfield, "Liberal executive may ask Copps to bow out," *The Globe and Mail*, September 24, 2003; accessed at www.globeandmail.com.

67. Campbell Clark and Stephanie Nolen, "Liberals get impressive warm-up act," *The Globe and Mail*, November 5, 2004; Gloria Galloway, "Chrétien goodbye an exercise in logistics," *The Globe and Mail*, November 13, 2004 (both accessed at www.globeandmail.com).

68. In July 2002 the three Cabinet ministers in the running (Allan Rock, Sheila Copps, and John Manley) publicly disclosed the amounts and sources of donations to their leadership campaigns. Martin considered making a similar disclosure, to avoid the appearance of excessive secrecy (and possible conflict-of-interest allegations), but decided against it. He argued that people and businesses had given money to his campaign without being aware that their names would be made public. He also alleged that donors who depended on the federal government for their livelihoods might be subject to retribution from the Chrétien government (e.g., cancellation of contracts). Delacourt, *Juggernaut*, 255–56.

69. John C. Courtney, "Recognition of Canadian Political Parties in Parliament and in Law," *Canadian Journal of Political Science*, XI:1 (March 1978), 33–60.

70. Leon D. Epstein, *Political Parties in the American Mold* (Madison: University of Wisconsin Press, 1986), 155–58.

71. The spending limits for candidates in the most recent general election, issued by Elections Canada on June 28, 2004, range from just about $70 000 to a little over $90 000 depending on the geographical size and registered voting population of the electoral district. They average out to approximately $80 000. The 2004 candidate spending limits are available online at www.elections.ca/ele/38e/limcan/can_limit.pdf.

72. In the original version of Bill C-24, the limit was 50 percent of the previous constituency maximum. The Standing Committee on Procedure and House Affairs, which reviewed the Bill, lowered the percentage at the urging of female MPs.

73. For more information about this ruling, see Heather MacIvor, *The Charter of Rights and Party Politics: The Impact of the Supreme Court Ruling in* Figueroa v. Canada (Attorney General (Montreal: Institute for Research on Public Policy, May 2004); available online at www.irpp.org.

74. The Christian Heritage Party, which failed to nominate 50 candidates in the 2000 election and thus lost its registered status, had contested federal elections since 1988. The Libertarian Party and the Progressive Canadian Party (a rump of former Progressive Conservatives opposed to the merger with the Canadian Alliance) were new to politics.

75. Donations to the Natural Law Party in 2003 were considerably lower than those for the Marxist–Leninists, at just over $9000. However, the Natural Law Party reregistered itself during 2003, so its figures for that year do not really count.

76. The various stages in the legislative process are explained in Dossier 5.1.

77. Elections Canada, "Chief Electoral Officer of Canada Announces Amounts to be Paid to Registered Political Parties for 2004," press release, December 11, 2003; accessed at www.elections.ca.

78. Kim Lunman, "NDP to double election chest to $12 million," *The Globe and Mail*, February 9, 2004; accessed at www.globeandmail.com.

79. John Ibbitson, "Your vote has extra value for your party," *The Globe and Mail*, May 25, 2004; accessed at www.globeandmail.com.

80. Alan Siaroff, "Two-and-a-Half Party Systems and the Comparative Role of the 'Half,'" *Party Politics*, 9:3 (2003), 273.

81. R. Kenneth Carty, William Cross, and Lisa Young, *Rebuilding Canadian Party Politics* (Vancouver: UBC Press, 2000) 3–4.

82. For a further discussion on these factors, see Herbert Kitschelt, *The Logics of Party Formation: Ecological Politics in Belgium and West Germany* (Ithaca, NY: Cornell University Press, 1989); and Keith Archer and Faron Ellis, "Opinion Structure of Party Activists: The Reform Party of Canada," *Canadian Journal of Political Science*, XXVII (1994), 277–308.

83. Peter Mair, "Party Systems and Structures of Competition," in Lawrence LeDuc, Richard G. Niemi, and Pippa Norris, eds., *Comparing Democracies: Elections and Voting in Global Perspective* (Thousand Oaks, CA: Sage, 1996).

84. James Bickerton, Alain-G. Gagnon, and Patrick J. Smith, *Ties that Bind: Parties and Voters in Canada* (Toronto: Oxford University Press, 1999), 46.

85. Bickerton, Gagnon, and Smith, 47.

86. Bickerton, Gagnon, and Smith, 47.

87. Keith Archer and Faron Ellis, "Opinion Structure of Party Activists: The Reform Party of Canada," *Canadian Journal of Political Science*, XXVII:2 (June 1994), 281–82.

88. Neil Nevitte, André Blais, Elisabeth Gidengil, and Richard Nadeau, *Unsteady State: The 1997 Canadian Federal Election* (Toronto: Oxford University Press, 2000), Chapter 8.

89. Faron Ellis, "The More Things Change . . . The Alliance Campaign," in Jon H. Pammett and Christopher Dornan, eds., *The Canadian General Election of 2000* (Ottawa: Carleton University Press, 2001), 62.

90. Ellis, 64–65.

91. Ellis, 68.

92. Ellis, 83–84.

93. André Turcotte, "Fallen Heroes: Leaders and Voters in the 2000 Canadian General Election," in Pammett and Dornan, eds., *The Canadian General Election of 2000*, 285.

94. Allison Dunfield, "Alliance, Tories head back in co-operative mood," *The Globe and Mail*, September 15, 2004; accessed at www.globeandmail.com.

95. Drew Fagan, "The motivating force? Fear of Paul Martin," *The Globe and Mail*, October 16, 2003; Drew Fagan, "Burden of bridge-building fell on leaders," *The Globe and Mail*, October 17, 2003 (both accessed at www.globeandmail.com).

96. Brian Laghi and Drew Fagan, "Let's pick leader by February, Alliance tells Conservatives," *The Globe and Mail*, September 19, 2003 (accessed at www.globeandmail.com); Sean Gordon, "'Swords will point at Liberals,'" *Ottawa Citizen*, October 17, 2003 (accessed at www.canada.com).

97. Excerpted from Stephen Harper and Peter MacKay, "Agreement-in-principle on the establishment of the Conservative Party of Canada," October 15, 2003; accessed at www.pcparty.ca (the site no longer exists), 1–3.

98. In December 2003 an Ontario Superior Court judge dismissed the suit. He ruled that the PC merger process conformed to the requirements in the *Canada Elections Act* for two registered parties to become one. See *Ahenakew v. MacKay*, December 5, 2003 (available at www.canlii.org).

99. "The PC Party of Canada outlines its ratification process," news release, October 28, 2003; accessed at www.pcparty.ca (the site no longer exists).

100. Jeff Sallot, "Orchard vows to stop new memberships," *The Globe and Mail*, October 20, 2003; accessed at www.globe andmail.com.

101. Allison Dunfield, "95.9% of Alliance voters agree to merger," *The Globe and Mail*, December 5, 2003; accessed at www.globeandmail.com.

102. Luma Muhtadie, "Tories vote to unite the right," *The Globe and Mail*, December 6, 2003; accessed at www.globeandmail.com.

103. Andrew Willis, "United right wins Street's hearts, wallets," *The Globe and Mail*, October 17, 2003; Brian Laghi, "Tories push corporations for cash," *The Globe and Mail*, December 2, 2004 (both accessed at www.globeandmail.com).

104. André Bernard, "The Bloc Québécois," in Alan Frizzell, Jon H. Pammett, and Anthony Westell, eds., *The Canadian General Election of 1993* (Ottawa: Carleton University Press, 1994), 81–82.

105. Manon Cornellier, *The Bloc* (Toronto: Lorimer, 1995), 17.

106. Cornellier, 157.

107. Richard Nadeau, André Blais, Elisabeth Gidengil, and Neil Nevitte, "Why Did the Liberals Win in Quebec?," 2 (available on the Canadian Election Study Web site: www.fas.umontreal.ca/pol/ces-eec).

108. Rhéal Séguin, "Liberals can no longer afford to ignore the Bloc," *The Globe and Mail*, May 15, 2004; accessed at www.globeandmail.com.

109. Jane Taber, "Martin tries to buoy caucus," *The Globe and Mail*, March 11, 2004; accessed at www.globeandmail.com.

110. Carty, Cross, and Young, 207.

111. This was a particular problem for the Progressive Conservatives in the 2000 federal election campaign. See Paul Attallah and Angela Burton, "Television, the Internet, and the Canadian Federal Election of 2000," in Pammett and Dornan, eds., *The Canadian General Election of 2000*, 229.

112. Delacourt, *Jugggernaut*, 265.

113. Ibid., 196.

114. The descriptions of the first three party systems are taken from R. Kenneth Carty, "Three Canadian Party Systems: An Interpretation of the Development of National Politics," in Perlin, ed., *Party Democracy in Canada,* 15–30. See also Carty, Cross, and Young. The description of the fourth party system is original to this volume, although based on the analysis of Carty, Cross, and Young. Note that some of the dates have been changed, to reflect the argument of this chapter.

115. Stephen Clarkson, "The Liberal Threepeat: The Multi-System Party in the Multi-Party System," in Pammett and Dornan, eds., *The Canadian General Election of 2000,* 15.

116. André Siegfried, *The Race Question in Canada* (Toronto: McClelland and Stewart, 1966 [1906]), 114.

117. See Duverger.

118. Siegfried, 136.

119. William T. Stanbury, *Money in Politics: Financing Federal Parties and Candidates in Canada,* volume 1 of the collected research studies for the Royal Commission on Electoral Reform and Party Financing (Toronto: Dundurn Press, 1991), 27–28.

120. Carty, "Three Canadian Party Systems," 19.

121. Brodie and Jenson, *Crisis, Challenge and Change.*

122. Carty, "Three Canadian Party Systems," 20.

123. Carty, "Three Canadian Party Systems," 19–21.

124. Although the anti-party sentiment of the Progressives contributed to their political demise, it led to the name of the Progressive Conservative Party. In 1943 John Bracken, premier of Manitoba from 1922 to 1943, was persuaded to move to federal politics and lead the Conservative party. Bracken had led the Manitoba Progressives, and his anti-party views had contributed to the formation of a "Liberal–Progressive" coalition, which won three successive provincial elections in the 1930s. In 1941 Bracken invited all parties in the Manitoba legislature to join in a coalition government, and all but a handful of members did so. In 1943 the same anti-party sentiment led Bracken to demand the addition of "Progressive" to the name of the Conservative Party as the price of agreeing to lead that party at the national level. Bracken never led his renamed party to victory, however, and thus never had the opportunity to attempt to replicate at the federal level his provincial success in promoting interparty cooperation.

125. Michiel Horn, "The LSR, the CCF, and the Regina Manifesto," in William J. Brennan, ed., *Building the Co-operative Commonwealth: Essays on the Democratic Socialist Tradition in Canada* (Regina: Canadian Plains Research Centre, 1984), 25–41.

126. Gad Horowitz, *Canadian Labour in Politics* (Toronto: University of Toronto Press, 1968).

127. C.B. MacPherson, *Democracy in Alberta: Social Credit and the Party System,* second ed. (Toronto: University of Toronto Press, 1962); Alvin Finkel, *The Social Credit Phenomenon in Alberta* (Toronto: University of Toronto Press, 1989).

128. On the establishment of the Dominion Conservative Association and the first party headquarters in Ottawa, see Larry A. Glassford, *Reaction and Reform: The Politics of the Conservative Party under R.B. Bennett, 1927–1938* (Toronto: University of Toronto Press, 1992), Chapter 3; the history of the extraparliamentary Liberal party is described in Reginald Whitaker, *The Government Party: Organizing and Financing the Liberal Party of Canada, 1930–58* (Toronto: University of Toronto Press, 1977), Chapter 1.

129. Carty, "Three Canadian Party Systems," 23.

130. David E. Smith, "Party Government, Representation and National Integration in Canada," in Peter Aucoin, ed., *Party Government and Regional Representation in Canada,*

volume 36 of the collected research studies for the Royal Commission on the Economic Union and Development prospects for Canada (Toronto: University of Toronto Press, 1985), 1–68.

131. Smith, 25.

132. Desmond Morton, *The New Democrats 1961–1986: The Politics of Change* (Toronto: Copp Clark Pitman, 1986).

133. The NDP's strategy has not been entirely successful, for a number of reasons. First, unions have not provided the level of support that was anticipated at the time of the party's founding. Second, the Canadian workforce is not highly unionized. Less than 40 percent of those who are employed belong to a union. Of those who do, many belong to public-sector unions, which are prevented by law or convention from directly supporting a particular party. Third, many union members ignore the suggestions of their union leadership in political matters. There are countless reasons for voting for one party or another, and the wishes of one's union leadership do not always prevail. Finally, in many constituencies, the NDP is not electorally competitive, and it has never formed the government nationally. For many voters, supporting a third party is viewed as a wasted vote. See Keith Archer, *Political Choices and Electoral Consequences: A Study of Organized Labour and the New Democratic Party* (Montreal and Kingston: McGill–Queens University Press, 1990).

134. Clarkson, "The Liberal Threepeat," 31.

135. David M. Farrell, "Campaign Strategies and Tactics," in Lawrence LeDuc, Richard G, Niemi, and Pippa Norris, eds., *Comparing Democracies: Elections and Voting in Global Perspective* (Thousand Oaks, CA: Sage, 1996), 176.

136. See Harold D. Clarke, Jane Jenson, Lawrence LeDuc, and Jon H. Pammett, *Absent Mandate: Interpreting Change in Canadian Elections,* 2nd edition (Toronto: Gage, 1991), especially Chapter 3.

137. Carty, Cross, and Young, 218.

138. Carty, Cross and Young, 219.

139. See Lawson and Merkl, eds., *When Parties Fail.*

4 ELECTIONS AND VOTING

LEARNING OBJECTIVES

- *explain* the differences among the major categories of electoral systems;
- *analyze* and *evaluate* the arguments in favour of a more proportional electoral system for Canada;
- *describe* and *evaluate* the current election-finance regime;
- *identify* and *describe* the long-term and short-term factors that influence Canadian voting behaviour.

INTRODUCTION

This chapter brings together three central themes in this book:

1. the importance of regionalism as a motivating force in Canadian politics;
2. the influence of institutions on political behaviour, specifically the incentives for parties and voters that are imposed by our current electoral system; and
3. the ongoing debate about the nature and reform of our political institutions. As political values change, so do the criteria by which Canadians evaluate their national institutions. In the 1970s and 1980s, the debate over electoral reform focused on the need to overcome territorial divisions; in the 1990s, the focus shifted to the representation of women and other nonterritorial groups in Parliament. The changing contour of the electoral-system debate in Canada illustrates one major difficulty in adapting political institutions: the lack of a consensus over the goals of reform. At the same time, the entire system of representative democracy—which rests on fair, competitive elections to Parliament—is increasingly subject to critique from populists and other direct-democracy advocates.

This chapter explains the role of elections in our national politics, describes and evaluates the operation of Canada's electoral system, and examines the patterns in Canadian voting behaviour.

Elections and Democracy

Our system of government is an "indirect" democracy. Citizens do not govern themselves directly; instead, they elect representatives to govern them. In this way, the consent of citizens is secured, however indirectly and imperfectly.[1] Periodic competitive elections based on universal adult **suffrage** are the crucial distinction between democratic and nondemocratic governments. But although every democratic state holds elections, the ways in which those elections are conducted vary widely. As we will see later in this chapter, there are dozens of different electoral systems in use around the world. Most of these fall into three distinct categories:

1. single member (one legislator per constituency);
2. **proportional representation (PR)** (multimember constituencies, with the seats distributed according to the parties' respective vote shares); and
3. mixed systems, which combine the first two principles.[2]

Different electoral systems can have varying effects on the composition of the legislature and the political executive, the number of parties in the party system, the incentives for parties seeking to win seats, and the behaviour of voters.

In a **general election,** the entire House of Commons is dissolved and all 308 seats are filled simultaneously. A **by-election** occurs when a single seat becomes vacant (e.g., the incumbent MP resigns), and a special vote is held to fill it. In either case, the prime minister asks the governor general to issue a writ of election, which sets the date on which ballots will be cast. (This is the origin of the phrase "dropping the writ" to describe the official start of an election campaign.) The prime minister normally decides when to call a general election (see Chapters 5 and 6). If the government is defeated in the House of Commons, the prime minister may submit his resignation to the governor general and thus trigger an early election. But when the prime minister controls a majority in the House of Commons, he has almost complete discretion over the timing of dissolution. There are only two constraints on this power:

1. The campaign is limited by law to 36 days.
2. No Parliament may last longer than five years, except in extraordinary circumstances, as spelled out in section 4 of the *Charter of Rights.*

An election call is usually preceded by weeks or months of anticipation and speculation. By the time the prime minister meets the governor general at Rideau Hall and obtains his or her signature on the writ of dissolution, campaign preparations are well under way. The major parties have nominated candidates in at least some of Canada's 308 constituencies, raised money to fight the campaign, and planned their electoral strategies on the basis of survey data gathered by their pollsters. Most major parties begin each election campaign with a reliable base in the electorate. The purpose of the campaign period, from the viewpoint of a party strategist, is to persuade "soft" supporters to remain loyal while winning over converts from the other parties and from among the pool of undecided voters. From a less partisan perspective, election campaigns are supposed to benefit the political system in two ways: by mobilizing apathetic voters to go to the polls and by allowing voters to set the broad outlines of government policy for the next few years. As we will see in this chapter, however, Canadian election campaigns do not live up to these ideals. We begin by examining the link between elections and public policy.

Elections and Public Policy

If Canadians are increasingly demanding a role in policy-making, through **referenda** and other direct-democracy devices, one reason may be the weak connection between the parties' election promises and the policies that they subsequently adopt in government. As we have seen, national governments are increasingly constrained by global economic conditions and supranational agreements. However, they still enjoy a wide latitude in some policy fields (e.g., criminal law[3]) within the fiscal limitations imposed by world capital and investment markets. Therefore, it is incorrect to assume that elections are irrelevant in the era of globalization.[4] When power changes hands in an election, the new governing party can impose its distinct priorities in many policy fields.

The connection between a party's pre-election platform and its post-election priorities can be understood in either of two ways: the agenda model and the mandate model.[5] The agenda model predicts that a party in government will seek to enact the specific policies that it promised during the most recent campaign. For example, if the Conservative platform includes a pledge to lengthen prison sentences for violent crimes, the party is committed to amend the existing penal legislation after taking office. The pledge is more than a campaign ploy to win votes; it reflects a genuine desire to "crack down" on criminals. A comparative study of 10 Western democracies found that the agenda effect is weaker in Canada than in most other countries—largely because of our single-party governments and single-member electoral system.[6]

The mandate model takes a broader view of the link between parties and policies. It has three primary elements:
1. "the belief that elections carry messages about problems, policies, and programs—messages plain to all and specific enough to be directive";
2. the claim that "certain of these messages must be treated as authoritative commands" to the party that wins an election; and
3. the assumption that "governments should not undertake major innovation in policy or procedure, except in emergencies, unless the electorate has had an opportunity to consider them in an election and thus to express its views."[7]

It is customary for newly elected governments, particularly new governments with large majorities in Parliament, to claim a mandate from the people to implement their platforms. The belief that the governing party has the legitimate authority to enact the will of the people is a powerful political tool. But in most cases, at least in Canada, it is a false belief. Neither the agenda model nor the mandate model provides an accurate account of the relationship between policy and elections. There are at least four reasons why Canadian general elections do not automatically set the policy agenda, or create specific policy mandates for governments:

1. The claim that voters use their ballots to express specific policy preferences is simply inaccurate. While the parties' varying approaches to critical issues do affect election outcomes, that effect is too small and too diffuse to constitute a clear and specific command. As we will see in later sections of this chapter, Canadian voters are influenced by a host of factors—party loyalty, social cleavages, impressions of the various leaders—and they are as likely to interpret party platforms through these lenses as they are to make up their minds about parties on the basis of their policy pledges.[8] In any case, elections are not referenda. They are designed to elect the people who will sit in Parliament, not to resolve particular policy disputes.[9] Therefore, the relationship between elections and public policy is indirect at best.

2. For the most part, Canada's brokerage parties (see Chapter 3) avoid making specific promises that might alienate potential voters. They rely instead on vague, leader-centred campaigns that build broad electoral coalitions and leave the winning party with the maximum flexibility in government.[10] Without a clear and consistent choice among party principles, voters cannot express their preferences by casting ballots for party candidates. The 1988 and 1993 elections were unusual, in the sense that the Liberals and PCs staked out clear and distinct positions on one or more crucial issues. In 1988 the PCs were forced to call an election on their free trade deal with the United States (the FTA), when the Liberal majority in the Senate refused to ratify the deal without consulting the electorate. Even in that campaign, which was dominated by a single issue to an extraordinary degree, the PC victory did not produce a clear-cut mandate for the FTA.[11] In 1993 the Liberals issued the first *Red Book,* an unusually detailed platform with which they invited voters to hold them accountable.[12] Jean Chrétien repeatedly told his audiences that if his government failed to keep its promises, it should lose the next election. While the *Red Book* won votes for the Liberals as a symbol of accountable and honest government,[13] its detailed contents made little impact on voters. Since the mid-1990s, the campaign platforms of the major parties have generally contained more partisan rhetoric than policy detail.

3. Canadian governments do not feel bound to await new instructions from the voters before undertaking significant changes in policy. While a government may pay a political price for a major "U-turn," there is no written or unwritten rule to deter it from breaking its promises. In 1974 Pierre Trudeau campaigned against a legislated "freeze" on wages and prices; in 1993 Jean Chrétien campaigned against the North American Free Trade Agreement (NAFTA) with the United States and Mexico. Both subsequently reversed themselves: Trudeau

imposed wage and price controls, and Chrétien signed the NAFTA deal without the significant improvements in labour and environmental protection he had demanded during the campaign.

4. Finally, both models overlook the practical difficulties that prevent a party in government from keeping its promises. As LeDuc points out, "Even politicians who are determined to carry through on their commitments may encounter difficulty in discerning a specific electoral message and translating it into effective public policy."[14] Shortly after winning the 1993 election, Prime Minister Chrétien told his new Cabinet that they would spend the first half of their mandate fulfilling their *Red Book* promises.[15] Unfortunately for the Liberals, the country's fiscal situation forced them to cut program spending, slash transfers to the provinces, and scale back Employment Insurance benefits—policies not anticipated in the *Red Book*. At least in that instance, the Liberals wrote the *Red Book* in the expectation that they would win the election; the policies were crafted, in part, with an eye to practicality. The same could not be said of the Ontario New Democrats, who were astounded when they won a majority in the 1990 provincial election. Their campaign platform, the "Agenda for People," had promised billions of dollars' worth of new spending on social programs, environmental protection, and infrastructure. Almost immediately after the election, Premier-elect Bob Rae began to distance himself from his party's promises. The "Agenda for People" was an effective tool for motivating NDP activists and supporters, but it was not a practical "blueprint for governing."[16] As one member of the NDP caucus put it, "We . . . had no notion that we would ever have to implement it."[17] When parties accustomed to the freedom of opposition run up against the reality of governing, the policies they adopted so enthusiastically may be revealed as impractical and potentially damaging. Under those circumstances, there is something to be said in favour of broken campaign promises.

If we conclude that elections do not determine the direction of public policy, then what exactly do they do?

- At the very least, competitive elections allow citizens to remove a government that has failed to live up to expectations and to replace it with an alternative government. In this way, citizens hold their rulers to account for their use of power. The prospect of losing the next election can act as a brake on a government that might otherwise abuse its power or trample the rights of its citizens.
- Elections are almost always used to select the members of the legislative branch (except in appointed upper houses, such as the Canadian Senate). In some countries, including the United States, selected executive and judicial offices are also filled by election. Popular election makes the exercise of state power legitimate, by signifying the consent of the governed.
- Elections allow voters to express their broad political preferences, even if they do not transmit specific policy choices.
- Finally, elections provide voters with the opportunity to engage directly with their political institutions. They use the electoral system to elect MPs, some of whom will sit in the Cabinet and one of whom will become (or remain) the prime minister.

Whatever its imperfections, representative democracy has at least one cardinal virtue: it brings the citizens into close contact with the state, at fairly regular intervals. Unfortunately, as we will see later in this chapter, fewer and fewer Canadians are taking advantage of that opportunity.

THE CONDUCT OF CANADIAN ELECTIONS

As we argued earlier, any state that claims to be a democracy must hold regular, free, fair, and competitive elections. To ensure fairness, an election must be organized and administered by a nonpartisan agency with nothing to fear from the loss of the incumbent party. Elections Canada operates at arm's length from the government of the day. The Chief Electoral Officer, who cannot be removed from office without just cause, reports directly to Parliament (in practice, to the Standing Committee on Procedure and House Affairs). While the governing party controls the content of the *Canada Elections Act*—the legislation that gives Elections Canada its authority and sets the rules by which it operates—it cannot be seen to pursue an electoral advantage denied to the other registered parties.[18] The Chief Electoral Officer is forbidden to vote in Canadian elections and referenda, to preserve an aura of impartiality.

In addition to the formal rules that guide Elections Canada and its officials, there are informal (and often unwritten) rules for the parties and candidates who participate in campaigns. Together, the formal and informal rules provide a complete picture of Canada's electoral system in operation.

■ The Formal Rules: The *Canada Elections Act*

Until recently, Canadian parties were subject to comparatively little formal regulation (Chapter 3). In most respects, constituency associations were treated as private clubs. Their internal operations fell outside the scope of the *Canada Elections Act,* whose rules about **agency, disclosure,** and spending limits applied only to candidates and not to the local party organizations that nominated them. There were no spending limits on nomination contests. Indeed, constituency associations were described as the "'black hole' in the current regulatory regime."[19]

All that changed on January 1, 2004, when Bill C-24—*An Act to Amend the* Canada Elections Act *and the* Income Tax Act *(Political Financing)*—became law. The Bill extended the regulatory regime to constituency associations ("electoral district associations," or EDAs in legal terminology). Every constituency association of a registered party has to file its own registration with Elections Canada. Only registered associations can accept donations and spend money.[20] This means that a constituency association that does not register cannot run an election campaign. The agency and disclosure provisions that used to apply only to national party organizations now apply at the local level. A registered constituency association must appoint an official agent, who is responsible for receiving donations and submitting an audited annual report of financial transactions to Elections Canada. (The constituency associations are also affected by the new rules for nomination contests, which are briefly discussed in Chapter 3.)

The new provisions for constituency associations operate independently of the existing rules for candidates and their campaign teams. Whereas the constituency rules are always in effect, those that apply to candidates only operate during (and after) the 36-day campaign period. Any candidate who received at least 10 percent of the valid votes cast in her constituency is eligible for reimbursement of up to 60 percent of the electoral and personal expenses incurred by her campaign.[21] To qualify for the reimbursement, the candidate's official agent must submit a report to Elections Canada detailing the revenues received by the campaign, election expenditures, and personal expenses incurred by the candidate.[22] Any surplus funds remaining after election day must be transferred to the bank account of the local constituency association affiliated with the registered party represented by the candidate. Over time, in well-organized constituency associations with popular incumbent MPs, those surplus funds can build up into very substantial amounts; in the early 1990s, some Progressive Conservative associations held assets of up to half a million dollars.[23]

The same regulatory principles also apply to registered parties:

- *Agency:* The registered party must, as a condition of registration, appoint an official agent (e.g., the Federal Liberal Agency of Canada), which is responsible for issuing tax receipts to donors and keeping complete records of revenues and expenditures;[24]
- *Disclosure:* The party's official agent must submit an annual fiscal report to Elections Canada, including the source and amount of each donation,[25] as well as a special report on each election campaign that details the revenues and expenditures of the national party organization[26] (candidates do not have to submit an annual report);
- *Spending limits:* The amount that a registered party can legally spend on its national campaign is determined by the number of candidates who run under its banner, and by the number of voters in the constituencies where those candidates are nominated;[27]
- *Public reimbursement of election expenses:* A registered party that receives at least 2 percent of the valid national vote, or at least 5 percent of the valid vote in the constituencies where it ran candidates, is eligible for a reimbursement of 50 percent of its allowable election expenses if it complies with the reporting requirements of the Act (the figure for the 2004 general election was 60 percent);[28] and
- *Tax credits for political donations:* A donation of $25 or more to a registered party, a registered constituency association, or an official candidate is eligible for a tax credit, which reduces the amount of income tax owing to the federal government (e.g., a donation of $400 to the official agent of a candidate entitles the donor to deduct $300 from his or her income tax).[29]

In addition, registered parties are subject to the broadcasting provisions of the *Canada Elections Act*. The key elements of the election broadcast rules are as follows:

- During the campaign period, every Canadian broadcaster—independent radio stations and radio and TV networks—must make 6½ hours of prime time available for purchase by the registered parties for their election advertising. That time is divided among the registered parties on the basis of their seat percentages in the Commons, their share of the vote in the previous general election, and the number of candidates each party nominated during the last campaign period. The allocation of time among the parties is determined by the Broadcasting Arbitrator, an official appointed by the Chief Electoral Officer before each election. No single party may receive more than 50 percent of the total broadcasting time.[30]
- Every radio and television network must provide free airtime to the registered parties in proportion to the allocation of paid airtime just described.
- Broadcasters and publishers may not charge inflated rates for campaign advertising; in other words, they cannot gouge the parties for extra money during an election.

Before 1974, when the *Election Expenses Act* took effect, parties and candidates were not required to disclose the amounts and sources of their revenues or to restrict their campaign spending. It may seem strange that parties would deliberately impose restrictive laws on themselves, but they had good practical and political reasons to do so:

- The cost of campaigning had soared in previous years, as electoral politics became increasingly capital-intensive. Party volunteers on the ground, who gave their time and effort freely to the cause, were being replaced by professional consultants, television advertising, public-opinion polling, and other costly innovations. A comparison between the 1972 and 1974 campaigns is instructive. The 1972 campaign produced a minority Liberal government, the fourth minority in 10 years (the others were elected in 1962, 1963, and 1965); it fell after two years in office, during which time it had been supported by the NDP. In the 1974 federal election, the last one held before the new regulations took effect, the Liberals spent 7 percent more than they had in 1972; PC spending rose by 20 percent, while NDP spending rose by more than one-third.[31] Overall, candidates for the three major parties reported expenditures of over $10.4 million in the 1974 campaign.[32] (Note, however, that almost 20 percent of major-party candidates in 1974 did not file fiscal returns, so these figures are incomplete.)
- As the previous point suggests, the problem of rising campaign costs was magnified by the frequency of elections during the preceding decade. Although the election of a Liberal majority in 1974 marked the end of a period of fragmentation and instability in the national party system—there have been only two minority governments since then, the PC minority of 1979–80 and the 2004 Liberal government—this could not have been foreseen at the time.

- The NDP exacted several policy concessions from the Liberals in exchange for supporting the 1972–74 minority, one of which was the *Election Expenses Act*. Rising campaign costs, and the frequency of general elections, were especially onerous for the NDP, which did not have access to the generous corporate contributors who supported the Liberals and PCs. Whereas Liberal candidates reported nearly $5 million in total spending in 1974, and PC candidates over $4.2 million, NDP candidates reported a total expenditure of less than $1.3 million.[33] The New Democrats were at a competitive disadvantage, which worsened as campaign costs escalated. Without spending limits, direct public reimbursements, and incentives for individual donors, the gap between the NDP and the brokerage parties would likely have widened over time, despite the loyal support of several labour unions. Beyond the immediate self-interest of the party, the NDP was ideologically committed to democratic reform. All in all, "The passage of the new act was part of the price it elicited in return for its support of the government."[34]

- Repeated election-expense scandals in Canada and elsewhere increased public cynicism and created a political climate conducive to reform. The Watergate scandal in the United States, which destroyed the presidency of Richard Nixon in 1974, revolved around the illegal use of campaign funds by the Committee to Re-Elect the President (also known as "CREEP"). Politicians throughout the Western democracies scrambled to avoid Nixon's fate by enacting (apparently) tough new laws concerning campaign finance.

- Finally, there had been a general trend toward reform of campaign finance in Canada since the early 1960s. The Quebec government cleaned up its election finance laws in 1963,[35] prompting the creation of a federal Advisory Committee on Election Expenses (the Barbeau Committee) in 1964. Its 1966 report, which laid the foundations for the 1974 Act, sat on a shelf until political circumstances forced the Trudeau government to adopt its recommendations.

In any case, some of the restrictions imposed by the 1974 Act and its subsequent amendments were more apparent than real. The introduction of C-24 closed many of the loopholes in the *Canada Elections Act*. For the first time, constituency associations, leadership races, and nomination contests are regulated by law. Some loopholes remain, many provided by the definition of "election expenses":

- There are no restrictions on spending by parties and candidates before the campaign officially begins. Not surprisingly, the "operating expenses" of the major parties—especially the governing party, which presumably has some idea of when the next election will be called—often rise dramatically in the months before an election, as organizers "bank" the resources they intend to use during the upcoming campaign. In 2003, for example, the federal Liberal Party reported "operating and administrative" expenditures that were nearly double those reported in 2002. Additionally, they reported over 10 times as much pre-election spending, and $1.5 million more in fundraising costs, compared to a year earlier.[36]

These figures suggest that the Liberals planned their 2004 campaign well ahead of time, and circumvented the election spending limits by incurring expenses before the campaign period officially began.

- The definition of "election expenses" excludes fundraising, the cost of creating party policies and campaign strategies,[37] and other expenditures that do not "directly promote or oppose a registered party, its leader or a candidate during an election period."[38] However, polling and research costs are now factored into the calculation of "election expenses" under section 407 of the amended Act.

- The distinction between the "personal" and "election" expenses of candidates is insufficiently clear. The 2000 Act imposed the disclosure requirement on "personal" expenses, and gave the Chief Electoral Officer the power to limit such expenses, but it also provided reimbursements for both types of expenditure.

The far-reaching reforms in Bill C-24 were surprising, because governments rarely impose stringent new rules on themselves unless forced to do so by a severe political crisis (recall the earlier discussion of the Watergate scandal). The 1991 Report of the Royal Commission on Electoral Reform and Party Financing had called on the government to extend the regulatory regime to constituency associations, a demand echoed by Chief Electoral Officer Jean-Pierre Kingsley. The impetus for change was the determination of former Prime Minister Jean Chrétien to leave a political legacy when he retired in 2003. The amendments to the *Canada Elections Act* were a key part of that legacy. It is too early to gauge the significance of their impact on Canadian elections.

DOSSIER 4.1 The *Election Expenses Act* and Its Impact on Political Parties in Canada

Contrary to the impact of the *Federal Election Campaign Act* in the United States, which stimulated the campaign-financing activities of ideological, corporate, and interest-group political action committees, the Canadian *Election Expenses Act* has consolidated the position of the three major parliamentary parties. Despite the successful constitutional challenge against the ban on third-party spending by the right-wing National Citizens' Coalition, there is as yet no sign of the PAC [Political Action Committee] phenomenon in Canada. Furthermore, there is little evidence that minor parties or independent candidates have benefited from the controls . . . In the light of the foregoing, it may be concluded that the reform of Canadian party finance reinforced the party orientation of the Canadian electoral system through the creation, with the help of public funding and tax incentives, of a regular, reliable and predictable source of funds for institutionalized parties.

Source: Reprinted with permission from Khayyam Zev Paltiel, "Political Marketing, Party Finance, and the Decline of Canadian Parties," in Alain-G. Gagnon and A. Brian Tanguay, eds., *Canadian Parties in Transition: Discourse, Organization, Representation* (Toronto: ITP Nelson, 1989), 348.

Liberal leader Paul Martin shakes hands with supporters during the 2004 election campaign. (© CP/Tom Hanson)

◼ The Informal Rules: Getting Out the Vote

A general election in Canada is really 308 separate elections held on the same day. Each constituency elects one MP from among the various candidates. Most are nominated by party constituency organizations; others are independent (or "nonaffiliated") candidates. Every constituency campaign must do at least three things, and do them well, if it hopes to succeed:

1. It must identify its committed supporters.
2. It must win over undecided voters and those weakly committed to other parties or candidates.
3. It must "pull" its voters out to the polls on election day.

There are two traditional ways of identifying real and potential supporters: the door-to-door **canvass** and the telephone canvass. Volunteers spend long hours contacting voters, either on the doorstep or by phone. Although the Internet may become an important tool for this purpose, it has not yet replaced the traditional methods. Both types of canvass are labour-intensive; they require large numbers of dedicated foot soldiers to contact the voters and an organization to collect and process the information they provide.

Elections Canada divides every constituency into small territorial units called "polls," which determine where a given elector will cast his or her ballot. The polling divisions are also used by the parties to target and keep track of their canvassing efforts. If a particular poll voted heavily for the Liberals in the previous election, the Liberal campaign manager and the canvass chair may send fewer volunteers to that neighbourhood; that way, they can concentrate their scarce resources in a neighbouring poll where the vote was evenly split last time. A poll that has always voted NDP by a wide margin may receive only a token canvass, because it will be perceived by the Liberals as a lost cause. Each poll is assigned to a "poll captain," who organizes the volunteers and collects their canvass reports. As the volunteers go from door to door or work down their phone lists, they sort the voters on their lists into categories. They often use different-coloured highlighters to indicate which voters are strongly committed, which are wavering, which are undecided, and which cannot be persuaded to support their candidate.

When election day rolls around, the Get Out the Vote (GOTV) organization swings into action. The volunteers at the candidate's headquarters have colour-coded voters' lists, which contain all the information collected during the canvass. They keep track of their committed and potential supporters: Which ones have voted? Which ones haven't? This information is provided by the "inside workers," who represent their party at the polling stations and report back to headquarters as they cross the names off their own lists. Supporters who have not yet voted receive phone calls from headquarters. Have they forgotten to vote? Do they need a lift to the polling place, a baby-sitter for their children, or some other type of assistance? In a close contest, where every vote counts, a well-organized and well-staffed GOTV effort can make the difference between winning and losing.[39]

ELECTORAL SYSTEMS

Table 3.8 in the previous chapter raised several important questions about the fairness of Canada's electoral process:

- Why did the Liberal Party form three successive majority governments with between 38 and 43 percent of the popular vote? And why did it form a majority government (155/301 seats) with 38 percent in 1997 and a minority (135/108 seats) with 36.7 percent in 2004?
- Why did the Canadian Alliance win only two seats in Ontario in 2000, despite winning almost one-quarter of the votes in that province, and almost all the seats in Alberta with just under 60 percent of the vote?

- How can a party with only 14 percent of the national vote form Her Majesty's Loyal Opposition with 54 seats—as the BQ did in 1993—while the Progressive Conservative Party, with 16 percent of the vote, won only two seats?
- Why, despite shifting partisan allegiances among a majority of voters, did the Liberals govern Canada for most of the twentieth century?

Many of the answers to these questions lie in the workings of Canada's electoral system. The impact of electoral systems on party systems is one of the clearest and most dramatic examples of how institutional rules shape political outcomes.

In all representative democracies, there is a set of rules known as the electoral system, which prescribes how citizen preferences, expressed through votes, are translated into seats in a legislative assembly. In interpreting the outcome of elections, most people focus on the distribution of seats in the legislature. However, the way in which preferences are expressed, and the rules used to aggregate those preferences, can have an important bearing on how seats are distributed among legislative parties. In other words, the parliamentary seats awarded to each party may give a misleading picture of its relative strength in the electorate. Electoral systems are not neutral. Electoral outcomes are affected by the electoral system itself; they are not solely determined by the preferences of citizens in a democracy.

There are three major dimensions of electoral systems:
1. the ways in which voters express their preferences (e.g., choosing among parties, or voting for an individual candidate);
2. the ways in which constituency boundaries are drawn; and
3. the **electoral formula** (the method by which votes are cast, counted, and translated into results).[40]

When a country establishes its electoral system, or adopts a new one, it must decide how to structure each of these dimensions. Those decisions can affect electoral outcomes, sometimes profoundly. As we saw in Chapter 3, the electoral system is one of the political institutions that directly affects the party system as a whole and the individual parties within it. As we will see in the following sections, the incentives set by these three dimensions of the electoral system shape the behaviour not only of political parties and elected officials, but also of voters.

Expressing Your Preference

How do citizens express their opinions about candidates in an election? Voting is only one way. Citizens can also campaign actively for a favourite candidate, contribute money to the campaign, place campaign signs on their lawns, or attend meetings to demonstrate political support. However, these activities do not determine who wins or loses. The winner is not the candidate with the most money, or the most volunteers, or the most lawn signs. The preferences expressed when votes are cast are the only ones that count, the only ones that are counted. Suppose, then, that there are three candidates and that a voter likes candidate A, dislikes candidate B, and is indifferent to candidate C. To what extent is the voter able to express this range of feeling on the ballot?

The simplest and crudest way of expressing preferences on an electoral ballot is through a **categorical** choice. A categorical ballot allows the voter to choose one, and only one, of the candidates listed (see Figure 4.1). Given a choice between candidates A, B, and C, the voter may put an "X" beside one of them or beside none of them (thereby spoiling the ballot). Note that with this method the voter is able to express a preference for Green over both Doe and Smith, but is unable to express a second preference for either Doe or Smith. If the voter dislikes Doe more intensely than he likes Green, a categorical ballot may encourage strategic voting—that is, voting for Green in order to defeat Doe. Under this condition, the voter has made a complex calculation, little of which is communicated through the ballot. Categorical ballots are used in federal and provincial elections in Canada.

Alternatively, the ballot could present voters with an **ordinal** choice, which involves rank-ordering some or all of the candidates listed from most preferred to least preferred. As shown in Figure 4.2, the voter has rank-ordered all of the candidates listed on the ballot. In this way, the voter expresses a fuller range of preferences, by identifying the positioning of each candidate relative to the others. Whereas the categorical ballot has the virtue of simplicity, an ordinal ballot can take a long time to fill out and demand much greater information and sophistication from the voter. Counting ordinal ballots is considerably more complex and time-consuming than counting categorical votes, as later discussion of different electoral systems demonstrates.

FIGURE 4.1 THE CATEGORICAL BALLOT

DOE, John	( )
GREEN, Elizabeth	(X)
SMITH, Frederick	( )

FIGURE 4.2 THE ORDINAL BALLOT

CHAN, Dorothy	(1)
DOE, John	(4)
GREEN, Elizabeth	(2)
SINGH, Gurbinder	(5)
SMITH, Frederick	(6)
ZEFFIRELLI, Giovanna	(3)

Drawing the Boundaries

Federal constituency boundaries are drawn by independent commissions to avoid the appearance of partisan favouritism.[41] When a constituency is deliberately designed to improve a particular party's electoral chances, the result is called **"gerrymandering."** As the Supreme Court noted in 1991, "such factors as geography, demography and communities of interest"[42] must be taken into consideration when constituency boundaries are drawn. In the interests of fairness, however, there must be an effort to ensure that the population of each constituency does not deviate too greatly from a predetermined standard—say, 100 000 voters per district—and that none of the parties currently represented in the legislature can redraw the boundaries according to its own self-interest.

Each Canadian constituency elects one MP to the House of Commons, to represent the voters living within that precise geographical area. Single-member constituencies produce clear winners—except in the rare event of a tie—and reduce a complex array of preferences to the choice of a single individual. Other elected bodies based on single-member constituencies include the British House of Commons, the House of Representatives in both the United States and Australia, and Canada's provincial legislatures. The other alternative is to have multimember districts, in which as few as two and as many as a hundred or more members are selected from a single constituency. The Canadian Senate, although not elected, uses multimember provincial and territorial districts in all provinces except Quebec, which is divided into 24 Senate districts. At the provincial level, British Columbia retained a number of multimember districts until 1990. Other institutions based on multimember constituencies include the American and Australian Senates, the legislatures of Israel and many European countries, and some city councils in Canada. Proportional representation electoral systems are always based on multimember districts, which allow parliamentary seats to be distributed among the various parties in a way that corresponds to their respective levels of support in the electorate. Single-member systems, as we will see, do not.

Translating Votes into Seats

An electoral formula is the rule or set of rules used to determine when a candidate can be declared a winner. Each electoral formula answers two questions:
 1. How many votes are required to win a legislative seat?
 2. Is a party's share of seats in proportion to its share of the vote?

The answer to the first question depends on whether single-member or multimember districts are used. In the case of single-member districts, there are two main alternatives: plurality and majority. In a **single-member plurality (SMP) system,** the winner is the candidate who receives more votes than any other. The candidate need not (and often does not) obtain the support of a majority of the voters in the electoral district. The plurality system is used at the federal, provincial, and municipal levels in Canada.

Under a majority system, by contrast, the winner must receive at least 50 percent plus one of all valid votes cast. Because a single round of voting often fails to produce a majority winner, majority systems are somewhat more complex than plurality systems. There are two principal methods for ensuring that one candidate receives a majority of the vote:

1. run-off systems, which require a second round of voting (usually restricted to the top two candidates from the first ballot); and

2. ordinal systems, in which the voter rank-orders the candidates as described above. In an ordinal majority system, such as alternative vote (AV), the valid ballots are counted and a quota—in this case, 50 percent plus one of the total number of valid ballots—is calculated. When the preferences are recorded, the candidate with the fewest first-preference votes is eliminated and that candidate's second-preference votes are redistributed among the remaining candidates according to the distribution of references by the voters. The counting continues, with the elimination of candidates and the redistribution of votes, until one candidate reaches the quota.

In multimember districts, which elect two or more MPs, the electoral formulas are very different. One way of electing members for such districts is the party-list system (also called **"list-proportional representation,"** or **list-PR**). Citizens vote for party lists, not for individual candidates; the parties are then awarded parliamentary seats in proportion to their shares of the vote. In a 100-seat district, for example, a party would draw up a ranked list of 100 candidates. If that party received 30 percent of the vote, it would receive 30 percent of the seats, which it would fill with the top 30 candidates on its list. The 150 seats in the lower house of the Netherlands are elected from one national constituency.

When citizens vote directly for individual candidates in a multimember district—as they do under a single transferable vote, or STV, system—each winning candidate must receive a predetermined quota of the valid votes cast. Most such quotas are slightly higher than the proportion of the district's seats represented by the one seat the candidate hopes to fill. In other words, one seat would represent 12.5 percent of an eight-member district, and the quota of votes required to fill that seat would be set at just over 12.5 percent. Voters rank the candidates on an ordinal ballot, and if the distribution of first preferences does not fill all of the seats, unused lower preferences are successively counted until all the seats are filled.

As to the second question concerning electoral formulas—whether a party's share of legislative seats will be proportional to its share of the vote—the answer depends on the type of electoral system in use. List-PR translates the vote share for each party list into a proportional share of seats in Parliament. STV in multimember districts also achieves a degree of proportionality, although that degree varies with the number of seats per constituency. The greater the number of MPs in a given district, the more proportional the result. Canada's SMP system does not produce proportional representation. Indeed, all single-member systems distort the translation of votes into seats to a greater or lesser degree. Suppose, for example, that the same three parties contest every district in an election based on the single-member plurality system. In order to win a seat, a party's candidate need only garner more votes than his or her competitors. If those opponents split the opposition vote evenly, a candidate can win with just over one-third of the vote. If the same party wins in this manner in every district, it could win 100 percent of the seats with only 35 to 40 percent of the vote. This hypothetical example, though extreme and improbable, illustrates the distorting effect of SMP.

Both proportional representation and the single-member plurality system have their defenders and their critics.[43] Proportional representation has the obvious merit of ensuring that a party's strength in the legislature is roughly equivalent to its popularity among the electorate. On the other hand, some kinds of PR, especially the party-list system, can encourage political parties to split into smaller factions (see Chapter 3). They also decrease the likelihood of any one party controlling a majority of legislative seats. As we will see in Chapters 5 and 6, the political executive must be able to rely on the support of a majority of members in the lower house of Parliament in order to carry out its responsibilities. Because it does not manufacture artificial majority governments, unlike SMP, list-PR increases the likelihood of **coalition** governments: Cabinets made up of ministers from two or more parties. Although some critics of list-PR argue that it promotes political instability and leads to the formation of weak and fragile governments, countries such as Sweden and Germany have enjoyed lengthy periods of stable coalition government.

A growing number of electoral systems combine two or more different electoral formulas. Most of these **mixed electoral systems** divide the national legislature into two categories: some MPs represent single-member constituencies, while the rest are elected from national or regional party lists. The voter casts two ballots on voting day, one for a constituency MP and the other for a party list. The proportionality of a mixed system depends on two factors: (1) whether each party's share of the seats in Parliament is based solely on the list vote, and (2) the ratio of list MPs to constituency MPs. A system in which the list votes determine seat shares is called "mixed-member proportional," or MMP. Conversely, in a mixed-member majoritarian system, the seat total for each party is the sum of the constituency seats plus the list seats. In the latter case, the larger the percentage of list seats, the more proportional the translation of vote shares into seat shares.

Most Canadian advocates of electoral reform favour some type of mixed system. In April 2004 the Law Commission of Canada recommended the adoption of an MMP system in which one-third of MPs would be elected from provincial lists (plus three seats from the territories).[44] The minister responsible for Democratic Reform referred the Law Commission report to the House of Commons Standing Committee on Procedure and House Planning, as part of "a broad review of the electoral process."[45] The release of the report coincided with important developments in five provinces:

- In British Columbia, a Citizens' Assembly was considering whether to recommend a new voting system for the province. If it did, the preferred alternative would be subjected to a referendum held concurrently with the May 2005 provincial election.[46] The Assembly chose STV.

- The Conservative premier of Prince Edward Island announced in May 2004 that he would appoint a commission to propose a new electoral system and conduct a public-education campaign; a referendum would be held by the end of 2005. This announcement followed the December 2003 tabling of a report by Justice Norman Carruthers, who called on the province to adopt some form of MMP.[47]
- The Charest government in Quebec committed itself to electoral reform,[48] although it seemed to consider parliamentary reform as a higher priority.
- In Ontario, the McGuinty Liberal government established a Democratic Reform Secretariat shortly after it took office in late 2003. One of the stated goals of the secretariat was to foster "an open debate on our electoral process, leading to a referendum on electoral reform."[49]
- Finally the government of New Brunswick set up a Commission on Legislative Democracy in late 2003. The Commission's mandate from Premier Bernard Lord was explicit: "To examine and make recommendations on implementing a proportional representation electoral system for the New Brunswick Legislative Assembly."[50] In early 2005, it recommended an MMP system.

It seems likely that one or more of the provinces will experiment with electoral reform in the near future. If the experiment succeeds, we could see a new electoral system at the federal level by the end of this decade. Institutional reforms often occur in the provinces and then spread to Ottawa. During the 2004 federal election campaign, NDP leader Jack Layton identified a national referendum on electoral reform as a crucial condition for his party's support of a minority Liberal government. Because the New Democrats fell one seat short in the 2004 election (see Chapter 5), their bargaining power is less than Layton might have expected. The Liberals, like most governing parties, are reluctant to change an electoral system that often gives them artificial majorities in Parliament. But if the Martin government faced a crucial parliamentary vote and needed the support of the NDP to survive, it might agree to Layton's condition.

Competing Concepts of Representation: Territorial versus Nonterritorial

Whereas the electoral systems used in most Western countries are designed to provide proportional representation for different parties—as surrogates for the various social and ideological groupings in the electorate—Canada's SMP system is designed to represent defined geographic territories. It gives every Canadian voter an elected representative in Parliament who is responsible for protecting the various interests of his or her constituents. (See the discussion of constituency "casework" in Chapter 5.) One of the chief complaints about SMP is that it exaggerates regional cleavages at the expense of effective national integration[51] (see "Does the Electoral System Encourage Regional Discord?" on page 167). But while territorial representation is still the guiding principle of Canada's political institutions—especially federalism and parliamentary government—it is increasingly challenged by nonterritorial concepts of representation based on gender, ethnicity, and ideology (see Chapter 2). Table 4.1 compares the proportion of female legislators in several Western democracies, to

TABLE 4.1 **THE REPRESENTATION OF WOMEN IN NATIONAL PARLIAMENTS, SELECTED COUNTRIES, JULY 2004**

COUNTRY	% OF WOMEN IN LOWER HOUSE OF PARLIAMENT	TYPE OF ELECTORAL SYSTEM
Rwanda	48.8	List-PR
Sweden	45.3	List-PR
Denmark	38.0	List-PR
Finland	37.5	List-PR
Netherlands	36.7	List-PR
Norway	36.4	List-PR
Cuba	36.0	SMM
Spain	36.0	List-PR
Belgium	35.3	List-PR
Costa Rica	35.1	List-PR
Argentina	34.0	List-PR
Austria	33.9	List-PR
South Africa	32.8	List-PR
Germany	32.2	MMP
Iceland	30.2	List-PR
New Zealand	28.3	MMP
Switzerland	25.0	List-PR
Australia	24.7	AV
Canada	21.1	SMP
Luxembourg	20.0	List-PR
Portugal	19.1	List-PR
United Kingdom	17.9	SMP
Israel	15.0	List-PR
United States	14.3	SMP
Greece	14.0	List-PR
Ireland	13.3	STV
France	12.2	SMM
Italy	11.5	Mixed
Japan	7.1	MMP
World Average	*15.7*	—

Source: The Representation of Women in National Parliaments, Selected Countries, July 2004. Inter-Parliamentary Union: www.ipu.org/wmn-e/classif.htm; accessed December 2004. Reprinted with permission from the House of Commons.

illustrate the impact that different electoral systems may have on nonterritorial representation.

Current debates about reforming Canada's electoral system revolve around both territorial and nonterritorial issues.[52] The territorial issues include the following:

- Should SMP be replaced with a mixed system, to produce a Parliament that more accurately reflects the distribution of party support across the regions?
- Would a more proportional electoral system remove the incentives for parties to appeal to regional resentments and reduce the divisiveness of Canadian politics?
- Would the incorporation of list-PR into the existing SMP system give too much power over candidate selection to national or provincial party elites, at the expense of the local constituency activists?

More recently, nonterritorial representation has become an equally pressing issue in the debate over electoral reform. The central questions include the following:

- Should there be special seats in the House of Commons (or the Senate) for Aboriginal peoples? If so, how many should there be, and how would they be filled?[53]
- As Table 4.1 shows, women make up about 21 percent of the Canadian House of Commons—well above the world average for female representation, but far less than the proportion of women in the electorate (roughly 51 percent). If we decide to reform the electoral system in order to increase the number of women in Parliament, should we do this through separate (though geographically overlapping) constituencies for men and women, with each gender electing its own member? Or should there be two members, one a woman and one a man, elected by both genders in each constituency? Or—as some advocates of electoral reform argue[54]—would the adoption of a more proportional electoral system encourage Canadian parties to nominate more women in winnable seats, thus improving female representation without special quotas?

As noted earlier, in 2004 the Law Commission of Canada recommended the adoption of an MMP system. It argued that a 2:1 ratio between constituency MPs and members elected from provincial party lists would improve both territorial and nonterritorial representation in the House of Commons:

> It would reduce the regional imbalances in the legislative caucuses of all the major parties. It would promote fairness, and encourage demographic representation by encouraging the entry of new voices into the legislature, particularly those of currently under-represented groups . . . In turn, it would help to energize and invigorate this country's parliamentary democracy.[55]

THE UNREFORMED CANADIAN ELECTORAL SYSTEM

As we have seen, Canadians use the single-member plurality system to elect their MPs (and provincial legislators). We mark a single "X" on a categorical ballot, which is counted together with the others cast in our particular polling division. The candidate who wins more votes than any other, regardless of the actual proportion received, is declared elected. SMP has four principal advantages, according to its defenders:

1. the simplicity of casting and counting the votes;
2. the speed with which a winner is declared;
3. the stability of single-party majority governments; and
4. the direct relationship between an MP and the voters who live in his or her constituency.

In addition to those previously discussed, SMP's alleged disadvantages include:

- SMP discourages voters from "wasting" their votes on smaller parties and independent candidates and eventually destroys parties that do not have distinct regional bases of support;
- SMP encourages voters to vote strategically (see above); and
- By giving no value to ballots cast for candidates other than the winner in each particular constituency, SMP lowers voter turnout.

Does Every Vote Count?

Table 4.2 demonstrates the disproportionality between the parties' vote shares and seat shares under SMP. It presents the results of each federal election between 1945 and 2004 as the ratio of each party's vote share to its share of seats. A ratio of 1.0 indicates that a party's seat percentage equalled its vote percentage (e.g., 30 percent of all seats and 30 percent of all votes). A ratio greater than 1.0 indicates that the party received a higher percentage of seats than votes—in effect, that it received an unfair advantage from SMP—whereas a ratio less than 1.0 indicates that it was penalized by our electoral system. Column 1 displays the vote and seat shares for the party that "won" each election, column 2 displays the results for the second-place party, and so forth.

Until the 1993 election, both the Liberals and Conservatives were fairly well served by the electoral system. In 13 of the 18 elections since 1945, the Liberal Party's share of seats was greater than its share of the popular vote. Likewise, the Conservative Party's share of seats exceeded its popular vote in 12 of the 18 elections. The party most consistently penalized by the electoral system was the NDP, which regularly received fewer than two-thirds of the seats it would have won had the same votes been cast under a system of proportional representation. One of the more striking features of these data is the degree to which parties are overrewarded once their percentage of the vote approaches 50. On the occasions when a party received around 50 percent of the vote (Liberals in 1949, Conservatives in 1958 and 1984), the electoral system worked to produce a legislative landslide. For example, in 1949 the Liberals received 73.7 percent of the seats on the basis of 49.5 percent of the votes, for a ratio of 1.49. In 1958, the Conservatives received 78.5 percent of the seats based on 54 percent of the votes, for a ratio of 1.45, while in 1984 they received 74.8 percent of the seats based on 49.7 percent of the votes, for a ratio of 1.51.

TABLE 4.2 RATIO OF POLITICAL PARTIES' VOTE SHARES AND SEAT SHARES, 1945–2004

YEAR	1	2	3	4	5
1945	Lib 1.24	PC 1.00	CCF 0.73	SC 1.29	–
1949	Lib 1.49	PC 0.53	CCF 0.37	SC 1.03	–
1953	Lib 1.32	PC 0.62	CCF 0.77	SC 1.06	–
1957	Lib 0.97	PC 1.09	CCF 0.88	SC 1.09	–
1958	PC 1.45	Lib 0.55	CCF 0.32	SC 0	–
1962	PC 1.17	Lib 1.01	NDP 0.53	SC 0.97	–
1963	Lib 1.17	PC 1.09	NDP 0.49	SC 0.76	–
1965	Lib 1.23	PC 1.13	NDP 0.44	Cdt 0.72	–
1968	Lib 1.29	PC 0.87	NDP 0.49	SC 1.21	–
1972	Lib 0.93	PC 1.16	NDP 0.66	SC 0.75	–
1974	Lib 1.24	PC 1.02	NDP 0.39	SC 0.82	–
1979	Lib 1.01	PC 1.34	NDP 0.52	SC 0.46	–
1980	Lib 1.18	PC 1.13	NDP 0.57	–	–
1984	PC 1.51	Lib 0.51	NDP 0.57	–	–
1988	PC 1.33	Lib 0.88	NDP 0.72	–	–
1993	Lib 1.46	BQ 1.37	Ref 0.94	NDP 0.39	PC 0.04
1997	Lib 1.34	Ref 1.03	BQ 1.36	NDP 0.64	PC 0.35
2000	Lib 1.40	CA 0.86	BQ 1.18	NDP 0.51	PC 0.33
2004	Lib 1.19	CP 1.08	BQ 1.41	NDP 0.39	–

Legend:

Lib:	Liberal Party	SC:	Social Credit Party
PC:	Progressive Conservative Party	Cdt:	Créditiste
CCF:	Co-operative Commonwealth Federation	BQ:	Bloc Québécois
NDP:	New Democratic Party	Ref:	Reform
CA:	Canadian Alliance	CP	Conservative Party of Canada

Note: Very small parties and independents are excluded.

Sources: F. Leslie Seidle, "The Canadian Electoral System and Proposals for Its Reform," in Alain-G. Gagnon and A. Brian Tanguay, eds., *Canadian Parties in Transition: Discourse, Organization, Representation* (Scarborough: ITP Nelson, 1989), 251. Reprinted with permission; calculated from data from Chief Electoral Officer of Canada, *Thirty-Fourth General Election, Report of the Chief Electoral Officer, 1988;* Appendices (Revised), (Ottawa, 1988), 20–21. Reprinted with permission of the Minister of Supply and Services Canada, 1994. Data from 1993, 1997, and 2004 elections taken from the website of Elections Canada: www.elections.ca. Data for the 2000 election taken from Jon H. Pammett and Christopher Dornan, eds., *The Canadian General Election of 2000* (Ottawa: Carleton University Press, 2001), Appendix.

In addition to magnifying the size of election victories, the electoral system can also make the difference between winning and losing. In 1957 and 1979, the Liberal Party received more votes than any other party but the Conservatives won more seats. The data in Table 4.2 show that, in both elections, the Conservatives translated votes into seats more effectively than did the Liberals; in both cases, the governor general invited the Conservatives to form a minority government.

In the 1993 federal election, the Canadian electoral system created one of the least proportional results ever recorded in a Western democracy. The Liberal Party received 60 percent of the Commons seats based on 41.1 percent of the vote—an abnormally high ratio of 1.46. At the other extreme was the Conservative Party, which won two Commons seats (0.67 percent) on the basis of 16 percent of the votes, for a representation ratio of 0.04. In other words, the Conservative Party received 4 percent of the seats to which it would have been entitled in a system of proportional representation. Parties that aspire to a national base of support but finish well behind the winner are severely penalized under Canada's electoral system. The NDP, which had national aspirations in 1993, had a low representation ratio of 0.39.

The distorted translation of votes into seats is more than a violation of abstract or mathematical rules of fairness; it may also be a violation of voting rights. While the Supreme Court stated in 1991 that section 3 of the *Charter* does not guarantee absolute parity of voting power, the majority added that "A system which dilutes one citizen's vote unduly as compared with another citizen's vote runs the risk of providing inadequate representation to the citizen whose vote is diluted."[56] There can be little question that votes cast for smaller parties, and for parties that are less competitive in a particular region, are diluted relative to those of voters who support the winning party (either nationally or regionally). Table 4.3 displays the number of votes required to elect an MP for each of the major parties in the 1993 and 2004 general elections.

TABLE 4.3 THE NUMBER OF VOTES CAST PER MP ELECTED, CANADA'S MAJOR NATIONAL PARTIES, 1993 AND 2004

PARTY	1993	2004
Liberal	31 601	36 675
BQ	33 838	30 966
Reform/Conservative*	49 578	40 350
NDP	103 869	111 397
PC	1 088 706	

*The Canadian Alliance and Progressive Conservative parties merged to form the Conservative Party of Canada shortly before the 2004 federal election. See Chapter 3.

ELECTIONS AND VOTING

If we take the chance of electing an MP as a reflection of the value of an individual vote, we find that in 1993 a Liberal vote was worth 34 times as much as a PC vote. Even in the 2004 election, which produced less dramatic distortions, three NDP votes counted for approximately as much as one Liberal vote.

Our single-member constituencies and plurality electoral formula, together with the way in which party votes are distributed across the country, profoundly affect the outcome of national (and provincial) elections. Table 4.4 displays the difference between the actual outcome of the 1993 election under SMP and the hypothetical outcome under a purely proportional system. The numbers in the bottom row were calculated by multiplying the number of seats in the Commons by the percentage of the national vote received by each of the five major parties. (Note that such hypothetical outcomes are inherently flawed by the assumption that each party would have received the same number of votes under an alternative electoral system; as noted earlier, SMP tends to reduce support for smaller parties.) Instead of forming a majority government (more than 148 of the 295 seats in the House at that time), the Liberals would have held a minority of the seats. A moderately proportional system, such as a mixed system, might have produced a slim majority with a more regionally balanced government caucus and a stronger Opposition.

How the Electoral System Affects the Party System

The relationship between electoral systems and party systems is one of the central themes in political science. The classic description of that relationship is Duverger's Law: single-member constituencies favour two-party systems, while list-PR favours multiparty systems (four or more parties in Parliament).[57] Proportional representation systems erect few barriers to smaller parties seeking election to Parliament; the **threshold of election** (the percentage of votes required to win a seat) is typically low, and the accurate translation of vote shares into seat shares ensures that most parties will secure at least some parliamentary representation. In contrast, electoral systems based on single-member constituencies tend to reduce the number of parties in Parliament and eventually in the party system as a whole. This "winnowing" effect has two dimensions:

1. *Mechanical effect:* Smaller parties are consistently denied their fair share of parliamentary seats and find it difficult to attract enough votes to establish themselves as major players in the party system.

TABLE 4.4   THE OUTCOME OF THE 1993 GENERAL ELECTION UNDER SMP AND PR (NUMBER OF SEATS PER PARTY OUT OF 295)

	LIBERAL	REFORM	BQ	NDP	PC
Actual	177	52	54	9	2
Proportional	121	56	40	21	47

2. *Psychological effect:* Over time, supporters of these smaller parties become discouraged and either switch to one of the larger parties or vote strategically to prevent the election of their least-favoured candidates.[58]

While there is ample evidence to substantiate Duverger's argument about the disincentives for multipartyism under SMP,[59] a puzzle remains: How do we explain the fact that Canada has not had a two-party system since 1921? The answer lies in the tendency of SMP to award a disproportionately large number of seats to parties whose support is regionally concentrated. Even smaller parties like the NDP, which run national campaigns, win most of their seats in their strongest regions (in this case, the Prairies and British Columbia). The same is true for India and the United Kingdom, which also use SMP. Therefore, the impact of SMP on the number of parties depends on an intervening variable: the size and mobilization of regional subcultures within the electorate.

Does the Electoral System Encourage Regional Discord?

The SMP system distorts the regional composition of party caucuses in the House of Commons. It over-rewards the party with the most votes in a given province, while denying other parties their rightful share of parliamentary representation. By artificially relegating entire regions to the Opposition benches, SMP has reinforced regional alienation in Canada. In the 1970s and early 1980s, the governing Liberals were all but shut out of the West, while the Progressive Conservatives were nearly invisible in Quebec, despite significant electoral support in each case. As a consequence, Western Canadians lacked significant elected representation in the government caucus and the Cabinet when the National Energy Program was introduced in 1980. Not only was the legislation less sensitive to regional concerns than it might have been, but the Liberal government lacked elected members to sell the package in the West. Distortions in the electoral system thus reinforced long-standing sentiments of regional alienation and further eroded the legitimacy of parliamentary institutions within the region. Similarly, in Quebec the electoral system contributed significantly to the "Tory syndrome"[60] or minority-party syndrome (see the "Categories of Party Members" section in Chapter 3): it bedevilled Conservative efforts to build the party within Quebec and to convince Canadian voters at large that the Progressive Conservatives were indeed a national party that could span linguistic divisions within the country.

For advocates of intrastate federalism (see Chapter 8), who wanted Canada's national political institutions to bridge our regional divisions, SMP became an obvious target. In addition to (or as an alternative to) promoting intrastate reforms to the Canadian Senate, it was often suggested that proportional representation would create truly national parliamentary caucuses—parties whose seats in various parts of the country would reflect the votes cast for them there, rather than the unnecessarily regionalized parties produced by the current electoral system.

Electoral reform to dampen the fires of regionalism seemed less necessary by 1984, when Brian Mulroney finally overcame the "Tory syndrome" to lead a Conservative government with strong representation from all parts of the country. Mulroney managed this feat largely by knitting together a national alliance that encompassed Quebec nationalists and alienated Westerners. But in 1993, as we saw in Chapter 3, this alliance came apart; Quebec nationalists left the Progressive Conservative Party for the Bloc Québécois, while Westerners migrated to the Reform Party. The impact of this regionalized system of party competition was exaggerated by the electoral system.

We conclude this discussion of the Canadian electoral system by emphasizing three key points:

1. The electoral system rewards parties whose votes are concentrated in particular regions while penalizing those whose votes are spread thinly across the country. The incentives for party strategists are clear: if you want to win the maximum number of seats in Parliament, you must target one or more regionally based subcultures and devote less attention to the rest of Canada. The implications of these incentives are twofold. First, they may encourage parties to inflame regional tensions and resentments as a way to mobilize and solidify their subcultural bases. Second, they elevate the importance of territorial concerns in Canadian politics at the expense of nonterritorial interests, such as gender and ethnicity. Consequently, our national political institutions do not reflect the demographic composition of the electorate, nor do they reflect the growing importance of nonterritorial concepts of political representation.

2. Instead of mobilizing voters, the electoral system tends to discourage Canadians from casting ballots. In so doing, it weakens the linkage between citizens and the state and erodes the legitimacy of our representative democratic institutions.

3. To the extent that categorical ballots stifle the expression of voters' true preferences and foster strategic voting, they distort the will of the people and prevent its reflection in our national political institutions.

As we will see in the next section, the reasons for nonvoting are not purely institutional. Nonetheless, the alarming drop in recent turnout rates justifies serious consideration of electoral reform.

VOTING AND NONVOTING

As Chapter 10 explains, the right to vote is one of the crucial sections of the *Charter of Rights*. Sections 3 to 5 are not subject to the section 33 legislative override, and the Supreme Court has set a higher standard for "reasonable limits" on democratic rights than those that apply to other sections of the *Charter*. Long before the *Charter* took effect in 1982, the **franchise** had been extended to women, Aboriginal Canadians, and other previously excluded groups. Since then, the courts have struck down laws that denied the franchise to prisoners, judges, and other groups. Despite the lack of formal legislative barriers to voting, some institutional impediments remain. One study for Elections Canada found that compulsory voting, flexible ballot options (e.g., voting by mail), and proportional electoral systems encourage higher turnout.[61] Canada has neither compulsory voting nor a proportional electoral system.

There are additional barriers to voting, arising from the attitudes and perceptions of citizens (especially younger citizens). A major survey of nonvoters concluded that "People are less likely to cast a ballot if they feel they have no influence over government actions, do not feel voting is an essential civic act, or do not feel the election is competitive enough to make their votes matter to the outcome, either at the national or the local constituency level."[62] One intriguing fact emerges from the survey: voters who were personally contacted by a party or a candidate were more likely to cast ballots than those who were not. The presence or absence of such contact had more influence on turnout than political cynicism, education, or income.[63] We might conclude that if the parties reached out to more voters, turnout would likely increase. Unfortunately, as we saw in Chapter 3, our parties have small and largely inactive memberships. Moreover, their growing reliance on capital-intensive campaign techniques has reduced the opportunities for direct engagement between local constituency workers and voters. While we should not put too much emphasis on any one explanation for declining turnout, this particular problem is—at least in principle—relatively easy to fix.

For a combination of reasons, the official turnout rate has fallen over the past six federal elections from 76 percent[64] to 61 percent,[65] the lowest in Canadian history. One partial exception to the claim that institutional factors no longer depress voter turnout is the evidence that young people were excluded from voting in 2000 by problems with the new *Permanent Register of Electors*. When Canadian citizens turn 18, they are not automatically registered to vote; they must submit a form authorizing Elections Canada to include their names in the list of eligible voters. The 2000 election marked the first time that the *Register* was used exclusively, in lieu of door-to-door enumeration. Whereas Canadians had never previously had to take the initiative to register, now many did. Even though citizens who were not in the *Register* could still vote, "being omitted from the *Register* apparently provided a psychological deterrent to voting for a substantial number of Canadians."[66]

Apart from the problems with the *Register*, which have been partially addressed since 2000, most of the institutional barriers to voting have been removed. Yet the active electorate in Canadian elections can change substantially from one election to the next. There is a continual flow of voters into and out of the electorate. For example, in any four-year election cycle, the electorate can change by as much as 25 percent as new voters enter and transient voters move into or out of the active electorate.[67] In addition, 10 to 15 percent of eligible voters never vote in elections. These are the "voluntarily disenfranchised" voters.

Until recently, little was known about the reasons for nonvoting. Three personal characteristics—age, education, and income—were believed to be powerful predictors of voting and nonvoting. In the 2000 election, less than one-quarter of the first-time voters (those who had turned 18 since the previous election) actually cast ballots. Among voters over 60, the turnout rate was more than 80 percent.[68] People with university degrees, and those in the highest income brackets, were more likely to vote than those with less education and income, although these effects appeared to be less significant than the impact of age.[69] After the 2000 federal election, concern about the low voter turnout prompted Elections Canada to commission the first major survey of nonvoters. It found that the primary reason for the rise of non-voting was the growing percentage of younger voters (those born after 1945) in the electorate.[70] In effect, older people with a strong tendency to participate in elections were being replaced by new voters with less political interest and a weaker sense of civic duty. While this finding is consistent with the analysis of political culture in Chapter 2, there was no support for the suggestion that "new social movements" are engaging younger Canadians in political activity. In general, people who participate in "old politics" by electing members to the House of Commons are also the ones who are most likely to become involved in other political activities.[71]

Among the nonvoters surveyed, a majority said that they had stayed home on voting day because they were not interested in the election. Other reasons included a lack of confidence in political parties, their leaders, and local candidates, and a belief that their vote didn't matter.[72] The authors concluded that administrative problems, and the *Register of Electors* in particular, were less of a deterrent than attitudinal and age-related factors. The key problem was that young Canadians felt less "commitment to the Canadian community" than their elders.[73] Under those circumstances, there was little that anyone—Elections Canada, party leaders, or institutional reformers—could do to reverse the trend. The authors predicted, accurately, that turnout would drop even further in the next federal election. Despite the closer competition between the two largest parties in 2004, which might have been expected to raise interest levels and encourage voters to cast ballots, the replacement effect within the electorate cancelled out any short-term gains.

THE CANADIAN VOTER

As we saw in Chapter 3, persistent subcultures within the electorate shape our national party system by influencing voting behaviour. But Canadian voters are not solely motivated by long-term factors such as class, region, partisanship, or ideology. Many cast their votes on the basis of short-term factors: economic evaluations, the parties' stands on key issues, or their perceptions of the party leaders. While the act of expressing a preference may be simple, at least in Canada, determining one's electoral preference can be a complicated process. In this section we will examine the major short-term and long-term determinants of Canadian voting behaviour, using the findings of the 2000 *Canadian Election Study* (CES) to illustrate their impact on election outcomes.

Long-Term Influences on Voter Choice

Social Cleavages

As we saw in Chapter 2, Western electorates are divided into subcultures along lines of social cleavage: class, religion, language, ethnicity, region, and gender. These demographic characteristics are relatively stable and persistent, underlying long-term patterns of voting behaviour. This is not to say that every member of the Canadian Auto Workers votes NDP, or that every woman votes for female candidates; nothing in voting behaviour is that simple. For a particular social cleavage to influence the way in which a person votes, certain conditions must be present:

- There must be a political party that reflects the interests and values of that particular group, either exclusively or as part of a broader electoral coalition (see Chapter 3).
- The cleavage must be politically salient—in other words, their identity as members of a particular group must be important enough to override other potential factors in voting choice, such as short-term issues and party leaders.
- The voters within the group must interpret political events and issues through the filter of the particular values associated with that subculture (e.g., Catholicism, feminism); in effect, they must be mobilized to see the world through the same lens.

In practical terms, the politically salient demographic characteristics of a given voter shape that voter's perceptions of political parties, issues, and leaders. These characteristics do not necessarily determine the person's vote, but they do influence the voter's judgments about the other long-term and short-term factors that affect voting choice.

In cross-national studies of voting behaviour, Canadian voters stand out from their European counterparts in two respects: the weakness of the class cleavage and the strength of regional cleavages.[74] Despite the presence of different socioeconomic classes in Canada, the class cleavage does not exert a significant influence on voting behaviour. Advocates of class voting consider this unusual cleavage pattern to be a sign of immaturity on the part of Canadian voters. They argue that the division between socioeconomic classes should take priority over all others. In reality, although a market economy may produce a fundamental conflict between the interests of those who own or control businesses and those who do not, the range of conflicting interests in a complex post-industrial society extends far beyond simple class conflict. Differences among various ethnic, linguistic, or religious groups; between those on the ideological left and right; between one region and another; between young and old, men and women, farmers and industrial workers, and many others are found in modern societies—and all of these differences may be reflected in the party system.

While the class cleavage is unusually weak in Canada, the regional cleavage is more pronounced than in many Western democracies. This should come as no surprise, given the discussions of regionalism throughout this book. While the class cleavage has weakened over the past few decades, the impact of regionalism on voting has grown.[75] (Recall the discussion of regional voting in the fourth party system in Chapter 3.) Two additional sociodemographic characteristics deserve mention: religious denomination and ethnicity. The impact of religion on voting is surprising, given the apparent decline of religious observance in Canadian society. In a country like the Netherlands, with a strong tradition of Catholic and Protestant parties, the persistence of the denominational cleavage is easier to understand. But during the twentieth century, the salience of religious issues in Canadian politics declined rapidly. There is no explicitly Catholic party, dedicated to promoting Catholic interests. Nonetheless, there are clear and consistent differences in voting behaviour among Canada's largest religious denominations. According to the 2000 *Canadian Election Study,* Catholics were 14 percent more likely than Protestants to vote Liberal and Protestants favoured the Canadian Alliance, while respondents who claimed no religion disproportionately supported the NDP.[76]

As for ethnicity, the Liberals are by far the most popular party among Canadians of non-European origin—a fact that helps to explain their dominance in Toronto, which is home to large numbers of first- and second-generation citizens—while the Alliance had an edge among descendants of Northern European immigrants.[77] In English Canada, the Liberals depend heavily on the support of Catholic and non-European voters: "Without [these two groups], the seven-point lead obtained by the Liberals over the Alliance outside Quebec would translate into a seven-point edge for the Alliance. In Ontario, the huge 28-point Liberal lead would shrink by almost half."[78]

Like the regional cleavage, the gender cleavage among Canadian voters is also becoming more significant over time. The Alliance was hampered in the 2000 campaign by its relative lack of appeal to female voters (especially in Ontario), while the NDP managed to hang on to official party status because women were almost twice as likely as men to support the party. This is a relatively recent phenomenon; before 1979, the gender gap worked against the NDP.[79] In other respects, Canada's female voters are very consistent: at least since 1974, the Liberals have been substantially more popular among women than men, while the reverse is true for the PCs.[80] In general, women for whom gender is a salient political variable (in practice, those who are moderately or strongly feminist in their values) tend to vote centre-left—i.e., Liberal and NDP.[81] The more socially conservative a party appears to be, the less it appeals to women: the gender gap among Canadian Alliance voters in 2000 was significantly greater than for Progressive Conservative voters, which implies that some women disliked the moral traditionalism espoused by Stockwell Day and his party.[82]

The cleavage structure in Quebec is simpler than that in English Canada. The two dominant cleavages are language—anglophone/allophone versus francophone—and age. Nonfrancophones overwhelmingly favoured the Liberals, while younger French-speaking voters supported the BQ.[83] The evidence is clear: Canadian voters are strongly, although not exclusively, influenced by the cleavage patterns in the electorate.

Values

The relationship between social cleavages and political values is complex. On the one hand, values can be shaped by membership in a particular subculture. As we have seen repeatedly, Western populists and Quebec nationalists have differing attitudes toward federalism. On the other hand, a particular set of values cannot automatically

A Suffragette rally, 1913 (© CP)

be attributed to every member of a given group—not all Catholics are pro-life, for example—nor can it be reduced to a set of subcultural biases. Finally, political values change over time (see Chapter 2), even when the makeup of the electorate remains fairly constant. They shift in response to historical events, institutional innovations, and long-term economic and social trends. While values are often related to social cleavages, therefore, these two factors may affect voting behaviour in different ways.

Before political values can affect voting behaviour, they must be mobilized by a political party or some other agency. Latent values—those that remain unexpressed or outside the public realm—do not play a role in politics. The core strategy of the Liberal campaign in 2000 was to mobilize latent fears about the Canadian Alliance and its new leader, Stockwell Day. To solidify the Liberal vote, party strategists crafted a campaign that pitted "Liberal values" against the socially conservative values of the Alliance.[84] The strategy succeeded, in part because Day's mixed messages about issues such as abortion and homosexuality made Liberal allegations of a "hidden agenda" more credible to many voters.[85]

According to Blais et al., the four core values in the Canadian electorate are "attitudes about free enterprise, moral traditionalism, and sympathy/antipathy towards racial minorities and feminism." In addition, voters are influenced by two "fundamental beliefs": "general disaffection with political parties and a sense of regional alienation."[86] Overall, these values and beliefs explained approximately 10 percent of voting choice in the 2000 election.[87] Voters who believed strongly in the value of free markets were more likely to support the Canadian Alliance or the Progressive

Conservatives; the Alliance also benefited from the support of moral traditionalists—e.g., people opposed to same-sex marriage—and those with negative feelings toward minorities and feminists. Conversely, the Liberals and New Democrats had a stronger appeal to voters who were ambivalent about free enterprise, who held less traditional views on morality, and who were sympathetic toward minorities and feminists. As the incumbent government, the Liberals suffered a loss in support among voters who were particularly cynical toward politics; they also bore the brunt of anger from voters who believed that their particular regions were shortchanged in Confederation.[88]

The sponsorship scandal that broke in early 2004 reinforced the anger and cynicism of many voters (see Dossier 6.2). During the first few weeks of the 2004 election campaign, it appeared that the scandal would cost the Liberals enough seats to relegate them to Opposition. In the end, other factors—likely including partisan attachment to the Liberals and concerns about a Conservative "hidden agenda"—gave them a plurality of seats in the Commons.

Stephen Harper's efforts to position his new Conservative Party as a moderate political force were undermined by a handful of "freelancing" MPs. Two caucus members made statements indicating that the party might attempt to restrict access to abortion if it formed a government; a third promised that his party would use the "notwithstanding clause" in the *Charter of Rights* to ban same-sex marriage. Harper tried to defuse the situation by disclaiming any intention of legislating on abortion, although he muddied the waters by speculating about allowing free votes on Private Members' Bills (see Chapter 5).[89] The Liberals seized on the "hidden agenda" supposedly revealed by the Conservative candidates' remarks, painting the Conservatives as extremists opposed to basic human rights.

Shortly after their disappointing performance in the June 28 election, some Conservative strategists argued that Liberal "fear-mongering" had scared Ontario voters away from the new party.[90] If this is true, it suggests that the Conservatives (or at least those who spoke out of turn) misread the values of a majority of Canadians. Another possible reason for the party's poor showing was the poor fit between the two parties that merged to form the Conservatives in late 2003. Supporters of the Canadian Alliance and the Progressive Conservatives held similar views on economic issues (i.e., the free market), but markedly different opinions on moral traditionalism, minorities, and feminism.[91] Despite optimistic predictions by party founders that "one plus one equals two"—i.e., that supporters of both founding parties would automatically vote for the new merged party—the Conservatives wound up with 29.6 percent of the vote, a full eight points lower than the two parties' combined share of 37.7 percent in 2000. The apparent defection of some former Progressive Conservative voters to other parties was no surprise; pre-merger surveys showed that most would pick the Liberals, not the Canadian Alliance, as their second choice.[92] Simplistic talk of "uniting the right" (Dossier 3.4) overlooked the obvious value differences between supporters of the two conservative parties.

The preceding discussion of values applies to English Canada. Quebec is a unique case. The most salient value cleavage in that province divides sovereigntists from federalists: the former vote overwhelmingly for the Bloc, while the latter support the Liberals. Other value cleavages are present, but they have little impact on voting choice.[93] There are two possible reasons for their lack of influence: either they are not fully mobilized, or they are less salient than other influences on voting choice. By late 2003, it appeared that this particular cleavage had lost much of its power. The BQ was trailing badly in the polls. A federalist government was in power in Quebec City. Separation seemed to have fallen off the political agenda. The BQ's remarkable comeback in the 2004 election (Dossier 3.5) does not necessarily signal a resurgence of sovereigntist sentiment, but it would be foolhardy to interpret the result as a mere reflection of short-term anger at the federal government.

Party Identification

On the surface, the Canadian electorate usually appears to be stable and consistent. With the exception of infrequent electoral "earthquakes," such as in 1958 and 1993, most elections produce little change in the relative vote shares of the major parties. Only the Liberal and Progressive Conservative parties have ever formed the government at the national level and in four of the ten provinces. In addition, there have been prolonged periods of one-party government both federally and provincially. The PCs governed continuously from 1867 to 1896, except for a brief stint in Opposition from 1873 to 1878; in the twentieth century, as we saw in Chapter 3, the Liberals spent far more time in government than in Opposition. This trend has been repeated, with variations, at the provincial level. The Union Nationale governed Quebec from 1936 to 1960, with the exception of the four years the party spent in Opposition during World War II. The Social Credit Party governed continuously in Alberta from 1935 to 1971 and in British Columbia from 1953 to 1991 (with the exception of three years of NDP government, from 1972 to 1975). The record for longevity in office belongs to Ontario's PC Party, which governed without interruption from 1943 to 1985.

However, this aggregate level of stability in Canadian voting behaviour is deceptive. First, it obscures the fact that the electoral system tends to over-reward parties with the greatest support and penalize others. Thus, majority governments may be based on population minorities, and shifting minorities at that. Second, the existence of aggregate stability in governing parties may hide considerable changes in the government's position relative to the legislature. For example, in 11 of the 17 federal elections from 1957 to 1997, the governing party changed hands or the same party held government but shifted between minority and majority status.

Third, and perhaps most important, one should not infer that the aggregate stability in Canadian election outcomes reflects consistency in the voting behaviour of individual Canadians. Indeed, the appearance of aggregate stability masks a relatively high level of volatility among individual voters. This volatility is illustrated by the experience of the former Progressive Conservative Party. When the PCs under Brian Mulroney won a landslide victory in 1984, their success did not represent a historic realignment of the electorate. Such realignments rarely happen in Canada. Instead, Mulroney benefited from high levels of short-term support on policy and leadership issues. Specifically, the Trudeau Liberals had alienated Quebec voters by imposing the *Constitution Act, 1982* over the objections of the provincial government; they had angered the West with the

National Energy Program; and they had acquired a reputation for arrogance and aloofness since taking power in 1968. The new PC government's precarious hold on its newfound supporters was illustrated by its dive in the public-opinion polls in 1987,[94] and by its fluctuating levels of support throughout the 1988 election campaign.[95] Although the party was re-elected in 1988, its victory owed more to the vagaries of the electoral system and the popularity of Mulroney's Canada–U.S. Free Trade Agreement in Ontario and Quebec, than to a long-term realignment from the Liberals to the PCs. The volatility of Canadian partisanship was evident in the 1993 election, when the PCs plummeted to 16 percent of the vote and two seats in the House of Commons. The 1993 election dispelled any doubts about a Progressive Conservative realignment in 1984.

Nonetheless, it would be wrong to assume that long-term attachments to a particular party play no part in Canadian voting behaviour. To explain long-term voting patterns, political scientists use the American concept of **party identification.**

A group of researchers at the University of Michigan, headed by Angus Campbell, conducted the first large-scale election studies. The portrait of the electorate that emerged from their surveys was surprising. They found that voters were less interested and involved in the campaign, and had a poorer understanding of the parties' positions on issues, than the researchers had anticipated. However, they also found that most voters had a psychological identification with one of the parties—they thought of themselves as Democrats or Republicans—and that these identifications had a strong effect on their vote.

Equally important was their analysis of the acquisition and durability of party identifications. For most voters, party identification was passed from generation to generation through the socialization process in the family. It was more likely to be an emotional tie to a party—a generalized feeling of like or dislike—than a rational opinion based on a critical appraisal of party policies. The importance of party identification for voting behaviour was twofold:

1. Research showed that this stable, enduring, emotional identification with a party was the single most important predictor of a person's voting behaviour—that is, party identification had a powerful, direct effect on voting.
2. Party identification significantly affected the ways in which voters thought about political issues and the candidates for office. In other words, most American voters in the 1950s did not become Democrats or Republicans because of their views on Dwight Eisenhower or Adlai Stevenson (respectively, the Republican and Democratic presidential candidates in 1952 and 1956); instead, they supported Eisenhower or Stevenson because they were already Republicans or Democrats, usually as a result of the political "cues" they had received from parents and others in their youth.

Research on the voting behaviour of Canadians has shown that partisanship operates differently in the Canadian context.[96] Identification with a political party in Canada is affected by federalism: many voters identify with different parties at the federal and provincial levels of government. In addition, party identifications are less stable, and Canadians are more likely to change their partisan self-image when they change their vote intention.[97] There is no Canadian equivalent to, for example, "Democrats for George Bush [George H. Bush, the Republican president from 1988 to 1992]," in which one retains a long-standing partisan identification while voting for another party.

The main reason for this difference between the two countries is institutional. Many U.S. states require voters to register as supporters of one of the political parties, so that they can participate in the state's primary elections to choose a presidential nominee for their party. There is no counterpart to this public declaration of partisanship in Canada; the *Register of Electors* (see above) does not record partisan affiliations. Moreover, general elections in the United States, both in presidential election years and in off-year congressional elections, usually feature a large and complex ballot. In addition to voting for candidates for the presidency, one may also participate in elections for the U.S. Senate, House of Representatives, governor, state legislatures, and a host of county and municipal offices. Party identification provides an efficient and effective way of managing a complex election process. It also provides a way to choose among the candidates running for less important offices (such as county sheriff) without having to depend on detailed information about these individuals (gathering and assessing such information can be relatively costly).

Elections in Canada are markedly different from their American counterparts. The typical Canadian ballot in a federal election has a short list of three to seven contestants for a single seat in the House of Commons. Most provincial election ballots are equally simple. In voting for a single office, there is a less pressing need for a party label to simplify electoral choice. There is also less of an institutional requirement to retain one's party identification if, in the current election, it proves inconsistent with candidate preferences.

As a result, analysts of voting in Canada developed a measure of partisanship that is sensitive to the way in which party attachments operate within our institutional framework. This measure is based on three components: stability, consistency, and intensity of attachment to a party. Stability of partisanship refers to its persistence over time—has one always identified with one party, or was there a period in which one felt closer to another party or to no party? Consistency is a measure of partisanship at the federal and provincial levels. Partisanship is consistent if the same party attachment is held at the two levels of government. Intensity refers to the strength of attachment and ranges from very strong to moderate to weak. Voters who have stable, consistent, and strong attachments to parties are called "durable partisans," and typically constitute between 34 and 37 percent of the electorate.[98] Those who deviate on one or more measures of stability, consistency, and strength of attachment are called "flexible partisans"; they constitute 63 to 66 percent of the electorate.

Because party identification is difficult to measure in Canada, there are conflicting estimates of its influence on Canadian voters. The 2000 *Canadian Election Study* employed a looser definition of partisanship—being "strongly disposed to support the same party at every election"—and found that 60 percent of those who voted in that election qualified as "partisans."[99] The gap between the figures produced by the two conflicting measures of partisanship—from less than 40 percent to almost two-thirds of voters—has important implications. The lower figure implies that election campaigns really matter, because a majority of voters approach the choice among parties with an open mind. The higher figure suggests that the outcome of an election is largely predetermined before the campaign even begins; a majority of the electorate has already decided for whom they will vote, and they will not respond to information that contradicts their preconceived ideas.

However large the proportion of party identifiers in the Canadian electorate may be, one fact is clear: among Canadian voters with a predisposition to support a particular party, the Liberals have a commanding lead, especially in Ontario.[100] The Canadian Alliance, like the Reform Party before it, had a solid core of partisans in the West, especially in Alberta and British Columbia. This base seems to have held firm after the merger of the Alliance and the PCs in 2003. For the moment, at least, the BQ is firmly entrenched in Quebec. Conversely, the New Democrat and PC "heartlands" in the electorate shrunk substantially between 1993 and 2000. In 1997, according to the *Canadian Election Study* team, the PCs could boast almost twice as many party identifiers as Reform (11.3 and 6.2 percent of the electorate, respectively);[101] in 2000 the Alliance could claim 13 percent of voters as durable partisans, while the PC share of the electorate had dropped to 8 percent.[102] This may help to explain the willingness of former PC leader Peter MacKay to negotiate a merger with Alliance leader Stephen Harper. The NDP could claim roughly 6 percent of voters as loyal partisans in 2000.[103] It is too early to tell whether the 2004 election, in which the NDP won nearly 16 percent of the vote, represents a long-term improvement in party fortunes or a short-term surge.

While partisan loyalties provide a degree of stability in the electorate, it is important to remember that most Canadian partisans are "flexible." We are "predisposed," not "predetermined," to vote for our favourite party.[104] In effect, partisanship operates as a political "default setting." In the absence of a compelling reason to vote against her preferred party, a flexible partisan will usually mark her ballot next to the name of that party's candidate. Every now and then, circumstances will conspire to provide such a "compelling reason." For example, a voter may decide that her party has been in government too long and "it's time for a change." A new leader may prove disappointing. If her party is in power, a scandal may shake her faith in the party's competence to govern.

These factors were in play in the 2004 election, according to pre-election polling. Some 66 percent of respondents to a May 2004 Ipsos-Reid poll agreed with the statement that "It's time for a change," compared to 29 percent who thought the Liberals deserved to be re-elected.[105] Prime Minister Paul Martin, who had been hugely popular when he first took office in December 2003, had slipped badly; by the time the election was called, almost half of respondents reported that their opinion of Martin and his party had worsened in the previous weeks.[106] This finding reflected public anger over the sponsorship scandal and the government's apparently inept response, together with a sense of disappointment that Martin had not lived up to his promises of change. Shortly after the campaign began, EKOS Research asked respondents who had voted Liberal in 2000 whether they intended to do so again; only 58 percent said "yes," well below the comparable figures for the other parties.[107] In the end, the Liberals won substantially more votes than anyone had predicted, suggesting that some Liberal identifiers returned to their "default setting" at the last moment.

In the 1990s, the volatility of Canadian voters caught the attention of political scientists at home and abroad. In the 1993 election, an unprecedented 42 percent of Canadian voters switched parties.[108] Three factors—the flexibility of Canadian partisanship, the large number of voters with no partisan attachment (44 percent, according to Blais et al.), and the strength of short-term forces (e.g., attitudes toward leaders and issues)—were credited with producing an unusually volatile electorate. In the 1997 and 2000 elections, however, aggregate stability in voting patterns returned. This stability was particularly marked among Liberal and Reform/Alliance supporters. Almost two-thirds (64 percent) of voters who supported the Liberals in 1997 voted for them again in 2000; the corresponding figure for the Reform/Alliance party was 80 percent.[109] The BQ also succeeded in retaining its 1997 support in 2000: 67 percent of its previous supporters voted again for the Bloc. (The PCs and the NDP were less successful, retaining 44 and 56 percent of their 1997 supporters, respectively.)

Even the 2004 election, which seemed likely to produce a significant vote swing from the Liberals to the new Conservative Party, produced a fairly consistent result. Canadian Alliance voters seem to have stayed loyal to the new Conservatives, while many Liberal voters "came home" after a mid-campaign flirtation with Stephen Harper. In hindsight, the last-minute return to the Liberals—especially in Ontario—might have been predicted. Partisanship played a major role in the 2000 election, when 85 percent of partisans voted for their "default" choice.[110] Some 86 percent of Liberal identifiers voted for "their" party, compared to 99 percent of Alliance supporters, over 90 percent of Bloc supporters, and almost 80 percent of NDP supporters.[111]

Blais et al. conclude that party identification "mediates a substantial fraction of the impact of sociodemographic characteristics and of core beliefs and values on the vote."[112] In other words, the effect of subcultural cleavages on voting behaviour is not expressed directly; rather, it shapes voters' attitudes toward the various parties, inclining them to vote consistently for the party that looks the most attractive when viewed through their particular demographic and ideological lenses. Catholics tend to vote Liberal, not because the Liberal Party actively promotes Catholic interests, but because Catholic families socialize their children to prefer the Liberals to all other parties. This does not mean that all Catholics vote Liberal, any more than it implies that all working-class Canadians vote for the NDP. Nevertheless, the long-term factors discussed in this chapter—demographic variables, political values, and party identification—do help to explain the extraordinary dominance of the Liberal Party in the twentieth and early twenty-first centuries. They also help us to understand why the Reform Party survived its 1993 breakthrough into the party system and its transformation into the Canadian Alliance (and subsequently the Conservative Party), and why the BQ—despite the uncertainties about its role in federal politics, which we discussed in Chapter 3—is still a key player in the politics of Quebec.

While these long-term factors help to explain the overall consistency in Canadian voting, they do not help us to understand the fluctuations in party support from election to election. True, the Liberals have stayed within a fairly narrow range—

between 36.7 and 41 percent of the vote—over the past four elections. But the Alliance vote rose from Reform's 20 percent in 1997 to almost 26 percent in 2000; the new Conservatives took almost 30 percent in 2004. The BQ lost to the Liberals in Quebec in 2000, for the first time since the party's founding in 1990, and then rebounded strongly in 2004. The vote share for the NDP has fluctuated in recent elections, from 7 percent in 1993 to 11 percent in 1997, down to 8.5 percent in 2000 and back up to 15.7 percent in 2004. How can we explain these changes in party fortunes? To answer that question, we need to look at the other side of the electoral equation: the short-term factors that produce sudden and occasionally radical shifts in voting behaviour.

■ Short-Term Influences on Voter Choice

It's the Economy, Stupid[113]

The way in which voters perceive the national economy influences their opinion of the incumbent governing party. It is generally believed that the fortunes of the governing party rise and fall with the economic health of Canadians. Comparative studies have found that "for every percentage point that real GDP [gross domestic product] grows in the election year, the major incumbent party stands to gain roughly 1.5 percent of the vote above its normal share."[114] In Canada, "everything else being equal, the vote for the incumbent party typically decreases by two points when the relative unemployment rate increases by one point."[115]

However, the relationship between economics and voting behaviour is neither straightforward nor inevitable. The governing party benefits from a strong economy only under two conditions:

1. The voters are willing to give it the credit for their current prosperity.
2. That prosperity has been achieved, at least in the public mind, through policies that are consistent with the values of a majority of voters (i.e., the social costs of an economic boom are not unacceptably high).[116]

Parties that have acquired a reputation for sound economic management are more likely to receive credit in good times and to ride out bad times. In Canada, the Liberals have benefited from such a reputation, while the NDP has suffered from a lack of credibility on fiscal issues. However, this does not mean that the Liberals won the 2000 election because the economy was prospering. Even though Canadians were considerably more upbeat about the economy in 2000 than they had been in 1997, that optimism did not translate into a major boost for the Liberal Party. Of the party's 41 percent share of the vote, Blais et al. attribute only 1 percentage point to economic issues.[117] One reason may be that the economy was less salient in the 2000 campaign than it had been in some previous elections (see Table 4.5). Another possible explanation is that Liberal supporters had the rosiest view of the economy, and most of them would have voted for the incumbent government anyway.[118] Additionally, few voters gave the Liberals credit for the rising employment and general prosperity.[119] Finally, those voters who were particularly concerned with economic issues did not necessarily perceive the Liberals as the best party to deal with those issues. As we will

TABLE 4.5 **MOST IMPORTANT ELECTION ISSUES, 1984–2000**

ISSUE	1984	1988	1993	1997	2000
Economy in general	17	2	8	4	3
Taxes	3	4	–	3	7
Government spending, deficit, budget	12	7	18	10	6
Unemployment, jobs	36	2	44	24	2
Free trade	–	88	2	–	–
National unity, regionalism, Quebec separatism	4	6	3	13	3
Resources, environment	2	9	1	1	2
Social issues (health = 31)	11	14	5	10	35
Government, trust, parties, accountability, leaders	26	7	10	3	8
All other issues	4	3	4	3	5
None, no important issues, don't know	25	5	10	29	29

Note: The number in each cell represents the percentage of respondents who named that particular issue as the most important in the campaign.

Sources: For 1984 and 1988, Harold D. Clarke, Jane Jenson, Lawrence LeDuc, and Jon Pammett, *Absent Mandate: Canadian Electoral Politics in an Era of Restructuring*, 3rd ed. (Toronto: Gage, 1996), 29. For 1993–2000, Jon H. Pammett, "The People's Verdict," in Christopher Dornan and Jon H. Pammett, eds., *The Canadian General Election of 2000* (Ottawa: Carleton University Press, 2001), 300.

see in the next section, a given party benefits from public concern with an issue only to the extent that voters' opinions are skewed toward a particular side of that issue. Because Canadians were not overwhelmingly convinced that the Liberals shared their views about economic issues in 2000, the incumbent party benefited less than it might have from a robust economy.

Issues

Voters' perceptions of specific issues—as distinct from their views about the economy in general—can change dramatically from election to election, as can the relative importance of a given issue. As Table 4.5 demonstrates, the issue that dominates one campaign—most obviously, free trade in 1988—can vanish before the next election call. The table illustrates at least three important facts about issue voting in recent Canadian elections:

- First, the salience of a given issue in a particular campaign is determined by short-term events, not just by its intrinsic long-term importance. For example, "trust" and "accountability" were important in the 1984 campaign, which brought the long reign of the Liberals to an ignominious end. Over time, Prime Minister Trudeau had acquired a reputation for being aloof and unresponsive, which is reflected in the "accountability" issue. His successor, John Turner, was badly damaged when Trudeau left him to make a long list of patronage appointments shortly before the election call. PC leader Brian Mulroney made patronage a central issue in the campaign, and scored a devastating blow in the English leaders' debate when Turner could not defend the appointments effectively. The salience of the unemployment issue rose in 1993, during a severe economic recession, while the prominence of the national unity question rose modestly in 1997 as a result of the 1995 Quebec sovereignty referendum (see Chapter 3). When new issues capture the public's attention, they seem to crowd out the old ones.

- Second, as the 1984 example demonstrates, the salience of an issue is determined both by preexisting public perceptions and by the parties' campaign strategies. By focusing on patronage, Mulroney elevated the importance of the issue in a way that benefited his party. Similarly, the Liberals focused on health care in 2000, not because their own record on the issue was particularly glowing (see the discussion of the Canadian Health and Social Transfer in Chapter 8), but because their pre-election polling found that the Canadian Alliance was vulnerable on the issue of "two-tier" medicine.[120] While voters were already concerned about the future of medicare, the Liberals heightened their anxiety in order to drive a wedge between the Alliance and the electorate. They followed suit in 2004, alleging that a Conservative government would restrict access to abortion and use the "notwithstanding clause" to weaken the *Charter of Rights*. There are, as yet, no data on the relative importance of these two issues in the campaign, but the Liberals' emphasis on the rights of women and minorities appeared to have helped them turn back the Conservative challenge.

- Third, Canadian elections are rarely fought over a single issue. (The 1988 "free-trade" election was an obvious exception.) In general, the government of the day will try to avoid calling an election when the voters are deeply preoccupied with one or two burning issues. In both 1997 and 2000, almost three out of ten voters could not name a single major issue; in such cases, the incumbent government faces a smaller risk that the issue of the day will blow up in its face.

It is rare for one political party to "win" the issue debate decisively. In most cases, the voters are divided over which party has the best approach to a particular problem. Nonetheless, issues can make an important difference in the outcome of an election. For this to happen, three conditions must be met:

1. The issue must be salient. In other words, large numbers of voters will think about that issue when deciding how to vote.
2. The issue must be linked to the parties. No matter how salient an issue may be to some voters, it will not structure the vote unless the parties are willing to stake out distinctive positions on it. Even when parties do take relatively clear and

distinctive positions on issues, the linkage may not be clear to all voters. For example, although research on the 1988 federal election has shown that one of the major effects of the campaign was to establish and solidify the connection between an individual's position on the Free Trade Agreement and that person's partisan support, a significant number of Canadians nonetheless voted for the party that opposed their own position on this key issue.[121]

3. The voters' opinions about the issue must be skewed. "Skewness" refers to the distribution of support on an issue. Opinion is skewed when significantly more people are on one side of an issue than the other. Alternatively, as was the case with the Free Trade Agreement issue in 1988, opinion is skewed if there are similar proportions of the electorate on either side of an issue but with one side linked to one party and the other side divided between two or more parties. In that instance, the PC government had negotiated the Free Trade Agreement with the Americans, and the party defended the deal vigorously. Voters who did not share this enthusiasm were split between the Liberals—whose credibility as crusaders against free enterprise was relatively weak—and the NDP, which had better ideological credentials for the anti–FTA fight but lacked credibility in other issue areas. In the end, the PCs were re-elected with a reduced majority.

Canadian elections rarely meet all of these conditions. Although several issues may be salient to voters during a given election, they may not be clearly linked to parties and the vote may not be skewed accordingly. Given the influence of the long-term factors discussed earlier and that of short-term factors yet to be discussed, the pool of voters who are open to persuasion on the basis of a single issue is relatively small.

One multivariate analysis of the 2000 election concluded that concerns about the survival of the publicly funded medicare program did have a modest impact on the result: "those in favour of the public health system were more likely to vote Liberal and less likely to support the Alliance. Clearly, the Alliance suffered from its perceived lack of support for the public health system."[122] Although the Alliance lost only 1 percent of the national vote because the Liberals successfully exploited the issue, "health is one of the reasons the party failed to make an inroad in Ontario."[123] The Alliance also lost about 1 percent of the vote to the NDP because it was perceived to be against reproductive choice, and gained 1 percent from the Liberals by calling for a more decentralized federal system (a popular stance in the West, as we have seen).[124] The net effect of issues on voting was quite small in 2000, partly because of a lack of skew and the absence of a single overriding issue.

Party Leaders

As their parties' chief spokespersons, particularly in an age of televised campaigning, party leaders can influence the voting behaviour of Canadians. As we noted in Chapter 2, popular evaluations of political leaders are increasingly unflattering. As captured and presented through the jaundiced eye of the media, party leaders usually become less popular the longer they remain in the public arena. Conventional wisdom holds that a popular leader may give his party a small boost, while an unpopular leader is an albatross around its neck.[125] But it would be wrong to overstate the importance of leader evaluations in voting choice. The available evidence suggests that the influence of party leaders on electoral behaviour has diminished since Pierre Trudeau left politics in 1984, and that no leader—however attractive or charismatic—can overcome the disadvantages posed by weak party organization and public hostility. In 1997, PC leader Jean Charest performed well in the two leaders' debates and ended the campaign as the most popular party leader in Quebec. But his party performed poorly on election day, partly because two-thirds of Quebec voters considered Charest to be "a one-man show."[126] There was no strong team of PC candidates and little party organization on the ground to capitalize on the leader's popularity. As Charest himself said after the campaign ended, "There were people knocking on our door, but there was nobody home to let them in."[127]

According to the authors of the 1988 *Canadian Election Study,* voters evaluate party leaders on two separate dimensions: competence and character.[128] Assessments of competence depend on perceptions of the leader as intelligent, knowledgeable, and able to provide strong leadership and a vision of Canada. The character of leaders is based on the extent to which they are perceived as moral, trustworthy, and compassionate. If a leader scores high on the competence index but falls short on character, as Brian Mulroney did in 1988, his party may still be able to win; after all, voters want a prime minister they can trust to do the job, even if they don't particularly want to invite him over for dinner. But over time, a serious deficit on the character dimension undermines public trust and can overcome even the most positive assessments of competence. Simply put, voters get tired of seeing someone on their television screens whom they dislike. On the other side of the coin, a likeable leader who does not appear to have the "right stuff" to lead the country may inspire affection, but will not draw many votes. In 1997, Charest was regarded by a majority of voters inside and outside Quebec as "all style and no substance," a perception that cost his partly almost 2 percent of the national vote.[129]

If the voters' evaluation of a leader is to benefit his or her party, three conditions must be met:
1. The leader must be significantly more popular or respected than the other leaders (otherwise the contending evaluations cancel each other out).
2. The leader's positive evaluations must be backed up by a strong party organization.
3. The other short-term factors that affect voting choice (the economy, issues) must be less salient than normal. In effect, opinions about party leaders may fill the vacuum left by a lack of issues.

In the 2000 campaign, the leaders had relatively little impact on the outcome. Although the Canadian Alliance tried to make leadership a central issue—by repeatedly condemning Prime Minister Chrétien as "arrogant," and presenting Stockwell Day as fresh and energetic—the salience of leadership did not increase appreciably over the two previous elections. In the first place, none of the five major-party leaders was significantly more or less well regarded than the others. By the end of the campaign, all five averaged between 45 and 48 points on the 100-point scale used by the CES team.[130] Note, however, that the evaluations of Day and BQ leader Gilles Duceppe varied widely, with some voters markedly more positive than others. In addition, voters in the various regions had quite different opinions about the aspiring prime ministers: Jean Chrétien was considerably more popular than Day in Ontario, while the reverse was true in the West.[131] Overall, while Stockwell Day appears to have been a liability to his party,[132] the net effect of leadership evaluations on the 2000 election was otherwise insignificant. Despite the downward trend in Day's popularity over the course of the campaign,[133] the Alliance still managed to increase its vote share and its seats in the Commons.

Similarly, Paul Martin became a liability for the Liberals in 2004. Surveys before and during the campaign showed a steep decline in voters' perceptions of his competence to govern. Those same surveys revealed a remarkable rise in the popularity of Stephen Harper, although some of that positive feeling may have dissipated after he refused to apologize for his party's unfair allegation that Martin defended child pornography.[134] Harper performed considerably better than expected, especially during the first half of the campaign, while Martin often appeared indecisive and inarticulate on the campaign trail. In the end, however, Harper's party received considerably fewer votes than the polls had predicted, especially in Ontario, while Martin's party staged a late comeback to form a minority government. We may conclude, therefore, that while party leaders receive the lion's share of the media attention during a campaign, their net impact on their parties' appeal to the voters is less than meets the eye.

Campaign Effects

Seasoned election watchers—journalists, party strategists, and political scientists alike—are convinced that a party that runs a sloppy, chaotic campaign quickly loses public support. Unfortunately, there is little statistical evidence to substantiate this belief.[135] Voters are rarely asked whether a leader's gaffe or an organizational miscue raised doubts in their minds about the party's fitness to govern and convinced them to vote for someone else. One possible indicator of a "campaign effect" on election outcomes is the timing of the vote decision. Voters who decide which party to support before the election call, or within the first two or three days of the campaign, are influenced more by long-term factors than by short-term factors. In effect, they do not need to wait to see how the campaign turns out; they are already predisposed to vote Liberal or BQ for the reasons discussed in the previous section, and they see no particular reason to consider the alternatives. Those who wait until the middle or the end of the campaign to decide which party to support are more likely to be influenced by short-term factors, including their perceptions of campaign competence. Table 4.6 compares the data on the time of voting choice for the past two federal elections.

Table 4.6 reinforces a point that has already been made: the Liberals have a marked advantage over all the other parties even before the campaign begins. Among those voters who decide which party to support either before or at the start of the

TABLE 4.6 **TIMING OF VOTE DECISION, 1997–2000**

PARTY/ELECTION	BEFORE ELECTION CALL (%)	WHEN CALLED (%)	DURING CAMPAIGN (%)	FINAL DAYS (%)
1997				
Liberal	44	45	28	41
PC	12	18	20	25
NDP	11	12	15	11
Reform	21	18	27	15
BQ	12	8	11	7
Total	54	10	13	23
2000				
Liberal	40	39	30	35
PC	8	9	21	18
NDP	9	11	12	12
Reform	28	30	31	22
BQ	14	10	3	8
Total	47	13	16	24

Note: In each cell, the number represents the percentage of respondents voting for each of the major parties who claimed to have made their voting decision at a particular stage of the campaign.

Sources: Jon H. Pammett, "The Voters Decide," in Alan Frizzell and Jon H. Pammett, eds., *The Canadian General Election of 1997* (Ottawa: Carleton University Press, 1998), 242; Jon H. Pammett, "The People's Verdict," in Jon H. Pammett and Christopher Dornan, eds., *The Canadian General Election of 2000* (Ottawa: Carleton University Press, 2001), 306.

electoral period, the Liberals hold a commanding lead. The data for the 2000 election suggest that voters turned against the Alliance because of its disappointing campaign, while rewarding the PCs and the NDP for their efforts. As the campaign wore on, PC leader Joe Clark was able to rescue his party from apparent oblivion. His strong performance in the leaders' debates was credited with turning the party's fortunes around.[136]

On the other hand, Stockwell Day and his team failed to live up to high initial expectations. The Alliance campaign did not quite seem to be "ready for prime time"; it was damaged by embarrassing mistakes, contradictory statements on party policy, and Day's unwillingness to "stay on message." Although the Alliance may have had an opportunity to win more seats in Ontario at the beginning of the campaign—thus achieving its primary goal—the problems in the campaign undermined its credibility as an alternative government and shook the confidence of voters. As the Alliance slipped in the polls, the morale of party workers on the ground weakened. By election day, some party officials were already blaming the new leader for the disappointing campaign. This illustrates one crucial point: a poor campaign can do more than affect the outcome of one election; it can leave scars on a party organization that take years to heal.

The 2004 election witnessed few major gaffes by any of the parties or their leaders. For the most part, the leaders "stayed on message," followed their scripts, and focused on their own platforms. There were some exceptions, most of them too early in the campaign to have much effect on the outcome. NDP leader Jack Layton laid the blame for the deaths of homeless people on spending cuts imposed by Paul Martin as Finance minister; this inaccurate and exaggerated claim probably did more harm to Layton than to its target.

As noted earlier, a few Conservative MPs engaged in harmful "freelancing" on divisive social issues. Their statements about abortion and same-sex marriage may have reassured some Canadian Alliance stalwarts that the new party spoke for them, but they also lent some credibility to the Liberals' "hidden agenda" attacks on Stephen Harper. Harper himself ran a remarkably smooth and error-free campaign, even though his brand-new team had had little time to prepare for the election. Unfortunately for Harper, his luck seemed to run out in the last two weeks before voting day. First, he unwisely speculated in public about forming a majority government, and let it be known that he had appointed a transition team to prepare for power. This was a gift for the Liberals, who had been trying to convince Canadians that a "protest vote" for the Conservatives might inadvertently help to elect a Harper majority. More generally, voters don't like to be taken for granted. Shortly after Harper's remarks, Conservative support in the polls started to slip. The second gaffe, mentioned earlier, was the release of an inflammatory and unfounded statement accusing Martin of supporting child pornography. Had Harper apologized immediately, the damage would have been contained. His refusal to do so may have convinced some voters that his party was mean-spirited and lacked judgment.

CONCLUSION

Elections are central to representative democracy. They provide the only opportunity for the citizens, en masse, to engage directly with their political institutions. Those institutions are the electoral system, which determines the expression of their preferences and sets incentives for voters to follow, and the House of Commons, whose members are elected in their separate constituencies. The outcome of a Canadian general election—the partisan makeup of the Commons—is the product of the interaction between the long-term and short-term factors that govern voting behaviour, and their translation by the electoral system. Nowhere else is the relationship between society and the state as clear and direct as it is on election day.

The conduct of Canada's general elections is subject to the same pressures for reform as those that affect all of our national political institutions. Citizens are turning away from electoral politics. Some are frustrated with an electoral system that "wastes" their votes and distorts their preferences. Others believe that their vote doesn't matter, largely because they perceive little difference among the parties. Many have given up on voting because they think politics is corrupt, distant, or simply irrelevant. Demands for greater direct participation in decision-making, together with the growing salience of nonterritorial forms of representation, have given new impetus to the campaign for reform of the electoral system and other national institutions.

The prospects for electoral reform depend on the willingness of other political institutions—specifically, the political executive whose power often rests on artificial majorities created by SMP—to accept changes that threaten their security. As we have seen repeatedly throughout this book, each of our national political institutions is affected by, and sometimes preserved by, the others. If our electoral system is to keep pace with changing democratic values, it must be reformed by the very political actors whose self-interest is served by the status quo. The same is true for some of the other possible reforms discussed in this book, including a reduction in party discipline and the introduction of a greater degree of direct democracy. Such reforms, in turn, would have far-reaching effects on the House of Commons, the political executive, and the incentives for voters. If institutional reform is blocked, the gap between the political values of some Canadian citizens and those reflected in our political system may widen.

The recent and apparently inexorable decline in voter turnout merits particular attention from would-be institutional reformers. Unfortunately, there are few obvious avenues for improvement. The recent study of nonvoting concludes that changes to the administration of elections would make little improvement. Few Canadians appear to make the connection between their electoral malaise and the flaws in SMP. The real barriers to participation are attitudinal, not institutional. Perhaps young people would find politics more engaging if they were given more opportunities to vote directly on the issues of the day, or if the parties used their websites in more creative ways. Reducing party discipline in the House of Commons might shorten the perceived distance between voters and their elected representatives (see Chapter 5). On the other hand, institutional reform may not be the most promising approach. A more concerted effort to educate young people about politics might inspire a sense of civic duty and involvement. The parties could make a stronger effort to contact young voters, and recruit more Canadians under 30 to run for office. There is no guarantee that any of these speculative suggestions would reverse the trend, but this much is clear: if younger Canadians continue to avoid the polling booth, the long-term implications for our democracy are worrisome.

GLOSSARY OF KEY TERMS

Agency: The legal requirement for registered parties and candidates to appoint an official agent, who is responsible for ensuring compliance with the election-expense rules in the *Canada Elections Act*.

By-election: A special election held to fill one seat in the Commons (e.g., after the death or retirement of the incumbent MP).

Canvass: The process by which party volunteers identify potential supporters during an election campaign; can be done face to face (knocking on doors) or over the telephone.

Categorical: A ballot structure that forces the voter to indicate a single preference among the available candidates.

Coalition: A Cabinet made up of ministers from two or more parties; the usual way of ensuring that the political executive is supported by a parliamentary majority in legislatures elected by proportional representation, where one party rarely wins more than half of the seats.

Disclosure: The legal requirement for registered parties to publicly disclose the amount and the source of all contributions.

Electoral formula: The method by which votes are cast, counted, and translated into the distribution of parliamentary seats.

Franchise: The right to vote in elections.

General election: The House of Commons is dissolved by a *Writ of Dissolution* (issued by the governor general on the advice of the prime minister), and every seat is filled by election on the same day.

Gerrymandering: Deliberately drawing constituency boundaries in a way that increases the electoral chances of a particular party or candidate.

List-PR: Proportional representation based on party lists; the voter marks a preference for one of the lists of candidates on the ballot, and the seats in Parliament are distributed among the parties on the basis of their vote shares (e.g., 30 percent of the vote in a ten-seat constituency entitles the party to three seats).

Mixed electoral system: A system that combines two or more electoral formulas in a single election (e.g., the New Zealand system, which uses SMP to elect some MPs and party lists to choose the rest).

Ordinal: A ballot structure that allows (or requires) the voter to rank-order some or all of the candidates listed.

Party identification: A long-term emotional attachment to a particular party, its policies, and its leader(s). Voters may form this attachment in childhood, through the absorption of their parents' political values. Throughout adult life, the voter perceives and interprets political events through the lens of party identification.

Proportional representation: The general name for electoral systems based on multimember constituencies, which are designed to translate the parties' vote shares into their seat shares in Parliament with as little distortion as possible.

Referenda: The plural of "referendum." See the discussion of direct democracy in Chapter 2.

Single-member plurality (SMP): The country is divided into territorial constituencies, each of which elects one MP; the winning candidate needs only a simple plurality of the votes; 50 percent plus one of the valid votes cast is not required.

Suffrage: The right to vote in elections, and to run for office.

Threshold of election: The percentage of votes required to win a seat under a given electoral system.

DISCUSSION QUESTIONS

1. What is an electoral system? How does it affect voters, political parties, and the composition of the House of Commons?

2. In your view, should the internal activities of Canadian parties be regulated by law? Should political parties and candidates receive public subsidies, either direct (reimbursement of election expenses) or indirect (tax credits)? Why or why not?

3. What are the key short- and long-term factors that affect voting choice in Canada? If you have voted in a previous federal or provincial election, which of those factors was foremost in your mind when you marked your ballot?

4. If you were eligible to vote in the last federal or provincial election but decided not to cast a ballot, what were the primary reasons for your decision not to vote?

SUGGESTED READINGS

Books and Articles

André Blais, Elisabeth Gidengil, Richard Nadeau, and Neil Nevitte, *Anatomy of a Liberal Victory: Making Sense of the Vote in the 2000 Canadian Election* (Peterborough, ON: Broadview Press, 2002).

Canada, Royal Commission on Electoral Reform and Party Financing, *Reforming Electoral Democracy* (Ottawa: Minister of Supply and Services, 1991).

Law Commission of Canada, *Voting Counts: Electoral Reform for Canada* (Ottawa: Minister of Public Works and Government Services, 2004).

Lawrence LeDuc, Richard G. Niemi, and Pippa Norris, eds., *Comparing Democracies: Elections and Voting in Global Perspective* (Thousand Oaks, CA: Sage, 1996).

Henry Milner, ed., *Making Every Vote Count: Reassessing Canada's Electoral System* (Peterborough, ON: Broadview Press, 1999).

Jon H. Pammett and Christopher Dornan, eds., *The Canadian General Election of 2000* (Ottawa: Carleton University Press, 2001).

William T. Stanbury, *Money in Politics: Financing Federal Parties and Candidates in Canada,* volume 1 of the collected research studies for the Royal Commission on Electoral Reform and Party Financing (Toronto: Dundurn Press, 1991).

Websites

The website of Canada's federal electoral agency, Elections Canada (www.elections.ca), provides a wealth of information. Click on "Electoral Law and Policy" to find the *Canada Elections Act* and background papers about recent amendments. Under "Election Financing," you can access the annual disclosure reports from Canada's registered parties, as well as their election-expense reports (and those of individual candidates). Updates to watch for: the disclosure of the parties' and candidates' election expenses; financial statements from electoral district associations, which should reveal the size of their "war chests"; and the number of registered parties.

The Law Commission's 2004 report and recommendations on electoral reform are available on its website (www.lcc.gc.ca), together with a series of background papers on electoral systems. Go to the website and click on "Electoral Reform."

For more information on electoral systems around the world, check the websites of the Inter-Parliamentary Union (www.ipu.org) and the International Federation for Electoral Systems (www.ifes.org).

NOTES

1. Canada, Royal Commission on Electoral Reform and Party Financing, *Reforming Electoral Democracy,* volume 1 (Ottawa: Minister of Supply and Services, 1991), 26.

2. The Institute for Democratic Education and Assistance categorizes electoral systems differently. It divides the systems in use around the world into plurality/majority, semi-PR, and proportional representation. The first category includes all of the single-member systems. The second comprises the "parallel" mixed systems and the single nontransferable vote. The third covers list-PR, single transferable vote, and mixed-member proportional. (The IDEA classification of electoral-system "families" is available at www.idea.int/esd/systems.cfm.) This classification, while more comprehensive and somewhat more accurate in detail, is too complex for the purposes of this book.

3. This does not mean that criminal law is unaffected by external pressures. Western countries rushed to adopt new anti-terrorism laws after 9/11, partly to reassure nervous citizens and partly in response to UN Conventions and other international obligations. In Canada's case, the federal government strengthened criminal sanctions against alleged terrorists and illegal immigrants as part of an overall strategy to keep the Canada–U.S. border open for trade.

4. For example, Keith Banting argues that Canadian social programs have been affected less by "convergence" with the United States and other trading partners than by the fiscal crisis of the mid-1990s (and, as we will see in Chapter 8, by the politics of federalism). Keith Banting, "Social Policy," in G. Bruce Doern, Leslie A. Pal, and Brian W. Tomlin, eds., *Border Crossings: The Internationalization of Canadian Public Policy* (Toronto: Oxford University Press, 1996), especially 50–52.

5. Lawrence LeDuc, "Elections and Democratic Governance," in Lawrence LeDuc, Richard G. Niemi, and Pippa Norris, eds., *Comparing Democracies: Elections and Voting in Global Perspective* (Thousand Oaks, CA: Sage, 1996), 349.

6. G. Bingham Powell Jr., *Elections as Instruments of Democracy: Majoritarian and Proportional Visions* (New Haven: Yale University Press, 2000). See also LeDuc, "Elections and Democratic Governance," 351.

7. Stanley Kelley Jr., *Interpreting Elections* (Princeton: Princeton University Press, 1983), 126–28.

8. Harold D. Clarke, Jane Jenson, Lawrence LeDuc, and Jon H. Pammett, *Absent Mandate: Interpreting Change in Canadian Elections,* 2nd edition (Toronto: Gage, 1991), 154; André Blais, Elisabeth Gidengil, Neil Nevitte, and Richard Nadeau, "Making Sense of the Vote in the 2000 General Election," paper delivered at the 2001 Annual Meeting of the Canadian Political Science Association, Quebec City; available at www.fax.umontreal.ca/pol/ces-eec.

9. Anthony King, "What Do Elections Decide?," in David Butler, Howard R. Penniman, and Austin Ranney, eds., *Democracy at the Polls: A Comparative Study of Competitive National Elections* (Washington: American Enterprise Institute for Public Policy Research, 1981), 200.

10. Clarke et al., 9–10.

11. Clarke et al., 147–48.

12. Edward Greenspon and Anthony Wilson-Smith, *Double Vision: The Inside Story of the Liberals in Power* (Toronto: Doubleday, 1996), 7.

13. Stephen Clarkson, "Yesterday's Man and his Blue Grits: Backward Into the Future," in Alan Frizzell, Jon H. Pammett, and Anthony Westell, eds., *The Canadian General Election of 1993* (Ottawa: Carleton University Press, 1994), 33–34.

14. LeDuc, 351.

15. Greenspon and Wilson-Smith, 7.

16. Patrick J. Monahan, *Storming the Pink Palace: The NDP In Power, A Cautionary Tale* (Toronto: Lester, 1995), 16.

17. David Reville, quoted in George Ehring and Wayne Roberts, *Giving Away a Miracle: Lost Dreams, Broken Promises, and the Ontario NDP* (Oakville, ON: Mosaic Press, 1993), 277.

18. This may explain why Bills containing amendments to the *Canada Elections Act* are routinely referred to the House of Commons Standing Committee on Procedure and House Affairs before second reading. This allows MPs from all parties to review and amend the legislation more thoroughly than usual. See the discussion of standing committees in Chapter 5.

19. William T. Stanbury, *Money in Politics: Financing Federal Parties and Candidates in Canada,* volume 1 of the collected research studies for the Royal Commission on Electoral Reform and Party Financing (Toronto: Dundurn Press, 1991), 9.

20. *Canada Elections Act,* as amended January 1, 2004, section 403.01.

21. *Canada Elections Act,* as amended January 1, 2004, sections 464–65.

22. *Canada Elections Act,* sections 451–56.

23. John Laschinger and Geoffrey Stevens, *Leaders and Lesser Mortals: Backroom Politics in Canada* (Toronto: Key Porter, 1992), 146–48.

24. *Canada Elections Act,* sections 415–16.

25. *Canada Elections Act,* sections 424–27.

26. *Canada Elections Act,* sections 429–34.

27. *Canada Elections Act,* sections 422–23.

28. *Canada Elections Act,* section 435.

29. Bill C-24, section 73.

30. The broadcasting rules are set out in the *Canada Elections Act,* sections 332–48. The allocations of airtime among the parties are available on the Elections Canada website: www.elections.ca.

31. Khayyam Zev Paltiel, "Campaign Financing in Canada and its Reform," in Howard R. Penniman, ed., *Canada at the Polls: The General Election of 1974* (Washington: American Enterprise Institute for Public Policy Research, 1975), 188.

32. Paltiel, Table 7-1, 186.

33. Paltiel, Table 7-1, 186.

34. Paltiel, 201.

35. Louis Massicotte, "Party Financing in Quebec: An Analysis of the Financial Reports of Parties 1977–89," in F. Leslie Seidle, ed., *Provincial Party and Election Finance in Canada,* volume 3 of the collected research studies for the Royal Commission on Electoral Reform and Party Financing (Toronto: Dundurn Press, 1991), 4.

36. Federal Liberal Agency of Canada, *Financial Statements,* December 31, 2003; available online at www.elections.ca/fin/rep/2003/liberal_2003.pdf.

37. Stanbury, "Regulating the Financing of Federal Parties and Candidates," in Alain-G. Gagnon and A. Brian Tanguay, eds., *Canadian Parties in Transition,* 2nd ed. (Scarborough: Nelson Canada, 1996), 391.

38. *Canada Elections Act,* section 407.

39. On the importance of local campaigns to the success of national parties, see: R. Kenneth Carty, William Cross, and Lisa Young, *Rebuilding Canadian Party Politics* (Vancouver: UBC Press, 2000), 171–72; David M. Farrell, "Campaign Strategies and Tactics," in Lawrence LeDuc, Richard G, Niemi, and Pippa Norris, eds., *Comparing Democracies: Elections and Voting in Global Perspective* (Thousand Oaks, CA: Sage, 1996), 179–80.

40. Douglas Rae, *The Political Consequences of Electoral Laws,* rev. edition (New Haven: Yale University Press, 1971), 16.

41. You can find maps of every federal constituency on the Elections Canada website: www.elections.ca. The site also provides information about the process of drawing electoral district boundaries. Click on "Electoral Districts" and follow the links to the "Federal Representation 2004" icon. It will take you to a Backgrounder entitled "Readjustment of Electoral Boundaries and Representation in the House of Commons."

42. *Reference re Provincial Electoral Boundaries (Sask.)* [1991] 2 S.C.R. 158.

43. The recent report of the Law Commission of Canada, *Voting Counts,* provides an excellent overview of this debate. Go to www.lcc.gc.ca and click on "Electoral Reform." In addition to the report itself, you will find background papers and studies on the topic of electoral reform.

44. The Commission recommended that the list seats be allocated according to the formula used to elect the Scottish Assembly. The complex calculations are very well explained in the Law Commission Report, 97–99.

45. Hon. Jacques Saada, "Letter to Nathalie Des Rosiers [President of the Law Commission of Canada]," April 7, 2004; accessed at the Law Commission website. Saada was subsequently moved to another portfolio in the July 2004 Cabinet shuffle; responsibility for Democratic Reform was reassigned to Mauril Bélanger, a more junior minister.

46. Information on the Citizens' Assembly, and useful learning resources, can be found at www.citizensassembly.bc.ca.

47. The Carruthers report and related documents are available at www.gov.pe.ca/electoralreform. The May 2004 announcement by Premier Binns was accessed at www.pei.cbc.ca from a link on the B.C. Citizens' Assembly website.

48. Jacques P. Dupuis, government House leader and minister for the Reform of Democratic Institutions, "Reform of Democratic Institutions: A Project with Three Aims," speech to the Institute for Research on Public Policy, September 10, 2003: www.mce.gouv.qc.ca.

49. The website of the Democratic Renewal Secretariat can be accessed directly from the Ontario Government site (www.gov.on.ca) or via the Ministry of the Attorney General.

50. The Commission's mandate, and other useful materials, can be found at www.gnb.ca (select the keyword "Democracy" in the Search database).

51. The definitive article is Alan C. Cairns, "The Electoral System and the Party System in Canada, 1921–1965," in Douglas E. Williams, ed., *Constitution, Government, and Society in Canada* (Toronto: McClelland and Stewart, 1988).

52. See Law Commission of Canada, *Voting Counts,* especially Chapters 2 and 4.

53. For a thorough discussion of this issue, see Robert A. Milen, ed., *Aboriginal Peoples and Electoral Reform in Canada,* volume 9 of the collected research studies for the Royal Commission on Electoral Reform and Party Financing (Toronto: Dundurn, 1991).

54. See Heather MacIvor, "Women and the Electoral System," in Manon Tremblay and Linda Trimble, eds., *Women and Electoral Politics in Canada* (Toronto: Oxford University Press, 2003); Donley Studlar, "Will Canada Seriously Consider Electoral Reform? Women and Aboriginals Should," and Thérèse Arseneau, "Electing Proportional Legislatures: Lessons from New Zealand," both in Henry Milner, ed., *Making Every Vote Count: Reassessing Canada's Electoral System* (Peterborough, ON: Broadview Press, 1999).

55. Law Commission of Canada, *Voting Counts,* 100–01

56. *Reference re Provincial Electoral Boundaries (Sask.)* [1991] 2 S.C.R. 158.

57. Maurice Duverger, *Political Parties: Their Organization and Activity in the Modern State,* translated by Barbara and Robert North (London: Methuen, 1964 [1954]), Book II, Chapter 1.

58. Duverger, 224–26.

59. André Blais and R. Kenneth Carty, "The Psychological Impact of Electoral Laws: Measuring Duverger's Elusive Factor," *British Journal of Political Science,* XXI (1991), 79–93.

60. George C. Perlin, *The Tory Syndrome: Leadership Politics in the Progressive Conservative Party* (Montreal and Kingston: McGill–Queen's University Press, 1980).

61. André Blais, Louis Massicotte, and Agnieszka Dobrzynska, *Why Is Turnout Higher in Some Countries Than in Others?,* (Ottawa: Elections Canada, March 2003); available at www.elections.ca/loi/tur/tuh/TurnoutHigher.pdf.

62. Jon H. Pammett and Lawrence LeDuc, *Explaining the Turnout Decline in Canadian Federal Elections: A New Survey of Non-Voters* (Ottawa: Elections Canada, March 2003), 1; available at www.elections.ca/loi/tur/tud/TurnoutDecline.pdf.

63. Pammett and LeDuc, *Explaining the Turnout Decline,* 25 (Table 17) and 28.

64. Alan Frizzell and Anthony Westell, *The Canadian General Election of 1984: Politicians, Parties, Press and Polls* (Ottawa: Carleton University Press, 1985), Table A1.

65. According to Elections Canada, 61.5 percent of eligible voters cast ballots in the 2004 general election. Go to www.elections.ca and click on "38th General Election" for details.

66. Pammett, "The People's Verdict," 311. Young people were particularly likely to be omitted from the *Register;* see Pammett and LeDuc, "Explaining the Turnout Decline," 66–67.

67. Harold D. Clarke, Jane Jenson, Lawrence LeDuc, and Jon Pammett, *Absent Mandate: Interpreting Change in Canadian Elections* (Toronto: Gage, 1991), 131.

68. Pammett and LeDuc, *Explaining the Turnout Decline*, 20, Table 14.

69. Pammett, "The People's Verdict," 312.

70. Pammett and LeDuc, *Explaining the Turnout Decline,* 21.

71. Pammett and LeDuc, 43.

72. Pammett and LeDuc, 66, Table 57.

73. Pammett and LeDuc, 44.

74. Russell J. Dalton, "Political Cleavages, Issues, and Electoral Change," in Lawrence LeDuc, Richard G. Niemi, and Pippa Norris, eds., *Comparing Democracies 2: New Challenges in the Study of Elections and Voting* (Thousand Oaks, CA: Sage, 2002), 193–94.

75. André Blais, Elisabeth Gidengil, Richard Nadeau, and Neil Nevitte, *Anatomy of a Liberal Victory: Making Sense of the Vote in the 2000 Canadian Election* (Peterborough, ON: Broadview Press, 2002), 91.

76. Blais et al., *Anatomy of a Liberal Victory,* 93.

77. Blais et al., *Anatomy of a Liberal Victory,* 94.

78. Blais et al., *Anatomy of a Liberal Victory,* 96.

79. Peter Wearing and Joseph Wearing, "Does Gender Make a Difference in Voting Behaviour?," in Joseph Wearing, ed., *The Ballot and Its Message: Voting in Canada* (Toronto: Copp Clark Pitman, 1991), 343.

80. Wearing and Wearing, 343.

81. Sylvia Bashevkin, *Toeing the Lines: Women and Party Politics in English Canada,* 2nd edition (Toronto: Oxford University Press, 1993), 56–61.

82. André Blais, Elisabeth Gidengil, Neil Nevitte, and Richard Nadeau, "Gender and the 'Fight for the Right,'" 2; available at www.fax.umontreal.ca/pol/ces-eec.

83. Blais et al., *Anatomy of a Liberal Victory,* 94–95.

84. Michael Marzolini, "The Politics of Values: Designing the 2000 Liberal Campaign," in Dornan and Pammett, eds., *The Canadian General Election of 2000,* 263–76.

85. Robert Benzie, "Tories pin blame on fear, rogue candidates," *Toronto Star,* June 30, 2004; accessed at www.thestar.com.

86. Blais et al., "Making Sense of the Vote in the 2000 Canadian Election," 7.

87. Blais et al., *Anatomy of a Liberal Victory,* 109.

88. Blais et al., *Anatomy of a Liberal Victory,* 109.

89. Allison Dunfield, "Tories wouldn't outlaw abortion, Harper says," *The Globe and Mail,* June 1, 2004 (accessed at www.globeandmail.com); Canadian Press, "We'd use notwithstanding clause: Tory MP," *Toronto Star,* June 25, 2004: accessed at www.thestar.com.

90. Robert Benzie, "Tories pin blame on fear, rogue candidates," *Toronto Star,* June 30, 2004: accessed at www.thestar.com.

91. Blais et al., *Anatomy of a Liberal Victory,* 203.

92. See, for example, Blais et al., *Anatomy of a Liberal Victory,* 77, Table 4.3.

93. Blais et al., "Making Sense of the Vote in the 2000 Canadian Election," 11.

94. Clarke et al., *Absent Mandate: Interpreting Change in Canadian Elections.*

95. Alan Frizzell, "The Perils of Polling," in Alan Frizzell, Jon H. Pammett, and Anthony Westell, eds., *The Canadian General Election of 1988* (Ottawa: Carleton University Press, 1989).

96. Subsequent analyses in the United States from the 1960s through the 1990s indicate that the importance of party identification was at its zenith during the relative calm of the 1950s.

97. Harold D. Clarke, Jane Jenson, Lawrence LeDuc, and Jon H. Pammett, *Political Choice in Canada* (Toronto: McGraw-Hill Ryerson, 1979).

98. Clarke et al., *Absent Mandate: Interpreting Change in Canadian Elections*, 48–49; Harold D. Clarke, Jane Jenson, Lawrence LeDuc, and Jon H. Pammett, "Voting Behaviour and the Outcome of the 1979 Federal Election: The Impact of Leaders and Issues," *Canadian Journal of Political Science*, XV:3 (1982), 517–52.

99. Blais et al., "Making Sense of the Vote in the 2000 Canadian Election," 12–13.

100. Blais et al., "Making Sense of the Vote in the 2000 Canadian Election," 13.

101. Neil Nevitte, André Blais, Elisabeth Gidengil, and Richard Nadeau, *Unsteady State: The 1997 Canadian Federal Election* (Toronto: Oxford University Press, 2000), 70.

102. Blais et al., "Making Sense of the Vote in the 2000 Canadian Election," 13.

103. Blais et al., *Anatomy of a Liberal Victory*, 119, Table 8.2

104. Blais et al., *Anatomy of a Liberal Victory*, 117.

105. Ipsos-Reid Canada, poll released June 1, 2004; accessed at www.ipsos-na.com.

106. Ipsos-Reid Canada, poll released June 1, 2004; accessed at www.ipsos-na.com.

107. EKOS Research, "Federal Election Part II: A Look at What Is Driving Federal Voting Intentions," press release, June 1, 2004, 1; accessed at www.ekos.com. The second-lowest figure was the 71 percent of former PC voters who said that they intended to vote for the new Conservative Party; this substantiates the argument about the conflict of values between the PCs and the Canadian Alliance.

108. Peter Mair, "Comparing Party Systems," in LeDuc, Niemi, and Norris, eds., *Comparing Democracies 2*, 103.

109. Pammett, "The People's Verdict," 295.

110. Blais et al., *Anatomy of a Liberal Victory*, 120.

111. Blais et al., *Anatomy of a Liberal Victory*, 121, Figure 8.3.

112. Blais et al., "Making Sense of the Vote in the 2000 Canadian Election," 15.

113. A reference to the famous sign in the Clinton "war room" during the 1992 American presidential campaign.

114. Helmut Norpoth, "The Economy," in LeDuc, Niemi, and Norris, eds., *Comparing Democracies*, 303.

115. Richard Nadeau and André Blais, "Explaining Election Outcomes in Canada," *Canadian Journal of Political Science*, 26, 775–90; summarized in Blais et al., *Anatomy of a Liberal Victory*, 129.

116. Norpoth, 299–318.

117. Blais et al., *Anatomy of a Liberal Victory*, 134.

118. Blais et al., "Making Sense of the Vote in the 2000 Canadian Election," 18.

119. Blais et al., *Anatomy of a Liberal Victory*, 133.

120. Marzolini, 268.

121. Richard Johnston, André Blais, Henry E. Brady, and Jean Crête, "Free Trade and the Dynamics of the 1988 Canadian Election," in Wearing, ed., *The Ballot and Its Message,* 321.

122. Blais et al., "Making Sense of the Vote in the 2000 Canadian Election," 21–22.

123. Blais et al., "Making Sense of the Vote in the 2000 Canadian Election," 22.

124. Blais et al., "Making Sense of the Vote in the 2000 Canadian Election," 24.

125. Nevitte et al., *Unsteady State,* 85.

126. Nevitte et al., *Unsteady State,* 87.

127. Jean Charest, remarks to the National Council of the Progressive Conservative Party of Canada, February 1998.

128. Richard Johnston, André Blais, Henry E. Brady, and Jean Crête, *Letting the People Decide: Dynamics of a Canadian Election* (Montreal and Kingston: McGill–Queen's University Press, 1992), 169–96.

129. Nevitte et al., *Unsteady State,* 87–88.

130. Blais et al., "Making Sense of the Vote in the 2000 Canadian Election," 28.

131. Blais et al., "Making Sense of the Vote in the 2000 Canadian Election," 29.

132. Blais et al., "Making Sense of the Vote in the 2000 Canadian Election," 30; Blais et al., *Anatomy of a Liberal Victory,* Chapter 12.

133. André Turcotte, "Fallen Heroes: Leaders and Voters in the 2000 Canadian Federal Election," in Dornan and Pammett, eds., *The Canadian General Election of 2000,* 285.

134. Canadian Press, "Harper won't apologize for remarks," *The Globe and Mail,* June 19, 2004; "An apology, Mr. Harper," *The Globe and Mail,* June 21, 2004 (both accessed at www.globeandmail.com).

135. See Nevitte et al., *Unsteady State,* 132; Farrell, 179–82.

136. Peter Woolstencroft, "Some Battles Won, War Lost: The Campaign of the Progressive Conservative Party," in Dornan and Pammett, eds., *The Canadian General Election of 2000,* 101–04.

5 PARLIAMENTARY DEMOCRACY AND THE LEGISLATIVE PROCESS

LEARNING OBJECTIVES

- *identify* the reasons for Cabinet dominance, adversarial politics, and excessive party discipline in the Canadian House of Commons, and *explain* why they persist;
- *explain* how a Bill becomes law in Canada;
- *explain* the functions of the House of Commons and the Senate, and *evaluate* the performance of our national legislative institutions;
- *explain* and *evaluate* some of the proposed reforms to Canada's Parliament.

INTRODUCTION

As we saw in Dossier 1.1, every government is divided into three branches: legislative, executive, and judicial. The legislative branch makes the laws that are implemented by the executive and interpreted by the judiciary. Strictly speaking, Canada's Parliament does not *make* laws, nor can it *propose* public expenditures. Government legislation, which comprises the vast majority of laws passed by Parliament, originates with the executive branch (see Chapter 6). **Money Bills**—formal authorizations to raise or spend public revenues—must be formulated by the Cabinet, and approved by the governor general, before they are introduced into the House of Commons.

Under the *Constitution Act, 1867,* law-making powers are divided between the Crown, the House of Commons, and the Senate. A government **Bill** is sponsored by the Crown, represented in this case by a particular Cabinet minister, and it must be given royal assent after its adoption by both Houses of Parliament. We will discuss the executive branch—the Crown, the political executive (Cabinet), and the permanent executive—in Chapter 6. This chapter focuses on our parliamentary institutions: how they operate, their place in the political system, and some of the debates over their possible reform.

As these words were written, Canada's national parliament faced two short-term challenges:

1. The June 2004 federal election produced a **minority government.** The Liberals won 135 of the 308 seats, well short of the 155 seats needed for a majority. For a brief time, it appeared that the New Democrats would win at least 20 seats, which would give the two parties a combined majority; in that scenario, as in the 1972–74 Liberal minority, the NDP would have exchanged its voting support for policy concessions. In the event, the New Democrats fell one seat short. Neither the Conservatives nor the Bloc Québécois showed much interest in supporting a minority Liberal government. So for the first time in a quarter-century, a prime minister had to govern without the assurance that his legislation or his financial measures would receive majority support in the House of Commons.

2. In December 2003, Prime Minister Paul Martin promised to reform the House of Commons. His Democratic Renewal Plan was fairly modest: to reduce party discipline in some (but not all) Commons votes, by instituting the British "three-line whip" system (see "Holding the Executive to Account" on page 234); to give committees more influence and autonomy in policy-making; and to improve relations between the Cabinet and Parliament.[1] During the brief third session of the thirty-seventh Parliament (February–May 2004), the Martin government took some steps to implement the Democratic Renewal Plan.[2] Unlike previous prime ministers who had promised to reform the Commons, Martin appeared to be sincere.[3] He had already made a significant contribution as Finance minister by empowering the Finance Committee to conduct pre-budget consultations.[4]

   It was not clear at the time of writing, however, whether the prime minister's commitment to Commons reform would survive the pressures of minority government. No governing party can reduce party discipline in its own ranks unless it enjoys a comfortable majority in the Commons. In a minority situation, every government MP must toe the party line or risk an early election—something that cash-strapped parties and exhausted MPs often prefer to avoid. On the other hand, minority government weakens Cabinet control over Commons committees.[5] Collectively, the Opposition parties hold more committee seats than the governing Liberals. Committees in the thirty-eighth Parliament had 12 regular members: 5 (42%) Liberals, 4 Conservatives, 2 Bloc Québécois, and 1 New Democrat. If the seven Opposition members worked together—especially when a Bill was referred to committee before second reading—they could force the government to accept their amendments to proposed legislation. So the current minority government could thwart Martin's plan to reduce party discipline in the chamber, even while accelerating the proposed shift of power to Commons committees.

These short-term challenges arose at a time when Canada's federal Parliament already faced serious long-term challenges. The first set of challenges came from outside Canada: (1) globalization; (2) the growing internationalization of public policy, via treaties and other binding agreements between national governments; and (3) the new emphasis on national security following 9/11. All of these external developments tend to restrict the power of national legislatures, either by reducing the autonomy of national governments as a whole (globalization) or by shifting power from the legislature to the executive branch. Some policies flowing from international agreements are subject to ratification by Parliament or must be enshrined in legislation; but most (e.g., the Kyoto Protocol) can be put into effect without the involvement of the legislative branch. (The same is true for agreements among Canada's federal and provincial governments, as Chapter 8 explains.)

To the extent that the "war on terrorism" has shifted the priorities of government from purely domestic issues toward national security and our relations with the United States—both of which fall under the Crown prerogative and are rarely subject to parliamentary review[6]—the House of Commons and the Senate have become marginalized in the national policy-making process. This trend could be reversed. Committees in both Houses could take a more active role in reviewing proposed treaties and ensuring that Canadian laws comply with our international obligations (see the discussion of Senate committees later in this chapter). They could also exert some influence over defence spending and administration, although the actual deployment of troops will likely remain within the Cabinet's purview.[7] For the moment, however, the internationalization of public policy—like the growing autonomy of provincial and local governments (Chapter 3)—appears to exacerbate the weakness of Parliament relative to the executive branch.

The second set of long-term challenges is domestic in origin, although mirrored in other Western states. "At the dawn of the millennium, Canada's system of parliamentary government is the target of sustained and serious criticism, perhaps the most sustained and serious in its long life."[8] This criticism has two primary sources: (1) the mismatch between the incentives imposed by an ancient institution, and the evolving attitudes of voters and **backbench** MPs; and (2) the widening gap between the theory of parliamentary democracy and the reality of Canadian politics and government.

In theory, Canada's Parliament performs the following functions:
- debating, improving, and ratifying the laws proposed by the Cabinet;
- holding individual Cabinet ministers accountable for the operation of their departments;
- holding the entire Cabinet accountable for the conduct of the executive branch;
- monitoring and controlling government expenditure by exercising the **power of the purse;** and
- representing the electorate in the national government.

Dossier 5.1 provides a brief sketch of Canada's legislative process, to illustrate the relationships among the various players.

The standard procedure for adopting a government Bill—let's call our hypothetical Bill C-x—is as follows:

- *First reading:* The sponsoring minister asks leave of the House to present Bill C-x, "An Act Respecting Y." The prefix C- before the number (e.g., C-68) means that the Bill originated in the Commons. A few government Bills are introduced in the Senate; they are designated by the prefix S- (e.g., S-2). Any Bill that requires the expenditure of public funds must originate in the Commons. The motion for first reading is a formality; there is no debate, and the House almost always assents. After first reading, the Bill is printed in both official languages and distributed to all MPs. The newly numbered Bill is placed on the Order Paper for future debate. An Order Paper lists all the items of business that could be considered by the House according to an established order.

- *Second reading:* On a day determined by the House leaders of the official parties (those with 12 or more MPs), Bill C-x is debated for the first time. Only the principle of the Bill may be debated at second reading; the details are left to later stages of the process. The sponsoring minister makes a speech defending the Bill, explaining its provisions and outlining the problem or problems the Bill is designed to address. The Speaker then recognizes the official Opposition critic assigned to the minister's department. The official Opposition critic presents her party's response to the Bill, focusing on the overall purpose of the legislation. The critics for the other Opposition parties follow. Other MPs may take part in the debate if they so choose. That choice usually depends on the relevance of the issue to their particular party or constituency, or the extent of their personal expertise on the subject matter of the Bill. After all MPs who wish to speak have had an opportunity to do so, the Speaker recognizes the sponsoring minister to respond to the critics and close the debate. Then the House votes on Bill C-x. When the government controls a majority of the seats in the Commons, its Bills are approved as a matter of routine. Once the House has voted in favour of a Bill at second reading, the principle of the Bill may not be changed at subsequent stages of the legislative process.

- *Committee stage:* The Bill is automatically sent to the appropriate standing committee of the House of Commons. Every department of the federal government is mirrored by a standing committee. If Bill C-x were sponsored by the minister of Justice, for example, it would be assigned to the Standing Committee on Justice, Human Rights, Public Safety and Emergency Preparedness. On occasion, Bills are sent to special legislative committees. (For more information about the committee system, see "Private Members' Business" on page 248.) The committee may hold public hearings on the Bill, summoning witnesses to testify about its possible effects. Most such witnesses are either policy experts or representatives of interest groups affected by the Bill. Once the hearings are concluded, the committee examines the Bill clause by clause. It considers amendments proposed by its members, or by witnesses, relying on advice from officials of the sponsoring department.[9] When the committee finishes its deliberations, it prepares a report to the House, including any amendments that were approved by a majority of the membership. In practice, committees in a majority Parliament adopt only amendments that the sponsoring minister has approved.[10] These amendments may not change the principle of the Bill, as adopted by the House at second reading, nor can they infringe on the Crown's prerogative by proposing additional public spending.[11] Ideally, the committee submits a consensus report with the agreement of all four parties; in practice, one or more Opposition parties often submit dissenting reports that reject the views of the government majority on the committee.[12]

- *Report stage:* The House debates the Bill as amended by the committee. Other amendments may be proposed from the floor by MPs who are not committee members. If the sponsoring minister considers a proposed amendment to be "friendly"—if, in other words, he believes that it would improve the legislation—he can accept the amendment without further ado. "Unfriendly" amendments are put to a vote of the House. Under a majority government, the House rarely accepts a change that does not meet with the Cabinet's approval; in a minority situation, a united Opposition can prevail over the objections of the minister (or initiate a bargaining process to reach a compromise).[13] If amendments are made to Bill C-x at report stage, either by the minister or by the House, the Bill is revised and reprinted.

- *Third reading:* The revised Bill is put to the House for a final debate and vote. As soon as it passes at third reading, the Bill leaves the Commons and goes to the Senate.

- *Senate:* The upper house follows a similar procedure to the Commons, with one major exception: because MPs cannot speak on the floor of the Senate (and vice versa), government Bills are sponsored by the government leader in the Senate. The Senate has the power to veto most Bills.[14] This power is rarely used—only five times between 1945 and 1999[15]—but its existence requires the government to take proposed Senate amendments seriously.[16] If the Senate amends Bill C-x and the Government refuses to accept those amendments,[17] the Senate usually (but not always) defers to the elected House. Sometimes the two Houses must work out a compromise before the Bill can proceed. After the Bill is passed by the Senate at third reading, it goes to the governor general for royal assent.

- *Royal assent:* The Crown's representative signs the Bill into law. The new law may take effect immediately or at a later date specified in its text.

As we will see in Dossier 5.2, some elements of this procedure may be varied with the consent of the Cabinet and a majority of the House. Since an amendment to the Standing Orders—the written rules of Parliament—in 1994, the government may refer a Bill to the appropriate standing committee before second reading.

In practice, the House of Commons does not carry out its duties—legislative, financial, or representative—as effectively as it might. There are at least three reasons for this gap between theory and practice:

1. The Commons—and, to a lesser degree, the Senate—is dominated by the political executive. While a degree of Cabinet dominance is the norm in parliamentary systems (otherwise the business of government would grind to a halt), "In no other British-type legislature has the shift of power to the executive proceeded further than in the Canadian federal House of Commons."[18] Legislators usually pass the laws proposed by the Cabinet with minor changes, if any, and little meaningful debate. The Cabinet also has the power to issue delegated laws—such as Orders in Council and Regulations—without ratification by Parliament.[19] (Regulations are discussed in greater detail in Chapter 6.) In most Parliaments, MPs lack the independence, experience, and expertise to hold the Cabinet accountable, either individually or collectively. The high turnover of MPs from election to election, especially on the Opposition side, weakens the capacity of the Commons as a whole. Members are overwhelmed by conflicting demands on their time and attention, which leaves little opportunity to challenge the executive. The Cabinet can force Government MPs to support its legislation by invoking the "**confidence convention**"; under a majority government, the only weapon available to Opposition MPs is the mobilization of public dissent. The power of the purse, traditionally an important bargaining chip for disgruntled legislators, has been reduced to empty ritual (see the discussion of the Estimates under "Parliament and the Public Purse" on page 227).

   Despite its poor public image, the Senate does a better job of legislating than the Commons. Because senators do not have the power to bring down a government, and they are not subject to election or re-election, they are more independent of the political executive and less constrained by party discipline. Unlike most MPs, senators generally remain in Parliament for long periods of time; this allows them to master parliamentary procedure and acquire policy expertise. Some senators are experts in public policy and administration even before their appointment, whereas most MPs are policy amateurs when they are sworn in.[20]

2. Strict **party discipline** prevents government MPs from openly challenging the Cabinet. It also denies Opposition MPs a meaningful opportunity to participate in policy-making, at least under a majority government. Party discipline constrains the autonomy of MPs at all stages of the legislative process, including committee work. There is one important exception: government MPs can express dissenting views in the weekly **caucus** meeting. Although these confrontations between ministers and backbenchers go on behind closed doors, which makes their influence difficult to measure, ministers may be forced to delay, amend, or withdraw proposed legislation by concerted opposition from their MPs. This power should not be overstated, however. Although one former minister claimed that "strong caucus opposition to any government proposal imposes an absolute

veto on that proposal,"[21] recent changes to House and Cabinet timetabling have reduced the power of government backbenchers. Whereas caucuses used to meet on the day before Cabinet, so that caucus feedback could be incorporated into Cabinet discussions of proposed legislation, Cabinet now meets on Tuesday mornings and the caucuses on Wednesdays.[22]

Although prime ministers routinely remind their Cabinets to pay attention to the views of government MPs,[23] ministers have little incentive to follow this advice. The longevity of their Cabinet careers depends on the prime minister, not their caucus colleagues. As noted earlier, senators are less subject to party discipline; consequently, they normally operate in a less adversarial way. This helps to explain why Senate committees are substantially more effective than their counterparts in the Commons.[24]

3. Neither the House of Commons nor the Senate represents the electorate as it was intended to do. Party caucuses in the Commons are dominated by artificial regional blocs created by the electoral system (see Chapter 4). Government MPs are divided into organized regional caucuses, which can have a major impact on policy behind closed doors.[25] In public, however, regional representation is stifled by party discipline. MPs do not reflect the demographic makeup of the electorate: they are disproportionately white, male, middle-aged, well educated, and prosperous. Note, however, that MPs work very hard on behalf of their ridings, and they spend most of their time helping individual constituents resolve problems with the federal bureaucracy. We will discuss their "**casework**" responsibilities later in this chapter. In other words, MPs may not represent Canadians in the pictorial sense; but they do their best to represent their constituents in tangible ways.

While senators are appointed to represent particular provinces, they are not perceived by the public as effective spokespersons for their regions. It is not clear that the Senate was designed for the aggressive defence of a particular province; instead, the division of Senate seats among regions was intended to give the smaller provinces a more powerful voice in the legislative process than they could have in the Commons. The upper houses in most federations are expressly designed to speak for the states or provinces; they enshrine the principle of intrastate federalism (discussed in Chapter 9).[26] When measured against the American Senate or the German Bundesrat, the Canadian Senate is usually found wanting. It is sometimes alleged that the Senate really represents corporate and business interests, rather than regional interests.[27] While it is true that some senators sit on the boards of large companies, the majority of them have no financial axe to grind; indeed, individual senators have been influential champions of the poor and disadvantaged.[28] More generally, there is no room in the British parliamentary tradition for the representation of particular class or economic interests.[29]

Executive dominance, party discipline, and the perceived failure of representation have reduced the effectiveness of Canada's legislative branch, relative to both the executive and the courts. As we saw in Chapter 2, Parliament has suffered a particularly steep decline in public confidence over the past three decades. The Commons has lost much of the legitimacy that one might expect an elected chamber to possess; the appointed Senate has never been particularly popular, and it is presently held in very low esteem.

Despite widespread public suspicion about the motives and abilities of our elected representatives, the truth is that MPs work very hard and make enormous personal and financial sacrifices in the name of public service. They divide their time between Ottawa and their constituencies, juggling a host of roles and responsibilities that often conflict with the expectations of the voters. A former Liberal MP described his job in the following terms:

> . . . at least three half-days each week in the House to ensure that a quorum was always maintained; attendance at major debates and divisions; attendance at question period "for both excitement and information"; membership in two standing committees and later, the [Chairmanship] of the Special Committee on Statutory Instruments; caucus meetings for three hours each Wednesday morning and caucus committee meetings in lunch and dinner breaks; twice-weekly French classes, "being determined to become bilingual," a one thousand-mile round trip each weekend to constituency and home in Windsor; approximately 200 public functions and 200 visits to the homes of constituents in each year; and a large volume of constituency business (some 5,500 cases a year).[30]

While MPs consider helping individual constituents to be the most important aspect of their jobs—perhaps because "casework" offers greater satisfaction than beating one's head against the brick walls of party discipline and Cabinet dominance—Canadians outside Parliament consider casework to be the least important.[31] This is only one example of the contradictions between the institutional incentives that shape MPs' behaviour, and voters' perceptions of their elected representatives. That conflict helps to explain declining public confidence in Parliament.[32]

As we saw in Chapter 1, institutions exert a powerful influence on the behaviour of those who operate within them. They set incentives for ambitious people who seek to advance their careers. An individual MP, no matter how determined, cannot resist those incentives for long. He or she must either give in and follow the institutional norms of behaviour, or leave Parliament. The experience of the Reform MPs elected in 1993 is instructive. Most were critical of the parliamentary system and determined to represent their ridings instead of toeing the party line. Formal critic positions were abolished, leader Preston Manning was symbolically relegated to the second row (even though the leader traditionally sits on the "front bench"), and the MPs repeatedly vowed to change the rules of Parliament. Within three years, the reverse had happened: they changed, while the rules remained intact. The unconventional caucus structure reduced Reform's effectiveness as an Opposition party, forcing them to acknowledge that "some parliamentary rules serve legitimate purposes."[33] While Reform's pledge to transform the House of Commons played a significant role in their rapid electoral success, it was based on a naive and simplistic approach to the institutional norms of parliamentary government.

The most important of those norms are Cabinet dominance, party discipline, and adversarial politics.

- The Cabinet must command the support of a majority of MPs in order to pass legislation and to remain in office. When the governing party holds a majority of the seats in the Commons, the prime minister (who is also the party leader) can generally count on remaining in office until he decides to call a general election (under the *Constitution,* no Parliament can last longer than five years in normal circumstances). In a minority Parliament, securing a majority of votes for proposed legislation, budget measures, or confidence motions requires the government to negotiate with the leaders of one or more Opposition parties. (Indeed, the leaders of the three Opposition parties demanded in September 2004 that the Standing Orders be amended, to restrict the confidence convention to financial measures and Bills expressly agreed by all parties to be questions of confidence in the government.[34]) In either case, the leaders of the governing party have a powerful incentive to keep their MPs in line. While a lost vote no longer spells the automatic resignation of the prime minister, it is a public political embarrassment and damages the credibility of the party in power. As a result, past prime ministers have often designated controversial Bills as "confidence votes," even though their defeat would not trigger a resignation under the constitutional conventions of parliamentary government (i.e., they are not money Bills).

- Political parties nominate candidates, campaign to elect MPs, and help to structure the voting patterns of the electorate (Chapters 3 and 4). The influence of party organizations on the recruitment of elected officials ensures that most MPs are committed partisans who owe a great political debt to their local constituency associations. This makes it harder for them to cross party lines, especially those on the government side of the House. Moreover, the news media are always ready to pounce on any hint of dissension within a party caucus. Journalists' enthusiasm for reporting conflict distorts what should be a normal part of parliamentary life: the exercise of individual conscience, or constituency representation, by an individual MP.

  Former Prime Minister Chrétien, who led three majority governments, used to keep rebellious backbenchers under control by threatening an early election in which they might lose their seats. He was widely regarded as the strictest party disciplinarian among recent prime ministers.[35] The result was "a compromise of ministerial accountability, a lack of significant parliamentary input into developing legislation, and a perception that government was far less open than it could, or should, have been."[36] While some measure of party discipline is an essential part of responsible Cabinet government, its excesses in the Canadian House of Commons weaken both the legitimacy and the legislative capacity of the institution.

- "Adversarial politics" refers to a particular style of political debate. Complex issues are reduced to two opposing sides, "yes" and "no"; the two sides bicker and belittle each other, instead of working together on constructive solutions. Adversarialism in the Commons is fostered by several features of the institution: the seating arrangements (see "Adversarial Politics and Party Discipline" on page 223); the confidence convention, which pits the governing "team" against an Opposition determined to bring it down; party discipline; the constant clash between the government's desire for speedy passage of its Bills and the constitutional prerogative of Parliament to review legislation and financial measures;[37] and the ever-present prospect of future electoral competition.

Collectively, these three norms of behaviour create a clear set of incentives for anyone who wants to become an MP, and for MPs who wish to secure leadership positions in their caucuses or Cabinet:

- To become a candidate, you must first become a member of a political party and demonstrate your attachment to its principles and goals. Your contacts with other party members, and your own experiences within the party organization, usually generate a strong sense of "team spirit" that shapes your behaviour and priorities. (This may be less true for some "star" candidates, who are recruited from outside the active party membership because of their prominence in some other field of endeavour; recent examples include business executive Belinda Stronach, now a Conservative MP, and former NHL goalie Ken Dryden, now a Liberal Cabinet minister.)

- Once elected, your chances of re-election rest on the fortunes of your party, not on your own individual efforts.[38] Similarly, your odds of either remaining in government or becoming part of a future government depend on the effectiveness of your leader and the popularity of your party as a whole. The fate of the "team" largely determines the political longevity of each individual member.

- A government MP who wishes to become a Cabinet minister—which most do[39]— must be a "team player," supporting the Cabinet and following the dictates of the prime minister with loyalty and enthusiasm. To publicly defy the prime minister is to risk immediate punishment and the loss of a promising political future. The turmoil in the Liberal caucus that followed the 2000 federal election can be attributed to the clash between two competing incentives: to stay loyal to incumbent Prime Minister Jean Chrétien, in the hope of an immediate promotion to Cabinet, or to support aspiring prime minister Paul Martin and wait for a Cabinet appointment in his future government.

- An Opposition MP who seeks a higher position in her caucus must be a vigorous critic of the government and a loyal supporter of the party leadership (at least in public). However, the enforcement of party discipline is less powerful on the Opposition benches. Without the carrot of immediate appointment, or the stick of the confidence convention, an Opposition leader must rely on team spirit and personal persuasion to win over rebellious MPs. Historically, Opposition leaders have been more vulnerable to revolts from their caucuses and extraparliamentary organizations than prime ministers.

This system of incentives does not reward independence of spirit, policy innovation,[40] or service to the constituency. As noted earlier, however, the latter is a high priority for most MPs: it does not guarantee re-election[41] or promotion, but it is often the most satisfying part of the job. No matter how dedicated their pursuit of a particular policy or how well informed their arguments, backbench MPs (both government and Opposition) have little if any power to shape legislation. Even Private Members' Bills (PMBs), which should give backbenchers direct law-making power, are given a low priority in House proceedings. While government MPs exercise some influence in the secrecy of the caucus room, they pay a high price for criticizing Cabinet decisions in public. Most MPs serve only one or two terms before leaving the Commons, either voluntarily or through electoral defeat. Just as they start to figure out the arcane rules of parliamentary procedure, and master one or two policy fields, they return to private life.

Because the institutional incentives are so powerful, and because they are embedded in the very structure of Parliament (as inherited from Britain and evolved in Canada), repeated efforts to reform our legislative institutions have had little effect. Some recent changes to Commons procedure were designed to give MPs a greater role in policy-making. In 1985–86 the committee system was strengthened, and new rules for Private Members' Bills were put in place. However, neither reform addressed the root causes of MPs' powerlessness—party discipline and executive dominance—and neither succeeded. Two more significant changes to the Standing Orders were adopted in 1994. First, standing committees were given the power to examine proposed legislation before second reading. This gives committees a chance to address the principle of the Bill, not just the technical details by which that principle will be achieved. The committee and report stages precede second reading, and MPs are freer to adopt amendments because the Cabinet has not yet committed itself or its backbenchers to a particular version of the Bill. Dossier 5.2 shows how this revised procedure works in practice.

Second, the 1994 reforms gave committees the power to investigate policy issues on their own initiative, and to draft Bills that address them. While these two reforms increased the potential policy influence of committees, that potential has not yet been realized. The Cabinet decides which Bills will be referred to committee after first reading, and it can ignore draft Bills originating in committee. Because Prime Minister Chrétien was reluctant to weaken his control over the legislative agenda, the new Standing Orders were rarely used during his tenure in office.

Prime Minister Martin promised, as part of his Democratic Renewal Plan, to refer all government Bills that were not subject to the "three-line whip" to the appropriate standing committees before second reading. To date, this promise has borne little fruit. Of the 37 government Bills introduced in the Commons during the third session of the thirty-seventh Parliament, 11 were referred to committee before second reading. Note, however, that 17 of the Bills had completed part of the legislative process before the House was prorogued in November 2003, so the actual proportion

C-2(R-*)—The Leader of the Government in the House of Commons—An Act respecting the election of members to the House of Commons, repealing other Acts relating to elections and making consequential amendments to other Acts.

- Introduced and read the first time—October 14, 1999
- Motion to refer the Bill to the Standing Committee on Procedure and House Affairs before Second Reading—Debated; adopted: October 19, 1999
- Order respecting report stage—December 2, 1999
- Reported with amendments—December 3, 1999
- Debated at report stage—December 7, 1999; February 14 and 22, 2000
- Time allocation at report stage and second reading, and at third reading—Notice: February 21, 2000; adopted: February 22, 2000
- Concurred in at report stage with further amendments and read the second time—February 22, 2000
- Debated at third reading—February 25, 2000
- Read the third time and passed—February 28, 2000

- Passed by the Senate; royal assent—May 31, 2000

Explanatory Notes

The designation "R-*" means that the Bill requires the expenditure of public funds; the "R" stands for "Royal Recommendation"—the Crown's request to Parliament for money.

The "Order respecting report stage" is a formal announcement that a committee will report back to the House on a given day and that its report will be debated shortly thereafter. This gives MPs a few days to prepare for the debate. The committee report on C-2, with amendments, was debated over three sitting days.

"Time allocation" is a procedural motion, introduced by the government House leader, which allows the government to limit the length of a debate. Once time allocation has been adopted by a majority of the MPs (in practice, by a disciplined majority of government MPs), the legislative process can speed up considerably. Less than a week after time allocation was imposed on February 22, Bill C-2 had moved through report stage, second reading, and third reading, and was sent to the Senate.

of new Bills referred to committee before second reading was 11/20. Of those 11, only 3 made it all the way through the process and received royal assent; 2 of those had been reported back without amendment by the committee.[42]

In fairness, the February–May 2004 parliamentary session was too brief and hurried to draw any firm conclusions about the prime minister's commitment to reform the Commons. However, the fate of the earlier attempts to empower backbench MPs and committees does not inspire great optimism about the fate of Martin's promises. If power does shift from the Cabinet to the Commons under Martin's leadership, it is more likely to be the result of minority government than of any deliberate reforms.

The declining influence of our legislative institutions, relative to the executive and judicial branches of government, cannot be reversed by tinkering with the Standing Orders. Nor can it be addressed by individual legislators or caucuses, as Reformers discovered after 1993. Effective reform of our national Parliament would require the following changes to the political system:

- weakening the institutional incentives that foster Cabinet dominance over the House of Commons, particularly the abuse of the confidence convention;
- greater tolerance on the part of ministers for the inevitable delays arising from genuine parliamentary deliberation;
- a more assertive and visible Senate; and
- a more representative Commons, chosen by a more proportional electoral system that encouraged the nomination of more female and visible-minority candidates and divided the seats more proportionally among the various parties (see Chapter 4).

The political barriers to reform are daunting. In particular, as we saw in Chapter 4, electoral reform is a frightening prospect for a governing party. There was no chance that Canada would adopt a more proportional electoral system as long as it was ruled by majority governments. However, the political calculus might be different under a minority government. In October 2004, the minority Liberal government agreed to submit the issue of electoral reform to the Standing Committee on Procedure and House Affairs. This proposal was made by the Conservatives and supported by all of the Opposition parties.

As for the Senate, any significant change (e.g., a more equal distribution of seats among the provinces) would require the support of all 10 provincial governments. As we will see in Chapter 9, Quebec opposes any constitutional change that would diminish its representation in national political institutions; therefore, a Triple-E Senate—*elected,* with *equal* provincial representation, and *effective* powers—is a remote possibility at best. Even if it were possible, an equal distribution of Senate seats among the provinces may not be desirable; it would not give any individual provincial delegation a veto over proposed laws, which raises doubts about its effectiveness, and provincial equality could reduce the legitimacy of the institution in the more populous regions.[44]

Given the political and institutional barriers to meaningful reform of our legislative branch, it is easy to understand why previous reforms have been confined to tinkering with the Standing Orders of the House of Commons (the Standing Orders are available on Parliament's website: www.parl.gc.ca).

These are not entrenched, and may be changed at any time by a majority vote of MPs. But such changes will have little effect, as long as the incentive structure for Cabinets and backbenchers remains intact.

One response to this stalemate is the demand for direct-democracy devices—referenda, initiatives, and recall—which would either supplement our legislative institutions or bypass them altogether (see Dossier 2.4). A less constructive response, one that partly explains the high turnover of Canadian MPs, is reflected in one MP's farewell speech to the House. His unusually blunt words captured the frustration of many of his colleagues, past and present (see Dossier 5.3).

Lee Morrison's disillusionment is not universal, but it is widely shared by MPs and their constituents. Among those who bemoan the "emasculation" of Parliament, some hearken back to a "golden age" in the nineteenth century when legislators were free to speak and vote according to their own convictions and the Cabinet was genuinely accountable to the House. Whether or not this "golden age" really existed, there is little doubt that the influence of our legislative institutions has diminished during the past century or so. The history of British parliamentary government is the story of a continual power struggle between the executive branch (as personified in the Crown) and the elected representatives of the citizens. In recent decades, the development of disciplined parliamentary parties and the growth of the federal government tipped the balance decisively in favour of the Cabinet. To understand the present state of Canada's legislative institutions, we need to look back at the evolution of parliamentary government in Britain.

DOSSIER 5.3 Lee Morrison on the House of Commons[45]

On October 20, 2000, shortly before the House was dissolved for the November general election, MP Lee Morrison bade farewell to the Commons. Morrison had been a member of the Reform caucus elected in 1993, whose hopes for a more open legislative process were dashed by their experiences on Parliament Hill. He had decided not to seek a third term, for reasons that are abundantly clear in his remarks:

Mr. Lee Morrison (Cypress Hills–Grasslands, Canadian Alliance): Mr. Speaker, this will probably be my last day in the House.

I will not regret leaving what has become, under Liberal management, a totally dysfunctional institution. I will not miss the thrill of making well-researched speeches in a virtually empty room. I will not miss working long hours on irrelevant ministerially guided committees. I will not miss the posturing. I will not miss the emasculated government members howling because they do not understand the difference between intelligent heckling and boorish noise. Perhaps it is their subconscious recognition of their own political impotence that drives them to act like hyperactive children.

I do not know what I will be doing for the next few years, but whatever it is I expect that I will be dealing with grown-ups. I am sure that it will be more useful than this past seven years that I have spent in this rubber-stamp Parliament.

I shall not look back.

THE HISTORY AND EVOLUTION OF PARLIAMENTARY INSTITUTIONS[46]

> *One of the strengths of the parliamentary system lies in its traditions and the rules that have evolved over the years. At the same time, Parliament is an adaptable institution, with a capacity to respond to changed circumstances and new demands . . . Procedural rules must be assessed continually and, when necessary, updated. Change is an on-going characteristic of a parliamentary process—not for its own sake, but change that is positive and considered.*[47]

As you read the historical material in this section, you may wonder how it is relevant to today's Canadian Parliament. The reasons are threefold:

1. Unless you understand the constitutional conventions that shape our legislative and executive institutions, you may find their rules and structures perplexing and arbitrary. Once you understand their origins, they become easier to grasp.

2. The history of the Westminster system demonstrates the flexibility of political institutions based on convention and precedent, rather than deliberate constitutional engineering. While institutional adaptation to changing circumstances is slow and difficult, the history of parliamentary government suggests the possibility of future reform.[48]

3. British parliamentary institutions evolved through a long series of power struggles among the Crown, the people, and the legislature that links the two sides. The powers of the Crown are now exercised by the executive branch, both political (the Cabinet) and permanent (the federal public service), and by the judiciary. Canada's Parliament, particularly the House of Commons, is still caught between the conflicting expectations of the other two branches of government, on the one hand, and the electorate on the other. As the policy-making powers of the executive and judicial branches expand, the independent role of Parliament diminishes. As the political values of subcultures within the electorate change, legislators are measured by new standards of performance—and, as we saw in Chapter 2, they are increasingly found wanting. Debates over future reform of the Commons and the Senate can be understood only within this institutional and cultural context.

Most of Canada's national political institutions were inherited from Britain. Our system of responsible government is enshrined in the preamble to the *Constitution Act, 1867,* which gave the new Dominion "A Constitution Similar in Principle to that of the United Kingdom." Such a constitution requires a bicameral Parliament (two separate chambers). The "lower house," elected by the citizens on the basis of "representation by population," controls the public purse and holds the Cabinet to account. In Canada, as in Britain, the lower house is called the House of Commons. Most Cabinet ministers are members of the lower house. The unelected upper house is intended to serve two legislative purposes: to check the power of the Cabinet, and to give "sober second thought" to proposed laws that may have been rushed through the lower house without adequate examination.[49] Canada's upper house, the Senate, is appointed by the prime minister; its members serve until their seventy-fifth birthdays. Britain's upper house, the House of Lords, was traditionally composed of hereditary peers. The eldest son of an aristocrat inherited his father's lands, his title, and his seat in the Lords. During the twentieth century the proportion of hereditary peers shrank, as prime ministers appointed growing numbers of "life peers": lords with honorary titles that could not be passed down to their descendants. In 1999, Britain's Labour government abolished hereditary seats in the upper house; henceforth, all members of the House of Lords will be appointed by the prime minister, just like Canadian senators (although the latter do not receive aristocratic titles).

Britain's "Westminster model" of parliamentary government, which Canada inherited in 1867, gradually took shape over several centuries. Its structure and rules evolved in response to particular historical events, which are briefly described here. The first British Parliament was summoned by King Edward I in 1295. The word "Parliament" is an anglicized version of the French "parlement," or "talking place." Edward invited the peers of the realm, together with representatives of the "commoners" and the Church, to the Palace of Westminster to discuss his cash-flow problem. After King John signed the *Magna Carta* ("great charter") in 1215, the Crown could not raise taxes "without the consent of the Kingdom."

England's tax base was primarily agricultural, although the towns were gaining in economic clout as manufacture and trade grew. The economy of rural England was controlled by landed aristocrats, while the towns were run by guilds. The Church was also an economic force in its own right: its vast landholdings, and the revenues from its parishioners, made it a tempting target for a cash-strapped king. Instead of asking each individual landowner, guildmaster, and bishop for money, it was more efficient to gather them all in one place. In exchange, those assembled presented petitions to the king, seeking redress of local grievances and asking him to settle disputes. The petitions were the forerunner of today's parliamentary Bills. Resolving disputes was part of the Crown's judicial power; the king, as the font of justice, moved his court around the kingdom to hear local cases. We still refer to the institution that dispenses justice as a "court."

The crowd that descended on the Palace of Westminster was too large to sit in the Great Hall, so it was divided into two separate groups: the Lords (including the bishops) and the Commons. The latter met in the chapel, where the benches were arranged in rows down the length of the building, each side facing the centre aisle. To this day, "Westminster" Parliaments use the same seating plan (see Figure 5.1).

King Edward's "model Parliament" was a great success, and the experiment was repeated whenever the Crown needed money (which was quite often, especially during wartime). By 1320, the separation of the two chambers had become a permanent arrangement. By 1340, the Crown had formally conceded the "power of the purse" to the Commons. When kings wanted money, they first had to agree to the demands of Parliament. The "power of the purse" remained the crucial bargaining chip in struggles between the Crown and the legislature. In 1376 the Commons refused to grant "supply"—i.e., tax revenues—to King Edward III, and it elected a

FIGURE 5.1 FLOOR PLAN OF THE CANADIAN HOUSE OF COMMONS

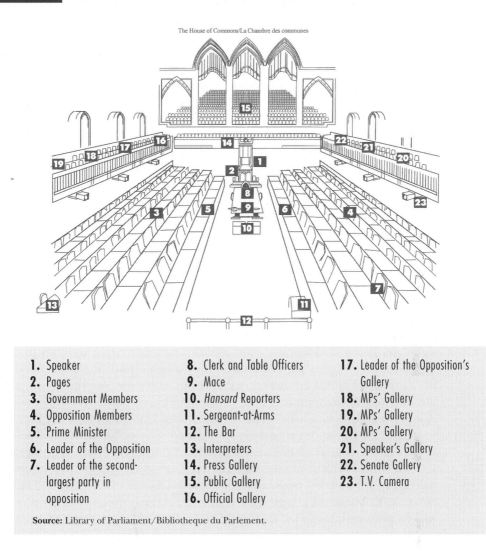

The House of Commons/La Chambre des communes

1. Speaker
2. Pages
3. Government Members
4. Opposition Members
5. Prime Minister
6. Leader of the Opposition
7. Leader of the second-largest party in opposition

8. Clerk and Table Officers
9. Mace
10. *Hansard* Reporters
11. Sergeant-at-Arms
12. The Bar
13. Interpreters
14. Press Gallery
15. Public Gallery
16. Official Gallery

17. Leader of the Opposition's Gallery
18. MPs' Gallery
19. MPs' Gallery
20. MPs' Gallery
21. Speaker's Gallery
22. Senate Gallery
23. T.V. Camera

Source: Library of Parliament/Bibliotheque du Parlement.

Speaker to deliver the bad news.[50] Over time, the Speaker became the liaison between the Commons and the Crown. He chaired parliamentary debates, and reported their results to the king. Members of the Commons addressed their remarks to the Speaker (and not to each other), a practice that survives today. Parliamentary procedure prohibits members of the Commons (who are commonly referred to as members of Parliament, or MPs for short) to speak to each other directly; they must refer to each other in the third person, as "the Honourable Member" from a particular constituency.

English monarchs were happy to cooperate with Parliament when it suited their purposes. A king or queen with a shaky claim to the throne would seek a formal declaration from Parliament recognizing the legitimacy of his or her rule. The most notorious of these declarations is *Titulus Regius* of 1483, which proclaimed Richard III as the lawful ruler of England and declared his nephews—the sons of the late King Edward IV and the true heirs to the throne—to be illegitimate. The legal and factual grounds for *Titulus Regius* were dubious at best, and Richard is now suspected of murdering his nephews in the Tower of London during his brief reign. By that time, two new parliamentary conventions had emerged: the consent of both Houses of Parliament was required for a law to take effect, and there were informal rules for the election of MPs. These were a far cry from today's **universal suffrage**—only a few wealthy men could vote, and they often chose corrupt members who took bribes in exchange for supporting particular Bills. There were no political parties in the modern sense of the word, merely loose parliamentary factions dominated by particular nobles. In the exercise of its executive functions, the monarch relied on his Privy Council. This small group of aristocrats and churchmen was not accountable to Parliament.

The Tudor monarchs (1485–1603) maintained the old relationship between the Crown and Parliament: they summoned Parliament to Westminster at their pleasure (usually when they needed money). However, Elizabeth I (1558–1603) shrewdly recognized the symbolic importance of the Commons as the "voice of England," and used the chamber to strengthen her ties to the people. Her successor, James I, founded the Stuart dynasty (1603–1714). The Stuarts believed that their "divine right" to rule entitled them to govern as absolute monarchs, and they disdained the legislative authority of the Commons. They avoided Parliament whenever possible, relying instead on tax revenues that lay within the Crown's prerogative. When they did summon Parliament, they were confronted by a Protestant majority deeply suspicious of the Catholic Stuarts. The tension boiled over in 1642, when King Charles I burst into the Commons chamber with a group of armed henchmen. They intended to murder, or at least to threaten, the MPs who stubbornly refused to grant supply without concessions from the king. The MPs had been tipped off, and the chamber was empty. (Almost 500 years later, representatives of the Crown are still forbidden to enter the Commons; Canada's governor general reads the Speech from the Throne, which opens each session of the Canadian Parliament, in the Senate Chamber.) After this incident, Parliament declared war on the king. The English Civil War ended in 1649 with the execution of Charles I and the establishment of a republic.

After the Stuarts were restored to the throne in 1660, they managed to avoid further bloodshed. But in 1688, Charles' brother James II was forced to abdicate. Parliament and the nobility invited his daughter Mary and her husband, Prince William of Orange (the ruler of the Netherlands), to rule England and Scotland in his place. In 1689 the new monarchs signed the *Bill of Rights,* which formally established a limited, or constitutional, monarchy and recognized Parliament as the chief law-making body in the realm. In effect, the Crown was no longer above the law; both the monarch and the Privy Council were subject to the laws made by Parliament. Privy councillors would require the support of Parliament, although there was as yet no formal mechanism to hold them accountable. Over time, the Privy Council evolved into the Cabinet: a subcommittee of the Commons and Lords that exercised the Crown's executive powers on behalf of the monarch. By the turn of the eighteenth century, constitutional convention required the monarch to give royal assent to any law passed by Parliament.

In 1714, after the death of the last Stuart monarch, an obscure German prince came to the British throne. Because George I spoke little English, he could not chair Privy Council meetings. In his place, the Council appointed a prime minister. Although officially *primus inter pares* (first among equals), the prime minister gradually became the dominant figure in the political executive. He chose the other members of the Cabinet (which were then formally appointed by the king or queen), he ensured that the Commons would support his Cabinet and grant supply to pay for its policies, and he advised the monarch on the exercise of the Crown's prerogative powers.

During the nineteenth century, the British House of Commons was transformed in two important ways. First, the electorate was expanded from a few wealthy magnates to most of the adult male population. Second, and resulting from the first, disciplined political parties appeared. There had been two contending factions in the Commons, the Whigs and the Tories; the former favoured a more democratic political system, while the latter supported the Crown. With the expansion of the franchise, these parliamentary factions were forced to seek political support across the country. The United Kingdom was already divided into electoral districts (called **constituencies** or ridings), each of which returned one MP to Westminster. Now the two parties (renamed the Liberals and the Conservatives) had to establish political organizations in each riding, to win the support of the newly enfranchised voters.

As the party organizations outside Parliament became stronger, so did party discipline inside Parliament. By the late nineteenth century, Britain's Parliament had assumed a familiar form. The prime minister was the leader of the party that held the most seats in the Commons. He hand-picked members of his caucus to serve in Cabinet, and kept his backbenchers in line with bribes and threats. The government sat at the Speaker's right side. The other party or parties in the Commons, known collectively as the Opposition, sat on the opposite side of the House, facing the government caucus. The largest party on the Speaker's left was the official Opposition, responsible for keeping the government accountable and providing a constructive alternative to the party in power. The Speaker chaired the debates and kept order in the House. The king or queen was a figurehead, with no active role in politics. The Crown's prerogative powers of appointment, legislation, and royal assent remained, but the monarch had lost the discretion to use them as he or she saw fit. The Cabinet reigned supreme.

This was the system of parliamentary government that Canada inherited in 1867. By 1896, as discussed in Chapter 3, a disciplined two-party system had evolved. The prime minister was, if anything, an even more commanding figure in Canada than in Britain, partly because the Liberal and Conservative parties were quite similar ideologically; the leaders, not party principles, became the focus of electoral campaigning. In the twentieth century the power of the political executive vis-à-vis Parliament was further strengthened by the explosive growth of the federal government and the ever-increasing complexity of public policy. Nowadays, the prime minister of Canada is as powerful domestically as any head of government in the world. Some observers argue that the very nature of our political system has been transformed: instead of parliamentary government, we now have prime-ministerial government. We will return to the question of prime-ministerial power in Chapter 6. For now, we will turn to the political resources of the House of Commons and Senate in the continuing struggle between the legislative and executive branches.

THE HOUSE OF COMMONS

Representativeness

Public evaluations of MPs' representativeness focus on two separate issues: Who are they, and what do they do? The answers to these questions are important, notwithstanding the earlier comments about the relative powerlessness of MPs in the legislative process. When MPs are perceived as effective representatives, the House has the legitimacy to support and to challenge the executive branch. If they are perceived as unrepresentative and out of touch with important subcultures, the legitimacy of Parliament suffers.

The debate over the meaning and purpose of parliamentary representation reflects the conflicting political values discussed elsewhere in this book. Three specific conflicts may be identified:

1. Should MPs speak for the national political community as a whole, or for their particular regions? In the trustee model of parliamentary representation, members of the Commons are elected to give voice to the collective will of the nation. They have more information and experience about national issues than their constituents do, and they should exercise their own judgment instead of taking orders from the voters. The opposing view, which has particular appeal for Western populists, treats MPs as delegates from their ridings, whose speeches and votes should reflect the majority opinion of their electors.[51]

   Neither model reflects the reality of the Canadian House of Commons. MPs generally vote according to party, not their own judgment or the will of their constituents. The delegate model is both impractical and unconstitutional, in the sense that it undermines the disciplined parties on which effective Cabinet government ultimately depends. In any case, the division of legislative responsibility between two Houses of Parliament assigns different representational tasks to the Commons and the Senate. The former represents the national electorate. It is elected, at least in theory, on the basis of representation by population ("rep by pop," for short). Although each MP serves a defined geographic area—or, more precisely, the people who live within it—he or she is expected to be more than simply a mouthpiece for local concerns. Collectively, members of the Commons make binding decisions in the national interest. Meanwhile, the Senate was intended to represent the various regional populations—as distinct from provincial governments—in the national legislative process. As we have seen, few Canadians believe that the upper house has been effective in this regard. In reality, the Senate has often used its legislative powers to amend proposed laws in order to make them more sensitive to the particular needs of one or more regions.[52] The government has rejected some of these amendments. This raises an important question: Is the Senate responsible for laws that ignore regional concerns, or should we blame governments that (unlike the Senate) do not include members from every region?

2. Is parliamentary representation confined to the territorial interests embodied in the "government's constitution," or does it also involve the nonterritorial interests embodied in the "citizens' constitution" (Chapter 9)? For example, who does a Liberal Jamaican Canadian female MP from Toronto really represent in Parliament: Visible minorities? Women? The Liberal Party? The government? Her particular constituency? The entire Toronto area? The province of Ontario? Any or all of the above? The claim that she represents women or visible minorities reflects the **numerical** or **pictorial** approach to political representation. From this perspective, parliamentary institutions should be microcosms of the Canadian electorate, with the same balance of demographic characteristics found in the broader population. The claim that she represents the Liberal Party, and the government that it controls, reflects the partisan model of representation. Most candidates for the House of Commons are long-time members of their respective parties who are wholeheartedly committed to the goals and principles of their political "teams." Responsible Cabinet government requires that the political executive maintain the support of the House, which means in practice that government backbenchers must vote in favour of the initiatives put forth by their party leaders. While partisan representation is the strongest institutional norm faced by most MPs, its legitimacy among voters has diminished in recent decades.

The claim that the female MP from Toronto represents her region—in this case, the City of Toronto or the Province of Ontario—reflects the territorial approach to representation. She is expected to promote the interests of her region, by lobbying for increased government spending in that area and by expressing local concerns about proposed legislation. Finally, the claim that she represents her constituency reflects both a territorial and a functional understanding of representation. She must speak on behalf of her entire riding within Parliament, while working hard for individual constituents who request her assistance.

In practice, every MP has to juggle at least three conflicting representational tasks: partisan, territorial, and functional. Female MPs, and those who belong to particular demographic minorities, face additional demands for representation. In recent years, the Senate has become the more "representative" House in the pictorial sense: "The patronage prerogative lets the Prime Minister compensate somewhat for imbalances of gender and race in the elected House."[53] Whereas the proportion of women in the House of Commons has been stuck at just over 20 percent since 1997, no such "glass ceiling" is apparent in the Senate; recent prime ministers have increased the percentage of women in the upper house to around one-third.[54] In a similar vein, members of visible minorities and Aboriginal Canadians make up a considerably higher proportion of the Senate than the Commons.[55]

3. Is the whole idea of representative democracy outdated? In other words, should we continue to elect MPs to speak and vote on our behalf, or should we take advantage of new technologies to make public decisions for ourselves through referenda and initiatives? As we saw in Chapter 2, direct democracy is an increasingly popular alternative to a parliamentary system that fails to meet the expectations of many Canadians. The success of the Reform Party (subsequently the Canadian Alliance, now the Conservative Party) in Western Canada and parts of Ontario is based, in large measure, on its critique of party discipline and Cabinet dominance. Many Reform/Alliance voters favoured the delegate model of representation, condemning MPs who follow the party line as traitors to the people who elected them. At the very least, direct democracy advocates argue that voters should have the power to recall MPs who do not represent their interests effectively (see Dossier 2.4). However, the political force of arguments for populist reform (or bypass) of Canada's legislative institutions has diminished in the past few years, as the Reform Party morphed into the Canadian Alliance and then the Conservative Party; the latter's statement of principles makes no mention of plebiscitary democracy or recall votes.

In the public mind, Canada's legislative institutions have not kept pace with changing political values. Evolving notions of representation, together with increasing skepticism about "top-down" politics, have apparently alienated many voters from their elected representatives. The institutional norms of Cabinet dominance, party discipline, and adversarialism evolved over centuries. In moderation, they make responsible government possible; in excess, they damage the reputation of both Houses of Parliament—notwithstanding the fact that each norm is considerably weaker in the Senate than in the Commons. Without a clear public consensus about the meaning of political representation and a better understanding of the institutional incentives that shape the behaviour of our elected officials, the mismatch between MPs' behaviour and the expectations of voters will likely continue.

Rep by Pop?

There are currently 308 seats in the House of Commons. Provincial representation ranges from 106 seats in Ontario to 4 in Prince Edward Island and 1 for each of the three territories. While seats are distributed across the provinces in rough proportion to their respective shares of the national population, there are some important exceptions to "rep by pop" (the shorthand form of "representation by population"). Prince Edward Island and New Brunswick are over-represented in the House because of the "senatorial floor rule," a constitutional provision specifying that a province cannot have fewer MPs than it has senators.[56] Because of the practical problems associated with their size, the northern territories are also over-represented.[57] Manitoba, Newfoundland, Nova Scotia, Saskatchewan, and Quebec are perpetually guaranteed the same number of seats they held when the present redistribution scheme was adopted in 1985.[58] These provisions, together with practical limits on the overall size of the Commons, have penalized the three provinces whose population has grown substantially since 1985; if seats were allocated strictly according to population, Ontario would have 117 seats rather than 106, British Columbia would have 40 rather than 36, and Alberta would have 31 rather than 28.[59]

The Representation of Nonterritorial Groups

Historically, most MPs have been white males from professional and business backgrounds. Although the demographic composition of the national and provincial legislatures is changing, it does not fully reflect the diversity of Canada's population. The under-representation of women has been a matter of concern since the 1970s (see Chapter 4); more recently, there have been complaints about the scarcity of visible-minority and Aboriginal MPs, and MPs with disabilities.[60]

The proportion of women and visible minorities in Parliament is not just an issue of abstract fairness or "political correctness." While there are no guarantees, it is sometimes argued that a "critical mass" of female legislators (15 percent or higher) can raise the level of debate and produce better legislation.[61] But female MPs and senators who wish to represent Canadian women in more than a numerical way face a number of obstacles. They are divided along party lines, constricted by party discipline, and disproportionately concentrated in "touchy-feely" Cabinet portfolios and standing committees (the "pink-collar ghetto" of public policy).[62]

Some women have brought a strong feminist sensibility to Canadian politics; Kim Campbell's work on the "rape shield" as Justice minister is a good example (see "The Transformation of Judicial Review in the *Charter* Era" in Chapter 10). Others abhor feminism and refuse to identify themselves as spokespersons for Canadian women in general. The situation of women in the House of Commons illustrates a central flaw in the numerical or pictorial approach to representation: unless the designated "representatives" actively seek to promote the interests of "their" groups, however they define those interests, they are little more than "tokens." It can be argued that some male MPs, such as the NDP's Svend Robinson (former MP for Burnaby–Douglas),[63] have been more effective advocates of gender equality than the nonfeminist women in the House.

◼ Casework: The MP as Constituency Representative

While there is considerable confusion about the numerical aspects of parliamentary representation, few MPs have any doubt about their importance as constituency representatives. Constituency service has two dimensions:

1. The MP is an informal ombudsman[64] for individual constituents who become entangled in disputes about pensions, Employment Insurance, passports, agricultural subsidies, and a myriad of other program areas in which the federal government plays a role. This is the "casework" aspect of parliamentary service.

2. MPs lobby the government for program spending and public services that will benefit their constituencies as a whole. Examples include public works, job-creation funds, and the location of federal government offices outside Ottawa.

Most parliamentary candidates have extensive backgrounds in volunteer community service, in addition to their partisan activities.[65] Many are inspired to run for public office as a result of their community involvement. At least half of all MPs cite constituency service as the most important factor in their initial decision to seek election.[66]

On average, most MPs devote significantly more time to constituency service than to any other aspect of their jobs, including legislative work and policy development.[67] (Committee chairs are often an exception to this rule.[68]) Even those who were motivated to run because of other factors, such as partisanship or policy interest, quickly become active ombudsmen. There are at least three reasons for the emphasis on constituency work:

- First, MPs fear the electoral consequences of neglecting their constituents. There is some evidence that dedicated service boosts the odds of re-election,[69] although this "personal vote" does not become an important factor until after the first two terms in office.[70] This is hardly surprising, given the low priority that most Canadians attach to personal assistance from their MPs. Whether or not good service brings rewards, however, MPs are convinced that "a failure to engage in district work can kill members politically."[71]

- Second, MPs whose Cabinet ambitions are thwarted or their policy preferences ignored can still find job satisfaction in helping their constituents. Changing government policy is a slow process with no guarantee of success, but cutting through red tape on behalf of a voter brings instant gratification to both parties.

- Third, constituency service is not constrained by party discipline. It is true that government MPs have more frequent access to ministers, which can make it easier to resolve particular cases. But in general, Cabinet members and public servants assist all MPs without discrimination on the basis of party.

Despite the enormous time and effort that most MPs invest in their constituencies, most Canadian voters perceive them as unresponsive and unconcerned. Between 1965 and 1993, the percentage of respondents who agreed that "Those elected to Parliament soon lose touch with the people" rose dramatically. Over the past decade, popular sentiment has become marginally more positive. Whereas 76 percent of respondents to a 1990 survey perceived MPs as "out of touch," that figure fell to 69 percent in 2000.[72] This improvement in the public perception of MPs is difficult to explain, but perhaps it can be attributed in part to the experiences of constituents.

Members of the public who are cynical towards federal politicians constitute the majority of citizens who have not had to turn to their MP for assistance. For many voters, their member of parliament is the buffer between them and a faceless or far-removed system of government. They leave their MP's constituency office feeling that they have a voice in Ottawa to represent their specific interests and needs.[73]

Adversarial Politics and Party Discipline

Public discontent with the House of Commons goes well beyond concerns about representativeness. We have seen that as the political values of the population change, institutions that embody older values may suffer a loss of legitimacy. The behavioural norms at the heart of parliamentary democracy are increasingly out of step with public opinion, particularly adversarial politics and party discipline.

Adversarial Politics

The very architecture of Parliament encourages mutual hostility: government and Opposition MPs confront each other across a centre aisle, their physical disposition signalling that there are two opposing sides to the issue at hand and little if any common ground. The most basic rules and procedures of parliamentary debate encourage this clash of opposing teams. The objective of parliamentary debate is not to reach a compromise solution, not to find the best possible outcome, but

Deborah Grey of the Democratic Representative Coalition stands during Question Period as other members of the coalition and the Progressive Conservative Party look on in the House of Commons (September 19, 2001). (© CP/Tom Hanson)

PARLIAMENTARY DEMOCRACY AND THE LEGISLATIVE PROCESS

rather to present two vigorously opposing points of view, with the electorate left to judge. The adversarial character of the House shapes its most basic operating rules and procedures.

It would be incorrect, however, to attribute the public conflict among parliamentary caucuses entirely to the rules of Parliament. While institutional norms and structures do have a powerful influence on individual and group behaviour, there are other reasons for the adversarial nature of the Commons. As we have seen, the length and trajectory of Canadian political careers are strongly influenced by an MP's relationship to his or her party. Most MPs are enthusiastic partisans, imbued with a powerful "team spirit." They genuinely believe that their particular party has the best answers to the public questions of the day, and they wish to support and assist the other players on their team. In a high-pressure situation such as Question Period (QP), these emotions come to the fore in boisterous and sometimes undignified ways. Perhaps because the overwhelming majority of Canadians—84 percent, according to a 2000 survey[74]—have never belonged to political parties, they find these noisy partisan displays puzzling and distasteful. In a 1997 survey, fully 90 percent of respondents agreed with the statement that "Canadian parties bicker too much"; 59 percent accused the parties of dividing the country, instead of bringing people together.[75]

The public perception of MPs as brawling combatants is greatly exaggerated. In private, many parliamentarians from different parties like and respect each other, and they can work together harmoniously. Because the television cameras in the Commons chamber must focus on the member who is speaking at a given moment, viewers rarely witness the off-camera chats between members of differing partisan stripes. News reporters prefer to cover conflict, not cooperation; consequently, Canadians receive a distorted picture of the Commons. Journalists focus on the fireworks provided by the 40-minute daily Question Period,[76] which is held every day that the House is in session. Members of the Cabinet, including the prime minister, are grilled by Opposition MPs about the public issues of the day. Symbolically, at least, QP gives the Opposition a chance to hold the government accountable to the House and to the electorate. Its effectiveness in this regard is open to debate. A former public official points out that "There are few instances where sustained opposition attacks have severely damaged a government or caused it to change its policy."[77] Questions by government backbenchers are much less frequent. They are usually employed to set up favourable statements by ministers: "Would the minister of Finance please explain to the House how he has been so successful in wrestling inflation to the ground, easing unemployment, and setting Canada on the path to economic prosperity?"

Question Period is valued by Opposition MPs and journalists because it forces ministers, day in and day out, to respond to their critics. It is the best opportunity for Opposition parties to mobilize the public and draw media attention to problems in government policy and performance. As we will see in Chapter 6, the top levels of the executive branch—both political and permanent—spend much of their time protecting the prime minister from embarrassing questions by Opposition MPs. Chapter 7 describes the close working relationship between the Opposition and the

At 2:15 p.m., four times each week, 11:15 on Fridays, the Speaker of the House of Commons calls for oral questions. The leader of the official Opposition rises in his place, is recognized by the Speaker, and begins the day's grilling of the government. Nowhere else in the world, even in the "Mother of Parliaments" in the United Kingdom, is the entire government held to daily account in such a fashion, being subjected to questions about virtually any of its programmes and policies.

Amid applause and shouts of encouragement from his caucus colleagues, and catcalls and heckling from those opposite, the Opposition Leader calls on a member of the Cabinet to respond to some matter of urgent and pressing need, some great calamity that has befallen Canada since the day before, a question about which the Government has received no official notice.

Usually to similar noise and action, that Cabinet minister, or the prime minister, will rise and respond, stating that whatever has exercised the member opposite has been solved already, will be taken under advisement, or, most often, is not really of any consequence or importance to any except those who have been less favoured by the voters. The rhetorical barbs fly in both directions, reminding us why the benches of the House are set two sword-lengths apart. The process of question and answer, supplementary and reply, is repeated 10 to 12 times, in this apparent free-for-all that is the pinnacle of government accountability in Canada—the daily question period.

According to the rules and to tradition, the Speaker of the House controls question period, which is known as QP to the gaggle of insiders who seemingly make it the central concern of their life. The Speaker will see a member rising in his place and call on the MP to direct a question to the government. Any Member can be called on, in any order, from any party. To those watching the live broadcasts at home this appears to be what is occurring.

But for those on the floor of the House, or in its galleries, there is another reality. While many Members may indeed be rising in their places, the Speaker is calling them not as he sees them, but from lists supplied by the House Leaders of the two opposition parties. These lists are often amended as QP progresses, changes called to the Speaker from House Leaders—who sometimes appear more like baseball managers signaling their on-deck batters and runners to bunt, steal, or run—by waving arms, pointing, nodding and stepping into the fray as the moment dictates. . . .

So, even though it may appear to be mayhem to the uninitiated, the degree of management that goes into the planning of question period is considerable. The effort to get the right "spin" onto an issue, to attract the attention of the media and of the government, consumes a great deal of time for a large number of people every day the House is in session, an effort that goes unnoticed, perhaps intentionally so, by those who watch from the outside.

Source: Reprinted with permission from Michael Kalnay, "Managed Mayhem: Question Period in the House of Commons," *Parliamentary Government*, 8, no. 4 (Summer 1989), 3–6.

news media, who share and exploit juicy revelations about government mistakes. Any Cabinet minister or senior public servant who exposes the prime minister to embarrassment in QP can expect to suffer political consequences.

Although Opposition MPs have strong incentives to make the prime minister look bad, the Cabinet and central agencies have equally strong incentives to make the prime minister look good. They also have the means at their disposal to minimize the political damage inflicted in QP. Experienced ministers can evade questions by ridiculing the Opposition, a skill at which former Prime Minister Chrétien excelled. Central agencies often refuse to share detailed information about policy and administration with Opposition MPs,[78] although they may be forced to comply with Access to Information requests filed by parliamentarians or journalists.[79] Over the long term, the entire House of Commons pays a price for short-term victories in QP: while journalists love to see ministers squirm, the media coverage of Question Period captures MPs in their most adversarial and abrasive temper and further erodes public confidence in parliamentary institutions.

Party Discipline

We have seen that MPs have powerful incentives to follow the party line, even though many voters perceive strict party discipline as illegitimate. Between 1990 and 2000, the percentage of Canadians who believed that MPs should vote freely, instead of along party lines, rose from 72 to 77 percent.[80] The very term "party discipline" suggests—incorrectly—that MPs are forcibly prevented from breaking ranks, under threat of punishment. It is true that an MP, especially a government MP, who votes against his or her party on an important issue pays a high price. Any chance of a Cabinet appointment may be lost and access to key decision-makers curtailed. Prized committee assignments are taken away. When committee chairs were appointed by the prime minister (pre-2002), they risked being fired for insubordination. Projects and programs of interest to a dissident MP's constituency may be threatened. Thus, the incentive structures of Parliament reinforce party discipline in a variety of ways. It is also true that votes in the House are orchestrated by the party "whips," a term that reinforces the negative connotations of party discipline.[81]

In most cases, however, parliamentarians willingly vote with their parties; while MPs are aware of the sanctions just listed, they rarely incur them by breaking ranks in public.[82] There are at least three reasons why MPs choose to follow the party line:

1. They believe that they are morally obliged to keep their campaign promises. Where a particular Bill relates directly to their party's platform, or to its core principles, most MPs feel duty-bound to express the views of their party.[83]
2. Party discipline shields MPs from vocal and aggressive minority interests.[84] In such cases, an MP may believe that his party's position is a more faithful reflection of majority opinion, or he may simply wish to deflect the blame for offending voters on one (or all) sides of a contentious issue.[85]

3. If every member of a caucus votes with the party leadership, all of them are protected from constituency reprisals. When one or more MPs defy the whip and vote against their party, their teammates are left exposed to public criticism.[86] Therefore, backbenchers often pressure each other to toe the party line, instead of relying on caucus officers to twist arms.

In moderation, party discipline is necessary for the smooth operation of government. A Cabinet that cannot depend on the support of its caucus cannot govern effectively. Canadians who fail to understand the workings of responsible parliamentary government may perceive their MPs as "trained seals" who slavishly place the interests of their party above the interests of their constituents and even their principles. In fact, MPs constantly lobby for their constituency and regional interests in caucus and in meetings with Cabinet ministers and bureaucrats. Unfortunately, these lobbying efforts take place behind closed doors. Therefore, they do not enhance the public's image of Parliament.

◼ Parliament and the Public Purse

The established procedures for handling supply in the House of Commons are based on two fundamental principles. If it is to continue with its activities, Government must have some assurance that its requests for funds be answered by certain fixed dates. Parliament, on the other hand, must be assured reasonable opportunity to examine these requests before they are granted. The first principle recognizes the need for an efficient, smoothly functioning government, the second the importance of accountability, a central tenet of parliamentary democracy.[87]

As we have seen, the lower house in a Westminster Parliament has the constitutional right to control the public purse. However, the Crown retains the power to propose spending and revenue measures. In other words, money Bills and taxes must be *approved* by the House of Commons, but they cannot be *proposed* by anyone other than a member of the Cabinet. These British constitutional conventions are entrenched in sections 53 and 54 of the *Constitution Act, 1867*. The process by which Parliament approves the Cabinet's tax and spending plans is divided into two parts: Ways and Means motions, which authorize the Crown to collect revenues; and Supply motions, which authorize spending on the hundreds of different programs and services provided by the federal government.[88] The spending approved by Parliament takes two forms: the annual Main Estimates, which must be approved by May 31 of each year, and two subsequent sets of Supplementary Estimates, which allow the government to alter its original spending plans (within limits) in response to unforeseen events. The first set of Supplementary Estimates must be passed before December 10, and the second before March 26.[89]

Because public finance is crucial to the operations of government, majority Governments control with an iron hand the Business of Supply, the official name of the process by which the government asks Parliament to appropriate (or authorize) the funds required to meet its financial obligations. This control takes two forms. First, the deadlines are strictly enforced in the Chamber (under the normal rules of debate, and in Committee of the Whole) and in standing committees. Second, the government's preferred allocation of funds to particular programs is preserved intact—even though the Standing Orders allow some modifications at the committee stage.[90] While the current procedures give the executive branch greater stability and predictability in its financial arrangements, they have deprived the House of Commons of one of its key constitutional functions: "It is reassuring to know that government and the vast array of services it provides can continue to function free of interruption, yet it is enormously troubling, to say the least, that the vast sums of money spent by government are subjected to only perfunctory parliamentary scrutiny."[91] However, minority governments may find the Supply deadlines more difficult to enforce.[92] If they choose, the Opposition parties can delay voting on the Estimates, in order to force the government to make concessions on other matters.

Ideally, the Business of Supply allows MPs to develop expertise about the machinery of government. It also gives them a golden opportunity to hold the political and permanent executives accountable to the electorate for their policies, their spending plans, and the overall expenditure of tax dollars. Because MPs have the final word on public spending, their advice should be sought early in the budget process; that advice should be based on full and complete information, to which the parliamentarians apply their own experience and expertise in public policy.[93] None of these ideal conditions exists in Canada. The first principle described in the above quotation has triumphed over the second: the quest for administrative efficiency has all but eliminated Parliament's power to hold the executive accountable for its use of public funds.

- Every year, on or before March 1, the Main Estimates are tabled in the Commons and referred to the appropriate standing committees. Each committee must report back to the House no later than May 31. If committee members miss the deadline, they are deemed to have reported the Estimates without amendment. As a result, there is little incentive for committee members to devote scarce time and energy to reviewing the government's spending plans.[94] Each item in the Estimates is treated as a separate motion, called a vote. The committee can deal with a vote in one of three ways: it can approve the proposed expenditure, reduce the amount to a specified figure, or reject it altogether.[95] Committees may not increase the amount allocated to any item; only the Crown can propose new expenditures. Nor can committees reallocate funds from one vote to another. Because of these restrictions, and the constraints imposed by party discipline in a majority government, MPs devote little time and effort to the Estimates. In 1990, for example, the 20 standing committees held fewer than 50 meetings on the Estimates, and none reported back to the House.[96] Matters had improved somewhat by 2001, when 10 committees reported on the Main Estimates, but none proposed any amendments, despite their formal power to do so.[97]

- The fiscal year is divided into three "supply periods," ending on December 10, March 26, and June 30. For each period, the government tables an *Appropriation Act* authorizing its overall expenditure. These general spending measures, unlike the detailed Estimates, are handled in Committee of the Whole (see "The Committee System" on page 245). The speed with which the Committee of the Whole disposes of these Acts does not inspire confidence in Parliament's scrutiny of government spending. The first *Appropriation Act* for the 2000–01 fiscal year is a typical case. In a few hours on a single day, the Act was introduced and read the first time; read the second time and referred to a Committee of the Whole; considered in Committee of the Whole; reported without amendment; concurred in at report stage; read the third time and passed.[98] This process may be admirably efficient, but it does not permit meaningful deliberation or accountability.

- In recent years, committees have been given more opportunity to participate in the formulation of future spending plans. The pre-budget consultations conducted by the Standing Committee on Finance are the most important part of this process; other standing committees also propose new spending initiatives in their policy reviews, which may be taken into consideration by the government as it crafts the next year's budget. The pre-budget work of committees is an important opportunity for interest groups and individual Canadians to express their views and lobby for their spending priorities; in 2001, for example, the Finance Committee heard from almost 250 witnesses.[99]

  However, the actual influence of the committee reports seems to be limited. As we have seen, a majority government can block any committee that seeks to challenge its fiscal plans (although, as noted earlier, committees may have more power in minority Parliaments). Moreover, few MPs are experts in the technical details of public finance. They have little opportunity to master the arcana of fiscal management. After repeated demands from committees, public servants in the Treasury Board Secretariat (TBS) have made some effort to clarify and explain the Estimates and related documents. But these efforts have not gone far enough, in the opinion of the Standing Committee on Government Operations and Estimates. In some cases, TBS officials have invoked Cabinet confidentiality (Chapter 6) as a reason for withholding information from Parliament; elsewhere, experts have argued that the Royal Recommendation process prevents the TBS from sharing details with MPs.[100] More generally, public servants from the various departments have an enormous advantage over MPs: years of experience, an intimate knowledge of past and present policy, and extensive control over the flow of information. They may also have a vested interest in particular spending priorities and the means to defend them against the most determined opposition. In short, they have no incentive to provide clear information to Parliament.[101]

Widespread dissatisfaction with the current system has provoked repeated calls by MPs for greater control over government finance. One recent proposal for reform has already produced some significant improvements in Parliament's oversight of the executive. In 1998 the Standing Committee on Procedure and House Affairs (SCPHA) recommended the creation of a new Standing Committee on the Estimates.[102] The proposed committee would review and report on the Estimates process and assist the other standing committees in their consideration of the votes for their particular departments. Proponents of the reform identified three advantages of assigning a group of MPs to work on the Estimates full-time: it would allow the other committees to focus more effectively on the other parts of their mandates (reviewing legislation and investigating policy issues); it would create a pool of MPs with specialized knowledge of public finance; and it would give the Estimates committee an overview of the government's tax and spending programs, resulting in a broader perspective on each individual vote.

The new Standing Committee on Government Operations and Estimates (SCGOE) was established in May 2002. Its mandate was not exactly as the SCPHA had recommended, insofar as the Estimates for specific government departments were still automatically referred to other standing committees. However, the SCGOE mandate contained three significant items: it had the power to review any Estimates that it considered to be important; it was empowered to propose further reforms to the Estimates process; and it was given the power to review the spending of the Privacy Commissioner and other officers of Parliament.[103]

The new committee set to work with a will. Within a year, it had tested some of the recommendations put forward in previous reports. Its sixth report summarized the results of those tests, and called on the government to amend the Estimates process. Among other things, it demanded greater clarity and openness from the TBS and other departments; it suggested that each standing committee be given the information needed to prepare properly for reviewing the Main and Supplementary Estimates; and it called for sanctions on committees that failed to devote adequate attention to the government's spending plans (thus creating an incentive to offset the "deeming" rule).[104] The government's official response to the report accepted most of the recommendations, and set out procedures for putting them into practice.[105]

While the long-term benefits of these recommendations may well be significant, it was a short-term project of the Estimates committee that captured public and media attention in the spring of 2003. This was an intensive review of the Office of the Privacy Commissioner, which fell under the specific mandate of the SCGOE. For the first time, a senior public official—then-Commissioner George Radwanski—was forced from office by a parliamentary committee. The "Radwanski affair" is described in Dossier 5.5.

While Parliamentary scrutiny of public spending is often sporadic and superficial, there is one notable exception. The Public Accounts Committee (PAC) is a standing committee of the House empowered to review the government's handling of public money. Unlike the other standing committees, which review Estimates for the next fiscal year, the PAC focuses on previous government spending. Historically, the PAC is unique among parliamentary committees: most standing committees are chaired by government MPs, who (until recently) were chosen by the prime minister. The PAC is the only committee chaired by a member of the official Opposition.

In late 2002, an Opposition motion to amend the Standing Orders garnered the support of a majority of MPs; it allowed committees to elect their own chairs without interference from the prime minister. Under the new rules, the committee elects a chair and two vice chairs at the beginning of each session of a new Parliament. The

In March 2003, the Standing Committee on Government Operations and Estimates began to investigate spending in the Office of the Privacy Commissioner (OPC). By June, whistleblowers in the OPC were secretly contacting the committee. They alleged that the Privacy Commissioner, George Radwanski, was spending lavishly on his own travel and entertainment; that he hired and promoted on the basis of favouritism, contrary to the rules set by the Public Service Commission; and that he mistreated employees whom he did not like.[106] These accusations of financial mismanagement and abuse of personnel caught the committee's attention, partly because of heightened public concern about these issues in the wake of the sponsorship scandal (Dossier 6.2).

The Estimates committee chair, Liberal MP Reg Alcock, began an investigation into the allegations against Radwanski. The SCGOE held a series of hearings, some public and some *in camera*, to determine the extent of the problems. The *in camera* meetings heard from employees of the Privacy Commissioner, who feared for their jobs if their comments were made public. Radwanski, a former journalist, defended himself vigorously at every opportunity. He charged that the investigation was a political witch-hunt, and that he had done nothing wrong. There might have been a grain of truth in his claim that the committee was motivated by politics, and not simply by concern for the public purse; after all, Radwanski had been hand-picked by Prime Minister Chrétien, whereas Alcock (like some other Liberals on the committee) was a prominent supporter of Paul Martin.

Additionally, the Liberal majority might have been tempted to scapegoat a public official in order to rehabilitate an image that had been tarnished by allegations of corruption.

Whatever the motivations for beginning the investigation, the Estimates committee hearings produced testimony and documentary evidence to substantiate the whistleblowers' claims. To make matters worse, it was discovered that Radwanski, or someone on his staff, had deleted a paragraph from a document before submitting it in evidence to the committee, and that steps had been taken to disguise the alteration of the document. Moreover, Radwanski claimed that he had submitted all information relating to his travel and hospitality expenses during a specified period of time; this claim was contradicted by evidence obtained from public servants in his office, which showed that Radwanski had incurred at least $90 000 in expenses that he had failed to disclose to the MPs.[107]

The committee's report detailed Radwanski's frequent indulgence in costly meals and travel at public expense, and questioned whether all of these expenditures were necessary for him to carry out his job. It also described the tense and sometimes hostile atmosphere that he created in the Office of the Privacy Commissioner, an atmosphere that the report described as "authoritarian" and "bullying."[108] Altogether, the SCGOE investigation produced a stinging indictment of Radwanski's tenure in office. Even before the report appeared, the Commissioner bowed to intense public pressure and resigned. In September 2003 the Public

(cont'd)

Service Commission echoed the criticism of Radwanski's hiring practices, and announced that it would investigate seven potentially fraudulent hiring decisions.[109] The following day, Auditor General Sheila Fraser issued a report that found Radwanski guilty of "abus[ing] the public treasury for the benefit of the former Commissioner and a few senior executives";[110] she formally requested a criminal investigation by the RCMP. Radwanski continued to deny any wrongdoing, claiming that he was the victim of a "smear campaign" and a "vicious personal attack."[111]

The fallout from the Radwanski debacle has affected the entire federal government. The fact that a standing committee stuck together across party lines, flexed its political muscles, and brought down a senior public official sets a potentially valuable precedent for the future. It may give other committees an incentive to take their financial accountability roles more seriously, knowing that their reports can have a real impact on the executive branch.

However, the Radwanski affair also provides a cautionary tale for would-be crusading committee chairs. After Alcock was named president of the Treasury Board in December 2003, he quickly alienated the federal public service with his aggressive style. The tough-minded (albeit fair-minded) way in which he spearheaded the investigation of Radwanski had sent a chill through the permanent executive, which deepened when Alcock immediately banned new hiring and initiated an expenditure-review process to cut federal spending.[112] Although some of his new measures (particularly the appointment of departmental comptrollers, discussed in Chapter 6) may turn out to be beneficial, Alcock's image as a "bureaucrat-basher" provoked resistance and hostility in the ranks. Before Prime Minister Martin appointed his second Cabinet in July 2004, media reports suggested that Alcock's reappointment as president of the Treasury Board could trigger the resignations of several senior public servants.[113] Alcock kept his job, but responsibility for the expenditure review was quietly shifted to Revenue Minister John McCallum.[114]

chair and one of the vice chairs comes from the governing party, while the other vice chair is drawn from one of the Opposition parties.[115] The exceptions are the PAC, which is still chaired by an Opposition MP, and the new Standing Committee on Government Operations and Estimates, which is chaired by a Liberal MP but whose vice chairs (at least, in the spring of 2004) were both from the Opposition side (one Conservative, one BQ).[116] The independence of the PAC from the government is usually compromised by the fact that a majority of its members are from the governing party. Under a minority government, the PAC can operate with fewer constraints.

Although the PAC is the official parliamentary "watchdog" of government spending, it lacks the resources to monitor a huge and complex executive branch. It relies on the experts in the Office of the Auditor General for detailed information about the activities of the permanent executive.[117] The auditor general is an officer of Parliament, who reports to the House at least once a year. These reports attract intense media coverage for their scathing and occasionally bizarre stories of fiscal mismanagement. The PAC draws considerably less attention, but its cooperation with successive auditors general has enhanced Parliament's control of the public purse.

The downside of the "power of the purse" is the risk that partisan rancour and scandal-hungry reporters will distort the process of fiscal accountability (Dossier 5.6).

DOSSIER 5.6 The "Billion-Dollar Boondoggle" That Never Was

In the mid-1990s, the newly created department of Human Resources Development Canada (HRDC) administered programs costing more than $50 billion annually. Approximately $3.3 billion of the total was spent on grants and contributions to agencies outside the federal government: provincial and local governments, private-sector companies, and volunteer agencies working with young people, the illiterate, and the unemployed.[118] One such program was the $100 million Transitional Jobs Fund (TJF), which was designed to promote job creation in areas of high unemployment. To access the TJF funds, companies and community agencies would submit grant proposals to local HRDC offices. The private-sector partners were expected to invest their own money, which would be supplemented by TJF grants. The proposals were evaluated by the front-line public servants, according to flexible criteria that allowed them to tailor the program to local needs. Unusually, proposals submitted in a particular federal constituency were also reviewed by the local MP; in most cases, they required the approval of the provincial government before the money could be released.[119]

In 1998 HRDC undertook an internal audit of selected grants and contributions programs—those involving local companies and volunteer agencies—whose combined annual budget totalled $1 billion. The audit was undertaken in response to concerns about financial management and control of the program (see Dossier 6.7). Senior managers at HRDC headquarters reviewed a sample of 459 project files from the various grants and contributions programs. The results were troubling. Most of the files were incomplete, lacking one or more of the required documents.[120] The sloppy paperwork at the local HRDC offices made it impossible, in some cases, for the central office to determine whether the conditions attached to the grants had been met, and the money allocated to the projects properly spent.

In early 1999, the then-minister of HRDC, Jane Stewart, took the unusual step of making the internal audit public. The news media and the Opposition in the House of Commons pounced on the results. They jumped to the conclusion that the entire $1 billion in annual grants and contributions had been mismanaged. Within the first 24 hours, the legend of the "billion-dollar boondoggle" was born. Question Period became a daily ordeal for Stewart, who faced furious attacks from the Reform Opposition—egged on by the *National Post* newspaper and other media outlets.[121] Stewart and her senior officials

(cont'd)

were called on the carpet before the Standing Committee on Human Resource Development. Opposition MPs alleged that the TJF, in particular, had been disproportionately targeted to Liberal ridings. There were loud calls for the prime minister to fire Stewart and her former deputy, Mel Cappe (then recently promoted to Clerk of the Privy Council). Prime Minister Chrétien aggressively defended his Cabinet colleague and her department. His favourite tactic was to remind the Commons that several Opposition MPs had participated in the TJF review process, and that their ridings had benefited from the program.[122] The "billion-dollar boondoggle" dominated the parliamentary agenda and the news coverage of national politics for several weeks.

Neither the Opposition nor (for the most part) the Press Gallery paid much attention to the actual results of the audit, or to the remedial measures that HRDC had already taken by the time those results were released to the public. In all the excitement about the alleged "Liberal slush fund" and the "missing" billion dollars, few people seemed to notice the conclusion of a follow-up audit of 17 000 program files: there was no missing money—every grant could be accounted for. The HRDC management did identify some debts owing to the government from individual program sponsors. The outstanding debt totalled $65 000—a far cry from $1 billion.[123] Neither the news media nor the Opposition wanted to hear this conclusion, or to report the "boring" details of the department's corrective plan. "This information was downplayed and largely ignored because it was significantly different from the original storyline that $1 billion had been lost."[124]

◼ Holding the Executive to Account

In a parliamentary democracy, the legislative branch is supposed to hold the executive branch accountable to the electorate. While the Commons has little direct control over the permanent executive—apart from committee scrutiny of Order-in-Council appointments, including deputy ministers and ambassadors—it does have the constitutional right to remove the political executive from office. If the House defeats a money Bill or passes a motion of no confidence in the government, the government is deemed to have lost the support of the House. (Defeat in the Senate does not affect the status of the government, because the Senate is not a "confidence chamber.") Recall that executive power in Canada is still vested in the Crown, which delegates that power to a Cabinet with the support of the Commons. If that support is lost, constitutional convention requires the prime minister to relinquish executive power and seek a new mandate from the electorate. In practice, however, a prime minister who loses a vote on a money Bill has two options:

1. He can resign immediately and ask the governor general to dissolve the House for a general election. Technically, the governor general has the right to refuse the request and ask another party leader to form a government. This option has not been used since 1926;[125] as a matter of constitutional convention, its revival

is extremely unlikely. Most recently, the minority Conservative government of Joe Clark lost a budget vote in the House in December 1979. Clark promptly resigned and called an election, which resulted in a Liberal majority.

2. He can clarify the intention of the House by moving an immediate motion of confidence. If the motion fails, then he has no choice but to resign. If it carries, however, the prime minister can claim that the defeat of the money Bill was unintentional and remain in office. The minority Liberal government of Lester Pearson lost a budget vote in early 1968, while most of his Cabinet ministers were absent from the House. The Liberals were in the midst of a leadership race, and several of the ministers were campaigning across the country. Pearson accused the Conservatives of deliberately engineering the vote to take advantage of his party's disarray and refused to resign.[126] He won a nonconfidence motion nine days later.

While the "confidence convention" is the Achilles' heel of a minority Cabinet, the reverse is true for a majority government. A Cabinet that controls a majority in the Commons can invoke the "confidence convention" to keep its MPs in line, even though defeat in the House is rarely a realistic threat. By treating every vote as a question of confidence in the government—a practice that is neither required nor sanctioned by parliamentary tradition[127]—the Cabinet can bludgeon reluctant MPs into supporting controversial legislation. In the 1998 debate over the government's compensation package for hepatitis C victims, the opposition Reform Party introduced an amendment that was explicitly not framed as a confidence test; the government insisted that it was, thereby taking advantage of an opportunity to snuff out revolt within its own ranks.

Despite the insistence of previous prime ministers to the contrary, failure to pass an ordinary Bill does not signal a loss of confidence in the government. If the parliamentary session ends before final reading and royal assent—if, for example, the House is dissolved for a general election—the Bill simply dies. There are no consequences beyond the fact that the proposed legislation is not put into place, and the legislation can be reintroduced in the next session of Parliament. If it is a Private Members' Bill, or if it is subjected to a free vote in which MPs and senators are not constrained by party discipline, the same conclusion applies.

The "confidence convention" has been turned on its head. What was once a powerful weapon for legislators in their struggle to hold the political executive to account has become an effective shield against dissent within the governing party. Recognizing this distorted approach to "confidence" as a barrier to Commons reform, the McGrath Committee in the mid-1980s called on the Cabinet to adopt the looser British approach (the McGrath Committee was an all-party committee that proposed substantial changes for the House of Commons). When a government in Westminster introduces a Bill, it assigns the legislation to one of four categories:

1. A three-line whip is a matter of confidence. This designation applies to money Bills and any other Bill that is central to the legislative agenda of the government.
2. A two-line whip applies to Bills that the government considers important but not crucial.

3. A one-line whip signals that the government is prepared to accept dissent and even defeat. It will modify the Bill if necessary to secure passage in the House.
4. A free vote allows government MPs to vote according to their consciences, or the wishes of their constituents, where these conflict with the party line.

The defeat of a Bill in the British House of Commons is rarely interpreted as the death knell of the government.[128] Party discipline is less heavy-handed than in Canada, and government MPs enjoy greater autonomy from the Cabinet. While this approach weakens the conventional power of legislators to remove the political executive from office, the fact is that such removals are already extremely rare. The McGrath Committee enjoined Canadian governments to acknowledge this fact and give their MPs more freedom to express their opinions.

> *In a parliament with a government in command of a majority, the matter of confidence has really been settled by the electorate. Short of a reversal of allegiance or some cataclysmic political event, the question of confidence is really a fait accompli. The government and other parties should therefore have the wisdom to permit members to decide many matters in their own deliberative judgement. Overuse of party whips and of confidence motions devalues both these important institutions.[129]*

In his 2003 Democratic Renewal Plan, Prime Minister Martin pledged to adopt the British approach to votes of confidence. He promised Liberal MPs more freedom to decide how they would vote on some government legislation. Few Bills were debated during the brief parliamentary session between his swearing-in and the 2004 election, so it is difficult to determine whether Martin kept his promise. As these words were written, it was not yet clear whether the minority government would adhere to the three-line model.

Just as the Commons has lost much of its power to hold the entire Cabinet to account, it has also been deprived of its conventional right to withdraw confidence from an individual Cabinet minister. As we will see in Chapter 6, each minister is responsible to the House for the operation of her department. In theory, this means that the exposure of corruption, widespread incompetence, or a single catastrophic error on the minister's watch triggers her resignation from the government. In practice, this constitutional convention is honoured more in the breach than in the observance. Cabinet ministers do resign from time to time, but these resignations are almost always triggered by revelations of personal misconduct or foolishness, not by problems within their departments. The contrast between Andy Scott and Jane Stewart is instructive:

- Andy Scott was solicitor general in 1998, when the Public Complaints Commission of the RCMP was investigating allegations of excessive force against protesters at the APEC Summit in Vancouver.[130] On an airplane in November of that year, an NDP MP overheard Scott predicting the outcome of the RCMP inquiry. After several days of intense criticism from the media and Opposition MPs, Scott resigned as solicitor general on the grounds that his apparent prejudgment of the inquiry had undermined public confidence in the fairness of the process.[131] The truth of the matter appears to have been rather different: Scott's inept handling of the embarrassing airplane incident, not the ethical questions raised by his ministerial performance, cost him the support of the prime minister and the government caucus. In the absence of an effective parliamentary check, Cabinet ministers need only retain the confidence of the prime minister. Scott lost that confidence, and he had no choice but to resign.[132]

- Jane Stewart was minister of Human Resources Development in late 1999, when the auditor general revealed that sloppy record-keeping in a job-creation program had allowed millions of dollars in spending without proper accountability or controls. Despite weeks of bitter attacks from the Opposition, Stewart kept her portfolio and was reappointed as minister of Human Resources Development after the November 2000 general election.[133] There are two likely reasons for her survival: the prime minister continued to support her, and there were suggestions that her predecessor in the portfolio might be responsible for the problems in her department.[134]

Two lessons may be drawn from these case studies. First, the confidence of the prime minister—not Parliament or the voters—is the most powerful determinant of a Cabinet minister's longevity. When that prime minister leads a majority government, accountability to Parliament is practically a nonissue. Even in a minority Parliament, keeping a minister loyal (and thus ensuring his vote for government legislation) may be more important than respecting the Commons' right to hold him accountable. Second, a Cabinet minister will pay a political price for personal error or wrongdoing, but not for the mistakes of officials in her department. With the severing of the accountability link between the political and permanent executives, the Commons has lost its constitutional power to hold the government responsible to the electorate. There are several institutional reasons for this failure of accountability:

- First, the prime minister has every incentive to protect the executive branch from parliamentary criticism. When he controls a majority of seats, he has the tools—party discipline, the confidence convention, and the control of the Commons and its committees—to protect his government very effectively. (We will return to this topic in Chapter 6.)

- Second, the Canadian House of Commons has an unusually high turnover rate of MPs. Put another way, most backbench MPs serve only one or two terms before retirement or defeat. Consequently, "a strong, solidly entrenched Prime Minister faces an insecure and transient House of Commons."[135] Few parliamentarians stick around long enough to master the details of policy and public administration, which greatly reduces their effectiveness as watchdogs.

- Third, government MPs face powerful pressures to support the Cabinet. While they can, and do, express reservations about particular policies and ministers in the privacy of caucus, they are unlikely to issue public demands for accountability.

- Fourth, apart from their opportunities to embarrass Cabinet ministers (in QP, for example), Opposition MPs are powerless against a majority government. Even in a minority situation, they must work together across party lines to exert real power. Moreover, the government controls the flow of information from the permanent executive to the House of Commons. If they so choose, Cabinet ministers (and especially the prime minister) can deny MPs access to the documents they need to hold the political executive accountable.

- Fifth, Canada's parliamentary institutions have changed relatively little since 1867, whereas the executive branch has been transformed beyond recognition. The proliferation of departments, agencies, and programs has made effective accountability all but impossible. While the permanent executive has become larger and more complex, it has also become increasingly impervious to political control.[136] As we will see in Chapter 6, the growing power of central agencies and the increasing popularity of "partnerships" with the private sector raise serious questions about democratic accountability in the federal government.

THE SENATE

Sober Second Thought: The Legislative Role of the Upper House

The Senate was created to perform a legislative role similar to that performed by the House of Lords in Britain, though the two institutions have different social and political foundations. The appointed Senate was to be a chamber of "sober second thought," wherein legislation passed by the House of Commons could be re-examined to ensure that minority interests—regional, linguistic, or political—were adequately protected.[137]

As we saw earlier, Prime Minister Martin has pledged to reform the House of Commons. He promised to give government MPs greater independence from Cabinet by weakening the confidence convention in some circumstances, and to give committees a greater role in policy-making. Although this will likely surprise most readers, Canada already has a national parliamentary chamber with effective committees, weaker party discipline, and a more consensual approach to legislating. That chamber is the Senate. In all the rhetoric about abolition, Triple-E, and other proposals, one fact is regrettably overlooked: the Senate and its committees play a valuable role in the legislative process. Senators review and amend legislation, using their own expertise and their excellent committee work to improve flawed Bills. Their relative independence from the Cabinet, and their freedom from constituency work and electoral considerations, allows them to operate in a more consensual and deliberative way than MPs. Without attracting much public attention, the Senate has quietly taken on several important tasks that the Commons cannot or will not do. These include scrutinizing regulations, examining Bills for potential conflicts with the *Charter of Rights,* and hearing from witnesses who might not have had an opportunity to appear before the more harried Commons committees.[138]

However, legislation originating in the House already carries the stamp of democratic approval before reaching the Senate. As a result, Senate debate on noncontroversial Bills is often perfunctory. Legislative procedure in the Senate is identical to that in the House, but the hurdles are lower at each stage. Many Bills reach the Senate so late in the parliamentary session that the delay entailed in any detailed examination would be tantamount to a veto; the Bills would die when the parliamentary session ended. In most cases, the Senate defers to the Commons. Thus, the legislative coordination of the House and Senate has been achieved by the joint institutional recognition of the House's greater democratic legitimacy. (However, this does not always ensure that the Senate will follow the government's schedule. Sixteen Bills died on the Order Paper when Parliament was dissolved for the 2004 general election; some had been passed by the Commons, but the Senate rebelled against the short time frame and refused to rush its legislative review.[139])

Although the Senate's lack of public legitimacy has made it the "junior partner" in the national Parliament, its formal powers are almost identical to those of the House of Commons. It has an absolute veto on ordinary legislation and a suspensive veto on constitutional amendments.[140] While money Bills cannot be introduced in the Senate, the upper house can defeat money Bills initiated in the Commons. For the reasons just explained, however, the Senate rarely vetoes legislation passed by the House.[141] It is more willing to amend legislation, although it does so less than 10 percent of the time.[142] Both Houses must agree on the version of a Bill to be passed at third reading; where a discrepancy arises, as when the Senate amends a Bill after passage by the Commons, it must be resolved. When the government accepts a Senate amendment, it asks the Commons to vote for a motion to amend the law as the Senate sees fit. If the government rejects the amendment and the written reasons for it that the Senate appends to the changed Bill, it rarely if ever resorts to the formal dispute-resolution mechanism: a conference of the two houses (in practice, the MPs and senators on the committees that reviewed the Bill). Instead, the Leader of the Government in the Senate usually holds informal discussions with his or her opposite number in the Commons, and perhaps with the sponsoring minister, to try to work out a compromise. Where no compromise can be reached, the Senate usually—but not always—defers to the Commons.

Thus, the potential problem associated with an appointed chamber having formal powers roughly equivalent to those of the elected chamber is usually avoided by the restraint shown by senators in the exercise of their formal powers. The principle of democracy underlies the convention of senatorial restraint. Senators lack the political legitimacy of elected MPs, and so they are wary of thwarting the will of the Commons.

In some cases, however, senators lose their diffidence toward the "other place" (their term for the House of Commons). When governments change, opposing majorities in the House and Senate are almost guaranteed due to the appointment process and the lags it produces. Because senators are appointed until age 75, those appointed by any given prime minister are likely to remain in place well after the governing party has changed in the House.[143] So there is a good chance that a new governing majority in the House will face an opposition majority in the Senate. Such was the case after the 1984 and 1993 elections, when the caucuses of the former governing parties were suddenly dominated by senators. Partly for partisan reasons, these senators flexed their legislative muscles and decided to block controversial government legislation.[144] In 1988, Liberal senators delayed the Conservative government's free trade deal with the United States and forced the prime minister to call an election on the issue; after the Conservatives won a second majority, the senators capitulated and passed the enabling Bill. Conservative senators repeatedly challenged Liberal legislation between 1993 and 1997, at a time when there were only two Conservative MPs and the party was in danger of disappearing altogether. When senators confront the elected House, their actions raise important questions about democratic and responsible government. However, the problem usually takes care of itself over time, as Opposition senators retire and the prime minister appoints supporters of his party to replace them.

One notable exception to the low status of the Senate is the work of its committees. These are typically "more knowledgeable and more familiar with the subjects and the potential impact of legislation" than their Commons counterparts.[145]

> *Membership on committees in the Upper House is stable, thus allowing members to develop expertise and experience in their areas of responsibility. Free of the constraints imposed by constituency duties, Senators are able to devote more time to committee work. Partisanship on Senate Committees is less pronounced and their actions and recommendations less threatening to government. Collectively, these attributes allow committees of the Senate to offer useful insights into problems facing Canadian society and to suggest creative ideas for their solution. Even some of the Senate's harshest detractors readily acknowledge the useful role performed by the Upper Chamber's committees.[146]*

Three standing committees merit particular attention here. The first is the Standing Joint Committee for the Scrutiny of Regulations (SJCSR), which reviews the detailed regulations made by public officials in the process of implementing the laws passed by Parliament. It is composed of 10 MPs and 5 senators, and co-chaired by a government member and an Opposition member. The senators tend to be the most active members of the committee, because they are not preoccupied with more politically sensitive matters (such as constituency work). Although the SJCSR can examine only about one-quarter of the thousand or so regulations issued each year, its analyses carry considerable weight because it has the power to recommend that a particular regulation be revoked. Under the Standing Orders, a recommendation to revoke a regulation is deemed to have been adopted by Parliament unless a minister files a formal objection within 15 sitting days after the report has been tabled.[147] The SJCSR has used this power sparingly, usually in relation to potential violations of the *Charter of Rights*. However, the threat of revocation can often persuade the executive branch to amend regulations where necessary.[148]

The Standing Committee on National Finance often does a more thorough job of reviewing the annual Main Spending Estimates than the Commons committees—despite the fact that the Commons, and not the Senate, holds the "power of the purse."[149] The Standing Committee on Human Rights was established in May 2001.[150] Its mandate is to ensure that federal legislation conforms to the *Charter*—a task that it shares with the Standing Committee on Legal and Constitutional Affairs—and to the international human rights instruments that Canada has signed since 1945.[151]

Several of its members also belonged to the Special Senate Committee on Bill C-36, the *Anti-Terrorism Act* (Chapter 10). That special committee heard from a multitude of witnesses and produced a thoughtful and thorough report on the issues raised by the new police powers. Although the government had used its majority in the Commons to push the Bill through, despite serious concerns about its impact on rights (particularly those of particular minorities), the all-party report of the Special Senate Committee forced the minister of Justice to accept some (though not all) of its amendments.[152] Other special committees have tackled difficult and complex policy issues ranging from postsecondary education to the legalization of marijuana.[153] While the government of the day is under no obligation to enact their recommendations into law, the high quality of these reports often exerts a long-term influence on public policy. Unlike the members of Royal Commissions and other formal inquiries, senators remain directly engaged in the legislative process after their reports are issued. They can call upon ministers and public servants to follow up on their recommendations, and use their leverage to ensure that their proposals are at least considered.[154]

Most Canadians are unaware of the contributions made by Senate committees. The upper house rarely attracts the attention of the news media and the public. The exceptions to this neglect are usually unflattering; most news stories about the Senate concern conflicts between the two Houses of Parliament (which should be treated as a normal part of the legislative process), or scandals over the conduct of individual senators (e.g., persistent absenteeism). The fact that many senators can claim an expertise in public policy unmatched by most MPs, and the diligence with which they carry out their legislative and investigative work, are rarely mentioned.

In a recent analysis of the upper house, C.E.S. Franks suggested that Canada has not one but three upper houses: the real Senate, which makes important but little-known contributions to the legislative process; the Senate portrayed by its critics, a failed institution that serves no useful purpose (especially in the area of regional representation); and a hypothetical reformed Senate, which changes its shape with the fashion of the moment.[155] The current vogue, as noted earlier, is for a Triple-E Senate. We will discuss the pros and cons of this proposal at the end of this chapter.

Regional Representation in the Senate

The need for sober second thought was not enough to justify a second legislative chamber in Canada. (Nor was it important enough to sustain provincial second chambers, which have now disappeared from the central and eastern provinces and were never constituted in the West.) For the Fathers of Confederation, the Senate was the product of a political compromise without which the country might never have come into being.[156] The Maritime colonies wanted assurances that their perspectives would not be drowned out by the larger Commons delegations from Ontario and Quebec; the latter insisted that it must be over-represented in the upper house, to protect the francophone population against the ever-growing English majority. The Fathers of

Confederation looked to the American Senate for inspiration.[157] The Senate, unlike the British House of Lords, was a federal chamber within which each state, regardless of its population, had two representatives. At first, American senators were indirectly elected by their state legislatures. Since 1911, American senators have been directly elected by the voters in their respective states.

Yet the Canadian Senate, while it was meant to reflect the same federal principles as its American counterpart, did not reflect the specifics of the American model. First, Canadian senators are not selected by provincial legislatures or governments; they are appointed by the prime minister, usually without consulting the provincial governments.[158] Second, Canadians opted for equal representation by region rather than equal representation by province. Thus, in 1867, Ontario, Quebec, and the Maritimes were each given 24 Senate seats. When a 1915 constitutional amendment recognized Western Canada as a senatorial region, it too was assigned 24 seats, divided equally among the four western provinces. Representation for Newfoundland in 1949 and for the two northern territories in 1975 was added to the initial regional allocation of seats. In 1999 the new Territory of Nunavut also received a Senate seat; this brought the total number of senators to 105.

Table 5.1 reveals the idiosyncratic distribution of seats among the provinces. Alberta, Ontario, and British Columbia have the weakest proportional representation in the existing Senate. These provincial inequities are defended on the ground that the Senate provides for equal regional representation, but even regional equality in

TABLE 5.1 DISTRIBUTION OF SENATE SEATS, 2004

PROVINCE	NO. OF SENATE SEATS	POPULATION PER SENATOR*
Newfoundland/Labrador	6	85 500
Prince Edward Island	4	34 000
Nova Scotia	10	91 000
New Brunswick	10	73 000
Quebec	24	301 500
Ontario	24	475 500
Manitoba	6	186 500
Saskatchewan	6	163 000
Alberta	6	496 000
British Columbia	6	651 000
Yukon	1	29 000
Northwest Territories	1	37 000
Nunavut	1	27 000

*Population figures based on 2001 census; rounded up or down to the nearest 500 for clarity.

the Senate takes some strange twists. The West, for example, is under-represented in the Senate relative to its share of the national population; the region has 30 percent of the national population (according to the 2001 census) but only 23 percent of the Senate seats. Atlantic Canada, with less than 8 percent of the national population and almost 29 percent of the Senate seats, is the primary beneficiary of Senate representation based on regional equality, a principle that was jettisoned in any event when Newfoundland's Senate seats were added to rather than drawn from the preexisting Maritime allotment.

The Senate's perceived failure to represent the regions is not solely the result of its unequal composition. Its lack of democratic legitimacy, combined with partisanship—which, although weaker than partisanship in the House of Commons, is still an important institutional norm—have prevented the upper house from expressing the distinct concerns of Canada's regions. Behind closed doors, government senators join their Commons colleagues in lobbying for the interests of their provinces or territories. But this representative role, like their legislative role, goes unnoticed by most voters.

In summary, the Senate reflects a fundamental ambiguity in the institutional structure of the Canadian federal state. It was designed to fulfill both the legislative role of the British House of Lords and the federal role of the U.S. Senate. To perform these functions effectively requires some tradeoff, some compromise, of both.[159] Consequently, the Senate has come under sustained and growing attack from those who see it as an affront to democratic values, to federal principles, or to both. Lost in the rhetoric about the "imaginary" and hypothetical Senates is the reality of the Senate's work.

THE LEGISLATIVE PROCESS

Orderly debate and voting depend on the enforcement of rules and the efficient resolution of disputes. At the same time, parliamentary debate must permit the expression of diverse opinions. This is a difficult balancing act, especially in a Parliament with four official parties. The Speaker of the House is caught between a government that expects speedy passage of its legislation on the one hand, and three Opposition parties with varying ideologies on the other. The success with which the Speaker and the Standing Orders ensure a balance among the contending parties is interpreted differently by the government and the Opposition. At the same time, MPs are caught between institutional incentives that foster adversarialism and party discipline, and an electorate whose acceptance of these parliamentary norms has waned substantially in recent decades.

Government Bills

Refer to Dossier 5.1 for the procedure by which most government Bills are passed. This section fleshes out that summary by focusing on two central themes: the characteristics of parliamentary debate and the role of the committee system in the legislative process.

Characteristics of Parliamentary Debate

As we have seen, most legislation originates in the executive branch. At first reading, the government serves notice to the House, and through the House to the country, that the Bill has been placed on the legislative agenda. Substantive debate begins with second reading, at which time the Bill is discussed in principle. The government also signals the importance it attaches to the Bill, and thus the extent to which the constraints of party discipline will apply in the subsequent debate.

Unless the government holds a minority of the seats and needs the support of other parties to pass legislation, parliamentary debate is not intended to change the minds of MPs.[160] (According to one former MP, "the purpose of most debates in the House of Commons is not to enlighten but to beat one's opponents to death by dullness."[161]) The real audience is outside the House. Government and Opposition MPs try to persuade the public that the Bill should be passed or defeated and that it resolves—or fails to resolve—a problem of pressing importance to the national community. The debate is therefore symbolically important, even though votes in the House may not change as a consequence. It is through parliamentary debate and through the public record of that debate in *Hansard* (the official transcript of the debates in Parliament), that MPs inform and educate the public. While the content of specific debates may be trivial, the role of parliamentary debate in a representative democracy is potentially crucial.

A majority government rarely loses a vote at second reading. Whatever the MPs on either side of the House think of a particular Bill, party discipline ensures that government backbenchers will turn out to support it. Therefore, Opposition MPs who oppose a particular piece of legislation cannot veto it. They are left with two alternatives:

1. First, they can try to embarrass the government into delaying or withdrawing the Bill. Their weapons include Question Period, media scrums, leaked documents, and the mobilization of interest groups. Notable examples include the two pornography Bills introduced by the Mulroney government in 1985 and 1986. While the government had a huge majority and could easily have forced either Bill through the House, it quickly became clear that there was no public consensus on the issue. Both Bills quietly died on the Order Paper—i.e., they were dropped from the agenda without coming to a vote.[162]

2. Second, they can bring Parliamentary business to a halt, thus drawing attention to the failings of the Bill and mobilizing public dissent. In the end, a determined government will almost always prevail. Time allocation (see Dossier 5.2) allows a majority government to limit debate at each stage of the legislative process and circumvent the tricks of the Opposition. Nonetheless, delaying tactics do attract public attention to the alleged faults of a Bill. Although the House of Commons sits for an average of 175 days a year, the parliamentary timetable is always tight. At any given time, there are dozens of government Bills and up to 30 Private Members' Bills and motions on the agenda, not to mention committee reports, Question Period, and other House business.

Each sitting of Parliament follows a preset script, beginning with prayers by the Speaker and proceeding through tabling of documents, introduction of Bills, notice of motions, presenting petitions, and so forth. At each stage of this process, Opposition MPs can take advantage of the rules to tie up the House for hours or days at a time. In November 1999 the Reform Opposition tried to stall the Bill ratifying a land claim treaty with the Nisga'a people of British Columbia. The most successful tactic was the presentation of hundreds of petitions, which delayed the start of the debate. The government imposed time allocation and forced the Bill through second reading and into committee. At report stage the Reform caucus presented hundreds of separate amendments to the Bill, each of which had to be read individually. (The Speaker has the discretion to group amendments together for voting, so that the House does not waste time voting separately on each one, but the reading of the amendments was still an effective delaying manoeuvre.) Although the Bill eventually passed, Reformers reaped the political rewards of delaying legislation that outraged many of their constituents.

The legislative process is more complicated under a minority government. The Cabinet cannot count on the automatic approval of its legislation. Instead, the government House Leader must negotiate with one or more Opposition parties to build support for each Bill and motion. In the process, the government often has to compromise: it may be required to amend certain Bills in exchange for Opposition votes, or abandon legislation altogether if it cannot work out a deal. Moreover, an Opposition party can sometimes force the government to introduce legislation that it would not otherwise have done. The 1972–74 minority Liberal government, which relied on voting support from the NDP caucus, passed at least two laws—the *Foreign Investment Review Act* and the *Election Expenses Act*—that were high-priority items for the New Democrats.[163]

The Committee System

A great deal of the work of Parliament is carried out in committees. Indeed, one of the reasons that there are often so few members in the Chamber is that many of them are attending committee meetings. It is not uncommon for there to be 50 or even 60 meetings during the course of a week, and 20 to 25 meetings on a particular day.[164]

After second reading, Bills are sent to committee for detailed, clause-by-clause examination. Since the Standing Orders were amended in 1994, the government may choose to refer a Bill to committee before second reading (see Dossier 5.2), although this option has rarely been exercised until recently. Whereas the entire House of Commons debates each government Bill for an average of eight hours, a committee can spend "many dozens of hours examining a Bill, hearing from witnesses and considering amendments."[165] While committees may not have as much immediate impact on the content of legislation as they might wish, they do perform two important political functions:

- By holding public hearings, either in Ottawa or across the country, they give interest groups and others who may be affected by the proposed legislation direct access to the policy process.[166]
- In so doing, they help to legitimize the legislative process and the laws that it produces.

Generally speaking, Commons committees fall into five categories:

1. *Committee of the Whole:* The entire House becomes a committee. The strict rules of parliamentary debate are relaxed, and members may discuss issues in a freer and less formal way. "Members are not required to be in their assigned seats, but can congregate around the Table . . . this facilitates intimacy and an exchange of views by participants."[167] The House usually goes into Committee of the Whole during the examination of supply Bills. Before 1968, the Estimates were examined in Committee of the Whole; refer back to the discussion of possible reforms to the Estimates procedure in "Parliament and the Public Purse."

2. *Standing Committees:* Specialist committees are established at the beginning of a Parliament (i.e., as soon as the House reconvenes after a general election) and remain in place until the House is dissolved. Each department of the federal government is monitored by a separate standing committee (see Table 5.2). The partisan composition of the committees corresponds to that of the Commons as a whole. Under a majority government, each Committee has a majority of members from the government party, with representation from the Opposition parties roughly in proportion to the size of their caucuses. In a minority Parliament, the Opposition parties collectively control a majority of the seats (although the governing party retains the largest single share). Each committee is chaired by a government MP, with the exception of the Public Accounts Committee (refer back to "Parliament and the Public Purse"). The committee chairs are now elected by the membership; before 2002, they were chosen by the prime minister. The formal powers and responsibilities of a standing committee are extensive: to examine matters referred to it by the House, including Order-in-Council appointments, Bills, and pressing policy issues; to report its findings and recommendations back to the House; to hold public hearings, summon witnesses, and "send for" all necessary documents; and to delegate these tasks to any subcommittee that it sees fit to establish.[168]

3. *Legislative Committees:* These are temporary committees, established for the sole purpose of examining a particular Bill. They are struck immediately after second reading and dissolved as soon as they have reported the Bill back to the House with or without amendments. Legislative committees were first created in 1985, on the recommendation of the Special Committee on House of Commons Reform (the McGrath Committee). In practice, the membership of legislative committees overlapped considerably with that of the standing committees in the same policy field, and the difficulty of scheduling meetings for dozens of standing and legislative committees created delays in the legislative process. Since the early 1990s, legislative committees have rarely been used. One notable exception is the

TABLE 5.2 **HOUSE OF COMMONS STANDING COMMITTEES, OCTOBER 2004***

NAME OF COMMITTEE
Aboriginal Affairs and Northern Development
Access to Information, Privacy and Ethics
Agriculture and Agri-Food
Canadian Heritage
Citizenship and Immigration
Environment and Sustainable Development
Finance
Fisheries and Oceans
Foreign Affairs and International Trade
Government Operations and Estimates
Health
Human Resources, Skills Development, Social Development and the Status of Persons with Disabilities
Industry, Natural Resources, Science and Technology
Justice, Human Rights, Public Safety and Emergency Preparedness
Liaison
National Defence and Veterans Affairs
Official Languages
Procedure and House Affairs
Public Accounts
Status of Women
Transport

***Source:** House of Commons Standing committees. From www.parl.gc.ca/committee/CommitteeList.aspx?SelectedElementid=e2_ &Lang=1&ParlSession=381. Reprinted with permission from the House of Commons. Retrieved October 2004.

Legislative Committee on Bill C-20 (the *Clarity Bill*), which was necessary because the sponsoring minister—the minister of intergovernmental affairs—does not have a separate department, and so there was no standing committee assigned to examine his Bills.

4. *Joint Committees:* Standing or special committees with members from both Houses of Parliament. Standing joint committees include the Committee on Scrutiny of Regulations and the Committee on Official Languages.

5. *Special Committees:* These committees are established to study and report on a particular issue, and then dissolved. Some are composed entirely of MPs (e.g., the 2001 Special Committee on the Modernization and Improvement of the Procedures of

the House of Commons), while special joint committees include both MPs and senators. Special joint committees played important roles in the megaconstitutional politics of the 1980s and 1990s (see Chapter 3).

Majority governments restrict the power of Commons committees in two ways:

1. The government majority on each committee ensures Cabinet control of its deliberations.
2. The constraints of party discipline that apply to the House as a whole operate within its committees as well, though often to a lesser degree. The adversarial style of QP is often absent; the chair sets the tone for the committee, and can encourage collegiality among the members. The lack of partisan posturing on committees is partly the result of media neglect; there are fewer incentives to indulge in adversarial behaviour in the absence of television cameras. (Note, however, that the House adopted an amendment to the Standing Orders in May 2001, permitting television coverage of committee meetings; this may have led to increased adversarialism in committee deliberations.) Even on the most collegial committees, however, amendments are moved, discussed, and voted on within the constraints of party discipline and with the understanding that the Bill has already been approved in principle by the House.

Successive reforms to the committee system have been guided by the assumption that backbench MPs should have a greater role in law-making. None of these reforms has worked as well as its creators hoped, because they could not overcome two key institutional norms: Cabinet dominance and party discipline. Unless and until a government decides to free its backbenchers from these constraints—a decision that would run counter to the self-interest of the Cabinet—no reform to the committee system can give MPs the independent policy influence that many of them crave.

Private Members' Business

Although the government has the sole right to introduce money Bills, backbenchers may propose other types of legislation. MPs and senators have the opportunity to introduce Private Members' Bills (PMBs) and motions, thereby initiating policy debate independently of the government. Although the Standing Orders governing Private Members' Business have been reformed in recent years to give MPs more opportunity to raise issues for debate, few PMBs ever pass into law. Between October 1999 and October 2000, when Parliament was dissolved for an election, 312 PMBs were given first reading. Only three of those were enacted into law, one of which was a carryover from the previous session of Parliament. The other two were relatively trivial: MPs proposing changes to the names of their constituencies. Many of the PMBs that died on the Order Paper in October 2000 were thoughtful, constructive, and well researched. Their potential benefits for Canadians were squandered.

At the beginning of the parliamentary session, the names of all MPs who have given notice of Private Members' Bills or motions are placed in a drum. Thirty names are chosen at random by the Deputy Speaker, to determine which items of

Private Members' Business will be placed on the order paper. Fifteen Bills and fifteen motions are listed in the order of precedence. Each is granted one hour of House debate during Private Members' Hour (between 5 and 6 p.m., Monday through Thursday). Each item is dropped from the Order Paper after one hour of debate, whether or not it has come to a vote. After 15 of the 30 have been dropped, another draw is held to bring the total number back up to 30 items in order of precedence.

Although most PMBs die after a single hour of debate, there are exceptions. After the 30 MPs are chosen in the draw, they must submit their proposed Bills or motions to the Standing Committee on Procedure and House Affairs. The Subcommittee on Private Members' Business selects 10 of the 30 items—5 Bills and 5 motions—as "votable items." Votable items must meet certain criteria, which are spelled out in the Standing Orders:

- They must be well drafted (usually with the assistance of the House of Commons Law Clerk and the Department of Justice).
- They must be constitutional: consistent with the division of powers and the *Charter*, and respectful of the Crown's prerogative over the raising and spending of public money.
- They may not be either trivial or redundant—in other words, they cannot duplicate a government Bill or another PMB.

Votable items are debated at second reading for up to three hours, after which they must be put to the House for a decision. The three hours of debate are not scheduled on consecutive days; votable PMBs bounce around the Order Paper in an arbitrary and often unpredictable way. A PMB that passes at second reading is referred to a committee, which must report back to the House within 60 sitting days. (The committee may request a 30-day extension, but if it fails to report within that time the Bill is deemed to have been reported without amendment.) Report stage is limited to one hour and forty-five minutes (also on random days) and must be immediately followed by third reading. If the PMB is adopted at third reading, it goes to the Senate.

Despite the stated purpose of the 1986 reforms to Private Members' Business—to enhance the legislative role of backbench MPs—the government can still quash a Bill or motion it deems to be unacceptable. As long as the governing party retains its control of the House, through a disciplined majority of MPs, few members will see their Bills and motions come to fruition unless they are supported by the Cabinet.

THE QUEST FOR INSTITUTIONAL REFORM

As we saw in Chapters 2 and 3, conflicting and evolving political values pose challenges for Canada's political institutions. This is particularly true for Parliament, both because of its recent loss of legitimacy and because the Commons is at the heart of Canadian representative democracy. The Senate has attracted criticism on several fronts from the moment of its creation. Fads in Senate reform come and go, but one theme remains constant: the Senate as currently constituted has few defenders. The debate over reforming the Commons is both more recent and more consistent. The goals of reformers are summarized in a June 2001 report on House reform:

> There is a general desire to re-assert the pre-eminence of the House of Commons, and increase its effectiveness and efficiency. Members want to increase the accountability of individual Ministers and the Government as a whole, and increase the opportunities for parliamentary influence in the legislative process. There is a feeling that individual Members of the House of Commons need to be empowered, and the role of the Speaker, as the servant of the House and its spokesperson, enhanced. A balance needs to be achieved between the Government's interests in implementing its legislative agenda, and the Opposition's interests in questioning and criticizing the Government. Similarly, other competing interests need to be reconciled, such as the inevitable tensions between individual Members and their parties, and between the chamber and its committees, to name but two. Parliamentary debate should be enhanced, by creating opportunities for more meaningful dialogue and increasing the relevance of the parliamentary processes.[169]

Both Houses of Parliament should be reformed to enhance their effectiveness as legislative bodies, as watchdogs over the executive, and as representative institutions. But the precise nature of those reforms, and how they are to be accomplished, are subject to considerable debate.

Senate Reform

As we will see in Chapter 9, Senate reform is widely perceived—especially in Western Canada—as the solution to a variety of political and institutional problems. The movement for Senate reform has focused on enhancing regional representation, with little attention to the legislative and investigative aspects of the Senate's work. Most of the recent proposals have sought to make the Senate a more effective vehicle for intrastate federalism (see Chapter 9). In the late 1970s and early 1980s, the prevailing model was a House of the Provinces (modelled on the German Bundesrat). Provincial governments would send delegations that would vote as a bloc on instructions from their government. Such a chamber would allow provincial governments to review the legislative activities of the House of Commons, particularly the use of the federal spending power in areas of exclusive provincial jurisdiction. The emphasis was on the representation of provincial *governments*, as opposed to provincial *electorates*, within the national legislative process.

By the mid-1980s, the fashion had changed. The House of the Provinces model was replaced by the Triple-E Senate (see Chapter 9). Advocates argued that an elected Senate would remedy the democratic failings of the existing upper house, while a Senate with equal representation from all provinces would enshrine the "equal provinces" vision of Canada. They claimed that the role of provincial governments and premiers on the national stage would be diminished, and regional alienation would be addressed in a number of ways:

- The election of senators would strengthen ties between citizens and their national government.
- An equal number of seats for all provinces would give "outer Canada" sufficient legislative clout to counterbalance central Canadian domination of the House of Commons.
- An effective Senate would ensure that regional representatives would in fact be heard in Ottawa.

Support for an elected Senate, although not necessarily for an equal or effective Senate, gained additional momentum from public discontent with parliamentary institutions and executive federalism. Public opinion is divided between those who support the direct election of senators and those who support the Senate's abolition. What is clear, however, is that few Canadians support the status quo. The controversy over Senator Andrew Thompson, who attended less than 5 percent of the Senate sittings in the 1990s while maintaining a full-time residence in Mexico, fuelled public anger.[170] Nonetheless, the status quo continues, with little sign of governmental enthusiasm for even modest reform. The Senate is still appointed, not elected. The Senate still has formal legislative powers virtually equal to those of the House. It is still based on an antiquated formula of regional representation that makes little sense to most contemporary Canadians. It is still an institution that attracts unrelenting public criticism and no discernible public support.

This should not lead automatically to the suggestion that the existing Senate is worthless or that senators do not provide reasonable value in return for their salaries and perks. As discussed in previous sections of this chapter, the Senate sometimes plays a valuable role in the legislative process; more recently, it has taken on a more active role in the investigation of public policy issues and the oversight of the executive. Its strengths lie in its differences from the House of Commons. Because the Senate does not hold the fate of the government in its hands, and its members are not subject to election or re-election, the chamber is more independent and less adversarial than the "other place."

The more consensual and unhurried style of the Senate has enhanced its effectiveness as a legislative chamber. The primary obstacle to even greater effectiveness is the appointment process, which diminishes its legitimacy as a legislative institution and creates a public perception of senators as time-serving party hacks. Paradoxically, however, the fact that senators are appointed and not elected can be viewed as an important asset. As we have seen, the composition of the Senate more closely approximates Canadian society than does that of the Commons. The prime minister can, if he so chooses, appoint distinguished public servants, former Cabinet ministers, community activists, and others with a wealth of expertise. When the appointment power is used sensibly, the result is a legislative chamber whose collective knowledge and experience far exceeds that of the elected MPs.

In all likelihood, the Triple-E proposal would fail to secure its chief goal—the promotion of regional perspectives in the national Parliament—while reducing the Senate's value as a legislative body. If senators were elected for fixed, renewable terms, the reformed Senate would impose the same institutional incentives that handicap the Commons: strong partisanship, high turnover, and amateurism. There is little evidence to support the claim that regional representation in national politics should be performed exclusively by the upper house of Parliament.[171] Indeed, as we will see in Chapter 8, intergovernmental relations are becoming increasingly institutionalized, although there is still no effective mechanism for holding executives to account for the deals struck among themselves.

On the other side of the debate, the New Democratic Party and other left-wing critics have long argued that the Senate should be abolished altogether. As we have seen, however, the dominance of the Commons by the federal Cabinet points up the need for a chamber of "sober second thought" to prevent hasty or ill-conceived Bills from becoming law. Moreover, abolishing the Senate shares at least one failing with the Triple-E proposal: it would require a unanimous amendment to the *Constitution*. For political reasons, the province of Quebec is unlikely to agree to any change that would diminish its representation in the national Parliament.[172]

More promising and practical suggestions for reform have been advanced by proponents of nonconstitutional change. The independence of senators from the government of the day could be enhanced by excluding government senators from the weekly caucus meeting. A new Senate committee could be established to review the details of proposed treaties between Canada and other states. In the era of globalization and internationalization, a legislative body with the time and the expertise to examine the implications of treaties for Canadian law and policy makes considerable sense.[173] An independent and nonpartisan appointment commission, similar to the one adopted in the United Kingdom, could ensure the continuing quality of Senate appointments while removing the taint of partisan patronage.[174] Perhaps most important, the Senate should make every effort to explain to the public, the government, and the media what it does and how well it does it. Given the near-certainty that the institution will persist in its current form for at least the foreseeable future, there is much to be said for educating the public about its strengths and contributions.

Reform of the House of Commons

The Senate has not been the sole target of parliamentary reform. The House of Commons has also come under criticism both from the public and from parliamentarians themselves.[175] Here the primary concern, one that goes to the core of parliamentary democracy, has been the pervasive impact of Cabinet dominance, adversarialism, and party discipline on the procedures of the House and on the capacity of the House to function as a representative institution.

Public discontent with party discipline is not a new phenomenon, especially in Western Canada. Ever since the Progressives swept into Parliament in 1921, Western protest parties—including the CCF, Social Credit, and the Reform/Alliance—have targeted party discipline as a priority for institutional reform. The problems that any significant reduction in party discipline might pose for responsible government, and indeed for electoral empowerment, are largely ignored. As we have seen throughout this chapter, some degree of adversarialism and party discipline is inherent in responsible parliamentary government. Both arise from the very architecture of British legislative institutions, and are reinforced by the incentive structures of representative democracy and party politics. To eliminate adversarialism and party discipline—assuming that such a thing were possible—would be to undermine the authority of the political executive and make it difficult for voters to determine which group of politicians should be rewarded or punished for its conduct in government. So despite the problems caused by the excesses of Cabinet dominance, the reality is that sweeping reform of the legislative branch may be neither practical nor, in some respects, desirable.

Despite these obstacles to reform, the internal procedures of the House of Commons have evolved considerably over time and will continue to evolve. Despite its long pedigree, parliamentary government is a remarkably flexible institution that can evolve to meet new challenges and unique social conditions.[176] Unfortunately, most of the reforms discussed in this chapter have been noticed only by MPs and aficionados of Parliament Hill. They have done little to address public dissatisfaction with the House and the behaviour of MPs, or the more general discontent with the responsiveness and representativeness of parliamentary democracy. The most effective way to enhance the legitimacy of the Commons and the Senate may not be to destroy a system of responsible government that has evolved over centuries. Rather, the answer could lie in a better-educated electorate, which understands the conflicting institutional incentives for their elected officials and appreciates the less publicized contributions of MPs and senators. But given the anti-institutional bias of some journalists, well-informed and sympathetic reporting of elected legislators may be too much to ask (see Chapter 7).

CONCLUSION

It should now be clear that the practice of Canadian parliamentary government does not conform to the theory presented at the beginning of this chapter. Because the House of Commons is subordinate to the executive branch, there is little it can do to hold the Cabinet accountable to the electorate. Instead of *making* laws, the best that MPs and senators can to is to *improve* or *delay* laws. While MPs devote much of their time and energy to serving their constituents, they do not represent the public in a demographic sense. Collectively, they lack the experience and the expertise to monitor the implementation of public policy. The incentives for parliamentarians, most of which are imposed by outside forces (principally the prime minister and the political parties), reward obedience and adversarialism while punishing independence and public cooperation.

Perhaps the most important lesson of this chapter is that the performance of any single institution within a political system is affected by its relationships with other institutions. Chapters 3 and 4 examine the processes by which MPs are recruited and elected, processes that contribute to the weakness of the lower house. Chapter 6 describes the centralization of power in the political and permanent executives and explains its implications for political accountability. Chapter 7 reveals that the "watchdog" function of the Commons has largely passed to the news media, while policy influence has shifted to interest groups outside Parliament. In Chapter 10, we will examine the power of the courts to make law in the *Charter* era.

Once we understand the impact of Canada's other national political institutions—the executive, the judiciary, pressure groups, the news media, the party system, and the electoral system—on our legislative branch, we may conclude that our MPs and senators are doing the best they can under difficult conditions. If Canadians are dissatisfied with their national Parliament, this could mean that our elected and appointed representatives are not living up to our expectations. On the other hand, it could simply prove that our expectations are unrealistic. In this context, it is useful to return to the discussion of international trends at the beginning of this chapter. To the extent that national governments bind each other through executive agreements, the sphere of law-making controlled by Parliament shrinks. The federal government's increased attention to Canada–United States relations worries some MPs (e.g., those opposed to Canadian participation in the proposed missile defence shield[177]), but they are powerless to block cross-border agreements between officials in the two countries—especially when the executive that negotiated the agreements controls a majority of Commons seats.[178]

Since 9/11, significant changes have been made to border security, immigration policy, and laws relating to terrorism. Some of these changes required no parliamentary involvement; indeed, some may not have been fully disclosed to Parliament, because the federal executive seems increasingly prone to invoking national security as a reason for withholding information. Many of the new measures on immigration and terrorism did require amendments to federal legislation, several of which were highly controversial. The 2001 *Anti-Terrorism Act* raised the most serious concerns about the rights and freedoms of people living in Canada (Chapter 10). In the end, all of the 9/11 measures passed through the House of Commons—then controlled by a Liberal majority—with few if any amendments, despite unusually frank public protests by some government backbenchers and Cabinet ministers.[179] The *Anti-Terrorism Act* (then Bill C-36) had a rougher ride in the Senate (particularly, as noted above, in the special committee), but it passed with some of the amendments demanded by senators.

The point is that even on the occasions when Parliament has a role to play in national security policy, its effectiveness is limited by Cabinet dominance and the strict discipline imposed on government MPs. The lack of parliamentary power was clearly illustrated by the Commons debate on Bill C-36: "The government invoked closure, which limited Parliament to two days of debate when the Bill was reported back to the House of Commons, and one day of debate [at] third reading."[180]

If the current focus on national security persists, or increases as a result of further terrorist attacks, MPs and senators may find themselves relegated to the role of spectators. Citing national security concerns, the various actors in the executive branch (the RCMP, the Canadian Security and Intelligence Service, immigration arbitrators) will likely continue to deny requests for sensitive information. This practice hampers the effectiveness of parliamentary committees, which cannot conduct adequate reviews of policy and spending decisions without a full knowledge of the issues. In effect, current international developments will reinforce the domestic trends discussed in this chapter, particularly Cabinet dominance over the legislative branch. That dominance could be offset, to a degree, by the dynamics of minority government. But in a climate of public fear and official secrecy, even the most determined Opposition may find it difficult to hold the executive to account.

GLOSSARY OF KEY TERMS

Backbenchers: Members of the House of Commons who do not belong to the Cabinet of the day. Backbenchers make up almost 80 percent of the Commons. All Opposition MPs are backbenchers, as are roughly half of government MPs. The proportion of government backbenchers in the thirty-eighth Parliament is unusually low. As of September 2004, there were 39 Cabinet ministers and 28 Parliamentary Secretaries, who are also sworn as members of the Privy Council under changes introduced by Prime Minister Martin. So almost exactly half of Liberal MPs—67/135—are not backbenchers. In a majority government, and before Parliamentary Secretaries were given Privy Council status by the current prime minister, it was more usual for two-thirds or more of the governing caucus to sit as backbenchers.

Bill: A draft law introduced into Parliament by a minister of the Crown (i.e., a Cabinet minister), or by a private member (a backbench MP). After the Bill has received royal assent, it becomes a statute (another word for "law").

Casework: The services provided to individual constituents by an MP and his or her staff. Anyone in Canada who encounters a problem with the federal government—e.g., citizenship, Employment Insurance, or the Canada Pension Plan—can seek assistance from the local office of his representative in the House of Commons. Casework is the most time-consuming, and often the most satisfying, of the many tasks assigned to MPs.

Caucus: The parliamentary contingent representing each of the various parties in Parliament. For the Liberals and Conservatives, caucus includes both MPs and senators. The NDP and the Bloc Québécois have no Senate representation. The caucuses meet separately on Wednesday mornings when the House of Commons is in session. The Liberal caucus is divided into regional caucuses, which often meet just before the full caucus. Within the secrecy of the caucus meeting, MPs and senators can speak freely about political and policy issues. Once the meeting ends, all members of caucus are expected to keep the discussions confidential.

Confidence convention: In a British parliamentary system, the Cabinet can remain in office only as long as it enjoys the support of the House of Commons for its policies and money Bills. If the Cabinet loses a vote on a money Bill or a key piece of legislation, constitutional convention requires the prime minister to tender the resignation of his government to the Crown (in Canada, the governor general). In practice, there are no legal sanctions for violating a convention (see Chapter 8); therefore, a prime minister may choose to stay in office and try to pass a vote of confidence in the House instead of resigning immediately. Prime ministers sometimes rely on a misinterpretation of the confidence convention to persuade their backbench MPs to support government legislation.

Constituency: An electoral district that sends one or more members to the national or provincial legislature. In Canada, also called a "riding." The word "constituency" may also be used to refer to an informal group within the electorate that expects a particular MP to speak on its behalf. Therefore, we might say that a female MP from Halifax has three constituencies: her particular riding, women, and the Atlantic region as a whole.

In camera: Latin for "in a closed room." When a parliamentary committee holds a closed meeting, the proceedings of which are not to be disclosed to the public, the meeting is said to be *in camera.*

Minority government: One party holds a plurality of the seats in the House of Commons (i.e., more than any other party), but not an absolute majority. Because the Commons works on the principle of majority voting, a minority government cannot pass legislation or financial measures without the support of some Opposition MPs. It may secure this support by striking a bargain with one or more Opposition parties, or it can try to win over individual MPs on a case-by-case basis. If it cannot do either, it risks defeat in the House (e.g., by losing a budget vote); in that circumstance, constitutional convention normally requires the prime minister to submit his or her resignation to the governor general. Moreover, a government with a minority in the House cannot dominate Commons committees, where seats are allocated according to the parties' respective shares of the House.

Money Bill: A formal authorization by the House of Commons to the Cabinet (technically, the Crown) to raise or spend public revenues. Ways and means Bills authorize the Crown to raise money; appropriations Bills authorize the spending of public funds.

Numerical/pictorial representation: The idea that the demographic characteristics of a particular political body (such as a legislature) should mirror those in the population at large. For example, women make up slightly over half of the Canadian electorate; therefore, a numerically representative House of Commons would also be 51 percent female.

Party discipline: The requirement that individual legislators vote according to the wishes of their leaders (or of the party caucus as a whole). Party discipline is strongest on the government side of the House, partly because of the confidence convention, but it affects MPs and senators from all parties. While discipline is somewhat weaker in the Senate, which is not a confidence chamber, few senators are willing to break ranks in public. Party discipline affects the behaviour of MPs on parliamentary committees, not just on the floor of the Commons or the Senate.

Power of the purse: The right of the House of Commons to approve or reject money Bills proposed by the Cabinet. That right is grounded in British constitutional convention. It was entrenched in section 53 of the *Constitution Act, 1867.*

Universal suffrage: Every citizen has the right to vote in parliamentary elections, without regard to wealth, gender, or social status.

DISCUSSION QUESTIONS

1. Briefly explain the differences among the major concepts of political representation discussed in this chapter. Which do you find the most appealing, and why?
2. How does a Bill become law in Canada?
3. Explain the roles and functions of the standing committees of the House of Commons. How could their effectiveness be enhanced?
4. Where do adversarialism and party discipline come from? How do they affect the operation of our legislative branch of government?

SUGGESTED READINGS

Books and Articles

David C. Docherty, *Mr. Smith Goes to Ottawa: Life in the House of Commons* (Vancouver: UBC Press, 1997).

C.E.S. Franks, *The Parliament of Canada* (Toronto: University of Toronto Press, 1987).

David A. Good, *The Politics of Public Management: The HRDC Audit of Grants and Contributions* (Toronto: University of Toronto Press/The Institute of Public Administration of Canada, 2003).

Serge Joyal, ed., *Protecting Canadian Democracy: The Senate You Never Knew* (Montreal and Kingston: McGill–Queen's University Press/Canadian Centre for Management Development, 2003).

David McInnes, *Taking It to the Hill: The Complete Guide to Appearing Before (and Surviving) Parliamentary Committees* (Ottawa: University of Ottawa Press, 1999).

Donald J. Savoie, *Governing from the Centre: The Concentration of Power in Canadian Politics* (Toronto: University of Toronto Press, 1999).

F. Leslie Seidle and David C. Docherty, eds., *Reforming Parliamentary Democracy* (Montreal and Kingston: McGill–Queen's University Press, 2003).

Websites

The Parliament of Canada website (www.parl.gc.ca) is a gold mine of information about the last three parliaments (numbers 36–38, at time of writing). It provides the full text of government and Private Members' Bills, the Standing Orders, *Legislative Summaries* prepared by the Library of Parliament, and committee minutes and reports.

NOTES

1. Canada, Office of the Prime Minister, *Democratic Reform,* news release, December 12, 2003; Canada, Privy Council Office, *Ethics, Responsibility, Accountability: An Action Plan for Democratic Reform* (Ottawa, February 2004) (accessed at www.pm.gc.ca, September 2004).

2. The government accepted recommendations from two Commons committees—Government Operations and Estimates, and Procedure and House Affairs—for amendments to the Standing Orders. Most of these related to the process for reviewing the annual Estimates, and the procedure governing Private Members' Bills. The government also made good on its promise to refer more Bills to committee before second reading, as discussed later in this chapter.

3. Martin had good reason to be committed to parliamentary reform: he had won the support of a majority of Liberal MPs during his leadership fight with Jean Chrétien (discussed in Chapter 3), in part by promising them a greater role in policy-making under his prime ministership.

4. For a description of this process, see Peter Dobell and Martin Ulrich, *Parliament's Performance in the Budget Process: A Case Study* (Montreal: Institute for Research on Public Policy, May 2002), 8–10; available online at www.irpp.org.

5. On the impact of minority status on the government caucus and committee dynamics, see Peter Dobell, *What Could Canadians Expect from a Minority Government?* (Montreal: Institute for Research on Public Policy, November 2000); available online at www.irpp.org.

6. Douglas L. Bland and Roy Rempel, *A Vigilant Parliament: Building Competence for Effective Parliamentary Oversight of National Defence and the Canadian Armed Forces* (Montreal: Institute for Research on Public Policy, February 2004), 8; available online at www.irpp.org.

7. Bland and Rempel, 47–54.

8. Jennifer Smith, "Debating the Reform of Canada's Parliament," in F. Leslie Seidle and David C. Docherty, eds., *Reforming Parliamentary Democracy* (Montreal and Kingston: McGill–Queen's University Press, 2003), 150.

9. David McInnes, *Taking It to the Hill: The Complete Guide to Appearing Before (and Surviving) Parliamentary Committees* (Ottawa: University of Ottawa Press, 1999), 71.

10. Dobell, *What Could Canadians Expect from a Minority Government?*, 12.

11. McInnes, 70.

12. The growing incidence of minority reports in recent years is a bad sign for committees. A lack of consensus weakens the political impact of committee recommendations, and makes it easier for the government of the day to ignore proposals with which it does not agree. See Peter Dobell, *Reforming Parliamentary Practice: The Views of MPs* (Montreal: Institute for Research on Public Policy, December 2000), 26–27; available online at www.irpp.org.

13. Dobell, *What Could Canadians Expect from a Minority Government?* 12–13.

14. The exceptions are proposed constitutional amendments, over which the Senate has a suspensive veto; it can delay their passage for up to 180 sitting days, but it cannot block them altogether.

15. Mark Audcent, "The Senate Veto: Opinion of the Law Clerk and Parliamentary Counsel" (Ottawa: Senate of Canada, 1999), 63, quoted in David Smith, "The Improvement of the Senate by Nonconstitutional Means" in Serge Joyal, ed., *Protecting Canadian Democracy: The Senate You Never Knew* (Montreal and Kingston: McGill–Queen's University Press/Canadian Centre for Management Development, 2003), 244.

16. Paul G. Thomas, "Comparing the Lawmaking Roles of the Senate and House of Commons," in Joyal, ed., *Protecting Canadian Democracy*, 198.

17. Most Senate amendments are technical in nature. They reflect the policy expertise of individual senators, and the higher quality of most Senate committee reviews. The majority of amendments are accepted by the government. See C.E.S. Franks, "The Canadian Senate in Modern Times," in Joyal, ed., *Protecting Canadian Democracy*, 151–88.

18. Dobell, *Reforming Parliamentary Practice*, 8.

19. Most laws passed by Parliament authorize the Crown to make any regulations necessary for their implementation. For example, a Bill that establishes a Crown corporation will contain provisions empowering the Cabinet to appoint directors to its board. Although regulations, as a matter of constitutional convention, should not usurp the power of Parliament (for example, by imposing new taxes or expenditures, or creating new criminal offences), there is little Parliament can do when the Cabinet decides to interpret its delegated legislative powers very broadly. Source: Privy Council Office, *Cabinet Directive on Law-Making* (Ottawa, March 1999), section 2; to access this document online, go to www.pco-bcp.gc.ca and enter "Cabinet Directive on Law-Making" in the Search window.

20. Lowell Murray, "Which Criticisms Are Founded?," 139; Franks, "The Canadian Senate in Modern Times," 164–65 and 169–73; Thomas, "Comparing the Lawmaking Roles," 201–06; all in Joyal, ed., *Protecting Canadian Democracy*.

21. Mark MacGuigan, quoted in Robert J. Jackson and Doreen Jackson, *Politics in Canada*, 3rd edition (Scarborough, ON: Prentice Hall, 1994), 347.

22. Donald J. Savoie, *Governing from the Centre: The Concentration of Power in Canadian Politics* (Toronto: University of Toronto Press, 1999), 93.

23. Savoie, 262.

24. Thomas, "Comparing the Lawmaking Roles", 212–25.

25. Paul G. Thomas, "Parties and Regional Representation," in Herman Bakvis, ed., *Representation, Integration and Political Parties in Canada*, volume 14 of the collected research studies for the Royal Commission on Electoral Reform and Party Financing (Toronto: Dundurn Press, 1991), 219–24.

26. Ronald L. Watts, "Bicameralism in Federal Parliamentary Systems," in Joyal, ed., *Protecting Canadian Democracy*, 67–104.

27. Colin Campbell, *The Canadian Senate: A Lobby from Within* (Toronto: Macmillan, 1978).

28. Thomas, "Comparing the Lawmaking Roles," 210–11.

29. Janet Ajzenstat, "Bicameralism and Canada's Founders: The Origins of the Canadian Senate," in Joyal, ed., *Protecting Canadian Democracy*, 11.

30. Mark MacGuigan, quoted in Jackson and Jackson, 350.

31. David C. Docherty, *Mr. Smith Goes to Ottawa: Life in the House of Commons* (Vancouver: UBC Press, 1997), 190.

32. Docherty, *Mr. Smith Goes to Ottawa*, 191–92.

33. Docherty, *Mr. Smith Goes to Ottawa*, 157.

34. Jane Taber, "Tories, NDP and Bloc unite to demand more clout," *The Globe and Mail*, September 10, 2004; accessed online at www.globeandmail.com.

35. David C. Docherty, "Conclusion: Can Canada Learn Some Lessons?," in F. Leslie Seidle and David C. Docherty, eds., *Reforming Parliamentary Democracy* (Montreal and Kingston: McGill–Queen's University Press, 2003), 231.

36. David C. Docherty and Stephen White, "Parliamentary Democracy in Canada," *Parliamentary Affairs*, 57:3 (2004), 613–29, 622.

37. Dobell, *Reforming Parliamentary Practice*, 9–10.

38. As we will see later in this chapter, there is some evidence of a "personal vote" for veteran MPs. However, this does not develop until after an MP has won two consecutive elections—which most fail to do. See Docherty, *Mr. Smith Goes to Ottawa*, 212.

39. Docherty, *Mr. Smith Goes to Ottawa*, 101.

40. Note, however, that some government backbenchers regard policy expertise as a prerequisite for Cabinet appointment. Therefore, they perceive a strong incentive to demonstrate a thorough grasp of at least one field of public policy. See Docherty, *Mr. Smith Goes to Ottawa*, 128.

41. Docherty, *Mr. Smith Goes to Ottawa*, 173.

42. Bills C-18 and C-21, both sponsored by the minister of Finance, received brief examinations from the Standing Committee on Finance. The Standing Committee on Procedure and House Affairs made two technical amendments to Bill C-3, *An Act to amend the* Canada Elections Act *and the* Income Tax Act. Information about these Bills, and the status of government Bills at the end of the thirty-seventh Parliament, is available on www.parl.gc.ca.

43. Source: "Status of House Business: Sunday, October 22, 2000," *Government Bills*, Commons, Bill C-2. Available online at www.parl.gc.ca under "Bills," 36th Parliament, second session (retrieved March 2001).

44. Jack Stilborn, "Forty Years of Not Reforming the Senate—Taking Stock," in Joyal, ed., *Protecting Canadian Democracy*, 31–66.

45. 36th Parliament, 2nd Session, *Hansard*, Number 133, Friday, October 20, 2000, 1105–10; obtained online at www.parl.gc.ca (retrieved March 2001).

46. The primary source for this section is Colin Pilkington, *Representative Democracy in Britain Today* (Manchester: Manchester University Press, 1997), Chapter 1. See also David C. Docherty and F. Leslie Seidle, "Introduction," in Seidle and Docherty, eds., *Reforming Parliamentary Democracy*, 5–7.

47. *Report of the Special Committee on the Modernization and Improvement of the Procedures of the House of Commons*, June 1, 2001, paragraph 5.

48. For a useful summary of reforms to parliamentary government in several former British colonies, see David C. Docherty and F. Leslie Seidle, "Introduction," in Seidle and Docherty, eds., *Reforming Parliamentary Democracy*, 3–19.

49. Ajzenstat, "Bicameralism and Canada's Founders," 3–8.

50. In tribute to the courage of past Speakers, who sometimes risked their necks when they had to tell the king that the Commons refused his requests for money, modern Speakers traditionally put on a show of reluctance when they are sworn in to office.

51. Docherty, *Mr. Smith Goes to Ottawa*, 143–44.

52. Thomas, "Comparing the Lawmaking Roles," 206–09.

53. Murray, "Which Criticisms Are Founded?," 147.

54. Gil Rémillard with Andrew Turner, "Senate Reform: Back to Basics," in Joyal, ed., *Protecting Canadian Democracy*, 121.

55. In late 2000, visible minorities and Aboriginals accounted for roughly 7 percent of MPs and 10 percent of senators. See Jonathan Nagle, "Appendix: Database and Charts on the Composition of the Senate and House of Commons," in Joyal, ed., *Protecting Canadian Democracy*, Chart C-1, 326.

56. *Constitution Act, 1867,* section 51(A).

57. The Supreme Court's discussion of geographic limitations on voting equity is summarized in Chapter 10.

58. *Constitution Act, 1867,* section 51(2). Cf. Elections Canada, "Representation in the Federal Parliament," in J. Paul Johnston and Harvey E. Pasis, eds., *Representation and Electoral Systems: Canadian Perspectives* (Scarborough, ON: Prentice Hall, 1990).

59. According to the 2001 census, which is the basis for calculating current provincial seat entitlements, Canada's population is a little over 30 million. Dividing the total by 308 seats yields an average population per constituency of 97 426. That average was divided into the populations of Ontario, British Columbia, and Alberta to estimate the number of seats given in the preceding sentence.

60. For a discussion of this issue, see Paul Howe and David Northrup, *Strengthening Canadian Democracy: The Views of Canadians* (Montreal: Institute for Research on Public Policy, July 2000), 10–22; available online at www.irpp.org.

61. See, for example, Louise Carbert, "Governing on 'The Correct, the Compassionate, the Saskatchewan Side of the Border,'" in Jane Arscott and Linda Trimble, eds., *In the Presence of Women: Representation in Canadian Governments* (Toronto: Harcourt Brace, 1997), 161–64.

62. Heather MacIvor, *Women and Politics in Canada: An Introductory Text* (Peterborough, ON: Broadview Press, 1996), Chapters 8 and 9. See also Lisa Young, "Fulfilling the Mandate of Difference: Women in the Canadian House of Commons," in Arscott and Trimble, eds., *In the Presence of Women*, 82–103.

63. Robinson represented a British Columbia constituency in the Commons for a quarter-century. He left politics in early 2004, after confessing to the theft of a piece of jewellry from an auction house.

64. An ombudsman is a public official empowered to investigate citizen complaints about treatment received from, and within, the bureaucracy. While not authorized to investigate complaints about the general nature of public policy, an ombudsman has a wide range of investigative powers relating to the administration of public policy.

65. Docherty, *Mr. Smith Goes to Ottawa,* 251.

66. Docherty, *Mr. Smith Goes to Ottawa,* 121.

67. Docherty, *Mr. Smith Goes to Ottawa,* 129.

68. Dobell, 23.

69. John Ferejohn and Brian Gaines, "The Personal Vote in Canada," in Bakvis, ed., *Representation, Integration and Political Parties in Canada*, 295–96.

70. Docherty, 212–13.

71. Docherty, 194.

72. Howe and Northrup, "Strengthening Canadian Democracy: The Views of Canadians," 9.

73. Docherty, 264.

74. Howe and Northrup, Table 19, 31.

75. Harold D. Clarke, Allan Kornberg, and Peter Wearing, *A Polity on the Edge: Canada and the Politics of Fragmentation* (Peterborough, ON: Broadview Press, 2000), 189.

76. Canada, House of Commons Standing Committee on Organization and Procedure, *Minutes,* November 20, 1975, 9–10.

77. David A. Good, *The Politics of Public Management: The HRDC Audit of Grants and Contributions* (Toronto: University of Toronto Press/Institute of Public Administration of Canada, 2003), 161.

78. Savoie, 340.

79. Savoie, 289–90. See also Good, *The Politics of Public Management,* 58–59.

80. Howe and Northrup, "Strengthening Canadian Democracy," 31, Table 19.

81. The whip is an MP charged with orchestrating the legislative behaviour of his or her partisan colleagues. Whips on both sides of the House are appointed by their respective party leaders and ensure that enough members turn up to vote, that committees are staffed, and that legislative procedures run as smoothly as partisan debate allows.

82. The incidence of public dissension in government ranks was unusually high during the thirty-seventh Parliament (2000–04). The most obvious explanation is the nasty battle over the Liberal leadership between Paul Martin's supporters and those of then-Prime Minister Chrétien. A less obvious, but intriguing, explanation is that the turnover at the 2000 general election was much lower than the average; a "critical mass" of MPs with one or two terms in Parliament under their belts may have felt emboldened to challenge the Cabinet in a way that less experienced members may not. This explanation also applies to the Opposition, particularly the Canadian Alliance. Dobell, *Reforming Parliamentary Practice,* 4.

83. Docherty, *Mr. Smith Goes to Ottawa,* 148.

84. Docherty, *Mr. Smith Goes to Ottawa,* 150.

85. Docherty, *Mr. Smith Goes to Ottawa,* 160.

86. Docherty, *Mr. Smith Goes to Ottawa,* 169–70.

87. *The Business of Supply: Completing the Circle of Control,* 51st Report from the Standing Committee on Procedure and House Affairs, House of Commons, October 1998, 1.

88. House of Commons, *Précis of Procedure,* section 13.

89. Canada, House of Commons, Standing Committee on Government Operations and Estimates, *Meaningful Scrutiny: Practical Improvements to the Estimates Process* (Ottawa, September 2003), 29.

90. Dobell, *What Could Canadians Expect from a Minority Government?,* 14.

91. *The Business of Supply: Completing the Circle of Control,* 1.

92. Dobell, *What Could Canadians Expect from a Minority Government?,* 13–16.

93. *The Business of Supply: Completing the Circle of Control,* 3.

94. *Meaningful Scrutiny,* 1.

95. House of Commons, *Précis of Procedure,* section 13, (a)(i).

96. *The Business of Supply: Completing the Circle of Control,* 17.

97. Dobell, *Parliament's Performance in the Budget Process,* 15.

98. "Status of House Business: Sunday, October 22, 2000," *Government Bills,* Commons, Bill C-30 (R). The "R" designates a money Bill that has been "recommended" by the governor general.

99. Dobell, *"Parliament's Performance in the Budget Process,* 9.

100. *Meaningful Scrutiny,* 13, 19–27, and 33–34.

101. Good, *The Politics of Public Management,* 196.

102. *The Business of Supply: Completing the Circle of Control,* Recommendation 1.

103. Standing Orders of the House of Commons, s.108(3)(c).

104. *Meaningful Scrutiny,* 37–41.

105. *Government Response to 6th Report of the Standing Committee on Government Operations and Estimates,* 2004; available on the committee's website (go to www.parl.gc.ca, click on "Committee Business," and follow the links).

106. Standing Committee on Government Operations and Estimates, *Matters Relating to the Office of the Privacy Commissioner* (Ottawa, June 23, 2003), 15–16.

107. *Matters Relating to the Office of the Privacy Commissioner,* 13.

108. Ibid., 16.

109. Canada, Public Service Commission, *Audit of the Office of the Privacy Commissioner* (Ottawa, September 2003); accessed online at www.psc-cfp.gc.ca/centres/opc/report-rapport_e.htm.

110. Canada, Auditor General of Canada, *Report on the Office of the Privacy Commissioner of Canada* (Ottawa: September 2003); accessed online at www.oag-bvg.gc.ca/domino/reports.nsf/html/20030930ce.html.

111. Allison Dunfield, "Auditor cites 'failure of control' by Radwanski," *The Globe and Mail,* September 30, 2003 (accessed at www.globeandmail.com).

112. Graham Fraser, "Alcock aims to mend fences in public service," *Toronto Star,* July 21, 2004 (accessed at www.thestar.com).

113. John Ibbitson, "Public service still waiting for Martin's agenda," *The Globe and Mail,* July 13, 2004 (accessed at www.globeandmail.com).

114. The Expenditure Review Sub-Committee of the Treasury Board (the Cabinet Committee, not the permanent Secretariat—see Chapter 6) was chaired by Alcock when it was established in December 2003. In July 2004, when the new post-election Cabinet was sworn in and the Cabinet committees reconstituted, McCallum was named the chair of the subcommittee; Alcock wasn't even listed as a member, despite the obvious logic of including the resident of the Treasury Board on one of its subcommittees.

115. Standing Orders of the House of Commons (accessed September 2004), section 106(2). In the third session of the thirty-seventh Parliament, most of the vice chairs were drawn from the Conservative Party (the official Opposition), but the New Democrats and the Bloc Québécois had one each.

116. In September 2004 the three Opposition leaders agreed that in the upcoming Parliament, both vice chairs should be Opposition MPs (one from the official Opposition Conservatives, and the other from either the New Democratic or Bloc Québécois caucus). The exceptions would be the standing committees on Public Accounts, Government Operations and Estimates, and a proposed new committee on Privacy, Access to Information and Ethics; each of these would be chaired by an Opposition member, with the two vice chair positions divided between the Liberals and another Opposition caucus. At the time of writing, this recommendation had not been acted on.

117. C.E.S. Franks, *The Parliament of Canada* (Toronto: University of Toronto Press, 1987), 239.

118. Good, *The Politics of Public Management,* 4–5.

119. Ibid., 36.

120. Ibid., 53.

121. Ibid., 71.

122. Ibid., 110.

123. Savoie, *Breaking the Bargain*, 149.

124. Ibid., 74.

125. In 1925, Liberal Prime Minister Mackenzie King dissolved Parliament for a general election. The voters returned fewer Liberals than Conservatives (104 to 115). According to constitutional convention, King should have resigned immediately and allowed the governor general, Lord Byng, to call upon Conservative leader Arthur Meighen to form a government. Instead, King stayed in office and delayed the return of Parliament for as long as he could. Finally, in 1926, he had to summon the Commons so that his government could secure the funds it needed to operate. Within a short time, his government was defeated in the House. Instead of resigning, King went to Lord Byng and asked him to dissolve Parliament for another election. Byng refused, accepted King's resignation, and called on Meighen to form a government. Meighen's government lasted only a few days; after it too was defeated, Byng dissolved Parliament. In the ensuing election, King turned the governor general's actions into the central campaign issue. He was re-elected with a majority. The "King-Byng crisis" may have established a new constitutional convention in Canada: that the governor general must accept the advice of a prime minister to dissolve Parliament for an election, even when there is an alternative government available.

126. John C. Courtney, *The Selection of National Party Leaders in Canada* (Toronto: Macmillan, 1973), 222.

127. *Report of the Special Committee on Reform of the House of Commons* (the McGrath Report) (Ottawa: Minister of Supply and Services, 1985), 7.

128. Franks, *The Parliament of Canada*, 114.

129. *Report of the Special Committee on Reform of the House of Commons* (the McGrath Report) (Ottawa: Minister of Supply and Services, 1985), 9–10.

130. The Asia–Pacific Economic Conference met in British Columbia in 1997. The presence of former Indonesian President Suharto, who was widely suspected of violating human rights in his country, triggered protests. At one demonstration, RCMP officers pepper-sprayed peaceful protesters without adequate warning. The Hughes Report on the incident is available on the website of the Commission for Public Complaints Against the RCMP (www.cpc-cpp.gc.ca), under "Reports and Publications."

131. Karen Busby, "Raising the Dough: Funding for Lawyers at Public Inquiries," in W. Wesley Pue, ed., *Pepper in Our Eyes: The APEC Affair* (Vancouver: UBC Press, 2000), 173.

132. Andy Scott returned to Cabinet in December 2003.

133. Jane Stewart left politics in 2004, after being dropped from Cabinet when Paul Martin took over as prime minister.

134. Good, *The Politics of Public Management*, 76.

135. Franks, *The Parliament of Canada*, 24; see also 74–75.

136. Franks, *The Parliament of Canada*, 228.

137. Ajzenstat, "Bicameralism and Canada's Founders," 6–7.

138. Murray, "Which Criticisms Are Founded?," 138–39.

139. John Ibbitson, "Parliament's work is not done," *The Globe and Mail*, November 5, 2003; accessed at www.globeandmail.com.

140. See section 47(1) of the *Constitution Act, 1982*. Because the Senate has only a suspensory veto, not an absolute veto, over constitutional amendments, it cannot block its own reform. In recent years, some government Bills have explicitly weakened the Senate's

power to block or suspend legislation adopted by the Commons. See Serge Joyal, "Introduction," in Joyal, ed., *Protecting Canadian Democracy*, xx.

141. In 1991 the Senate split 41–41 over the Mulroney government's Bill to recriminalize abortion, following the 1988 *Morgentaler* ruling from the Supreme Court (Dossier 10.2). Under Senate rules, a tied vote is equivalent to a defeat. This rare Senate veto of a high-profile government Bill raised little public protest, likely because the Bill had little support from either the "pro-life" or "pro-choice" camps.

142. Franks, "The Canadian Senate in Modern Times," 172; Thomas, "Comparing the Lawmaking Roles," 202–03.

143. The problem of partisan "hangover" in the Senate was mitigated, to a degree, by former Prime Minister Chrétien's penchant for appointing senators who were already in their late sixties or early seventies. Over a quarter of his appointees were over the age of 70, compared to roughly 1 percent each for prime ministers Trudeau and Mulroney. (See Nagle, "Appendix," in Joyal, ed., *Strengthening Canadian Democracy*, 326–27.) While Chrétien's preference for older senators made political sense, because it allowed him to appoint more people in a shorter period of time, it may have undermined the longevity of tenure, which is one of the great strengths of the upper house.

144. Murray, "Which Criticisms Are Founded?," 134–35; Franks, "The Canadian Senate in Modern Times," 155–68.

145. Franks, *The Parliament of Canada*, 169.

146. Brian O'Neal, *Senate Committees: Role and Effectiveness* (Ottawa: Library of Parliament Research Branch, June 1994), 2; endnotes omitted.

147. Sections 123–128 of the Standing Orders.

148. Thomas, "Comparing the Lawmaking Roles," 212–14.

149. Thomas, "Comparing the Lawmaking Roles," 222–23.

150. Rémillard and Turner, "Senate Reform," 123–24.

151. The committee's mission, and its rationale for taking international human rights instruments into account, are contained in its December 2001 report. The report, entitled "Promises to Keep: Implementing Canada's Human Rights Obligations," is available online at www.parl.gc.ca. Go to "Committee Business," click on "Senate Committee List," and follow the links to the Standing Senate Committee on Human Rights. The second report was issued during the first session of the thirty-seventh Parliament.

152. Kent Roach, *September 11: Consequences for Canada* (Montreal and Kingston: McGill–Queen's University Press, 2003), 66–69.

153. The report of the Special Committee on Illegal Drugs, issued in September 2002, recommended that the simple possession of cannabis (marijuana) be decriminalized. The report is available on the Senate Committees website; go to www.parl.gc.ca and follow the links (the report was listed in the Committee Archives under the second session of the thirty-seventh Parliament).

154. Thomas, "Comparing the Lawmaking Roles," 220.

155. Franks, "The Canadian Senate in Modern Times," 152.

156. Ajzenstat, "Bicameralism and Canada's Founders," 15.

157. See Jennifer Smith, "Canadian Confederation and the Influence of American Federalism," *Canadian Journal of Political Science*, XXI:3 (September 1988), 443–64.

158. The brief exception to this rule came during the three years between the initial signing of the Meech Lake Accord in 1987 and its collapse in June 1990. During this interregnum, Prime Minister Mulroney agreed to make Senate appointments from lists submitted by provincial governments.

159. On the dilemmas created by competing institutional expectations of the Senate, see Jack Stilborn, "Forty Years of Not Reforming the Senate," in Joyal, ed., *Protecting Canadian Democracy*, 31–66.

160. C.E.S. Franks, "The 'Problem' of Debate and Question Period," in John C. Courtney, ed., *The Canadian House of Commons: Essays in Honor of Norman Ward* (Calgary: University of Calgary Press, 1985).

161. Franks, "The 'Problem' of Debate and Question Period," 9.

162. Robert Campbell and Leslie A. Pal, *The Real Worlds of Canadian Politics: Cases in Process and Policy* (Peterborough, ON: Broadview Press, 1989), 140–41 and 149.

163. Alan Whitehorn, *Canadian Socialism: Essays on the CCF-NDP* (Toronto: Oxford University Press, 1992), 92 and 168; F. Leslie Seidle, "The Election Expenses Act: The House of Commons and the Parties," in John C. Courtney, ed., *The Canadian House of Commons: Essays in Honour of Norman Ward* (Calgary: University of Calgary Press, 1985), 116–17.

164. Standing Committee on Procedure and House Affairs, *Nineteenth Report*, 37th Parliament, 1st Session (April 2001), 2.

165. McInnes, 14.

166. Leslie A. Pal, "Advocacy Organizations and Legislative Politics: The Effect of the Charter of Rights and Freedoms on Interest Lobbying of Federal Legislation, 1989–91," in F. Leslie Seidle, ed., *Equity and Community: The Charter, Interest Advocacy and Representation* (Montreal: Institute for Research on Public Policy, 1993), 121.

167. *Report of the Special Committee on the Modernization and Improvement of the Procedures of the House of Commons*, June 1, 2001, paragraph 29.

168. House of Commons, *Précis of Procedure*, section 14 (b); available online at www.parl.gc.ca (retrieved July 2000).

169. *Report of the Special Committee on the Modernization and Improvement of the Procedures of the House of Commons*, June 1, 2001, paragraph 6.

170. Under pressure from his colleagues, who voted to suspend him without pay, Thompson resigned his Senate seat in 1997. See Joyal, "Introduction," xviii.

171. Stilborn, "Forty Years," 55–59.

172. As discussed in Chapter 9, the late Quebec premier Robert Bourassa did accept a Triple-E Senate as part of the Charlottetown Accord. However, he insisted that Quebec be compensated for its loss of Senate seats by receiving a permanent 25 percent share of the Commons. This tradeoff angered English Canadians, who felt that Quebec was getting too much, while some Quebeckers feared that they would lose too much power in national politics.

173. Rémillard and Turner, "Senate Reform," 128.

174. David E. Smith, "The Improvement of the Senate by Nonconstitutional Means," in Joyal, ed., *Protecting Canadian Democracy*, 258–59.

175. See, for example, Jennifer Smith, "Debating the Reform of Canada's Parliament," 150–67; Howe and Northrup, *Strengthening Canadian Democracy*, 22–24; Dobell, *Reforming Parliamentary Practice.*

176. Docherty and Seidle, "Introduction," 3–17.

177. Some Liberal backbenchers, many of them women, spoke out strongly against the government's August 2004 decision to bring the proposed "missile shield" under the mandate of NORAD (the North American Aerospace Defense Command). Information about the new mandate of NORAD is available from the Department of National Defence (www.forces.gc.ca).

178. The split within the Liberal caucus over the proper degree of policy cooperation with the American government (and the Bush administration in particular) is well discussed in Louis Pauly, "Canada in a New North America," in Peter Andreas and Thomas J. Biersteker, eds., *The Rebordering of North America Integration and Exclusion in a New Security Context* (New York: Routledge, 2003), 90–109.

179. Kent Roach, *September 11: Consequences for Canada* (Montreal and Kingston: McGill–Queen's University Press, 2003), 65–66.

180. Roach, 67.

THE POLITICAL EXECUTIVE AND THE PERMANENT EXECUTIVE

- *identify* the key players in the federal government's political and permanent executives, and describe their different roles;
- *explain* how the Cabinet operates;
- *explain* the process by which government legislation is drafted and approved;
- *describe* and *evaluate* recent changes to Canada's permanent executive, including the blurring distinction between politics and administration, and the recent emphasis on service delivery to "clients."

INTRODUCTION

The Canadian executive is by far the largest and most powerful of the three branches of government. Indeed, when we refer casually to "the federal government," we usually mean the executive branch alone. Unlike the judicial branch, which consists of one type of institution (the courts), or the legislative branch, which is made up of two primary institutions (the House of Commons and Senate), the executive comprises a complex and sprawling array of institutions and programs. In its simplest terms, Canada's national executive can be divided into three primary structures:

1. the **Crown,** represented by the governor general (appointed for a five-year term by the prime minister);
2. the political executive (the prime minister and Cabinet); and
3. the permanent executive (the **federal public service**).

The **political executive,** as the name suggests, includes the MPs (and one or more senators) from the governing party who sit in Cabinet at the pleasure of the prime minister (and, technically, the House of Commons). The **permanent executive** consists of career public servants who work in **central agencies, line departments, Crown corporations,** and other components of the federal government.

The governor general symbolizes the prerogative powers of the British monarch. Over the centuries, her role in the executive branch has diminished from broad discretionary powers to a largely ceremonial function. Nonetheless, and despite the power of the constitutional principle of democracy, it is unwise to overlook the reserve and emergency powers of the Crown.[1] Normally, the executive powers of

DOSSIER 6.1 Central Agencies versus Line Departments

In general, line departments are large service-delivery organizations with a limited jurisdiction. They are responsible for a functional area of government policy such as agriculture, health, or transportation. Each is headed by a Cabinet minister, although ministers do not have the time or the expertise to actually run their departments. The real head of the department is the deputy minister. This terminology is confusing, inasmuch as it suggests that the deputy is a politician like the minister. In fact, the deputy minister is a senior public servant, who is responsible for the policy and administrative activities of the department. Each line department is divided into several branches, each of which reports to an assistant deputy minister. Typical branches include Policy, Programs and Services, Research, Corporate Services, and Intergovernmental Liaison.

Most of the public servants who work in each department occupy either line positions or staff positions. Line employees are linked directly to the rest of the permanent executive by the Privy Council Office (PCO), to which they report. Staff employees deliver programs and services to the public and manage the internal operations of the department. In effect, line employees participate in making the policies that the staff employees implement. A list of line departments can be found in the right-hand column of Dossier 6.3 on page 287.

Central agencies, by contrast, are small in size but powerful in jurisdiction. Their responsibilities cut across the functional areas of government; they focus on coordinating policy, not delivering services. Because of the distinct responsibilities of central agencies, their personnel are different from those in line departments. The staff of central agencies, sometimes called "superbureaucrats," are less likely to be career public servants and more likely to move from one agency to another. They tend to be more highly educated than their counterparts in the line departments and often have considerable career experience outside the bureaucracy (e.g., business or academia). The four key central agencies are the PCO, the Prime Minister's Office (PMO), the Department of Finance, and the Treasury Board Secretariat (TBS). Although Finance appears to be a line department, it is actually a central agency: it coordinates the annual budget process, which determines the policy priorities of other departments.

the Crown are exercised by the prime minister, his Cabinet, and the central agencies that report directly to him. In theory, the permanent executive carries out the orders of the political executive, subject to the laws passed by Parliament. In practice, senior public servants—especially those in the Privy Council Office and the Department of Finance—exercise enormous influence over Canadian public policy. That influence is based on two primary factors:

1. their mastery of the complex and often challenging details of policy and governance, a mastery that most temporary Cabinet ministers cannot hope to match; and

2. institutional incentives that concentrate administrative power in the central agencies.

Collectively, the three elements of the executive branch perform key government functions:

- Drafting, approving, enacting, and enforcing regulations made under the law-making authority delegated by Parliament.
- Initiating, drafting, sponsoring, and implementing the laws passed by Parliament.
- Making and executing agreements with other governments—provincial as well as foreign—often without the approval of Parliament.
- Raising, allocating, and spending public funds, nominally with the consent of Parliament, and monitoring that spending to ensure that it remains within the approved limits and has the desired effect.

Most of the activity in the executive branch is guided by laws and policies that have been in effect for decades, and by constitutional conventions inherited from Britain. Although the proposal of new legislation and policy attracts most of the attention from the media and the public, these innovations are only a small part of what Canada's executive actually does.

Our discussion of the executive branch ties together several of the concepts raised in other chapters:

- Chapter 1 argues that political institutions create incentives for the actors who operate within them. The concentration of power at the centre of Canada's executive branch creates strong incentives for Cabinet ministers to carry out the wishes of the prime minister and for public servants in line departments to follow orders from central agencies. The overriding incentive of the political and permanent executives is the same: to make the prime minister, and by extension the entire government, look good. Potentially embarrassing mistakes must be avoided whenever possible; if they cannot be avoided altogether, they must be either hidden from public view or managed appropriately. The result is a culture of caution, secrecy, and deference to the prime minister. Recently, New Public Management (NPM) and other approaches to "reinventing government" have emphasized different incentives: serving "clients" efficiently, reducing costs, and cutting "red tape." These goals may be well suited to the private sector; indeed, their advocates are often inspired by business and market models of organization. The problem is that they are not always congruent with the imperatives of public administration, especially the need to account to the public for the use of tax dollars.[2]

- Chapter 1 also outlined the constraints imposed on the federal government by globalization, internationalization, and the aftereffects of 9/11. The extent of these constraints may be significant, although they should not be overstated. It is certainly true that the federal government cannot set its own fiscal and monetary policies in isolation from global forces, although it is incorrect to suggest that this is a new phenomenon. Canada has always been a trading nation, acutely sensitive to world markets for its commodities. Similarly, one could argue that the creation of supranational agencies such as the North American Free Trade Agreement (NAFTA) or the World Trade Organization has actually empowered the executive in some ways. The federal government—as distinct from Parliament—represents Canada on these international bodies; it is solely responsible for implementing many, if not most, of the policies that flow from them. Moreover, what appears initially to be a constraint on government action (e.g., the Kyoto Protocol) can turn out to be a powerful political resource: the federal executive can claim, in response to critics inside and outside Parliament, that it has no choice but to enact the policies to which it has committed itself in front of the whole world.

  Finally, the renewed emphasis on Canada–U.S. relations in the wake of the 2001 terrorist attacks appears to have had some effect on Canadian policy. As noted in Chapter 5, for example, the federal Cabinet has been forced to harmonize security and immigration policies with those of the United States, or risk catastrophic delays to cross-border trade flows. On the other hand, former Prime Minister Chrétien resisted intense political pressure from Washington to send Canadian soldiers to Iraq. This suggests that the Cabinet is determined to retain full sovereignty over national policy wherever possible.[3] Moreover, as mentioned in Chapter 5, the new emphasis on national security tends to strengthen the autonomy of the executive branch from parliamentary oversight and control.

- In Chapter 2, we discussed worsening public perceptions of political institutions. Canada's political executive, like those in other Western states, has responded to growing criticism of government in two ways. First, it has concluded that the problem lies with the permanent executive, the "bureaucrats" whom people love to hate. As a result, it has engaged in several rounds of "reform" to the public service, with mixed results. Second, it has placed ever-greater emphasis on the service-delivery aspect of government. This makes sense, because the legitimacy of public institutions is directly related to their success in meeting the needs of citizens.[4] For example, the apparent "crisis" in Canada's health care system is focused on long waiting lists for diagnostic testing and surgery, the shortage of family doctors, and horror stories about patients lingering in pain for hours in overcrowded emergency wards. The arcana of managing the system itself, particularly the complex public financing arrangements, attracts far less public attention. Consequently, the federal government stressed waiting times and primary health care in its September 2004 meeting with the provinces and territories. In exchange for new funding, most of which was targeted toward the service-delivery issues just identified, it demanded that the provinces set meaningful "benchmarks" for performance and provide annual reports on their progress toward meeting those goals. This is all consistent with the "client-driven" approach to public management, which has become increasingly influential in recent years. The unique feature of the September 2004 health-care deal, in this context, is Ottawa's refusal to endorse an expanded role for the private sector in the delivery of health care. In other policy fields, where the political taboo against business involvement is less powerful, the federal government has embraced public–private partnerships of varying types. The primary motivations seem to be the desire to reduce service-delivery costs, and the attractions of the NPM approach to government.

- Chapter 5 discussed the dominance of Cabinet over the legislative branch. MPs who wish to become members of the political executive have strong incentives to toe the party line, even at the risk of alienating voters. For the small number who do make it into Cabinet, the institutional incentives to defer to the prime minister and his senior advisers are even stronger than for backbench MPs: the constitutional conventions of Cabinet secrecy and collegiality muzzle dissenters, while the PM's power to "fire" unsatisfactory ministers gives him considerable control over his Cabinet. However, as Chapter 5 notes, the current minority Parliament reduces the autonomy of the Cabinet and raises the possibility of genuine accountability to the legislature.

- In Chapter 8 we discuss the distinction between written constitutional law and constitutional conventions. The power of the prime minister (PM) and Cabinet is largely based on British constitutional convention, not on the Canadian constitutional text. With few formal constraints on his power, the PM enjoys a remarkable degree of authority within the political and permanent executives.

- Chapter 8 also explains how Canadian federalism constrains the law-making capacity of the federal executive, while concentrating much of the remaining power in the hands of the Cabinet and prime minister. The political and permanent executives cannot act unilaterally in most policy areas; they must coordinate their work with their provincial counterparts (see the discussion of intergovernmental relations in "No More Watertight Compartments: Intergovernmental Relations in Canada" in Chapter 8). This process of **executive federalism** allows the First Ministers and other members of the executive branch to bypass their respective legislatures, except in the case of constitutional amendments. Finally, Chapter 8 describes Ottawa's fiscal dominance in the federation; fiscal federalism is managed by the national central agencies, most of which are under the direct control of the prime minister and the minister of Finance.

- Chapter 10 discusses the new constraints on executive and legislative power in the *Charter* era. The enhanced policy-making role of the courts, especially the Supreme Court, diminishes the autonomy of the political and permanent executives. However, the executive branch has adjusted to the *Charter;* it routinely reviews proposed laws, regulations, and procedures to insulate its decisions against review (and possible nullification) by the courts.

In addition to the broad themes just identified, this chapter makes two primary arguments about the executive branch of Canada's national government. First, the prime minister, supported by the PMO and the PCO, dominates both the political and permanent executives. The only other member of the Cabinet who enjoys special prestige is the Finance minister—whose department is a central agency in its own right—and even he is clearly subordinate to the PM. (As of October 2004, there had never been a female finance minister at the federal level.) As the power of Cabinet shifts to the PM and the central agencies, as the public service relies increasingly on contracting-out and other business-inspired practices, and as middle managers are eliminated for budgetary reasons, the accountability of the executive branch to Parliament becomes ever more tenuous.[5]

As we saw in Chapter 5, the sheer size and complexity of the federal government makes it impossible for inexperienced MPs to hold the executive accountable to the electorate. In recent years, as the central agencies have acquired ever-greater authority to coordinate national policy-making, their secretiveness and their close relationship to the prime minister have concentrated power at the centre of government to an unusual degree. This trend has recently been exacerbated by international treaties and the post-9/11 security environment. All in all, the implications for representative democracy are worrisome.

The second argument is that the traditional distinction between politics and administration has lost much of its appeal, at least for Cabinet ministers. In the British model of government, there was a clear division of responsibility between the political executive and the permanent executive. Ministers, individually and collectively, made policy. They were driven by partisan political incentives—particularly the desire for re-election—to choose those policy alternatives that benefited the electorate (or at least their particular constituency). The menu of choices was prepared by public servants who were the acknowledged experts in policy and governance. Once the decisions were made by the "political masters," the administrative servants got on with the task of putting them into practice. In the NPM jargon of the 1990s, the ministers steered the ship of state; they left the rowing to the public servants within their departments.[6] The Cabinet was responsible to Parliament, and ultimately to the public, for the broad outlines of policy. The public servants were ultimately responsible to the minister, and through him or her to Parliament, for the administrative operation of government. They could not be held to account directly, either by legislators or by the electorate. They were assumed to be anonymous, nonpolitical, and loyal to the Crown rather than to the party in power.[7]

This traditional relationship between the political and permanent executives has come under attack in the past two decades. The attack has taken two forms. First, and most obviously, ministers have become increasingly unwilling to take the blame for alleged errors or mismanagement within their departments (see Dossier 6.5 on page 305). Second, the boundary between political decisions and administrative decisions has become fuzzy and, in a few cases, appears to have been ignored altogether. Two recent episodes illustrate the problem: the now-defunct Transitional Jobs Fund in the former Human Resources Development department (Dossier 5.6), under which MPs helped to decide which projects in their ridings should receive funding; and the "sponsorship scandal" in Public Works and Government Services, in which government contracts for advertising and other work were given to firms that had donated money to the Liberal Party. In the latter case, the normal controls on the contracting-out process appear to have been circumvented, or ignored, by the public servant in charge of the Sponsorship Program (Dossier 6.2).

In practical terms, the traditional distinction between politics and administration is generally acknowledged to be a false dichotomy. As we will see throughout this chapter, members of the political and permanent executives work closely together at all stages of policy development and implementation. To succeed in their jobs, senior public servants (e.g., deputy ministers and the staff of central agencies) must be aware of, and sensitive to, the political incentives under which Cabinet members operate—especially, but not exclusively, the overriding importance of protecting the prime minister. At the same time, the "political masters" must be conscious of the legal, fiscal, and practical constraints on the permanent executive. Nonetheless, the traditional distinction has considerable normative value. When politics intrudes too deeply into the permanent executive, as it may have done in the Sponsorship Program, the results can be troubling.

THE STRUCTURE OF CANADA'S EXECUTIVE BRANCH

The Crown and Governor General

The *Constitution Act, 1867* vests the executive power in the Crown (section 9). That power is formally exercised by "the Governor in Council"—i.e., the governor general acting on the advice of the **Privy Council** (section 12). In the provincial setting, the lieutenant governor holds many of the same formal executive powers, plays the same ceremonial roles, and occupies the same position in the legislative process as does the governor general in Ottawa. Yet while the Crown's executive powers are vast, they are usually exercised only on the advice and consent of the Cabinet. In practice, this means that the political executive makes the decisions, which are then formally ratified by the Crown's representative. Strictly speaking, the "Privy Council" does not exist; every Cabinet minister, past and present, has been sworn in to the Privy Council, and they retain that status after they leave the political executive. The Privy councillors who really matter are the small group (between 30 and 40) who belong to the Cabinet of the day.

The governor general symbolizes the separation of the political and permanent executives. Although the prime minister is the political head of the government, the formal executive authority of the state transcends the political personalities of the day and resides in the Crown. (In contrast, the president of the United States is not only

Shortly after the 1995 sovereignty referendum in Quebec, former Prime Minister Chrétien decided that the federal government and its symbols (especially the Canadian flag) should be more visible in that province. As part of a broader plan to coordinate and improve communications across the federal government, the department of Public Works and Government Services Canada (PWGSC) established a new Sponsorship Program to raise the profile of the federal government, to be administered by PWGSC's Communications Coordination Services Branch (CCSB). Ottawa would contribute money to community events (some outside Quebec), in return for prominently displayed advertisements.[8] Between 1997 and 2003, the Sponsorship Program contributed roughly $250 million to almost 2000 events; of that amount, more than $100 million was spent on production fees and commissions to communications and advertising firms.

In October 2000, an internal audit of the Sponsorship Program appeared on the PWGSC website.[9] Among other things, it found that "The processes used by CCSB to select and contract with the Communications Agencies . . . did not fully comply with the spirit or the letter of Treasury Board rules and directives."[10] The processes for tendering contracts were subjective, undocumented, and appeared to be heavily weighted in favour of two or three companies. One of the companies that appeared to enjoy the favour of the program's executive director, Chuck Guité, was Groupaction of Montreal. Moreover, there was little evidence to show that Canadians had received value for the monies that those companies

had received. After months of questioning from Opposition MPs, and questions in the media about possible conflicts of interest, then-PWGSC Minister Alfonso Gagliano was removed from the Cabinet and appointed ambassador to Denmark. He was replaced by Don Boudria, who was forced to publicly acknowledge in March 2002 that Groupaction had been paid over a million dollars for two identical reports that were of poor quality.

In May 2002 the auditor general issued a special report on the Sponsorship Program and three of the contracts that it had awarded to Groupaction. The report showed that there was no documentation to demonstrate why any of the examined expenditures had been necessary, or why Groupaction had received contracts at the discretion of Executive Director Guité that should have been subject to public competition.[11] At a news conference, Auditor General Sheila Fraser declared that "Senior public servants broke just about every rule in the book," and announced that she had asked the RCMP to investigate possible criminal wrongdoing.[12]

The "Sponsorship Scandal" was now at its peak, both in the media and in Question Period. Much was made by some Opposition MPs and news outlets about the "Liberal-friendly ad firms" who received money under the program. In 1999, for example, Groupaction—whose former head was charged with fraud related to the sponsorship program in May 2004, together with Guité—contributed a little over $50 000 to the Liberals.[13]

Following the release of the May 2002 report, the auditor general and her staff had undertaken a wide-ranging review of federal sponsorship and advertising programs. She was due to report to Parliament in November 2003; shortly before the expected release of the comprehensive study, Prime Minister Chrétien prorogued Parliament. The new report would have to wait until after Prime Minister Martin called the House back to work in February 2004—which meant, of course, that he would have to answer publicly for the findings. (As an officer of Parliament, the auditor general cannot issue reports to the public when the Commons is not in session.)

The conclusions in the report were highly damaging, especially the findings about the complete personal discretion that Guité exercised over contracts and the allegations that other federal departments and some Crown corporations had colluded in covering up the transfer of money to advertising agencies.[14] There was little to suggest that the money paid to the advertising and communications firms, including Groupaction, provided any value to Canadians; instead, there was ample evidence to show that the normal accounting and contracting procedures established by the TBS to ensure accountability and probity in public spending had been consistently disregarded.

Martin and his advisers referred the February 2000 report to the House of Commons Standing Committee on Public Accounts, which quickly turned into an unproductive partisan slanging match as an anticipated federal election loomed. Martin also set up a Commission of Inquiry, cancelled the Sponsorship Program, and took other steps to try to contain the political damage from the auditor general's findings.[15] But within a few weeks after the report was issued, the Liberals had fallen more than 10 points in national surveys (from around 50 percent to below 40 percent among decided voters). The scandal hurt the Liberals as they prepared for a spring election, which was put off until late June as the fallout continued. According to the preliminary findings of the 2004 *Canadian Election Study,* the "Sponsorship Scandal" was the single most important reason why the Liberals were reduced to a minority and flirted with defeat.[16]

The Commission of Inquiry into the scandal, headed by Justice John Gomery, was initiated in February 2004 and started public hearings in September 2004. The commission received internal government documents dating back to 1999, one of which described the TBS's dealings with Groupaction as "wretched experiences" and complained, "Not only do they charge exorbitant amounts for work they do not perform, but the work they do perform is, at best, incompetent."[17]

Gomery also heard allegations that Chuck Guité had been hand-picked to head the Sponsorship Program by then-Public Works Minister David Dingwall, despite concerns that had already been raised about Guité's managerial abilities.[18] Perhaps most important, the inquiry was told that a former Clerk of the Privy Council, Jocelyn Bourgon, had written a memo to then-Prime Minister Chrétien to underline his personal accountability for monies spent under his national unity initiative.[19] A few days later, the current Clerk, Alex Himelfarb, refuted any suggestion that Chrétien was legally responsible for the Sponsorship Program or any of its difficulties.[20] At the time of writing, Chrétien had not yet been called as a witness.

the political head of the American government but also its formal and symbolic head.) Even if this distinction between the head of state and the head of government is irrelevant to most Canadians, it has important practical consequences for the operation of government. By carrying much of the ceremonial load that would otherwise fall on the shoulders of the prime minister, the head of state frees the head of government to get on with the business of running the country.

In the United States, the ceremonial burden of a head of state is shared by the vice president. Vice presidential nominees are usually chosen to "balance the ticket" by representing a region (and perhaps an ideological faction) different from that represented by the presidential candidate. Ideally, however, a presidential nominee chooses a partisan running mate with the experience and the competence to replace him in case of death, incapacity, or impeachment. Because Canada's governor general has no partisan, electoral, or administrative role to play, the selection criteria are rather different. He or she is a symbolic bridge between the major linguistic and cultural communities in Canada; consequently, the office alternates between anglophone and francophone appointees, and the governor general must be fluent in both official languages. More recently, the selection of governors general and lieutenants governor has reflected new criteria for political representation, particularly gender and ethnicity. Adrienne Clarkson's 1999 appointment as governor general was symbolically important in two ways: she was the second woman to hold the post, and the first Chinese Canadian.

The governor general is the Crown's representative in Canada. Except for the rare occasions when the British monarch pays a visit, the governor general carries out the formal duties associated with the Crown. The most important of these ceremonial duties are as follows:

- appointing the prime minister and swearing in the Cabinet (although, as we have seen, the governor general merely ratifies the choices made elsewhere);
- delivering the Speech from the Throne, which sets out the government's legislative agenda at the beginning of each session of Parliament;
- dissolving Parliament and issuing a proclamation for a general election (again, this power is exercised only on the advice of the prime minister);
- bestowing Royal Recommendations on bills that authorize the raising or spending of public money (section 54 of the *Constitution Act, 1867*); and
- giving royal assent to legislation that has been adopted by both Houses of Parliament (although, in practice, the Chief Justice of the Supreme Court often performs this task).[21]

The Crown's representative in Canada has lost the executive powers that were routinely exercised by British officials before Confederation. Nonetheless, the institution of the governor general provides a potential check on the power of the political executive. She retains the reserve power to reject the advice of the Cabinet and the emergency power to keep the government running in a severe national crisis (for example, the sudden death or resignation of a prime minister). While there are alternative models for a head of state—such as the elected presidents of the United

Governor General Adrienne Clarkson during an Inspection of the Guard at Rideau Hall in Ottawa, June 2001 (© CP/Jonathan Hayward)

States and France—the Crown possesses the advantage of political neutrality. The Crown's representative must act in the best interests of the country, not of a particular political party. Beginning in the 1970s, Rideau Hall (the official residence of the governor general) was occupied by a series of former politicians. However qualified these individuals might have been, their appointment raised doubts about their impartiality in a possible political crisis. The appointment of former journalist Adrienne Clarkson implies at least a temporary return to political neutrality. (You can visit the governor general's website at www.gg.ca.)

In 2003, Clarkson and her husband (author John Ralston Saul) became the targets of public criticism for their spending habits. The House of Commons Standing Committee on Government Operations and Estimates, which had recently forced the Privacy Commissioner to resign over allegations of overspending (Dossier 5.5), turned its attention to the substantial increase in spending by Rideau Hall since Clarkson's appointment. The MPs were particularly incensed by a three-week trip to

Russia and Scandinavia, with a planned budget of over $1 million. Clarkson and Saul had invited nearly three dozen artists, writers, and businesspeople to accompany them on their travels. The governor general's staff defended the trip, pointing out that the initiative had come from the Department of Foreign Affairs and International Trade, which was also footing the bill.[22] Nonetheless, the public image of an imperious and spendthrift head of state damaged Clarkson's credibility. In the end, the committee backed down and did not formally criticize her spending—even when it was revealed that the trip cost more than $5 million.[23] So despite the officially nonpolitical status of the governor general, even she can get caught up in the partisan machinations swirling around Parliament Hill.

THE POLITICAL EXECUTIVE

When Britain granted responsible government to its North American colonies in the 1840s, the exercise of executive power shifted from the Crown to a council with the support of the legislature. In 1867, responsible government was entrenched in the preamble to the *Constitution Act, 1867* (see "Constitutional Conventions: The Unwritten Constitution" in Chapter 8.) In principle, responsible government means four things:

1. The Cabinet is collectively responsible to the House of Commons, and the prime minister must resign as soon as his government loses the confidence of Parliament.
2. Individual ministers are responsible to Parliament for the conduct of their departments.
3. Ministers are responsible to the Crown, on whose behalf they exercise authority.
4. Ministers are responsible to one another, in the sense that all must adhere to collective decisions.

In practice, as we saw in Chapter 5, Canadian ministers are no longer responsible to the House of Commons in any meaningful way, either collectively or individually. They are, however, directly responsible to the prime minister as the head of government, and they are responsible to their Cabinet colleagues. The principle of Cabinet solidarity means that Cabinet deliberations are held in secret, Cabinet documents are secret, and ministers who cannot support Cabinet decisions must resign. The constraints of Cabinet solidarity on ministerial behaviour reinforce the constraints of party discipline to which all MPs are subject.

The Prime Minister

As noted in Chapter 5, the origins of the prime ministership were relatively modest: Britain's Privy Council needed an English-speaking chairman. Over time, as party politics evolved, the British prime minister became the leader of a disciplined parliamentary majority and acquired the use of the Crown's prerogative to select Cabinet ministers.

Today, Canada's prime minister is among the most powerful heads of government in the world (at least domestically). Because the PM's power is based on constitutional convention (as opposed to written law), and because the scope of the Crown prerogatives that he exercises is so vast, he "has no outer limits defining his political authority within the Government."[24] His control of Parliament, at least in a majority government, ensures legislative approval for his priorities. In a very real sense, the prime minister *is* the government. Canada's prime ministers are listed in Table 6.1.

The specific powers of the PM are impressively broad:

- He has full discretion over the machinery of government. The PM can create, merge, or abolish departments, establish new agencies and programs, and change the size and structure of the Cabinet whenever he wishes. The evolution of one particular department illustrates the process. In 1993, Kim Campbell reduced the size of the Cabinet from 36 to 25 ministers and merged several departments into so-called "superministries." The new Department of Human Resources Development Canada (HRDC) included the former Department of Labour, the Employment section of Employment and Immigration, the Student Loans program from the defunct Secretary of State Department, and other related agencies and activities.

  After the scandal over alleged mismanagement of public funds by HRDC in the late 1990s (see Dossier 6.7 on page 316), it became evident that the department was simply too large to manage effectively.[25] In December 2003 the department was broken up into two new entities: Human Resources and Skills Development, and Social Development. A more important change reflected the new Martin government's emphasis on national security and Canada–U.S. relations (reflected in the new structure of Cabinet; see Dossier 6.4 on page 296). Martin created a new department, called Public Safety and Emergency Preparedness Canada (PSEPC). It houses the former Solicitor General's Department (including Corrections Canada, the National Parole Board, and the RCMP) and the Canada Border Services Agency (which previously was the Customs branch of the Canada Customs and Revenue Agency). Also included is the office of Critical Infrastructure Protection and Emergency Preparedness, previously located in the Department of National Defence.[26] PSEPC brings together most of the federal government's activities relating to emergency management, national security, law enforcement, and crime prevention.[27] Its creation is part of "the most sweeping changes in the government's national security structure since the start of the Cold War."[28] (Other elements of this initiative are discussed elsewhere in the chapter.)

- The prime minister chooses all Cabinet ministers, senators, and Supreme Court justices.[29] While the PM normally consults knowledgeable advisers about each appointment, the final decision is his alone. There are conventional constraints on the appointment of Cabinet ministers—most notably, they must be members of the government caucus—but within those constraints the prime minister has complete latitude to appoint (or disappoint) whomever he wishes.

TABLE 6.1 **PRIME MINISTERS OF CANADA, 1867–2004**

NAME	POLITICAL PARTY	TERM OF OFFICE
Macdonald, Sir John Alexander	Conservative	July 1, 1867–November 5, 1873 October 17, 1878–June 6, 1891 (died in office)
MacKenzie, Sir Alexander	Liberal	November 7, 1873–October 8, 1878
Abbott, Sir John	Conservative	June 16, 1881–November 24, 1892
Thompson, Sir John	Conservative	December 5, 1892–December 12, 1894 (died in office)
Bowell, Sir Mackenzie	Conservative	December 21, 1894–April 27, 1896
Tupper, Sir Charles	Conservative	May 1, 1896–July 8, 1896
Laurier, Sir Wilfrid	Liberal	July 11, 1896–October 6, 1911
Borden, Sir Robert	Conservative	October 10, 1911–October 11, 1917
Borden, Sir Robert	Unionist*	October 12, 1917–July 9, 1920
Meighen, Arthur	Conservative	July 10, 1920–December 28, 1921 June 29, 1926–September 24, 1926
King, William Lyon Mackenzie	Liberal	December 29, 1921–June 28, 1926 September 25, 1926–August 6, 1930 October 23, 1935–November 14, 1948
Bennett, Richard	Conservative	August 7, 1930–October 22, 1935
Saint-Laurent, Louis	Liberal	November 15, 1948–June 20, 1957
Diefenbaker, John	Conservative	June 21, 1957–April 21, 1963
Pearson, Lester	Liberal	April 22, 1963–April 19, 1968
Trudeau, Pierre	Liberal	April 20, 1968–June 3, 1979 March 3, 1980–June 29, 1984
Clark, Joe	Conservative	June 4, 1979–March 2, 1980
Turner, John	Liberal	June 30, 1984–September 16, 1984
Mulroney, Brian	Conservative	September 17, 1984–June 24, 1993
Campbell, Kim	Conservative	June 25, 1993–November 3, 1993
Chrétien, Jean	Liberal	November 4, 1993–December 11, 2003
Martin, Paul	Liberal	December 12, 2003–

* During World War I, the country was deeply divided over the question of whether or not Canadian men should be conscripted (i.e., drafted against their will) to fight overseas. The Conservative Cabinet was joined by English-speaking Liberals in the Union Government and was able to impose conscription after the 1917 federal election.

- Unlike senators and judges, whose tenure is protected by law, Cabinet ministers can be fired by the prime minister at any time. While individual firings are rare, PMs usually "shuffle" their Cabinets every year or two. Weak ministers whose ineptitude has embarrassed the government may be "shuffled out." In January 2002, for example, Prime Minister Chrétien fired Alfonso Gagliano from the Cabinet in response to public criticism of the sponsorship scandal. A more wholesale housecleaning usually accompanies the swearing-in of a new prime minister from the incumbent governing party. Of the 39 ministers in Martin's first Cabinet in December 2003, only 17 had served in the previous Chrétien Cabinet. (Some of those survivors were later defeated in the June 2004 election, or left out of the second Cabinet when it took office in July 2004.) The two primary reasons for the December purge were Martin's desire to project the image of a new government, and the need to reward supporters of his leadership (while getting rid of stalwart Chrétien supporters).[30]

- The PM also appoints Parliamentary Secretaries: MPs who assist Cabinet ministers in the performance of their duties. Until recently, the role of Parliamentary Secretaries was ill-defined. They could not attend meetings of the Cabinet or Cabinet committees, because they did not take the Privy Council Oath. Their primary tasks were to sit on the Commons committees that monitored their departments, and report back to the minister; they also undertook some public duties, standing in for a minister who had to be elsewhere. Parliamentary Secretaries were routinely shuffled every two years, often into committee chair positions (which, until 2002, were also appointed by the prime minister.)[31] When he became prime minister, Martin revamped the position. Parliamentary Secretaries are now sworn into the Privy Council, enabling them to attend meetings of Cabinet and its committees. They receive specific policy mandates from the prime minister, which may be supplemented by additional duties delegated by their ministers.[32] To reflect the new importance of their portfolio responsibilities, the two-year rotation of Parliamentary Secretaries has been abandoned.[33] The job of Parliamentary Secretary is widely seen as a steppingstone to Cabinet, and it is coveted by ambitious government backbenchers. The PM's appointment prerogative, together with the confidence convention discussed in Chapter 5, ensures that most of his MPs follow the party line.

- The PM, as the leader of the party with the most seats in the Commons, has a democratic legitimacy denied to the rest of the Cabinet. His public profile is by far the highest of any minister. The news media focus on the activities of the PM, which can be a mixed blessing. But the important point is that would-be challengers have difficulty raising their public profiles, unless—like Paul Martin did until January 2002—they occupy the Finance portfolio. However, Finance is traditionally regarded as the graveyard of political ambition; with a few notable exceptions, including Jean Chrétien, ministers of Finance rarely rise to the prime ministership. The reasons for this are not entirely clear, although it may be that the Finance minister's role as "bad cop" during economic recessions damages the popularity of the incumbent.

- The PM decides when to call elections.[34] During the campaign, national party leaders dominate the news coverage. When his party wins a majority, the PM takes the credit. He can silence dissent in Cabinet and caucus by reminding ministers and MPs that many of them were elected on his coattails. Even in the face of electoral setbacks, such as the 2004 Liberal minority, the PM rarely faces reprisals from his party.[35] Although he may be subject to a leadership-review vote at a party convention—for which the PM can mobilize enormous political resources, so that rarely poses a serious threat to his or her position—there is no formal mechanism in Canada for the caucus or Cabinet to fire an ineffective leader. (Contrast this security to the fate of former British PM Margaret Thatcher, whose caucus threw her out of office in 1990.)
- The most powerful central agency in the Canadian government, the Privy Council Office, reports directly to the PM. The Clerk of the Privy Council is both the deputy minister to the PM (who has the sole discretion over the Clerk's appointment[36]) and the top official in the federal public service. The Clerk recommends the hiring, transfer, and firing of deputy ministers and other senior public servants. He or she also monitors the entire permanent executive, through frequent meetings with deputy ministers, as well as the political executive, through the PCO note-takers who attend all Cabinet and Cabinet committee meetings. Every morning the Clerk briefs the PM on current developments in the executive branch. The close working relationship between the PM and the Clerk has at least two advantages for the PM: he has access to information about all departments and agencies, which the other ministers do not share, and he effectively controls the person to whom every senior public servant is directly accountable.
- The PCO handles all the paperwork for the Cabinet and its committees. It sets meeting agendas, takes and distributes the minutes, and prepares briefing materials on the issues to be resolved. The Clerk provides all these materials to the PM and submits proposed agendas for his approval. The PM can add or delete agenda items as he wishes, which gives him an absolute veto over the policy direction of the government.
- The PM chairs Cabinet meetings and summarizes the discussions. No formal votes are taken in Cabinet; the PM's summary is the only official record of the deliberations. As such, it sets out the overall policy of the government and directs the operations of the executive branch. While a PM usually "goes with the flow" on low-priority issues, he can occasionally ignore an opposing majority and declare a consensus in support of his own position on a high-priority issue.[37]
- The PCO is also responsible for preparing the mandate letters received by ministers when they are sworn in to Cabinet. These letters explain the responsibilities of Cabinet office, describe the major issues relating to the specific portfolio, and set out the PM's priorities in that policy field.[38] Some portfolios are not expected to be politically sensitive or to generate much policy innovation during a given mandate. In those cases, the minister may be advised to manage existing policies and programs, not to rock the boat. The deputy minister also receives a copy of the letter. Because the Clerk advises the PM on deputy ministerial appointments,

deputies have a powerful incentive to stick to the mandate and keep their ministers in line as best they can. While most mandate letters are pro forma, the PM does read and amend them before they are sent out. He can change a department's mandate and priority if he sees fit.[39]

- The PM has his own central agency, the Prime Minister's Office, which straddles the line between the political and permanent executives. Whereas the PCO provides nonpartisan policy and operational advice, the PMO serves as the "political antennae" of the PM. It enhances the PM's authority over the Cabinet, the government caucus, and the party organization outside Parliament. (See "The Prime Minister's Office" on page 300.)

- Although the PM does not have a specific portfolio, he is traditionally responsible for three policy fields: foreign affairs and security, national unity, and federal–provincial relations. On those issues, the Cabinet usually defers to the PM. He receives advice and assistance from the deputy minister for Intergovernmental Affairs, a Senior Foreign Policy Advisor, and a National Security Advisor, all of whom work in the PCO. The PM can participate in constitutional negotiations, trade talks, and informal meetings with premiers without interference from the Cabinet.

- As globalization shifts decision-making power from national governments to supranational agencies, the PM's position as the head of Canada's government acquires even greater importance. He meets with other world leaders, collectively or individually, striking agreements that bind the federal government without the necessity of Cabinet or parliamentary approval. Examples include World Summits, the Organization of American States, and the World Trade Organization.

- Finally, the PM can intervene in any issue that particularly interests him, or that threatens to become a problem for his government. As soon as a particular issue is identified as a prime ministerial priority, the machinery of government mobilizes to serve his will. As a former senior adviser to Brian Mulroney put it, when his boss focused on a particular issue "no one stood in the way inside the government and we always got what he wanted."[40] No Cabinet minister can enact a policy without the PM's support; conversely, prime ministers can—and sometimes do—override ministers whose preferences clash with their own. The PM is also the final umpire in conflicts between ministers.

These powers are subject to few constraints, most of them informal:

- The PM cannot act unconstitutionally. While the scope of executive power at the federal level is poorly defined, it is limited by the division of powers and by judicial review of the *Charter*. In particular, sections 4 and 5 of the *Charter* require prime ministers to seek a new mandate from the electorate at least once every five years and to submit annually to the scrutiny of Parliament.

- The PM seeks to avoid controversy and embarrassment whenever possible. The Opposition in the Commons, together with the media, can grill the PM over real or apparent errors in policy and administration. Preventing or "managing" such errors consumes much of the PM's scarce time and attention—and that of his senior officials in the "apolitical" PCO.

- A wise PM will recognize the limits of his political capital and use it sparingly. For example, the power to summarize Cabinet discussions in a way that conflicts with the views of the majority should be exercised sparingly. Otherwise, the PM risks a public revolt against his leadership and ultimately the collapse of the government.[41]

- Because of the scarcity of time, a PM can pursue only a few priorities. All other issues must be either delegated to the Cabinet, or ignored. Pierre Trudeau's priorities included the *Constitution,* the threat of Quebec sovereignty, inflation, and foreign affairs. Brian Mulroney also focused on constitutional and national-unity issues, as well as free trade with the United States.[42] Although Jean Chrétien came to office in 1993 promising to downplay megaconstitutional politics, he was forced to respond to the national-unity crisis provoked by the 1995 Quebec referendum (see Chapter 9). His other priorities included international trade—both multilateral negotiations through summit meetings and informal contacts with foreign buyers on Team Canada missions—and deficit and debt reduction. Toward the end of his decade as prime minister, Chrétien focused on his "legacy" projects. These included a new campaign-finance law (discussed in Chapters 3 and 4) and stronger ethics rules for government officials. Paul Martin's top priorities appear to be health care, improved relations with the United States, and safeguarding the budget surpluses resulting from his policies as Finance minister. While all of these men might have liked to do more during their tenure, it must be recognized that time is the single greatest constraint on a PM's power.[43]

It should be clear that the prime minister is not just *primus inter pares* ("first among equals") except perhaps when he or she attends meetings of First Ministers.[44] Even then, the federal spending power in areas of provincial jurisdiction ensures that the PM's goals often take priority over the demands of the premiers. (See the discussion of the Social Union Framework Agreement in Chapter 9.) Among his Cabinet colleagues, the PM's preeminence is unquestioned. He sets the agenda, has the final say on high-priority issues, and enjoys a broad overview of government activities that is denied to other ministers. (The minister of Finance is a partial exception to this last point, because of his responsibility for the budget process; he is, in effect, second among equals.)

While it is sometimes argued that Canada has a prime-ministerial government rather than Parliamentary or Cabinet government (recall "The History and Evolution of Parliamentary Institutions" in Chapter 5), this claim is somewhat exaggerated. The federal government is too large and too complex to be directed by a single individual, even when backed by the resources of the PCO and PMO. In the trench warfare of public policy formulation and administration, Cabinet ministers retain real influence and discretionary power. The PM's scarce time, energy, and attention are carefully rationed out to a relatively few areas of special interest, political sensitivity, or expertise. While the House of Commons rarely exercises its full power to hold the Cabinet accountable, the fact that such a power exists constitutes a potential constraint on prime-ministerial discretion. That potential is sometimes realized in a minority parliament: if the prime minister is unable or unwilling to compromise with

DOSSIER 6.3 The Federal Cabinet in Order of Precedence, September 2004

All members of the Cabinet, except the prime minister, are entitled to the prefix "The Honourable" before their names; the prime minister is styled "The Right Honourable." These prefixes have been omitted in this table for reasons of space.

NAME	PROVINCE	PORTFOLIO
Paul Martin	Quebec	Prime Minister
Jacob Austin	British Columbia	Leader of the Government in the Senate
Jean-C. Lapierre	Quebec	Transport
Ralph E. Goodale	Saskatchewan	Finance
Anne McLellan	Alberta	Deputy Prime Minister; Minister of Public Safety and Emergency Preparedness
Lucienne Robillard	Quebec	President of the Queen's Privy Council for Canada; Minister of Intergovernmental Affairs
Stéphane Dion	Quebec	Environment
Pierre Stewart Pettigrew	Quebec	Foreign Affairs
Andy Scott	New Brunswick	Indian Affairs and Northern Development; Federal Interlocutor for Métis and Non-Status Indians
James Scott Peterson	Ontario	International Trade
Andrew Mitchell	Ontario	Agriculture and Agri-Food
William Graham	Ontario	National Defence
Albina Guarnieri	Ontario	Veterans Affairs
Reginald B. Alcock	Manitoba	President of the Treasury Board; Canadian Wheat Board
Geoff Regan	Nova Scotia	Fisheries and Oceans
Tony Valeri	Ontario	Leader of the Government in the House of Commons
M. Aileen Carroll	Ontario	International Cooperation
Irwin Cotler	Quebec	Justice and Attorney General
Judy Sgro	Ontario	Citizenship and Immigration
Ruben John Efford	Newfoundland and Labrador	Natural Resources
Liza Frulla	Quebec	Canadian Heritage; Status of Women
Giuseppe (Joseph) Volpe	Ontario	Human Resources and Skills Development
Joseph Frank Fontana	Ontario	Labour and Housing

(cont'd)

Scott Brison	Nova Scotia	Public Works and Government Services
Ujjal Dosanjh	British Columbia	Health
Ken Dryden	Ontario	Social Development
David Emerson	British Columbia	Industry
Ethel Blondin-Andrew	Northwest Territories	Minister of State: Northern Development
Raymond Chan	British Columbia	Minister of State: Multiculturalism
Claudette Bradshaw	New Brunswick	Minister of State: Human Resources Development
John McCallum	Ontario	National Revenue
Stephen Owen	British Columbia	Western Economic Diversification; Minister of State: Sport
Joseph McGuire	Prince Edward Island	Atlantic Canada Opportunities Agency
Joseph Robert Comuzzi	Ontario	Minister of State: Federal Economic Development Initiative for Northern Ontario
Mauril Bélanger	Quebec	Deputy Leader of the Government in the House of Commons; Minister Responsible for Official Languages; Minister Responsible for Democratic Reform; Associate Minister of National Defence
Carolyn Bennett	Ontario	Minister of State: Public Health
Jacques Saada	Quebec	Economic Development Agency of Canada for the Regions of Quebec; Francophonie
John Ferguson Godfrey	Ontario	Minister of State: Infrastructure and Communities
Tony Ianno	Ontario	Minister of State: Families and Caregivers

Note: The order of precedence is determined by two primary factors: length of Cabinet service (the most senior ministers are listed above their less experienced colleagues, regardless of the importance of their respective portfolios) and alphabetical order. If two or more ministers are sworn in for the first time on the same day, they are listed according to the first letter of their surnames. For example, Stéphane Dion and Pierre Pettigrew joined the Cabinet simultaneously; Dion precedes Pettigrew alphabetically. Although the PM is always at the top, regardless of the other two factors, no other portfolio determines the order of precedence.

Source: The Federal Cabinet Members, http://pm.gc.ca/eng/NEW_TEAM.asp. Retrieved July 2004. Reproduced with the permission of the Minister of Public Works and Government Services, 2004. Courtesy of the Privy Council Office.

backbench MPs—both on his own side of the House and in Opposition—he risks losing a vote of confidence and the prospect of resignation. As we will see in the next section, the PM cannot govern alone; he relies heavily on the other members of the Cabinet.

■ The Rest of the Cabinet

As we noted earlier, the PM has the power to arrange the Cabinet in any way he wishes. As of September 2004, the Martin Cabinet included 39 ministers. The last Chrétien Cabinet had only 28 members, because Chrétien had distinguished between senior ministers and junior Secretaries of State; the latter were not designated as members of the Cabinet. Martin has abandoned this distinction, treating all ministers and ministers of State as full members of Cabinet.[45] Each minister is responsible for a particular policy field, or **portfolio,** within the executive branch; that responsibility may be shared with one or more ministers of State, as directed by the prime minister. A minister is usually the political head of a line department, solely responsible to Parliament "for all aspects of his or her portfolio, even in situations where the Minister is assisted by Ministers of State."[46] However, two ministers are responsible for central agencies (the minister of Finance and the president of the Treasury Board) and one, the minister for Intergovernmental Affairs, has no separate department or agency. The leaders in the House and Senate coordinate the legislative activities of the government, and are not responsible for particular policy fields (although the government leader in the House normally sponsors amendments to the *Canada Elections Act*).[47] All ministers and ministers of State are bound by the constitutional convention of collective responsibility.

Ministers of State used to play a largely ceremonial role: announcing new policies, visiting government-funded projects in Canada and overseas, and substituting for senior ministers when necessary. Under Prime Minister Martin, they all receive a mandate letter outlining their specific responsibilities within their minister's portfolio.[48] Despite their expanded role in the new government, one fact about ministers of State is consistent: by expanding the number of positions within the Cabinet, they give the PM more scope for regional and demographic representation—not to mention rewarding political supporters. (See Table 6.2 on page 292.)

Political science students are sometimes surprised to learn that few members of the Cabinet are chosen for their expertise in a particular field of policy. There are obvious exceptions: the minister of Finance requires experience and connections within the business community, while the Justice minister must be a member of the Bar. But in general, Cabinet ministers are appointed for reasons unrelated to their professional backgrounds. Every Cabinet contains at least one minister who is clearly in over his or her head, but whose appointment satisfies one or more of the criteria discussed below. In contrast, the American president must look outside Congress for his Cabinet secretaries; the separation of powers in the American *Constitution* forbids legislators to serve in the executive branch. This gives the president a huge pool of potential Cabinet appointees, whereas the Canadian PM is restricted to his or her party caucus (both the Commons and the Senate). A president can boost his political standing and strengthen his Cabinet by appointing policy experts and respected public figures; for example, President George W. Bush won political points by selecting former General Colin Powell as his first Secretary of State.

The criteria for inclusion in Canada's political executive are based on four primary principles:

1. constitutional convention;
2. regional and demographic representation;
3. seniority; and
4. the prospective minister's political (and perhaps personal) relationship to the prime minister.

As a matter of constitutional convention, a Cabinet minister must be either an MP or a senator from the prime minister's party. On rare occasions, the PM will appoint a Cabinet minister from outside Parliament; in that case, the minister must win a seat in the Commons at the earliest opportunity, usually through a by-election (a special election held to fill a single seat in the Commons). After the shock of the 1995 Quebec referendum, Prime Minister Chrétien appointed Stéphane Dion and Pierre Pettigrew to his Cabinet to strengthen his Quebec contingent. Both easily won by-elections shortly thereafter. Had either man lost, constitutional convention would have required him to resign from the Cabinet.[49]

The principles of responsible government limit the number of senators who can sit in the Cabinet. Although the government leader in the Senate is always a member of the Cabinet, senators cannot appear on the floor of the Commons; hence, ministers drawn from the Senate weaken the Cabinet's daily accountability to the House. In special circumstances, however, additional senators have held Cabinet posts. For example, the Progressive Conservative government elected in 1979 included only one MP from Quebec. Prime Minister Joe Clark appointed two Quebec senators to his Cabinet, to boost that province's representation. Similarly, Prime Minister Pierre Trudeau used Western Canadian senators to provide regional representation in the Cabinet after the 1980 election, which returned two Liberal MPs from Manitoba and none from the other Western provinces.

Regional representation has dominated Canadian Cabinet-making since Confederation. There are two distinct principles at work:

1. The Cabinet must include at least one minister from each region, and preferably one from each province. This poses problems for a PM whose party is weak in particular areas of the country. Ontario and Quebec usually dominate federal Cabinets; the smaller provinces provide fewer ministers, although this does not necessarily imply a lack of influence within the political executive. Powerful regional ministers from provinces such as Alberta (Anne McLellan) or Saskatchewan (Ralph Goodale) can become political "patrons" within their regions, securing program spending and infrastructure projects through close ties to the PM. A province that elects only one or two government MPs may find itself with a lacklustre minister, but this is not always the case.

Prime Minister Paul Martin, Governor General Adrienne Clarkson, with the federal Cabinet at Rideau Hall in Ottawa, July 2004 (© CP/Jonathan Hayward)

2. Certain portfolios are traditionally awarded to particular regions. Fisheries and Oceans is reserved for ministers from the East and West coasts. Finance and Industry are often associated with Ontario,[50] while Justice and Public Works are disproportionately awarded to Quebeckers.[51]

The practice of awarding portfolios on the basis of region, rather than policy expertise, is usually defended on three grounds:

- First, the Cabinet is the supreme body where competing regional claims are brokered. In effect, the Cabinet is the highest intrastate institution within the Canadian federal state ("intrastate" means "within the state").
- Second, regional ministers have historically played a key role in linking the provincial political communities with the national executive.[52]
- Third, the national government must reflect the two national linguistic communities. This means in practice that Quebec ministers must be sufficiently numerous to reflect the "two-nations" vision of the political community.

Table 6.2 provides a regional breakdown of the federal Cabinet as of September 2004. Note that Ontario, which currently supplies 60/135 Liberal MPs (44 percent), accounts for a slightly smaller share of the Cabinet. Quebec is over-represented in relation to its share of Liberal MPs, primarily because of the representational conventions discussed above.

TABLE 6.2 **GEOGRAPHIC REPRESENTATION IN THE FEDERAL CABINET, SEPTEMBER 2004**

PROVINCE/TERRITORY	NUMBER OF MINISTERS	% OF CABINET
Newfoundland/Labrador	1	2.56
Prince Edward Island	1	2.56
New Brunswick	2	5.13
Nova Scotia	2	5.13
Quebec	9	23.08
Ontario	15	38.46
Manitoba	1	2.56
Saskatchewan	1	2.56
Alberta	1	2.56
British Columbia	5	12.82
Territories	1	2.56
CANADA	39	100/100

Source: Prime Minister of Canada website: www.pm.gc.ca.

While the major language and religious groups have been represented in Cabinet since Confederation, gender and ethnicity are more recent considerations. The first woman was appointed to Cabinet in 1957 (Ellen Fairclough), and the first nonwhite minister was appointed in 1979 (Lincoln Alexander). Since the 1970s, prime ministers have tried to include at least one woman and one member of a visible minority group in each Cabinet. In short, the federal Cabinet has come to be seen as a mirror, if an imperfect one, of Canadian society. Partly because citizens expected to find their reflection in the composition of the Cabinet, the Cabinet grew in the 1970s and 1980s as Canadian society became more complex. By the early 1990s, there were 40 ministers in the Mulroney Cabinet.

The seniority criterion receives less public attention than the representational issues just discussed, but it has greater practical significance for the operation of the political executive. Generally speaking, the prime minister prefers to appoint experienced MPs rather than newcomers. Where he has no choice—because he leads a new government with a high proportion of rookies, or he has only a few MPs from a particular region or demographic group—the prime minister may be forced to appoint an unknown quantity. But where he has a choice, he will naturally prefer to elevate people who have proven themselves to be politically skilled. While some rookie MPs have excelled in Cabinet, inexperienced ministers are more accident-prone than their more seasoned colleagues.[53] On the whole, the Cabinet usually comprises the most experienced group of MPs in the Commons; the backbenchers on both sides are less seasoned and therefore less effective in holding the Cabinet to account.[54]

The purely political criteria for Cabinet appointment are more difficult to define than the first three, but they are often equally important.

- Caucus members who played key roles in the prime minister's successful campaign for the party leadership are often rewarded with Cabinet posts. Prime ministers like to surround themselves with trusted allies.
- The candidate who finished second in the most recent leadership contest, if she remains in politics, is virtually guaranteed a senior portfolio. (The most recent exception is Sheila Copps, who was dropped from Martin's first Cabinet and then lost a bitter nomination battle with a Martin loyalist.) However, her caucus supporters may be shut out of Cabinet unless they are entitled to portfolios for other reasons (e.g., regional representation or seniority in the party).
- Prominent caucus members from different ideological perspectives may be included in the Cabinet, in order to avoid alienating factions within the party organization. However, their experience in Cabinet is often frustrating, especially when they find themselves on the opposite side of an issue from the PM and his advisers. Lloyd Axworthy, a powerful regional minister under Pierre Trudeau, lost several key battles with Paul Martin during the first Chrétien government. Although he was a leading member of the Liberal left wing, he could not protect his Human Resources Development portfolio against the 1995 cutbacks.[55] After scoring some notable successes as minister of Foreign Affairs in the second Chrétien government, he retired from politics in 2000.

To summarize: the conventions governing the selection of Cabinet ministers tend to reduce the influence of the political executive vis-à-vis the permanent executive. The seniority criterion partially offsets the weakening effect of the representational criteria, while the impact of the political criterion is mixed: although a loyal Cabinet strengthens the hand of the PM, the inclusion of weak ministers for partisan reasons diminishes the effectiveness of the political executive as a whole. Those few ministers who enter the Cabinet with a solid grasp of their portfolios, extensive political experience, a clear set of priorities, and the support of the PM can bend their departments to their will. Most end up, if not the captives of their public servants, very dependent on them for expert advice about policy and governance.[56]

■ The Operation of Cabinet Government

Individual Cabinet Ministers

A Cabinet minister is expected to play several roles, some political and some administrative. A Cabinet minister:

- Is a member of Parliament (in rare cases, a senator) and, like any MP, must keep in touch with the constituency and serve its needs. Even ministers with safe seats—such as Herb Gray in Windsor, who won 13 consecutive elections between 1962 and 2000—know that they cannot afford to neglect their ridings. Ministers with perilous seats, such as Deputy Prime Minister Anne McLellan in Edmonton, know that their continued presence in Cabinet depends on their re-election.

- Is a member of the government caucus. The caucus meets weekly when Parliament is in session, and Cabinet ministers are expected to attend. (But recall from Chapter 5 that the caucus meets the day after the weekly Cabinet meeting, which reduces its potential influence on ministerial deliberations.)

- Sits on at least one Cabinet committee. Although these smaller groups are more efficient than the full Cabinet (see the following section, "Cabinet Committees"), their meetings still consume a great deal of time and energy.

- Must attend the weekly meeting of the full Cabinet (see "The Full Cabinet" on page 298).

- Is the political head of a line department. While the day-to-day administrative and policy tasks are handled by the deputy minister and other public servants, the minister must stay abreast of all major developments in the portfolio. Failure to do so can result in an embarrassing public slip-up at Question Period or in a media scrum.

- Is expected to maintain good relations with the important "client groups" associated with the department. For example, the minister of Justice needs to pay attention to the Canadian Bar Association; if the minister fails to appear at its annual convention or fails to consult its members about pending legislation, loss of the association's cooperation and goodwill could result.

- Sponsors all legislation that originates in the department. In addition to making speeches in the House, the minister must appear before the parliamentary Committee that examines each minister's Bills and evaluates proposed amendments.

- Is a prominent member of a national political party. At the very least, ministers are expected to make speeches at fundraising dinners and other party events across the country, and to participate in party conventions.

- Must devote considerable time and effort to media appearances, even though a Cabinet minister has a lower profile than the PM. Public announcements of new policies, the daily scrum after Question Period, interviews, and "photo ops" require intense preparation.

Given these multiple and conflicting demands, individual ministers are too busy to give much time and attention to any one role. As a result, they rely heavily on their senior departmental officials and the central agencies for information and advice on policy-making.[57] This is particularly true for new ministers, whose previous work experience rarely prepares them for the complexities and frustrations of government. The relationship between the minister and his or her deputy is fraught with tension on both sides: a minister who disregards the advice of the deputy is unlikely to be effective in Cabinet, while a deputy who sides too often with his or her minister risks losing face with the Privy Council Office.[58]

Cabinet Committees

Much of the work of Cabinet takes place in Cabinet committees. As Cabinets expanded from a handful of ministers in 1867 to 30 or more in the 1970s, they became too large and unwieldy to make collective decisions in an efficient manner. Apart from the Treasury Board, which dates back to Confederation, Cabinet committees are a relatively recent invention. Their primary purpose is to ease the burden on the full Cabinet by assigning particular policy and administrative responsibilities to smaller groups of ministers, who discuss new proposals and emerging issues in detail. In addition to reviewing proposed program changes, spending targets, and draft legislation, committees are expected to resolve interdepartmental disputes and coordinate government policy. They are assisted by officials from the PCO and from the relevant line departments, and, when necessary, by the PM. All committee decisions are sent to the full Cabinet for review; as we will see, however, prime ministers discourage their ministers from questioning committee decisions.

The number of committees has fluctuated over the years, as prime ministers experimented with different models of Cabinet decision-making. During the second Mulroney government (1988–1993) there were 11 standing committees, including Priorities and Planning, Operations, Expenditure Review, and Environment. In theory, these committees coordinated government policy across the line departments. In practice, most were undermined by the excessive workload of the ministers and by the low priority awarded them by the PM. Priorities and Planning (and later, Operations) were essentially "inner Cabinets": small groups of senior ministers who controlled the overall direction of government policy. The sheer number of committees placed huge demands on ministers, and left them little choice but to accept the recommendations of officials from the central agencies and the line departments.

When he took power in 1993, Chrétien sought to return to the more personalized, less bureaucratic decision-making style of the 1960s. His preference for smaller Cabinets allowed him to dispense with an "inner Cabinet," at least during his first mandate. He relented in June 1997, as part of a general reorganization of Cabinet decision-making following the government's disappointing performance in the federal election of that year. The Special Committee of Council was responsible for "the Government's overall legislative planning and for specific legislative issues requiring decisions by Cabinet."[59] At the same time, Chrétien set up an ad hoc Government Communications Committee that "look[ed] at Government-wide communications issues, and work[ed] to ensure consistency in how all parts of the Government reach out to better inform and listen to Canadians."[60] By the end of Chrétien's term as prime minister, his Cabinet had only five standing committees. In contrast, his successor created eight standing committees and one subcommittee; these are described in Dossier 6.4.

Cabinet committees enjoy a good measure of autonomy. Their decisions need not be ratified or even discussed by the full Cabinet, although it is informed of all committee activities. At the weekly Cabinet meeting, the fourth item on the agenda

The Chrétien Cabinet had two policy committees—Economic Union and Social Union—and three administrative committees: Treasury Board, the Special Committee of Council (SCC), and Government Communications. When Paul Martin was sworn in as prime minister in 2003, he exercised his prerogative to reorganize the political executive. He retained the Treasury Board, which is enshrined in legislation, but all of the other existing committees were abolished and replaced with a more complex committee structure.

Martin returned to the Mulroney model: a large Cabinet with two "inner Cabinets" to coordinate policy-making. He set up a Priorities and Planning Committee, responsible for the government's "strategic direction and priorities,"[61] and an Operations Committee to provide "the day-to-day coordination of the implementation of the government's agenda, including policy, House planning, urgent issues, and communications."[62] The Operations Committee also screens proposed policies and laws, deciding which ones should proceed to further discussion, and "directs issues to policy committees" as appropriate.[63] It is assisted by a Deputy Secretary to the Cabinet for Operations and Domestic Affairs.[64]

In the new Cabinet structure, there is a clear distinction between the five policy committees and the four operational committees (the two just discussed, plus the Treasury Board and its Sub-Committee on Expenditure Review). The policy committee with the broadest mandate is Domestic Affairs, which effectively replaces Chrétien's Economic Union and Social Union Committees. The Domestic Affairs Committee

"considers, in an integrated manner, economic and environmental policy issues."[65] Aboriginal issues were assigned to a separate Aboriginal Affairs Committee, reflecting Martin's emphasis on this particular file; unusually for a prime minister, Martin chairs this committee. Unlike Chrétien, who had no separate Cabinet body devoted to foreign policy, Martin has two: the policy committees on Global Affairs and Canada–U.S. relations. The latter is also chaired by the prime minister. Like the Aboriginal Affairs Committee, the Canada–U.S. committee is supported by a new PCO Secretariat.[66] Straddling the divide between domestic and foreign policy is the new Security, Public Health and Emergencies Committee. The creation of these three new committees demonstrates the impact of 9/11, SARS, and other recent crises on the operations of Canada's national government. The flexibility of our Cabinet structure allows the prime minister to reorganize the political executive in response to emerging issues.

Unlike the policy committees, which rely on individual line departments and the Privy Council Office for assistance, the Treasury Board is supported by its own central agency, the Treasury Board Secretariat. By law, the Treasury Board has six members, including the president of the Treasury Board (who chairs the committee). The vice chair is the minister of Finance. In addition, six Cabinet ministers are designated as alternates to the Treasury Board. The board "focuses on overall government management. That includes attention to proper and effective use of public funds, ensuring that the Government of Canada manages its employees well, and bringing the highest quality service to Canadians."[67] Martin's Treasury Board also has a Sub-Committee on Expenditure Review, responsible for reallocating funds "from lower to higher priority programs."[68] It was ordered to conduct a review of all existing government activities and identify potential cost savings. Finally, the Treasury Board is responsible for reviewing all proposed regulations. (See the discussion in "Regulations" on page 307.)

Under the 2003 system, responsibility for reviewing Order-in-Council appointments—apart from Supreme Court justices and other high-profile positions—also rests with the Treasury Board.

The Governor in Council population consists of more than 3,500 appointees. There are approximately 1,000 federally appointed judges, some 100 heads of mission, including Ambassadors and High Commissioners, as well as some 500 full-time and 1,900 part-time appointees in a wide array of agencies, boards, commissions, Crown corporations and Government departments. These appointees include deputy ministers, heads of agencies and members, CEOs of Crown corporations and directors, and returning officers. Their responsibilities are diverse, ranging from making quasi-judicial decisions and socio-economic development recommendations to the management of large, diversified corporations.[69]

The deputy PM, the Finance minister, and the president of the Treasury Board may participate in any Cabinet committee as ex-officio (i.e., nonvoting) members. Apart from chairing the Canada–U.S. and Aboriginal Affairs Committees, the PM takes no official role in the committee system. As noted previously, he has full access to all records of committee discussion, and the discretion to send an issue back to committee for re-evaluation if he does not believe that its decision will be approved by the full Cabinet.[70]

is an appendix containing committee reports. Although ministers have the right to challenge committee decisions, PMs frown on those who exercise it. In nearly every case, the Cabinet rubber-stamps the decisions of its standing committees. During the first Chrétien government (1993–97), only three committee decisions were challenged in Cabinet.[71] In those rare cases, the PM will send the controversial issue back to the committee instead of allowing the Cabinet to overrule its decision.

There are two final points about Cabinet committees. First, although the PM does not sit on most committees, he controls their operations at a distance. He appoints the chair of each committee, favouring ministers with an instinct for avoiding trouble and resolving disputes in private. The committees are staffed by PCO officials, who report directly to the Clerk of the Privy Council, who, in turn, reports to the PM, informing him of any problems on a committee. If there is reason to suspect that a committee report will cause tension in Cabinet, the PM can simply delete that item from the Cabinet agenda.[72] Second, the committee system complicates the representation of regional interests within the national government. Given that the most representative body—the full Cabinet—is less central to the process, the smaller and less representative committees have become more critical. The role of regional ministers has become more difficult in the decentralized Cabinet.

The Full Cabinet

In media coverage of the federal government, it is commonplace to encounter such phrases as "the Cabinet met to decide." The truth is very different:

> *Cabinet is not where decisions are made. Rather, it is where briefings are presented, infor-*
> *mation is shared, and where the prime minister and certain ministers provide a general*
> *tour d'horizon. The issues that keep surfacing at regular Cabinet meetings include the*
> *Government's fiscal position, national unity, the Government's political standing, and*
> *foreign affairs. These issues do not lend themselves to Cabinet decisions.*[73]

Cabinet ministers rarely engage in detailed policy debates during their weekly meetings. Instead, they discuss political issues raised by the PM, they hear presentations from ministers and their deputies about particular areas of concern (e.g., a slide show from the minister and deputy minister of Finance about the current state of the economy), and they ratify Order-in-Council appointments that have already been determined.[74]

As noted earlier, there are no formal votes in Cabinet. Voting makes sense as a decision-making technique only if all participants are considered equal. But on each particular issue, the influence of the ministers varies according to their departmental responsibility. For example, the ministers of Defence and Foreign Affairs carry more weight in a Cabinet discussion of Canadian forces in NATO than the ministers of Justice or Natural Resources. Some have a greater regional interest than others: a minister from Saskatchewan might contribute less to a discussion of fishing bans and the protection of cod stocks than his colleagues from Atlantic Canada. Some ministers are, or are perceived to be, more seasoned and politically astute than others. Simply taking a vote would impose an artificial and unproductive equality.

Voting in Cabinet would produce clear winners and losers, logrolling, and possibly long-standing factions, and would thus disrupt the collegiality of the ministers. Perhaps most important, it would reduce the weight of the PM to one vote. This would not only undercut his capacity for leadership but would also fly in the face of the real differences in status, electoral importance, and power between the prime minister and ministers. Cabinet decisions are therefore made by consensus; the PM summarizes the consensus, and ministers are expected to accept his summation or resign from Cabinet. This decision-making style reflects the basic institutional reality of responsible government: because the Cabinet speaks with a single voice, the search for consensus is an institutional necessity.

All federal Cabinet and committee discussions and related documents are subject to strict secrecy.[75] To some degree, this secrecy is a function of the issues themselves; public disclosure could undermine national security, or unfairly benefit private interests. More important, secrecy allows a frank discussion within Cabinet while still retaining Cabinet unity before the Commons, the media, and the electorate. Only with the conventions of secrecy in place can the Cabinet speak with a single voice and thus maintain collective responsibility. However, the Cabinet is far from leakproof: "one can find a number of instances in which ministers have flouted the long-standing norms of cabinet secrecy and solidarity, without any apparent harm to their careers."[76]

The downside of Cabinet secrecy is that regional and group representation takes place behind closed doors and out of view of the electorate. The institutional barriers to public representation of regional and demographic interests allow provincial premiers and pressure groups to claim this role as their own. We will return to the issue of pressure-group involvement in policy-making in Chapter 7.

THE PERMANENT EXECUTIVE

Central Agencies

The Privy Council Office

The senior officials of the PCO are at the heart of the federal decision-making process and wield considerable policy and political influence. As we have seen, the Clerk of the Privy Council is the most senior public servant in the federal government. The Clerk's responsibilities are threefold:

1. As the prime minister's deputy minister, the Clerk provides advice and support to the prime minister on a full range of responsibilities as head of government, including management of the federation.
2. As the secretary to the Cabinet, the Clerk provides support and advice to the ministry as a whole and oversees the provision of policy and secretariat support to Cabinet and Cabinet committees.
3. As the head of the public service, the Clerk is responsible for the quality of expert, professional, nonpartisan advice and service provided by the public service to the prime minister, the ministry, and to all Canadians.[77]

As we will see in "The Political and Permanent Executives in the Policy-Making Process" later in this chapter, the PCO is directly involved at every stage of the government's legislative planning. It is also responsible for the regulatory policy of the federal government and for intergovernmental affairs. It is staffed by the most experienced public servants in Ottawa, many of whom are posted to the PCO for short periods before returning to their line departments. Although its activities attract little public attention, the PCO is at the heart of power in both the political and permanent executives.

The Privy Council Office plays a key role in the elaboration of Government policy, supporting the Prime Minister in providing leadership and direction to the Government. This role also involves coordination. The Privy Council Office must work closely with line departments, as well as with the Prime Minister's Office, the Treasury Board Secretariat and the Department of Finance to ensure that new proposals are consistent with the Government's overall objectives and policies, and that all affected interests have been consulted. Once a decision is reached by Cabinet, the Privy Council Office ensures that it is communicated to the affected departments and oversees its effective implementation.[78]

Although the distinction between logistical support and policy advice—in effect, between administration and politics—is clear in principle, in practice the two are intertwined. The Clerk is responsible to the PM for both the smooth running of the Cabinet system and the quality of the government's legislation. Because the Clerk has the authority to promote or demote public servants and answers only to the PM, the importance of the PCO in both the political and permanent executives cannot be overstated.

The Prime Minister's Office

Unlike the PCO, which is staffed entirely by career public servants, the PMO is primarily a political and partisan body. Its size and structure are entirely at the discretion of the incumbent prime minister. Pierre Trudeau, who served as PM from 1968 until 1984, inherited a small administrative and correspondence unit. He expanded the PMO to include policy analysts, regional desks, and political advisers. Trudeau envisioned his office as a "counterweight" to the policy advice of the PCO and the line departments, and a centre for planning and coordination within the federal government.[79] Although its success in meeting these goals was mixed, no subsequent PM has completely reversed Trudeau's expansion of the PMO. The creation of a central agency to provide independent partisan and political advice reduced the influence of the government caucus, while reinforcing the already considerable power of the PM over the operations of the executive branch.

The tasks of today's PMO are threefold:

1. The administrative section supports the nonpartisan work of the PM as the head of government. It is responsible for travel, scheduling, correspondence, and other administrative matters.

2. The legislative staff supports the PM in his role as leader of the government in the House of Commons. The legislative assistant prepares the PM for the daily Question Period when the House is sitting, monitors the news to identify likely avenues of Opposition attack, coordinates the government's overall Question Period strategy (with the staff of the government leader in the Commons), and suggests suitable answers to all possible questions. Where necessary, the legislative assistant prepares background information for the PM to take to the House.

3. The political staff assists the prime minister in his role as leader of the governing party. They brief the PM about the political implications of current issues, handle his constituency work, and keep him in touch with the Cabinet and the party.[80]

To be effective, the PMO must work closely with the PCO. The latter controls the information on which the PM's effectiveness as head of government depends, while the former is responsible for advising the PM on "priorities, political strategy and tactics, and political dimensions of policy initiatives."[81] As discussed at the beginning of this chapter, the normative distinction between political decision-making and administration is not always clear in practice. The relationship between the PMO and PCO illustrates the practical difficulty of drawing a line between the two approaches. A PCO official who lacks political sensitivity will find his policy advice ignored, however sound his grasp of the issues and the process. The new Cabinet papers system introduced in early 2004 appears to reflect this reality: Ministerial Recommendations approved by the PCO must now include "political perspectives, risks and strategies to address them . . . and communications considerations."[82] These are not the traditional tasks of the permanent executive; in theory, the responsibility for providing political analyses of proposed policies rests with the PMO and the ministers' political staffers. On the other side, a PMO official who does not understand how the federal government works is of little value to the PM. In 1971, a former Clerk observed that each office had a unique mandate:

> The Prime Minister's Office is partisan, politically oriented, yet operationally sensitive. The Privy Council Office is non-partisan, operationally oriented yet politically sensitive . . . What is known in each office is provided freely and openly to the other if it is relevant or needed for its work, but each acts from a perspective and in a role quite different from the other.[83]

Today, this functional distinction between the PCO and the PMO appears to be eroding.

The Department of Finance

Finance occupies a unique position among the departments of the federal government. On the one hand, it is a line department with responsibility for a particular policy portfolio. Its policy experts monitor developments in the Canadian and global economies and advise the government on appropriate responses to current economic trends. Finance also manages particular programs and services; for example, its Federal–Provincial Relations and Social Policy branch delivers the Canada Health Transfer, Canada Social Transfer, and equalization payments to the provinces (see Chapter 8). In this sense, it resembles Agriculture and Agri-Food Canada and Health Canada. On the other hand, Finance operates as a central agency with overall responsibility to coordinate fiscal policy. In that role, it prepares the annual federal budget. The Chrétien government's emphasis on budget-cutting in the mid-1990s elevated the status of Finance even further, because it required the department to sign off on any new spending proposals (which gave it effective veto power over other departments). The annual budget became "the government's major policy statement," restricting the program activities of all departments and forcing reluctant public servants to implement the priorities of the PM and the minister of Finance.[84] Even now, after several years of surplus budgets, Finance retains its central position within the federal executive.

The work of the Economic and Fiscal Policy Branch is dominated by the annual budget process. Usually in February,[85] the finance minister presents the federal budget to the House of Commons. The Budget Speech is the culmination of months of effort, beginning in October when Finance releases budget consultation papers to the public and the minister makes an "Economic Statement" to the Standing Commons Committee on Finance. The committee holds public hearings to consult with interest groups and individuals, while the minister seeks input from the business and financial communities. Traditionally, the budget process was wrapped in a thick blanket of secrecy. Leaks that might provide an economic advantage to certain groups—for example, the banking sector—were avoided at all costs. As Finance minister, Paul Martin ended this tradition, preferring instead to consult widely and to build up political support for the budget before its formal introduction in the House.

As the budget takes shape, the Cabinet and its committees evaluate the proposed spending and revenue targets. Under the new Cabinet structure, this task would likely be carried out by the Domestic Affairs Committee and Treasury Board.[86] Finance officials and the PCO's Liaison Secretariat for Macroeconomic Policy advise ministers about the strategic and economic implications of the draft budget and its spending targets for each department. After extensive economic and political analysis, the minister delivers the speech. His officials keep a close eye on its fiscal impact, and prepare to make any necessary adjustments to their overall revenue and spending plans.

The Treasury Board Secretariat

While Finance sets the broad outlines of economic and fiscal policy, the Treasury Board Secretariat oversees the detailed spending estimates tabled in the House every March. It works closely with Finance during the budget process, advising on expenditure targets and advising Cabinet committees about possible reallocations of funding. (The TBS was part of the Finance department until the 1930s, and the two agencies still share personnel and administrative resources.) The TBS is also responsible for estimating the likely cost of new policy or program initiatives. In setting expenditure targets for individual departments and programs, the TBS relies on the business plans submitted by deputy ministers.[87] Once the budget and the detailed Estimates have been submitted to the House, the TBS monitors departmental spending and keeps the PCO informed of any problems.

The TBS is also "the employer and general manager of the public service."[88] It works with the Public Service Commission (PSC)—an arm's-length agency that reports to Parliament—to ensure that public servants are properly recruited and trained.[89] The TBS and the PSC establish broad policy guidelines for the public service, which are implemented by the administrative branches within the various departments and agencies of the federal government.

When the Martin government took office in December 2003, it "remandated" the TBS as part of its plan to reduce government expenditure. The TBS is now "responsible for continuous reallocation and realignment of spending from lower priorities to higher priorities,"[90] as determined by Cabinet and its committees.

■ Line Departments

As we have seen, each line department is responsible for policy and programs in a particular field, such as transport, agriculture, or human resources development. Within each department, until recently, a strict hierarchy prevailed. The deputy minister was at the top, followed by a handful of assistant deputy ministers and increasing numbers of people in the lower levels. This hierarchical structure was supposed to facilitate a unity of command in which each bureaucrat has one person to whom he or she is directly answerable. Tasks within the organization are fragmented to facilitate an efficient division of labour. Recruitment or selection to the organization, and promotion within it, are based on merit.

In principle, each line department limits its activities to those matters that fall within its specialized jurisdiction. Accountability to Parliament is ensured by the appointment of a political head or "minister." While each department focuses on a specific area, efficient government requires that policy and administration be coordinated to avoid contradiction and duplication. In theory, that coordination is provided by the Cabinet. Civil servants are nonpartisan professionals who implement the policy goals set for them by their political masters. Moreover, to secure their independence and impartiality, civil servants, like judges, are granted security of tenure.

This model of public administration comes at a cost: continuity and hierarchy often prevail over responsiveness and innovation. Since the 1970s, successive efforts to "reform" Canada's public service have been aimed at redressing that balance.[91] Red tape was to be cut, front-line managers empowered, and public-sector approaches to administration replaced with private-sector "management" practices. These reforms failed, for the most part, because the incentives for private-sector managers are in conflict with the culture of the permanent executive—or at least the senior officials in Ottawa.[92] As we have seen, their longevity in office is determined by their ability to make their political masters look good, not by the quality of their service to the public; in consequence, they tend to "manage up."[93] A different culture prevails among the front-line managers and service-delivery staff outside Ottawa. They "manage down," focusing their efforts on the "clients" whom they serve every day. In effect, therefore, the recent emphasis on service delivery at all levels of the permanent executive is an attempt to extend the "managing down" culture from the bottom of the organizational pyramid to the highest levels.

Recent fashions in governance, particularly the New Public Management (NPM) model, were supposed to break down central control and "red tape," freeing front-line managers to deliver services and form partnerships with the local private-sector and voluntary groups (the "third sector").[94] They are expected to produce "results," not follow rigid bureaucratic procedure. The overall goal is to make government operate more like a business by "increasing the autonomy of public sector managers to better serve citizens."[95] In the process, however, government can seriously erode its capacity to manage programs and ensure accountability for the spending of public money. We will discuss the NPM in "Changing Approaches to Fiscal Management" later in this chapter.

The Federal Public Service

The institutional culture of the public service is based on at least three key principles:
1. Public servants must be politically neutral. They cannot allow their personal opinions about a given policy or government to affect their judgment.
2. Public servants know that their chances for promotion depend on their adherence to the rules and standards laid down by the Clerk of the PCO—not on their obedience to the dictates of their ministers.
3. Public servants control the knowledge and information on which policy-making and governance depend.

The second and third principles reduce the power of the Cabinet over the permanent executive, while effectively enhancing the PM's dominance over his ministers. While the political executive sets the priorities of the government and approves the broad outlines of proposed policy, the permanent executive takes care of day-to-day management and determines the details and the implementation of the government's legislative program.

A central theme of this chapter is the accountability of the executive branch to Parliament, so a brief discussion of the accountability of public servants is in order. We saw in Chapter 5 that Cabinet ministers no longer obey the constitutional convention of individual responsibility. In other words, they do not resign from the Cabinet because of errors made by their departments. If the ministers are no longer accountable, can their officials be made responsible for the minister's misdeeds? The answer is uncertain. Historically, ministers accepted the blame because they were perceived to be the "political masters" of their departments. More recently, as ministers' limited role in departmental administration has become public knowledge, deputy ministers have found themselves answering to parliamentary committees—and occasionally to the media—for mistakes and problems in their departments.[96] Traditionally, only the minister was accountable to Parliament. In 1990, the PCO issued instructions to public servants who had been called to appear before parliamentary committees. Officials, including deputy ministers, were warned against divulging confidential information, engaging in debate about alternative policies, or violating their ministers' "full confidence in the loyalty and trustworthiness of those who serve them." An official who placed her duty to Parliament above her duty to the minister would violate "the fundamental principle of responsible government, namely that it is Ministers and not public servants who are accountable to the House of Commons for what is done by the Government."[97]

Over the past 50 years, the traditional distinction between the minister's political role and the deputy minister's administrative role has become patently unrealistic.[98] Ministers increasingly acknowledge their reliance on public servants, for policy advice as well as administrative assistance, and the impossibility of keeping track of every decision made in a huge and complex organization. Given this acknowledgment, why should they take the fall for an error made by a public servant? This change in ministerial attitudes toward their officials became crystal clear in 1991, during the

Mohamed Al-Mashat had been Iraq's ambassador to the United States, and his country's primary spokesman in the West, during the 1990–91 Gulf War.[99] A few months after the war ended, the media revealed that Al-Mashat had been granted landed immigrant status in Canada. The Opposition demanded the resignations of Joe Clark and Barbara McDougall, respectively the ministers of External Affairs (now Foreign Affairs) and Immigration. Clark and McDougall refused to take responsibility for the incident, pinning the blame instead on an associate deputy minister of External Affairs. That ADM happened to be Raymond Chrétien, the nephew of then-Opposition leader Jean Chrétien. The Clerk of the PCO forced him to apologize publicly for his department's political error in accepting Al-Mashat's application to enter Canada.[100] Raymond Chrétien's treatment by his minister and by the Clerk sent a chill through the entire permanent executive:

Senior executives now heard a mixed message from the Government: We want you to take risks, we expect you to make mistakes sometimes; but if you screw up, we may hang you out to dry publicly. The refusal of ministers Joe Clark and Barbara McDougall to take responsibility in the traditional manner for departmental errors reinforced public service caution and scepticism about taking risks.[101]

"Al-Mashat Affair" (see Dossier 6.5). In an apparent attempt to shield officials from parliamentary persecution, in 2003 the PCO produced new guidelines for deputy ministers. The document distinguishes between accountability and "answerability": the former involves the risk of sanctions for poor performance or wrongdoing; the latter refers only to "the duty to explain and inform."[102] The effect of this distinction is to deny that public servants can be held personally liable for any errors or wrongdoing in their departments.

As the scope and intensity of government activity grew, particularly after World War II, the federal public service mushroomed. In 1929, Ottawa had 42 790 civil servants on the payroll. The single largest departments at the time were the Post Office (10 871), National Revenue (5771), and Marine and Fisheries (4283). There were more convicts in Canadian penitentiaries than there were civil service employees in most federal government departments.[103] By 1975 the federal government employed 273 000 civil servants, more than six times the 1929 number. Over the past quarter-century, and particularly in the 1990s, that growth was partially reversed. At the federal level, close to 50 000 employees left the public service between 1995 and 1998 as part of the Program Review initiated by the Finance department. Between 1996 and 1997 alone, there was a net drop of 13 581 or 6.5 percent, to a total of 194 396. However, that figure understates the full scope of federal government employment. Including members of the RCMP and the military, the federal executive branch payroll stood at 450 000 in early 2004.[104]

The "downsizing" of the permanent executive can be traced to two primary factors. First, cutbacks to federal spending since 1980 have forced departments to cut programs and lay off the staff employees who administered them. Second, the influence of the NPM model in government circles transformed the traditional approach to public administration (see "Changing Approaches to Fiscal Management" on page 311). Whereas post-war governments were expected to provide services directly to the public (which implies a large permanent coterie of public servants), today the public sector is regarded as a strategic partner that establishes policy frameworks for others to follow. Some services and programs have been contracted out to the private sector, which bears many of the costs associated with employment (such as pay and benefits). In this new, streamlined permanent executive, public servants are expected to perform only those functions that the private sector cannot carry out: policy-making, coordination, and financial reporting. As we will see toward the end of this chapter, however, the Canadian experience of "reinventing government" has not been entirely positive. When the purpose and structure of a large and complex institution change too rapidly, it may lose its ability to perform its existing tasks—such as ensuring accountability for the spending of public funds—as effectively as it once did. (See Dossier 6.7 on page 316 for an example.)

Services and Programs

Most of the high-profile and costly government programs—health care, social assistance, and education—are delivered by the provinces, with financial assistance from Ottawa (Chapter 8). However, the federal line departments still oversee a wide range of programs and services to Canadians, as the following examples attest:

- Public Safety and Emergency Preparedness Canada is responsible, among other things, for Corrections Canada (which operates the federal prison system) and the RCMP.
- Agriculture and Agri-Food Canada provides financial assistance to farmers who suffer poor yields or declining prices for their harvests.
- Health Canada tests new drugs and medical devices before they reach the market.
- Social Development Canada provides funding for local job-creation projects and community training initiatives. It also manages the Employment Insurance and Canada Student Loans programs.
- International Trade Canada assists Canadian exporters in reaching foreign markets.
- Foreign Affairs Canada issues passports to citizens who wish to travel abroad.

Many of these programs and services are delivered by regional offices, some—such as the Summer Career Placements Program—by temporary employees, and others by full-time public servants. Still other programs are delivered by private-sector companies and managed by public servants; for example, Canada Student Loans are obtained from chartered banks, subject to the guidelines and regulations set by the federal government. Private-sector partnerships and alternative service delivery are discussed in more detail in "The Evolving Executive" later in this chapter.

◼ Regulations

Regulations are a form of law, often referred to as delegated or subordinate legislation. Like Acts, they have the same binding legal effect and usually state rules that apply generally, rather than to specific persons or things. However, regulations are not made by Parliament. Rather, they are made by persons or bodies to whom Parliament has delegated the authority to make them, such as the Governor in Council, a minister or an administrative agency. Authority to make regulations must be expressly delegated by an Act. Acts that authorize the making of regulations are called enabling Acts.[105]

When Parliament approves a government Bill, it delegates to the executive the power to make any regulations necessary for its implementation. This delegated law-making authority should not be overly broad, and it should not usurp Parliament's right to amend the details of legislation.[106] Most regulations are made by public servants in the line departments and central agencies, subject to the approval of the Governor in Council (i.e., the Cabinet). New legislation should contain the text of the regulations that will be required to put it into effect; regulations made under existing legislation cannot exceed the authority granted by the relevant law. All new regulations must be examined by legal counsel in the Justice department and the PCO, they must be registered with the Orders in Council Division of the PCO for review by the Special Committee of Council, and they must be published in the weekly *Canada Gazette*.[107] The criteria for approving or rejecting draft regulations are set out in the regulatory policy of the Government of Canada:

- Regulatory authorities must demonstrate both that a problem or risk exists and that federal intervention is justified.
- All possible alternative means—whether regulatory or nonregulatory—of addressing the problem or risk have been considered.
- Stakeholders—industry, labour, consumer groups, professional organizations, other governments, and interested individuals—have been consulted on all phases of the identification of problems and the development of the regulatory solution.
- Intergovernmental agreements must be respected and opportunities for intergovernmental coordination exploited.
- Benefits and costs of the regulatory interventions under consideration have been assessed, the benefits justify the costs, and limited government resources are used where they will do the most good.
- Adverse impacts on the economy must be minimized.
- Systems are in place to manage regulatory resources effectively.
- Compliance and, when appropriate, enforcement policies must be implemented.
- The regulators have the resources for monitoring compliance and enforcing the regulations.[108]

Once a regulation has been published in the *Canada Gazette,* it is tabled with the Standing Joint Committee on Statutory Instruments. While this group of MPs and senators has the formal power to review any and all Orders in Council, its limited resources prevent it from undertaking a detailed examination of more than a quarter of them. In a sense, therefore, Parliament colludes in the shift of law-making power from the legislative branch to the executive.

Although the purpose of the regulatory policy is to minimize government interference in economic and social activity, Canada remains a highly regulated society. In addition to the regulations enforced by government departments, there are several regulatory agencies—statutory bodies "charged with responsibility to administer, to fix, to establish, to control, or to regulate an economic, cultural, environmental, or social activity by regularized and established means in the public interest and in accordance with general policy guidelines specified by the government."[109] What we watch on television and hear on the radio is determined by broadcast regulations established by the Canadian Radio-television and Telecommunications Commission (CRTC). Marketing boards set the prices and production quantities of chickens, eggs, turkeys, milk, and a host of other farm and agricultural products. The medicines we take, the vehicles we drive, even our food and water are subject to government standards and regulations.

From the perspective of the neoconservative political ideologies that began to dominate public affairs in the 1980s, it is not clear why government regulations are preferable to the rules that emerge from private transactions (e.g., contracts). Coupled with this skepticism about bureaucracy was a concern with the aggregate social cost of regulation. Why should regulations protect the Canadian publishing industry, say, or dairy producers? Such regulation allows these sectors to profit—or, to put it in policy terms, it encourages Canadian writing and protects the family farm and security of Canadian food supplies, but at what cost to others?

Increasingly, regulation is also constrained by international agreements. The North American Free Trade Agreement, for example, forces Canadian authorities to treat American and Mexican companies exactly as they would Canadian companies—thereby eliminating a host of discriminatory regulations that used to protect Canadian industries. Agricultural marketing boards feel pressure to open access to (cheaper) foreign supplies, and even the protections for cultural institutions are hedged and constrained. The World Trade Organization, a host of United Nations bodies, and the Multilateral Agreement on Investment are examples of international bodies and agreements that (with Canadian participation and support) gradually limit the old practices of regulation.

Technological changes, globalization, and the prominence of more ideologically conservative governments in the 1980s all contributed to the sense that the last decade has been one of massive deregulation. In specific sectors, such as transport, this perception is accurate. Transport Canada, the federal department responsible for aviation, railways, and marine traffic, houses a Programs and Divestiture Branch whose mandate includes "the transfer of ports, harbours, and airports to communities and other interests."[110] The federal government set up a nonprofit corporation, NAV CANADA, to take over its air-traffic control services. Similarly, the Economic Development and Corporate Finance branch of the Finance department houses a

Privatization, Crown Corporations, and Defence unit, the responsibilities of which include "the disposition of the Government's Crown commercial holdings."[111]

However, the reduction of direct regulation by the federal government does not imply the end of regulation altogether. Some federal regulatory activities have been shifted upward to international agreements such as NAFTA and international agencies such as the World Trade Organization; others have moved downward, to the provincial governments (e.g., the devolution of labour market training in the late 1990s). In other cases, regulatory activities that once were undertaken by government departments have been shifted to private, noncommercial agencies. Government is not out of the regulatory game; it is simply changing the rules and its strategies.

THE POLITICAL AND PERMANENT EXECUTIVES IN THE POLICY-MAKING PROCESS

Laws proposed by the executive branch fall into three categories:
1. routine (e.g., the annual federal budget);
2. improving (amendments to existing legislation to update it or to make it more effective); and
3. innovatory (new laws or policies designed to achieve a particular purpose).

When a line department proposes a Bill, it must justify the addition of new legislation to the existing body of federal law. If the purpose of the Bill can be achieved in a more efficient way—e.g., by issuing new regulations under existing delegated authority—the PCO will advise against proceeding with the Bill.

Most Bills are initiated by the policy branch within a particular line department. Immediately after the Speech from the Throne, at the beginning of a new session of Parliament, the assistant secretary to the Cabinet for Legislation and House Planning sends a letter to all deputy ministers requesting a list of Bill proposals. Under the new procedures introduced in December 2003, the first stage is the preparation of a two-page Issue Brief for review by the Operations Committee of Cabinet. In a single sentence, this document must describe the policy issue to be addressed. It also identifies "Strategic Considerations," including possible environmental, intergovernmental, regional, or international implications of accepting or rejecting the proposed policy; summarizes the views of the government caucus and Parliament as a whole; describes the funding implications, the way in which the minister expects to proceed, and expected outcomes; and suggests "Communications Considerations" (e.g., the timing of the proposal in relation to future federal–provincial or international meetings).[112] The required format for the Issue Brief demonstrates the heightened importance of international and provincial governments in national policy-making, as well as the close connection between policy and politics. Its brevity reflects Martin's goal to speed up decision-making at the Cabinet level.

The Operations Committee determines whether the proposed policy will go ahead. Together with the Priorities and Planning Committee, it decides which of the approved Issue Briefs should be turned into proposed legislation during the upcoming or current parliamentary session. The House of Commons operates on a tight schedule. Relatively few Bills can be debated, scrutinized, and passed within a given session of Parliament (which normally lasts for about two years). Therefore, Cabinet must be careful not to overload Parliament; it must decide which bills to introduce early in the session, when the chances of passage are greatest. In general, high-priority items are those that implement key policy promises in the Throne Speech, the annual budget, or the party platform;[113] those required by international or federal–provincial agreements; or those that address pressing public issues, such as criminal justice or economic conditions.

When a department is notified that the Cabinet has given priority to its Issue Brief, the experts in its policy branch prepare a Memorandum to Cabinet (MC). The MC is designed to secure "policy approval and an authorization for the Legislation Section of the Department of Justice to draft the bill."[114] Ideally, a department should follow four steps in preparing an MC:

1. Analyze the policy issue to be addressed, and compare alternative solutions to the one proposed in the Bill.
2. Consult its client groups, other departments, and other governments that may be affected by the Bill.
3. Determine and justify the impact of the proposed Bill.
4. Calculate the resources required to implement the Bill.[115]

As of December 2003, each MC must be accompanied by the written approval of the Departmental Comptroller and the Comptroller-General of Canada. These positions were established by the Martin government as a step toward "effective control, oversight and monitoring systems on public expenditure."[116] This innovation may be, at least in part, a response to the problems in the Human Resources Development and Public Works departments (Dossiers 6.2 and 6.7).

Prime Minister Martin also revamped the rules governing MCs. He introduced three new formats, replacing the "one size fits all" approach of past prime ministers.[117] The first and shortest format is reserved for policy issues that are considered to be noncontroversial. It consists of a five-page Ministerial Recommendation (MR), which sets out the sponsoring department's proposed course of action on a particular issue and analyzes it from several perspectives: political, practical, legal, regional, indicators of success, cost, and public reaction.[118] The MR is a Cabinet document, subject to strict secrecy.

The second format, which will apply to most MCs, supplements the MR with a six-page background/analysis document. This should be written in such a way that, if it eventually becomes public, it will not compromise Cabinet confidentiality. It explains why the minister believes that the proposed policy is necessary, and discusses its possible effects on other federal policies and on the public at large. The third format is reserved for policies that are likely to be subjected to "extensive consultation beyond government."[119] The MR will be supplemented with a discussion paper, which can be as long as necessary; it is expected to set out genuine alternatives that will set the agenda for discussions with "stakeholders."

The draft MC, with or without supporting documents, is submitted by the sponsoring department to the PCO for review. If it meets with the approval of the PCO, it goes to both the Operations Committee and the appropriate policy committee of Cabinet (i.e., Domestic Affairs or Global Affairs). As we have seen, the decisions of Cabinet committees are almost always accepted by the full Cabinet. After the MC has been accepted by Cabinet, it is sent to the Justice department for drafting in proper legislative form.

The Legislation Section at Justice must follow several guidelines when drafting bills for Parliament:

- First, the draft bill must be constitutional.
- Second, it must be consistent with both the civil law of Quebec and the common-law system in the other provinces.
- Third, it must be drafted simultaneously in both English and French; because both official-language versions are equally authoritative, "it is not acceptable for one version to be a mere translation of the other."[120]

Most government Bills include three main elements:

1. the preamble, which sets out the purpose of the bill (these sections are not enforceable);
2. the substance of the legislation, which consists either of amendments to existing laws or new legislative provisions; and
3. schedules containing draft regulations and any other information required to put the substance of the Bill into effect.

When the drafting is complete, the Bill is sent to the Legislation and House Planning Secretariat of the PCO. This secretariat distributes the Bill to the government leader in the House of Commons and to the other members of the Operations Committee. If it meets with their approval, the Bill returns to the relevant policy committee of Cabinet where the government leader "seeks delegated authority to arrange for the introduction of the bill in either the House of Commons or the Senate."[121] Once this authority has been granted, the government leader and the sponsoring minister sign off on the bill and prepare to introduce it in Parliament. The assistant secretary to the Cabinet for Legislation and House Planning notifies the Clerk of the House or Senate that the Bill will be introduced, and the government leader meets with the other House leaders in the Commons to work out the legislative timetable.

THE EVOLVING EXECUTIVE

Changing Approaches to Fiscal Management

The creation of Canada's welfare state after World War II vastly increased both the federal and provincial public sectors. Since the 1970s, fiscal constraints and attacks by conservative ideologues have led successive federal governments to downsize the permanent executive through cutbacks, deregulation, and privatization. The New Public Management model seeks to shift program and service delivery from the public to the private sector wherever possible, while reducing the regulatory burden on the economy and replacing hierarchical organization with flexible and decentralized management. One example of an NPM-inspired initiative in Canada is the program review undertaken by the Chrétien government in 1994.

▨ The "New Public Management" and the Problem of Accountability

While the fiscal benefits of NPM, program review, and the EMS have been impressive, their impact on public administration and accountability may be less positive. In practice, transferring "activities or programs . . . in whole or in part to the voluntary sector" means giving public money to outside agencies to deliver public services. In some cases, "improving efficiency" means contracting-out program delivery and support functions to the private sector. The official name for this approach is "alternative service delivery" (ASD). According to the TBS policy on ASD:

> *Citizens expect value for money, accountable and transparent governance, quality, timely and efficient service, and a public sector that can help to put the right social and economic fundamentals in place. For any ASD option—including partnership—the proponent should be able to make a persuasive business case from the perspective of the citizen as client, taxpayer and/or user.*[122]

The NPM focus on "getting government right"—i.e., reducing public sector activities to those that can be carried out only by government agencies—is one of two reasons for the current popularity of the ASD approach:

> *Creativity, a citizen-centred service orientation and a focus on results . . . are not the exclusive domain (or responsibility) of service agencies. Whenever it is sensible, possible and in the public interest to do so, it is the responsibility of all government organizations and managers to forsake the status quo and consider the partnership option.*[123]

The other reason is the need to reduce government spending by shifting the overhead costs of program delivery to outside agencies.

The results of NPM have been mixed. Hiring temporary employees on contract undermines the accountability of the public service, which is based on the assumption that staff personnel are full-time professionals. At least as alarming is the loss of financial accountability arising from the transfer of tax revenues to voluntary and private-sector agencies. When public money is spent by someone other than a public servant, to whom is that person accountable? The problems encountered by Human Resources Development Canada in the 1990s provide a well-publicized example of the accountability deficit created by NPM—although, as explained in Dossier 5.6, the actual

When Paul Martin became Finance minister in 1993, he knew that the federal deficit was a problem, but he was not convinced that the solution would require drastic cuts in expenditure. He thought that economic growth would meet the Liberals' deficit target of 3 percent of GDP. His officials spent a year convincing him that the target could not be met that way and were vindicated when the initial 1994 deficit projections proved to be significantly higher than first thought. In the spring of that year, Martin had to convince his Cabinet colleagues to implement a spending freeze. At this point Martin received strong support from Prime Minister Chrétien, and the freeze was imposed. The urgency of the country's fiscal problems, combined with a severe currency crisis in Mexico that raised the spectre of a similar crisis in Canada, convinced the key players in the political and permanent executives that the deficit had to be addressed immediately. Tinkering with small cuts would not be sufficient; it was time to make tough decisions about the priorities and capacities of the federal government.

During the 1993 election campaign, Liberal candidate (and former senior PCO official) Marcel Massé had called for a thorough review of federal programs. He argued that "getting government right" required Ottawa to reduce its activities to those that only it could do well, while "overhauling the delivery of public services and political institutions to make them more responsive" and devolving some powers to the provinces.[124] After his first budget failed to reduce the deficit, Martin threw his full support behind Massé's proposal and put the Department of Finance in charge of the process. The PCO assigned each department to review its programs and provided a framework for evaluation. The framework consisted of six "tests":

1. Does the program or activity continue to serve a public interest?
2. Is there a legitimate and necessary role for government in this program area or activity?
3. Is the current role of the federal government appropriate, or is the program a candidate for realignment with the provinces?
4. What activities or programs should or could be transferred in whole or in part to the voluntary sector?
5. If the program or activity continues, how could its efficiency be improved?
6. Is the resultant package of programs and activities affordable within the fiscal restraint? If not, what programs or activities should be abandoned?[125]

As each department reviewed its programs, it would be required to prepare a "business plan" for the programs that remained. Those plans would be reviewed by a central committee of deputy ministers; if the plans were not satisfactory, they would be sent back for revision. In at least one case, when a department refused to cut the minister's pet program, the committee eliminated it anyway.[126] This decision reflects the reality of program review: the first five "tests" were largely disregarded in favour of the "fiscal restraint" guidelines referred to in the sixth. Finance officials

(cont'd)

told departments how much spending to cut, and they had to juggle their activities to meet the targets. The final decisions, in every case, were made by the PM and the minister of Finance, not by the program experts in the line departments.[127] (Note, however, that the NPM principles reflected in the first five tests had an enormous impact after the cuts had taken effect, when it became impossible to deliver public services without contracting out to, or forming partnerships with, the private sector.)

The spending cuts identified by the program review, together with the transfer cuts announced in the 1995 federal budget, had an enormous impact on Canada's permanent executive.

[U]nder the program review 45,000 public service and military positions were eliminated. Long-established programs like Freight Rate Assistance and transportation subsidies for Western farmers were also eliminated, and major reductions were implemented in various agricultural and industrial subsidies. A further $1 billion in spending cuts were made in defence and $500 million in foreign aid . . . New cuts were introduced to the unemployment insurance program and to federal-provincial transfers in the social policy area. Seventy-three boards, commissions, and advisory bodies were shut down. All in all, $29 billion in cuts were announced. By 1996–97 program spending would be reduced to 13.1 percent of GDP, the lowest level since 1951.[128]

The political impact of the cuts was almost equally significant. The Cabinet and the government caucus were deeply divided.[129] Left-leaning Liberals derided the cuts as a violation of Liberal values. The PM had to intervene repeatedly to get reluctant ministers, MPs, and senators on board. By the summer of 1995, when veteran MP Warren Allmand was fired from his committee chair position for voting against the budget, everyone in Ottawa knew that the Finance minister had the full support of the PM. From that point forward, Martin and the Department of Finance began to drive the entire government agenda.

While the fight over the program review was at its height, in February 1995, the government announced a new budget process: the Expenditure Management System (EMS). In effect, the EMS further strengthened the central agencies—especially the PCO and Finance—while reinforcing the dominance of the PM and the minister of Finance over their Cabinet colleagues. In essence, the Department of Finance and the TBS set annual and long-term expenditure targets for each department and agency. The long-term targets permit strategic planning by department officials. Subject to the fiscal constraints imposed at the centre, each department is required to submit an annual business plan to the TBS: "Using the business planning approach, departments set out their strategies for changing their businesses to reflect Budget targets and government priorities."[130]

To ensure compliance with the EMS program, Finance and the TBS made four crucial changes to the federal spending process:

1. There were no "policy reserves"—i.e., pots of money squirrelled away in case of a shortfall or a new initiative during the fiscal year. Departments wishing

to develop new programs would have to find the funds internally, usually by cutting something else. One exception was the National Unity Reserve, established by Prime Minister Mulroney. It was revived after the 1995 Quebec referendum, and became the basis for the troubled Sponsorship Program in Public Works.

2. A contingency reserve was established by the minister of Finance to cover unexpected expenditures. Unlike the former policy reserves within the line departments, it was controlled directly by the Finance minister.

3. Treasury Board had a small operating reserve to lend to departments, on the strict condition that loans would be repaid. There would be no free lunch for a department that overspent its target.

4. Forecasts for economic growth, interest rates, and revenues were deliberately conservative. The annual budget projections were based on the worst-case scenario, to avoid committing the government to overly optimistic spending targets.

Together, these measures strengthened central control over public spending and forced departments to stay within their annual budgets.

Program review, EMS, and the new fiscal strategies paid off handsomely. By late 1997 it seemed clear that the federal government was headed toward a budget surplus, and the February 1998 budget confirmed that Ottawa's fiscal fortunes had been reversed. This success was partly the result of good luck; a booming economy produces higher tax revenues and makes fewer demands on government assistance programs. Nonetheless, the institutional and process changes adopted after the 1994 federal budget allowed the Finance department to take full advantage of economic growth to balance the budget and begin to pay down the national debt. The story of the budget process under the Chrétien government highlights two important themes of this chapter:

- First, the full support of the prime minister ensures the implementation of policy initiatives, even those that depart radically from his party's platform. Without the political might of Jean Chrétien and his willingness to establish the necessary organizational structures, neither program review nor the EMS would have succeeded.

- Second, central agencies with the backing of the PM can prevail over a majority of unhappy Cabinet ministers and government MPs. The power to make and implement policy decisions has shifted decisively from the "political masters" to their nonpartisan "servants" in the PCO, the PMO, TBS, and Finance. As long as the Privy Council Clerk and the PM set the incentives for ambitious politicians and public servants, neither the political nor the permanent executive will be fully accountable to Parliament, to the electorate, or indeed to anyone other than the prime minister.

financial deficit was a tiny fraction of that reported by the media and the Opposition. As Dossier 6.7 explains, while the "billion-dollar boondoggle" may have been fictional, the problems created by NPM and the budget cuts of the 1990s were real.

The problems at HRDC appear to have contributed to a more critical attitude toward business models in government. In early 2004 the TBS issued a document describing the approach of the Martin government to public-sector management. It states clearly that "Private sector models of customer service and shareholder interests do not fit the much more complex public sector management environment,

---

DOSSIER 6.7 Accountability Problems at Human Resources Development Canada

As we have seen, Human Resources Development Canada (HRDC) was established in 1993. It was the product of a merger between several departments and programs. Shortly after the creation of the new department, while its managers were still working out the details of the merger, its senior officials were caught up in the program review and EMS exercises. According to the auditor general, the NPM mantras of "empowerment" and "business practices" took priority over basic departmental functions:

> During the mid- to late 1990s, the Department emphasized the importance of cutting red tape, empowering front-line staff, and increasing the delegation of authority . . . In contrast, the Department placed little emphasis on the importance of maintaining key financial and management controls. Appropriate controls and monitoring by management must accompany the effective empowerment of front-line staff.[131]

A former senior HRDC official recalls that the budget cuts imposed in the mid-1990s fell disproportionately on the middle-management staff within the department,

because the federal government insisted that service delivery be maintained. As a result, personnel responsible for ensuring "financial and program compliance" disappeared.[132] The impact of the staff cuts was reinforced by the devolution of labour market training programs to the provinces, which created immensely complex management structures even as the people responsible for operating them were leaving the public service.[133] These developments weakened HRDC's capacity to monitor its own activities, particularly at the local level. According to the auditor general, "there was not enough emphasis on maintaining essential controls while red tape was being reduced and service improved."[134]

Under these circumstances, the NPM model—particularly its emphasis on public–private partnerships (PPPs)—appeared particularly attractive. Under the influence of private-sector management models, the federal government deliberately "loosen[ed] both financial and administrative controls," not just in HRDC but in several departments.[135] Instead of relying on public servants to deliver all of its programs and services, HRDC would entice private-sector companies and agencies to establish and pay for job-creation and training schemes by making grants and contributions available to participants.[136] The funding criteria would be flexible. Local HRDC staff members worked with their private partners to design programs, which they would then help to approve and to administer.

This decentralization of decision-making authority posed two practical problems. First, it became nearly impossible for staff at HRDC headquarters in Hull—at least those who survived the cuts—to ensure that the program conditions (e.g., the timely filing of documents) were being met. Second, there was no central record of how the grants and contributions were being spent. Financial accountability broke down, according to the auditor general:

We found a widespread lack of due regard to probity in spending public funds and to achieving desired results. Several practices in the four programs we examined were unacceptable. These included lack of adherence to program terms and conditions, inadequate project selection processes, breaches of authority, payments made improperly, and inadequate monitoring.[137] . . . Program staff often made informal arrangements with sponsors that were not reflected in formal amendments to written agreements. Some of these informal arrangements were documented; others were agreed to orally or even implicitly. Some of the arrangements were contrary to the conditions established in the written agreement or to departmental and Treasury Board policies.[138]

The experience of HRDC illustrates two failings of the NPM model. First, the decision to pursue PPPs was taken without adequate consideration for the "ambiguous allocations of responsibility" that result.[139] When the traditional approach to accountability within the public service—the clear chain of command from the deputy minister all the way down to the front-line service workers[140]—gives way, it must be replaced by some new accountability mechanism.[141] Little thought appears to have been given to this problem in the enthusiasm for business models.[142]

The internal audit conducted by HRDC, in response to growing concerns about the lack of central oversight, is not a perfect mechanism. It occurs after the problems have already arisen, and does little to prevent them; moreover, it is not really an "audit" in the sense that it tracks only the completeness of files, not the actual spending of money.[143]

Second, and more broadly, the incentives that shape the work of public servants are very different from those under which private-sector managers operate. In particular, public servants know that they are accountable to Parliament—through their ministers—for their use of public money. They are required to keep detailed and accurate records of their activities, and to obey a complex and often contradictory set of criteria (e.g., transparency, efficiency, and equity).[144] According to Canada's leading expert in public administration, "Borrowing the vocabulary and management practices of a private sector soaring in prestige and confidence does not change the obvious fact that managing government operations in a parliamentary democracy and running a business are two vastly different things."[145]

where your 'customer' is a client with services expectations, a taxpayer who wants value for money, and a citizen with both rights and obligations."[146]

CONCLUSION

As we saw in Chapter 5, the legislative branch within the national government is supposed to hold the executive accountable to the voters. The members of the political executive are also members of the legislative branch. They must obtain the approval of Parliament for their proposed legislation and fiscal plans, and they cannot continue to exercise the prerogative powers of the Crown without the confidence of the Commons. By answering to Parliament for their actions, they allow our elected representatives to hold the permanent executive accountable for its policy and spending choices.

In practice, the incentives set by Canada's political institutions make a mockery of this textbook picture of governance:

- Ambitious politicians know that they must support the PM, just as ambitious public servants have to win the approval of the Clerk of the Privy Council. The resulting concentration of power at the centre of the political and permanent executives weakens accountability.
- Senior "line" officials, together with their counterparts in the central agencies, monopolize two vital resources: information about public policy and knowledge of governance. Inexperienced Cabinet ministers, overwhelmed by conflicting demands on their time and attention, are no match for experienced public servants. The supremacy of the political executive over the permanent executive is now, in some cases, a constitutional fiction.
- In recent years, with the growing popularity of business models for public administration, the incentive structure for public servants has changed. Partly as a result, the permanent executive—and consequently, the political executive—is less accountable to Parliament for its disbursement of public funds. When the auditor general issues a scathing report and the Opposition mounts a sustained attack on wasteful government spending, the PM must respond. Otherwise, the weakening of fiscal accountability goes unnoticed.

Most Canadians pay little attention to the workings of the executive branch, despite its size and its enormous impact on our daily lives. It conducts its business behind closed doors, out of the media spotlight. Ironically, the daily dramas in the House of Commons attract the lion's share of public notice, despite their relative unimportance compared to the executive branch. This does not mean, however, that the weakness of the legislative branch has gone unnoticed. Canadians whose efforts to change public policy through the parliamentary process have been frustrated often turn to the courts for redress, as we will see in Chapter 10. Increasingly—and perhaps partly as a result of the value changes noted in Chapter 2— they are also turning to single-interest organizations to express their demands to governments. We will examine the power of the media and pressure groups in the next chapter.

GLOSSARY OF KEY TERMS

Central agencies: Those departments within the federal government whose primary responsibility is to monitor and coordinate policy-making and implementation across the entire executive branch. The four primary central agencies are the Privy Council Office (PCO), the Prime Minister's Office (PMO), the Treasury Board Secretariat (TBS), and the Department of Finance.

Crown: The source and symbol of executive power in Canada. As a former British colony, Canada inherited "a *Constitution* similar in Principle to that of the United Kingdom." Although most of the Crown's powers are now delegated to the political executive, and particularly to the prime minister, the residual and emergency powers of the Crown are vested in the governor general, who must approve all spending measures before they are submitted to the House of Commons. In addition, the Crown's representative formally appoints the political executive and signs Bills passed by the legislative branch into law.

Crown corporations: Public agencies that provide goods and services to a particular clientele. Examples include the CBC, VIA Rail, and—at one time—Air Canada. Crown corporations are ultimately responsible to the federal government, but they are normally operated at arm's length from the political executive. Canada's Crown corporations were originally established to provide goods and services that were too costly for the private sector, such as national railways and coast-to-coast broadcasting. In recent years, many have been privatized (sold to the private sector), partly because of complaints about unfair competition and partly to raise money.

Executive federalism: A style of policy-making in which the executive branches of the various governments in the Canadian federation negotiate directly with each other. The most obvious illustration of executive federalism is megaconstitutional politics, in which First Ministers—the premiers and the prime minister—meet behind closed doors to hammer out amendments to the *Constitution*. Executive federalism is often criticized as being undemocratic, because it usually takes place in secret, and as a threat to the power of the legislative branch. In most cases, deals struck between the executive branches of two or more governments are never submitted to Parliament or the provincial legislature for ratification.

Federal public service: Another name for the permanent executive. The federal public service includes the line and staff employees of all federal government departments, both inside and outside Ottawa.

Line departments: Departments within the federal government that make and implement policy in particular fields, such as agriculture, transport, and foreign affairs. Line departments deliver services to the public, whereas central agencies normally serve other government organizations.

Permanent executive: The federal public service. In principle, the permanent executive is politically neutral; as the name suggests, it remains in place when the governing party changes. It is organized hierarchically, with the Clerk of the Privy Council at the top. Within each department, the permanent executive is headed by the deputy minister.

Political executive: The Cabinet of the day. Often referred to, in colloquial terms, as "the government."

Portfolio: The traditional term for the policy assignment given to a particular Cabinet minister or secretary of state. For example, Finance Minister Ralph Goodale is said to hold the "Finance portfolio."

Privy Council: The historic term for the political executive. The *Constitution Act, 1867* refers to the executive branch of government as "the Governor in Council; the Crown's representative, the governor general, exercises supreme executive power on the advice of the Government of the day." In reality, as we have seen repeatedly, the governor general is an essentially ceremonial figure. The power of the Crown is exercised by the political executive: the prime minister and his or her Cabinet. The Privy Council does not exist, for all practical purposes, even though the central agency that serves the Cabinet is still called the Privy Council Office. The Privy Council is a constitutional fiction; the Privy Council Office is not.

DISCUSSION QUESTIONS

1. Distinguish between the political executive and the permanent executive, and briefly describe the relationship between them. What roles do they play in the creation of public policy? How has the relationship changed in recent years?

2. Why is Canada's prime minister such a powerful head of government? What is his relationship to the rest of the Cabinet?

3. When the prime minister chooses his Cabinet, what criteria does he use to decide which MPs will become ministers and which will not? In your opinion, do these criteria make sense? Why or why not?

4. What do Cabinet committees do? What resources are available to assist them in their work?

5. Briefly explain the roles and responsibilities of the four primary central agencies. In your opinion, are they too powerful? Why or why not?

6. Briefly describe the recent changes created by the emphasis on alternative service delivery. What are their implications for Parliament's control of the public purse?

SUGGESTED READINGS

Books and Articles

Herman Bakvis, *Regional Ministers: Power and Influence in the Canadian Cabinet* (Toronto: University of Toronto Press, 1991).

David A. Good, *The Politics of Public Management: The HRDC Audit of Grants and Contributions* (Toronto: University of Toronto Press, 2003).

Edward Greenspon and Anthony Wilson-Smith, *Double Vision: The Inside Story of the Liberals in Power* (Toronto: Doubleday Canada, 1996).

Donald J. Savoie, *Breaking the Bargain: Public Servants, Ministers, and Parliament* (Toronto: University of Toronto Press, 2003).

Donald J. Savoie, *Governing from the Centre: The Concentration of Power in Canadian Politics* (Toronto: University of Toronto Press, 1999).

David E. Smith, *The Invisible Crown: The First Principle of Canadian Government* (Toronto: University of Toronto Press, 1995).

Websites

Information about the Privy Council Office is available in the "Publications" section of its website: www.pco-bcp.gc.ca.

Many of the changes that Paul Martin made to the federal government since he became prime minister are described and explained on his website: www.pm.gc.ca.

Individual departments and agencies of the federal government have their own websites; to find them, go to the main government site (www.gc.ca) and click on "About Government" and then "Departments and Agencies" for an alphabetical listing of all departments and agencies and direct links to their sites.

NOTES

1. David E. Smith, *The Invisible Crown: The First Principle of Canadian Government* (Toronto: University of Toronto Press, 1995), 59.

2. Christopher Pollitt, "New Forms of Public Service: Issues in Contemporary Organizational Design," in Thomas J. Courchene and Donald J. Savoie, eds., *The Art of the State: Governance in a World Without Frontiers* (Montreal: Institute for Research on Public Policy, 2003), 217.

3. Athanasios Hristoulas, "Trading Places: Canada, Mexico, and North American Security," in Peter Andreas and Thomas J. Biersteker, eds., *The Rebordering of North America: Integration and Exclusion in a New Security Context* (New York: Routledge, 2003), 35.

4. Pollitt, "New Forms of Public Service," 232.

5. David A. Good, *The Politics of Public Management: The HRDC Audit of Grants and Contributions* (Toronto: University of Toronto Press, 2003), 32–38.

6. The metaphor of "steering" and "rowing" comes from David Osborne and Ted Gaebler, *Reinventing Government* (New York: Addison-Wesley, 1992); quoted in Donald J. Savoie, *Breaking the Bargain: Public Servants, Ministers, and Parliament* (Toronto: University of Toronto Press, 2003), 11.

7. Savoie, *Breaking the Bargain*, Chapter 3.

8. Canada, Office of the Auditor General of Canada, *November 2003 Report—Matters of Special Importance, 2003* (Ottawa: Minister of Public Works and Government Services Canada, 2003), Chapter 3, paragraph 3.6; available online at www.oag-bvg.gc.ca/domino/reports.nsf/html/20031103ce.html/$file/20031103ce.pdf.

9. This timeline relies, in part, on the time line prepared by CBC staff and posted on the corporation's website in fall 2004: www.cbc.ca/news/background/groupaction/timeline_origin.html.

10. PWGSC, *Directed Audit of the Management of Sponsorships at the Communications Co-ordination Services Branch (CCSB): Final Report* (Ottawa: PWGSC, October 2000), 2 (accessed online at www.pwgsc.gc.ca/aeb/text/archive/pfd/2000-723-e.pdf).

11. Office of the Auditor General, *Report to the Minister of Public Works and Government Services on Three Contracts Awarded to Groupaction* (Ottawa: Office of the Auditor General, May 2002); accessed online at www.oag-bvg.gc.ca/domino/reports.nsf/html/02sprepe.html.

12. Office of the Auditor General, *Report to the Minister of Public Works and Government Services on Three Contracts Awarded to Groupaction*, news release (Ottawa, May 8, 2002); accessed online at www.oag-bvg.gc.ca/domino/media.nsf/html/02prsp_e.html.

13. Groupaction Gosselin Communications Strategiques gave the party $15 680 in the 1999 fiscal year, while Groupaction Marketing contributed $36 239. The following year, the party reported donations of less than $7000 from both companies. Figures taken from the Registered Political Parties Fiscal Period Returns database maintained by Elections Canada: www.elections.ca.

14. Office of the Auditor General, *Matters of Special Importance*, 2003, Chapter 3, 11–20; accessed online at www.oag-bvg.gc.ca/domino/reports.nsf/html /20031103ce.html/$file/20031103ce.pdf.

15. The prime minister's official responses to the report were placed online at www.pm.gc.ca.

16. Elisabeth Gidengil, André Blais, Joanna Everitt, Patrick Fournier, and Neil Nevitte, "Down to the Wire," *The Globe and Mail*, July 15, 2004; accessed online at www.ces-eec.umontreal.ca/ces.html.

17. E-mail from Michael Calcott, Treasury Board Secretariat, to Evelyn Marcoux, Communications Co-ordination Services Branch (PWGSC), June 2, 1999; reproduced in the transcript of the Commission of Inquiry into the Sponsorship Program and Advertising Activities, September 22, 2004, 1537; accessed online at www.gomery.ca/en/transcripts.

18. Warren Kinsella, former Chief of Staff to the Hon. David Dingwall, minister of Public Works and Government Services, November 3, 1995; reproduced in the transcript of the Commission of Inquiry into the Sponsorship Program and Advertising Activities, September 15, 2004, 862–64; accessed online at www.gomery.ca/en/transcripts.

19. Clerk of the Privy Council, "Memorandum to the Prime Minister," December 18, 1996; reproduced in the transcript of the Commission of Inquiry into the Sponsorship Program and Advertising Activities, September 14, 2004, 672–76; accessed online at www.gomery.ca/en/transcripts.

20. Canadian Press, "Chrétien not legally responsible for Adscam: Official," September 27, 2004; accessed online at www.canoe.ca.

21. Smith, *The Invisible Crown,* 114 and 124–25.

22. Steven Chase, "MPs query Clarkson's costly tour," *The Globe and Mail,* September 19, 2003; accessed at www.globeandmail.com.

23. Kathleen Harris, "Clarkson's polar jaunt cost $5.3M," *London Free Press,* February 14, 2004; accessed online at www.canoe.ca.

24. Donald J. Savoie, *Governing from the Centre: The Concentration of Power in Canadian Politics* (Toronto: University of Toronto Press, 1999), 108.

25. Simon Tuck, "HRDC dies in overhaul of social policy mechanism," *The Globe and Mail,* December 13, 2003; accessed online at www.globeandmail.com.

26. Canada, Prime Minister's Office, *Changes to Government,* updated January 23, 2004; accessed online at www.pm.gc.ca.

27. Canada, Public Safety and Emergency Preparedness Canada, "Overview of the Organization," April 2004; accessed online at www.psepc-sppcc.gc.ca/about/overview_e.asp.

28. Douglas L. Bland and Roy Rempel, *A Vigilant Parliament: Building Competence for Effective Parliamentary Oversight of National Defence and the Canadian Armed Forces* (Montreal: Institute for Research on Public Policy, February 2004), 55; available online at www.irpp.org.

29. See the discussion of appointments to the Supreme Court in Chapter 10.

30. *The Globe and Mail* staff, "Cabinet prepares for purge," *The Globe and Mail,* December 11, 2003; accessed online at www.globeandmail.com.

31. Peter Dobell, *Reforming Parliamentary Practice: The Views of MPs* (Montreal: Institute for Research on Public Policy, December 2000), 14–15; available online at www.irpp.org.

32. Canada, Privy Council Office, *Governing Responsibly: A Guide for Ministers and Ministers of State* (Ottawa, 2003), 6; accessed online at www.pco-bcp.gc.ca.

33. Canada, Privy Council Office, *Ethics, Responsibility, Accountability: An Action Plan for Democratic Reform* (Ottawa: Privy Council Office, February 2004), 10; available online at www.pco-bcp.gc.ca.

34. As of September 2004, the governments of British Columbia and Ontario had introduced fixed election dates. There have been calls for a similar reform at the federal level, but nothing has come of them so far.

35. In September 2004, newspapers began to report rumours that two former Cabinet ministers, Martin Cauchon and Maurizio Bevilacqua, had launched unofficial leadership campaigns. Martin quickly denied the reports, and insisted that he had the full support of all members of the Liberal caucus.

36. There had been a few calls for the replacement of the current Clerk, Alex Himelfarb, prior to the swearing-in of the Martin government in December 2003; however, Martin made it clear that he valued Himelfarb's advice and would not consider replacing him.

37. Savoie, *Governing from the Centre,* 86.

38. Savoie, *Governing from the Centre,* 137–39.

39. Savoie, *Governing from the Centre,* 138.

40. Quoted in Savoie, *Governing from the Centre,* 318.

41. For example, a Cabinet revolt destroyed the Diefenbaker government in 1963. Although Diefenbaker led a minority government, which increased the danger of a split in

Cabinet, he refused to heed the advice of those ministers who opposed his stand on American nuclear weapons. The result was catastrophic: the government fell and Diefenbaker lost the ensuing general election. See Denis Smith, *Rogue Tory: The Life and Legend of John G. Diefenbaker* (Toronto: Macfarlane Walter and Ross, 1995), Chapter 12.

42. Savoie, *Governing from the Centre*, 318.

43. Savoie, *Governing from the Centre*, 108.

44. Savoie, *Governing from the Centre*, 348.

45. The Martin government's guidebook for Cabinet members is explicit on this point: "While a Minister of State does not have a portfolio independent of the Minister he or she assists, the Minister of State is Cabinet colleague and peer, not a subordinate, of that Minister." Privy Council Office, *Governing Responsibly*, 8.

46. Ibid., 6.

47. One of Martin's innovations in December 2003 was to appoint the government whip and deputy House leader to Cabinet; previously, this individual had no Cabinet rank. The elevation of the government whip to ministerial rank was part of Martin's plan to close the distance between the Cabinet and the Liberal backbench; see *Ethics, Responsibility, Accountability*, 9.

48. Privy Council Office, *Governing Responsibly*, 8.

49. For example, former Prime Minister Trudeau appointed a past president of the CBC to the Communications portfolio in 1978. Pierre Juneau subsequently ran in a by-election, and lost. He resigned his Cabinet seat immediately.

50. The current Martin Cabinet is an exception: the Finance minister is from Saskatchewan, while the Industry minister is from British Columbia. This reflects the prime minister's determination to increase his party's popularity in the Western provinces—although this strategy bore little fruit in the 2004 election.

51. The sponsorship scandal may have made it politically impossible to appoint a Quebecker to Public Works, at least for the time being. Current PWGSC minister Scott Brison is a former Progressive Conservative MP from Nova Scotia.

52. Herman Bakvis, *Regional Ministers: Power and Influence in the Canadian Cabinet* (Toronto: University of Toronto Press, 1991), 297.

53. Sharon L. Sutherland, "The Consequences of Electoral Volatility: Inexperienced Ministers 1949–90," in Herman Bakvis, ed., *Representation, Integration and Political Parties in Canada*, volume 14 of the collected research studies for the Royal Commission on Electoral Reform and Party Financing (Toronto: Dundurn Press, 1991), 336–37.

54. David C. Docherty, *Mr. Smith Goes to Ottawa: Life in the House of Commons* (Vancouver: UBC Press, 1997), 55.

55. Edward Greenspon and Anthony Wilson-Smith, *Double Vision: The Inside Story of the Liberals in Power* (Toronto: Doubleday Canada, 1996), Chapters 9 and 13–15.

56. Savoie, *Breaking the Bargain*, 165.

57. Savoie, 245.

58. Savoie, 253.

59. Privy Council Office, *Cabinet Directive on Law-Making*, Section 3, available online at www.pco-bcp.gc.ca/legislation/directive_e.htm; accessed June 2000.

60. Prime Minister of Canada's website: *The Cabinet:* www.pm.gc.ca; accessed June 2001.

61. Canada, Privy Council Office, *Memoranda to Cabinet* (January 2004); accessed online at www.pco-bcp.gc.ca/default.asp?Language=E&Page=Publications.

62. *Cabinet Committee Mandates and Membership,* July 20, 2004, 1; available online at www.pm. gc.ca/grfx/docs/Cab_committee-comite.pdf.

63. *Memoranda to Cabinet,* 1.

64. See the organizational chart of the PCO at its website: www.pco-bcp.gc.ca.

65. *Cabinet Committee Mandates and Membership,* 3.

66. Canada, Prime Minister's Office, *New Structures in the Prime Minister's Office and Privy Council Office,* December 12, 2003; accessed online at www.pm.gc.ca.

67. Prime Minister of Canada's website: *The Cabinet:* www.pm.gc.ca; accessed June 2001.

68. Canada, Treasury Board Secretariat, *Strengthening Public Sector Management: An Overview of the Government Action Plan and Key Initiatives* (Ottawa, March 2004), 12; accessed online at www.tbs-sct.gc.ca/spsm-rgsp/index_e.asp.

69. Privy Council Office, *A Guide Book for Heads of Agencies: Operations, Structures and Responsibilities in the Federal Government* (August 1999), Section II; available online at www.pco-bcp.gc.ca; accessed June 2001.

70. This new Cabinet structure was accompanied by significant changes in the system for preparing and managing Cabinet documents. Under the rules announced by the Privy Council Office in early 2004, documents from the public service that recommend a particular course of action will be kept as brief as possible. Confidentiality restrictions will apply only to Ministerial Recommendation (MR) sections; all other Cabinet documents should be drafted in a way that will permit their eventual release to the public. The changes are outlined in a Privy Council Office document entitled *Memoranda to Cabinet,* which is available on the PCO website: www.pco-bcp.gc.ca.

71. Savoie, *Governing from the Centre,* 128.

72. Savoie, *Governing from the Centre,* 265.

73. Savoie, *Governing from the Centre,* 127.

74. Savoie, *Governing from the Centre,* 262–63.

75. Since taking power in 2001, the Liberal government in British Columbia has opened Cabinet meetings to the media and the public. Video of the meetings is available on the BC government's website: www.prov.gov.bc.ca/prem/popt/cabinet. To date, no other Canadian government has taken such a significant step away from the British convention of Cabinet secrecy.

76. Bakvis, *Regional Ministers,* 286.

77. *The Role and Structure of the Privy Council Office:* www.pco-bcp.gc.ca; accessed June 2001.

78. Privy Council Office, *Decision-Making Processes and Central Agencies in Canada: Federal, Provincial and Territorial Practices* (Ottawa: PCO, 1998), Section 3; available online at www.pco-bcp.gc.ca/Decision/canada-e.htm; accessed June 2001.

79. Savoie, *Governing from the Centre,* 99.

80. Privy Council Office, *Decision-Making Processes and Central Agencies in Canada,* Section 2: accessed June 2001.

81. Privy Council Office, *Decision-Making Processes and Central Agencies in Canada,* Section 2; accessed June 2001.

82. Privy Council Office, *Memoranda to Cabinet* (January 2004), 3.

83. R.G. Robertson, "The Changing Role of the Privy Council Office," a paper presented to the 23rd Annual Meeting of the Institute of Public Administration of Canada on September 8, 1971 and published in *Canadian Public Administration,* XIV:4, 1971, 506.

84. Savoie, *Governing from the Centre,* 189.

85. At least until recently. Martin delivered a "mini-budget" in October 2000, just before the federal election, and did not present a full budget until December 2001.

86. However, a revenue-raising measure—the sale of as many as 300 office buildings owned by the federal government—was approved in September 2004 by the Operations Committee and the Expenditure Review Sub-Committee. It is not yet clear whether this will be the normal practice of the new Cabinet. Source: Drew Fagan and Jane Taber, "Ottawa plans to sell property to fund social spending," *The Globe and Mail,* September 21, 2004, A4.

87. Privy Council Office, *A Guide Book for Heads of Agencies,* Section VII; accessed June 2001.

88. Privy Council Office, *Decision-Making Processes and Central Agencies in Canada,* Section 3; accessed June 2001.

89. Savoie, *Governing from the Centre,* 223.

90. *Strengthening Public Sector Management,* 9.

91. Savoie, *Breaking the Bargain,* Chapters Five and Seven.

92. Ibid., 152.

93. Ralph Heintzman, "The Dialectics of Organizational Design," in Courchene and Savoie, eds., *The Art of the State,* 244.

94. Pollitt, 219.

95. Good, 50.

96. When the HRDC internal audit of the Transitional Jobs Fund became public in early 1999, the former deputy minister of the department, Mel Cappe (who had subsequently become the Clerk of the Privy Council), testified before the House of Commons Standing Committee on Human Resources Development. Cappe's appearance before the Committee became a media circus, as Opposition MPs looked for contradictions between his testimony and the minister's public statements on the audit. See Good, 82.

97. Canada, Privy Council Office, *Notes on the Responsibilities of Public Servants in Relation to Parliamentary Committees* (December 1990), 1; accessed online at www.pco-bcp.gc.ca.

98. See, for example, C.E.S. Franks, *The Parliament of Canada* (Toronto: University of Toronto Press, 1987), 245.

99. Savoie, 212.

100. Savoie, 303–04.

101. Gene Swimmer et al., "Public Service 2000: Dead or Alive?" in Susan Phillips, ed., *How Ottawa Spends 1994–95* (Ottawa: Carleton University Press, 1994), 172; quoted in Savoie, 212.

102. Canada, Privy Council Office, *Guidance for Deputy Ministers* (June 2003), 4; accessed online at www.pco-bcp-gc.ca.

103. *Canada Year Book, 1930,* 1008–12.

104. *Strengthening Public Sector Management,* 2.

105. Privy Council Office, "World of Regulations," Section 1, available online at www.pco-bcp.ca; accessed June 2001.

106. Privy Council Office, *Cabinet Directive on Law-making,* Section 2; accessed June 2000.

107. Privy Council Office, *World of Regulations,* Section 2; accessed June 2001.

108. Privy Council Office, *World of Regulations,* Section 2; accessed June 2001.

109. Kenneth Kernaghan and David Siegel, *Public Administration in Canada,* 3rd edition (Scarborough: ITP Nelson, 1995), 226.

110. See the Transport Canada website: www.tc.gc.ca.

111. Department of Finance, *Structure and Role* (Ottawa, December 1999), 12.

112. Canada, Privy Council Office, *Memoranda to Cabinet* (January 2004), 6; accessed online at www.pco-bcp.gc.ca.

113. Privy Council Office, *Decision-Making Processes and Central Agencies in Canada,* Section 1; accessed June 2001.

114. Privy Council Office, *Cabinet Directive on Law-making,* Section 4; accessed June 2000.

115. Privy Council Office, *Cabinet Directive on Law-making,* Section 2; accessed June 2000.

116. TBS, *Strengthening Public Sector Management,* 7.

117. *Memoranda to Cabinet,* 2.

118. *Memoranda to Cabinet,* 9–10.

119. *Memoranda to Cabinet,* 3.

120. Privy Council Office, *Cabinet Directive on Law-making,* Section 2; accessed June 2000.

121. Privy Council Office, *Cabinet Directive on Law-making,* Section 4; accessed June 2000.

122. Treasury Board Secretariat, *Alternative Service Delivery* (June 2001), "Introduction," available online at www.tbs-sct.gc.ca; accessed June 2001.

123. Treasury Board Secretariat, *Alternative Service Delivery* (June 2001), "Introduction"; accessed June 2001).

124. Greenspon and Wilson-Smith, *Double Vision,* 115.

125. Savoie, 175.

126. Greenspon and Wilson-Smith, 223–25.

127. Savoie, 183.

128. Savoie, 181.

129. Greenspon and Wilson-Smith, Chapter 14.

130. Government of Canada, *The Expenditure Management System of the Government of Canada* (Ottawa: Treasury Board Secretariat, August 1996); available online at www.tbs-sct.gc.ca; accessed June 2001.

131. Auditor General of Canada, *Annual Report* (Ottawa, April 2000), Chapter 2, paragraph 11.24.

132. Good, *The Politics of Public Management,* 34.

133. Ibid., 45.

134. Auditor General of Canada, *Annual Report,* Chapter 2, paragraph 11.9.

135. Good, 159.

136. Good, 136.

137. Auditor General of Canada, *Annual Report,* Chapter 2, paragraph 11.52.

138. Auditor General of Canada, *Annual Report,* Chapter 2, paragraph 11.77.

139. Pollitt, 219.

140. Savoie, *Breaking the Bargain,* 5 and 43.

141. Pollitt, 220–21.

142. Savoie, *Breaking the Bargain,* 146.

143. Good, 190–94.

144. Pollitt, 210–11; Good, 16.

145. Savoie, *Breaking the Bargain,* 152.

146. *Strengthening Public Sector Management,* 3.

7

NONGOVERNMENTAL ACTORS IN THE CANADIAN POLICY PROCESS

LEARNING OBJECTIVES

- *define* the term "policy community" and explain its importance in the policy-making process;
- *distinguish* between the **subgovernment** and the discourse community;
- *differentiate* among the different types of policy communities that operate in various policy sectors;
- *explain* the factors that determine the policy influence of a particular pressure group;
- *identify* and *explain* three institutional incentives that influence media coverage of Canadian politics;
- *explain* how the news media influence Canadian government and policy-making.

INTRODUCTION

Most chapters in this book describe either governmental institutions, such as the House of Commons, or formal political agencies like political parties. These entities are regulated by laws, both entrenched and nonentrenched. For the most part, the structures and operations of government institutions are open to public view. Their leaders can be held accountable to the Canadian public, to a greater or lesser degree, either by their members or by other agencies of government. For all of these reasons, they are easy to describe and analyze, although their day-to-day impact on public policy is less easy to measure.

The organizations discussed in this chapter, interest groups and the news media, are a different story. Their internal structures and operations are more opaque, and their influence on public policy (and, thus, on the lives of Canadians) more difficult to assess. The scholarly literature on journalists and their political impact is relatively extensive and increasingly sophisticated. The same cannot be said for the literature on interest groups. Some studies draw general conclusions from anecdotal evidence,[1] while others overstate group influence by overlooking alternative explanations for particular policy changes.[2]

The deficiencies in the literature, and the impossibility of drawing firm conclusions about the structures and influence of interest groups in particular, are necessarily reflected in this chapter. Readers should be aware that our knowledge about **nongovernmental organizations (NGOs),** including the news media, is often sketchy. There are some exceptions: interest groups that engage directly with the government in the public arena leave clear traces of their activities. These include testimony before standing committees of the House of Commons and the Senate, formal interventions before the courts, and legally mandated disclosures about lobbying activities and election campaign advertising. However, these data do not allow us to draw firm conclusions about the structures of the groups that engage in such activities, nor about their influence on policy outcomes. At best, we are entitled to make the same assumption about interest groups as we often make about companies that spend millions of dollars on consumer advertising: if they did not believe that such expenditures of time and money benefited them directly, they would refrain. In a similar vein, we can assume that journalists and their employers believe that political reporting influences political events, whether at the Cabinet level or within the electorate; otherwise, they would channel all of their resources into more lucrative activities, like covering sporting events and celebrity gossip.

With these caveats in mind, we turn to a discussion of NGOs and their participation in the policy process. The next section discusses interest groups, although it also indicates the contribution of some journalists to shaping policy discourse. The second half of the chapter focuses more directly on the mass media, and specifically on the ways in which journalists cover political news. The conclusion assesses the effects of globalization and internationalization on NGOs and their participation in the policy process.

INTERESTS, GROUPS, AND POLITICS

What Is an Interest Group?

An **interest group** is an organization of people who seek to promote a common goal. It may be local—e.g., a group of homeowners who protest against a proposed trash incinerator in their neighbourhood—provincial, national, or global (e.g., Amnesty International). The scope of interest-group organizing has widened significantly with the introduction of the Internet, which allows far-flung groups to form worldwide alliances and to mobilize like-minded individuals around the world very cheaply. Most interest groups are founded for nonpolitical purposes, although some are drawn into the policy-making process to protect the interests of their members. For example, people who enjoy hiking in the Rockies might establish an organization to allow them to communicate with like-minded individuals, to pool resources, or to achieve ends that they might not be able to achieve singly. It is easy to go hiking by yourself, but by joining a club you meet others with the same interest and perhaps find out about new trails. As a group, the hikers might be able to get discounts on transportation or equipment. None of this requires political action. It is certainly **collective action,** in that individuals are trying to act in concert, but it is not political. However, it is easy to imagine how this group's activities might become political. Hiking requires wilderness, and wilderness areas depend on government protection. Since it is in the interest of hikers to have a place to hike, it is also in their interest to persuade government to protect wilderness areas. This is the rationale behind the extensive political activities of groups such as the Sierra Club. Their members may not be interested in politics per se, but their shared interests (e.g., wilderness recreation) often require extensive pressure on government.

An interest group that devotes some or all of its resources to influencing public policy is called a **pressure group.** To be effective, a pressure group must be well organized and well resourced. Its structure and resources are determined, in part, by the size and wealth of its membership and by its policy goals. A group that represents a particularly powerful interest, that can count on ample and predictable financial support, and that shares the overall policy approach of the government will generally have an advantage over competing groups that do not share those characteristics. It would be incorrect, however, to overlook the role of the state in determining which groups are more powerful than others. In the late 1960s and 1970s, Canada's federal government deliberately mobilized latent interests in the electorate. It identified particular groups—official language minorities, women, ethnic minorities, and Aboriginal communities—and encouraged them to create their own pressure groups. State support for these embryonic organizations took two primary forms: positional and financial.[3]

> *Positional support means access for some groups and not others to information or to decision-makers or to a formal or quasi-formal role in decision-making . . . Usually, the organization will have to establish its credibility before it is granted this positional support, but once such support is granted, its position vis-à-vis its competitors in the policy field is considerably enhanced.*[4]

State financial support for pressure groups includes annual core funding, which covers the daily overhead costs of running an organization, and grants for individual projects. The process of applying for public funding consumes a substantial amount of the scarce time and energy that may be available to a volunteer organization or a non-profit agency. More seriously, in the view of some **advocacy** groups, to accept government funding might compromise their freedom to criticize state policy.[5] They fear **co-optation** into the policy agenda of the ruling party. Alternatively, they worry that an over-reliance on granting programs could distort their organizational priorities—a

Gun lobby rally on Parliament Hill, September 22, 1998 (© CP/Tom Hanson)

realistic fear, according to studies of Canadian women's groups and Aboriginal organizations.[6] Nonetheless, most eligible groups do apply for public funding. Unlike the United States, which has a well-developed network of private charitable foundations, Canadian pressure groups have few opportunities to secure funding from nonstate sources. "Groups clearly recognize the possibility of co-optation but prefer being vigilant recipients to pristine paupers."[7]

While it is easy to understand why an interest group would seek available funding from the state, it may be less easy to understand why a government would wish to subsidize groups that might be inclined to criticize its activities. According to Pal, there are at least two reasons for state funding of interest groups. First, a particular agency might seek to create a well-organized political constituency for its programs and services. Should the agency face a challenge to its autonomy or its finances, whether from inside or outside the federal government, such an external constituency may become a crucial resource in its self-defence campaign.[8] Second, from the perspective of the government as a whole, giving money to groups that will, in turn, demand even more public resources makes long-term strategic sense. Advocacy organizations whose primary purpose is to secure programs for disadvantaged social groups—

women, people with disabilities, Aboriginal peoples, and others—provide arguments to justify the continual expansion of the state.[9]

While those arguments serve the interests of the state during periods of prosperity, which helps to explain the boom in advocacy funding during the late 1960s and early 1970s, they tend to fall on deaf ears during periods of fiscal constraint. The spending cuts that began to affect the federal government in the 1980s go a long way to explain declining state support for advocacy groups since that time—not just directly, in the sense that government had less money to spend on core and project funding, but indirectly, because advocacy groups became more of a nuisance than a political resource.

Whether or not they receive funding from the state, pressure groups engage in the policy process in three distinct ways: lobbying, representation, and consultation.[10] **Lobbying** refers to one-way communication from a pressure group to the state actors in the relevant policy field. In other words, it describes the effort by a particular group to convince government decision-makers that its interests should be reflected in public policy. Lobbying occurs at the initiative of the pressure group, not at the invitation of the government. As we will see in Tables 7.1 and 7.2, lobbying is a major industry in Ottawa (and, to a lesser degree, in provincial capitals).

Representation is also a one-way street, although it is normally initiated by the state and not by the participating groups. When the federal government decides to establish a Royal Commission to investigate a particular issue, it usually gives the commission a mandate to hold public hearings. Those hearings attract pressure-group spokespersons, who seize the opportunity to set the policy agenda and to attract their share of the media coverage. Some publicly funded groups are expressly invited to submit briefs, as part of their overall mandate from the government. While Royal Commissions are increasingly rare policy tools, the 1986 reforms to the committee system in the House of Commons provide more frequent opportunities for interest representation. Between 1994 and 1998, more than 24 000 witnesses appeared before House of Commons and Senate committees.[11]

Unlike lobbying and representation, **consultation** is a two-way flow of communication, in which state actors and group representatives work together to resolve common problems. Like representation, consultation is initiated by the government; unlike representation, consultation normally implies "an ongoing process, not a one-off exchange of views."[12] Since the 1980s, consultations with stakeholders have become an increasingly important part of Canadian policy-making and program implementation. The need for consultation has grown still further, as federal departments have entered into partnerships with private and nonprofit agencies (recall the discussion of public–private partnerships in Chapter 6). The downsizing of the federal public service forced the government to rely more heavily on the specialized knowledge of its "client groups," knowledge that can be "bought" only in exchange for a seat at the policy table.

The balance between lobbying, representation, and consultation varies among the different policy sectors. In other words, the relationships between the state and pressure-group actors within a particular policy field—e.g., agriculture or health care—are largely determined by variables unique to that sector. The key variables include the following:

- "the autonomy and capacity of state agencies;
- the organizational development of sectorial interests;
- the relationships or networks that develop between state and societal actors";[13] and
- the nature of the policies that dominate that particular field.

The autonomy of the state agencies "refers to the degree of independence from societal groups possessed by state actors when they formulate policy objectives. The goals of an autonomous state, including its diagnosis of societal problems and the formulation of policy alternatives to deal with these, are internally generated and not simply reflective of societal interests or demands."[14] **Policy capacity** is determined by the availability to state actors of "sufficient institutional resources both to design policies that will realize [their] policy objectives and to implement these policies."[15] An autonomous state agency with a strong policy capacity is more likely to dominate its policy sector than one that relies heavily on its pressure-group partners for information and support. Those partners may be unified or fragmented, strongly organized or weak.

When the pressure groups in a given policy sector are united, perhaps by the creation of a "peak" organization that represents all the relevant interests in a coherent fashion, and they are well organized and well financed, they are likely to exert more influence in the policy process. The relationships among the state and nonstate actors are shaped by the characteristics of the particular agencies and groups involved in policy-making and implementation, and by the nature of the policies themselves. Distributive policies, that is, policies that allocate goods and services to individuals, tend to favour the state actors. Distributive policies are also less likely to require intense consultation than regulatory policies, which demand "a close working relationship between state and sectorial actors, including the sharing of information and responsibility."[16]

Collectively, the state and nonstate actors who operate within a given policy field are called the **policy community.** Much public policy-making in Canada occurs within policy communities. These are loosely defined groups, made up primarily of state actors and representatives of organized interests, which interact to shape public policy in a given sector over time.

Within a given policy community, we can distinguish two main elements: the subgovernment (the inner circle) and the **discourse community** (the outer circle). The subgovernment makes the actual policy decisions. It includes the relevant minister or ministers (and their ministers of State); the senior policy officials in their departments or agencies; provincial officials, where appropriate; and "representatives of the few interest groups whose opinions and support are essential."[17] This select set of pressure groups possesses the resources and the political clout to "meet the demands of subgovernment work":

> *day-to-day communication between agency officials and representatives of companies or groups; automatic group inclusion on advisory committees and panels of experts;*

invitations to comment on draft policy; participation on committees or commissions charged with long-range policy review; and continual formal and informal access to agency officials.[18]

The pressure groups in the subgovernment are those that participate regularly in consultation; they may also be involved in policy implementation and program delivery.

Groups and individuals that are excluded from the subgovernment are relegated to the second tier: the discourse community. They include academic specialists (in universities, think tanks, and private consulting firms), journalists with a particular interest in the policy field, and interest groups that lack the resources or the political legitimacy to secure an automatic place at the table where policy choices are made. The distinction between the subgovernment and the discourse community involves at least four criteria:

- the values and preferences of the group members;
- the organization and resources of the various groups seeking admission to the subgovernment (discussed in "The Uneven Playing Field: Pressure-Group Resources" on page 341);
- the perceived legitimacy of the group's leadership, in relation both to its members (its internal **mandate**) and to its position on the broader political spectrum (a group that espouses mainstream policy positions will more easily gain acceptance in the subgovernment than one that speaks for a "fringe" element in society[19]); and
- the ability of a particular pressure group to work cooperatively with other groups, which maximizes their collective resources and reflects a long-term commitment to the policy community.[20]

The boundary between the subgovernment and the discourse community is more or less porous—in other words, the subgovernment is more or less willing to admit previously unheard voices—depending on the policy field at issue and on the circumstances at a given time.[21] For example, in the 1990s the Reform Party successfully refocused the discourse on criminal justice away from the rights of suspects to the rights of victims. As the **political salience** of violent crime increased, victims' rights groups—which had been absent from the drafting of the legal rights in the *Charter*— became increasingly prominent in legislative battles over amendments to the *Criminal Code*.[22]

It is also important to recognize that decisions affecting a specific policy sector may be influenced by other policy communities.[23] In an era of fiscal constraint, governments have to make tradeoffs among competing policy priorities. In effect, they are forced to choose between the priorities of different policy communities. Consequently, decisions about health-care funding (e.g., the September 2004 commitment to increase the Canadian Health Transfer by $9 billion more than the federal government had planned) may limit alternative policies—for example, the national child-care program that the Liberals promised during the 2004 federal election campaign. Therefore, we cannot assess the policy influence of the Child Care Advocacy Association of Canada in isolation from developments in health care and other policy fields.

Once a pressure group gains access to the subgovernment, it must retain its position of influence by behaving in certain ways.[24] The institutional incentives for pressure groups within the subgovernment are particularly clear and powerful. Pressure groups must observe the norms of bureaucratic behaviour, which are followed by the public servants with whom they collaborate. These norms include discretion, cooperation (as opposed to confrontation), decision-making based on solid factual information and rational debate, and a clear understanding of the division of responsibilities within the political and permanent executives. A subgovernment pressure group that provides reliable information and advice to policy-makers, and represents its membership according to the norms and values of the permanent executive, can exercise significant and continuing influence within the policy process.

As noted earlier, the structure of a given policy community is shaped by the variables that are unique to that particular policy sector. In Canada, scholars have identified five types of **policy networks:**

1. pressure pluralist;
2. clientele pluralist;
3. corporatist;
4. concertation; and
5. state-directed.[25]

Pressure pluralist networks are dominated by autonomous state agencies. The pressure groups involved are relatively weak and fragmented; they must rely on lobbying and representation, because they are rarely invited to consult. In clientele pluralism, both state and nonstate actors are weak and dispersed; "agencies rely on associations for information and support and allow them to participate in policy-making."[26] Corporatist networks unite strong and autonomous state agencies with equally strong and united interests, who consult regularly on policy design and cooperate in policy implementation. Concertation is similar to corporatism, except that it involves one "peak" interest organization that enjoys an equal partnership with the relevant state agency.

Finally, a state-directed network, as the name suggests, pits an autonomous and capable government agency against a weak and fragmented set of interests. In some cases, the interests may be weak because they are still in the early stages of mobilization;[27] if and when they develop strong organizations and acquire significant policy capacity—perhaps as a consequence of state support—a new policy network will emerge.

In Chapter 6, we discussed the state agencies that participate in the various policy communities. Now we will take a closer look at the goals and structures of the nonstate actors. In general, pressure groups share four primary characteristics:

1. They seek to influence public policy in accord with the interests of their members.

2. They possess the necessary organization and resources to participate directly in the policy process (through representation and consultation).
3. They try to channel the diverse and often conflicting demands of their members into consistent policy positions.
4. They wish to "influence those who hold power rather than to exercise the responsibility of government."[28]

We will take a closer look at each of these four characteristics in turn.

◾ Pressure Groups and Public Policy

Pressure groups perform five essential functions in the Canadian political system:[29]
1. They promote the interests of their members in the policy process, in the media, and in negotiations with other groups (e.g., trade unions bargain collectively with employers on behalf of their members).
2. They provide a channel of communication between governments and their members, informing the latter about new debates and developments in public policy while keeping the former abreast of emerging problems that directly affect their members' interests.
3. They legitimate public policy by participating in its formation and persuading their members to accept the resulting programs and regulations.
4. Some pressure groups regulate their members on behalf of government agencies by monitoring compliance with the law and imposing sanctions for noncompliance.
5. Some pressure groups also participate directly in program implementation, either by entering into formal partnerships with government agencies (recall the discussion of the New Public Management program in Chapter 6) or by encouraging their members to cooperate with public servants (e.g., gathering crucial information about the impact of a program on a group's target clientele).

To succeed in these tasks, a pressure group must be accepted into the relevant subgovernment. As we have just seen, policy communities vary with the relationships among their members—in other words, the different policy networks within each community. On any given issue, participants in the relevant policy network will disagree about preferred outcomes and approaches. Each side of a particular question is represented by a specific policy network whose members share common assumptions and goals. Therefore, the policy community is not a simple collection of like-minded groups and individuals; it is divided among two or more policy networks, which may engage each other in bitter power struggles over contentious issues.

For example, the issue of genetically modified (GM) foods has become a matter of public concern in recent years. GM foods are the product of new, scientifically developed strains of wheat, canola, and other agricultural crops. The companies that created these new strains have manipulated the genetic codes of the seeds in order to achieve certain goals, such as higher yields; increased resistance to pests, diseases, and chemicals; and longer shelf life. The policy network in favour of GM foods includes the corporations that developed and patented the new seeds (e.g., Monsanto), farmers who share the goals of the GM developers, and food-processing companies (at least until recently). The policy network opposed to GM foods unites public-health advocates concerned about the possible side effects of eating "Frankenfood,"[30] organic farmers who worry about the contamination of their crops by "super-seeds," and environmentalists who fear that GM crops will destroy biodiversity and interfere with the natural balance of rural ecosystems. Within the federal government, the relevant agencies are deeply divided over the policy issues arising from GM food. Agriculture and Agri-Food Canada initially supported efforts to promote GM crops, whereas Health Canada was pressured by its client groups in the public-health field (and by some of its own scientists) to oppose licensing GM seeds for widespread use on Canadian farms.

Public-awareness campaigns by members of the anti-GM policy network sparked worldwide boycotts of food products made with GM crops, and drove a wedge between groups representing food-processing companies and their former allies on the pro-GM network. Pressure groups representing farmers, such as the Canadian Federation of Agriculture, are divided over the GM issue. Given the lack of consensus within the GM policy community, the opposing policy networks spent years battling to influence policy. In late 2001, the federal government tried to find a middle ground: Health Canada would be responsible for ensuring the safety of food products containing GM ingredients, while the responsibility for regulating the growth and labelling of GM foods was assigned to the Canadian Food Inspection Agency, an autonomous agency that reports to the minister of Agriculture and Agri-Food.[31]

Despite concerns about the secretive and possibly corrupting nature of that influence, pressure groups are an indispensable part of the policy process in Canada and elsewhere: "It is hard to imagine how we could organize policy debate if pressure groups, with their specialized knowledge, did not focus discussion in policy communities."[32] Nonetheless, there are legitimate questions about the extent of pressure-group power in policy-making:

- Do state agencies favour certain types of interests and downplay others? If so, what is the long-term effect on the legitimacy of our political institutions?
- Do pressure groups really speak on behalf of their members, or does their advice to policy-makers merely reflect the interests of their leaders and permanent staff?
- What are the implications of pressure-group influence within policy subgovernments for Parliament, political parties, and other democratic institutions? Should pressure groups be allowed to intervene directly in the democratic process, and, if so, to what degree?

Organization and Resources

There are two central points to be made about the organization of pressure groups in Canada:

1. The structure and functions of pressure groups are shaped by institutional incentives, especially those arising from federalism, responsible Cabinet government, and (in some cases) the *Canadian Charter of Rights and Freedoms*.

2. Not all pressure groups are created equal. Some control substantial resources, which may help them to gain access to the subgovernment, while others do not. Exploiting institutional norms and adapting to institutional incentives is neither easy nor automatic; it demands a high degree of organizational sophistication and financial support.

Institutional Incentives and Canadian Pressure Groups

Canada's federal system, and the regionalism that it both reflects and fosters, affects pressure groups in several ways. First, federalism complicates the process of public decision-making. As we explain in Chapter 8, the "watertight compartments" view of Canadian federalism is no longer accurate (if it ever was). Pressure groups concerned with health care, social assistance, and postsecondary education (to take just three examples) must operate at both the federal and provincial levels of government. The Canadian labour movement is a case in point. The Canadian Labour Congress, for example, is a federal body in that it is made up of both national and provincially based labour organizations.[33] Its policy capability (i.e., the degree to which the national body can arrive at independent positions that it can then impose on its members) is constrained by a variety of factors, of which federal structure is one. Although this decentralization of policy-making power provides more access points for organized interests—in other words, it gives them a greater number of opportunities to influence decision-making—the growing reliance on executive federalism since the 1960s has effectively excluded most nongovernmental actors from the policy process. Aboriginal "peak" organizations (those that represent a wide spectrum of Aboriginal Canadians, such as the Assembly of First Nations) are often invited to participate in discussions among federal, provincial, and territorial leaders, but other groups are rarely consulted in an official way.

In Chapter 8, we examine the growing autonomy and parity of Canada's provincial governments. As policy capacity shifts from Ottawa to the provinces, the institutional incentives for pressure groups change. When the federal government effectively eliminated conditions on transfer payments in 1995, when it introduced the Canadian Health and Social Transfer (CHST), the impact on pressure groups in health care and other affected fields was immediate:

> *Previously, the social services policy community was strongly oriented to the federal level, since Ottawa not only spent money in the field but was seen to be a leader. Now, as the core responsibility shifts to the provincial level, the corresponding policy communities will fragment and focus more on local/provincial dynamics.*[34]

A second characteristic of Canadian federalism is the presence of Quebec. While the presence of provincial governments requires national interest groups to organize themselves on a regional basis, the special circumstances in Quebec pose unique challenges for coordination. The practical difficulties created by two official languages are compounded by different social traditions. In the field of human rights, for example, Quebec has a rich tradition of Catholic overseas missionary work and social action that differs significantly from the English Canadian pattern. Consequently, many human rights organizations are split between Quebec and "Canadian" offices. Amnesty International, for example, whose "Canadian section" was established in 1973 as one organization, now has two branches, one in Montreal (francophone) and one in Ottawa (mostly anglophone). This "two-nations" approach to interest-group organization can threaten the unity of a national group, particularly when constitutional issues are on the table. The National Action Committee on the Status of Women (NAC) came close to a serious rupture during the public debate over the Meech Lake Accord, when Quebec feminist groups accused their "sisters" in English Canada of bigotry over their concerns about the implications of the distinct-society clause for gender rights.[35]

If federalism disperses power, responsible Cabinet government concentrates it. Decisions are made in the Cabinet, and ultimately by the prime minister, not by the legislative branch; parties are highly disciplined (and therefore closed to external influences); and decision-making is tightly controlled and often secretive. Under these conditions, interest groups have traditionally had few points of access. Cabinet ministers and senior officials have been the key actors in the political system; MPs and senators are less frequent targets of lobbying, although Prime Minister Martin's pledge to give backbench MPs more influence recently prompted some lobbyists to change their strategies.[36] Moreover, the current minority government is likely to increase lobbyists' attentions to MPs. As for public servants, they prefer to work with pressure groups that share their institutional norms. Therefore, access to the subgovernment has traditionally been the privilege of large, bureaucratized groups that possess knowledge and other essential resources.

As we saw in Chapter 5, there have been repeated attempts to reform the House of Commons in order to provide greater autonomy to backbench MPs. Recent reforms to the standing committee system have encouraged pressure groups to divert some of their attention from the subgovernment to the parliamentary arena. As a result, the scope of parliamentary consultations over major pieces of legislation has expanded dramatically. This is true of foreign and trade policy, where, for example, there are now annual consultations on broad policy and on human rights.[37] It also applies to the annual federal budget, which has been shaped since 1994 by consultations with the Standing Committee on Finance.[38] A major exercise such as the social security review in 1994 saw 1200 submissions from organizations and 40 000 completed "workbooks" from individual Canadians.[39] As noted earlier, thousands of Canadians appear before one or more standing committees of the House of Commons and Senate every year. For pressure groups that are excluded from the subgovernment, such an opportunity for representation may be their best chance to influence public policy. But as we saw in Chapters 5 and 6, a Cabinet that controls a majority of the seats in the Commons can disregard committee recommendations that do not conform to the priorities of the political executive and the central agencies.

Since 1982, the *Charter of Rights and Freedoms* has expanded the policy role of the courts (Chapter 10). Previously, groups disgruntled with a particular piece of legislation or policy could only lobby the legislative and executive branches of government. Now, if they have the resources, they can pursue *Charter*-based litigation in the hope of changing public policy. For example, the October 2004 Supreme Court hearings into the constitutionality of same-sex marriage attracted more than two dozen interventions—many from interest groups on both sides of the issue.[40] The day before the hearings began, two separate news conferences were held in Ottawa: one sponsored by groups favouring same-sex marriage and the other by opponents. Because the issue concerns section 15 of the *Charter*, the guarantee of equality rights, many of these groups would have been eligible for support from the federally funded Court Challenges Program (CCP). The CCP was established in 1985, shut down in 1992, and reinstated in an altered form in 1993.[41] Its purpose is to assist groups and individuals who wish to use either the equality rights or the official-language minority rights (sections 16–23) in the *Charter*. As the example of the same-sex marriage hearings demonstrates, *Charter* litigation fails at least as often as it succeeds; the groups on one side or the other were undoubtedly disappointed with the eventual outcome of the Court's deliberations. Moreover, public-interest litigation is enormously expensive, which makes it a risky strategy for advocacy groups with limited resources.[42]

■ The Uneven Playing Field: Pressure-Group Resources

In the early twentieth century, American political scientists coined the term "pluralism" to describe the relationships among interest groups and between the various groups and the state. The central assumption of pluralism was that groups competed with each other for resources and influence, under "rules of the game" that were fair to all players. The state was a neutral referee, enforcing the rules without systematically favouring any of the contending teams. Since the 1960s, pluralism has been largely discredited by clear evidence of bias on the part of government agencies. In other words, the rules of the pressure-group game are far from neutral. They give certain interests, and certain types of pressure groups, a clear advantage over others. We have already seen that groups whose interests dovetail with those of state actors exercise greater influence than those that are perceived, fairly or otherwise, as "fringe" or "protest" movements. What is less obvious, at least initially, is the organizational and resource base that distinguishes the groups that are admitted to the subgovernment from those that are not.

To achieve and retain a privileged place in the subgovernment, a pressure group must have both political salience and policy capacity. The political salience of a particular group is determined by several factors,[43] some of which have already been discussed:

- the size, cohesion, socioeconomic status, and political leverage of its membership;
- its willingness and ability to build coalitions with like-minded groups;
- its tangible resources (e.g., money) and its intangible resources (membership commitment, skilled leadership, and reputation);

- its ability to represent its membership effectively and to mobilize that membership in support of its political activities (e.g., letter-writing campaigns to politicians); and

- its effectiveness as a channel of communication between the government and its membership.

The policy capacity of a particular pressure group depends on its ability to use its political salience to advance its policy goals. A group with a large and wealthy membership may not automatically secure entry into the subgovernment on that basis. It must repeatedly demonstrate its value as a participant in the making and implementation of public policy. The key ingredients in policy capacity are:

- tangible resources: money, expert staff (in-house or contract lobbyists and policy specialists), and a stable, continuous organizational presence (e.g., a large national office in Ottawa); and

- intangible resources: expertise in both the substance of policy and the process of policy-making (not only the formal flow charts of political science textbooks but also the informal hierarchy of status and influence within the relevant departments and agencies); a reputation with ministers, senior officials, and other groups within the subgovernment; a track record of competent and reliable service to the subgovernment (providing reliable information, building support for new measures among the membership, assisting in the implementation of policy).

It would be misleading to assume that the tangible resources define the limits of the cost of policy participation; the intangible resources—especially policy expertise and service to the subgovernment—are enormously expensive and time-consuming:

When governments and their agencies decide that specific groups speak for a significant part of the population and that their views are legitimate, they turn to them frequently, inviting them to sit on advisory committees and consulting them on issues far afield from the immediate concerns of the groups themselves. Responding to these overtures takes considerable effort. Membership opinions may have to be elicited, or specialized knowledge tapped. More frequently, the organization may have to dedicate the time of its research staff to the government's question, diverting it from tasks more important to the group and its members. Even participation on advisory boards can siphon off valuable executive time . . . The cost of participation is the price the group pays for acceptance as a full-fledged member of the policy community.[44]

Groups that can afford to acquire the necessary expertise in the technical details of policy and the art of governance, while simultaneously providing the permanent and political executives with the necessary information, support, and regulatory assistance, may become and remain core members of the subgovernment. Indeed, a leading expert on Canadian government suggests that certain pressure groups are more influential than political parties, precisely because of their "research capacity," networking skills, and media savvy.[45]

Less well-endowed groups usually enjoy less influence, regardless of the intrinsic merits of their policy recommendations or the legitimacy of their members' concerns. As public financial support for advocacy groups shrinks, the subgovernment status of those groups is seriously threatened. While there may still be an important role for women's groups, Aboriginal groups, and other interests to play in policy-making, cuts to state grants in the late 1980s and 1990s have made it increasingly difficult for them to sustain the responsibilities of policy participation.

Business groups and associations are often at the centre of fears that public policy is being unduly affected by special pressures. Business has several advantages in policy-making that are denied to other types of groups:

- Given the capitalist nature of the Canadian economy, prosperity and jobs still depend on private-sector decisions about investment and development. If business is unhappy with taxes or social policies, the argument runs, it will invest elsewhere. This assumption alone ensures a more attentive hearing for groups like the Canadian Bankers' Association, the Council of Chief Executives, and the Canadian Chamber of Commerce.

- Business also enjoys financial resources well beyond the capacities of other groups. It can hire lobbyists (and deduct their cost as a business expense) and make substantial political contributions to parties.

- Many politicians are either drawn from the business community or have extensive social connections with members of that community. This gives the latter privileged access and a sympathetic hearing.

Ottawa and the provincial capitals have blossomed in recent years with companies and individuals who lobby government on behalf of others. For reasons of ideology and personal contacts, specific firms tend to be in favour with specific governments at any given time. For example, questions were raised about Prime Minister Martin's relationship with Ottawa-based Earnscliffe Research and Communications. Earnscliffe had two separate departments: "one did more traditional lobbying and consulting work with industries and private-sector interests; the other, the research arm, worked primarily with government departments and ministers' offices."[46] Several senior members of the firm's research department, and at least one of its lobbyists, played key roles in Paul Martin's campaign to replace Jean Chrétien as Liberal leader and prime minister between 2000 and 2003. The nasty and high-profile power struggle within the governing party drew public and media attention to Earnscliffe, and raised questions about potential conflicts of interest. One parliamentary reporter put it this way: "You could go to Earnscliffe to lobby for an item in the budget, fully aware that the other side was deeply involved in preparing that budget."[47] These questions grew more pointed after Martin became prime minister and some former Earnscliffe staffers joined his transition team and subsequently took positions in the Prime Minister's Office (PMO). To date, no allegations of conflict have been proven; Earnscliffe's senior partners insisted that there was no improper communication between the two halves of the business.

The corollary is that when governments are replaced, lobbying firms tend to be too.[48] Concerns that cronyism and business influence were ruling the corridors of power in Ottawa finally led to the 1985 *Lobbyists Registration Act.* The original legislation had some huge holes—for example, it narrowly defined lobbyists as those who actually arrange meetings or communicate with public officials on behalf of clients—but nonetheless for the first time yielded some hard information on the scope of the lobbying industry at the federal level. The 1985 Act distinguished between Tier I and Tier II lobbyists. A Tier I lobbyist "is an individual who, for payment and on behalf of a client, undertakes to arrange a meeting with a public office holder or to communicate with a public office holder in an attempt to influence the development, making or amendment of any federal law, regulation, policy or program or the award of any federal monetary grant or the award of any federal contract."[49] Tier II lobbyists act on behalf of their employer for the same ends (with the exception of awarding of contracts).

Amendments to the Act came into force on January 31, 1996, and were designed to elicit more comprehensive information about lobbyists and their activities. The Act was amended again in 2003, as part of the ethics package enacted by former Prime Minister Chrétien. The Act now provides for three categories of lobbyists, all of whom must register and file public reports of their lobbying activities:

1. A consultant lobbyist is an individual "who, for payment, on behalf of any person or organization," communicates with a public office holder with the intent to influence policy, obtain a financial benefit, or secure a federal contract. These are the professional, full-time "government relations" personnel employed by companies like Earnscliffe.
2. An in-house corporate lobbyist is a person who works for a commercial company (other than a lobbying firm), and who spends at least 20 percent of his or her working time on lobbying the federal government.
3. In-house lobbyists who work for the same organization and whose collective lobbying efforts constitute at least 20 percent of the overall activity of the organization.[50]

Table 7.1 displays the number of lobbyists in each category between 2000 and 2002. We may safely assume that many of the groups and individuals whose activities are summarized in this table are doing more than just lobbying when they engage with their chosen government departments. In order to achieve their short-term and long-term policy objectives, at least some of them must also participate in policy networks and communities through representation and consultation.

Under federal law, consultant lobbyists must file an annual report with Industry Canada, including the following information: the names of their clients, the amounts paid by their clients, the specific law or program that each client hoped to influence, and the persons in government with whom the lobbyist has been in contact. Less detailed information is required of the part-time lobbyists who fall under the "in-house" category. The law does not apply to appearances before parliamentary committees, submissions to public officials on the enforcement of laws or regulations, and submissions that are a response to a request. Therefore, the law does not allow us to

TABLE 7.1 **NUMBER OF ACTIVE LOBBYISTS IN THE THREE CATEGORIES, 2000–02**

CATEGORY	NUMBER OF ACTIVE LOBBYISTS 2000–01	NUMBER OF ACTIVE LOBBYISTS 2001–02
Consultants	788	858
In-house (corporate)	299	233
Organizations (senior officers)	356	351

Source: From *Lobbyists' Registration Act Annual Report* for the year ended March 31, 2002; available online from Industry Canada at www.strategis.ic.gc.ca/epic/internet/inlrel.nsf/en/lr01110e.html; accessed October 2004. Reproduced with the permission of the Minister of Public Works and Government Services, 2004.

gauge the degree to which pressure groups engage in representation or consultation—which, as we have seen, may be more likely to result in changes to public policy. Lobbying, in many cases, is a last resort. Nonetheless, the data provided by the Act give us a good indication of the policy areas that attract the greatest attention from pressure groups. Table 7.2 shows the top 20 subjects of lobbying at the federal level. The top three categories are business-related, which tends to reinforce concerns about the influence and resources of these interests.

Table 7.3 lists the federal departments and agencies that were the most frequent targets of lobbying in 2000–01 and 2001–02, according to the information filed by registered lobbyists in those years. It is no coincidence that four of the top departments—Industry, Finance, Foreign Affairs and International Trade, and Revenue Canada—are particularly important to the business sector.

Internal Relations with Pressure-Group Membership

We have seen that the characteristics of a pressure group's membership help to determine its political salience, although they are less crucial to its policy capacity. However, some interest constituencies may constrain the policy capacity of their leaders. Groups that refuse to cooperate with the government, or whose members fear co-optation into political institutions, will exercise less influence than those whose members are willing to accept the norms of the subgovernment. The leaders and staff of a pressure group must have a degree of latitude, so that they can participate effectively in the subgovernment without constantly facing accusations of selling out, or demands for consultation, from their members.

Pross describes the "vertical information problem" that can arise as a newly formed pressure group becomes more institutionalized, with leaders and staff taking on distinct roles and values from the people whose interests they are expected to express. The leaders, who interact directly with other members of the policy community, "become knowledgeable about the policy process, come to feel more effective in it, and consequently tend to move away from their followers."[51] At this point, the emerging political salience of the pressure group may be undermined by a perception

NONGOVERNMENTAL ACTORS IN THE CANADIAN POLICY PROCESS **345**

TABLE 7.2   **TOP 20 SUBJECTS OF LOBBYING, 2000–02**

SUBJECT OF LOBBYING	2000–01 RANKING	2001–02 RANKING
Industry	1	1
International Trade	2	2
Taxation and Finance	3	3
Environment	4	4
Transportation	8	5
Science and Technology	5	6
Health	6	7
Internal Trade	10	8
Consumer Issues	7	9
Energy	12	10
Employment and Training	9	11
Regional Development/Intellectual Property	13/14	12
International Relations	11	13
Government Procurement	16	14
Infrastructure	18	15
Agriculture	16	16
Small Business	17	17
Labour	19	18
Telecommunications	20	19
Aboriginal Affairs*	n/a	20

*Aboriginal Affairs was not among the 20 most frequently identified topics in 2000–01.

Source: From *Lobbyists' Registration Act Annual Report* for the year ended March 31, 2002; available online from Industry Canada at www.strategis.ic.gc.ca; accessed October 2004. Reproduced with the permission of the Minister of Public Works and Government Services, 2004.

among public officials that its constituency does not support the goals and tactics of the leaders. When this happens, officials wonder whether they can rely on the group's members to support the policies approved by their leaders, or to participate effectively in their implementation.

In sum, the leaders of pressure groups are caught in a dilemma. On the one hand, the demands of participation in the subgovernment cannot be met without the financial and moral support of their members. Nor will they be admitted to the subgovernment without a firm mandate from the grassroots of their organizations—"the express assignment of representative capacity to a group's leadership by its membership."[52] On the other hand, pressure-group leaders cannot respond quickly to requests for information and advice if they are required to seek the formal approval

DEPARTMENT OR AGENCY	2000–01 RANKING	2001–02 RANKING
Industry Canada	1	1
Finance Canada	2	2
Foreign Affairs and International Trade	3	3
Environment Canada	5	4
Transport Canada	7	5
Health Canada	6	6
Revenue Canada	4	7
Privy Council Office	8	8
Natural Resources Canada	10	9
Human Resources Development Canada	11	10
Public Works and Government Services Canada	9	11
Canadian Heritage	13	12
Agriculture and Agri-Food Canada	14	13
Treasury Board of Canada	12	14
Fisheries and Oceans Canada	15	15
National Defence	16	16
Justice Canada	17	17
Western Economic Diversification Canada	19	18
Indian and Northern Affairs Canada*	n/a	19
Canadian International Development Agency	18	20

*This department was not in the top 20 identified by lobbyists in their registrations for the 2000–01 period.

Source: From *Lobbyists' Registration Act Annual Report* for the year ended March 31, 2002; available online from Industry Canada at www.strategis.ic.gc.ca; accessed October 2004. Reproduced with the permission of the Minister of Public Works and Government Services, 2004.

of their members for every policy pronouncement. While it may be desirable in theory for leaders to be fully accountable to those in whose name they speak, it is clear that pressure-group leaders are most effective when they achieve the autonomy and the experience to participate in detailed policy-making.

Such leaders may also acquire the polish and the communications skills that allow them to use the news media to raise the profile of their group and its issues. Close ties between journalists and pressure-group leaders carry advantages as well as disadvantages. On the plus side, frequent media appearances by a group leader or spokesperson "may help to keep the movement's concerns before the public, and enhance its status in the eyes of policy makers."[53] The downside, particularly for advocacy groups with "radical" agendas, is that sustained media attention "may alienate policy makers, if the latter perceive the movement's tactics as illegitimate or embarrassing."[54] Further, and returning to the theme of the internal workings of pressure groups, "the transformation of activists into media celebrities can foster internal envy and resentment."[55] In summary, the institutional incentives for pressure groups seeking admission to the subgovernment pull their leaders and their members in different directions. The former must adapt to the requirements of policy-making and media relations, while the latter cannot allow leaders to lose touch with the concerns of those who gave them their mandate in the first place.

◼ Pressure Groups in Canadian Politics

The role of pressure groups in Canadian politics will likely increase in the next few years, for four reasons. First, while there seems to be growing optimism and some return to trust among the electorate, politicians and political parties are still held in low regard by most Canadians. Many groups, on the other hand, enjoy high levels of legitimacy. Second, as noted here and in Chapter 10, the *Charter of Rights and Freedoms* has given many groups new leverage in challenging public policy. Litigation is expensive and risky, but it has often been used successfully by women's groups, gays and lesbians, labour unions, and Aboriginal groups.

Third, for the time being, governments across the country are proclaiming the importance of consultation and partnership with "civil society." As we noted above, funding and support for advocacy organizations have in fact been in decline for the last decade; even as the delivery of social services shifts to the voluntary and charitable sectors, the financial and logistical support needed to make program delivery work do not. Nonetheless, consultation is "in" and policy-makers cannot avoid, even if they want to, connecting with a wide variety of organizations. Fourth and finally, as mentioned above, groups may be developing a new capacity for mobilization and for building networked coalitions through the use of new information technologies.

For some, further growth in pressure-group activity will make our politics hostage to shifting coalitions of "special interests." For others, the opposite is true: collective action in pursuit of shared goals is the foundation of the "social capital" required to support democratic institutions (see Chapter 2). (Note, however, that to the extent that the state funds advocacy groups that would otherwise lack the wherewithal to participate in policy-making, the growing numbers of interest associations reflect government priorities rather than a vibrant civil society.) In either event, the balance between political parties and pressure groups will be a challenging one. The problem is that our political institutions—from Parliament and federalism to the amending formulas of the *Constitution* itself—operate according to a logic that is relatively closed, hierarchical, and obviously representational. Referenda, consultations, and direct representation by groups and organizations of citizens assume, by contrast, that citizens want to act for themselves. If we are to do so effectively, and if we are to hold the state actors within policy communities to account for their decisions, we need complete and accurate political information. So we turn now to a second nongovernmental political institution that is supposed to provide us with that information: the Canadian news media.

Public servants march below Parliament Hill, August 15, 2001. (© CP/Fred Chartrand)

THE NEWS MEDIA

The mass media are as much a part of the democratic system as are Parliament, the Supreme Court, or provincial governments. And while these other institutions all operate within a system of checks and balances—MPs are accountable at election time, the power of the Supreme Court is circumscribed by law and thus by Parliament, and provincial governments must face the electorate and govern both with and against Ottawa—the mass media seem to have few such constraints. Increasingly in Canada, they have power without accountability. The responsibility for that failure, for that betrayal of public interests and public responsibility, falls on many shoulders.[56]

Strictly speaking, the news media do not constitute a single, unified institution analogous to the House of Commons or the Supreme Court. Nonetheless, the thousands of professionals who write, record, edit, and broadcast information and opinion about Canadian politics collectively constitute an entity with many of the characteristics of a formal institution:[57] shared norms and values, a hierarchy of power and status, clear incentives for ambitious participants, and a distinct role in the political system. Like other institutions, the news media both influence and are influenced by the political culture within which they operate. In this section, we will focus on three particular aspects of the news media: (1) the institutional characteristics of the major news media in Canada; (2) the degree to which news coverage influences Canadian citizens; and (3) the news media's impact on the operation and priorities of our three branches of government.

◼ The News Media in Canada: Institutional Characteristics

Broadly speaking, the news media occupy a middle ground between our political institutions and those whom they govern. Most Canadians have little direct experience of national politics. You may have shaken the hand of an MP or cast a ballot in an election, but in all likelihood, you have never attended a party convention or sat in the Commons gallery during Question Period. We depend on newspapers, magazines, radio, television, and the Internet for information and analysis about the policies, processes, and personalities that affect our lives. Ideally, this secondhand information about politics and government should be as accurate and comprehensive as possible if we are to carry out our responsibilities as informed and active citizens. In practice, political news is constrained and sometimes distorted by the institutional characteristics of the mass media in Canada and elsewhere.

With the notable exception of the Canadian Broadcasting Corporation (including the CBC website, Société Radio-Canada, *CBC Newsworld,* and Radio Canada International), Canadian media companies are privately owned. Even the CBC, a Crown corporation subsidized by Parliamentary appropriations, has become increasingly dependent on advertising revenues over two decades of deep spending cuts. Private ownership affects the ways in which media companies discharge their primary public service: the collection and dissemination of political information.

In the first place, privately owned news companies must make a profit for their owners and shareholders. To do this, they must keep their costs down while boosting their revenues. Investigative journalism is expensive, as are Ottawa bureaus and foreign correspondents. Therefore, local newspapers increasingly rely on wire services, press releases, and prepackaged news. Maximizing revenue means selling as much advertising as possible, at the highest rate the market will bear. Advertising rates depend on the number of people who read, watch, or listen to the company's product. The larger the audience or readership, the higher the profits. So most media companies have a strong incentive to downplay costly political coverage in favour of attention-grabbing scandal, conflict, and "news you can use."[58]

Competition among media companies translates into a battle for readers and ratings, a battle in which celebrity gossip and hyped-up crime stories often take priority over in-depth coverage and analysis of government and policy-making. Journalists who operate in a free market are required to "give the people what they want," not necessarily what they need. "For the most part, modern media organizations have tipped the balance toward treating their audience as consumers rather than citizens."[59] While this trend is fuelled, in part, by the perception on the part of news editors and producers that "the public is not interested in the complex issues that make up routine coverage of public bodies and the bureaucracy,"[60] we cannot blame shallow and superficial coverage of political events on the media alone.[61] In a culture where the Kobe Bryant trial and the love life of Jennifer Lopez attract greater public interest than electoral corruption or the process by which political leaders make the laws that directly affect our lives, it is hardly surprising that market-driven news producers focus on personalities at the expense of complicated issues.

While broadcasting, especially local broadcasting, is becoming more competitive, most local markets have only one, perhaps two, daily newspapers. In recent decades, ownership in the newspaper business has been concentrated in fewer and fewer hands: "Of all the capitalist countries in the world today, Canada has the highest concentration of media ownership . . . In 1998, Southam/Hollinger, Sun Media, Quebecor, Thomson, and Torstar controlled 87.3% of circulation."[62] At the same time, newspapers and national television networks are being absorbed into huge multibusiness conglomerates—which often seem to regard the news as just another "product." Critics of former Southam owner Conrad Black alleged that his erstwhile control of such a large share of the newspaper business—45 percent of daily circulation in Canada[63]—restricted the range of political viewpoints expressed in the media. In particular, they pointed to his strong conservative bias and his willingness to inject that bias into his newspapers, partly by hiring editors, publishers, and journalists who shared his political views.[64] It has also been alleged that Black's personal dislike of former Prime Minister Chrétien prompted his newspapers, especially the *National Post*, to wage a political vendetta against the Liberal government.[65]

However, Lord Black's proprietorship of Southam—now part of the CanWest MediaWorks conglomerate[66]—did heighten national competition in the newspaper business. In 1998 Black created the *National Post* to compete with *The Globe and Mail.* The *Post*'s lively prose, unabashed promotion of conservative politicians, and gleeful attacks on the governing Liberals sparked a new dynamic in Canadian politics. For example, the fierce competition between the two national newspapers affected the Liberal leadership battle between Prime Minister Chrétien and Finance Minister Paul Martin. Former Southam reporter Susan Delacourt recalls: "With heightened competition between the political reports on [Parliament] Hill, there was a rush to publish any or all tips or leaked information. It became far easier for strategists to plant their stories in the national press, sometimes just for mischief, sometimes to send messages to their rivals."[67] The newspaper wars also played a role in the clash between the Liberals and the Reform Opposition in the House of Commons in the late 1990s; reporters from the *Post* worked with Reform MPs to expose scandals in the management of public funds, to such an extent that "journalists became part of the story and were making their own news."[68] However, the *National Post* failed to turn a profit; its huge losses contributed to Southam's financial woes, which eventually forced Black to sell the newspaper chain to TV conglomerate CanWest Global (now CanWest MediaWorks).

The ideological biases of those at the top of the hierarchy—newspaper publishers and editors, and news producers on radio and TV—may influence the reporters who cover politics. While direct editorial intervention is rare, journalists know that a story that conflicts with the beliefs of their superiors may be rewritten or killed outright. In order to survive in "an organizational culture where promotions, higher salaries, and top assignments require a certain amount of team play,"[69] a reporter may decide not to cover a particular story or to cover it in a way that pleases management.

In addition to the constraints arising from private ownership, journalists are subject to other institutional incentives—some of which conflict with market impera-tives. First, they must follow the ethics and values of their profession. Until fairly recently, journalism was not considered to be a "profession" like law or medicine. In the past few decades, schools of journalism have sprung up across the country to train and socialize aspiring reporters. The core values of professional journalists include accuracy, the rapid transmission of information to the public, the investigation of public institutions, and the analysis of complex issues.[70] Although these ideals are not always followed in practice, to disregard them completely would ruin a reporter's career.

At the very least, a political story must be balanced between opposing viewpoints; a quotation or a video clip from one side of an issue must be followed by a similar con-tribution from the other side. The coverage of the national-unity issue in Canada pro-vides a possible exception to the "balance" rule: some federalist politicians have alleged that francophone Quebec journalists (including those at Radio-Canada) are overly sympathetic to the separatist cause.[71] Similar allegations of bias were levelled at the anglophone media during the 1995 Quebec referendum campaign. One telling indicator of the gulf between the perceptions of the two "media solitudes" is the coverage of the pro-Canada rally in Montreal shortly before the referendum vote: "CBC Newsworld estimated the crowd at 150,000, while RDI [the francophone equiv-alent of Newsworld] reported that only 30 or 40 thousand people had attended the rally."[72]

Second, reporters are subject to the competitive pressures of gathering and reporting news to a tight deadline. They cannot afford to miss out on a "hot" story. When a senior politician steps on a political land mine, the parliamentary press gallery turns into a pack of hungry wolves (Dossier 7.1).[73]

Once the "pack" seizes on its target, reporters pursue the unfortunate politician relentlessly, desperate for a new daily angle to keep the story alive. These "feeding frenzies" are motivated by more than simple blood-lust: reporters know that if they drop the ball on the big story of the day, they will face criticism from their colleagues and competitors as well as from their bosses.[74] The "pack" mentality also arises from the process of political reporting. Journalists spend hours or days crammed together in hallways, buses, planes, and other confined spaces with little to do except to wait for their prey and exchange the latest gossip and speculation. While a political scandal in Ottawa—for example, allegations that former Prime Minister Chrétien intervened improperly in dealings between a Crown lender and the owner of a hotel and golf course in his constituency—may generate little interest in the rest of the

The dynamic of Ottawa's pack-journalism culture is not easy to dissect. Reporters don't conspire to pursue the same story or personality. There are no head-office directives distributed to members of the parliamentary press gallery, as conspiracy theorists might imagine. Rather, the media will be seized with a single idea simultaneously and spontaneously, and then collectively pursue it to death. Media competition exaggerates this tendency, as rival reporters scramble to outdo each other. One story begets a follow-up story. One question in a scrum leads to another along the same lines. The morning chitchat on the Sparks Street Mall [a pedestrian thoroughfare a block south of Parliament Hill] turns into an item by lunch and an issue by pre-dinner drinks. Soon, the theme seeps into the wider culture.

country, it immediately becomes the only topic of conversation in the nation's capital. Members of the press gallery live for stories like this, just as their counterparts in Washington live in hopes of the next Monica Lewinsky scandal, however much this obsessive focus on wrongdoing and foolishness by political leaders may damage public support for politics (or journalism). The "pack" phenomenon also arises from the uncertainty inherent in deciding which events are "news" and which are not; reporters often watch each other for cues, finding safety in numbers.[76]

Third, many political reporters rely heavily on official "sources," including Cabinet ministers and senior public officials.[77] The daily "news cycle" is unforgiving, especially in an era of 24-hour news channels. A journalist must have immediate and secure access to informed sources, either to generate stories or to confirm information received elsewhere. The need to maintain cordial working relationships with powerful people places the reporter in a dilemma: if she "burns" a source, her access is over and other political actors may never trust her again; if she accepts a source's version of events uncritically, however, she becomes a mouthpiece for that individual or group and loses her credibility as a journalist.

In addition to the constraints imposed by market forces and institutional incentives, journalists who work in television are constrained by the technical requirements of the medium. A story with good "visuals" is more attractive to news producers than one without. Political developments that take place behind closed doors, in the absence of cameras, or that lack eye-catching visual symbolism or settings are difficult to convey on TV. Because television is primarily a visual medium, events that require extensive verbal explanation and context are given short shrift—whatever their intrinsic importance. "Talking heads" are considered boring; action and confrontation are not.

When a politician gives a speech or is interviewed on camera, the preferred length of the "clip" included in an individual story is 10 to 12 seconds. Clips have become shorter in recent years—an average of 7.8 seconds in the 2000 U.S. presidential race[78]—largely because of "the perceived attention span of viewers and the need to grab and hold the audience with sharp, fast-paced, action-oriented stories."[79] Most political and administrative issues are inherently complex and require substantial explanation if they are to be fully understood by nonspecialists. Such complexity is unsuited to the demands of television news. Small wonder, then, that coverage of the July 2001 G8 Summit in Genoa, Italy, focused on the riots in the streets outside the meeting, paying little attention to what the leaders of the world's richest countries were discussing inside. A riot is a good story for TV; a lengthy discussion of trade policy and developing countries' debt is not.

The institutional incentives that operate within the news media often produce shallow, sensationalistic coverage of politics and government. While there are obvious exceptions, including the CBC/Radio-Canada, *The Globe and Mail,* and *Le Devoir*, much of what passes for political reporting in this country is inadequate to inform and educate the public. Nor is there any reason to expect that matters will improve quickly. One survey of Canadian journalists found that the youngest respondents had a significantly different view of their profession from their older colleagues. They considered accuracy, investigative journalism, and policy analysis to be less important, while placing a greater emphasis on "entertainment and relaxation."[80] Nevertheless, the fact that younger journalists were considerably less skeptical toward "government and public institutions" than their elders may be a good sign (showing less of an anti-institutional bias) albeit surprising in light of the discussion of postmaterialism in Chapter 2. Reporters who came of age in the 1950s often deplore the anti-establishment attitudes and the cynicism of their baby boomer colleagues, accusing them of undermining the legitimacy of political institutions.[81] If the current generation of journalists does not share the postmaterialist values of their peers, we cannot yet know whether they will turn back the clock to an earlier era of deferential reporting, or become increasingly cynical in the process of "giving the people what they want."

◼ The Impact of News Coverage on Citizens

All institutions are required to create order out of chaos—to turn a welter of competing ideas, interests, priorities, and viewpoints into coherent action. For the news media, the "chaos" is the infinite number of events that happen every day. Only a few can be made to fit in the pages of a newspaper or the brief period of a newscast. The criteria editors and producers use to select which stories to cover are called **"news values."** These are politically significant, because the decision to cover one type of story entails a decision not to report other events that may be intrinsically important for citizens, but not as appealing to consumers.

Generally speaking, news values emphasize conflict, drama, novelty, and "human interest" over detailed policy analysis or descriptions of the political process.[82] For both technological and financial reasons, this is particularly true of television—by far the most popular news medium in Canada. Comparative studies reveal that Canadians are less likely to read newspapers, and more likely to obtain their news from television, than people in many other developed countries.[83] This imbalance contributes to relatively low levels of "civic literacy" in Canada, compared to countries whose citizens rely more on newspapers for their political information.[84]

When media analysts examine the impact of journalistic practices on the selection and presentation of news stories, they often focus on three particular concepts: agenda-setting, news frames, and priming. Agenda-setting refers to the alleged power of the news media to influence public perceptions of the relative importance of a given event. Studies of media effects have consistently found "a correlation between the frequency of a topic covered by the news media and its ranking in public opinion polls."[85] One Canadian study provides a more nuanced picture of the agenda-setting process: the degree to which media coverage shapes public perceptions varies with the type of issue involved. Perceptions of a problem like unemployment, which directly affects millions of Canadians, are less likely to be affected by media coverage than abstract issues beyond the daily experience of the average voter.[86]

In some cases, the media can heighten public awareness of an issue; growing public concern may then force governments to devote more attention to the problem than they might otherwise have done. On occasion, a dramatic event can capture the simultaneous attention of the media, the public, and policy-makers. When such a "political wave" hits, the news media can affect the policy responses of governments by "framing" the event in particular ways. Terrorist attacks are the best example of these "political waves."[87] While the 9/11 attacks in the United States would have had an extraordinary impact under any circumstances, the fact that millions of people watched (some in real time) as the hijacked planes flew into the World Trade Center towers must have strengthened the "political wave" that resulted. Indeed, the damage to the Pentagon, and the lives lost in that attack, appear to have left fewer psychological traces precisely because there was no video footage of the plane hitting the building.

The agenda-setting power of the media affects both leaders and voters. The political executive can be forced to respond to a media-generated perception of a problem, instead of to its objective reality. For example, "Notwithstanding the general decline in rates of violent crime, the media spotlight on 'youth gangs' and violent crimes involving young people helped place revisions to the *Young Offenders Act* on the Parliamentary agenda."[88] The long-term effect on the population at large may be even more significant in light of our dependence on the media for "secondhand" information about politics and government: "By directing audience attention towards some aspects of reality and away from others, the news media help to define reality for their audiences and to structure the public's perceptions of the political world."[89]

News frames are "those rhetorical and stylistic choices . . . that alter the interpretations of the topics treated and are a consistent part of the news environment."[90] Any given event can be presented and explained in a number of different ways. For example, a general election may be "framed" by journalists as a horserace among the party leaders, as a contest among ideologies and principles, as the supreme expression of Canadian democracy, or as a turning point in our national history. Each of these "frames" is based on a set of assumptions about politics, about the preexisting knowledge and beliefs of the audience, and about the motivations of the actors who "star" in the nightly newscast.

In both Canada and the United States, elections are most often "framed" as strategic battles between self-interested and perhaps dishonest politicians.[91] It is not entirely clear why journalists prefer this frame. One reason may be that it lends itself to television's need for arresting visual images and juicy "revelations" about underhanded political tactics; another possible explanation is that the "strategic" frame is consistent with the alleged cynicism and anti-institutional bias of the press corps. Whatever the reasons for its popularity, the decision to "frame" election campaigns as content-free horseraces "encourage[s] a trivialization of politics, and contribute[s] to a general decline in political discourse and the quality of political life."[92]

Another example of media "framing" is discussed in Dossier 5.6: the alleged "billion-dollar boondoggle" in the former Human Resources Development department. Once the news media, led by the *National Post*, had decided that an internal audit revealed widespread mismanagement and political corruption in the Grants and Contributions programs—whose annual cost totalled roughly $1 billion—no amount of damage control by the minister or her officials could overcome that perception. "The media reported new and unexpected negative events that reinforced the original storyline, and ignored those that did not."[93]

Whereas the concept of agenda-setting refers to the frequency with which the media cover a particular issue, "priming" goes a step further. The theory of media priming holds that news stories not only tell us what is important but also how we should think about it. The ways in which journalists tell "stories" about the world implicitly prescribe "the appropriate criteria for evaluation of persons, policies, or actions."[94] Specifically, voters are more likely to judge the performance of their political leaders in relation to issues that receive intense media scrutiny than they are to judge the government's handling of more obscure problems.[95] This may help to explain why, as we saw in Chapter 4, a handful of issues will tend to dominate voters' perceptions during each election campaign; those issues vary from election to election, depending in part on their relative visibility in the media.

The Effect of News Coverage on Canadian Political Institutions

Generally, it can be said that there are two types of reporters: those who see themselves as part of the institutions they cover, and those who believe that it's the media's job to crusade against the institutions where they work . . . Now, it is fair to say that for every one institutionally minded reporter in Ottawa, there is at least one reporter with an anti-institutional bent.[96]

For many observers, the role of the news media in Canadian politics has changed in recent years. Whereas the parliamentary press gallery was once "a narrator or an independent observer reporting and commenting on political events," it has become "a major political actor in its own right."[97] Its political role takes three forms. First, the news media provide the most important channel of communication between the state and the citizens. Today, governments have the capacity to communicate directly via the Internet; but the print and broadcast media remain the most important source of information for most Canadians, especially those who lack the resources required for Internet access.[98] As we have seen, news coverage of political events is not neutral; it is shaped by the institutional constraints on media workers and by the conventions of news coverage itself—agenda-setting, framing, and priming.

Second, reporters act as conduits of information and opinion *between* government actors.[99] During political crises, when politicians may not be in direct contact with each other, they communicate through the media. An ill-judged public statement by one participant may provoke another to respond with equal defiance, leading to a showdown that may have undesirable results. The near-collapse of the minority Liberal government in October 2004 demonstrated the consequences of communication via the press gallery. The leaders of the Conservative Party and the Bloc Québécois (Stephen Harper and Gilles Duceppe, respectively) told reporters that they would vote for a BQ sub-amendment to the Speech from the Throne; the Liberals responded, also via the media, that they would interpret such a result as a vote of nonconfidence and request the governor general to call an election immediately.[100] As the hours ticked away, both sides dug in their heels. They could not retreat from the hard-line positions they had taken publicly, without risking embarrassment and the loss of support from their MPs. The defeat of the government after four days in the Commons—a result that no rational person could seriously have wished—seemed increasingly possible. Finally, Prime Minister Martin invited Harper and Duceppe to his office for a face-to-face discussion. Shortly afterward, the BQ changed the wording of its sub-amendment to remove the offending passages. It passed unanimously, and a crisis was averted.[101] Had the three men met earlier, instead of indulging in macho posturing before the television cameras, it is unlikely that a crisis would have erupted so soon in the life of the thirty-eighth Parliament.

Third, the media's more aggressive coverage of politics and government has forced politicians and public servants to change the ways in which they work. For example, reporters often file access-to-information requests to obtain internal documents from government departments. A former policy adviser in the federal government recalls the "chilling" effect on policy-making: "I saw myself that officials are extremely leery of putting things on paper that they wouldn't like to see made public or find their way to the media, several months later, that could be embarrassing to the minister."[102] Now, that caution extends to e-mails as well as paper documents. Among the exhibits submitted to the Commission of Inquiry into the Sponsorship Program (Dossier 6.2) were several internal e-mails, which revealed that senior managers in the Treasury Board Secretariat and elsewhere had concerns about the program well before the alleged abuse of public money came to the attention of the media and the Opposition. More broadly, Canadian governments have been forced to adapt to the needs and values of the news media: the demand for instant answers, the tendency to put a negative "spin" on even the most innocuous events, and Cabinet ministers' fear of being perceived as either corrupt or incompetent.

The Legislative Branch

Much of the coverage of the House of Commons is focused on question period. This is only part—and, arguably, a distorted view—of the work of the House, and involves only a handful of Members. It is important that Canadians get a fuller picture. They need to be given an opportunity to see other MPs at work, and to see what committees are doing.[103]

Neither the House of Commons nor the Senate attracts much serious attention from the news media, despite the crucial role of legislative institutions as a forum for the discussion of national issues.[104] The daily Question Period in the Commons is the sole exception, not because of its intrinsic importance in the legislative process, but because "it has everything required for a good story":

There is no shortage of ten-second clips containing the needed quotient of personal vitriol and conflict. Personalities are magnified and issues condensed . . . For the prime minister and opposition party leaders, the daily dramatics of Question Period can have a corrosive effect. Instead of being shown in a dignified setting where their authority is respected, they are seen hurling accusations at each other and in shouting matches.[105]

Regular debates and committee hearings, despite their greater potential importance and (sometimes) content, are generally ignored by the media.[106] As one CBC reporter told the McGrath Committee in 1985, "By and large, once the lead-off speaker [of] each party has spoken, you know what every other speaker is going to say and, let us face it, you do not even go to hear them yourselves."[107] Reporters pay attention to debate or committees only when the system breaks down: an Opposition party tries to block legislation through procedural shenanigans, a government backbencher breaks with her party, or a committee hearing erupts in chaos. This distorted focus "encourages the worst aspects of parliamentary behaviour"[108] and likely contributes to the decline in public support for Parliament discussed in Chapters 2 and 5.[109] We might argue, therefore, that the emphasis on Question Period arises both from its congruence with the requirements of television—conflict, good visuals, and short, emphatic statements—and from its consistency with the anti-institutional bias of some journalists: "Parliament itself, inasmuch as it seems to have the atmosphere of a prize-fight—at least as presented on television—has dropped considerably in public esteem in recent years."[110]

Three further aspects of the media's relationship to Parliament deserve mention. First, reporters rarely give the Senate positive coverage, despite its valuable role in the legislative process (see "Sober Second Thought: The Legislative Role of the Upper House" in Chapter 5). If more Canadians understood and appreciated the work done by senators, the institution might enjoy greater public legitimacy. Second, journalists hostile to political authority have effectively usurped the role of the official (and Loyal) Opposition in the Commons.[111] The function of an official Opposition is not just to criticize the government of the day; it is to provide an alternative government, one that can be held accountable to the voters. Journalists cannot perform this function; all they can do is to undermine public faith in the wisdom and integrity of elected officials by devoting all their attention to undignified partisan name-calling while ignoring valuable legislative work.

Third, the media and the opposition parties often work together to get the most mileage out of Question Period. Opposition MPs attend morning tactics meetings, armed with piles of newspaper clippings and primed by watching videotapes of last night's newscasts. They use the headlines and the top stories to determine the content and order of their questions for that day. Don Newman, the Parliamentary bureau chief for CBC Television and formerly a reporter for *The Globe and Mail*, once remarked that "When you were writing your story you knew that you were writing Question Period the next day."[112] To the extent that reporters and Opposition MPs uncover genuinely important information about problems in the executive branch, their cooperation can provide the most effective guarantee of government accountability to the people. It can also bring down an individual Cabinet minister, as we saw in "Holding the Executive to Account" in Chapter 5 (the case study of former Solicitor General Andy Scott). On the downside, a close working relationship between journalists and Opposition MPs who share an ideological agenda and an antipathy to the government can produce distorted news coverage and turn Question Period into a pointless witch-hunt. As noted earlier, reporters for the *National Post* and other news outlets portrayed sloppy paperwork at Human Resources Development Canada as a "billion-dollar boondoggle" (Dossier 5.6). The *Post* collaborated with the Reform caucus, sharing documents obtained via access-to-information requests and, in turn, relying on Reform MPs "to provide context and set the agenda for the coming week."[113]

The prime minister and his central agencies measure their success not only by their accomplishments but also by their ability to "manage" media crises.

> *The work of the media by all accounts dominates the agenda of morning meetings between the prime minister and the Clerk of the Privy Council. What the evening news on national television reported the night before and what the headlines in morning newspapers say have a profound impact on question period, and by extension, on government operations.*[114]

Much of the cooperation between the media and the Opposition produces nothing but sound and fury: phony outrage, manufactured or exaggerated scandals, and questionable reporting. But on occasion, media cooperation with the auditor general and other parliamentary watchdogs can force the government to fix problems in policy or management that would otherwise have gone unaddressed.

The Executive Branch

Prime ministers and those who work for them devote enormous time and effort to "managing" problems. In other words, they try to keep potentially embarrassing mistakes and conflicts from reaching the media; if that fails, they want to "spin" the story in order to minimize the political damage. On occasion, the "spin" staff themselves become part of the story—usually in unflattering ways. In 2002, at the height of both the Liberal leadership battle and the newspaper war between the *Globe* and the *Post*, the director of communications in the Prime Minister's Office was forced to resign after making an indiscreet remark to a member of the press gallery. Françoise Ducros had alienated many reporters with her blunt style. Her fierce loyalty to then-Prime Minister Chrétien also put her at odds with leadership aspirant Paul Martin and his supporters.[115] At a NATO Summit, in a briefing with Canadian journalists, Ducros described U.S. President George W. Bush as "a moron." The Ottawa bureau chief for the *National Post* overheard the comment, and repeated it anonymously in a story on the Summit. The quote provoked an uproar in Ottawa and Washington, where the identity of the speaker became a hot question. "Ducros was 'outed' by all major media the very next day."[116] Had she fostered good working relations with the press gallery, it is doubtful that Ducros' off-the-record comment would have been published or her identity revealed. Despite Chrétien's continued loyalty to his employee, Ducros was forced to resign soon afterward. "Her departure was greeted with enormous relief by most political reporters."[117]

Most of the time, relations between the Prime Minister's Office and the news media are less strained. The communications staff members in the PMO are supported by media-relations teams in other ministers' offices, and increasingly by public servants sensitive to their concerns about news management. (Recall the discussion of the new Cabinet papers system, with its emphasis on communications strategies, in Chapter 6.)

Despite this new awareness of media attention, the slow and deliberate pace of bureaucratic decision-making is unsuited to today's media-driven politics: "[T]he breathtaking speed of television news is putting enormous pressure on government to make decisions quickly for fear of appearing indecisive and not in control—one of the worst fears for a head of government."[118] Thus the political and administrative dominance of the prime minister is further enhanced, as the media focus on his performance and give him and his advisers a strong incentive to control the information flow for the entire executive branch.

> *The electronic media can hardly follow a government process and they have little interest in describing how it works. They need to focus on political actors and the one that matters the most to their audiences. And the one that can provide an answer to any question in any policy field is the prime minister.*[119]

In reality, of course, the prime minister cannot control the entire federal government. He is surrounded by Cabinet ministers, senior public officials, and political advisers, each of whom has the power to expose errors or internal power struggles that might damage the prime minister's reputation and that of his government. Despite the strong ethos of discretion and confidentiality within the federal public service, leaks do happen. In some cases, a minister or an official will try to "spin" a controversial issue in the "right" way by calling a reporter.[120] In other cases, a minister who wants to test public reaction to a proposed policy will send up a "trial balloon"; if the initial public and media reaction is hostile, the minister will withdraw or amend the proposal. Ministers are wise to fear the power of the media; a minister who performs poorly in Question Period, or who fumbles her relationship with the press gallery, may find herself at the centre of a feeding frenzy. A Cabinet minister who becomes a public embarrassment to the prime minister may have a short career in the political executive. All the way down the line, from the deputy minister to the front-line service-delivery staff in a given department, public servants are keenly aware of the risks posed by today's competitive, nondeferential journalists:

> *[T]here is a limit to how many times the media or the opposition can uncover administrative foul-ups before the media begins to accuse the government of no longer being in control . . . Senior public servants intuitively know that their greatest risk is not whether their draft of a Cabinet document will be found lacking or if a program will perform poorly, but if a scandal or embarrassment erupts in full view of the media.*[121]

To some extent, the effective use of executive power rests on a reputation for fairness and competence. The media, through their ability to shape the secondhand picture of politics that Canadians receive, possess considerable latitude to shape that reputation.

The Judicial Branch

Until the 1980s, neither journalists nor their audiences paid much attention to the Supreme Court of Canada or the provincial Courts of Appeal. A trial judge might acquire some notoriety during a high-profile criminal case, but in general the judicial branch operated beyond the reach of the media spotlight. That obscurity came to an end in 1981, when television cameras were admitted into the Supreme Court chamber to cover the justices' ruling on the *Patriation Reference*. Shortly thereafter, the late Brian Dickson took over as chief justice. He set out to create a new working relationship between the court and the media.[122] Dickson appointed the first executive legal officer, responsible for briefing reporters on important rulings and ensuring that the court's decisions are reported accurately.[123] He also broke precedent by granting interviews to journalists and by permitting cameras within the private precincts of the Supreme Court building. Since 1997, the Canadian Parliamentary Affairs Channel (CPAC) has provided gavel-to-gavel coverage of court hearings on high-profile appeals and constitutional references.[124] These broadcasts may hold little appeal for nonexperts; the legal arguments are often difficult for the layperson to understand. Nonetheless, they offer a unique glimpse into the judicial policy-making process.

Despite the relatively harmonious working relationship between the court and the press—reflected in the Media Relations Committee, which brings together justices and reporters to resolve disputes—the Supreme Court has received more than its share of media criticism for its interpretations of the *Charter of Rights*. Rulings that appear to protect the due-process rights of the accused against the rights of actual or potential victims have been especially controversial. The court's reluctance to allow the introduction of improperly obtained evidence in criminal trials is sometimes portrayed as a callous disregard for public safety and an assault on the legitimate investigative powers of the police.[125] The fact that section 24(2) of the *Constitution Act, 1982* not only permits, but actually requires, judges to exclude tainted evidence is rarely mentioned (see Chapter 10). A handful of judicial rulings on the right to a fair trial—principally *Seaboyer* and *Askov,* which are discussed in Chapter 10—have provoked widespread media and pressure-group criticism of the court. Note, however, that when a *Charter* ruling attracts severe and sustained criticism from the media and from pressure groups, Parliament usually responds by amending or reintroducing the impugned law (see the discussion of the "rape shield" in "The Transformation of Judicial Review in the *Charter* Era" in Chapter 10). One might argue, therefore, that the media play an important role, both in the continuing dialogue between legislators and judges and in the improvement of our laws.

Perhaps the most hostile media response to a *Charter* decision (apart from the 1988 *Morgentaler* ruling) concerned the court's 1994 ruling in *Daviault.* It quashed a conviction for sexual assault on the ground that the accused was too drunk at the time of the offence to form the requisite criminal intent. In other words, he could not be found guilty because the Crown could not prove that he knew what he was doing when he committed the crime.[126] The ruling hit the front pages, amid howls of outrage from women's groups and victims' rights groups. The news coverage implied that the court had not only set the man free—when, in reality, it had ordered him to stand trial a second time—but had declared open season on women for any man who was physically capable of sexual assault while he was drunk enough to meet the standard of "extreme intoxication." Daviault's 65-year-old victim was confined to a wheelchair, a fact that sharpened accusations of callousness on the part of the justices (whereas, in law, the relative vulnerability of an adult victim generally plays little if any role in determining guilt). When the worst fears of the court's critics were confirmed, and five men were acquitted of sexual-assault charges under the *Daviault* doctrine within a year of the ruling, the media played up the theme that victims' rights were being ignored. Notably, however, "The six unsuccessful uses of the defence and the reversal on appeal of two of the five acquittals received less attention."[127] In this highly charged political and journalistic climate, it was hardly surprising that Parliament closed the *Daviault* loophole a year after the ruling.

Whenever the court hands down a ruling that infuriates lawyers, police, feminist groups, or other organized interests, reporters have a field day. All the ingredients of a good news story are right there: conflict, emotion, willing interviewees, and—in many cases—sympathetic victims or articulate pressure-group leaders who can personalize abstract issues very effectively. Increasingly, journalists rely on pundits to explain lengthy and often highly technical decisions to their readers or viewers. Morton and Knopff argue that these pundits, many of whom are law professors, are often biased in favour of the left-leaning "Court Party."[128] Whether or not this particular accusation is legitimate, it is certainly true that news values corrupt and distort the reporting of *Charter* decisions. The "pro–con" format of journalism, together with the media's preference for clarity and conflict, reduce the parties in difficult and complex constitutional cases to "winners and losers."[129] In the process, the subtleties of legal doctrine and the careful balancing of rights and interests are overlooked.

Relations between the Supreme Court and the media took a turn for the worse with the establishment of the *National Post* in 1999. According to one of the paper's columnists, Andrew Coyne, its editorial position is strongly and consistently anti-court: "The *Post* is against any attempt on the part of unelected judges to impose their will on a democratically elected legislature."[130] While the justice reporter for *The Globe and Mail*, Kirk Makin, agrees that the *Post* is "leading the charge" against the Supreme Court, he argues that the roots of journalistic hostility lie deeper: "Having demystified and demythologized every other institution in society, I see the media now turning a great deal of attention to judges, judicial behaviour, and actual judgments."[131]

Former Chief Justice Antonio Lamer acknowledged that the fear of widespread public and media criticism is having an impact on the court: "Judges are human beings. I would be remiss if I were to say that we are superhuman or that we are not influenced sometimes."[132] A survey of appellate judges in the early 1990s found that some were concerned about "the impact of media criticism that they could not respond to without themselves violating judicial independence." (See the words of the late Justice Sopinka in Dossier 10.6.) Others worried that "the inaccurate or sensationalist handling of judicial decisions by the media was in a sense putting pressure on them to make decisions that would result in a 'good press.'"[133] While there are legitimate concerns about the accountability of the Supreme Court in the *Charter* era, shallow and sensationalistic news coverage is not a constructive solution to the problem.

◼ The Effect of News Coverage on the Canadian Electorate

As we discussed in Chapter 2, the influence of the news media is a contentious issue in Canadian politics. Whereas political scientists in the early twentieth century believed that the tone and content of news coverage directly affected public opinion, most now believe that the relationship between news and opinion is more complex.

In the first place, media influence on voters varies with the degree of information and the strength of political conviction each voter possesses.[134] A news junkie with an intense interest in politics is more likely to be influenced by media coverage than his more apathetic neighbour, but only under certain conditions. Agenda-setting, framing, and priming appear to exert the strongest effects on "voters with high political interest combined with a high degree of uncertainty on the issues."[135] Once the voter makes up his or her mind, the prospect of media influence diminishes. One study of the 1993 election campaign found that the growth in the Reform Party vote occurred predominantly among voters who followed the news coverage diligently and who already shared Reform's preference for deficit reduction over social spending.[136] Equally well-informed voters who favoured social spending over deficit reduction—in other words, those who were predisposed to reject Reform's fiscal policies—did not change their voting intentions on the basis of the news coverage. "Only those voters predisposed to like the Reform Party platform and those likely to be aware of the news coverage recognized Reform's position on a key policy issue in 1993—the deficit—and became more likely to support the Reform Party."[137] Because most people either avoid or screen out information that conflicts with their beliefs, "the effects of the media will be stronger among people who are predisposed to accept [their] message."[138]

Second, Canadian evidence suggests that those who identify with a particular political party are more likely to follow the news than those who lack a personal investment in the political process.[139] If this is the case, two conclusions follow:

- As just noted, media coverage of politics can reinforce the opinions voters already hold, instead of imposing the opinions of journalists on their audiences.
- Not all news consumers are "blank slates" waiting for reporters to write on them; instead, many are active readers and viewers, who filter the news through their preexisting political values.

Third, although it is no longer widely believed that the news media can tell us what to think, evidence suggests that they can and do tell us "what to think about."[140] As we have seen, the news media help to set the political agenda by emphasizing certain stories—and certain types of stories—over others. Institutional incentives within media companies lead producers and editors to focus on individual political events— "episodes"—and to present them in a dramatic, personal, and confrontational way. When the "crisis" in Canada's health-care system became a hot story in 1999–2000, the complex underlying issues (changes in fiscal federalism, technological developments in hospital care, an aging population) were reduced to "human interest" stories about individual patients who waited hours for treatment or who had to go to the United States for life-saving medical procedures. While these stories are certainly worthy of attention, they should not squeeze out rational public discussion of the core problems and the possible solutions.

Fourth, we have seen that latent social cleavages must be mobilized if they are to play a significant role in politics (Chapter 2). Particular segments of the news media can help to mobilize subcultures, and to reinforce subcultural attachments that have already been formed. The example given above, of the discrepancy in the reporting of the 1995 Quebec referendum by anglophone and francophone journalists, illustrates a persistent problem in Canadian democracy: for whatever reason (overt bias, the need to appeal to audience preconceptions, journalistic reliance on official sources), Quebec francophone journalists tend to "frame" political events from a nationalist perspective, while their anglophone counterparts in the rest of Canada take an explicitly federalist stand on national-unity issues.[141] There are at least two worrisome implications:

1. The reinforcement of the Quebec nationalist subculture by at least some francophone journalists intensifies the mutual suspicion and misunderstanding between Quebeckers and other Canadians.
2. Each segment of the media "frames" national-unity crises—such as the demise of the Meech Lake Accord or the 1995 Quebec referendum—in distinct and sometimes mutually offensive ways. Not only do these contending "frames" make it

more difficult for political leaders to compromise in constitutional negotiations, they may also encourage Canadian citizens to reject any such compromise on the ground that "their" side has been shortchanged. In so doing, they create potent symbols of division and irreconcilable difference to add to the store of such symbols that are already available to unscrupulous political leaders. (Recall the discussion of symbolism in the Meech Lake Accord, in Dossier 1.5.)

CONCLUSION

This chapter has described the domestic political roles played by two nongovernmental actors: pressure groups and the news media. Increasingly, both are changing in response to globalization. As policy-making shifts from the nation–state to supranational bodies, advocacy groups are forming international, sometimes worldwide, coalitions with other state-based groups and with older transnational organizations. For example, Canada's Aboriginal organizations have forged strong links with similar groups in other countries, and with environmentalists. These alliances succeeded in forcing Canadian governments to change certain policies. For example, the James Bay Cree recruited American environmental activist Robert Kennedy Jr. to pressure U.S. states not to buy hydroelectric power from Quebec as a protest against provincial efforts to expand its power-generating facilities on Cree land.[142]

There is nothing new about international networks of activists; decades before the term was coined, NGOs took shape across borders to combat the slave trade and the oppression of women. "What *is* new is the recent explosion in numbers, activity, and visibility of international initiatives by civil society actors on a variety of issues, at least in part linked to the rapid expansion of globalization of communications, transportation, and production."[143] The attraction of global networks for domestic pressure groups is obvious: they "enable citizens who have only limited political voice within national political institutions to amplify their voice, and to highlight harms and injustices that might otherwise be neglected."[144] It must be noted, however, that transnational NGOs direct most of their lobbying efforts toward national and provincial states; supranational bodies are increasingly important, but they have not yet supplanted nation–states as the prime target of pressure groups.

Another recent development is the explosion of interactive communication technology, which has altered the information environment within which the news media have long operated. The erosion of national boundaries by computer networks has prompted both optimistic predictions of "global citizenship"—a possible curative for the "democratic deficit" of supranational organizations—and pessimistic forecasts of increasing terrorist activity by loosely knit international networks like Al-Qaeda. At the moment, the optimistic scenario seems unrealistic, both because Internet access is still concentrated among the wealthy[145] and because the growing commercialization of the Internet appears likely to squeeze out grassroots perspectives within a few years.[146] Whatever the future brings, media organizations will have to find ways of covering international events more effectively. This is particularly true for American news outlets, whose lack of attention to international affairs probably contributed to the pervasive sense of bewilderment in that country after 9/11. During the 2000 presidential election campaign, all of the major news organizations combined produced only 10 stories about U.S. foreign policy.[147] Unfortunately, the high cost of foreign reporting runs counter to the market-based approach to the news business discussed earlier in this chapter.

At the same time, both the Internet and the growing spate of specialty TV channels threaten to divide fragmented electorates into ever-smaller groups. Critics argue that "narrowcasting," whether via computer networks or satellites, undermines social cohesion and precludes concerted political action to hold elites accountable (whether national or supranational).[148]

Of course, the problem of unaccountable power is not confined to the formal institutions of policy-making. Neither pressure groups nor media companies can effectively be held accountable for the power they wield in Canadian and international politics. There are some limited exceptions to this rule. Pressure groups must disclose some of their activities to the public (Tables 7.1–7.3 in this chapter), although the information contained in the lobbyists' register tells us little or nothing about the internal structures of these groups or the effectiveness of their activities. Broadcasting companies are regulated by the Canadian Radio-television and Telecommunications Commission (CRTC). In rare cases, the CRTC can suspend the licence of a broadcaster that breaks the rules,[149] but in general, Canadian journalists are constrained only by their employers and by the informal norms of their profession. They cannot be held formally accountable to the public for the information they choose to present and the ways in which they choose to present it.

In contrast, governmental institutions and closely related bodies like political parties are subject to formal rules of operation and accountability. Some of those rules are entrenched in written constitutional texts; others are unwritten conventions of procedure. Their cumulative effect is to constrain the arbitrary power of the state and to hold political actors accountable—however imperfectly—to the electorate. We have already looked at parties and elections and at the legislative and executive branches of the national government, and the informal incentives under which the actors involved must operate. The following chapter examines the formal rules for the exercise of power in Canada, both written and unwritten. Chapter 9 analyzes recent attempts (mostly unsuccessful) to change those rules, while Chapter 10 describes the impact of the most significant rule change in recent years: the *Canadian Charter of Rights and Freedoms*.

GLOSSARY OF KEY TERMS

Advocacy groups: Movements that try to alter conventional perceptions of the political and social status quo, and/or to mobilize support for projects for political and social change. Examples include the women's movement, the Aboriginal rights movement, and the environmental movement.

Collective action: The organized pursuit of a shared goal by a group of people; can be formal and structured (a military unit in combat) or informal and loosely structured (neighbours gathering to protest a zoning change).

Consultation: A state-sponsored process of cooperation between one or more government agencies and select pressure groups. May include the development of public policy, the shared implementation of new programs, or alternative service-delivery arrangements.

Co-optation: The process by which a pressure group, which opposes certain elements of state policy, is induced to accept the ideology or the policy priorities of the government. The most powerful tool of co-optation is public funding, although some groups fear that a close working relationship with state agencies could have the same effect. Groups that oppose the status quo on principle fear that the exercise of power might erode their independence and even corrupt their leaders.

Discourse community: See the definition of **policy community** below.

Interest group: An organization of people who seek to promote a common goal.

Lobbying: The effort to influence public policy directly, by persuading decision-makers in the political and permanent executives to adopt the goals of a particular group or individual. May be public (media events, appearing before a Commons committee) or private (meeting with the assistant deputy minister responsible for that policy file).

Mandate: The authority vested in the leaders of a pressure group by its membership. If there are doubts about the congruence between the goals of the leaders and those of the membership, the political salience of those leaders will suffer.

News values: The criteria used by journalists to determine which events to cover and the "spin" they will apply to that coverage.

Nongovernmental organization (NGO):   A group that operates outside the formal structure of government, as defined in the *Constitution,* and that seeks to participate in the policy process (from agenda-setting to policy formulation, and, ultimately, implementation).

Policy capacity: The tangible and intangible resources that a pressure group can devote to its participation in the policy community. If it has sufficient policy capacity—e.g., expert knowledge and the resources to mobilize its members to implement a new program—it can become a member of the subgovernment.

Policy community: The mix of groups and individuals with a particular interest in a specific policy field. Divided into the **subgovernment** (inner circle) and the **discourse community,** a broader universe of groups and individuals "who have some knowledge of the policy issue in question and who collectively construct a policy discourse"[150] (outer circle). Usually contains one or more distinct policy networks. The structure and influence of the policy community in a given policy sector depends on three factors: the autonomy and policy capacity of the state agency or agencies, the strength of the pressure groups in that sector, and the relationship among the members of the subgovernment.

Policy network: The term used to describe the web of relationships among the members of a particular policy community.

Political salience: (1) The perceived legitimacy of a particular pressure group; the congruence between its goals and those of the government. (2) The importance accorded to a particular policy issue at a given time by the news media, pressure groups, respondents to opinion surveys, and/or politicians. The political salience of a particular issue at a given time is reflected in its position on the policy agenda: the most salient issues (e.g., health care) receive the greatest amount of government attention, whereas those with less salience may be ignored. The salience of an issue is not a function of its intrinsic importance. For example, environmental issues had relatively little salience in the early twenty-first century, despite the obvious dangers posed by climate change and expanding human population. They were eclipsed by fears of terrorism, the wars in Afghanistan and Iraq, and concerns about the apparent shrinkage of world oil supply, among other issues.

Pressure group: An interest group that devotes some or all of its resources to influencing public policy.

Representation: In the context of the policy community, representation is the midpoint between lobbying from the outside and consultations on the inside. Representation entails speaking on behalf of a particular interest, usually at the invitation of the state, but unlike consultation, it may not reflect a continuing and close working relationship between the pressure group and the government agencies in a particular policy field.

Subgovernment: The inner circle of the policy community. Includes the key pressure groups and members of the political and permanent executives, who work together to formulate and implement public policy in a specific area (e.g., health care or agriculture).

DISCUSSION QUESTIONS

1. Why are Canadians increasingly turning to pressure groups, rather than political parties, to represent their interests in federal politics?

2. Have you ever belonged to a pressure or advocacy group? If so, did you participate in efforts to influence political decision-makers? What were those efforts? In your view, did they succeed?

3. How often do you watch a television newscast? How many times a week do you read the front section of a newspaper? If you are a regular consumer of Canadian political news, what is your opinion of the information and analysis available from our media companies?

4. Try the following experiment: The next time a big political story breaks, make a point of either watching three different newscasts (e.g., *CBC Newsworld, CTV Newsnet,* CPAC or Global) or reading the coverage in three different newspapers (e.g., *The Globe and Mail,* the *National Post,* and the *Toronto Star*). Can you

identify different "spins" or "frames" in the coverage? Do the news values of each media organization differ? How might a habitual reader or viewer or listener of one paper or broadcast perceive politics differently from someone who chooses a different source for his or her daily news?

SUGGESTED READINGS

Books and Articles

W. Lance Bennett and Robert M. Entman, eds., *Mediated Politics: Communication in the Future of Democracy* (Cambridge, UK: Cambridge University Press, 2001).

Robert M. Campbell and Leslie A. Pal, *The Real Worlds of Canadian Politics: Cases in Process and Policy,* 3rd edition (Peterborough, ON: Broadview Press, 1994).

Joseph N. Cappella and Kathleen Hall Jamieson, *Spiral of Cynicism: The Press and the Public Good* (New York: Oxford University Press, 1997).

William D. Coleman and Grace Skogstad, eds., *Policy Communities and Public Policy in Canada: A Structural Approach* (Toronto: Copp Clark Pitman, 1990).

Susan Delacourt, *Juggernaut: Paul Martin's Campaign for Chrétien's Crown* (Toronto: McClelland and Stewart, 2003).

Michael Howlett, "Do Networks Matter? Linking Policy Network Structure to Policy Outcomes: Evidence from Four Canadian Policy Sectors 1990–2000," *Canadian Journal of Political Science,* 35:2 (June 2002), 235–67.

Paul Nesbitt-Larking, *Politics, Society and the Media: Canadian Perspectives* (Peterborough, ON: Broadview Press, 2001).

Leslie A. Pal, *Interests of State: The Politics of Language, Multiculturalism, and Feminism in Canada* (Montreal and Kingston: McGill–Queen's University Press, 1993).

A. Paul Pross, *Group Politics and Public Policy,* 2nd edition (Toronto: Oxford University Press, 1992).

Stuart N. Soroka, *Agenda-Setting Dynamics in Canada* (Vancouver: University of British Columbia Press, 2002).

David Taras, *The Newsmakers: The Media's Influence on Canadian Politics* (Scarborough, ON: Nelson Canada, 1990).

David Taras, *Power and Betrayal in the Canadian Media* (Peterborough, ON: Broadview Press, 1999).

Websites

Most of the major pressure groups in Canada and elsewhere have set up websites, either for themselves alone or shared with related organizations. Examples include the Child Care Advocacy Association of Canada (www.childcareadvocacy.ca);

Greenpeace International (www.greenpeace.org), which is linked to national Greenpeace sites; and the Canadian Council of Chief Executives, formerly the Business Council on National Issues (www.bcni.com). Industry Canada's Strategis website (www.strategis.gc.ca), devoted to Canadian business and consumer matters, provides information about the Lobbyists Registration System.

While most media companies have their own websites, there is a growing trend away from free access in favour of paid or unpaid registration. As of October 2004, both *The Globe and Mail* (www.globeandmail.com) and the *National Post* (www.nationalpost.com) required paid subscriptions from anyone wishing to read their full news content online. Canadian Press (www.canoe.ca) and the Canadian Broadcasting Corporation (www.cbc.ca) still allowed free access to their news content.

Many American news outlets, such as Microsoft's online *Slate* magazine (www.slate.com) and the Cable News Network (CNN) (www.cnn.com) were still free, as were some leading British newspapers, such as the *Guardian* (www.guardian.co.uk) and *The Independent* (www.independent.co.uk). Slate.com provides a daily summary of what has been covered by major U.S. newspapers.

NOTES

1. Kennith G. Hunter, "An Application of Herd Theory to Interest Group Behavior," *Administration and Society*, 34:4 (September 2002), 390.

2. For example, a recent—and generally excellent—study of policy networks in Canada implicitly attributes recent changes in federal funding for postsecondary education (PSE) to the relationship between government and nongovernment actors in that policy field. See Michael Howlett, "Do Networks Matter? Linking Policy Network Structure to Policy Outcomes: Evidence from Four Canadian Policy Sectors 1990-2000," *Canadian Journal of Political Science*, 35:2 (June 2002), 235–67. But among the policy changes listed in the study are the 1995 CHST and the subsequent increases in the amount of federal cash given to the provinces for health care and PSE. As explained in Chapter 8 of this book, the CHST was inspired by the federal Cabinet's determination to eliminate the national deficit, not by extraneous lobbying from the PSE sector. Moreover, the later increases in cash payments to the provinces were driven, not by the demands of universities, colleges and students, but by growing public concern over the delivery of health care.

3. Leslie A. Pal, *Interests of State: The Politics of Language, Multiculturalism, and Feminism in Canada* (Montreal and Kingston: McGill–Queen's University Press, 1993), 42.

4. Pal, 42.

5. Pal, 43.

6. Pal, 48–51.

7. Pal, 277.

8. Pal, 43.

9. Pal, 44–45.

10. Leslie A. Pal, *Beyond Policy Analysis: Public Issue Management in Turbulent Times*, 1st edition (Scarborough, ON: ITP Nelson, 1997), 213.

11. David McInnes, *Taking It to the Hill: The Complete Guide to Appearing Before (and Surviving) Parliamentary Committees* (Ottawa: University of Ottawa Press, 1999), 1.

12. Pal, *Beyond Policy Analysis,* 218.

13. William D. Coleman and Grace Skogstad, "Policy Communities and Policy Networks: A Structural Approach," in William D. Coleman and Grace Skogstad, eds., *Policy Communities and Public Policy in Canada: A Structural Approach* (Toronto: Copp Clark Pitman, 1990), 15.

14. Coleman and Skogstad, 15.

15. Ibid., 16.

16. Coleman and Skogstad, "Conclusion," in Coleman and Skogstad, eds., 318.

17. A. Paul Pross, *Group Politics and Public Policy,* 2nd edition (Toronto: Oxford University Press, 1992), 121.

18. Pross, 121.

19. Pross, 96.

20. Pross, 156.

21. Howlett found that the number of groups involved in trade and transportation policy shrank between 1990 and 2000, although the membership of the policy community remained relatively stable. In contrast, the number of groups with an interest in PSE and banking policy expanded over the same period, and the membership of the policy community was far less stable. See Howlett, "Do Networks Matter?," 254–59.

22. See Kent Roach, *Due Process and Victims' Rights: The New Law and Politics of Criminal Justice* (Toronto: University of Toronto Press, 1999), especially 48–50, 79–81, and 278–312.

23. Hunter, 394.

24. Pross, 147–54.

25. Coleman and Skogstad, 27; Pal, *Beyond Policy Analysis,* 203.

26. Pal, *Beyond Policy Analysis,* 203.

27. Coleman and Skogstad, 29.

28. Pross, 4.

29. Pross, 130–39.

30. Krista Foss, "Canadians Have Little Taste for GM Food," *The Globe and Mail,* August 30, 2001, A4.

31. The Health Canada "Action Plan" and related materials are available at www.hc-sc.gc.ca/food-aliment/mh-dm/ofb-bba/nfi-ani/e_novel_foods_and_ingredient.html. The regulations governing biotechnology, including GM foods, are laid down by Health Canada and implemented and enforced, in part, by the Canadian Food Inspection Agency, which reports to the minister of Agriculture and Agri-Food. Otherwise, the latter department has no formal responsibility for GM foods.

32. Pross, 218.

33. David Kwavnick, *Organized Labour and Pressure Politics: The Canadian Labour Congress, 1956–1968* (Montreal and Kingston: McGill–Queen's University Press, 1972).

34. Pal, *Beyond Policy Analysis,* 212.

35. Patrick J. Monahan, *Meech Lake: The Inside Story* (Toronto: University of Toronto Press, 1991), 141–42.

36. Campbell Clark, "Power corridor extends to Q Street," *The Globe and Mail,* January 5, 2004; accessed at www.globeandmail.com.

37. Robert M. Campbell and Leslie Pal, *The Real Worlds of Canadian Politics: Cases in Process and Policy,* 3rd edition (Peterborough, ON: Broadview Press, 1994), Chapter 4.

38. Evert A. Lindquist, "Citizens, Experts and Budgets: Evaluating Ottawa's Emerging Budget Process," in Susan D. Phillips, ed., *How Ottawa Spends, 1994–95: Making Change* (Ottawa: Carleton University Press, 1994), 91–128.

39. Herman Bakvis, "Shrinking the House of 'HRIF': Program Review and the Department of Human Resources Development," in Gene Swimmer, ed., *How Ottawa Spends, 1996–97: Life Under the Knife* (Ottawa: Carleton University Press, 1996), 142.

40. Luma Muhtadie, "Groups spar over same-sex marriage," *The Globe and Mail,* October 6, 2004; accessed online at www.globeandmail.com.

41. On the history of the CCP, see Ian Brodie, "Interest Group Litigation and the Embedded State: Canada's Court Challenges Program," *Canadian Journal of Political Science,* 34:2 (June 2001), 357–76.

42. For a more extensive discussion of interest-group interventions and public-interest litigation, see Heather MacIvor, *Canadian Government and Politics in the Charter Era* (Toronto: Nelson Thompson Learning, 2005), Chapter 6.

43. Pross, 101.

44. Pross, 155.

45. Donald J. Savoie, *Breaking the Bargain: Public Servants, Ministers, and Parliament* (Toronto: University of Toronto Press, 2003), 106.

46. Susan Delacourt, *Juggernaut: Paul Martin's Campaign for Chrétien's Crown* (Toronto: McClelland and Stewart, 2003), 87.

47. Ibid., 87.

48. John Sawatsky, *The Insiders: Government, Business, and the Lobbyists* (Toronto: McClelland and Stewart, 1987).

49. *Lobbyists Registration Act, Annual Report for the Year Ended March 31, 1992* (Ottawa, 1992), 5.

50. *Lobbyists Registration Act,* as amended by Bill C-15, *An Act to Amend the Lobbyists Registration Act,* sections 5–7; accessed at www.canada.justice.gc.ca.

51. Pross, 199.

52. Pross, 200.

53. Robert A. Hackett, *News and Dissent: The Press and the Politics of Peace in Canada* (Norwood, N.J.: Ablex Publishing Corporation, 1991), 23.

54. Ibid., 22.

55. Ibid., 22.

56. David Taras, *Power and Betrayal in the Canadian Media* (Peterborough, ON: Broadview Press, 1999), 4.

57. Timothy E. Cook, "The Future of the Institutional Media," in W. Lance Bennett and Robert M. Entman, eds., *Mediated Politics: Communication in the Future of Democracy* (Cambridge, UK: Cambridge University Press, 2001), 182–200.

58. Doug Underwood, "Reporting and the Push for Market-Oriented Journalism: Media Organizations as Businesses," in Bennett and Entman, eds., *Mediated Politics,* 99–116.

59. Ibid., 113.

60. Ibid., 101.

61. Robert M. Entman, *Democracy Without Citizens: Media and the Decay of American Politics* (New York: Oxford University Press, 1989), 10.

62. Nesbitt-Larking, 110.

63. Taras, *Power and Betrayal*, 18.

64. Ibid., 19 and 213; Nesbitt-Larking, 180.

65. David A. Good, *The Politics of Public Management: The HRDC Audit of Grants and Contributions* (Toronto: University of Toronto Press, 2003), 60.

66. The company was called CanWest Global until October 2004, when it was renamed as part of a management shakeup. Richard Blackwell, "CanWest shakes up its ranks with U.S. recruits," *The Globe and Mail*, October 5, 2004, B1.

67. Delacourt, 127.

68. Good, 70–71.

69. David Taras, *The Newsmakers: The Media's Influence on Canadian Politics* (Scarborough, ON: Nelson Canada, 1990), 14.

70. David Pritchard and Florian Sauvageau, "English and French and Generation X: The Professional Values of Canadian Journalists," in Harvey Lazar and Tom McIntosh, eds., *Canada, The State of the Federation 1998/99: How Canadians Connect* (Montreal and Kingston: McGill–Queen's University Press, 1999), 287.

71. Taras, *Power and Betrayal*, 142.

72. Ibid., 157.

73. See, for example, George Bain, *Gotcha!: How the Media Distort the News* (Toronto: Key Porter, 1994); Larry Sabato, *Feeding Frenzy: How Attack Journalism Has Transformed American Politics* (New York: Free Press, 1991).

74. Taras, *The Newsmakers*, 90.

75. Delacourt, 158–59.

76. Cook, 188.

77. Taras, *The Newsmakers*, 79–81.

78. Stephen J. Farnsworth and S. Robert Lichter, *The Nightly News Nightmare: Network Television's Coverage of U.S. Presidential Elections, 1988–2000* (Lanham, MD: Rowman and Littlefield, 2003), 81.

79. Taras, *The Newsmakers*, 102.

80. Pritchard and Sauvageau, 299.

81. Bain, 6–7.

82. Ibid., Chapter Four; Good, 63.

83. Henry Milner, *Civic Literacy: How Informed Citizens Make Democracy Work* (Hanover, NH: University Press of New England, 2002), Figures 7.2 and 7.3, 99–100.

84. Milner, Chapter 7; Henry Milner, *Civic Literacy in Comparative Context* (Montreal: Institute for Research on Public Policy, July 2001); available online at www.irpp.org.

85. Joseph N. Cappella and Kathleen Hall Jamieson, *Spiral of Cynicism: The Press and the Public Good* (New York: Oxford University Press, 1997), 51.

86. Stuart N. Soroka, *Agenda-Setting Dynamics in Canada* (Vancouver: University of British Columbia Press, 2002), 20–21 and 118.

87. Gadi Wolfsfeld, "Political Waves and Democratic Discourse: Terrorism Waves During the Oslo Peace Process," in Bennett and Entman, eds., *Mediated Politics*, 226–31.

88. Robert A. Hackett, "News Media's Influence on Canadian Party Politics: Perspectives on a Shifting Relationship," in Hugh G. Thorburn and Alan Whitehorn, eds., *Party Politics in Canada*, 8th edition (Toronto: Prentice-Hall, 2001), 382.

89. Ibid., 381.

90. Taras, *The Newsmakers,* 40.

91. Ibid., 39; Matthew Mendelsohn, "Television News Frames in the 1993 Canadian Election," in Helen Holmes and David Taras, eds., *Seeing Ourselves: Media Power and Policy in Canada,* 2nd edition (Toronto: Harcourt Brace, 1996).

92. Mendelsohn, 17.

93. Good, 83.

94. Nesbitt-Larking, 159.

95. Cappella and Jamieson, 52.

96. Susan Delacourt, "The Media and the Supreme Court of Canada," in Hugh Mellon and Martin Westmacott, eds., *Political Dispute and Judicial Review: Assessing the Work of the Supreme Court of Canada* (Toronto: Nelson, 2000), 31.

97. Savoie, *Breaking the Bargain,* 65.

98. On the "digital divide" between rich and poor, see Pippa Norris, *Digital Divide: Civic Engagement, Information Poverty, and the Internet Worldwide* (Cambridge: Cambridge University Press, 2001), especially Chapter 3.

99. Cook, 193.

100. Susan Delacourt, "The gloves come off," *Toronto Star,* October 6, 2004; accessed at www.thestar.com; Allison Dunfield, "Liberals could fall in evening confidence vote," *The Globe and Mail,* October 7, 2004; accessed at www.globeandmail.com.

101. John Ibbitson, "The madness stops as all sides back off," *The Globe and Mail,* October 8, 2004; accessed online at www.globeandmail.com.

102. Giles Gherson, comment on CBC Radio's "This Morning," December 3, 1997; quoted in Savoie, *Breaking the Bargain,* 50.

103. House of Commons, Standing Committee on Procedure and House Affairs, *Nineteenth Report* (November 1998), 1.

104. Bain, 250.

105. Taras, *The Newsmakers,* 108.

106. The 2003 hearings of the Standing Committee on Government Operations and Estimates into alleged overspending by former Privacy Commissioner George Radwanski are an exception to this rule (see Dossier 5.5). Radwanski is a former journalist, and therefore well known to the Press Gallery. Moreover, stories about mismanagement of public funds were particularly attractive in light of the sponsorship scandal. For a variety of reasons, the "water-cooler" appeal of the Radwanski hearings was higher than most issues investigated by parliamentary committees.

107. Quoted in C.E.S. Franks, *The Parliament of Canada* (Toronto: University of Toronto Press, 1987), 159; the square brackets were in the original.

108. Ibid., 159.

109. Taras, *The Newsmakers,* 108–09.

110. Ibid., 108.

111. Ibid., 63.

112. Ibid., 88.

113. Good, 76.

114. Donald J. Savoie, *Governing from the Centre: The Concentration of Power in Canadian Politics* (Toronto: University of Toronto Press, 1999), 342.

115. Delacourt, *Juggernaut,* 143.

116. Ibid., 302.

117. Ibid., 303.

118. Taras, *The Newsmakers,* 95.

119. Ibid., 96.

120. Ibid., 81–82.

121. Savoie, *Governing from the Centre,* 333.

122. Delacourt, "The Media and the Supreme Court of Canada," 32–33.

123. The executive legal officer's media responsibilities have been well described by a former incumbent. See James W. O'Reilly, "The Supreme Court of Canada and the Media," 42, *St. Louis University Law Journal* (1997–1998), 1189–1200.

124. Delacourt, "The Media and the Supreme Court of Canada," 34.

125. See, for example, Roach, 81 and 83.

126. *R. v. Daviault* [1994], 3 S.C.R. 63.

127. Roach, 178.

128. F.L. Morton and Rainer Knopff, *The Charter Revolution and the Court Party* (Peterborough, ON: Broadview Press, 2000), 136.

129. Ibid., 159.

130. Andrew Coyne, "The Charter under Attack," *National Post,* May 3, 1999; quoted in Delacourt, "The Media and the Supreme Court of Canada," in Mellon and Westmacott, eds., 36.

131. Ibid.

132. Quoted in Kirk Makin, "Lamer Worries about Public Backlash," *The Globe and Mail,* February 6, 1999, A1.

133. Ian Greene et al., *Final Appeal: Decision-making in Canadian Courts of Appeal* (Toronto: Lorimer, 1998), 184.

134. Robert M. Entman and Susan Herbst, "Reframing Public Opinion as We Have Known It," in Bennett and Entman, eds., *Mediated Democracy,* 207–08.

135. Nesbitt-Larking, 355–56.

136. Richard W. Jenkins, "The Media, Voters, and Election Campaigns: The Reform Party and the 1993 Election," in Joanna Everitt and Brenda O'Neill, eds., *Citizen Politics: Research and Theory in Canadian Political Behaviour* (Toronto: Oxford University Press, 2002), 215–31.

137. Ibid., 215.

138. Ibid., 218

139. R.H. McDermid, "Media Usage and Political Behaviour," in Frederick J. Fletcher, ed., *Media and Voters in Canadian Election Campaigns,* volume 18 of the collected research studies for the Royal Commission on Electoral Reform and Party Financing (Toronto: Dundurn Press, 1991), 66–67.

140. Bernard C. Cohen, *The Press and Foreign Policy* (Princeton: Princeton University Press, 1963), 13; quoted in Robert A. Hackett, "News Media's Influence on Canadian Party Politics: Perspective on a Shifting Relationship," in Hugh G. Thorburn and Alan Whitehorn, eds., *Party Politics in Canada,* 8th edition (Toronto: Prentice-Hall, 2001), 381.

141. Taras, *Power and Betrayal,* Chapter 6.

142. Will Kymlicka, "New Forms of Citizenship," in Thomas J. Courchene and Donald J. Savoie, eds., *The Art of the State: Governance in a World Without Frontiers* (Montreal: Institute for Research on Public Policy, 2003), 290.

143. L. David Brown, Sanjeev Khagram, Mark H. Moore, and Peter Frumkin, "Globalization, NGOs, and Multisectoral Relations," in Joseph S. Nye and John D. Donahue, eds., *Governance in a Globalizing World* (Washington, D.C.: Brookings Institution Press, 2000), 272.

144. Kymlicka, 291.

145. Norris, *Digital Divide,* Chapter 3.

146. Sparks, 87.

147. Farnsworth and Lichter, *The Nightly News Nightmare,* 51.

148. Oscar H. Gandy, Jr., "Dividing Practices: Segmentation and Targeting in the Emerging Public Sphere," in Bennett and Entman, eds., *Mediated Democracy,* 141–59.

149. The CRTC ran into controversy in July 2004, when it took the unusual step of revoking a broadcast licence. Some listeners had complained about CHOI-FM in Quebec City. Specifically, they claimed that the morning host on the radio station had made derogatory comments about particular ethnic groups. The commission determined that the station had violated the conditions of its licence, and refused to renew it. The decision outraged fans of the station, who marched on Parliament Hill in protest. The text of the July 2004 decision is at www.crtc.gc.ca/archive/ENG/Decisions/2004/db2004-271.pdf.

150. Howlett, "Do Networks Matter?," 248.

8

CONSTITUTION I: FEDERALISM

LEARNING OBJECTIVES

- *identify* and *explain* the essential components of a constitution, providing examples to illustrate each component;
- *explain* the origins and development of Canadian federalism, specifically the transition from independence to interdependence;
- *identify* and *explain* the reasons why Canadian federalism has become less hierarchical since the 1970s;
- *describe* and *evaluate* the impacts of "glocalization" on Canadian federalism.

INTRODUCTION: CONSTITUTIONAL LAW AND CANADIAN POLITICAL INSTITUTIONS

In Chapter 1, we defined a political institution as "An organization, usually grounded in constitutional law (either written or unwritten), that makes and/or enforces binding rules for the population of a particular territory." The first section of this chapter explains the general principles of constitutional law and their impact on our national political institutions. The rest of the chapter is devoted to two central elements of the Canadian *Constitution:* the federal system and intergovernmental relations. The next two chapters discuss the politics of **amendment** and the *Canadian Charter of Rights and Freedoms.*

The Nature and Purpose of a Constitution

Constitutions are the heart of democratic politics and government. They set the rules of the political game and clarify the relationships among the players. Three such relationships are particularly important:

1. the balance among the various branches of government: the scope of the executive, legislative, and judicial powers, and the processes for choosing the individuals who will exercise them;

2. the division of powers and responsibilities among the national government and the subnational governments (see the discussion of federal and unitary states in Chapter 1); and

3. the relationship between the state and the people: the rights and obligations of citizens, the shared values and symbols that legitimate political authority, and the collective aspirations of the political community.

■ The Four Elements of the Canadian *Constitution*

While we usually speak of a "constitution" as though it were a single document, the supreme law of a given society includes both written and unwritten rules of political conduct. The written *Constitution* includes **entrenched constitutional laws, nonentrenched**

TABLE 8.1   THE THREE RELATIONSHIPS GOVERNED BY THE CANADIAN *CONSTITUTION*

RELATIONSHIP	RELEVANT SECTIONS OF THE ENTRENCHED CONSTITUTION
Balance among the various branches of government: legislature, executive, and judiciary	*Constitution Act, 1867:* Preamble (responsible Cabinet government); Part III (executive power); Part IV (legislative power); Part VII (judicial power); section 132 (treaty-making powers)
	Constitution Act, 1982: Section 24 (judicial remedy for a breach of rights); section 33 (the "notwithstanding clause"); section 52 (the power of the courts to strike down laws that conflict with the *Constitution*)
Division of powers and responsibilities among the federal and provincial governments	*Constitution Act, 1867:* Part V (provincial constitutions); sections 57, 58, and 90 (reservation and disallowance of provincial laws); Part VI (distribution of legislative powers); section 109 (mineral rights and revenues assigned to the provinces)
	Constitution Act, 1982: Part III (equalization and regional disparities); Part V (amending formula)
Relationship between the state and the people	*Constitution Act, 1987:* Sections 37, 40–41, 50–52 (election of members of the House of Commons); section 92 (13) (property and civil rights); section 94 (uniformity of laws concerning civil rights)
	Constitution Act, 1982: Part I (*Canadian Charter of Rights and Freedoms*); Part II (Aboriginal rights)

laws, and **common law** (judicial rulings on the *Constitution*). The unwritten *Constitution* is made up of **constitutional conventions** that guide the behaviour of politicians and voters. We will discuss each of these four elements separately.

Entrenched Constitutional Law

The written *Constitution* overrides all other laws and binds all political actors (including citizens). Unlike ordinary statutes, constitutional laws are designed to remain in force for decades or even centuries. Consequently, the process of amending the *Constitution* is deliberately complex and difficult. In the first place, it often requires more than the usual legislative majority (50 percent plus one of those voting). Some countries require ratification (i.e., formal approval) by referendum. Second, in federal states, an amendment that affects the division of powers must be ratified by most or all the regional governments. These rules protect the *Constitution* against frivolous or unpopular amendments. In Canada, major amendments require the approval of both Houses of the federal Parliament and at least seven of the provincial legislatures (representing at least 50 percent of the population).[1] That **amending formula** was part of the *Constitution Act, 1982*. (For more information, see Dossier 9.1.) The *Constitution Act, 1867* did not contain a comprehensive amending formula. It was an ordinary British statute, passed by the Parliament at Westminster. Therefore, the British Parliament retained the power to amend it until 1982.

TABLE 8.2   **THE FOUR ELEMENTS OF THE CANADIAN *CONSTITUTION***

CATEGORY	PARTICULAR ELEMENTS	DEFINITION	EXAMPLES
Written	Entrenched laws	Constitutional documents and formal amendments	*Constitution Act, 1867* *Constitution Act, 1982*
	Nonentrenched laws	Ordinary federal laws that regulate the application of entrenched laws	*The Supreme Court Act, 1875* *The Indian Act, 1876* *The Bill of Rights, 1960* *The Constitutional Veto Act, 1996*
	Common law	Judicial interpretations of the *Constitution* by the Judicial Committee of the Privy Council (pre-1949) and the Supreme Court of Canada (1875–present)	*Edwards v. A-G Canada, 1929* (the "Persons Case") *The Patriation Reference, 1981* *The Secession Reference, 1998*
Unwritten	Constitutional convention	Unwritten, binding rules that constrain the behaviour of political actors; not enforceable by the courts, but violations may bring political sanctions	Executive power is exercised by the prime minister and Cabinet, not by the governor general

Entrenched laws are contained in the written *Constitution*. The two principal documents are the 1867 and 1982 *Constitution Acts* (see the Appendix). The *Constitution Act, 1867* (formerly called the *British North America Act,* or the "*BNA Act*") established the new Dominion of Canada. It defined the powers of the national political institutions, and divided jurisdiction over policy-making between the federal and provincial governments. However, it said very little about the relationship between states and citizens. Individual rights were omitted, and their protection tacitly left to Parliament and the British common law (in Quebec, the civil law). The only legitimating symbol was the Crown; there was no attempt to enshrine indigenous myths and symbols that might inspire and unite the new country. While the *Constitution Act, 1982* defined individual and group rights—in the *Canadian Charter of Rights and Freedoms,* and the subsequent sections on Aboriginal rights—it too was silent about shared values and symbols. Most national constitutions begin with a lyrical preamble about shared beliefs and collective aspirations. The preamble of the 1982 Act simply states that "Canada is founded upon the principles that recognize the supremacy of God and the rule of law."

Nonentrenched Law

Some laws and documents are considered to have semiconstitutional status, even though they are not formally entrenched.[2] These include:

- the *Supreme Court Act* of 1875, which established Canada's highest court of appeal and gave the executive branch the right to refer constitutional questions directly to the courts (these are called **reference cases**);
- the *Canadian Bill of Rights,* which was enacted by the Canadian Parliament as ordinary legislation in 1960 (discussed in Chapter 10);
- the *Canada Elections Act,* which regulates the national electoral system;
- the *Indian Act, 1876,* which consolidated pre-Confederation laws concerning Aboriginal Canadians and set out the way in which the national government would exercise its Crown prerogatives toward them; and
- *The Constitutional Veto Act* of 1996, which prohibits the federal Parliament from ratifying any future constitutional amendment that has not been approved by all five "regions."

While these are ordinary federal laws that may be amended or repealed by a simple majority of both Houses of Parliament, their subject matter is clearly within the constitutional realm. They spell out the details of the general rules for those who operate our political system.

Judicial Decisions

The third element of written constitutional law is the common law, also called "case law." This is the sum total of judicial interpretations of the *Constitution.* Entrenched constitutional law defines the powers and duties of institutions, levels of government, and citizens in broad terms, which remain in force for many years. Because the people entrusted with writing constitutions cannot anticipate the future, they deliberately use vague and general language to cover all possible circumstances. The precise meaning of the *Constitution* is left to judges, who must interpret these general principles and apply them to each unique situation. The process of authoritative constitutional interpretation is called **judicial review.**

Dossier 8.1 describes a famous example of judicial review, to illustrate the ways in which the meaning of a constitutional phrase can evolve to keep pace with changing public attitudes.

DOSSIER 8.1 The "Persons Case"

Section 24 of the *BNA Act* sets out the procedure for appointing senators. It reads, in part: "The Governor General shall from Time to Time . . . summon qualified Persons to the Senate." In 1927 the Supreme Court of Canada was asked to determine whether the word "Persons" included women. Until that time, no woman had ever been "summoned" to the Canadian Senate. The impetus for the Supreme Court reference was a lawsuit brought by five Alberta women against the Government of Canada. The "Famous Five"—Irene Parlby, Nellie McClung, Emily Murphy, Louise McKinney, and Henrietta Muir Edwards—were determined that Murphy should become the first female senator. Each was already a public figure in her own right.[3] Nellie McClung led the fight for female suffrage in Manitoba and later served in the Alberta legislature. Emily Murphy was the first female magistrate in the British Empire. Louise McKinney was the first woman in the British Empire to be sworn in as an elected legislator. Henrietta Muir Edwards and Irene Parlby were the chair and vice chair of the Legal Committee of the National Council of Women; the latter was also the second woman ever appointed to a provincial Cabinet (the first was in British Columbia). The "Famous Five" argued, with the support

of the Alberta government, that because women had won the right to vote and to run for elective office it made little sense to deny them appointment to the Senate.

The Supreme Court of Canada disagreed. The justices held unanimously that the word "Persons" did not include women. They relied on past legal precedents, which had denied women the right to hold public office, and on the intent of the Fathers of Confederation. Women were not legal "Persons" in 1867, so they could not be considered as such in 1928.

The case was appealed to the **Judicial Committee of the Privy Council (JCPC).** On October 18, 1929, the JCPC overturned the Supreme Court decision.[4] Declaring that "the exclusion of women from all public offices is a relic of days more barbarous than ours," the Law Lords refused to restrict the meaning of the *BNA Act* to the attitudes of 1867: "The *British North America Act* planted in Canada a living tree capable of growth and expansion within its natural limits . . . Their Lordships do not conceive it to be the duty of this Board to cut down the provisions of this Act by a narrow and technical construction, but rather to give it a large and liberal interpretation." They noted that sections 41 and 84 of the Act referred to the election of "Persons" to Parliament and

(cont'd)

the provincial legislatures; in that context, the word "Persons" now expressly included women (except Quebec). Therefore, the meaning of the word "Persons" was clearly adaptable to changing attitudes and circumstances. The JCPC concluded that "the word 'persons' in s. 24 includes members both of the male and female sex." The "Persons Case" was a legal triumph for Canadian women, although none of the victorious five was ever appointed to the Senate. On October 18, 2000, a monument to the "Famous Five" was unveiled on Parliament Hill—right next to the Senate Chamber.

Irene Parlby   Louise McKinney   Nellie McClung   Henrietta Muir Edwards   Emily Murphy

(© CP/Calgary Herald)

The doctrine of judicial review is an American invention. It is based on the ruling of U.S. Chief Justice John Marshall in the 1803 case *Marbury v. Madison*.[5] Marshall declared that the Supreme Court had the power to strike down laws that violated the *Constitution*. The claim that a court can overrule an elected legislature is alien to the British tradition of parliamentary supremacy, which gives the legislative branch the final word on public policy. But in a federation that divides the legislative power between two levels of government, there must be some mechanism to settle disputes. A supreme or constitutional court with the power to strike down laws is the most common such mechanism. Before the proclamation of the *Canadian Charter of Rights and Freedoms* in 1982, judicial review of our *Constitution* was largely confined to the division of powers (sections 91–95 of the *BNA Act*). We will discuss some of the most important division-of-powers cases later in this chapter. Since 1982, the courts have had the power to declare null and void any federal and provincial laws that infringe protected rights and freedoms; we will discuss judicial review of the *Charter* in Chapter 10.

Constitutional Conventions: The Unwritten *Constitution*

We have already seen that entrenched constitutional law is written in broad terms, to permit its application in changing circumstances. The unwritten element in Canada's *Constitution* is another source of flexibility. It allows constitutional law to

In *Attorney General of Manitoba et al. v. Attorney General of Canada et al.* (better known as the 1981 *Patriation Reference*), the Supreme Court of Canada was asked to determine the legality of the Trudeau government's proposal to amend the *Constitution* with the consent of only two provinces. Three of the dissenting provinces—Quebec, Manitoba, and Newfoundland—had solicited reference opinions from their own Courts of Appeal, all of which had declared the plan to be unconstitutional. The federal government appealed these rulings to the Supreme Court, which handed down its decision in September 1981. The central issue, in the absence of a written amending formula, was as follows: What were the constitutional conventions governing constitutional amendment? Specifically, is there a constitutional convention that requires either unanimous or substantial provincial consent to a constitutional amendment altering the division of powers between Ottawa and the provinces?

In its ruling, which essentially upheld the decisions of the three provincial Courts of Appeal, the majority on the Supreme Court provided an extended discussion of constitutional conventions. (See also Dossier 8.3.) According to the four justices in the majority, "The main purpose of constitutional conventions is to ensure that the legal framework of the *Constitution* will be operated in accordance with the prevailing constitutional values or principles of the period." Constitutional conventions allow our political institutions to adapt to changes in political culture, without the necessity of formally amending the written constitution.[6]

adapt to changes in the political environment—such as evolving cultural values or new socioeconomic conditions—without the need for formal amendment.[7]

> *Constitutional conventions are the means through which constitutional morality is brought into contact with political reality. For their meaning is dependent upon the configuration of power in a society and upon popular assumptions about how that power should be regulated.*[8]

While a constitution must be stable and durable, it cannot become rigid; the political system that it governs must be able to adapt to unforeseen circumstances, as the Supreme Court pointed out in 1981 (see Dossier 8.2).

Constitutional conventions are unwritten rules for political conduct. They are based on custom and precedent, although they are more than just practical expedients or automatic habits. Political actors obey a constitutional convention because they feel obliged to do so[9] and because it embodies important constitutional values or principles such as federalism and democracy (recall Dossier 1.3).[10] While the courts cannot enforce conventions, they may be called upon to determine whether a particular convention exists. When that happens, the judges may encounter a problem arising from an over-reliance on constitutional conventions to govern the political system: the fact that a convention, like beauty, is in the eye of the beholder.

In the 1981 *Patriation Reference,* the Supreme Court of Canada was asked to determine the legality of the Trudeau government's plan to amend the *Constitution* with the consent of only two provincial governments. The majority of the justices ruled that while such an amendment would be constitutional in law—without an amending formula, there were no written rules to be broken—it would violate a constitutional convention. The conventional requirement of substantial provincial consent, resting as it did on the principle of federalism, "cast a heavy mantle of political illegitimacy"[11] over the Trudeau plan.

The majority ruling sent the 11 senior governments back to the constitutional bargaining table in November 1981, resulting in an Accord that was signed by the federal government and all of the provinces except Quebec. That Accord led to the 1982 patriation of the Canadian *Constitution* and the entrenchment of both the *Charter of Rights* and an amending formula. The sovereigntist Quebec government refused to recognize the deal, and appealed to the Supreme Court to strike down the *Constitution Act, 1982.* Quebec argued that to proclaim an amendment without its consent would violate two constitutional conventions. The first was the convention of unanimous provincial consent to amendments that altered the division of powers between the two levels of government. The court had already declared, in the *Patriation Reference,* that no such convention

existed; it upheld that finding in the 1982 *Quebec Veto Reference.* The second was based on the "two-nations" vision of Canadian federalism—the Quebec nationalist claim that Confederation was a deal between two founding nations, English and French. Because Quebec is the homeland of the French "nation" in Canada, nationalists in that province claim the right to veto any proposed change to national institutions.

The justices dismissed the arguments of the Quebec government, ruling that there was no historical evidence to support the alleged convention of special status. The province's claim to a unilateral veto was declared to be unfounded in both law and convention. Quebec nationalists reacted with fury, charging that the Supreme Court was biased in favour of the federal government that appointed its members. Although the Court's decision may have been correct as a matter of law, the political fallout was damaging. If constitutional conventions are indeed a reflection of political culture, as argued earlier, it is reasonable to expect that different subcultures will interpret historical precedents in varying ways. It should not come as a surprise, therefore, that Quebec nationalists still claim the right to a veto over changes to the original "deal" on which Canada was founded. That claim became a central issue in the megaconstitutional politics of the late 1980s and early 1990s, as we will see in Chapter 9.

Over time, parts of a written constitution fall into disuse. Others, which may have been congruent with prevailing political values at the time of their adoption, lose their moral force as the political culture changes. New conventions evolve, which may directly contradict the entrenched constitutional law. These new conventions are added to the existing set of unwritten rules, which are unusually powerful in

Canadian politics. The text of the 1867 *Constitution* bears little resemblance to the way our political system actually works. For example, the *Constitution* gives the governor general virtually unlimited executive power: "a dictatorship, the autocratic rule of one central figure, acting in the place of the Sovereign, who governs the Dominion with little reference to, or control by the people. The only popular element is apparently supplied by a House of Commons, which meets when the governor desires, considers financial legislation which he recommends, and can be forced into an election whenever he deems it desirable."[12]

The reality is very different. As we saw in Chapter 1, Canada is a parliamentary democracy. The executive powers of the Crown are exercised by the prime minister and his Cabinet. While as a matter of law they merely "advise" the governor general, in practice he or she always defers to the "political executive." Any attempt by a governor general to exercise executive power without the consent of the Cabinet and the House of Commons would be an outrageous violation of democratic norms and constitutional conventions, even though it would be technically legal under the terms of the 1867 *Constitution*. In effect, "The critical underpinnings of democratic, responsible government in Canada are to be found not in the 'written' Constitution but in the constitutional conventions inherited from the United Kingdom."[13] While those conventions are not spelled out in the text of the *BNA Act*, they are enshrined in its preamble: "a Constitution similar in Principle to that of the United Kingdom." On that seemingly innocuous phrase rests the entire structure of responsible Cabinet government.

In contrast, Canada's federal system is based on a detailed division of powers within the written *Constitution*. The rules of the game are set out in black and white. But even here, conventions and nonentrenched written laws play a key role in the actual operation of federalism. As we will see in the remainder of the chapter, the existence of entrenched constitutional law is no guarantee against conflict, ambiguity, and the continual adaptation of political institutions to changing conditions.

THE FEDERAL SYSTEM IN CANADA: FROM INDEPENDENCE AND HIERARCHY TO INTERDEPENDENCE AND (PARTIAL) PARITY

The federation established in 1867, and entrenched in the *BNA Act,* was characterized by two key institutional qualities: (1) mutual independence (as opposed to interdependence) between the two levels of government, and (2) hierarchy (as opposed to parity).[14]

1. *Mutual independence:* With a few exceptions—notably the concurrent powers over agriculture and immigration (section 95)[15]—the national and provincial governments were expected to operate independently of each other. Each had its own defined policy fields, over which it exercised both legislative and executive/administrative authority. In other words, the province of Ontario could make laws in relation to primary education within its boundaries, and it could take whatever steps were necessary to put those laws into effect

(e.g., establishing local school boards). Equally as important, the provinces had access to their own tax bases; in theory, they could pay for their assigned responsibilities from their own revenues, without assistance from Ottawa. (As we will see, those revenues quickly proved inadequate in practice.)

2. *Hierarchy:* In the rare cases when the two levels of government rubbed up against each other in the management of their exclusive policy fields, the federal government was expected to be paramount. It possessed the power to delay or veto provincial laws, and the **residual power** to legislate in fields not explicitly controlled by the provinces (see Table 8.3). A clear hierarchy was established, in which Ottawa was expected to prevail over the provinces. Without a strong central government, it was feared, the new Dominion of Canada could not build a strong national economy; in the worst-case scenario, prompted by the recent horrors of the American Civil War, Confederation might collapse altogether.

TABLE 8.3   FEDERAL AND QUASI-FEDERAL ELEMENTS IN THE CANADIAN *CONSTITUTION*

FEDERAL ELEMENTS	CANADIAN EQUIVALENT
Division of legislative powers between national and subnational governments, set out in written constitutional law	Part VI of the *Constitution Act, 1867* (especially sections 91 and 92)
Representation of the subnational governments in the institutions of the central government	The Senate of Canada formally represents the provinces in the central government, although there is no rational division of seats among the provinces and the senators are appointed by the prime minister
A court with the authority to settle legal disputes	The Supreme Court of Canada
Intergovernmental relations	A complex network of contracts and agencies — mostly ad hoc, but increasingly institutionalized — that bring together members of the permanent and political executives in the 11 senior governments to work out conflicts and harmonize different policies
QUASI-FEDERAL ELEMENTS	CANADIAN EQUIVALENT
The national government may veto laws passed by the subnational governments	The reservation and disallowance powers of the lieutenants governor (sections 57, 58, and 90 of the *BNA Act*)
The residual power is vested in the national government	The preamble to section 91 of the *BNA Act*
The national government controls the lion's share of tax revenues	Sections 91 (3) and 92 (2) of the *BNA Act*

While independence, reflected in the division of policy fields and fiscal powers into "watertight compartments" was consistent with the classical model of federalism (Chapter 1), federal paramountcy was not. According to K.C. Wheare, author of the classic text on federalism, the Canadian *Constitution* is only "quasi-federal" because it gives the national government the power to intrude on the sovereignty of the provinces.[16] He argued, however, that the hierarchical elements in the *Constitution* had fallen into disuse because the political cost of exercising them would be too high. Therefore, "although Canada has not a federal constitution, it has a federal government."[17]

Perhaps because the *BNA Act* enshrined the principles of independence and hierarchy, the Fathers of Confederation did not foresee the need for an entrenched mechanism to settle disputes between governments. But by the time the Supreme Court of Canada was established by an act of the federal Parliament in 1875, Ottawa was already uneasy about provincial legislation that (it believed) violated the division of powers. Rather than employ the politically contentious reservation and disallowance procedures, the federal government decided to create a national court to referee intergovernmental disagreements. The *Supreme Court Act* included a reference provision, under which the federal government could leave the constitutionality of provincial laws to be determined by an independent body.[18] If the new court was intended to preserve federal paramountcy, it failed—not because of its own decisions, but because its rulings could be appealed to the JCPC in London. As we will see in "Judicial Review of the *BNA Act*" on page 392, the JCPC disapproved of the "quasi-federal" elements in sections 91 and 92 and did its best to put the provinces on a more equal footing in Confederation.

Canada was one of the earliest federations (following Switzerland and the United States), and the first to combine federalism with parliamentary institutions. There were no precedents from which to learn, which may help to account for several features of the *BNA Act* that have produced serious dysfunctions in our federal system:

- The *BNA Act* contains no formal dispute-resolution mechanism, and no provision for future amendment of the division of powers. Even the Supreme Court, as just noted, is the creation of Parliament; it is not entrenched in the *Constitution*, although section 101 of the *BNA Act* empowered the federal government to create such a court if it saw fit. An amending formula was finally created in 1982 (see Chapter 9), although its rigidity has made it extremely difficult to put into practice.

- The drafters of the *BNA Act* did not, and probably could not, foresee how soon the "watertight compartments" in sections 91 and 92 would collapse. In particular, the division of taxing powers and spending responsibilities between the two levels of government quickly proved to be impractical. Shortly after Confederation, the federal government began to transfer money to the provinces to pay for programs in concurrent fields (agriculture and immigration). Over time, the **federal spending power** expanded into exclusively provincial jurisdictions—most notably health care, postsecondary education (PSE), and social welfare. The "vertical imbalance" between the two levels grew during the first half of the twentieth century, as Ottawa's capacity to raise revenues outstripped that of the provinces, and the latter faced the soaring costs of social programs.

The federal spending power has no clear basis in the *Constitution,* unlike the equivalent powers in more recent federations. Indeed, Quebec governments have long argued that it violates the division of powers, inasmuch as Ottawa imposes conditions on fiscal transfers to the provinces and thus, in effect, legislates in provincial policy fields.[19] In the 1990s, Ottawa unilaterally slashed its transfer payments for health care and other social programs as it struggled to eliminate the federal deficit. In response, outraged provincial governments banded together and demanded greater independence in their exclusive jurisdictions. By the beginning of the current century, the "deficit wars" had given way to the "surplus wars."[20] Ottawa has regained the financial wherewithal to use its spending power for national purposes, imposing new conditions on social transfers in the process, while the provinces—still stinging from the "downloading" of the federal deficit—insist on retaining their new autonomy over social spending.[21] Consequently, our governments are involved in a tug of war: the federal government is trying to reassert a measure of paramountcy over the politically sensitive field of social policy, while the provinces are collectively asserting their right to set "national" standards in their own fields of jurisdiction. So although interdependence is now firmly established, the two senior orders of government are still battling over the degree of parity in the making of social policy.

- As **fiscal federalism** evolved and it became clear that governments would have to work together to make and implement policy, **intergovernmental relations (IGRs)** became a central focus of Canadian government and politics. The absence of any constitutional provision for collaborative policy-making between the two levels of government has resulted in the piecemeal evolution of **ad hoc** arrangements (e.g., the First Ministers' Conference). Newer federations have recognized the inevitability of IGRs, and made constitutional provision for permanent institutions to facilitate and enforce cooperation across jurisdictions. Perhaps the best known is the upper house of the German national Parliament, the Bundesrat, which is made up of delegations from the *Länd* (state) governments. A majority in the Bundesrat must approve any law that affects the activities of the *Länder.*

In the absence of such constitutional provisions, Canadian IGRs have fallen to the executive branch by default. They are conducted by First Ministers, ministers, and public servants, with little if any involvement by legislators or the wider public. Decisions reached via the processes of **executive federalism** are not enforceable by the courts;[22] at best, they may achieve the status of constitutional conventions (which, as we have seen, are also unenforceable). Therefore, participating governments have no real obligation to live up to their agreements. At the same time, executive federalism blurs the lines of accountability to Parliament and provincial legislatures, and to the various electorates represented at the bargaining table. It is therefore incompatible with "the logic of responsible government in a Westminster system."[23]

- The Fathers of Confederation appear to have assumed that the existence of a separate Quebec government would satisfy the aspirations of French Canadians. In fact, Quebec's status as one province among four (now ten) has been a source of bitter conflict since 1867. For most of the twentieth century, Quebec governments pursued two constitutional goals: (1) the recognition of Quebec as "une province pas comme les autres" (more recently, "a distinct society") and (2) greater autonomy from Ottawa.[24] In consequence, Quebec has refused to participate fully in IGRs in recent years. That strategy was modified, if not abandoned, with the election of Jean Charest's Liberal government in 2003. Nonetheless, Quebec's continuing rejection of the federal spending power in provincial policy fields, and its enduring suspicion of Ottawa, have helped to thwart recent efforts to place intergovernmental cooperation on a firmer legal footing (e.g., the creation of binding enforcement and dispute-resolution mechanisms).

- The federal system established in 1867 focused entirely on governments. There was no place for interest groups and individual citizens. As Canadian political culture has evolved, demands for direct participation have grown louder and deference to governments has waned (Chapter 2). The elite-driven processes of executive federalism have lost whatever legitimacy they may once have possessed. At the same time, Canada is bound by many of its international commitments, and by recent models of public administration,[25] to involve private actors in government decision-making. This creates a dilemma: on the one hand, a large majority of Canadians want their governments to stop fighting over money and powers[26]—which implies the creation of binding agreements backed up by a powerful enforcement mechanism. On the other hand, binding intergovernmental agreements, negotiated and enforced by executives, would necessarily constrain the powers of elected legislators, thus deepening the "democratic deficit."[27]

- In recent decades, Aboriginal organizations have claimed an inherent right to self-government; the federal government accepted this claim in 1995. Since then, many First Nations have achieved unprecedented sovereignty through new treaties and land claims agreements (involving Ottawa and the relevant provinces), while long-established band councils have gained a measure of additional autonomy and responsibility from the federal government. The logical conclusion of these developments is that Aboriginal leaders—band chiefs and/or the leaders of "peak" organizations—should play a formal role in IGRs.[28] Once the leaders of nongovernmental organizations (NGOs) received a place at the table in the 1990–92 constitutional negotiations, the demands of territorial governments to participate in IGRs on an equal footing with the provinces could no longer be resisted. While it may be perfectly reasonable, and even praiseworthy, to include Aboriginal groups and territories in IGRs, the difficulty of reaching consensus increases with every new participant.[29]

- Finally, the federal system was designed for an independent nation–state (although it took a few decades for Canada to gain full sovereignty from Britain). It was not intended to handle the complexities of globalization, which undermines "the tidy distinction between domestic and foreign."[30] As nation–states yield some of their sovereignty to supranational institutions, and as cities become more independent players in international affairs, the two-level model of federalism has become a four-level model (five, if we include regional organizations like the Annual Conference of New England Governors and Eastern Canadian Premiers). This new "multi-tiered" federalism greatly increases the complexity of relations between national and provincial governments,[31] which are now faced with new problems: Should provinces play a direct role in international negotiations that restrict their activities within their own jurisdictions? Can Ottawa fulfill its obligations under international treaties (e.g., the Kyoto Protocol on Climate Change) if one or more provinces refuse to cooperate? Should the federal government deal directly with municipalities, bypassing the provinces (which enjoy exclusive responsibility for municipal governments under the *BNA Act*)?

The institutions of federalism, as entrenched in the 1867 *Constitution,* are clearly inadequate to address the long-standing and emerging issues just canvassed. Over the decades, a multitude of nonconstitutional mechanisms—some ad hoc, others more stable and continuous—have evolved to deal with unforeseen circumstances and conflicts.[32] These include the First Ministers' Conference, ministerial and official committees, and intergovernmental Accords of various types. While these mechanisms may help to resolve immediate crises in the short term, they do not have the legal or constitutional muscle to ensure genuinely collaborative policy-making and implementation over the long term. In short, there is no institutional incentive for governments to respect each other's jurisdictions, or to work together productively on common problems. Recognizing the limits of nonconstitutional mechanisms, provincial governments have proposed formal amendments to the *BNA Act* since at least 1887.[33] As we will see in Chapter 9, however, the failure of the Meech Lake and Charlottetown Accords prompted Canada's political leaders to abandon large-scale constitutional reform in favour of "incremental political adaptation supplemented where necessary by specific constitutional adjustments."[34]

Students of federalism have traditionally focused their attention on the two senior levels of government. For example, they asked whether a particular federation had grown more centralized or decentralized over time—i.e., whether the power to make and enforce decisions had moved from the national government to the subnational (provincial) governments, or vice versa. The consensus is that Canada, despite its origins as a "quasi-federal" state, is now on balance "one of the most decentralized federations in the world."[35] Although the pendulum has swung back and forth, the general trend is clear: the centralized federation envisaged by Sir John A. Macdonald has been transformed almost beyond recognition.

While these traditional conceptions of federalism are not obsolete, their usefulness is diminishing. To say, for example, that Canada is a "decentralized" federation implies that the provinces have evolved into 10 autonomous fiefdoms, each pursuing its own independent policy agenda. This picture obscures the growing importance of interprovincial, and now provincial–territorial (PT), collaboration, most recently in the establishment of the Council of the Federation. At this point, the extent of this collaboration is limited; the chief goal of most PT meetings is to forge a "common front" against the federal government—a clear assertion of parity within the federation—not to make policy. This could change in the near future, largely because Quebec seems to be more willing to engage in interprovincial collaboration than in the recent past (indeed, Quebec initiated the council).

"Decentralization" also understates the mutual interdependence, not only between the federal, provincial, and territorial (FPT) governments, but also among nation–states, supranational organizations and agreements (e.g., the North American Free Trade Agreement, or NAFTA), municipal governments, Aboriginal governments, and NGOs. While the impact of these factors to date should not be overstated,[36] there is little doubt that the old functional boundaries between and within states are breaking down. Their erosion reinforces the preexisting trends away from independence and hierarchy, and toward interdependence and parity; it also magnifies the complexity of making and enforcing public policy, and brings new actors to the table. Hamish Telford cites some recent examples:

> The various crises that confronted Canada in the summer of 2003—SARS, mad-cow, West Nile Virus, the electricity blackout in Ontario—all illustrate that contemporary political problems spill over multiple jurisdictional boundaries, and require for resolution the collaborative efforts of local, provincial, federal and international agencies.[37]

To this list, one might add terrorism, trade disputes (e.g., the dispute between Canada and the United States over softwood lumber), and environmental protection issues. The point is that, in most policy fields, no single government can craft and implement programs without taking into account the effects on the agendas of other governments—provincial, national, local, foreign—or the constraints imposed by external factors over which that government has little if any control.

Over the years, Canadian federalism has continually adapted to changing conditions. At various times, the balance between independence and interdependence has shifted back and forth, as has the balance of power between Ottawa and the provinces. The period from 1945 to the mid-1970s is often called "cooperative federalism"; since the 1980s, it has been replaced by "collaborative federalism." In both periods, Ottawa transferred millions of dollars to the provinces to pay for programs in provincial jurisdiction; in other words, there was a high degree of fiscal interdependence. The key difference is the degree to which Ottawa can set priorities in provincial fields: "collaborative federalism envisages partnership and equality between orders of government, whereas co-operative federalism involves strong federal government leadership." This shift from hierarchy to relative parity is the direct result of cuts to federal transfer payments, and the gradual replacement of **conditional grants** with block grants since the 1970s.[38]

Before we turn to a more detailed discussion of the economic trends just described, we will consider three additional influences on Canadian federalism: the logic of the federal institutions themselves, judicial review of the division of powers, and changes in Canada's political culture, specifically Western regionalism and Quebec nationalism.

The Institutional Logic of Federalism

The erosion of independence and hierarchy is partially explained by the character of Canada's federal institutions themselves:

- First, federalism creates institutional incentives for the actors who operate within it. The establishment of provincial governments creates a focus for local political grievances and ambitions. In effect, ambitious provincial politicians have an incentive to "get the best deal" from the federal government, in order to prove their worth to the voters. Over time, the provinces have learned that "ganging up" on Ottawa is more effective than going it alone; one premier cannot credibly claim to be the equal of the prime minister, whereas 10 premiers (or 9, if Quebec refuses to participate) have a better chance to assert parity within Confederation.

- Second, the numerical balance between Ottawa and the provinces has changed dramatically since 1867. Between 1873 and 1949, six new provinces were added to the original four, each with its own local needs and conditions. As the number of provinces grew, Ottawa's dominance at the bargaining table shrank.[39] The recent entry of the territories and NGOs seems likely to reinforce this trend.

- Third, the division of jurisdictions in the *BNA Act*—which initially favoured the central government—has now tipped the balance of power toward the provinces. By the end of the twentieth century, federal powers over defence and railways were far less important than they had been in 1867, and most Canadians considered the provincial realms of health care and education to be the highest political priorities.[40]

So the federal system itself, combined with the growing number of provinces and the unforeseen effect of the division of powers, doomed "watertight compartments" and federal paramountcy over the long term.

Judicial Review of the *BNA Act*

The Judicial Committee of the Privy Council: Wicked Stepfathers or Kindly Uncles?

Until 1949, when appeals to London were abolished, Britain's Judicial Committee of the Privy Council (JCPC) was the final court of appeal for Canada. The JCPC was established in 1833 to hear appeals to the Crown against the decisions of colonial governments.[41] Its members were distinguished lawyers and judges who had either inherited or been appointed to seats in the House of Lords. Under the 1865 *Colonial Laws Validity Act,* an "imperial statute" could override a law passed by the Canadian Parliament when the two conflicted. The JCPC, as the highest court in the Empire, had the ultimate responsibility to determine whether or not Canadian laws conflicted with British laws, the most important of which was the *BNA Act*. The JCPC had the authority to overturn constitutional rulings of the Canadian Supreme Court, as well as the right to hear constitutional appeals directly from provincial courts. The Supreme Court was bypassed altogether in about half of the JCPC's cases on the *BNA Act*.[42] So judicial review of the Canadian *Constitution* in its crucial early years was primarily a British operation.

While the JCPC's impact on Canadian federalism is still a matter for heated debate, one point is clear: most of the Law Lords disapproved of the "quasi-federal" elements in the *BNA Act* and sought to diminish Ottawa's paramountcy. "From the late 1890s onward the Committee embarked on a course of giving the provincial powers over 'property and civil rights' [section 92 (13)] an expansive interpretation while narrowly limiting Parliament's general power related to 'Peace, Order and Good Government' [the Preamble to section 91] and the enumerated federal power over 'trade and commerce' [section 91(2)]."[43] In 1867, as noted earlier, the Fathers of Confederation had deliberately subordinated the provincial governments to the national government. In the "POGG clause" (peace, order, and good government), they gave Ottawa a broad residual power to legislate on all matters not expressly reserved to the provinces. The JCPC effectively reversed this relationship, interpreting section 92(13) ("Property and Civil Rights in the Province") as a residual-powers clause and restricting the application of the "POGG clause" to temporary national emergencies (e.g., war). Viscount Haldane, the JCPC's most influential advocate of provincial parity, boasted that he and his colleagues had transformed the Canadian *Constitution* by raising the status of the provinces to "equal authority co-ordinate with the Dominion" (i.e., the central government).[44]

The assault on the POGG clause began in 1896, with the *Local Prohibition Case*. The JCPC ruled that the residual power was strictly limited to "such matters as are unquestionably of Canadian interest and importance." It did not empower Ottawa to "encroach upon any class of subjects which is exclusively assigned to provincial legislatures by s.92." The Law Lords added that a broader interpretation of the POGG clause might "destroy the autonomy of the provinces."[45] The residual power was narrowed further in the 1922 *Board of Commerce* reference. Haldane declared that in a serious national emergency, the POGG clause might temporarily authorize the federal government to regulate property and civil rights; otherwise, these matters must be left exclusively to the provinces, which possess "quasi-sovereign authority" over them.[46] He elaborated on that ruling in 1923:

> In the event of war, when the national life may require for its preservation the employment of very exceptional means, the provision of peace, order and good government for the country as a whole may involve effort on behalf of the whole nation, in which the interests of individuals may have to be subordinated to that of the community in a fashion which required s.91 as providing for such an emergency. The general control of property and civil rights for normal purposes remains with the Provincial Legislatures. But questions may arise by reason of the special circumstances of the national emergency which concern nothing short of the peace, order and good government of Canada as a whole.[47]

Their Lordships insisted that the emergency powers granted by the POGG clause must be relinquished as soon as the national crisis was over.

By restricting the application of the POGG clause to wartime, the JCPC effectively forbade its use during peacetime. In the 1925 *Snider* case, the Lords repeated that only a severe national emergency could trigger the use of the residual powers.[48] When the Great Depression of 1929, combined with a serious Prairie drought, threw millions out of work and created near-famine conditions in Western Canada, the Bennett government brought in "New Deal" legislation to address the unemployment crisis. In 1937 the JCPC declared most of the "New Deal" laws **ultra vires,** on the ground that they dealt with property and civil rights. It dismissed the argument that unemployment was a national crisis severe enough to invoke the POGG clause.[49]

Critics of the JCPC were outraged by the "New Deal" decisions, which marked a return to the provincial bias of the Haldane period. In two 1932 rulings—the *Aeronautics Reference* and the *Radio Reference*—their Lordships had ruled in favour of the central government. Both cases turned on the federal government's power to implement international treaties. Did Ottawa, by virtue of signing a treaty with other sovereign states, acquire the capacity to legislate in areas of provincial jurisdiction in order to carry out its responsibilities under that treaty? In the *Aeronautics Reference,* Lord Sankey repudiated the Haldane doctrine in favour of a more centralist interpretation of the *BNA Act:*

> *While the Courts should be jealous in upholding the charter of the Provinces as enacted in s. 92 it must no less be borne in mind that the real object of the Act was to give the central Government those high functions and almost sovereign powers by which uniformity of legislation might be secured on all questions which were of common concern to all the Provinces as members of a constituent whole.*[50]

Sankey also supplemented the emergency powers doctrine by "reading in" to section 132 of the *BNA Act* an entitlement for the federal government to make laws in areas of provincial jurisdiction, where such laws were a necessary consequence of a foreign treaty. He concluded that "substantially the whole field of legislation in regard to aerial navigation belongs to the Dominion." In the *Radio Reference,* Viscount Dunedin agreed that the federal government must have the power to implement treaties. However, he located that power in the POGG clause, not in section 132.[51]

The 1937 *Labour Conventions Case* reversed the 1932 rulings, stripping Ottawa of the power to enforce international treaties in fields of provincial jurisdiction and returning to the JCPC's usual pro-province approach. Lord Atkin distinguished between treaty-making and treaty implementation, arguing that the former was an executive power and the latter a legislative responsibility.[52] Therefore, while the national executive had the right to negotiate and assent to foreign treaties, it could not endow the national Parliament with unlimited power to enact them into law. Atkin argued that neither of the 1932 cases constituted a binding precedent for "holding that legislation to perform a Canadian treaty is exclusively within the Dominion legislative power."[53] To accept that doctrine, he claimed, would "undermine the constitutional safeguards of Provincial constitutional autonomy." The federal government might negotiate treaties with other countries with the sole intent to override the division of powers in sections 91 and 92, and thus "clothe itself with legislative authority inconsistent with the constitution which gave it birth."[54] Atkin ended with a now-famous metaphor for Canadian federalism: "While the ship of state now sails on larger ventures and into foreign waters she still retains the water-tight compartments which are an essential part of her original structure." This ruling remains in effect,[55] forcing Ottawa to involve the provinces in the crafting of international treaties. Without *Labour Conventions*, globalization might well have restored federal paramountcy, as it appears to have done in Australia;[56] with *Labour Conventions*, the impact of Canada's international commitments in provincial fields is less clear (see "Federalism and 'Glocalization,'" on page 415).

As previously noted, there were some exceptions to the JCPC's pro-province jurisprudence. Perhaps the most influential was the 1946 *Canada Temperance Federation* case. Viscount Simon explicitly rejected Haldane's "emergency power" interpretation of the POGG clause and substituted a "national concern" doctrine.

> *In their Lordships' opinion, the true test [of constitutionality] must be found in the real subject matter of the legislation: if it is such that it goes beyond local or provincial concern or interests and must from its inherent nature be the concern of the Dominion as a whole [as in the Aeronautics and Radio references], then it will fall within the competence of the Dominion Parliament as a matter affecting the peace, order and good government of Canada, though it may in another aspect touch on matters specially reserved to the provincial legislatures.*[57]

Simon broadened the application of the residual power and restored to the central government some of the legal power that had been stripped away by previous rulings of the committee. Note, however, that the JCPC ignored this reformulation of the residual power in its remaining appeals, returning to the "emergency powers" approach favoured by Haldane. The full implications of the "national concern" doctrine were left for the Supreme Court of Canada to determine after 1949.

Although the actual impact of the JCPC's constitutional interpretations has attracted considerable criticism,[58] their Lordships have powerful defenders as well. Alan Cairns argues that "the provincial bias of the Privy Council was generally harmonious with Canadian developments," and that the JCPC's popularity with Quebec governments—which generally favoured provincial autonomy—may well have saved Canada from breaking up.[59] Contrary to the complaints of centralist lawyers that the committee had reduced the federal government to an empty shell, Cairns notes that "Canada was run in a highly centralist fashion" from 1945 until about 1960.[60] In practice, the federal government was far from helpless in the face of the JCPC's decisions. After the committee struck down the *Employment and Social Insurance Act* in 1937, the *BNA Act* was amended in 1940 to insert "Unemployment Insurance" in section 91. Given the strength of the other influences on Canadian federalism, Cairns concludes that "Judicial review scarcely seems to have been as important a determinant of constitutional evolution as has often been imagined."[61] But while the JCPC did not solely determine the evolution of Canadian federalism, it did set many of the rules under which the provincial and federal governments competed for power and resources.

The Supreme Court of Canada: Biased Umpire?

Appeals to the JCPC were abolished in 1949, and the Supreme Court became the final arbiter in constitutional disputes. The Court was still bound by the JCPC's rulings under the doctrine of *stare decisis,* which led some observers to expect that it would continue to interpret national powers narrowly. On the other hand, provincial governments worried about the loss of their supporters in London, and feared that a Canadian court appointed by the prime minister would favour Ottawa in jurisdictional disputes. Those fears have persisted, prompting repeated calls for provincial participation in the appointment of Supreme Court justices.[62]

Initially, those fears were confirmed. In its first definitive ruling on the division of powers, the Supreme Court relied on Viscount Simon's "national concern" doctrine to uphold a national law that affected property and civil rights.[63] The "national concern" approach was reinforced in 1967, when the court determined that control over offshore minerals was not expressly included in the *BNA Act* and thereby awarded it to the federal government under the residual power.[64] By 1988, the court had developed "a 'provincial inability' test which would justify federal legislation if it could be established that a particular problem required national treatment unobtainable through provincial co-operation."[65] The justices also relied on Simon's "national concern" doctrine: it can be used to justify permanent federal legislation (unlike the emergency powers doctrine); it "applies both to new matters which did not exist at Confederation and to matters which, although originally matters of a local or private nature in a province, have, since, in the absence of national emergency, become matters of national concern"; the problems addressed by the legislation must be clearly national in scope, and there must be serious potential consequences of provincial inability to address the problem.[66]

In subsequent cases, the court has backed away from the "national concern" doctrine under POGG because it "inevitably raises profound issues respecting the federal structure of our *Constitution*."[67] On the other hand, it has rejected the JCPC's subordination of the federal trade and commerce power to the provincial property and civil rights power,[68] and reasserted federal paramountcy over interprovincial trade.[69] However, that paramountcy is limited: the federal government may not encroach on provincial jurisdiction except as part of a broad regulatory scheme that is beyond the constitutional competence of the provinces (either individually or acting in concert).[70] As we will see in "Federalism and 'Glocalization,'" this tentative expansion of federal power over trade could have significant implications for the provinces in an era of binding trade agreements between national governments.

By the 1980s, the justices were trying to balance federal and provincial interests, partly in response to provincial attacks on the court's legitimacy.[71] However, this does not imply a return to the pro-provincial bias of the JCPC. Section 92 (13) is no longer treated as an implicit residual-powers clause that can trump Parliament's right to legislate in matters affecting the country as a whole. Instead, some observers argue that the Supreme Court has turned section 91 (27)—the power to make criminal law for the entire country—into an effective residual-powers clause for the federal government (Dossier 8.4).[72] In policy fields ranging from environmental protection[73] to tobacco advertising,[74] the court has recognized the right of the federal Parliament to make laws that define criminal offences and prescribe sanctions for noncompliance. However, Parliament cannot use the criminal-law power to "invade areas of exclusively provincial legislative competence" merely by "legislating in the proper form." It must have a very good reason for creating new criminal offences and sanctions in policy fields that would otherwise be exclusively or concurrently provincial.[75]

DOSSIER 8.4 The Reference re the *Firearms Act*

In 1995 the federal government introduced Bill C-68, the *Firearms Act*. The Act requires all gun owners to register their firearms with the federal government and to obtain licences for their legal use. In 1996 the Alberta government asked the province's Court of Appeal to rule on the constitutionality of the law. Under section 92 (13) of the *Constitution Act, 1867,* the provinces have jurisdiction over property and civil rights. Alberta argued that the Act was *ultra vires* the federal Parliament, because it regulated the property of gun owners. A majority on the Court of Appeal upheld the law. The Alberta government appealed the ruling to the Supreme Court of Canada.

The Supreme Court agreed with the Court of Appeal.[76] The justices ruled unanimously that the *Firearms Act* was primarily a criminal statute, because it was designed to prevent and punish the harmful use of firearms. As such, it was "a valid exercise of Parliament's jurisdiction over criminal law" (section 91 [27]). There was no federal intrusion on provincial powers, because "gun control has been the subject of federal law since Confederation." The justices rejected the provincial argument based on section 92 (13):

The Firearms Act does not trench on provincial powers such that upholding it as criminal law will upset the balance of federalism. The provinces have not established that the effects of the Act on provincial jurisdiction over property and civil rights are more than incidental . . . the mere fact that guns are property does not suffice to show that a gun control law is in pith and substance a provincial matter.

The court held that "A federal state depends for its very existence on a just and workable balance between the central and provincial levels of government . . . The question is not whether such a balance is necessary, but whether the 1995 gun control law upsets that balance." Because gun control was already a matter of federal jurisdiction, the justices concluded that the *Firearms Act* did not affect the division of powers. Despite the court's talk of "balance," the outcome might have been different under the JCPC, inasmuch as the Law Lords tended to favour the provinces in most jurisdictional disputes involving property and civil rights.

In general, we can conclude that the Supreme Court is more sympathetic to the national government than the JCPC had been. But the change has not been as extreme as provincial-rights advocates had feared. A 1979 study concluded that the justices had "favoured the provincial interest at least as often as they have favoured the federal interest";[77] this conclusion remains valid today.[78] However, portraying the court's approach to federalism as a zero-sum game is misleading. Instead of dividing powers into federal and provincial "watertight compartments," the court has often expanded the scope of shared, or concurrent, jurisdictions.[79] Its preference for concurrency over exclusive powers likely helps to explain the reliance on the criminal law power, rather than the POGG clause, as the basis for a federal role in environmental regulation. Unlike the POGG clause, which grants exclusive power to the national government, jurisdiction over the criminal law is shared between Ottawa (which writes the statutes) and the provinces (which administer, enforce, and prosecute).[80] In effect, the court has not deliberately expanded federal powers at the expense of the provinces, or vice versa; rather, it has expanded the power of government generally, and opened up new areas of overlap within which the two levels of government must cooperate.

There is at least one further reason to question the widely held view—at least among premiers, especially those from Alberta and Quebec—that the Supreme Court since 1949 has been biased toward Ottawa. The logic of the *BNA Act* itself, and the division of powers in particular, promotes a strong central government. Unlike the JCPC, which often seemed to disregard the express language of sections 91–92 in order to impose its own view of federalism, the Supreme Court of Canada has generally been faithful to the intentions of the framers.[81]

Even if the Supreme Court were unfairly biased in favour of Ottawa, as its critics allege, the provinces would still hold the political resources to overcome the effects of judicial review. Provincial "losses" at the Supreme Court have often been followed by "wins" in subsequent political bargaining with Ottawa. In 1978, for example, the Supreme Court struck down a Saskatchewan law imposing royalties on oil wells, on the ground that the royalty was an indirect tax and thus a violation of sections 91(3) and 92(2). Three years later, when Prime Minister Trudeau needed the support of Saskatchewan's NDP government for his plan to patriate the *Constitution*, he agreed to an amendment recognizing provincial rights to levy taxes on natural resources.[82] (This is now section 92A of the *Constitution Act, 1867;* see the Appendix to this book.)

The Political Culture of Federalism: Quebec Nationalism and Western Regional Alienation

A third influence on Canadian federalism is political culture (recall Chapter 2). Regionalism has always existed in the Maritime (now "Atlantic") provinces and the Western provinces. Since 1960, Western regionalism has been mobilized as a political resource. The inspiration for this "province-building" activity was the Quiet Revolution in Quebec. As regional grievances were mobilized by provincial governments, especially those of Alberta and British Columbia, provincial challenges to central power grew, and the legitimacy of the federal government diminished. The battles between the federal and provincial governments eventually culminated in the 1980–82 constitutional negotiations that produced the *Constitution Act, 1982* (see Chapter 9).

Quebec's demand for more powers arises, in large measure, from the central myth of Quebec nationalism: the belief that Confederation was a deal between two founding nations, French and English.[83] Quebec is the primary home of the French nation in North America; therefore, the Quebec government is that nation's chief institutional expression. The rest of Canada is the home of an English Canadian nation, which, as a majority in the federal Parliament, naturally controls the federal government. In short, Ottawa is primarily the government of English Canada, just as Quebec is the true government of the French nation. As we saw earlier, this "two-nations" myth implies that Quebec is not a province like the others; it requires special status and powers to protect it as a founding nation, and it has the right to negotiate changes to the federation one-on-one with the federal government. This myth, with its attendant symbols of humiliation and sovereignty (see Dossiers 1.5 and 2.3), drives Quebec's demands for independence and parity in the federal system.

It also underlies the recurring demand for constitutional recognition as a "distinct society," which was a crucial factor in the failures of the Meech Lake and Charlottetown Accords (see "Megaconstitutional Politics after 1982: From Meech Lake to Charlottetown" in Chapter 9). The Quebec nationalist claim to "distinct society" status has three implications:

1. It must be recognized in entrenched constitutional law. Otherwise, judicial review could not be counted on to protect the interests of the "founding nation" centred in Quebec.

2. The government of Quebec required special powers to protect its distinct language and culture. These included a veto over constitutional change and the right to socialize immigrants into francophone society. Quebec also demanded the right to "opt out" of any national **shared-cost programs** in provincial jurisdiction, and receive federal money to operate its own separate program (e.g., the separate Canada and Quebec Pension Plans).

3. Quebec required an assurance that national political institutions would reflect its special character and laws. While the Supreme Court of Canada, by convention, always includes three justices from the Quebec civil bar, the Quebec government wanted that requirement to be entrenched, along with an appointment process that gave it control over who those justices would be.

In many ways, Canada's *Constitution* already recognizes Quebec as a "distinct society." Britain's *Quebec Act* of 1774 granted the former French colonists the right to practise the Roman Catholic faith and to use civil law (as opposed to English common law) in their private disputes. The *BNA Act* perpetuated these rights. However, successive Quebec governments have argued that these protections are insufficient.

Western Canadians, especially those in Alberta and British Columbia, have long complained about central Canadian dominance in the House of Commons. Those complaints arise from two basic elements of our political system:

1. Seats in the House of Commons are distributed among the provinces in rough proportion to their shares of the national population (see "Rep by Pop?" in Chapter 5). Together, Ontario and Quebec account for over half of the seats in the House (181 of 308, or 59 percent), while the four Western provinces can claim less than one-third (92 of 308 seats, or 29 percent). While it is mathematically possible to form a majority government with very few Western seats—as the Liberals did in 1980—no party that seeks to form a government can afford to ignore the interests of Central Canada.

2. The numerical disadvantage of the Western provinces is reinforced by the conventions of party discipline and Cabinet solidarity. Even in government, Western MPs cannot openly address regional issues in a way that threatens their party's base in Ontario and Quebec. (These points are discussed in greater detail in Chapter 5.)

To make matters worse, from the Western perspective, the threat of Quebec separatism dominated the national political agenda during the last quarter of the twentieth century. A province that can credibly threaten to break up the country is likely, all other things being equal, to receive more than its fair share of attention and resources from the national government.

Western discontent with the federal system exploded in the 1970s, as the economic interests of Alberta oil producers clashed head-on with those of industrial Ontario and Quebec. When the world price of oil soared in the 1970s, Alberta grew rich while Central Canada stagnated. A new national-unity crisis erupted, which came to a head when the Trudeau government introduced the National Energy Program (NEP) in the fall of 1980. The NEP was designed to control the increase in oil prices, to provide greater oil tax revenues for the federal government, to Canadianize ownership of the oil industry, and to shift exploration from provincial lands to "Canada lands" in the North and offshore.

The NEP brought Western resentment of Canada's political institutions to a head. It was introduced by a national Liberal government that held only two seats in Western Canada—both in Manitoba—but that nonetheless commanded a solid national majority. Thus, even to Western Canadians outside Alberta, the NEP demonstrated a serious flaw in parliamentary institutions. Moreover, the NEP's bitter reception in the West also demonstrated what can happen when the national government lacks elected members to sell its programs in a region.

In 1984, Western Canadians voted massively for the Progressive Conservatives. They hoped that a federal Cabinet with a large Western contingent would be more sensitive to regional concerns. That hope ended in 1986, when the Mulroney government awarded a major contract for the maintenance of CF-18 aircraft to a Montreal firm, despite the fact that a cheaper and technically superior bid had been submitted by a Winnipeg firm. For many Westerners, this event brought into even sharper focus the flaw in Canada's parliamentary regime: even when the West was solidly represented on the government benches, Ontario and Quebec would always carry greater weight in a chamber based on representation by population, and Western members of the government party would be silenced by party discipline and Cabinet solidarity. So powerful was the Western discontent with the CF-18 contract that it became the galvanizing event in the formation of a new political party—the Reform Party, which entered national politics under the slogan "The West Wants In."[84]

As we will see in Table 9.1, the Quebec nationalist agenda for institutional reform overlaps with the Western regionalist agenda in one key respect: both want to carve out the broadest possible sphere of fiscal and legislative autonomy for provincial governments. However, the two agendas contradict each other in an equally fundamental way: whereas Quebec nationalists claim special status for their province, Westerners—like most "English" Canadians—believe that Canada is composed of 10 equal provinces. Whereas Quebec's constitutional agenda is driven by nationalism, that of the Western provinces is fuelled by regional alienation and populist rejection of our representative democratic structures. Nonetheless, both subcultures agree on one central point: Canada's national political institutions do not adequately serve regional interests.

Although the two subcultures agreed on one possible solution to the problem—shifting more powers from Ottawa to the provinces—they disagreed over the other: to reform our national institutions in order to enhance their capacity to express and accommodate regional interests. Political scientists refer to these two competing approaches—parity and reform to national institutions, respectively—as **interstate federalism** and **intrastate federalism.**

- Interstate federalism resolves regional conflict through negotiations between heads of government (e.g., First Ministers' Conferences or the Council of the Federation). Provincial premiers are not just the heads of regional governments; they are national political figures in their own right, as the designated spokespersons for regional interests in federal politics. Claims to provincial parity are the logical accompaniment to interstate bargaining.
- Intrastate federalism is designed to resolve regional conflicts by reflecting regionalism within the institutions of the central government; regional electorates choose their national representatives, often members of the upper house of the federal Parliament, bypassing their premiers.

In general, Quebec nationalists favour interstate federalism. It is analogous to the intergovernmental negotiations among national leaders, which fits the "two-nations" vision of Confederation. Western regionalists tend to prefer intrastate solutions, which would enhance the representation of the smaller provinces within the national political system.

Whatever form Canada's federal system may take in the future—some options are discussed in Chapter 9—its current legitimacy is clearly linked to the strength of regionalism in various parts of the country. A 2002 survey asked Canadians whether their national, provincial, or local government gave them "the most for their money."[85] Respondents in Atlantic Canada were the most likely to name the national government (36.6 percent), whereas those in Quebec and Alberta disagreed. Some 22 percent of Quebec respondents thought they received the best value from the federal government (almost exactly the same percentage as Ontario), while only

7.8 percent of Albertans felt the same way. (Note, however, that regional samples in national surveys are often too small to provide completely reliable results.) Conversely, Albertans were by far the most likely to identify the provincial government as the best value provider (44.4 percent), compared to 35.7 percent in Quebec and 29 percent across the entire national sample. It is probably fair to conclude, as the authors of the survey did, that these findings reflect more than simple regional sentiment. The high score for the national government in the Atlantic sample is a logical result of that region's dependence on federal transfers and **equalization,** whereas Alberta's oil wealth makes it a net (and sometimes reluctant) contributor to the fiscal system.[86]

However, a different question revealed a consistent regional pattern of opinion toward the various levels of government. Respondents in Quebec and the two westernmost provinces reported feeling less "trust and confidence" in the federal government than those in the Atlantic region, the Prairies, and Ontario.[87] These findings suggest that Quebec nationalism and Western alienation undermine public support for the national government in those regions of the country. If this is correct, it may help to explain why successive governments in Ottawa have tried to respond to regionally based demands for constitutional change—with little success, as we will see in Chapter 9.

▨ Fiscal Federalism: The Key Reason for Interdependence and Parity

The economic disparities among Canada's governments and regions have always affected the balance of powers in Canada's federal system. The hierarchical federation established in 1867 depended on continual economic growth, which would allow the federal government to carry out its nation-building program. That program was seriously threatened by the recessions of the 1870s and 1880s, as was the legitimacy of the new national government among citizens who had never fully accepted the loss of their colonial independence.[88] As the fiscal resources of the federal government shrank, so did its paramountcy over the provinces. Back in 1887, the first premiers' conference demanded more money from Ottawa to meet their constitutional responsibilities.[89] Over the past century, the degree to which the national government can assert paramountcy in provincial jurisdictions has been largely determined by its taxing and spending capacity at a given time. When Ottawa reaps sufficient revenues from taxation, and distributes them among the provincial governments via cash transfers, it can set priorities in provincial policy fields; it is the dominant partner in Confederation. When its revenues shrink—because taxing power shifts to the provinces, because of economic recession, or because of high interest payments on the public debt—so do its cash transfers to the provinces and, consequently, its power to intervene in provincial areas such as health care, PSE, and social welfare. In short, the federal spending power, and Ottawa's ability to determine priorities in provincial policy fields, varies with the amount of money that Ottawa can actually spend.

Collectively, the financial relationships between the federal and provincial governments are called "fiscal federalism." (The word "fiscal" refers to public finance.)

While fiscal federalism is hardly the sexiest topic in political science, it does have a direct and significant impact on the lives of Canadians. For example, postsecondary tuition fees continue to rise in most provinces, partly because of the 1995 Canada Health and Social Transfer (discussed later in this chapter). Concern about the future of the health-care system was a central issue in the 2000 and 2004 federal elections. Welfare recipients have seen their benefits slashed by provincial and municipal governments desperate to reduce their social assistance costs in the wake of federal transfer cuts (and, in the case of some provinces, for ideological reasons as well). So while fiscal federalism may appear dull, its effects are anything but.

An Unbalanced Federation

The 1867 *Constitution* gave the provincial governments jurisdiction over education, health care, and social welfare. At the time, these were not particularly important or costly areas of public policy. Private and religious charities delivered social services, especially in Quebec, and governments spent relatively little to fill the gap. Ottawa was responsible for the big-ticket items of the late nineteenth century: railways and defence. It only made sense to give the central government the lion's share of tax revenues. However, section 118 of the *BNA Act* (now repealed) provided for an unconditional transfer to the provinces, at a rate of 80 cents per capita, in compensation for the taxing powers that the provinces had ceded to Ottawa. Almost immediately, the Atlantic provinces began to press (often successfully) for more generous unconditional grants from the national government. These early block grants were the precursors of the current equalization program (see the next section).[90] The horizontal imbalance among the new provinces was already apparent. Despite the reality of national transfers to the provinces, every effort was made to preserve the "watertight compartments" in sections 91–92.

Within 50 years of Confederation, the vertical imbalance between the two levels of government had become acute. The unconditional transfers continued, and were gradually enriched; the first conditional grants were introduced in 1912.[91] The sum total of transfer payments proved completely inadequate during the Great Depression of 1929–39, which placed enormous demands on the social services provided by provincial and private agencies, while gutting provincial (and federal) revenues. The provinces demanded a dramatic increase in financial assistance from Ottawa. The fiscal crisis of the 1930s prompted the federal government to appoint a Royal Commission—called the Rowell–Sirois Commission after its chairmen—to recommend improvements. The commission issued its report in 1940, when Canada was fully engaged in World War II. Two of its key recommendations were (1) to centralize taxing powers in Ottawa, in order to prevent federal–provincial tax competition and the exhaustion of available revenues, and (2) to make the ad hoc system of unconditional fiscal transfers permanent.[92] The commission was strongly opposed to conditional grants, mostly for practical reasons; it argued that joint administration of social programs would provoke intergovernmental conflict and destroy the "watertight compartments" that were still perceived as the bulwarks of federalism.[93]

The combination of World War II and the Rowell–Sirois Report brought significant and lasting changes to the fiscal relationship between the two senior levels of government.[94] Under the 1940 tax-rental agreement, the provinces gave Ottawa complete control over personal and corporate income tax.[95] The cost of participating in a global conflict was staggering, as was the centralization of policy-making power required to mount a national wartime effort. The consolidation of taxing powers in Ottawa may have begun as an emergency measure, but it persisted until 1957, with the consent of all the provinces except Quebec (and, initially, Ontario).[96]

After peace was restored in 1945, the federal government turned its attention to a new goal: the management of the national economy through Keynesian fiscal and monetary policies. In effect, the Keynesian model of government (named after Lord John Maynard Keynes, a British economist) was designed to prevent future economic crises like the Great Depression of the 1930s. It prescribed strong central control over employment, inflation, and public spending. At the same time, the federal government was planning for an unprecedented expansion in the size and activities of the public sector. The "welfare state" would provide income security and health care to every Canadian who needed help. Postsecondary education would grow rapidly, as Canada's young people prepared themselves for life in the new, information-based economy. Together, the Keynesian approach to government and the growth of the welfare state gave the federal government a reason to maintain its wartime control over tax revenues.

The welfare state also prompted a massive expansion in the scope of the federal spending power. While public-health insurance and other social programs were largely federal initiatives, most of the programs and services were delivered by the provinces. Increased funding for health care, social welfare, and PSE prompted rapid growth in provincial public sectors. As their roles and responsibilities expanded, provincial governments became increasingly dependent on federal funds. Thus, the federal government became heavily involved in financing programs within the legislative jurisdiction of provincial governments. In order to maintain its control of income tax, while ensuring that the 10 provincial governments carried out its wishes, the federal government developed the complex modern system of fiscal federalism. It collected income taxes from every Canadian—except those in Quebec, which has long collected its own income tax[97]—and distributed part of the proceeds to the provincial governments on the condition that their programs met the criteria set by Ottawa. In effect, the federal government used its spending power to determine provincial programs, spending priorities, and standards. By attaching conditions to the receipt of federal funding, Ottawa was able to legislate indirectly in provincial fields of jurisdiction. Thus the era of cooperative federalism witnessed the persistence of hierarchy, even as policy-making became ever more interdependent.

The Evolution of Fiscal Federalism, 1945–95: From Conditional Grants to the Canada Health and Social Transfer

As discussed earlier, fiscal federalism evolved to address two major imbalances in the revenues of Canada's 11 senior governments: a vertical imbalance between Ottawa and the provincial governments (discussed above), and a horizontal imbalance among the 10 provinces. Per-capita income levels in the three "have" provinces—Ontario, British Columbia, and Alberta—are significantly higher than those in the seven "have-not" provinces. Without subsidies from Ottawa, the provincial governments in the Atlantic region, Quebec, and the Prairies would be unable to provide services comparable to those available to Canadians in the wealthier parts of the country.

The equalization program, established in 1957, reduces this horizontal imbalance. Its importance is reflected in its entrenchment in section 36 of the *Constitution Act, 1982*. The purpose of equalization, as described in section 36, is "to ensure that provincial governments have sufficient revenues to provide reasonably comparable levels of public services at reasonably comparable levels of taxation."[98] In simple terms, the federal government gives each province a fixed percentage of the income tax collected in its territory. The "have-not" provinces receive an additional transfer to "top up" these tax revenues, which is calculated on a per-capita basis.[99] The equalization transfer brings the total per-capita revenues for each "have-not" province almost up to the average per-capita revenues of the five "middle-income" provinces. In 2004–05, equalization payments ranged from almost $1800 per capita for Prince Edward Island to less than $500 for Saskatchewan.[100] In 2002–03, equalization accounted for more than 20 percent of provincial revenues in the Atlantic region, 10 percent in Quebec, and 19 percent in Manitoba.[101] Note that equalization does not promote federal paramountcy, because there are no conditions attached to the federal money; nor does it necessarily affect interdependence.

Provincial governments have long complained about the equalization formula, which produces unpredictable and often substantial fluctuations in revenue from year to year. Consequently, it is difficult for provincial Finance ministers to make accurate revenue projections when they prepare their annual budgets. The formula's complexity sometimes leads to errors in the collection and processing of data; these can produce a nasty surprise for a province that has already received its transfer for a fiscal year, only to be told to repay part of the money later on.[102] In its 2004 budget, the federal government took steps to reduce the fluctuations and impose more stability on the equalization program;[103] however, it rejected the provinces' call to include Alberta in the "average," arguing that it could not afford the higher payments that inevitably would result.[104]

Shared-cost programs address the vertical imbalance between the revenues and the spending responsibilities of each government.[105] During the heyday of cooperative federalism in the 1950s, the principal form of cost-sharing was the conditional or matching grant. Ottawa would offer money to the provinces to offset the costs of new programs in health care, PSE, and social welfare. For every dollar spent on these programs, Ottawa would reimburse the province 50 cents (in the case of a matching grant). But the reimbursement was conditional: the provincial program had to meet criteria set by the federal government. As noted earlier, this meant that the federal spending power was used to legislate indirectly in provincial jurisdictions. The provinces spent lavishly on new hospitals, universities, and social-assistance programs, thus committing Ottawa to ever-larger reimbursements. While the direct transfer of federal cash gave the national government effective paramountcy, at least in the broad sense of setting policy priorities, it made controlling the federal budget virtually impossible; the spending decisions were being made elsewhere. Accountability was also an issue, because the federal Parliament—which is constitutionally responsible for monitoring and approving the spending plans of the executive branch—had no role in fiscal federalism.

By the 1970s, the federal government was losing its economic preeminence in the federal system. The provinces had gained enormous power and policy-making capacity as their social programs grew. At the same time, the Keynesian approach to government was discredited by a prolonged economic slump that began with the 1973 oil price shock. As faith in national economic management eroded, so did the basis of Ottawa's claim for "a large enough share of the tax system" to control the economy.[106] Meanwhile, the federal government faced new and growing constraints on its spending power: after almost three decades of annual budget surpluses, it consistently incurred deficits after 1974.[107] Over time,

> an accumulation of federal government deficits and rising debt-service costs . . . reduced its ability to undertake new spending initiatives and hence to shape and influence provincial spending patterns through the use of federal–provincial matching grants or other cost-sharing programs. The federal government even found it difficult to maintain its commitments for existing joint programs.[108]

In response to its fiscal crisis, the federal government gradually reduced its cash transfers to the provinces; in the process, it gave up much of its control over provincial policy-making. The transition from cooperative to collaborative federalism began in 1977, when Ottawa negotiated the Established Programs Financing (EPF) framework with the provinces. Cash grants for health care and PSE were replaced, in part, by **"tax points."** Instead of collecting income taxes and then sending the money to the provinces, under the extended wartime tax-rental agreement, the federal government agreed to let the provinces collect their own income taxes and decide how to spend the revenues.

By reducing its direct cash transfers, the federal government hoped to regain control over its own expenditures (which would not be determined by provincial priorities), and to shift more financial responsibility for health care, PSE, and welfare to the provinces.[109] To the extent that direct transfers were replaced by tax points, EPF was a program of **block funding**, not conditional funding. By reducing its cash subsidies, the federal government effectively gave up control over programs in provincial jurisdiction; at one stroke, it reduced both hierarchy and, to a lesser degree, interdependence.

The other major cost-sharing program was the Canada Assistance Plan (CAP), which was established in 1966 to provide conditional grants to the provinces for their social-assistance programs. Ottawa paid 50 cents for every dollar of eligible provincial welfare expenditures.[110] As the federal purse strings tightened, CAP became a serious obstacle to budget management. In 1990, at the same time that Ottawa froze the cash portion of its EPF transfers, it set a 5 percent "cap on CAP" for the wealthiest provinces. Alberta, British Columbia, and Ontario would no longer receive an automatic reimbursement of 50 percent of their welfare costs; the federal contribution would increase by a maximum of 5 percent a year, regardless of provincial spending. The "cap on CAP" took effect at the start of a serious recession, which hit Ontario particularly hard and placed unusual demands on its welfare system. As the CAP transfer shrank and the cost of social assistance rose, the federal contribution to welfare costs in Ontario fell from 50 to 25 percent.[111]

The trend from conditional to block funding continued into the 1990s. Successive federal governments were forced by fiscal constraints to reduce the cash portion of shared-cost programs and rely more heavily on tax points. The 1995 Canada Health and Social Transfer (CHST), which replaced EPF and CAP, was the culmination of this trend. Then-Finance Minister Paul Martin pledged to "complete the gradual evolution away from cost-sharing to block funding of programs in areas of provincial responsibility."[112] This pledge was motivated, not by the desire to erode federal paramountcy, but by the urgent need to rescue the Canadian economy from impending disaster.[113] There are at least three important things to note about the CHST:

- First, it was a block grant. The only conditions attached to the funding were the observance of the principles of the *Canada Health Act*—public administration, comprehensiveness, universality, portability, and accessibility—and the prohibition of provincial residency requirements for social assistance. If a province violated either of these conditions, it risked a federal "claw-back" of funds.[114] However, Ottawa gave up any right to dictate the types of programs that the provinces could deliver in these fields.

- Second, each province was free to allocate the CHST among the three components (health care, PSE, and social welfare) as it saw fit. In practice, given the strong political constituency supporting the health-care system, this meant that PSE and welfare were left relatively unprotected. When the federal government introduced the CHST, it predicted that the provinces would spend 43 percent of the total transfer on health care;[115] by 2004, the federal estimate had risen to 62 percent. This suggests that the fears of postsecondary institutions and social-welfare advocates were correct. Moreover, the CHST monies went into general provincial revenues, not directly into social programs; if they so chose, provinces could spend their CHST dollars on other policy priorities.

- Third, the amount transferred under the CHST was substantially smaller than the total of the two programs it replaced. Without consulting the provinces, the federal government cut its transfers by one-third over the first two years of the CHST.[116] Over time, under the initial CHST formula, the cash portion of the transfer would shrink relative to the value of the tax points. Within a year, Ottawa had recognized the implications of this trend for its ability to impose national standards, and announced that cash transfers would not fall below a certain percentage of the total CHST package.

The political fallout from the CHST was enormous. Janice MacKinnon, a former Finance minister in Saskatchewan, describes the 1995 federal budget as "a watershed in Canada's history":

> Years of wrangling at constitutional tables had not changed federal–provincial fiscal relations as dramatically as this one budget did. While constitutional proposals had been the subject of intense debate, and even of a referendum, the wholesale changes made in 1995 were unilateral decisions, made with no national debate, except in the private discussions of the finance ministers. The Canada of the past, in which a strong federal government funded and set national standards for health and social programs, was swept aside in favour of a more decentralized federation, in which the provinces became the main guardians of the programs most Canadians cherished.[117]

Provinces wondered why they should have to follow national standards, imposed by a federal government that had slashed its cash transfers, in their own fields of jurisdiction.

By the time Martin presented the 1999 federal budget, two things had changed: (1) Ottawa's fiscal position had improved dramatically, and (2) health care had become the dominant issue in Canadian politics. Martin announced immediate and substantial increases in cash transfers under the CHST—all of which would be targeted to health care. This marked the beginning of Ottawa's efforts to reassert itself in provincial policy fields: it was the first time since 1977 that the federal government had expressly earmarked funds for health care.[118] (Note that while health care dominated public and intergovernmental discussion, the virtual elimination of federal funding for social assistance was often overlooked.[119])

For the next several years, the 11 senior governments wrangled over health-care funding. The provinces got a boost from the 2002 report of the federally sponsored Romanow Commission on Health Care,[120] which called on Ottawa to underwrite at least 25 percent of provincial health expenses through cash transfers—not tax points or a blend of the two.[121] Provincial governments, claiming that federal cash transfers amounted to roughly 15 cents for every dollar of health-care spending, demanded that Ottawa come up with more money to close the "Romanow gap."

In February 2003 the First Ministers concluded the Accord on Health Care Renewal, under which the federal government "topped up" health transfers by more than $2 billion in 2003–04. Ottawa also created a new Health Reform Transfer (HRT), which was targeted to primary health care (i.e., family doctors), home care, and "catastrophic drug coverage." The budget for the HRT was $16 billion over five years. The provinces pointed out that this one-time infusion of cash would help them to rebuild their delivery systems, but there was no guarantee that the added operating costs associated with this new infrastructure would be matched by Ottawa in future years.[122]

Another element of the 2003 Accord was a revamped CHST. On April 1, 2004, the CHST was divided in two: the Canada Health Transfer (CHT), accounting for

62 percent of the former total CHST payment, and the Canada Social Transfer (CST), worth the remaining 38 percent. The stated purpose of dividing the CHST in this manner was to "enhance the transparency and accountability of federal support for health while continuing to provide provinces and territories with the flexibility to allocate funds among social programs according to their respective priorities."[123] Romanow had recommended a targeted CHT, in order to ensure that the provinces actually spent federal money on health care—not on tax cuts, lawnmowers, or other unrelated items.[124]

From Ottawa's perspective, a separate health transfer makes good political sense: it allows the federal government to show the public exactly how much money it spends on health care, instead of giving the provincial governments a block grant for all social programs and letting them decide how to spend it. In effect, Ottawa will now determine exactly how many federal dollars each province can spend on hospitals and other delivery systems. The provinces complained that Ottawa had fixed the 62–38 split between the CHT and CST arbitrarily, without consulting them; this was a direct violation of the 1999 Social Union Framework Agreement (SUFA), which requires the federal government to consult the provinces before making any significant changes to shared-cost programs.[125] (We will discuss the SUFA in Chapter 9.)

In March 2004, after announcing yet another funding increase for health care in its latest budget, the federal government claimed that its direct provincial transfers— under the CHST, the Health Reform Transfer, and other rubrics—amounted to 32 percent of provincial health-care spending in 2003–04. After factoring in equalization and direct federal spending on health (e.g., the delivery of services to Aboriginal Canadians on reserves), "the federal government is providing about $34 billion a year, or about 40% of all national public spending on health care in Canada."[126] As usual, the provinces begged to differ. At the July 2004 meeting of the Council of the Federation, the premiers argued that the new federal funding was insufficient. They echoed Romanow's call to raise the cash transfer portion of the CHT to cover 25 percent of their health care costs.[127]

This call for more cash, and fewer tax points, is somewhat puzzling, especially coming from the premiers. The cash portion is already projected to grow to two-thirds of the CHT in 2007–08, compared to a little over half in 2003–04.[128] More important, a greater reliance on cash transfers could strengthen Ottawa's case for more direct federal involvement in policy-making on health care. As we have seen, more federal cash equals more federal control. Since the federal deficit disappeared in the late 1990s, Ottawa has steadily increased the number of conditions on transfer payments and taken other steps to reassert federal paramountcy in provincial jurisdictions.[129] The unilateral withdrawal of federal cash from shared-cost programs in the 1995 budget produced an unprecedented degree of parity in the policy fields dearest to Canadians' hearts.[130] Why would the provinces continue to demand greater infusions of money from Ottawa and risk a revival of federal paramountcy? The answer may lie in the 1999 SUFA, which recognizes the legitimacy of the federal spending power while imposing conditions on its use in provincial jurisdictions (see Chapter 9).

Unfortunately for the provinces, the federal government has already imposed unilateral changes on health-care transfers without following the notice and consultation requirements in the SUFA.

The overriding importance of the health-care issue in recent years has provoked heated battles between the federal and provincial governments. The recurring conflicts over money and control, fuelled by a competition for political credit (and damage control), have thrown a harsh light on our federal institutions. Ottawa and the provinces cannot even agree on the size of their respective contributions to health-care costs, let alone the proper use of the federal spending power or the enforcement of intergovernmental agreements. The source of these failings can be traced to our ad hoc system of IGRs, in which decisions are made by consensus (as opposed to formal voting rules), and to the refusal of Canadian governments to yield even a modicum of their individual sovereignty to an enforcement body.[131] Compared to other federal states, Canada's IGR mechanisms are undeveloped and ineffective; as a result, "Canada has been less well-equipped to manage the contemporary challenges of interdependence than most federations."[132] We will explore these problems in the next section.

NO MORE WATERTIGHT COMPARTMENTS: INTERGOVERNMENTAL RELATIONS IN CANADA

If the fiscal imbalance between the two levels of government has had a marked impact on the evolution of Canadian federalism, so has the practical overlap between the powers listed in sections 91–95 of the *Constitution*. The scope of modern government was unimaginable to the Fathers of Confederation. Today the federal and provincial governments are active in fields that are not explicitly assigned by the *Constitution* to either order of government. Matters such as consumer protection, multiculturalism, and environmental protection do not fall easily into "watertight compartments." As a result, governments—more specifically, members of the political and permanent executives—work together constantly to develop and implement policies in virtually every field of activity.

Historically, the key intergovernmental relationships have been those (1) between the national government and one or more provincial governments and (2) among the provinces themselves. Relations in the former category are now labelled "FPT," for "federal, provincial and territorial"; the shorthand for the latter is "PT." In legal and constitutional terms, the three territories do not enjoy the status of provinces; they are created and controlled by the federal government. Strictly speaking, therefore, Ottawa's relationship to Nunavut or Yukon is not "intergovernmental." Nonetheless, the leaders of their governments are now included in most meetings of the First Ministers, and they have been full participants in the Annual Premiers' Conference (now the Council of the Federation) since 1991.[133]

In the Canadian federation, as noted earlier, relationships among the various governments are managed by the executive branch of government. Members of the political and permanent executives meet regularly to share information, hammer out agreements, and try to resolve disputes. These activities are collectively called "executive federalism." The formal relations among the executives of Canada's senior governments occur at three distinct levels:

1. *Peak:* First Ministers' Meetings (the leaders of some or all FPT governments), the Council of the Federation, and bilateral meetings between two or more government leaders.

2. *Ministerial:* Some or all of the FPT or PT Cabinet ministers responsible for a particular policy field; for example, the Canadian Council of Ministers of the Environment (FPT) or the Council of Ministers of Education, Canada (PT).

3. *Official:* The FPT or PT public servants who make and enforce policy in a specific field; for example, the Deputy Ministers' Committee, which supports the work of the Canadian Council of Ministers of the Environment.[134]

Peak Institutions

The peak institution, at the FPT level, is the First Ministers' Conference (FMC). (After the failure of the intergovernmental bargaining over the Meech Lake and Charlottetown Accords, these events were renamed First Ministers' Meetings, or FMMs, perhaps to lower public expectations by presenting a more relaxed image.[135]) The first official FMC was the 1906 Dominion–Provincial Conference on fiscal relations; the second was held in 1918, and the third in 1927.[136] The FMC did not become a regular event until after the fiscal crisis of the Great Depression, which prompted a Royal Commission to recommend frequent Dominion–Provincial Conferences, with a permanent secretariat to coordinate IGRs. When the welfare state began to take shape after World War II, FMCs became annual events. While their official purpose was to discuss fiscal relations, and especially the creation of national shared-cost programs in provincial policy fields, they quickly became the most prominent arena for federal–provincial combat. By the 1960s, the Quiet Revolution in Quebec had sparked a more aggressive attitude on the part of several premiers. The agenda now included oil and gas pricing, constitutional amendment, and provincial demands for more powers and greater autonomy from Ottawa (i.e., both independence and parity).

Despite the increasingly hostile dynamic, the First Ministers met 21 times between 1971 and 1983. (The 1980–82 constitutional negotiations are discussed in Chapters 9 and 10.) Over time, "Meetings became more structured, with an agenda defined well in advance and greater follow-up."[137] The Canadian Intergovernmental Conference Secretariat (CICS) was created in 1973, to provide logistical support for FMCs and other intergovernmental meetings. Its limited mandate left the responsibility for agenda-setting, compliance, and policy development to the individual governments; there was no genuinely intergovernmental mechanism for dispute resolution and enforcement. During this period, some premiers played to the television cameras; they aggressively challenged the legitimacy of the federal government, and claimed an equal right to speak for Canadians. Although he agreed to a provincial request to entrench FMCs in the *Constitution Act, 1982*—albeit only for a limited time—Prime Minister Trudeau came to loathe them.[138] His successor, Brian Mulroney, promised Canadians a new era of intergovernmental harmony and cooperation. He chaired several FMCs on social and economic issues, Aboriginal concerns, and constitutional reform. (The latter, which produced the Meech Lake and Charlottetown Accords, are discussed in Chapter 9.) The contentious constitutional debates ultimately poisoned the relationship between Ottawa and the provinces. Consequently, little was accomplished at the other FMCs.

Under the Chrétien government (1993-2003), formal gatherings of government leaders were infrequent. Prime Minister Chrétien chaired only seven formal gatherings of the FPT First Ministers. Unlike the highly charged and media-driven FMCs of the 1970s and 1980s, these were private and relatively low-key FMMs.[139] None was devoted to constitutional change; as we will see in Chapter 9, the defeat of the Charlottetown Accord in 1992 led Canada's governments to pursue nonconstitutional avenues for resolving conflicts within the federation. Therefore, the FMMs of the Chrétien era produced agreements and Accords—on internal trade, the social union, and health-care renewal—which were, at best, morally binding on all governments. Few of these deals carried the imprimatur of the Quebec government, which was controlled during most of this period by the separatist Bloc Québécois.

For the most part, Chrétien preferred to discuss matters of shared concern in less public and formal settings. During the late 1990s, Chrétien led several "Team Canada" trade missions to foreign countries. He would invite premiers and business leaders to accompany him, using his prestige as the prime minister of Canada to entice foreign businesspeople to strike deals with Canadian entrepreneurs. During the lengthy airplane trips to and from the "Team Canada" destinations, Chrétien would hold informal talks with the premiers on board. There are no written records of these conversations, but it is reasonable to assume that the participants found it somewhat easier to reach an understanding in the absence of television cameras and entourages anxious to score political points.

Prime Minister Paul Martin, like former Prime Minister Mulroney, came to office promising a new era of FPT collaboration. The preceding discussion of the recent wrangles over health-care funding does not bode well for this commitment; few provincial governments have forgotten that Martin was the architect of the now-notorious 1995 federal budget. The tense dynamic between Ottawa and the provinces will likely persist, despite the presence of Liberal governments in Ontario, Quebec, and British Columbia.

In September 2004, the much-anticipated Health Care Summit of the FPT First Ministers nearly broke down over money. At the August meeting of the Council of the Federation, the premiers had demanded that the federal government allocate a total of $13 billion per year to health-care spending. Ottawa countered by offering substantially less money. At the start of the September 2004 Summit, the premiers submitted a revised plan calling for an additional $5.2 billion in annual health-care funding.[140] After the first day of the three-day Summit, no agreement between the governments seemed possible. Finally, in the early hours of the last day, the federal government agreed to spend an additional $18 billion on health care over the following six years, and exempted the province of Quebec from most of the reporting requirements imposed on the other provinces in exchange for the new funding.[141]

The federal government promised the provinces that it would negotiate a separate agreement on equalization payments at a First Ministers' Meeting in October. This time, the talks failed to produce a deal. Danny Williams, the Conservative premier of Newfoundland and Labrador, walked out of the meeting before the talks even started. He and Nova Scotia Premier John Hamm claimed the prime minister had promised that the federal government would not penalize their provinces for their growing oil and gas revenues by cutting their equalization payments, and then reneged on that promise just before the October meeting. Faced with the possible defection of at least one Liberal MP from Newfoundland, the prime minister tried to negotiate a deal with the two Atlantic premiers.[142] In February 2005, Prime Minister Martin finally signed Accords with Williams and Hamm—which prompted immediate calls for similar deals from other premiers.

As for the FMC as an institution, it has no more legal or constitutional status than it had in 1906. It lacks "a set of fixed rules and procedures, an established organization, and a set of distinct incentives, disincentives and constraints that are capable of influencing or shaping the behaviour and strategies of political actors."[143]

Until 2003, the peak institution at the PT level was the Annual Premiers' Conference. Since its inception in 1960, the APC had held annual meetings to discuss issues of common importance. It was chaired, on a rotating basis, by each of the provinces in turn. It lacked a permanent secretariat or staff, relying instead on whatever resources the host government for each year could provide. The turnover of premiers and territorial leaders varied: sometimes there was considerable continuity from one year to the next, while other annual meetings turned into get-acquainted sessions for new members. As a result, the institutional memory of the APC was unreliable and it could not pursue goals that required more than a year or two to accomplish.

The initiative for the new Council of the Federation came from the Quebec Liberal Party, which proposed a more institutionalized forum for interprovincial cooperation in its 2001 report on Quebec's place in Canada.[144] In spring 2003, Quebec elected a federalist government for the first time in almost a decade. The new premier, Liberal Jean Charest, immediately made the Council of the Federation a top priority. Its purpose, according to the December 2003 founding agreement, is to create a formal and stable structure that can exercise effective "leadership on national issues of importance to provinces and territories." The council will meet at least twice a year and will receive and consider reports from PT ministerial and official committees (discussed below). A steering committee, made up of deputy ministers responsible for intergovernmental relations, and a permanent secretariat will carry out the work of the council between the twice-yearly meetings of the PT government leaders.[145] In principle, they will be responsible for monitoring progress on the strategic goals set by the council and for helping to identify shared priorities for future interprovincial collaboration.

In practice, however, the Council of the Federation may amount to little more than "a slightly more formalized APC." If this is the case, "it will likely serve only to reinforce the current tendency of premiers to get together principally to fashion a common position against Ottawa" in the never-ending battle over money and power.[146] This pessimistic assessment overlooks one positive aspect of the council: the full participation, indeed the leading role, of Quebec. After years of sitting on the sidelines or backing out of intergovernmental agreements at the last minute,[147] the new Liberal government in Quebec has become the strongest advocate of "collaborative federalism." Whether it can sustain this position, in the face of growing unpopularity at home and Ottawa's increasingly assertive use of the federal spending power, is uncertain.

In addition to these national peak institutions, the Council of Atlantic Premiers and the Western Premiers' Conference meet at least once a year. (The latter includes the territorial leaders.) These regional PT groups have established working relationships with their counterparts in neighbouring U.S. states (the Western Governors' Association and the New England Governors, respectively[148]). Since 9/11, the primary focus of the annual cross-border meetings has been trade and border security, although the PT leaders and governors also deal with economic development, environmental policy, and energy issues (the latter gaining particular importance after the August 2003 blackout in eastern North America). The Western premiers and territorial leaders have also demanded a seat at the table in international trade negotiations,[149] a request that Ottawa has yet to fully accept.

Ministerial and Official Councils

The peak institutions of executive federalism receive considerable media coverage. However, most of the actual work is accomplished at the ministerial and official levels. The FPT and PT ministers responsible for particular policy sectors meet regularly, as do their deputy ministers and other senior civil servants. Some of these are national councils, others are regional forums. In 2003, the CICS reported 47 FPT and PT ministerial meetings, compared to 43 meetings of officials. These numbers are consistent with the yearly averages since 1974.[150] (Note that the CICS data are incomplete; they do not necessarily include intergovernmental meetings of officials.) There is a growing trend for PT ministers and officials to meet without their federal counterparts, ostensibly to coordinate work on purely provincial matters. In reality, these gatherings—whether peak, ministerial, or official—seem to be less concerned with interprovincial issues and more focused on forging a "common front" against Ottawa.[151] The CICS data are revealing: FPT meetings of ministers and/or officials are often preceded by a gathering of the provincial and territorial participants. This pattern suggests a provincial awareness of the danger of a federal "divide and conquer" strategy, such as the manoeuvre by Prime Minister Trudeau that led to the adoption of the *Constitution Act, 1982* (Chapter 9).

At present, some ministers and officials are abandoning the traditional ad hoc approach to intergovernmental relations. In some sectors, they have established more or less formal and institutionalized procedures for collective decision-making and the sharing of information. At the FPT level, the best example is probably the Canadian Council of Ministers of the Environment (CCME). It is co-chaired by the federal Environment minister and a provincial minister; the latter position rotates annually among the PT governments. The CCME has a permanent secretariat in Winnipeg, with a staff averaging eight full-time positions. The secretariat oversees the work of several committees of deputy ministers and other officials. The council also collaborates with the Council of Energy Ministers on shared files, including air quality and climate change.[152]

Of the purely PT organizations, the Council of Ministers of Education, Canada (CMEC) is the oldest and most well established. It was created in 1967 to provide a forum for interprovincial cooperation and a clearing-house for information about new policy challenges.[153] Although the CMEC has long had a secretariat, its functions have been restricted to administrative tasks. The agenda of the CMEC fluctuated from year to year, in response to emerging issues and crises. At the annual meetings, most of the time was devoted to information-sharing; there was no mechanism to set strategic goals or to follow up on previous agreements. The CMEC reviewed its structure and operations in 2003–04, with one primary goal: to become a partner with Ottawa and the Council of the Federation in policy-making and implementation.

In addition to the formal intergovernmental meetings just described, there are countless informal contacts between ministers and officials. Most of these arise in the day-to-day business of administering policy in shared jurisdictions. Some involve specialists in intergovernmental relations, most of whom work in discrete departments (e.g., the Federal–Provincial Relations Office in Ottawa); others involve policy experts looking for "best practices" and other useful advice, or members of the various intergovernmental committees that do the heavy lifting for the political executives. As the number of FPT and PT councils and forums has grown in recent years, so has the volume of intergovernmental agreements (numbering somewhere between 1500 and 2000 in 2003[154]). These require constant contacts among the officials charged with implementing them.

One final point on IGRs: it is difficult to gauge the degree of nongovernmental participation in these meetings. As we noted at the beginning of our discussion of federalism, Aboriginal groups and other NGOs have demanded seats at the table when matters of particular importance to them are discussed. To date, these demands do not appear to have met with much success. Aboriginal leaders have been invited to participate in FPT meetings of ministers and officials responsible for Aboriginal affairs; they were also involved in the 2003 meeting of the FPT Ministerial Council on Social Policy Renewal, which reviewed the SUFA (Chapter 9). But they were barred from the first two meetings of the Council of the Federation, despite a public appeal by the leader of the Assembly of First Nations for inclusion in the July 2004 discussions on health care. At present, the status of Aboriginal and non-Aboriginal NGOs seems to depend on the political will of the senior governments. There is no formal provision for their participation in IGR institutions.

■ Federalism and "Glocalization"

In the coming years, relations between the federal and provincial governments will be further complicated by the participation of two additional levels of government: supranational and municipal. It is often argued that globalization has shifted policy-making and enforcement authority upward to supranational agencies, and downward to local bodies (hence the new buzzword "glocalization"[155]). Any transfer of power to Canadian cities should not be overstated; although some world capitals are becoming semiautonomous "city regions,"[156] our municipalities remain "what they have always been: mechanisms by which local people arrange for public infrastructure and the provision of local public services."[157] Nonetheless, they appear set to become key players in the politics of Canadian federalism. The growing interdependence of policy-making and -implementation means that global decisions, as well as national and provincial decisions, have direct impacts on local communities. For example, international commitments to reduce agricultural subsidies—commitments that the United States, among other key producers, see fit to ignore—have worsened the damage caused by poor weather, volatile markets, and the discovery of "mad cow disease" in one Alberta animal in 2003. The effects are felt most acutely at the local level:

> *Economic hardship strains marriages, which burdens local social services; it affects the behavior of children in school; it reinforces rural–urban migration, which erodes the social capacity of cities, while leaving rural localities languishing in anomie.*[158]

Given the severity of these local problems, it is both unfair and unrealistic to expect municipal governments to deal with them unassisted. It may be equally unfair to deny local governments an opportunity to participate in provincial, national, and even global decision-making, particularly where environmental and immigration issues are involved. In recognition of this fact, and of the growing political independence of cities, Ontario Premier Dalton McGuinty signed a memorandum of understanding with the Association of Municipalities of Ontario (AMO) in August 2004. It guarantees a role for AMO representatives in future intergovernmental discussions with possible ramifications for urban governments.[159] Toronto's city council was outraged by the agreement, which it interpreted as a denial of the city's special status as the largest urban government in Canada. Its mayor and several councillors argued that Toronto should be able to deal directly with the federal government. McGuinty tried to reassure the city's leaders that the memorandum did not forestall direct relations between Toronto and Ottawa, but the dispute threatened to split the AMO.

The current federal government under Paul Martin has put cities at the centre of its policy agenda, despite the fact that municipal institutions fall under provincial jurisdiction (section 92[8]).[160] Cities and towns have no independent constitutional status. They are legal creations of their provincial governments, although they receive much of their funding from property taxes and other local sources. In the 1970s the Trudeau government dabbled unsuccessfully in urban affairs; it established a department responsible for cities, which accomplished little and was finally disbanded in the early 1980s.

Canada's largest cities bore the brunt of federal and provincial "downloading" in the 1990s, especially with regard to social assistance. They have struggled to maintain their existing infrastructure—e.g., roads, waterworks, and public transit—while their expanding populations have demanded new facilities. The implications of the fiscal crisis in municipal governance are profound. Most Canadians (almost 80 percent in the 2001 census[161]) live in cities or towns. They need safe housing and streets, clean drinking water, and adequate policing. Canada cannot meet its international environmental commitments, notably the Kyoto Protocol on Climate Change (discussed later in this chapter), unless millions of Canadians switch from private vehicles to public transit.

Faced with these problems, Martin promised a "new deal for cities" when he took office in December 2003. He appointed a Parliamentary Secretary to the Prime Minister with special responsibility for municipal affairs; this position was upgraded to a Ministry of State in the July 2004 Cabinet. In early 2004 Martin made good on his earlier pledge to exempt municipal governments from the federal goods and services tax (GST) on their purchases; the federal government predicted that this would amount to a $7 billion saving for all cities over the next 10 years.[162] In the 2004 federal election campaign, he unveiled a package of policies aimed at helping municipalities and giving them a formal role in national politics (e.g., by consulting with mayors during the annual pre-budget consultations).[163] However, the March 2004 budget failed to give cities what they really wanted: a share of the federal tax on gasoline. Martin and his Finance minister, Ralph Goodale, argued that the national government could not afford to give up the tax, even though pump prices at the time were at near-historic high levels because of jitters in the world oil market over the war in Iraq. The thrust of all these promises—delivered and otherwise—was simple: Ottawa would do whatever it could, within its own jurisdiction, to address the fiscal crisis of local governments.

A tax break is one thing; the direct transfer of money from the federal government to municipalities is considerably more problematic. Although provincial governments have accepted federal participation in specific urban projects—e.g., inner-city redevelopment or upgrading the facilities surrounding ports[164]—they are less welcoming toward proposals for long-term federal funding of municipal activities. Provincial governments argue that if Ottawa wants to give money to cities, it "should all flow through provincial governments so that the latter can ensure that [it] is used in accordance with provincial priorities and policies."[165] Future federal efforts to subsidize cash-strapped cities will likely complicate the emerging three-way relationship, in which the provinces will try to remain the "middleman."

At the supranational level, the NAFTA and other binding treaties between states may alter the balance of power between subnational governments (e.g., American states or Canadian provinces) and national governments. Before the 1980s, international trade agreements usually focused on **tariff** barriers to the import of foreign goods. Under section 91 of the *BNA Act,* the federal government had jurisdiction over tariffs and other import policies. The global push toward open markets forced states to reduce or eliminate tariffs. Recent rounds of trade negotiations, whether at the World Trade Organization (WTO) or within particular regions—such as the European Union (EU) or North America (e.g., NAFTA)—have focused on **nontariff barriers** to trade, many of which fall under provincial jurisdiction. Recall that under the JCPC's *Labour Conventions* ruling, the federal government has the power to make binding treaties but lacks the power to implement them in fields assigned to the provinces under section 92. Consequently, the new emphasis on reducing nontariff barriers has forced the federal government to seek provincial cooperation in the negotiation and implementation of trade deals with other countries.[166] Although the premiers do not enjoy formal standing with the WTO and other bodies, the division of jurisdictions in the *BNA Act* gives them considerable capacity to frustrate the implementation of trade treaties that impinge—as most do—on their policy fields.[167]

To date, the level of intergovernmental conflict in trade matters has been relatively low.[168] This could change, as the PT leaders—nationally, regionally and individually—become more aggressive in their pursuit of independent relationships with other countries and U.S. states. (One interesting symbol of this aggression is the renaming of Alberta's IGR department: it is now the Department of International and Intergovernmental Relations.) At its first meeting in July 2004, the Council of the Federation unanimously demanded "full provincial and territorial participation in Canada's international activities that affect their jurisdiction and responsibilities, including development of positions, involvement in negotiations, and management of disputes."[169] This demand makes some sense, given the increasing emphasis in global trade talks on culture, education, and other provincial jurisdictions. Ottawa, unsurprisingly, does not quite see it this way. It generally denies provincial governments their own seats at the bargaining table, preferring instead to consult with the provinces on national priorities and implementation mechanisms.[170] Even when there are no binding international agreements at stake, the federal government is determined to "maintain its exclusive role in international affairs"; for example, "it excluded Ontario from the joint Canada–U.S. inquiry concerning the electricity blackout in the summer of 2003."[171]

Canada's participation in global environmental Accords has already provoked sharp and highly public disagreements. The 1997 Kyoto Protocol on Climate Change is the most recent irritant between Ottawa and the provinces, especially Alberta. Before the Kyoto talks, the federal government had promised the provinces that it would agree to reduce Canada's emissions of "greenhouse gases" (particularly carbon dioxide) to 1990 levels by the year 2010. During the negotiations with other states, Canada agreed to additional cuts in emissions.[172] The provinces were placated by a promise from the federal minister of the Environment that Kyoto would not be ratified if the costs were too high. For the next five years, while the federal government considered whether to ratify the Protocol, the senior governments worked together to develop a plan to implement Canada's commitments on climate change. The collaboration was fairly harmonious, but it produced few results. The main reason for the lack of progress was the opposition of eight provinces (Manitoba and Quebec were the exceptions).[173]

When, in September 2002, former Prime Minister Chrétien suddenly announced that his government would ratify the Kyoto Protocol by the end of the year, the Government of Alberta reacted with fury and defiance. Premier Ralph Klein argued that the Kyoto agreement, which bound Canada to reduce its emissions of "greenhouse gases" (particularly carbon dioxide) to 1990 levels by 2010, would inflict severe damage on the fossil-fuel industries in his province. Alberta's economy is driven by oil and natural gas; the extraction and refining of these commodities produces significant amounts of carbon dioxide. Moreover, meeting the Protocol targets would require Canadians to burn less fossil fuel in their cars, furnaces, and power plants, thus shrinking the domestic market for Alberta oil and gas. After U.S. President George W. Bush had announced in 2001 that his country would not ratify Kyoto, which freed American fossil-fuel producers and consumers from complying with its provisions, Klein's arguments[174] found receptive ears outside Alberta. Why, some Canadians wondered, should they have to pay the high cost of meeting the Kyoto emission targets when their American competitors did not? And what was the point of ratifying Kyoto when the world's largest producer of greenhouse gases refused to make it work?

The opposing provinces demanded that Ottawa pay the full cost of meeting the Kyoto targets; when Ottawa refused, they boycotted a meeting of FPT energy and environment ministers. The House of Commons subsequently passed a symbolic resolution in favour of ratification, but only after the prime minister cracked the whip on his Liberal backbenchers. Alberta, British Columbia, and Ontario have initiated their own "Action Plans" on climate change, bypassing the Kyoto process. In any event, enforcing the Kyoto Protocol was a moot point until it was ratified by countries that collectively produce at least 55 percent of the world's greenhouse gases; it took effect in February 2005.

The impact of Canada's federal system on our participation in global economic and environmental treaties has received considerable attention. Less obvious, although no less significant, are the potential effects of globalization on the division of powers between Ottawa and the provinces. Those effects will likely vary across policy fields. One recent study of NAFTA's Chapter 11 rules, which regulate **foreign direct investment (FDI),** suggests that their enforcement will shift some power from the provinces to Ottawa. The FDI provisions require Canadian governments to treat American and Mexican companies as though they were domestically owned. They effectively prohibit the imposition of laws and regulations that put foreign-owned companies at a disadvantage, relative both to locally owned companies and to the jurisdiction in which the company is based. These might include labour standards and benefits, environmental regulations, or local procurement policies. If an individual or corporate investor believes that a Canadian government has violated Chapter 11, that investor can seek a legal ruling from a NAFTA tribunal. If the tribunal rules in favour of the investor, the tribunal can order the national government to pay monetary damages—even if the alleged violation of the NAFTA treaty was committed by a provincial government. In effect, the federal government is liable, as a signatory to NAFTA, for provincial laws over which it has no direct control.[175]

Damage awards ordered by NAFTA tribunals are enforceable in the domestic courts of the host country. The Supreme Court of Canada would have to decide whether the costs of breaching Chapter 11 should be borne by the federal government or by the province that lost the case. In the process, it would surely be asked whether the federal government could legislate in areas of provincial jurisdiction in order to ensure future compliance. As we saw in the earlier discussion of Supreme Court jurisprudence on the trade and commerce clause of section 91 (page 396), the court has recently extended the federal government's power to regulate internal trade. Moreover, the post-1949 revival of the "national concern" doctrine could have an impact on jurisprudence; under NAFTA and other binding trade agreements, "subject matters that would have traditionally fallen into provincial power now take on an importance that transcends provincial boundaries."[176] Therefore, globalization could produce "an expansion of federal powers that could intrude deeply into areas of exclusive provincial jurisdiction," partly as a result of Supreme Court rulings arising from NAFTA appeals.[177] This could signal at least a temporary revival of federal paramountcy. On the other hand, the fact that the national government has to take provincial concerns into account when it negotiates such agreements in the first place implies a greater degree of parity than meets the eye.[178]

Whatever the long-term impact of NAFTA on provincial jurisdictions, one broader point is clear; the territorial logic of federalism is in direct conflict with the nonterritorial logic of globalization. Whereas provincial jurisdiction—e.g., section 92(13): control over "Property and Civil Rights in the Province"—is territorially bound, NAFTA and other trade treaties transcend (indeed, tend to erode) political and geographic borders.[179] As the nation–state yields more of its sovereignty to supranational organizations, it also loses some of its authority to actors outside the formal constitution: "the private sector, communities and civil society."[180]

Territorial forms of organization are also under assault from new technologies, including the Internet.[181] The ease and low cost of communication in cyberspace reduce the political salience of territory, and provoke public impatience with the "boundary maintenance" that preoccupies political leaders in federations. They also allow nonstate actors to form networks and share information without regard for geographic distance or administrative demarcations. As Pierre Marc Johnson (a former premier of Quebec) recently observed, "a data transfer that used to cost $150,000 in 1970 only cost 12¢ in 1999."[182] If knowledge is power, as it surely is in the information economy, then the rapid and cheap diffusion of knowledge implies that national and provincial states are losing some of their capacity to resist challenges to their authority. "In short, [new communication technologies] give federalism the dated look of a concept designed for a territorial and segmented political world that is rapidly disappearing."[183]

Paradoxically, another recent global phenomenon—the "war on terror"—has temporarily reversed the erosion of international borders,[184] but it also has the potential to empower the national government at the expense of the provinces. A renewed emphasis on national security "will heighten the relative importance of the federal government in the eyes of citizens," and require—or permit—the federal government to respond with policies that trench on provincial jurisdictions.[185]

One possible example is the emerging national policy on public health. Whereas the delivery of health care, as we have seen, is an exclusively provincial field, the creation and management of public-health programs (education, prevention, coordination) is shared between Ottawa and the provinces. Early in the new century, public health became a matter of urgent national concern. The 9/11 attacks provoked fears of bioterrorism, which were fuelled by subsequent panics over anthrax and other biological weapons. In 2003, Canada suffered a serious outbreak of SARS (severe acute respiratory syndrome), which killed several people and hurt tourism (especially in Toronto). SARS also highlighted Canada's vulnerability to new global epidemics, and revealed the shortcomings of our public-health system—in particular, the lack of coordination among the federal and provincial governments and the effects of sustained underfunding. In October 2003 the National Advisory Committee on SARS and Public Health recommended the creation of a National Agency for Public Health, headed by a new chief public health officer.[186] The committee's chair, Dr. David Naylor, called the lack of intergovernmental collaboration during the SARS crisis "a national embarrassment," a sentiment later endorsed by the Ontario Commission of Inquiry into the outbreak.[187]

In September 2003, before the National Advisory Committee issued its report, the federal, provincial, and territorial (FPT) Health ministers met to discuss public health. They agreed to "clarify roles and responsibilities for preventing and responding to public health threats," while respecting jurisdictional boundaries, and to strengthen intergovernmental coordination in advance of the next epidemic.[188] The language of the agreement does not indicate that Ottawa would take the lead role in public health; the provincial Health ministers appear to have assumed that jurisdiction would remain in their hands. In December 2003, however, incoming Prime Minister Paul Martin created a new Cabinet portfolio, the Ministry of State for Public Health, and appointed Dr. Carolyn Bennett to the position. Her mandate was to create a new Canada Public Health Agency, a centrepiece of the February 2004 Throne Speech.

While the agency will operate under the aegis of Health Canada, its creation appears to be related to the simultaneous announcement of a new federal Department of Public Safety and Emergency Preparedness. Significantly, the discussion paper issued by Bennett in the spring of 2004 begins, "Over the past three years [i.e., since 2001], concerns have grown about the capacity of Canada's public health system to anticipate and respond effectively to public health threats."[189] Although the letter refers to West Nile virus and "mad cow disease" (bovine spongiform encephalopathy, or BSE) as well as SARS, neither was perceived as a significant threat to Canada until 2002 at the earliest. The implicit connection between the new federal assertiveness in the field of public health, and the post-9/11 concern about bioterrorism, is made explicit in the Naylor report:

> Compounding the challenges of dealing with emerging and re-emerging infectious diseases is the threat of the accidental or intentional release of biological agents as highlighted by the intentional release of anthrax spores in the USA in the Fall of 2003.[190]

Naylor also offered some interesting comments about federal jurisdiction:

> From a constitutional perspective, public health is primarily a provincial concern. However, the federal government has authority to legislate aspects of public health owing to its powers over, variously, the criminal law, matters of national concern for the maintenance of "peace, order and good government," quarantine provisions and national borders, and trade and commerce of an interprovincial or international nature.[191]

The references to the criminal law power and the "national concern" branch of POGG indicate a link between national security, on the one hand, and public health on the other.[192] It appears that the federal government wanted to assume the leading role in a policy field that is, at the very least, a shared jurisdiction with the provinces, and found a convenient justification in post-9/11 security concerns.

CONCLUSION

At Confederation, Canada's federal system was characterized by independence and the paramountcy of the national government. Today, it is a highly interdependent system in which the provinces and territories claim parity with Ottawa. In the absence of a dominant central government, federations cannot function properly without strong mechanisms for coordination, collaboration, and the enforcement of mutual agreements. As this chapter has demonstrated, the absence of such mechanisms in Canada has produced decades of intergovernmental bickering and little effective cooperation (at least at the peak level of IGRs). As we will see in Chapter 9, there has been no shortage of proposed reforms to bring Canada's federal institutions up to date. Since 1992, however, the emphasis has shifted from the high-stakes game of constitutional amendment to the gentler arena of nonconstitutional renewal; some of the developments discussed in this chapter, notably the Council of the Federation, illustrate these incremental and nonbinding processes.

There is little prospect that Canadian federalism will ever return to its hierarchical roots, despite the current fiscal strength of the federal government. Granted, two current developments—the "new deal" for cities and a larger post-9/11 role for the federal government—seem to indicate the desire of the Martin government to reassert federal paramountcy. A third, the potential impact of NAFTA on the division of powers, could make that task easier. Ironically, Martin himself provided the biggest impetus toward parity when he cut transfers to the provinces in his 1995 budget. Now that the "deficit wars" of the 1990s have given way to the "surplus wars" of this decade, the federal Liberals want to re-establish a degree of hierarchy by using the federal spending power.

However, the provincial governments have solidified their united front against Ottawa. They are adamant in their refusal to surrender the parity that they achieved, at a high cost, during the downsizing and "downloading" of the 1990s. Chapter 9 traces the current struggle to rewrite the rules for IGRs, in which the federal government seeks to formalize the spending power and the provinces insist on safeguarding their exclusive jurisdiction over social policy.

GLOSSARY OF KEY TERMS

Ad hoc: A Latin term meaning "temporary" or "expedient." For example, the prime minister may establish an ad hoc committee of ministers to deal with a short-term issue, and disband it after it reports its recommendations back to the full Cabinet.

Amending formula: The formal process for changing a written constitution. The formula is usually included in the constitution itself. Amending a constitution is a complex and difficult process, requiring a broad consensus among the key players in the political system. Because the constitution sets out the rules of the political game, and it is intended to provide continuity and stability to the political system, the amending formula must protect the written constitution against changes that are purely temporary in nature, or that violate the core principles on which the political system is based (e.g., democracy and federalism).

Amendment: Any proposed or actual alteration in the wording of a written constitution. An amendment can insert one or more new provisions into the constitution, it can delete one or more existing provisions, or it can rewrite part of a constitution to keep it up to date with changing circumstances.

Block funding: A fiscal transfer from Ottawa to one or more provinces that imposes few, if any, conditions on the way the money is to be spent. For example, the 1995 CHST provided money for health care, PSE, and social assistance, without specifying the percentages to be spent in each policy field.

Common law: The collective term for the body of judicial rulings on a particular subject; e.g., the due-process rights of suspected criminals or the division of powers between governments.

Conditional grants: Transfer payments from Ottawa to one or more provinces, which come with strings attached. The recipient provinces must spend the money as directed by the federal government, or risk losing some or all of the transfer.

Constitutional convention: An unwritten principle of political practice, which gradually acquires binding force over time. It may evolve to fill a gap in the written constitution, or it may directly contradict the legal text. Conventions provide greater flexibility than the written constitution, allowing national institutions to adapt to changes in political culture. Unlike written constitutional law, conventions cannot be enforced by the courts; their violation may be punished only in the political arena.

Entrenched constitutional law: Written legal provisions that have been ratified through the appropriate amending formula, and that take priority over ordinary laws in case of a conflict.

Equalization: The federal government collects tax revenues from the richer or "have" provinces (usually British Columbia, Alberta, and Ontario) and distributes them among the poorer or "have-not" provinces (the other seven). The purpose of equalization payments is to ensure that every provincial government can provide "reasonably comparable" services to its citizens, without regard to the size of its tax base. Equalization payments may be used for any purpose; they are not conditional. The system was entrenched in the *Constitution Act, 1982* (section 36).

Executive federalism: The collective term for the relations among the political and permanent executives of Canada's senior governments.

Federal spending power: Ottawa's use of fiscal transfers to determine provincial priorities in areas of provincial jurisdiction, particularly health care, postsecondary education, and social assistance. It arises from the federal powers to tax (section 91[3]), to regulate public property (section 91[1A]), and to spend federal funds as it sees fit (section 106).[193] The taxing power provides Ottawa with more money than it needs to carry out its own constitutional responsibilities. The spending power allows Ottawa to transfer those excess revenues for purposes outside its areas of jurisdiction. The federal spending power is not explicitly defined in the *Constitution*.

Fiscal federalism: The term used to refer to the flow of money—both cash and tax points—from Ottawa to the provinces and territories. That money is supposed to redress both the vertical imbalance between the two senior levels of government, and the horizontal imbalance among the "have" and "have-not" provinces.

Foreign direct investment (FDI): Refers to any business or other undertaking that operates in Canada and is owned (in whole or in part) by non-Canadians.

Intergovernmental relations (IGRs): In a federation, frequent conflicts flare up between two or more levels of government. The processes for resolving those conflicts at the political level (as distinct from court rulings on the division of powers) are collectively termed "intergovernmental relations." In Canada, IGRs entail more than the resolution of conflicts over jurisdiction and resources: joint policy-making and implementation are also involved.

Interstate federalism: A political system in which regional and intergovernmental conflicts are resolved by bargaining among the various political units. Interstate federalism is premised on the belief that the premiers are the most effective spokespersons for their respective regions. It is analogous to international diplomacy, in which sovereign states negotiate solutions to their common problems. Literally, "interstate" means "between states."

Intrastate federalism: A political system in which regional and intergovernmental conflicts are resolved within representative national institutions. For example, the upper house of the German federal Parliament (Bundesrat) is made up of delegations from the *Länd* (state) governments, a majority of whom must approve all legislation proposed by the national executive. In an intrastate federation, unlike an interstate federation, the premiers are not the sole legitimate representatives of their respective regions. The task of representing the regions in national politics is carried out by national, not provincial, politicians. "Intrastate" means "within the state."

Judicial Committee of the Privy Council (JCPC): A panel of British Law Lords, appointed by the Crown to act as the final court of appeals for the Empire (later the Commonwealth). Any apparent conflict between a British law (e.g., the *BNA Act*) and a statute adopted by a former colony could be given a definitive resolution only by the JCPC. Canada abolished the right of appeal to Westminster (the common name for the British government) in 1949; since then, the Supreme Court of Canada has been the highest court of appeal in Canadian law.

Judicial review: The process by which courts provide authoritative interpretations of law. Generally speaking, the judicial review of a particular law can be triggered in one of two ways: by a normal court case (criminal or civil), in which a dispute arises over a general issue of law (which must be settled during the appeals process, as described in Chapter 10), or by the reference procedure, in which the executive branch poses a direct question to the courts. In constitutional terms, judicial review is the interpretation of the *Constitution* (usually the written text, although a reference question may focus on a particular constitutional convention) and its application to a specific case. Before the *Charter of Rights* was proclaimed in 1982, most judicial review of the *Constitution Act, 1867* revolved around the division of powers between the federal and provincial governments; since 1982, judicial review has expanded to include questions about the precise meanings of rights and freedoms (see Chapter 10).

Nonentrenched law: An ordinary statute (either federal or provincial, but usually federal) that supplements the entrenched *Constitution* by applying a general principle to specific circumstances. Example: the *Canada Elections Act,* which sets out the rules and procedures by which Canadians exercise their democratic rights. Unlike entrenched constitutional law, nonentrenched laws may be amended through the normal legislative process; they do not take priority over regular statutes.

Nontariff barriers: Laws and policies that protect local producers of goods and services from competitors in other provinces or countries. These include government procurement policies that favour local suppliers; licensing regimes for service providers that restrict foreign access to local markets; and regulations that discourage the flow of goods, services, and direct investment across provincial or national borders (e.g., the imposition of stricter labour or environmental standards in one jurisdiction relative to another).

Reference cases: Court rulings on legal or constitutional issues that do not arise from lower-court appeals. In a reference case, the executive branch of government submits a question to the judicial branch for a definitive resolution. Governments may initiate reference cases in order to prevent future conflict between governments—by clarifying the division of powers in a federation, for example—or in an effort to resolve an issue that has already provoked disagreement. The 1981 *Patriation Reference* and the 1998 *Secession Reference* are the best-known examples, although there have been reference cases concerning the division of powers since the days of the JCPC.

Residual power: In a federal system, the written constitution divides existing policy jurisdictions between the two levels of government. It must also provide for the allocation of jurisdictions that were omitted by the drafters, and of unforeseen policy areas that may emerge long after the constitution takes effect, in order to avoid unresolvable disputes. The mechanism that allocates authority over unspecified policy areas is called the "residual power." It is normally assigned to one level of government or the other. In Canada, the residual power is assigned to the federal government by the preamble to section 91 of the *BNA Act* (the "POGG clause").

Shared-cost programs: The federal government pays part of the cost for provincial programs concerning health care, postsecondary education, and social assistance. When federal money comes with strings attached, requiring provinces to adapt their federally funded programs to standards set by Ottawa, it is called a **conditional grant.** Conditional grants allow Ottawa to use its spending power to influence policy-making in areas of provincial jurisdiction, usually to ensure that provincial programs follow national standards (e.g., the five principles of the *Canada Health Act*). In recent years, conditional grants have been phased out and replaced with block funding: the federal government contributes to provincial programs without specifying how the money will be spent, or in what specific areas.

Stare decisis: Latin for "the decision stands." In English common law, the doctrine that judges are bound to follow previous interpretations of the law (by higher courts, or by the same court). Over time, judicial precedents build up into a body of case law that shapes the application of the law for decades or even centuries to come.

Tariff: A policy mechanism that protects domestic producers (e.g., farmers and manufacturers) from competition by overseas producers. In essence, a tariff is a tax imposed by the national government on goods imported from other countries. The tariff raises the price of the imported item, so that it becomes more expensive to purchase than the equivalent domestically produced item. The lower purchase price encourages domestic consumers to buy goods produced in their own country, even though the actual production cost may be higher (and the goods of lower quality) than the competing foreign imports.

Tax points: The term used to describe the percentage of income tax revenue that Ottawa allocates to the provinces. One percent of tax revenue equals one tax point. Under tax rental agreements, the federal government sends each province a sum of money equal to the specified percentage of income tax collected in that province each year. Tax collection arrangements allow the provinces to set their own income tax levels, although the Canada Revenue Agency actually collects the taxes and remits the difference to the provincial government (except in Quebec, which collects its own share of income tax). In effect, the transferal of tax points from Ottawa to the provinces is an indirect form of block funding; Ottawa has no say over how a provincial government spends its own tax revenues, even those that the federal government collects on its behalf.

Ultra vires: Latin for "beyond the power of." When a court rules that a particular law does not belong within the constitutional jurisdiction of the government that adopted it (e.g., Ottawa or a province), it declares the law to be *ultra vires.* Once a law has been declared *ultra vires*, it immediately ceases to have any force or effect. Before 1982, a law that was *ultra vires* the federal Parliament might be *intra vires* (within the proper jurisdiction, and therefore constitutional) if enacted by a provincial government, and vice versa.

DISCUSSION AND REVIEW QUESTIONS

1. Briefly describe each of the four elements of the Canadian *Constitution*. Give an example of each. How does each element affect our political system?

2. Briefly define "judicial review," and explain how it differs from the British institutional tradition.

3. How have the rulings of the JCPC and the Supreme Court of Canada affected the balance of power between the federal and provincial governments? How great is their impact?

4. How has Canada's system of fiscal federalism changed since the 1970s? What is the historical significance of the CHST?

5. Briefly explain the meanings of "interdependence" and "parity" in the context of Canadian federalism.

SUGGESTED READINGS

Books and Articles

Herman Bakvis and Grace Skogstad, eds., *Canadian Federalism: Performance, Effectiveness, and Legitimacy* (Toronto: Oxford University Press, 2002).

David Cameron and Richard Simeon, "Intergovernmental Relations in Canada: The Emergence of Collaborative Federalism," *Publius: The Journal of Federalism*, 32:2 (Spring 2002).

Alain-G. Gagnon and Hugh Segal, eds., *The Canadian Social Union Without Quebec: Eight Critical Analyses* (Montreal: Institute for Research in Public Policy, 2000).

Roger Gibbins, *Regionalism: Territorial Politics in Canada and the United States* (Toronto: Butterworths, 1982).

James Ross Hurley, *Amending Canada's Constitution: History, Processes, Problems and Prospects* (Ottawa: Minister of Supply and Services Canada, 1996).

Harvey Lazar, ed., *Toward a New Mission Statement for Canadian Fiscal Federalism* (Montreal and Kingston: McGill–Queen's University Press/Queen's University School of Policy Studies, 2000).

J. Peter Meekison, Hamish Telford, and Harvey Lazar, eds., *Reconsidering the Institutions of Canadian Federalism* (Montreal and Kingston: Institute of Intergovernmental Relations/McGill–Queen's University Press, 2004).

François Rocher and Miriam Smith, eds., *New Trends in Canadian Federalism*, 2nd edition (Peterborough, ON: Broadview Press, 2003).

John T. Saywell, *The Lawmakers: Judicial Power and the Shaping of Canadian Federalism* (Toronto: University of Toronto Press/Osgoode Society for Canadian Legal History, 2002).

Websites

The Canadian Intergovernmental Conference Secretariat, an agency of the federal government, maintains a website (www.scics.gc.ca) listing all major intergovernmental meetings that took place in recent years. There are links to major documents (statements or agreements) produced by or at these meetings. This website is an excellent resource on fiscal and executive federalism.

The federal Department of Finance provides a wealth of information about the fiscal relations between the federal and provincial/territorial governments. Go to www.fin.gc.ca and click on the "Transfer Payments to Provinces" icon. You can also access these pages from the website of the Intergovernmental Affairs Secretariat within the federal Privy Council Office; go to www.pco-bcp.gc.ca and click on "Other PCO Sites: Intergovernmental Affairs."

For a different perspective on IGRs, check out some of the provincial sites. Alberta's Department of International and Intergovernmental Relations (www.iir.gov.ab.ca) is an excellent source of information. Most provincial IGR sites are less informative, although the BC site provides useful links to other governments (go to www.portaltest.bc.ca and enter "intergovernmental" in the Search window). See also the Ontario site (www.mia.gov.on.ca) and the Quebec site (www.mce.gouv.qc.ca).

NOTES

1. This is the "general amending formula" contained in section 38 of the *Constitution Act, 1982*. See the Appendix to this book.

2. James Ross Hurley, *Amending Canada's Constitution: History, Processes, Problems and Prospects* (Ottawa: Minister of Supply and Services Canada, 1996), 2.

3. Grant MacEwan, *Mighty Women: Stories of Western Canadian Pioneers* (Vancouver: Greystone Books, 1995 [1975]).

4. *Henrietta Muir Edwards and Others v. Attorney General for Canada and Others*, JC 1929, in Richard A. Olmsted, ed., *Decisions of the Judicial Committee of the Privy Council*, volume 2 (Ottawa: Queen's Printer, 1954).

5. *Marbury v. Madison*, 5 U.S. 137 (1803); available online at www.findlaw.com.

6. *Supreme Court of Canada, Attorney General of Manitoba et al. v. Attorney General of Canada et al.* [the Patriation Reference], in Peter H. Russell, Rainer Knopff, and Ted Morton, eds., *Federalism and the Charter* (Ottawa: Carleton University Press, 1989 [1981]), 739.

7. For an excellent discussion of the divergence between constitutional text and political practice in Canada, see Jennifer Smith, "The Constitutional Debate and Beyond," in François Rocher and Miriam Smith, eds., *New Trends in Canadian Federalism*, 2nd edition (Peterborough, ON: Broadview Press, 2003).

8. Vernon Bogdanor, "Introduction," in Vernon Bogdanor, ed., *Constitutions in Democratic Politics* (Aldershot, UK: Gower, 1988), 6.

9. Russell, Knopff, and Morton, 740.

10. Ibid., 743.

11. Peter H. Russell, "The Supreme Court Decision: Bold Statecraft Based on Questionable Jurisprudence," in Peter H. Russell et al., *The Court and the Constitution: Comments on the Supreme Court Reference on Constitutional Amendment* (Kingston: Queen's University Institute of Intergovernmental Relations, 1982), 1.

12. R. MacGregor Dawson, *The Government of Canada,* 5th edition, rev'd Norman Ward (Toronto: University of Toronto Press, 1970), 59.

13. Hurley, 11.

14. These dichotomies are taken from J. Peter Meekison, Hamish Telford, and Harvey Lazar, "The Institutions of Executive Federalism: Myths and Realities," in J. Peter Meekison, Hamish Telford, and Harvey Lazar, eds., *Reconsidering the Institutions of Canadian Federalism* (Montreal and Kingston: Institute of Intergovernmental Relations/ McGill–Queen's University Press, 2004), 4.

15. Other concurrent powers were less explicit: sections 91 and 92 awarded legislative powers over criminal law and marriage to Ottawa, while the administration of those laws was left to the provinces.

16. K.C. Wheare, *Federal Government,* 4th edition (London: Oxford University Press, 1963), 19.

17. Ibid., 20. Note, however, that the powers of reservation and disallowance are still included in the Canadian *Constitution.* While some provincial governments have argued that these sections have lost their legal effect through disuse, the federal government disagrees. See Hurley, 15.

18. Smith, "The Constitutional Debate and Beyond," 54–55.

19. Hamish Telford, "The Federal Spending Power in Canada: Nation-Building or Nation-Destroying?," *Publius: The Journal of Federalism,* 33:1 (Winter 2003), 24–27.

20. On the conflict over federal surpluses, see Geoffrey E. Hale, "Managing the Fiscal Dividend: The Politics of Selective Activism," in Leslie A. Pal, ed., *How Ottawa Spends, 2000–2001: Past Imperfect, Future Tense* (Toronto: Oxford University Press, 2000), 59–60 and 67–68.

21. The three territories have separate fiscal relationships with Ottawa, which will not be discussed here. For information on Territorial Formula Financing, which makes up the large majority of public revenues in the three territories, go to www.fin.gc.ca and click on "Transfer Payments to Provinces."

22. However, they are subject to judicial review, which implies the possible evolution of full judicial enforcement; see Chapter 9.

23. David Cameron and Richard Simeon, "Intergovernmental Relations in Canada: The Emergence of Collaborative Federalism," *Publius: The Journal of Federalism,* 32:2 (Spring 2002), 66–67.

24. Alain Noël, *The End of a Model? Quebec and the Council of the Federation* (Kingston and Montreal: Institute for Intergovernmental Relations/Institute for Research on Public Policy, 2003), 2; available online at www.irpp.org.

25. Especially the New Public Management; see Chapter 6.

26. In a 2003 survey by the Centre for Research and Information on Canada (CRIC), 70 percent of respondents thought that "improved federal–provincial cooperation" should be a high priority for the new prime minister. The same proportion believed that both levels of government were equally to blame for the persistent conflicts between them; only 42 percent believed that the federal and provincial governments worked well together.

See CRIC, "Canadians' Priorities: More Money for Health Care, Education; and Improved Federal/Provincial Cooperation," October 28, 2003; available online at www.cric.ca.

27. Cameron and Simeon, 66–67.

28. See, for example, Frances Abele and Michael J. Prince, *Counsel for Canadian Federalism: Aboriginal Governments and the Council of the Federation* (Kingston and Montreal: Institute for Intergovernmental Relations/Institute for Research on Public Policy, 2003), 2; available online at www.irpp.org. See also Abele and Prince, "Aboriginal Governance and Canadian Federalism: A To-Do List for Canada," in Rocher and Smith, eds.; Abele and Prince, "Alternative Futures: Aboriginal Peoples and Canadian Federalism," in Herman Bakvis and Grace Skogstad, eds., *Canadian Federalism: Performance, Effectiveness, and Legitimacy* (Toronto: Oxford University Press, 2002).

29. Cameron and Simeon, 63.

30. Douglas M. Brown, *Getting Things Done in the Federation: Do We Need New Rules for an Old Game?* (Kingston and Montreal: Institute for Intergovernmental Relations/Institute for Research on Public Policy, 2003), 3; available online at www.irpp.org.

31. Ronald L. Watts, *Comparing Federal Systems,* 2nd edition (Montreal and Kingston: Institute of Intergovernmental Relations/McGill–Queen's University Press, 1999), 69–70. See also Ronald L. Watts, *Intergovernmental Councils in Federations* (Kingston and Montreal: Institute for Intergovernmental Relations/Institute for Research on Public Policy, 2003), 3; available online at www.irpp.org.

32. See Jennifer Smith, "The Constitutional Debate and Beyond" and "Informal Constitutional Development: Change by Other Means," in Bakvis and Skogstad, eds.

33. J. Peter Meekison, "The Annual Premiers' Conference: Forging a Common Front," in Meekison, Telford, and Lazar, eds., 143.

34. Watts, *Comparing Federal Systems,* 123.

35. Ibid., 119.

36. Richard Simeon, "Important? Yes. Transformative? No: North American Integration and Canadian Federalism," in Harvey Lazar, Hamish Telford, and Ronald L. Watts, eds., *The Impact of Global and Regional Integration on Federal Systems* (Montreal and Kingston: Institute for Intergovernmental Relations/McGill–Queen's University Press, 2003).

37. Hamish Telford, *Expanding the Partnership: The Proposed Council of the Federation and the Challenge of Glocalization* (Kingston and Montreal: Institute for Intergovernmental Relations/Institute for Research on Public Policy, 2003), 2; available online at www.irpp.org.

38. Harvey Lazar, "In Search of a New Mission Statement for Canadian Fiscal Federalism," in Harvey Lazar, ed., *The State of the Federation 1999–2000: Toward a New Mission Statement for Canadian Fiscal Federalism* (Montreal and Kingston: Institute for Intergovernmental Relations/McGill–Queen's University Press, 2000), 29.

39. Alan C. Cairns, "The Judicial Committee and its Critics," in Douglas E. Williams, ed., *Constitution, Government, and Society in Canada: Selected Essays by Alan C. Cairns* (Toronto: McClelland and Stewart, 1988), 59–60.

40. Among respondents to the 2003 CRIC poll, greater spending on health care and education were by far the highest policy priorities (named by 73 and 70 percent, respectively).

41. Donald V. Smiley, *The Federal Condition in Canada* (Toronto: McGraw-Hill Ryerson, 1987), 48.

42. Peter H. Russell, Rainer Knopff, and Ted Morton, "Introduction," in Russell, Knopff, and Morton, eds., *Federalism and the Charter* (Ottawa: Carleton University Press, 1989), 6.

43. Smiley, 49.

44. Viscount Haldane, "The Work for the Empire of the Judicial Committee of the Privy Council," *Cambridge Law Journal,* 1 (1923), 150; quoted in Cairns, "The Judicial Committee and Its Critics," 90.

45. *Attorney General for Ontario v. Attorney General for Canada* [Local Prohibition Case], JC 1896, in Olmsted, volume 1, 355–56.

46. In re *The Board of Commerce Act, 1919,* and the *Combines and Fair Prices Act, 1919,* JC 1922, in Olmsted, volume 2, 250–51.

47. *Fort Frances Pulp and Power Company v. Manitoba Free Press,* JC 1923, in Olmsted, volume 2, 313–14.

48. *Toronto Electric Commissioners v. Snider,* JC 1925, in Olmsted, volume 2, 408–09.

49. Reference re *Employment and Social Insurance Act,* JC 1937, in Olmsted, volume 3, 217.

50. In re *The Regulation and Control of Aeronautics in Canada,* JC 1932, in Olmsted, volume 3, 724.

51. In re *Regulation and Control of Radio Communications in Canada,* JC 1932, in Olmsted, volume 3, 25.

52. *Attorney General for Canada v. Attorney General for Ontario* [the Labour Conventions Case], JC 1937, in Olmsted, volume 3, 200.

53. *Labour Conventions* Case, 203.

54. Ibid., 204.

55. Whether it will continue to do so is an open question. Some scholars suggest that the Supreme Court has been nibbling away at the *Labour Conventions* doctrine, and may overturn it altogether in the near future. See John T. Saywell, *The Lawmakers: Judicial Power and the Shaping of Canadian Federalism* (Toronto: University of Toronto Press/Osgoode Society for Canadian Legal History, 2002), 298–301.

56. Harvey Lazar, Hamish Telford, and Ronald L. Watts, "Divergent Trajectories: The Impact of Global and Regional Integration on Federal Systems," in Lazar, Telford, and Watts, eds., 17.

57. *Attorney General of Canada v. Canada Temperance Federation,* JC 1946, in Russell, Knopff, and Morton, eds., 120.

58. See, for example, Frank R. Scott, "The Privy Council and Mr. Bennett's 'New Deal' Legislation," and "Centralization and Decentralization," in Frank R. Scott, *Essays on the Constitution: Aspects of Canadian Law and Politics* (Toronto: University of Toronto Press, 1977), 90–101 and 260–72, respectively.

59. Cairns, "The Judicial Committee and Its Critics," 61–63.

60. Ibid., 80.

61. Ibid., 80–81.

62. The appointment process became an issue in the 2004 federal election. Shortly before the campaign began, the Justice Committee in the House of Commons reviewed the process (discussed in Chapter 10). In the campaign itself, Conservative leader Stephen Harper demanded that the pool of candidates be restricted to nominees put forward by provincial governments. The federal government did not follow this advice when it appointed two new justices from Ontario in August 2004.

63. *Johannesson v. West St. Paul,* S.C.R. 1952, in Russell, Knopff, and Morton, eds., 134–35.

64. Reference re *Offshore Mineral Rights of British Columbia,* S.C.R. 1967, in Russell, Knopff, and Morton, eds., 150.

65. Russell, Knopff, and Morton, "Comment on *The Queen v. Crown Zellerbach Canada Ltd.,* 1988," in Russell, Knopff, and Morton, eds., 273.

66. *R. v. Crown Zellerbach Canada Ltd.* [1988] 1 S.C.R. 401.

67. *R. v. Hydro-Québec* [1997] 3 S.C.R. 213, paragraph 110.

68. Reference re *The Farm Products Marketing Act (Ontario),* S.C.R. 1957, in Russell, Knopff, and Morton, eds., 142–43.

69. *Attorney General of Manitoba v. Manitoba Egg and Poultry Association* (Chicken and Egg Reference), S.C.R. 1971, in Russell, Knopff, and Morton, eds., 152–61.

70. *General Motors of Canada Ltd. v. City National Leasing* [1989] 1 S.C.R. 641.

71. Russell, Knopff, and Morton, "Introduction," 9.

72. Gerald Baier, "Judicial Review and Canadian Federalism," in Bakvis and Skogstad, eds., 27; Gerald Baier, "The Law of Federalism: Judicial Review and the Division of Powers," in Rocher and Smith, eds., 126–27; A. Wayne MacKay, "The Supreme Court of Canada and Federalism: Does/Should Anyone Care Anymore?," *Canadian Bar Review,* 80:1–2 (March–June 2001).

73. *R. v. Hydro-Québec.*

74. *RJR-MacDonald Inc. v. Canada (Attorney General)* [1995] 3 S.C.R. 199.

75. *R. v. Hydro-Québec,* paragraph 121.

76. Supreme Court of Canada, Reference re *Firearms Act (Can.),* S.C.R. 2000 (www.lexum.umontreal.ca).

77. Peter W. Hogg, "Is the Supreme Court of Canada Biased in Constitutional Cases?," *Canadian Bar Review,* 57 (1979).

78. Baier, "The Law of Federalism," 127–28.

79. MacKay, 268; Saywell, 254.

80. MacKay, 274–75; Saywell, 284–87.

81. Saywell, 271.

82. Russell, Knopff, and Morton, "Comment on *Canadian Industrial Gas and Oil Ltd. v. Government of Saskatchewan,* 1978," in Russell, Knopff, and Morton, eds., 188–89.

83. Daniel Johnson, *Égalité ou Indépendance* (Montreal: Les Éditions de L'Homme Ltée, 1965).

84. See Tom Flanagan, *Waiting for the Wave: The Reform Party and Preston Manning* (Toronto: Stoddart, 1996), Chapter 3.

85. Richard L. Cole, John Kincaid, and Andrew Parkin, "Public Opinion on Federalism in the United States and Canada in 2002: The Aftermath of Terrorism," *Publius: The Journal of Federalism,* 32:4 (Fall 2002), Table 3, 129.

86. Cole, Kincaid, and Parkin, 130.

87. Ibid., 142.

88. Cairns, "The Judicial Committee and its Critics," 95, 97.

89. Meekison, "The Annual Premiers' Conference," 143.

90. Peter A. Cumming, "Equitable Fiscal Federalism: The Problems in Respect of Resources Revenue Sharing," in Mark Krasnick, ed., *Fiscal Federalism,* volume 65 of the collected research studies for the Royal Commission on the Economic Union and Development Prospects for Canada (Toronto: University of Toronto Press, 1986), 50–51.

91. Canada, *Report of the Royal Commission on Dominion-Provincial Relations,* volume 1, abridged by Donald V. Smiley (Ottawa: Carleton University Press, 1963 [1940]), 210.

92. Richard Simeon and Ian Robinson, *State, Society, and the Development of Canadian Federalism,* volume 65 of the collected research studies for the Royal Commission on the

Economic Union and Development Prospects for Canada (Toronto: University of Toronto Press, 1986), 106.

93. *Report of the Royal Commission on Dominion–Provincial Relations,* 210–14.

94. See Lazar, "In Search of a New Mission Statement for Canadian Fiscal Federalism," 7–10.

95. Smiley, 171.

96. Telford, "The Federal Spending Power in Canada," 32–33; Cumming, 53.

97. Telford, "The Federal Spending Power in Canada," 33.

98. Paul A.R. Hobson and France St-Hilaire, "The Evolution of Federal–Provincial Fiscal Arrangements: Putting Humpty Together Again," in Lazar, ed., *Toward a New Mission Statement for Canadian Fiscal Federalism,* 163.

99. Edith Boucher and Arndt Vermaeten, "Changes to Federal Transfers to Provinces and Territories in 1999," in Lazar, ed., *Toward a New Mission Statement for Canadian Fiscal Federalism,* 139–40.

100. Canada, Department of Finance, "Backgrounder: Equalization Program," March 2004; accessed online at www.fin.gc.ca/fedprov/eqpe.html. Note: British Columbia, which is usually a "have" province, has qualified for small equalization payments in recent years; it received less than $200 per capita in 2004–05.

101. "Strengthening the Equalization Program: Perspective of the Finance Ministers of the Provinces and Territories," September 2003, 4; available online at www.scics.gc.ca.

102. In 2001–02, the federal government paid an extra $3.4 billion in equalization to four provinces because of an accounting error by Revenue Canada. Prime Minister Chrétien demanded that the provinces repay the money, much of which had already been spent. His then-Finance minister, Paul Martin, argued that the money should be forgiven and directed toward health care. Thus the accounting error caused a major political conflict, not only between governments, but also within the federal Cabinet. Susan Delacourt, *Juggernaut: Paul Martin's Campaign for Chrétien's Crown* (Toronto: McClelland and Stewart, 2003), 232–34.

103. Canada, Department of Finance, "Backgrounder: Equalization Renewal 2004–05 to 2008–09," March 2004; accessed online at www.fin.gc.ca/fedprov/eqre.html.

104. "Strengthening the Equalization Program," 6.

105. It should be pointed out that the "vertical imbalance" of revenues and responsibilities, which is an article of faith for the provincial governments, is vigorously contested by Ottawa. The federal Department of Finance argues that both levels of government have access to all the revenues they need, and points out that several provinces have recently cut income taxes—implying that any shortfall in provincial revenue-raising capacity arises from politics, not from the *BNA Act.* See Canada, Department of Finance, "The Fiscal Balance in Canada: The Facts," March 2004; available online at www.fin.gc.ca/facts/fbcfacts8_e.html.

106. Lazar, 10.

107. Stephen Laurent and François Vaillancourt, *Federal-Provincial Transfers for Social Programs in Canada: Their Status in May 2004* (Montreal: Institute for Research on Public Policy, July 2004), 4; available online at www.irpp.org.

108. Ibid.

109. Hobson and St-Hilaire, 162–63.

110. Ibid., 166.

111. Ibid., 167.

112. Quoted in Hobson and St-Hilaire, 167.

113. Janice MacKinnon, *Minding the Public Purse: The Fiscal Crisis, Political Trade-Offs, and Canada's Future* (Montreal and Kingston: McGill–Queen's University Press, 2003), Chapter 1.

114. In November 1995, for example, the federal government held back over $400 000 of its planned cash payment to Alberta; it claimed that an equal amount had been charged to patients by private clinics in the province, which violated the nonprofit element of the public administration criterion. Andrew C. Tzembelicos, "Chronology of Events July 1995–June 1996," in Patrick C. Fafard and Douglas M. Brown, eds., *Canada: The State of the Federation, 1996* (Kingston: Institute for Intergovernmental Relations, 1997), 258.

115. Keith Banting and Robin Boadway, "Defining the Sharing Community: The Federal Role in Health Care," in Harvey Lazar and France St-Hilaire, eds., *Money, Politics and Health Care: Reconstructing the Federal-Provincial Partnership* (Montreal and Kingston: Institute for Research on Public Policy and Institute for Intergovernmental Relations, 2004), 13.

116. Alain-G. Gagnon and Hugh Segal, "Introduction," in Gagnon and Segal, eds., 2.

117. MacKinnon, x.

118. Laurent and Vaillancourt, 10–11.

119. Hobson and St-Hilaire, 175.

120. Roy Romanow is a former NDP premier of Saskatchewan and a passionate defender of publicly funded health care. He is also a savvy veteran of intergovernmental conflict, having played a key role in the 1980–82 constitutional negotiations (as we will see in Chapter 9).

121. Canada, *Building on Values: The Future of Health Care in Canada* [the "Romanow Report"], (Ottawa: Minister of Government Works and Public Services, November 2002), 69.

122. "Federal/Provincial/Territorial Fiscal Relations in Transition: A Report to Canada's Western Premiers from the Finance Ministers of British Columbia, Alberta, Saskatchewan, Manitoba, Yukon, Northwest Territories and Nunavut," June 2003, 6; available online at www.scics.gc.ca.

123. Canada, Department of Finance, "Backgrounder: Canada Health Transfer," March 2004; available online at www.fin.gc.ca/fedpriov/chte.html.

124. Report of the Commission on the Future of Health Care in Canada, 67; Laurent and Vaillancourt, 11.

125. "Federal/Provincial/Territorial Fiscal Relations in Transition," 11–12.

126. Canada, Department of Finance, "Federal Support for Health Care: The Facts," March 2004; available online at www.fin.gc.ca/facts/fshc6_e.html.

127. Council of the Federation, "Premiers' Action Plan for Better Health Care: Resolving Issues in the Spirit of True Federalism," July 30, 2004, 2; available online at www.scics.gc.ca.

128. "Backgrounder: Canada Health Transfer," 3.

129. Laurent and Vaillancourt, 16–18.

130. Pierre Marc Johnson with Karel Mayrand, "Citizens, States and International Regimes: International Governance Challenges in a Globalized World," in Thomas J. Courchene and Donald J. Savoie, eds., *The Art of the State: Governance in a World Without Frontiers* (Montreal: Institute for Research on Public Policy, 2003), 376.

131. Brown, *Getting Things Done in the Federation.* In 2002 the First Ministers agreed to a dispute-resolution process in the health-care field, to deal with issues like the Alberta–Ottawa fight over private for-profit clinics and the resulting federal "clawback." However, the final decision in any given dispute rests with the federal Health minister, which calls into question the genuinely intergovernmental nature of the process. For

details, see Health Canada, *Fact Sheet: CHA Dispute Avoidance and Resolution;* available online at www.hc-sc.gc.ca/english/media/releases/2002/health_act/cha.htm.

132. Watts, *Intergovernmental Councils in Federations,* 8–9.

133. Meekison, "The Annual Premiers' Conference," 147.

134. For more on the CCME and its operation, see Julie M. Simmons, "Securing the Threads of Co-operation in the Tapestry of Intergovernmental Relations: Does the Institutionalization of Ministerial Conferences Matter?," in Meekison, Telford, and Lazar, eds., 285–311.

135. Martin Papillon and Richard Simeon, "The Weakest Link? First Ministers' Conferences in Canadian Intergovernmental Relations," in Meekison, Telford, and Lazar, eds., 144.

136. Papillon and Simeon, 116–17.

137. Ibid., 119.

138. The requirement was contained in section 37, which was repealed automatically in 1987. See Appendix, footnote 98.

139. Papillon and Simeon, 123.

140. *Provincial–Territorial Backgrounder,* September 14, 2004; accessed at www.scics.gc.ca/pdf/800042010_e.pdf.

141. Campbell Clark, "Brinksmanship nearly scuttled health deal," *The Globe and Mail,* September 20, 2004.

142. Brian Laghi and Jane Taber, "PM tries to pacify Williams," *The Globe and Mail,* October 28, 2004.

143. Papillon and Simeon, 125.

144. J. Peter Meekison, *Council of the Federation: An Idea Whose Time Has Come* (Kingston and Montreal: Institute for Intergovernmental Relations/Institute for Research on Public Policy, 2003), 1; available online at www.irpp.org.

145. "Council of the Federation: Founding Agreement," December 5, 2003; accessed online at www.scics.gc.ca.

146. Gregory P. Marchildon, *The Health Council of Canada Proposal in Light of the Council of the Federation* (Kingston and Montreal: Institute for Intergovernmental Relations/Institute for Research on Public Policy, 2003), 5; available online at www.irpp.org.

147. Quebec is not a participant in the new Health Council of Canada, or in any of the other recent FPT health agencies (e.g., Canadian Blood Services). See Marchildon, 5. Quebec participated in the PT negotiations leading up to the Social Union Framework Agreement, but refused to sign the final FPT accord (see Dossier 9.4).

148. The Province of Quebec participates in the Annual Conference of New England Governors and Eastern Canadian Premiers, but not in the Council of Atlantic Premiers meetings.

149. J. Peter Meekison, "The Western Premiers' Conference: Intergovernmental Co-operation at the Regional Level," in Meekison, Telford, and Lazar, eds., 199.

150. The data for 2003 are available on the Canadian Intergovernmental Conference Secretariat website (go to www.scisc.gc.ca and click on "Conference Information"); the historical data are from Simmons, Table 1, 289.

151. Meekison, "The Annual Premiers' Conference," 157; Simmons, 290.

152. For more information, see the Council's website: www.ccme.ca.

153. The history and purpose of the CMEC are described in its December 2003 *Framework for the Future* document, available online at www.cmec.ca. Appendix D of the document also contains a very useful analysis of the CCME and other FPT bodies.

154. Johanne Poirier, "Intergovernmental Agreements in Canada: At the Crossroads Between Law and Politics," in Meekison, Telford, and Lazar, eds., 427.

155. Thomas J. Courchene, "Glocalization: The Regional/International Interface," *Canadian Journal of Regional Science,* 18:1 (Spring 1995).

156. Michael Keating, "The Territorial State: Functional Restructuring and Political Change," in Courchene and Savoie, eds., 339–40.

157. Andrew Sancton, "Municipalities, Cities, and Globalization: Implications for Canadian Federalism," in Bakvis and Skogstad, eds., 268.

158. Telford, *Expanding the Partnership,* 4.

159. Simon Tuck and Katherine Harding, "Cities can sit in on Ottawa talks, province promises," *The Globe and Mail,* August 24, 2004 (accessed at www.globeandmail.com); Gillian Livingston, "New deal won't hurt big cities: McGuinty," Canadian Press, August 25, 2004 (accessed at www.canada.com).

160. Some observers argue that provincial jurisdiction over municipalities does not prevent the federal government from intervening in urban affairs, any more than the provincial responsibility for hospitals prohibits Ottawa from putting conditions on transfer payments for health care. The real barrier to federal involvement in cities is a lack of political will and financial wherewithal. See Roger Gibbins, "The Missing Link: Policy Options for Engaging Ottawa in Canada's Urban Centres," in Meekison, Telford, and Lazar, eds., 412.

161. Data retrieved online, at http://geodepot.statcan.ca/Diss/Highlights/Page11/Page11_e.cfm.

162. Canada, "Speech from the Throne," February 2, 2004, 12.

163. Liberal Party of Canada, *Moving Canada Forward: The Paul Martin Plan for Getting Things Done* (Ottawa, May 2004), 31; accessed online at www.liberal.ca.

164. Sancton, 264.

165. Ibid., 264.

166. Grace Skogstad, "International Trade Policy," in Bakvis and Skogstad, eds., 160.

167. It should be noted that the Council of Ministers of Education Canada (CMEC) has long been the principal Canadian voice in international agreements relating to education policy, despite being a purely PT organization. See the CMEC website for more information: www.cmec.ca.

168. Skogstad, 161–62.

169. "Premiers Announce Progress on Key Initiatives," news release, July 30, 2004, 3; available online at www.scics.gc.ca.

170. Skogstad, 162–65.

171. Telford, *Expanding the Partnership,* 3.

172. Kathryn Harrison, "Passing the Environmental Buck," in Rocher and Smith, eds., 337–38.

173. Harrison, 338. See also Mark S. Winfield, "Environmental Policy and Federalism," in Bakvis and Skogstad, eds., 133.

174. Alberta, "Alberta stands firm on pledge to protect economy against impact of Kyoto Protocol, Klein says," news release; accessed online at www.gov.ab.ca/home/index.cfm?Page=350.

175. Mark A. Luz and C. Marc Miller, "Globalization and Canadian Federalism: Implications of the NAFTA's Investment Rules," *McGill Law Journal,* volume 47 (2001–02), 984.

176. Luz and Millar, 985.

177. Ibid., 988.

178. Simeon, "Important? Yes," 154–56.

179. One recent dispute, which fell outside the purview of NAFTA, illustrates the complexity of "multitiered" federalism under globalization. In 1999, the Ontario government of Mike Harris leased the 407 toll highway to a private consortium controlled by a Spanish company. In 2004 the consortium raised the toll rates, which it claimed it had the right to do under the terms of the lease. The new premier, Dalton McGuinty, argued that the province had the power to veto any rate increases as it saw fit. In retaliation, the Spanish government asked the European Union (EU) to raise the issue with Canadian officials during negotiations over a proposed Canada–EU trade agreement. Concerned that the talks might be derailed by the dispute, Canada's minister of Trade asked McGuinty to reconsider his opposition to the toll increase. At the time of writing, the clash between Ontario and the Spanish consortium had not been resolved. Associated Press and Canadian Press, "Working to end Ontario row over toll road, EU says," *The Globe and Mail,* August 12, 2004; Richard Mackie, "McGuinty shrugs off highway toll spat," *The Globe and Mail,* August 12, 2004 (both accessed at www.globeandmail.com).

180. Johnson and Mayrand, 375.

181. Roger Gibbins, "Federalism in a Digital World," *Canadian Journal of Political Science,* 33:4 (December 2000).

182. Johnson and Mayrand, 374.

183. Gibbins, "Federalism in a Digital World," 674.

184. Peter Andreas and Thomas J. Biersteker, eds., *The Rebordering of North America: Integration and Exclusion in a New Security Context* (New York: Routledge, 2003).

185. Ronald L. Watts, "Managing Interdependence in a Federal Political System," in Courchene and Savoie, eds., 147.

186. *Learning from SARS: Renewal of Public Health in Canada* (Ottawa: Health Canada, October 2003); available online at www.hc-sc.gc.ca.

187. Marina Jimenez and Brian Laghi, "Squabbling abetted SARS, panel says," *The Globe and Mail,* October 8, 2003 (accessed at www.globeandmail.com); Hon. Mr. Justice Archie Campbell, "The SARS Commission Interim Report: SARS and Public Health in Ontario" (Toronto, April 15, 2004); available online at www.hc-sc.gc.ca.

188. Annual Conference of Federal–Provincial–Territorial Ministers of Health, news release, September 4, 2003, 1; accessed online at www.scics.gc.ca.

189. *Strengthening the Pan-Canadian Public Health System,* discussion paper (Ottawa: Health Canada, 2004); available online at www.hc-sc.gc.ca.

190. *Learning from SARS,* 2.

191. Ibid., 2.

192. The reference in the Naylor report to "national concern," as opposed to "emergency," is also intriguing. Because SARS was clearly an "emergency" within the meaning of the POGG jurisprudence from both the JCPC and the Supreme Court, it would serve to justify only a temporary federal intrusion into provincial jurisdiction. "National concern," on the other hand, could underpin a permanent federal role that goes beyond anything envisioned by the provinces in September 2003.

193. Peter Hogg, *Constitutional Law of Canada,* 3rd edition (supp.) (Toronto: Carswell, 1992), 6–16.

9

CONSTITUTION II: FROM "MEGACONSTITUTIONAL POLITICS" TO "NONCONSTITUTIONAL RENEWAL"

- *describe* and *explain* megaconstitutional politics in Canada;
- *explain* the failure of the Meech Lake and Charlottetown Accords;
- *summarize* the Supreme Court's ruling in the *Secession Reference*, which declared a unilateral declaration of independence by a province to be unconstitutional, and compare it to the texts of the federal *Clarity Bill* and Quebec's Bill 99;
- *explain* the recent emphasis on nonconstitutional renewal of the federation, and *summarize* the most important developments flowing from it.

INTRODUCTION: REWRITING THE RULES OF THE CANADIAN FEDERATION

Almost as soon as Confederation took root, its rules for the conduct of government came under challenge. Some provinces, particularly Ontario and Quebec, claimed that the division of powers in sections 91 and 92 imposed too many restrictions on their revenues and policies. As more provinces joined the federation, their divergent perspectives on government and society produced more calls for reform. Beginning with the first Premiers' Conference in 1886, provincial governments demanded formal **amendments** to the *Constitution*. Before 1982, there was no official **amending formula** in the Canadian *Constitution*. In legal terms, the power to change the *BNA Act* rested with the British Parliament—although it was clearly understood that no such change would be carried out except in response to a request from the federal government. The tricky question was the degree of provincial consent to such a request: Did it require the unanimous consent of the provinces, a majority of the provinces, or even less?

These unanswered questions did not prevent the amendment of the *BNA Act* between 1867 and 1982. In 1940, for example, the provinces agreed to transfer responsibility for Unemployment Insurance to the federal government; the resulting amendment is enshrined in clause 2A of section 91. Subsequently, the federal government was granted control over pensions, via amendments passed in 1951 and 1964 (clause 94A). In all cases where the division of powers was amended, the federal government secured the unanimous agreement of the provinces before proceeding to the British Parliament—even while refusing to formally acknowledge that unanimity was required.[1] While altering the text of the *BNA Act* was hardly a routine procedure, it was clearly achievable.

The eventual creation of an amending formula might have been expected to make the process easier, by reducing intergovernmental disputes about decision rules and the role of the various players. Instead, it appears to have produced a constitutional stalemate.[2] The general amending formula (Dossier 9.1) has been successfully invoked only once, in 1983. Two attempts to use the unanimity formula—the Meech Lake and Charlottetown Accords—ended in spectacular and embittering failure. The Charlottetown Accord, which was rejected in a 1992 referendum, brought at least a temporary respite from megaconstitutional politics. No one had any appetite for yet another round of haggling, horse-trading, and public protest. Instead of amending the entrenched *Constitution* to address provincial (and Aboriginal) grievances, Canada's governments would attempt to solve problems and resolve disputes through nonconstitutional renewal (NCR).

The high-profile constitutional wars of recent decades have obscured an important fact about Canadian politics: most adjustments to our system of government—particularly the relationships among the senior governments—have occurred without formally amending the *Constitution*. These adjustments were, and are, incremental and often ad hoc. Many began as short-term solutions to immediate practical problems, which persisted for decades by the force of institutional inertia. They include the federal spending power in provincial jurisdictions, executive federalism, and the complex structure of intergovernmental relations (all discussed in Chapter 8). Some incremental adjustments have now been recognized as unwritten constitutional conventions; others have been enshrined in formal written agreements among governments.[3]

There have always been significant differences between the prescriptions in the entrenched *Constitution* and the political practices followed by Canadian governments.[4] In large measure, these arise from the persistence of British constitutional conventions, which were formally imported into Canada by the "Preamble" to the *BNA Act* ("a government similar in Principle to that of the United Kingdom"). As we argued in Chapter 8, conventions provide a useful degree of flexibility in the operations of government; they allow our institutions to adapt to changing social conditions and attitudes without requiring the difficult and contentious formal amendment process. The same might be said of written intergovernmental agreements, although—as we will see later in this chapter—few (if any) of these have proven particularly effective in practice. Their implementation depends almost entirely on the political will of the participants, a shaky foundation at best.[5] Unlike amendments to the entrenched *Constitution,* neither conventions nor intergovernmental agreements are subject to enforcement by the courts. As yet, there are no effective mechanisms for decision-making, enforcement, or dispute resolution. Their absence reveals the limitations of an NCR strategy, and suggests that the current suspension of mega-constitutional politics cannot persist indefinitely.[6]

This chapter traces the various efforts to reform Confederation in response to political and social change. It begins with an analysis of megaconstitutional politics between 1960 and 1992, focusing on two driving forces for constitutional change: Quebec nationalism and Western regionalism. Following an account of the Charlottetown Accord, the failure of which terminated 30 years of megaconstitutional politics, the chapter summarizes the shift to nonconstitutional renewal in the 1990s. It deals with three key issues: (1) the crisis provoked by the 1995 Quebec sovereignty referendum, which nearly destroyed Confederation; (2) the desire (partly provoked by globalization) to forge a stronger **economic union;** and (3) the pursuit of a collaborative **social union.** Because the last issue received considerable attention in Chapter 8, the discussion in this chapter is confined to the 1999 Social Union Framework Agreement (SUFA)—an attempt to craft new rules for the management of social policy.

"MEGACONSTITUTIONAL POLITICS": DEBATING CANADA'S POLITICAL INSTITUTIONS

Megaconstitutional Politics before 1980: Quebec Nationalism versus Western Regionalism

Since 1960, constitutional politics in Canada has revolved around complex and divisive questions:

- Is Canada a partnership of two founding nations (the Quebec vision) or a Confederation of 10 equal provinces?
- Should constitutional politics revolve around territorial cleavages, such as regionalism, or around nonterritorial cleavages such as language, gender, and Aboriginality?
- Do our rights as citizens belong to each of us as equal individuals, or as members of particular groups?
- How should we make decisions about the nature of the Canadian community? Should we leave the process of constitutional amendment to the political elites (the "governments' constitution" approach), or should citizens have the right to participate in constitution-making in a meaningful way (the "citizens' constitution" approach)?
- Finally, who should bear the rising costs of social programs, how should the money be spent, and who should decide?

Constitutional politics from 1867 to about 1960 rarely involved open challenges to the very legitimacy of the existing *Constitution*. Amendments to the entrenched *Constitution* were limited in scope, addressing particular, well-focused issues. They occurred occasionally, one by one, not in packages large enough to raise questions about the legitimacy of the entire constitutional structure. On the whole, pre-1960 constitutional politics was an elite-driven process of improving Canada's existing political institutions, not a public and passionate debate over their very legitimacy.

Quebec's Quiet Revolution signalled the end of this elite-dominated and incremental constitutional politics. The mobilization of Quebec nationalism into an aggressive separatist movement challenged the entire political system. While Quebec's demands received the highest priority, rising Western regionalism and populism also forced the federal government to respond. In addition, the Liberal governments of Lester Pearson (1963–68) and Pierre Elliott Trudeau (1968–79 and 1980–84) had their own constitutional agenda:

- First, the federal government wanted to "patriate" (literally, "bring home") the Canadian *Constitution*. As we have seen, the 1867 *BNA Act* was an ordinary statute of the British Parliament, not a Canadian law, and it could not be amended by Canadian parliamentarians.
- Second, the absence of a written amending formula was an embarrassing anomaly that had to be addressed.
- Third, Trudeau was determined to entrench a *Charter of Rights*.[7] Such a *Charter* would not only protect the rights and freedoms of individual Canadians but also counteract the growing force of regionalism. A *Charter* would be a unifying symbol for Canadians in every province, not least for those in Quebec.

Between 1960 and 1971, there were two failed rounds of constitutional bargaining. The 1964–65 round—which did result in an amendment to give Ottawa powers over pensions—was an attempt to create an amending formula, while the 1971 *Victoria Charter* also included a few entrenched rights and some minor changes to the division of powers between Ottawa and the provinces. The *Victoria* amending formula required, in addition to the consent of the federal government, the consent of Ontario, Quebec, any two Eastern provinces, and two Western provinces having at least 50 percent of the Western population.[8] Quebec's opposition, based in part on the federal government's refusal to provide financial compensation for provinces that "opted out" of amendments transferring powers to Ottawa, doomed both processes.

The 1976 election of Quebec's first separatist government provoked intense concern outside the province and inspired dozens of proposals for institutional reform. In 1978, as electoral defeat loomed, Trudeau introduced Bill C-60. The bill contained a *Charter*, an amending formula, and **intrastate** reforms to national institutions. The most important of the institutional reforms was the replacement of the Senate with a House of the Provinces, which would comprise delegations from the provincial governments. The bill encountered fierce opposition, including a constitutional challenge in the courts, and it died when the House of Commons was dissolved for the 1979 election. The Progressive Conservatives formed a minority government, Trudeau announced his retirement from politics, and the constitutional issue was placed on the back burner. When the PC government was defeated in the House of Commons in December 1979 on a budget vote, Trudeau withdrew his retirement. He led the Liberals to a majority government in February 1980, shortly before the Parti Québécois government held the first Quebec sovereignty referendum.

The *Constitution Act, 1982*

As both the prime minister and a Quebecker, Trudeau was in a position to offer Quebeckers something in return for defeating separation—which was now called sovereignty-association, a mix of political independence and economic union—in the referendum. What he offered was a vague promise to renew Canada's *Constitution*.[9] When 60 percent of Quebeckers voted "no," Trudeau immediately kicked off another round of constitutional negotiations. The first stage culminated in a First Ministers' Conference (FMC) in September 1980.[10]

Many Quebeckers believed that Trudeau had promised to devolve powers to the provinces. Indeed, when federal and provincial officials met to set the agenda for constitutional discussions, the reallocation of powers was included as a priority item. Trudeau also proposed reforms to the Senate and the Supreme Court, an entrenched *Charter of Rights*, and an amending formula based on the regions. But the political situation had changed dramatically in two years, to the detriment of the provinces. By September 1980 Trudeau had been re-elected with a majority, and the PQ government had lost the referendum and faced a tough election battle within the year. Trudeau revoked the concessions he had made to the provinces in Bill C-60, and re-imposed his preferred centralist view of Confederation. Many Quebeckers felt that Trudeau had broken his promise of constitutional renewal. That sense of betrayal, coupled with the preexisting conflict between Quebec nationalism and the equal-provinces vision of Confederation, doomed the September 1980 FMC to failure.

Shortly thereafter, Trudeau decided to proceed with his constitutional project unilaterally—i.e., without the consent of the provinces. He argued that unanimous provincial consent was not legally required to amend the division of powers. Because it was not entrenched, the principle of unanimous provincial consent lacked the status of constitutional law. If it existed at all, the unanimity rule was a constitutional "convention," and conventions were unenforceable. Legally, according to this view, Ottawa was entitled to transmit requests for amendment to Britain unilaterally, and that is precisely what it proposed to do. The federal package would not address all the matters that had been on the constitutional agenda, only those that Trudeau considered essential: patriation; the *Victoria Charter* amending formula, plus the option of a national referendum to override the provincial governments; and the entrenchment of a *Charter of Rights*. The referendum proposal was the clearest indication of

Trudeau's strategy to undermine the premiers' opposition by going over their heads to the Canadian electorate. Although two of the provinces, Ontario and New Brunswick, supported Ottawa's initiative, the other eight provinces mounted vigorous opposition. Having lost the independence referendum, the PQ government felt compelled to participate in the attempt to reform the Canadian *Constitution;* despite this concession, it never abandoned its long-term sovereigntist inclinations.

The so-called "Gang of Eight" provinces challenged Ottawa's unilateralism in the courts, arguing that (1) the convention of provincial consent existed and (2) it was legally binding. The dissident premiers signed an Accord on April 16, 1981, setting out their counterproposals to the Trudeau package. They demanded an amending formula based on provinces, not on regions. Any future changes to the division of powers would require the consent of at least seven provincial legislatures representing at least 50 percent of the national population (the seven–fifty rule); up to three provinces could "opt out" of the amendment, which would not apply within their borders. This "Alberta formula" reflected the "governments' constitution," in contrast to the "citizens' constitution" reflected in Trudeau's referendum proposal. Quebec demanded, as the price of its signature to the Accord, full financial compensation for any province that opted out of amendments transferring provincial powers to Ottawa. This meant that a province would not be penalized for opting out when Ottawa taxed all Canadians for programs that did not apply in that province. The Gang of Eight also proposed a very limited *Charter of Rights,* whose weak guarantees echoed the 1960 *Bill of Rights.* Under pressure from Opposition parties in the House of Commons, Trudeau agreed to postpone any unilateral action pending a court ruling. In September 1981 the Supreme Court ruled that while Ottawa was legally entitled to proceed unilaterally, its package would be unconstitutional in political terms unless it received "substantial" provincial consent. (See Dossiers 8.2 and 8.3.)

In November 1981, Ottawa and the provinces made one last attempt to reach a deal. They hammered out a compromise package that became the basis of the *Constitution Act, 1982.* The first major compromise was a tradeoff between parliamentary supremacy and entrenched rights. Parliamentary supremacy implies the possibility of policy variation among provinces in matters within their jurisdiction. Applying the same entrenched rights to both orders of government, by contrast, constrains policy variation across provincial jurisdictions. It also gives the Supreme Court the power to strike down provincial laws that conflict with the *Charter,* a right that is also enjoyed by the U.S. Supreme Court. The provinces accepted the *Charter* reluctantly, in exchange for the power to override some of its provisions. Section 33 of the *Constitution Act, 1982* allows a legislature to declare that a particular law will operate "notwithstanding" the fundamental freedoms in section 2, the legal rights in sections 7–14, or the equality rights in section 15. The premiers hoped to use this remnant of parliamentary supremacy to protect their jurisdictions against the *Charter*'s nationalizing standards. In practice, negative public reaction to the "notwithstanding clause" has raised the political cost of a section 33 declaration to unacceptably high levels outside Quebec.

The second major compromise involved the *Charter* and the amending formula.[11] In essence, the Gang of Eight swapped its preferred amending formula—minus compensation for opting out in most cases—for a stronger version of the *Charter* than they had previously been willing to accept. Although Trudeau's referendum proposal was scrapped, it played a crucial role in the November 1981 negotiations. When the First Ministers reached a deadlock, Trudeau suggested that it be broken by submitting the two contending packages to a national vote. Quebec Premier René Lévesque endorsed that suggestion, thus alienating the other seven dissenting premiers and destroying the Gang of Eight. With the common front shattered, the other seven premiers were free to make a deal with Ottawa. The deal-maker was Ottawa's decision to accept both the notwithstanding clause and the seven–fifty formula. (See Dossier 9.1 for a synopsis of the 1982 amending formulas.) Trudeau also sweetened the deal for the Western provinces by inserting section 92A into the 1867 *Constitution*, guaranteeing the provinces a measure of control over the exploitation of their nonrenewable natural resources.

DOSSIER 9.1 The 1982 Amending Formulas

To make sense of recent megaconstitutional politics, an understanding of the amending formula (or formulas) adopted in 1982 is critical. As noted earlier, entrenched constitutions may be altered only by special procedures. These procedures are spelled out in Part V of the *Constitution Act, 1982,* which can be found in the Appendix to this book. Here is a brief synopsis of the various sections and their application in the Meech Lake and Charlottetown rounds of constitutional negotiation.

Sections 38–40 set out the *general* amending formula. Unless otherwise specified, amendments to the Canadian *Constitution* must be ratified by resolutions of both Houses of the federal Parliament and the legislatures of at least seven provinces containing at least 50 percent of the population (the seven–fifty rule). In practice, this means that the Atlantic and Prairie provinces cannot pass an amendment over

the objections of Ontario, Quebec, and British Columbia. An amendment under the general formula that reduces provincial powers must be approved by a majority of the members of each legislature, not just a majority of those present at the time of the vote. A provincial legislature that objects to a proposed amendment may formally reject it by a majority vote of its members, which ensures that the amendment will not apply to that province. The seven–fifty rule is subject to a three-year time limit; in other words, if the first legislature approves the amendment on January 1, 2006, the others must follow suit by January 1, 2009, or the amendment dies unratified.

Finally, any amendment in this category that transfers powers over education or culture to the federal Parliament must be accompanied by an offer of financial compensation to any province that rejects it. Matters subject to the general amending

(cont'd)

formula are listed in section 42. The formula was used successfully in 1983 to amend sections 25 and 35 of the *Constitution Act, 1982*.[12] The amendments clarified and extended the scope of Aboriginal rights (see sections 25, 35, and 35.1 in the Appendix).

Section 41 lists the subjects that can be amended only with the *unanimous* approval of all 10 provincial legislatures and the two federal Houses. The unanimity rule applies to the powers of the Crown, the composition of the Supreme Court, the two official languages, and section 41 itself. In other words, the extension of the unanimity rule requires unanimous consent. This became a crucial issue in both the Meech Lake and Charlottetown rounds, because the only practical way to give Quebec a veto over all future amendments was to extend the unanimity rule (in effect, giving every province a veto). We will discuss the interaction between Quebec's demands for additional powers and the equal-provinces principle in the following pages. Section 41 has never successfully been used to amend the *Constitution*.

Section 43 permits a constitutional amendment affecting one or more provinces, but not all of them, with the consent of the provincial legislature(s) concerned and the federal Parliament. This section was used six times between 1982 and 2001: three changes to Newfoundland's religion-based education system (1987, 1997, and 1998),

once to alter the organizational basis of Quebec's school boards from religion to language (1997), once to entrench equal status for francophones and anglophones in New Brunswick (1993), and once to permit the construction of the fixed link to Prince Edward Island (1994).

Sections 44 and 45 give the federal and provincial governments the right to amend their own constitutions. Section 44 has been used twice: to amend the procedure for distributing Commons seats among the provinces (the *Constitution Act, 1985* [Representation]), and to create a Senate seat for the new Territory of Nunavut (the *Constitution Act, 1999* [Nunavut]). Section 46 allows a legislature that has already ratified a proposed amendment to rescind (i.e., revoke or withdraw) its consent before the amendment takes effect. One of the crucial milestones in the Meech Lake saga was the revocation of Newfoundland's consent to the Accord in April 1990. Finally, section 47 limits the power of the Senate to a suspensory veto. In other words, the Upper House of the federal Parliament can delay a constitutional amendment but it cannot kill it outright. This provision was applied to the 1997 amendment regarding Newfoundland's education system; the Senate refused to approve the amendment, but its refusal was overridden by a second vote of approval in the House of Commons.

The Quebec government rejected the November agreement, and refused to sign it. Lévesque could not accept a package that neglected his province's decentralizing demands and implemented Trudeau's centralizing agenda instead. When the other seven members of the Gang of Eight reached a deal with Ottawa, Quebec felt betrayed. The perceived betrayal was worsened by the fact that the agreement was hammered out at a late-night meeting (known in Quebec as the "night of the long knives") to which the Quebec delegation had not been invited.[13]

Quebec raised several objections to the package, including the fact that the new seven–fifty amending formula would deprive the province of what it considered its traditional veto over constitutional change. True, this formula had been proposed by the Gang of Eight (of which Quebec was a member), but Quebec had agreed to the formula somewhat hesitantly, hoping thereby to cement the united front required to derail the constitutional process completely. If its own project were scuttled, Ottawa would certainly not consent to implement the Gang of Eight's alternative project, which was limited to simple patriation by way of the seven–fifty amending formula, and Quebec would be off the hook.[14] There is some indication that Lévesque might reluctantly have agreed to the package if full compensation had been restored, but this would have been completely unacceptable to Ottawa and would thus have killed the deal. Unwilling to see their compromise deal unravel, the other premiers refused Lévesque's request. Lévesque then bitterly announced that his government could not accept the Accord.[15] Despite Quebec's opposition (see Dossier 8.3), the federal government asked Britain to enact the new package. The resulting *Constitution Act*—featuring both the new *Charter of Rights* in Part I (sections 1–34) and the new amending formula in Part V (sections 38–49)—came into force on April 17, 1982.

Even before the *Charter* was enacted, it weakened the "governments' constitution" and gave new prominence to groups of citizens for whom territorial politics were irrelevant. Women, Aboriginal peoples, ethnic groups, people with disabilities, and seniors all sensed the advantages of constitutional recognition; they lobbied hard, and often successfully, for entrenched group rights. (We will return to the battle over the wording of the *Charter* in Chapter 10.) The influence of "Charter Canadians"— the groups with a particular stake in entrenched rights[16]—was not felt in the crafting of the 1982 amending formulas, which was purely the product of horse-trading among governments. Inevitably, it excluded nongovernment actors from future constitutional amendments, most explicitly by rejecting Trudeau's referendum proposals. If the *Charter* entrenched the "citizens' constitution," the amending formulas entrenched the "governments' constitution" and elite accommodation. The tension between these competing visions of Canada led to the failure of subsequent attempts to amend the *Constitution*.

Although the 1982 entrenchment of the *Charter* represented the triumph of Trudeau's vision of Canada—a strong central government representing a national community of equal citizens—it did not end megaconstitutional politics. The Quebec nationalist myth of two nations, which had provoked recurring constitutional crises since 1960, was not reflected in the 1982 reforms. Indeed, both the *Charter* and the new amending formula constituted a forceful denial of the two-nations theory. Ever since, Quebec governments have denied the legitimacy of the 1982 *Constitution Act* and demanded further constitutional changes to protect the province's distinct society. Similarly, while the *Charter* was a nationalizing response to Western regionalism, it did not address the intrastate agenda or devolve powers to the provincial governments. The continuing strength of Quebec nationalism and Western regionalism would

Queen Elizabeth II signs the *Constitution Act, 1982,* as Prime Minister Pierre Elliott Trudeau looks on. (© CP/Ron Poling)

provoke subsequent rounds of constitutional negotiation, but they would no longer have the playing field to themselves. The new "Charter groups" would mobilize against any perceived threat to their entrenched status, while the long-standing grievances of Aboriginal groups would ultimately force federal and provincial governments to respond.

Megaconstitutional Politics after 1982: From Meech Lake to Charlottetown

Having explored the relationship between political institutions and political values (Chapter 1), recent changes in Canadian political values (Chapter 2), and the strains inherent in Canada's federal system (Chapter 8), we are now ready to understand the megaconstitutional politics of the 1980s and 1990s. (Recall the definition of "megaconstitutional politics" in Chapter 1.) While territorial cleavages remained important, they were joined by growing public interest in equal rights and direct democracy arising from the value changes discussed in Chapter 2. These conflicting political values, and the proposed institutional reforms arising from them, are briefly summarized in Table 9.1.

There are at least two striking features of the demands listed in this table. First, the tension between the two primary subcultures (Quebec nationalism and Western regionalism) remains as sharp as ever. While the decentralizing demands arising from

TABLE 9.1   CORE THEMES OF MEGACONSTITUTIONAL POLITICS, 1982–92

SPECIFIC DEMAND	ORIGIN	CATEGORY	EXAMPLES
Constitutional recognition of Quebec as a distinct society	Quebec nationalism	Territorial	Meech Lake: "distinct-society" clause; Charlottetown Accord: "distinct-society" clause
Decentralization of powers over culture, immigration, and economic development	Quebec nationalism, regionalism	Territorial	Meech Lake: provincial opt-out of constitutional amendments with full compensation; entrenchment of existing Ottawa–Quebec agreements over immigration
			Charlottetown: withdrawal of the federal government from labour market training
Restrictions on federal spending power in provincial jurisdictions	Quebec nationalism, regionalism	Territorial	Meech Lake: provincial opt out of new shared-cost programs with full compensation
Intrastate federalism	Quebec nationalism, regionalism	Territorial	Meech Lake: provincial role in selection of Supreme Court judges and senators; entrenchment of the Supreme Court
Quebec veto over future constitutional amendments	Quebec nationalism	Territorial	Meech Lake: extension of the unanimity formula
Triple-E Senate	Regionalism	Territorial	Charlottetown: Triple-E Senate
Constitutional recognition of provincial equality	Regionalism	Territorial	Meech Lake: extension of Quebec's demands to all 10 provinces (except the distinct-society demand)
Aboriginal self-government	Aboriginal rights	Nonterritorial	Charlottetown: Aboriginal self-government
Direct democracy	Value change (postmaterialism and populism)	Nonterritorial	Charlottetown: referendum on Accord
Group rights	Value change	Nonterritorial	*Charter of Rights and Freedoms* Charlottetown: *Social Charter*

Quebec nationalism overlap with those arising from regionalism, the others are directly contradictory. If Quebec is recognized in the *Constitution* as a "distinct society," how can all 10 provinces be treated equally? Second, the nonterritorial reforms conflict with the territorial proposals. Intrastate federalism is based on relations between heads of governments, whereas direct democracy seeks to bypass "backroom deals" by vesting power directly in the people. Aboriginal self-government contradicts the territorial integrity of provinces, and may threaten the rights of other groups. Finally, populist demands for direct democracy based on majority opinion can undermine special legal protections for minority groups. We will explore the impact of the megaconstitutional conflicts in this section.

Bringing Quebec Back In

Although the Quebec government has never formally approved the *Constitution Act, 1982*, its provisions apply as fully in that province as they do in the rest of Canada. Ten days after the Supreme Court of Canada rejected Quebec's claim to veto the November 1981 deal (see Dossier 8.3), Quebec's National Assembly passed a resolution setting out the conditions for its acceptance of the November deal:

1. *It must be recognized that the two founding peoples of Canada are fundamentally equal and that Québec, by virtue of its language, culture and institutions, forms a distinct society within the Canadian federal system and has all the attributes of a distinct national community;*

2. *The constitutional amending formula*
   (a) *must either maintain Québec's right of veto or*
   (b) *be in keeping with the Constitutional Accord signed by Québec on April 16, 1981 [the Gang of Eight Accord] whereby Québec would not be subject to any amendment which would diminish its powers or rights, and would be entitled, where necessary, to reasonable and obligatory compensation.*[17]

This resolution established Quebec's bargaining position in future constitutional negotiations. After the separatist Parti Québécois government was defeated in December 1985, the Liberal government of Premier Robert Bourassa set out five conditions under which the Quebec government would agree to sign the *Constitution Act, 1982*. If the federal government and the other nine provinces would agree to Quebec's proposed amendments, the province's symbolic exclusion from the new *Constitution* would end. The five demands were as follows:

1. constitutional recognition of Quebec's "distinct society";
2. restoration of Quebec's constitutional veto;
3. greater control over immigration;
4. a role in selecting future senators and Supreme Court justices from the province (together with the entrenchment of the Supreme Court); and
5. restrictions on the federal spending power in areas of provincial jurisdiction.

- *August 1984:* Progressive Conservative leader Brian Mulroney promises to bring Quebec "back into the Canadian constitutional family."
- *September 1984:* Mulroney becomes prime minister.
- *December 1985:* The PQ government is defeated and a federalist Liberal government takes power in Quebec.
- *May 1986:* The Quebec government sets out five conditions for its acceptance of the *Constitution Act, 1982;* the federal government accepts the five conditions and sets out to sell them to the other provincial governments.
- *August 1986:* The premiers agree to negotiate on the basis of Quebec's demands.
- *April 1987:* The First Ministers hammer out a deal at Meech Lake, Quebec.
- *June 1987:* The First Ministers approve a legal text of the Meech Lake deal; Quebec ratifies the legal text, setting the three-year clock in motion.
- *September 1987:* Saskatchewan ratifies the Accord.
- *October 1987:* New Brunswick election won by Frank McKenna, who opposes the Accord; House of Commons ratifies the Accord.
- *December 1987:* Alberta ratifies the Accord.
- *April 1988:* Manitoba election produces a minority Progressive Conservative government, with the Liberals led by Meech opponent Sharon Carstairs holding the balance of power in the legislature.
- *May–July 1988:* Prince Edward Island, Nova Scotia, British Columbia, Ontario, and Newfoundland ratify the Accord.
- *December 1988:* Quebec government announces that it will use section 33 to override a Supreme Court decision striking down a ban on English-only commercial signs; outraged reaction in English Canada.
- *April 1989:* Newfoundland election won by Clyde Wells, who refuses to accept the "distinct-society" clause.
- *March 1990:* New Brunswick proposes, and Ottawa accepts, a "parallel Accord" to address the concerns of Meech critics while preserving the 1987 deal intact.
- *April 1990:* Quebec rejects a parallel Accord that could weaken Meech's protection of its distinct society; Newfoundland rescinds its approval of the Accord.
- *May 1990:* Parliamentary Committee recommends a "parallel Accord"; federal Cabinet Minister Lucien Bouchard quits in protest, and later forms the Bloc Québécois.
- *June 1990:* After six days of heated negotiations, the First Ministers work out a "parallel Accord" without the full approval of Wells; Manitoba legislator Elijah Harper refuses to allow the legislature to vote on the ratification motion; the Accord is ratified in New Brunswick, but Wells adjourns the Newfoundland legislature without a vote, and the Accord dies on June 23; Quebec erupts in anger, and federalist Premier Robert Bourassa announces

(cont'd)

that he will hold a referendum on sovereignty unless Quebec's demands are addressed in another round of constitutional talks.

- *November 1990:* Ottawa establishes the Spicer Commission to investigate the constitutional priorities of the ROC ("rest of Canada").
- *January 1991:* Publication of the Allaire Report, calling for a massive decentralization of powers to the provinces.
- *March 1991:* Publication of the Bélanger–Campeau Report, recommending a Quebec sovereignty referendum by October 1992 unless the ROC makes an acceptable offer of constitutional change.
- *September 1991:* Ottawa releases its proposed constitutional package, entitled *Shaping Canada's Future Together.*
- *October 1991:* Special joint committee begins ill-fated public hearings on the federal proposals; after weeks of disarray, it finally gets back on track.
- *March 1992:* Release of special joint committee report, which is quickly rejected by Quebec; talks begin among the ROC First Ministers and Aboriginal leaders.
- *May 1992:* Federal government introduces referendum legislation; talks nearly break down over Triple-E Senate.
- *July 1992:* ROC First Ministers announce a deal; Quebec agrees to discuss it, but not to formal negotiations.
- *August 1992:* Quebec formally returns to the bargaining table; accepts Triple-E Senate in exchange for a perpetual guarantee of 25 percent of the Commons; at final meeting in Charlottetown, all First Ministers sign the Accord and kick off referendum campaign.
- *September 1992:* "Yes" campaign runs into trouble, as the unpopularity of Prime Minister Mulroney rubs off on the Accord.
- *October 1992:* Quebec voters decide that the Accord does not go far enough, while ROC voters conclude that the Accord gave Quebec too much; the Accord is rejected by voters in Nova Scotia, Quebec, the four Western provinces, and Yukon.

The first two demands reflect only the Quebec nationalist agenda, while the other three also arise from the regionalist demand for greater provincial autonomy. Both the Meech Lake and Charlottetown Accords gave the Quebec government what it wanted. Unfortunately, the "two-nations" vision had little appeal outside Quebec, where the "equal-provinces" vision dominated public perceptions of federalism. The "distinct-society" clause in Meech, and a special provision in Charlottetown to offset Quebec's objections to a "Triple-E" Senate, led directly to the defeat of both Accords.

When Meech died, the Quebec government refused to participate in any future constitutional negotiations as one province among ten equals. Instead, the province would pursue a two-nations strategy. Quebec would wait until the rest of Canada came up with its own constitutional proposal, and then negotiate on a nation-to-nation basis. In the meantime, Quebec would undertake its own public consultations on the *Constitution* and develop its own positions. The resulting "two-track" process—one track in Quebec and the other in the ROC—began in the fall of 1990 and culminated with the announcement of the Charlottetown Accord in August 1992.

The "Quebec track" featured two sets of public consultation on future constitutional options: the constitutional committee of the provincial Liberal Party, chaired by Jean Allaire, and the Bélanger–Campeau Commission. The latter was a broad-based task force with members from all parties in the Quebec National Assembly as well as the private sector. The Allaire Committee was more highly nationalistic and decentralist than the Bélanger–Campeau Commission, but both bodies proceeded on classic Quebec nationalist assumptions.

For its part, the federal government established the Citizens Forum on Canada's Future (popularly known as the Spicer Commission, after its chairman) and a joint committee of the Senate and House of Commons on constitutional amendment, chaired by Gérald Beaudoin and Jim Edwards. The Spicer Commission found considerable discontent with the political process, particularly the secretive and unaccountable backroom deals of First Ministers. This finding reflected both the increasing influence of postmaterialist and populist sentiments, and the declining public satisfaction with representative political institutions. Concerns about the legitimacy of the constitutional process were shared by the Beaudoin–Edwards Committee, which recommended that any future constitutional deal be submitted to the public in a referendum. The Spicer Report also found that most Canadians outside Quebec preferred a strong central government, contrary to the assumptions of both Quebec nationalists and regionalists.

Matters were brought to a head in May 1991, when the National Assembly, in response to the Bélanger–Campeau recommendations, passed a law requiring a provincial referendum on sovereignty no later than October 28, 1992. The federal government responded in the fall of 1991 by releasing a new set of constitutional proposals, *Shaping Canada's Future Together*.[19] While the federal proposals were primarily a response to Quebec's ultimatum, their substance was shaped by the fallout from Meech Lake. Political leaders in the ROC sought to avoid the perception of a reform package driven mainly by Quebec's concerns, emanating from private negotiations of First Ministers, and presented for legislative approval as a seamless and unalterable web. The outcome of the "Canada Round" had to reflect both the "citizens' constitution" and the "governments' constitution," while satisfying populist demands for direct democracy and the equal-provinces vision of the ROC.

The ROC package, particularly the Triple-E Senate, directly contradicted the Quebec nationalist agenda. On the other hand, the purpose of the ROC process was to devise a package that would satisfy Quebec. Predictably, it failed to do so. Despite his reservations about certain parts of the deal, particularly the Triple-E Senate, Premier Robert Bourassa eventually agreed to sign what became the Charlottetown Accord. He accepted the Triple-E Senate in exchange for a guarantee that Quebec would hold 25 percent of the seats in the House of Commons in perpetuity (i.e., even if its share of the national population fell well below that figure).

Regionalism: Provincial Equality and Intrastate Federalism

As we have seen, the Meech Lake Accord was designed to meet Quebec's five conditions for signing the *Constitution Act, 1982*. But the process by which it was created and the content of the Accord were also shaped by the principle of provincial equality. Quebec's demands, apart from the distinct-society clause, were extended to the other provinces on an equal basis. Thus, Quebec's demand for a say in Supreme Court appointments became a general right of provinces to submit lists of potential Supreme Court appointees, from which Ottawa would select the winning candidate. Similarly, Quebec's desire for a constitutional role in immigration policy became the right of all provincial governments to negotiate constitutionally entrenched agreements "relating to immigration" with the federal government. Quebec's proposal to restrict federal spending power gave rise to a general provincial right to opt out of national shared-cost programs with "reasonable compensation" from Ottawa. Finally, Quebec's demand for a veto over future constitutional amendments resulted in a proposal to expand the list of subjects that could be amended only with unanimous provincial consent, thus effectively extending a veto to every province. This strategy not only respected the equality of the provinces but also ensured the unanimous agreement of the other premiers to Quebec's demands, because it guaranteed that every player (with the possible exception of the federal government) would win.

Had the Accord been entrenched, it would have decentralized powers to all of the provinces. Indeed, it has been aptly described as "a provincialist revenge against the nationalizing thrust of [the *Charter*]."[20] It was the attempt by proponents of the old governments' constitution to regain some of the ground they had lost in 1982. It reflected the governments' constitution not only in its content but also in the way it was formulated and presented to the public.[21] It was simply assumed that the 1982 amending procedures would be implemented in the old way—by interstate negotiations among the First Ministers. Thus, the Accord was worked out behind closed doors by the prime minister and the premiers and presented to the public as an unalterable fait accompli.

By 1987, when the Meech Lake negotiations opened, interstate proposals had to compete with those inspired by intrastate federalism. The idea was to reform national institutions—particularly the Senate and the Supreme Court—in order to make the federal government more sensitive to provincial concerns, thereby forestalling further demands for decentralization.

Because the Supreme Court, with its alleged pro-Ottawa bias, was the umpire in intergovernmental conflicts, provincial governments demanded a role in Supreme Court appointments. As we have seen, those allegations of bias are not entirely credible. Nonetheless, it did (and does) seem strange that in a federal state, the national government enjoys a monopoly over the membership of the highest constitutional court.

As we saw in Chapter 5, the Senate has never provided effective regional representation in Ottawa. After considering several alternative models, most Senate reformers eventually adopted the "Triple-E" (elected, equal, and effective) proposal. An elected Senate would inject a greater element of democracy into the national

Parliament, while a chamber with equal representation from all the provinces would offset the dominance of Ontario and Quebec in the House of Commons. An effective Senate, at least in theory, would give the elected representatives of the regions the power to influence legislation.

While the intrastate approach had great appeal in the West, it was regarded with suspicion in Quebec. Quebec wanted a say in appointing Supreme Court justices, but it rejected a Triple-E Senate that would entrench the equal-provinces principle. Under the current *Constitution*, Quebec controls nearly one-quarter of the seats in the upper house (24 of 104). A Triple-E Senate would reduce the Quebec contingent to just under one-tenth of the total. This reduction in the province's parliamentary representation was unacceptable to the Quebec government. In this respect, as in others, the constitutional aspirations of Quebec nationalism were directly opposed to those of the other nine provinces. This contradiction proved fatal to both Accords.

The "Citizens' Constitution": Direct Democracy, Group Rights, and "New Politics"

"Charter Canadians" were strongly opposed to any constitutional amendment that appeared to threaten their protected rights. As postmaterialist values and populist demands for direct democracy grew, the *Constitution* was redefined. It was no longer the exclusive property of governments, a matter of no interest except to politicians, lawyers, and academics; it was now a powerful symbol for hundreds of thousands of Canadians. The clash between citizens and governments helped to defeat Meech and prompted the referendum on Charlottetown that rejected the First Ministers' handiwork.

Both the content and the process of Meech jeopardized the newly won constitutional status of the "Charter groups." The Accord favoured territorial over nonterritorial interests. Feminists worried that Quebec might use the "distinct-society" clause to infringe women's rights—in effect, that a more restrictive approach to gender equality could prove to be part of Quebec's distinctiveness.[22] Aboriginal peoples wondered why only Quebec deserved constitutional recognition as a distinct society within Canada. Critics believed that the Meech Lake process treated the *Constitution* as the property of political elites, to amend as they saw fit. "Charter groups" reacted furiously. The *Constitution* belonged not to governments but to citizens, they argued, and citizens had to be involved in its amendment. These groups had been major players in the amendments of 1982 and they resented being shut out of the process now.

In their battle against Meech, "Charter groups" were assisted by two features of the 1982 amending formulas:

1. Certain elements of the *Constitution* could be amended only with the unanimous consent of the federal and provincial governments, while others required the consent only of Ottawa and seven provinces having 50 percent of the Canadian population. The amendments contained in the Meech Lake Accord fell into both categories. For example, entrenching the right to opt out of shared-cost programs with financial compensation fell under the seven–fifty formula, while amendment of the amending formulas themselves—to meet Quebec's demand for a veto, by extending the unanimity rule—required unanimous consent.

Instead of dividing the Accord into two packages corresponding to the two different amending formulas, it was presented as a "seamless web" that had to be passed as a whole or not at all. This meant simultaneously meeting the requirements of the unanimity and seven–fifty amending formulas. The latter imposes a three-year deadline for ratification. Consequently, the Accord had to be ratified by all 10 provincial legislatures and the federal Parliament within three years. The three-year clock starts running when the first legislature passes a proposed amendment. Canada's First Ministers had signed the Meech Lake Accord on June 3, 1987, and Quebec's legislature approved it on June 23. Thus, opponents of Meech could sink the entire package by persuading even a single province not to ratify the Accord before midnight, June 23, 1990.

2. Constitutional deals struck by First Ministers had to be ratified by federal and provincial legislators. First Ministers with disciplined legislative majorities can usually pass whatever they like in the legislature in a very short time. But the ratification process was delayed by legislative hearings in some provinces, and two of the First Ministers lost power before they could ratify the Accord. A third, Newfoundland's Brian Peckford, steered the Accord through the legislature before losing an election. That approval was later rescinded by the new premier, Clyde Wells. These developments gave the "Charter groups" opposed to Meech the time they needed to mobilize public opinion against the Accord. The longer they could delay final approval, the more likely it was that some province would refuse to ratify it before the deadline.[23] In the end, two provincial legislatures were denied the opportunity to vote on the Accord before the June 23, 1990, deadline.

Canada's political leaders learned a lesson from the failure of Meech. The "Canada Round," at least in the early stages, reflected the logic of the citizens' constitution in several respects:

- First, the federal government sought public feedback for its constitutional proposals; it tried to prevent the rejection of a potential deal as the product of closed-door intergovernmental negotiations.
- Second, a special joint committee of the Senate and House of Commons (the Beaudoin–Dobbie Committee) held extensive public hearings on the federal package.
- Third, when the special committee ran into logistical problems and an indifferent public response, the federal government organized five conferences across the country in early 1992, to invite discussion of various parts of the package.

All of this delayed the onset of traditional intergovernmental negotiation by First Ministers and emphasized public participation and consultation. The citizens' constitution prevailed, at least temporarily, over the governments' constitution.

Intergovernmental negotiation could only be delayed, however. The amending formula, as part of the governments' constitution, requires the consent of federal and provincial legislatures. While political executives could no longer ratify constitutional amendments without the consent of their legislatures, the First Ministers would still be the key players in the actual negotiations. Those negotiations began shortly after the Beaudoin–Dobbie Committee reported at the end of February 1992, and continued throughout the summer.

Although the interstate bargaining went on behind closed doors, the federal minister for Constitutional Affairs worked hard to keep the media and public informed. The 10 First Ministers (the prime minister and the premiers of the ROC provinces) were joined at the table by teams from the territories and four national Aboriginal organizations. Aboriginal peoples had played a leading role in the death of the Meech Lake Accord. This time, they would participate in the bargaining process. These features of the negotiations reflected efforts to graft the "citizens' constitution" onto an amending procedure formally based on the "governments' constitution." Despite these efforts, some "Charter groups" (particularly women's groups) complained of their exclusion from the negotiations. In a particularly dramatic objection of this kind, Aboriginal women's groups, alleging that their interests were not adequately represented by the male-dominated Aboriginal organizations admitted to the negotiations, asked the courts to force the federal government to fund their participation in the Charlottetown process. The federal government refused to grant this request; this refusal was later upheld by the Supreme Court.[24]

The tension between direct democracy and executive federalism was evident in both the content and the process of the Accord. Under the proposed revisions of the 1982 amending procedures, some matters, such as reform of the Senate, were to be shifted from the seven–fifty category to the unanimity rule. However, the actual process of amendment would remain in the hands of political elites. Although the text of the Charlottetown Accord reflected the governments' constitution, its ratification would recognize the citizens' constitution. The Accord would be submitted to the electorate in a referendum. There was no provision for a referendum in the 1982 amending formula; its results would not be legally binding on the politicians, but they would certainly carry political weight. Recall that Quebec was already committed to holding a referendum on sovereignty in October 1992. The provincial government changed the question: instead of asking Quebeckers to approve sovereignty, they would ask them to accept the Charlottetown Accord. British Columbia and Alberta had also committed themselves to consulting their populations through referenda, and Ottawa had passed legislation enabling a national referendum. Ottawa and Quebec arranged separate referenda, held under Quebec's law in that province and the federal law in the rest of Canada. Both were held on October 26, 1992. It would seem that minor constitutional amendments can still be passed without such a referendum, but most observers agree that the October 1992 referendum established a new constitutional convention.[25] In future, major amendments of the megaconstitutional scope and significance of the Charlottetown Accord will almost surely be ratified by the voters, and not just by the legislative and executive branches of the two levels of government.

The Accord was rejected by a majority of the voters in a majority of provinces, including Quebec. There were many reasons for its failure, but the bottom line was that voters were less willing than political leaders to compromise their political values and aspirations. As Peter Russell puts it, "The Charlottetown Accord was defeated because, outside Quebec, it was perceived as giving Quebec too much, while inside

CONSTITUTION II: FROM "MEGACONSTITUTIONAL POLITICS" TO "NONCONSTITUTIONAL RENEWAL"

Quebec it was perceived as not giving Quebec enough."[26] In other words, the conflict between the two-nations vision of Canada and the equal-provinces principle was unresolved. It might have worked, if the electorate had been willing to leave constitutional matters in the hands of the politicians. As Canada's political culture becomes less deferential and more participatory, resolving disputes over core political values becomes increasingly difficult, if not impossible.[27]

Aboriginal Rights

The Meech Lake Accord was finally ratified in New Brunswick, after the adoption of the "parallel Accord," but it failed to pass in Newfoundland and Manitoba. In the latter province, Aboriginal discontent with the Meech process sealed the fate of the Accord. At the eleventh hour, the difficulties of minority government had been overcome and the leaders of all parties agreed to ratification. By then there was not enough time to pass the necessary motion while respecting all the procedures of the Manitoba legislature. Those procedures could be suspended and passage expedited, but only with the unanimous consent of all members of the legislature. Elijah Harper, a prominent Aboriginal member of the legislature who reflected the Aboriginal community's opposition to Meech, repeatedly refused to consent to expedited procedures. Aboriginal peoples were upset by the exclusion of their leaders from the Meech Lake process, and by the possibility that the distinct-society clause would infringe Aboriginal rights. The fact that the Accord did not pass in Newfoundland was at least partly due to the perception in that province's legislature that Harper's resistance had already killed it in Manitoba. That a single legislator could effectively derail a major constitutional amendment is surely one of the more dramatic illustrations of the power of institutional rules.

By the summer of 1990, when the Meech Lake Accord died unratified, Aboriginal issues had risen to the top of the political agenda. A confrontation between Aboriginal activists and Quebec Provincial Police at Oka, Quebec, turned into a lengthy standoff between Mohawk warriors and the Canadian Armed Forces. The "Oka crisis" forced non-Aboriginal leaders to recognize the depth of Aboriginal discontent with the legal and constitutional status quo, as did Elijah Harper's role in the death of Meech, with the result that Aboriginal groups became key players in the negotiation of the Charlottetown Accord. Their leaders sat at the bargaining table with the First Ministers, and they won the agreement of all 11 governments to a plan for Aboriginal self-government.

The participation of Aboriginal leaders reflected a general acceptance of the claim that Aboriginal peoples, like Quebeckers, constituted distinct societies within Canada. The Charlottetown Accord recognized Aboriginal peoples as "the first peoples to govern this land," with "the right to promote their languages, cultures and traditions and to ensure the integrity of their societies." Moreover, Aboriginal peoples would express their distinctiveness through their own governments, governments to which they had an inherent right and that were said to be "one of the three orders of government in Canada" and thus of equal status with the government of Quebec. That government could not accept equal constitutional status for Aboriginal "nations," which contradicted the "two-nations" myth of Quebec nationalism.

Elijah Harper blocking the Meech Lake Accord in the Manitoba Legislature (© CP WFP/Wayne Glowacki)

Nonetheless, by leaving the details of self-government to be worked out after the Accord was ratified, the federal government succeeded in obtaining Quebec's approval for the package. Although the outcome of the October 1992 referendum was widely perceived as a rejection of Aboriginal aspirations by non-Aboriginal voters, the truth is rather different: a significant majority of Aboriginal peoples themselves voted against Charlottetown, because the proposed changes did not go far enough.[28] The parallel with the Accord's rejection in Quebec is unmistakable.

"NONCONSTITUTIONAL RENEWAL": MEGACONSTITUTIONAL POLITICS BY OTHER MEANS

The public rejection of the Charlottetown Accord left Canadians with a profound sense of constitutional weariness and a marked distaste for megaconstitutional politics. However, it did nothing to address the demands for institutional change that had driven the two previous rounds of bargaining. Quebec still wanted Ottawa to vacate shared policy fields, including labour market training. At the same time, most provincial governments agreed that the use of the federal spending power in provincial jurisdictions should be restricted in some way, so that Ottawa could no longer impose its own priorities in health care, postsecondary education (PSE), and social welfare. Business groups demanded freer domestic markets for goods, services, and labour, which meant eliminating or reducing provincial barriers to trade and mobility.

These forces for change gained added impetus in 1995, after two events shook the federation to its core. First, the Quebec sovereignty referendum came within a whisker of breaking up the country. Proving that Canadian federalism could work, even without large-scale constitutional change, became a preoccupation of the Chrétien government. Second, the federal budget ended the existing system of transfer payments to the provinces and replaced it with the Canadian Health and Social Transfer (CHST). As we saw in Chapter 8, the unilateral decision to slash transfers and rewrite the rules of fiscal federalism infuriated the provinces. They banded together in self-defence, and demanded a more formalized and collaborative process for decision-making on social policy. (This dynamic subsequently produced the Council of the Federation, discussed in Chapter 8.)

These pressures for change, combined with the cautious and incremental attitude of the Chrétien government, produced a wide-ranging strategy of nonconstitutional renewal.[29] As we will see in the next section, the federal government's "Plan A" strategy for dealing with Quebec sovereignty includes legislated promises to respect Quebec's distinct society and its claim to a veto. Other items on the Meech Lake and Charlottetown agendas were partly addressed by formal intergovernmental agreements. By the end of the twentieth century, Ottawa and the provinces had negotiated agreements on shared management of the economic and social union. These developments are summarized in Table 9.2.

Table 9.2 reveals the lack of progress on some megaconstitutional demands since the suspension of constitutional negotiations in 1992. The key difference between high-priority and low-priority items appears to be the receptiveness of the federal government to particular demands. When Ottawa perceives an opportunity to gain political ground by passing a law or participating in an FPT agreement, it does so. For instance, the Agreement on Internal Trade was popular among business groups frustrated by internal barriers to trade and labour mobility. The *Constitutional Amendments Act* was a key part of the "Plan A" strategy to minimize the political damage from the 1995 Quebec sovereignty referendum. However, federal concessions are strictly limited in scope and likely to be ignored when they become politically inconvenient (like the SUFA restrictions on the federal spending power).

Throughout this period, the government of Quebec was, at best, an intermittent participant in the federation. While it often sent observers to intergovernmental meetings, and it endorsed the agreement on the economic union, Quebec did not sign the 1999 SUFA. This points up one of the key differences between megaconstitutional politics and the more recent NCR strategy:[30]

TABLE 9.2 NONCONSTITUTIONAL RESPONSES TO MEGACONSTITUTIONAL DEMANDS, 1992–2004

SPECIFIC DEMAND	NONCONSTITUTIONAL RESPONSE
Constitutional recognition of Quebec as a distinct society	1995 resolution in the House of Commons, recognizing Quebec's distinctiveness
Decentralization of powers over culture, immigration, and economic development	Beginning in 1996, Ottawa negotiated specific arrangements with each province for labour market training; more collaborative approach to policy-making; under the Agreement on Internal Trade (AIT), provinces and Ottawa share responsibility for managing the economic union[31]
Restrictions on federal spending power in provincial jurisdictions	Social Union Framework Agreement (SUFA); has done nothing to prevent unilateral federal spending and policy-making in provincial jurisdictions
Intrastate federalism	No progress; continuing provincial demands for a role in appointing Supreme Court justices and senators denied
Quebec veto over future constitutional amendments	1996 *Constitutional Amendments Act*
Triple-E Senate	No progress
Constitutional recognition of provincial equality	No progress; both *Constitutional Amendments Act* and SUFA violate equal-provinces principle[32]
Aboriginal self-government	Completion of several land claims and treaty negotiations; recognition of "inherent right to self-government" by federal government; some efforts to include Aboriginal "peak" organizations in PT and FPT processes
Direct democracy	No progress; populism seems to be a waning force in Canadian politics[33]
Group rights	No progress

In earlier periods, Ottawa and at least some of the provinces would have gone to great lengths to avoid "isolating Quebec." Today, governments appear to have reluctantly accepted that they must get on with business even if Quebec absents itself or assumes observer status only.[34]

The 2003 election of a federalist Liberal government in Quebec promised to end the province's self-imposed isolation. Early in his mandate, Premier Jean Charest initiated the creation of the Council of the Federation (Chapter 8). However, Quebec has shown no interest in signing the SUFA, or joining the various intergovernmental agencies responsible for health-care policy. This is cause for concern, because it implies that the federation can get along just fine without a key province. The recent practice of "9-1-1" federalism, in which nine provinces and Ottawa strike deals without Quebec's support, may set a poor precedent for the future.

The NCR strategy differs from the megaconstitutional approach in other ways as well. Constitutional amendments, once entrenched in the text, are subject to judicial enforcement. Intergovernmental agreements are not, unless they are enshrined in federal or provincial legislation.[35] (It should be noted, however, that judicial enforcement is not a panacea for intergovernmental conflict. As we saw in Chapter 8, political actors can bypass court rulings; Chapter 10 explains the limitations on courts' enforcement powers.) The Supreme Court of Canada has twice ruled against plaintiffs who sought to challenge government decisions made under the Canada Assistance Plan (CAP).[36] In the 1991 *Reference Re Canada Assistance Plan (B.C.)*, the court considered the legality of the 1990 "cap on CAP" (Chapter 8). A unanimous court agreed that a cost-sharing agreement was justiciable—that is, open to judicial review—but it determined that the British Columbia government could not expect judicial relief for the federal government's unilateral decision to limit transfer payments.[37] The 1993 *Finlay* case dealt with a challenge by a Manitoba welfare recipient. He argued that the provincial government had violated the terms of the CAP agreement when it deducted money from his welfare cheques to recover an earlier overpayment. The majority on the court disagreed, holding that "the conditions attached to the federal government's contribution are not designed to dictate the precise terms of the provincial legislation, but rather to promote legislation which achieves substantial compliance with the objectives of CAP."[38]

In both cases, the court was reluctant to interpret the terms of intergovernmental agreements in a way that would require it to intervene directly. This reluctance arises, in part, from the federal principle; the justices have consistently recognized the legitimacy of divergent provincial policies to meet local needs, and allowed considerable flexibility to provincial policy-makers.[39] It is also grounded in the principle of parliamentary supremacy: agreements flowing from the process of executive federalism are not binding on the legislatures of the participating governments, unless they are subsequently ratified by legislators or enshrined in enabling statutes.[40] But the court rulings may also reflect the uncertain legal status of intergovernmental deals that are not enacted into constitutional amendments. Unless they contain effective mechanisms for enforcement and dispute resolution, agreements and Accords have little (if any) power to constrain the decisions of governments.

Another difference between the constitutional and nonconstitutional strategies is that the former create permanent rules for political conduct; the latter lead to temporary arrangements that can be revoked (or ignored) when political circumstances change. On the positive side, nonconstitutional change allows flexibility in the resolution of intergovernmental conflict; a short-term crisis, such as the 1995 CHST, can be resolved by negotiating new rules for both orders of government. If the crisis passes, the temporary arrangements—which may or may not be useful for other purposes—can be allowed to lapse.

The potential downside of NCR is the political uncertainty generated by impermanent arrangements. A long-standing political problem, like Quebec separatism, may require a permanent constitutional solution; anything less could be perceived as an inadequate stopgap. But this does not mean that nonconstitutional mechanisms are useless. They can have symbolic significance. They can set political precedents that ensure their survival long after an immediate crisis has passed. For example, Jennifer Smith argues that the 1996 *Constitutional Veto Act* (discussed in the next section) cannot be revoked by a future Parliament without heavy political costs.[41]

The examples of NCR discussed here are the products of a particular set of circumstances. The political will that produced them is the best guarantee that they will remain in place and work effectively. At this point, the political will to follow the terms of the economic union agreement seems to persist, though largely because private-sector groups are pushing the internal-trade agenda. The SUFA may be a different story. The forces that encouraged the institutionalization of fiscal federalism—in particular, the "deficit wars" of the 1990s—are waning. As of August 2004, Alberta had retired its debt and was awash in oil revenues. Under those circumstances, the province was in a position to refuse federal transfers for health care and set up its own system, free from even the notional constraints imposed by the *Canada Health Act*. The defection of a key province from a national social program could undermine the political will of the other participants even further.[42]

Nonconstitutional Responses to Quebec Nationalism

The renewed focus on Quebec's constitutional aspirations began with the 1994 election in Quebec of the Parti Québécois, under the leadership of hard-line separatist Jacques Parizeau. The Parizeau government announced that it would hold a referendum on independence in the first year of its mandate. This referendum, which took place on October 30, 1995, plunged Canada into the deepest of its modern megaconstitutional crises.

Parizeau initially wanted to hold a referendum on outright independence. However, the polls showed that Quebeckers were not prepared to vote for sovereignty without some form of continuing association with Canada.[43] Although many francophones were convinced that their "nation" could not reach its full potential within Canada, their fears about the economic costs of complete separation outweighed their nationalism.[44] As in 1980, therefore, a compromise position was worked out. Ultimately, Parizeau's Parti Québécois agreed with the federal Bloc Québécois and the provincial Parti Action Démocratique (the third party in the Quebec legislature) that Quebeckers should be asked whether the province "should become sovereign, after having made a formal offer to Canada for a new economic and political partnership." Note that sovereignty was conditional only on an "offer" of partnership, not on Canada's acceptance of that offer. If partnership negotiations broke down, Quebec could unilaterally declare its independence. The compromise among the three parties was enshrined in Bill 1 (see Dossier 2.3), which would become law after a successful referendum on sovereignty.

Even with an ambiguous question, campaign polls in the early fall of 1995 showed the sovereigntists trailing. Becoming desperate, Parizeau effectively turned the leadership of the "yes" campaign over to the more charismatic Lucien Bouchard, leader of the Bloc Québécois. Officially, Bouchard was appointed Quebec's chief negotiator

---

DOSSIER 9.3 The Quebec Referendum Questions in 1980 and 1995

In the 1980 and 1995 referenda on sovereignty, PQ governments posed questions that were carefully crafted to maximize the "yes" vote. Instead of asking outright "Do you want Quebec to separate from Canada?"—a question that, according to polling data, would produce a strong "no"—both questions fudged the issue by referring to "economic association" and "partnership." The 1980 question also requested not outright sovereignty, but merely a "mandate to negotiate." Soft nationalists who wanted a renewed federalism, not a complete separation, could still vote "yes" in the hope that this would strengthen Quebec's bargaining position vis-à-vis the federal government.

Although the PQ has always argued that the questions were perfectly clear to the voters, federalists accuse the separatists of trying to trick or confuse Québécois voters into voting "yes." Such an outcome, they argue, could not be regarded as a genuine expression of political will and would not have to be respected by the ROC. Judge for yourself.

Question asked at the 1980 referendum:
The Government of Québec has made public its proposal to negotiate a new agreement with the rest of Canada, based on the equality of nations; this agreement would enable Québec to acquire the exclusive power to make its laws, administer its

taxes, and establish relations abroad—in other words, sovereignty—and at the same time, to maintain with Canada an economic association including a common currency; any change in political status resulting from these negotiations will be submitted to the people through a referendum; on these terms, do you agree to give the Government of Québec the mandate to negotiate the proposed agreement between Québec and Canada?

Question asked at the 1995 referendum:
Do you agree that Québec should become sovereign, after having made a formal offer to Canada for a new Economic and Political Partnership, within the scope of the Bill respecting the future of Québec and of the agreement signed on June 12, 1995?

At its August 2004 convention, held while the PQ was in Opposition, the party voted to adopt a new strategy. Whenever it returned to power in the province, the PQ would hold a third referendum on sovereignty. This time, the question would be absolutely clear, along the lines of "Do you want Quebec to become a separate country?"[45] Although the PQ refuses to accord any legitimacy to the *Clarity Bill,* it is difficult to imagine that the party would have abandoned its cautious *étapiste* (step-by-step) approach to separation if the federal government had not forced it to do so.

in the anticipated post-referendum partnership negotiations with Canada, but everyone understood that he was now in charge of the referendum campaign itself. An effective campaigner, capable of rousing public emotions, Bouchard soon turned the tide and recaptured momentum for the "yes" side. Sensing a looming disaster, Prime Minister Jean Chrétien, who had been content to lie low for much of the campaign, stepped into the fray in its latter stages. A long-time opponent of the constitutional recognition of Quebec as a distinct society, Chrétien now committed his government to pursuing a distinct-society provision. He also agreed to promote a Quebec veto over constitutional amendments.

In any event, the separatists lost the referendum—but only by a whisker. Whereas about 60 percent of Quebeckers had voted "no" in the 1980 referendum, the result in 1995 was 50.6 percent "no" and 49.4 percent "yes" (with a voter turnout of over 90 percent). The difference between the vote totals was just over 50 000. Francophones voted 60 percent "yes" (up from 50 percent in 1980) while anglophones and allophones voted over 90 percent "no," provoking an embittered Jacques Parizeau to declare on referendum night that the sovereignty option had been defeated by "money and the ethnic vote." Shortly thereafter, Parizeau resigned as premier and Lucien Bouchard left federal politics to become the new leader of the PQ and premier of Quebec. Disappointed by the referendum loss but buoyed by how close they came to winning, the Parti Québécois promised to hold yet another independence referendum at an opportune time in the future, when the "winning conditions" are in place.

Given the close call of 1995, the separation of Quebec has become a more seriously imagined reality for most Canadians.[46] On one hand, this has led to renewed efforts to win the "hearts and minds" of Quebec nationalists. On the other hand, it has led to tough-minded thinking about precisely how separation and disengagement can and should occur. The two approaches have become known as "Plan A" (the reconciliation option) and "Plan B" (the "tough love" option).

The Chrétien government's immediate post-referendum strategy was based on Plan A. In particular, the government soon made good on its promise to do something about "distinct society" and the Quebec veto. On the distinct-society front, the House of Commons quickly passed a resolution recognizing Quebec as a "distinct society within Canada." The resolution declared that the House itself would "be guided" by the reality of Quebec's distinct society and "encourag[ed] all components of the legislative and executive branches of government to take note of this recognition and be guided in their conduct accordingly."[47] In other words, Quebec's distinctiveness would be a guiding principle not only for parliamentarians but also for all federal government bureaucrats. Although this commitment was not entrenched, it could be seen as the first step toward an entrenched recognition of the "two-nations" vision.

In early 1996, the federal government also gave Quebec a veto over constitutional amendments by "lending" its veto to Quebec. Under the *Constitutional Amendments Act*,[48] Ottawa would pass a constitutional resolution only if it had first been approved by Quebec, Ontario, British Columbia, two of the Prairie provinces having 50 percent of the Prairie population, and two of the Atlantic provinces having 50 percent of that region's population. As so often in the past, a proposal designed for Quebec was extended to other provinces in order to ensure its acceptance in the ROC, although this particular proposal reflected the regionalist vision of Canada rather than the equal-provinces approach. Ironically, the 1996 veto legislation makes the exercise of the general amending formula even more difficult; even if the political will to revive constitutional negotiations existed, there would be little chance of a positive outcome.

In addition to the distinct-society resolution and the veto legislation, Ottawa's Plan A strategy for placating Quebec included some administrative decentralization of jurisdictions. In the 1996 Throne Speech, Ottawa announced that it would withdraw from the field of labour market training and transfer funds for that purpose to the provinces.[49] The federal government also committed itself to negotiate a new intergovernmental agreement on Canada's social union, which would give the provinces more influence over the federal spending power (see "The 1999 Social Union Framework Agreement" on page 473). In effect, the Chrétien government was trying to accomplish Quebec's Meech Lake agenda without amending the *Constitution*.

Should Quebec decide to leave despite the blandishments of Plan A, it could not be allowed to unilaterally set the rules for its own departure. To protect its own interests, Canada needed to set clear and demanding rules and conditions under which secession could take place. By demonstrating the difficulties and costs involved in separation, such rules might cause Quebeckers to think twice before voting "yes" in the next independence referendum. This was Plan B, which included three main elements:

1. Although Quebec was entitled to separate, a unilateral declaration of independence (UDI) would be illegal under both Canadian constitutional law and international law. If Quebec wished to respect the rule of law, and to ensure its global recognition as a sovereign state, separation could be achieved only through an amendment to the existing Canadian *Constitution*. Since such an amendment would require the consent of other Canadian legislatures, including the Parliament of Canada, the details of disengagement—e.g., the division of the debt—would have to be negotiated first, while Quebec was still part of Canada, not after a UDI. As part of this dimension of its Plan B strategy, the Chrétien government referred the question of the legality of a UDI to the Supreme Court of Canada (see Dossier 1.3).

2. Federal Intergovernmental Affairs Minister Stéphane Dion rejected Quebec's argument that a 50 percent plus one "yes" vote in an independence referendum would be sufficient to trigger even a legal secession process. "Secession, the act of choosing between one's fellow citizens," argued Dion, "is one of the most consequence-laden choices a society can ever make." It is one of those "virtually irreversible changes that deeply affect not only our own lives but also those of future generations," and should thus be subject to more than an ordinary majority decision rule. "It would be too dangerous," he continued, "to attempt such an operation in an atmosphere of division, on the basis of a narrow, 'soft' majority . . . which could evaporate in the face of difficulties." A more substantial consensus would have to be shown.[50]

3. Dion raised the contentious issue of the partition of Quebec. If Quebec could separate from Canada, he suggested, parts of Quebec might with equal legitimacy secede from Quebec and remain in Canada. Dion highlighted the right of Quebec's Aboriginal peoples to remain in Canada. This example was no doubt strategically chosen; immediately before the 1995 referendum, three Aboriginal nations held their own votes on whether to stay in an independent Quebec. "The Cree voted 96% No; the Inuit voted 95% No; and the French-speaking Montagnais voted an astonishing 99% No."[51] Clearly, there would be pressure for the partition of Quebec, and Dion asserted that no one could "predict that the borders of an independent Quebec would be those now guaranteed by the Canadian Constitution."[52]

The ROC provinces also played a role in the evolving and shifting balance between the Plan A and Plan B responses to the separatist threat. Especially important in this regard was the so-called Calgary declaration, which emerged from a September 1997 meeting in Calgary of all provincial premiers and territorial leaders except for the premier of Quebec. The Calgary declaration set out a series of principles to guide public consultation on strengthening the Canadian federation. One of these principles involved the recognition of the "unique character" of Quebec society, an obvious reformulation of the distinct-society principle. This extension of an olive branch to Quebec became a prominent part of the Plan A strategy.

Inevitably, however, the Calgary declaration balanced its support of "unique character" with simultaneous support of the equal-provinces view. Thus, one of the principles insisted that "all provinces, while diverse in their characteristics, have equality of status," and another declared that "if any future constitutional amendment confers powers on one province, these powers must be available to all provinces." Once again, we encounter the now time-honoured strategy of giving to all provinces whatever is given to Quebec.

The Calgary declaration, in other words, embodied the tension between Quebec nationalism and Western regionalism that the Meech Lake and Charlottetown Accords had failed to resolve. Despite this, the declaration was widely supported in a variety of public consultations undertaken by provincial governments, and by mid-1998 the legislatures of all provinces and territories other than Quebec had passed, or intended to pass, resolutions supporting the declaration. The House of Commons passed a similar resolution. Even the Reform Party, which was the only federalist party to oppose the Charlottetown Accord, endorsed the Calgary declaration. Indeed, it was the Reform Party (later the Canadian Alliance, now the Conservative Party) that introduced the Commons resolution supporting the declaration.

The widespread support for the Calgary declaration is surely explained in part by the fact that it is merely a set of principles for discussion, not a proposed set of constitutional amendments. The stakes are thus much lower, and the tensions between competing principles easier to fudge or ignore. The history of recent megaconstitutional politics suggests that any attempt to incorporate the Calgary declaration into the entrenched *Constitution* would meet the same fate as the Meech and

Charlottetown Accords. Despite the Calgary rhetoric about Quebec's "unique character," and the shock of the referendum result, public opinion in the ROC was strongly opposed to constitutional recognition of "distinct-society" status or a special Quebec veto. "At the end of 1995, only 22 percent of people in ROC regarded Canada as a 'pact between two founding groups,' while 75 percent agreed that it is 'a relationship between ten equal provinces.'"[53]

By the fall of 1998 the Calgary declaration had receded into the background of Canadian politics. Attention was focused instead on the Supreme Court's pending judgment in the *Secession Reference*. Nearing the end of its mandate, the Quebec government was considering the timing of an election, and many observers speculated that Premier Bouchard was anxious to use a pro-Ottawa judgment by the court as the pretext for an election call. Quebec had portrayed the reference as an illegitimate tactic by Ottawa to impose its will in a matter that only Quebeckers could decide, and had thus refused to participate in the case. (Ottawa had to appoint an *amicus curiae,* or "friend of the court," to present Quebec's side of the argument.) The PQ government was waiting to pounce on a predictably anti-secessionist judgment by "Ottawa's Court."

The court did not oblige Bouchard. As in the 1981 *Patriation Reference,* it gave enough to both sides to make it difficult for either to simply reject the judgment. The court did conclude that Quebec had no legal right to secede unilaterally, that a legal separation would require a negotiated constitutional amendment, as Ottawa had maintained. On the other hand, the court ruled that if a "clear" referendum question yielded a "clear" result in favour of secession, the rest of Canada had a constitutional obligation to negotiate in good faith with Quebec. The court also implied that such negotiations had to be open-ended enough to include options other than simple separation—"sovereignty association," perhaps, or a "new partnership." This was too good for Quebec nationalists to pass up. No longer could the federal government argue that Canada was indivisible. No longer could it refuse to negotiate a new "partnership" with Quebec, on the basis that separation was a simple in-or-out proposition. Instead of rejecting the decision, therefore, the Quebec government tried to turn it to its advantage, emphasizing the parts it liked and de-emphasizing other parts.

The court left several key questions to be answered by politicians. What exactly was a "clear" referendum question? Did it have to be simpler and more direct than the 1980 and 1995 questions, as Ottawa maintained, or were those questions perfectly acceptable, as the PQ government argued? And what percentage of the voters would constitute a "clear" majority in a secession referendum? Would 50 percent plus one suffice, as Quebec had always insisted, or would a more substantial majority be required to break up the country, as Stéphane Dion regularly argued? A clear result on a clear question was necessary to trigger the constitutional "obligation to negotiate," said the court, but whether either the question or the result was sufficiently clear was a matter for political, not legal, judgment. In effect, the judges asked the questions; political leaders would supply the answers. In 2000, as Dossier 9.4 explains, the House of Commons did just that.

In December 1999 federal Intergovernmental Affairs Minister Stéphane Dion introduced Bill C-20 in the House of Commons. The *"Clarity Bill,"* as it was quickly dubbed, provided some of the answers to the political questions posed by the court. In particular, it addressed the issues of a "clear majority" and a "clear question." It gave the House of Commons the power to determine whether a provincial referendum question on secession was sufficiently clear to provide "a clear expression of the will of the population of a province on whether the province should cease to be part of Canada and become an independent state."[54] In a pointed rebuke to the PQ, the *Clarity Bill* condemned the 1980 and 1995 referendum questions: "a clear expression of the will of the population of a province that the province cease to be part of Canada could not result from

(a) *a referendum question that merely focuses on a mandate to negotiate without soliciting a direct expression of the will of the population of that province on whether the province should cease to be part of Canada; or*

(b) *a referendum question that envisages other possibilities in addition to the secession of the province from Canada, such as economic or political arrangements with Canada, that obscure a direct expression of the will of the population of that province on whether the province should cease to be part of Canada."[55]*

If the House of Commons determined, after consultations with Opposition parties,

Aboriginal groups, and other interested parties, that the question was not sufficiently clear, the federal government would not enter into negotiations on secession following a "yes" majority. Nor would Ottawa be obliged to negotiate if the "yes" majority was too small, or if it did not represent a majority of the entire electorate. The Bill does not define "a clear majority" precisely, although Dion has repeatedly declared that 50 percent plus one is an insufficient basis to break up the country. Finally, the Bill set out the mandatory subjects to be negotiated: "the division of assets and liabilities, any changes to the borders of the province, the rights, interests and territorial claims of the Aboriginal peoples of Canada, and the protection of minority rights."[56] In effect, the federal government warned Quebec voters that they could not take the existing provincial borders for granted; if anglophone or Aboriginal communities wanted to remain in Canada, they could count on Ottawa's support.

The Quebec government reacted angrily to the *Clarity Bill,* and quickly tabled a legislative response. Bill 99 effectively declared the *Secession Reference* inapplicable to Quebec, and proclaimed "the right of the Québec people to self-determination."[57] Section 4 defined a "clear majority" as "a majority of the valid votes cast, namely fifty percent of the valid votes cast plus one." There was no reference to the percentage of the overall electorate. Bill 99 concluded with the defiant assertion that "No other parliament or government may reduce the powers, authority, sovereignty or legitimacy of the National Assembly, or impose constraint on the democratic will of the Québec people to determine its own future." This refusal to accept the Supreme Court ruling in its entirety was hardly surprising. One month before the tabling of the *Clarity Bill,* Quebec's Intergovernmental Affairs minister had publicly condemned the *Secession Reference* as "a federally orchestrated strategy which sought to use the highest court of the land to obtain the answers that the federal government was looking for in response to questions of its own devising."[58] Nor is it surprising that a separatist government would respond with hostility to the Plan B strategy, the centrepiece of which was the Supreme Court reference. As a matter of law, however, it seems clear that Quebec is bound by the terms of the *Clarity Bill* in the event of a future "yes" vote in a referendum on sovereignty.

◾ Strengthening the Economic Union: The 1994 Agreement on Internal Trade

In every federation, a balance must be struck between the legitimate diversity of provincial priorities, including the promotion of local economic interests, and the maintenance of a strong national economy. Reconciling these competing goals is often a difficult process. In political terms, the immediate benefits of enacting policies that benefit local farmers, industries, and professionals are usually irresistible. The same cannot be said for collaborating with other governments to harmonize policies and eliminate barriers to commerce and labour mobility.

As far back as 1940, the Rowell–Sirois Commission identified provincial nontariff barriers as a potential threat to Canada's economic growth. By the 1980s, as the Canadian and American economies became more integrated, Ontarians were discovering that it was easier to do business in Michigan than in Quebec. Business leaders pressured the federal and provincial governments to dismantle the complex network of internal-trade barriers that had grown incrementally over the past century. Broadly speaking, these barriers were of two types:

1. discriminatory policies that deliberately excluded out-of-province competition (e.g., laws that restricted construction work to provincial unions, or forbade the sale of beer brewed in another province); and
2. otherwise legitimate regulations that differed from those in other provinces, thereby making it more difficult for workers and industries to set up shop.

Many barriers in the second category were imposed, not by provincial governments themselves, but by self-regulating professional bodies whose standards for accreditation were too narrowly drawn; for example, requiring an occupational therapist to hold a particular postsecondary qualification that was offered only at an institution in that province. Some of these variations among provincial standards—those pertaining to lawyers—had been eliminated by court rulings under the mobility rights clause of the *Charter* (section 6);[59] most were unaffected.

Both the "Quebec Round" and the "Canada Round" of negotiations featured discussions of the economic union, although these received less attention than Quebec's specific demands. The search for a binding intergovernmental solution to internal-trade barriers received added urgency from the failure of the Charlottetown Accord. The Mulroney and Chrétien governments were anxious to show the provinces, especially Quebec, that federalism could be made to work without formal constitutional change.[60] In late 1992 the Progressive Conservative Industry minister initiated the process by tabling a proposed *Statement of Principles* for collaborative management of the economic union. Negotiations among the FPT trade ministers began shortly thereafter and proceeded without interruption when the federal government changed hands. In July 1994 the new Liberal prime minister signed the Agreement on Internal Trade (AIT), along with the 10 premiers. The AIT took effect on July 1, 1995.[61]

The agreement requires the federal and provincial governments to do certain things, and to refrain from doing others.[62] First, governments are expected to eliminate existing trade barriers, either by abolishing discriminatory practices (e.g., local preference in government procurement) or working with other governments to harmonize divergent policies (e.g., labour qualifications or environmental regulations). In many cases, this requires them to work closely with groups in the private sector—an example of the "multitiered" federalism discussed in Chapter 8. Second, they must avoid establishing any new practices that may be perceived by other provinces as unfair or discriminatory—for example, offering subsidies to businesses that bring new jobs into the province. However, there are exceptions to the AIT rules: governments can still pursue development initiatives for their poorest regions. This is an important loophole: unemployed workers desperate for a job can vote, whereas an intergovernmental agreement cannot.

Third, the parties to the AIT agreed to establish a Committee on Internal Trade, made up of ministers from the 11 governments. This committee is responsible for monitoring the implementation of the agreement and conducting an annual review to determine priorities for future improvement. Unfortunately for advocates of a stronger economic union, the committee has been hampered by two institutional problems. The first is that it makes decisions by consensus, which means that an individual province can block a particular decision that it perceives as contrary to its interests.[63] Second, the committee's members—which include the ministers of Industry, Intergovernmental Affairs, and Economic Development—do not enjoy a monopoly over the policies that affect the agreement. There are separate intergovernmental committees with responsibility for labour, communications, transport, and many other policy fields directly related to the mandate of the Committee on Internal Trade. This diffusion of decision-making power hampers the effectiveness of the AIT.[64] However, there are recent indications that all departments within the senior governments have begun to take their agreement seriously when they review proposed policies.[65] If this is accurate, it suggests a more coordinated approach to internal trade across departments, and the possibility that the members of the Committee on Internal Trade can operate with the confidence that the governments they represent will honour their commitments.

Fourth and finally, the signatory governments established an Internal Trade Secretariat. The ITS, based in Winnipeg, does not report to any individual government; instead, it reports to all of the FP governments.[66] It is a genuinely intergovernmental institution; however, it lacks the teeth to enforce the AIT effectively. Enforcement is left to a dispute-resolution mechanism that can be triggered by either a government or a private-sector individual or company. If the parties to a particular dispute over internal trade cannot negotiate a resolution within a specified time, the case is referred to a panel for resolution. Panel decisions are nonbinding, so a government that is found to have violated the AIT is not required to abide by its ruling.[67]

It has been argued that a government in that position would have a strong political incentive to abide by the panel's decision, if only to ensure smooth trading relations with other governments in the future.[68] On the other hand, there may be a stronger political incentive to ignore panel rulings that, if followed, could jeopardize local jobs and, thereby, local votes. To offset these protectionist forces would require a very powerful intergovernmental agency with a binding dispute-resolution mechanism or, alternatively, a ministerial committee in which decisions could be made by a majority, rather than a consensus. Given the realities of Canadian federalism, especially the equal-provinces principle, neither seems likely.

For some observers, "progress in implementing the AIT has been disappointing, at best. Most of the targets and goals included at its signing have not been met."[69] However, the Internal Trade Secretariat paints a rosier picture: its 2003 annual report shows that most of the 11 governments are meeting their reporting obligations under the agreement, although other responsibilities imposed on individual provinces, or on the parties as a whole, are lagging behind the original deadlines. Notably, negotiations with professional bodies and municipalities to implement the labour mobility provisions were still underway almost a decade after the AIT took effect.[70]

In many sectors, however, internal trade and labour mobility are considerably freer today than they were in 1995. When the interests of the private-sector "stakeholders" are served by freer trade within Canada, the AIT has provided a framework for ensuring that their goals are met. Elsewhere, businesses, unions, or professional organizations have resisted changing a status quo that suits their own interests.[71] Consequently, the impact of the agreement varies from sector to sector. For example, FPT governments had worked to harmonize highway and transport policies for over two decades before the AIT was signed; as a result, the interprovincial trucking sector is highly integrated across Canada.[72] In this instance, the removal of internal-trade barriers was clearly a priority of both governments and the businesses involved in the trucking industry. Under those circumstances, policy harmonization in this sector would likely have occurred without the AIT.

In the long run, the symbolism of the AIT may be at least as important as its practical effects on internal trade. The negotiation of the agreement, and its unanimous acceptance by all 11 FP governments, placed the 11 senior governments on an equal footing in the management of Canada's economic union. Instead of invoking its powers under section 91 of the *Constitution Act, 1982*—the responsibility to regulate trade and commerce, or the "national concern" branch of the residual power—the federal government agreed to share the governance of internal trade with the provinces.[73] While the AIT shares the failings of other nonconstitutional mechanisms, including the lack of effective enforcement and dispute resolution, its mere existence seems to reflect a shared determination to make the federation work.

▪ The 1999 Social Union Framework Agreement: Institutionalizing Intergovernmental Relations?

In February 1999, shortly before the federal budget that began to restore CHST transfers for health care, the federal government and nine of the ten provinces signed the Social Union Framework Agreement (SUFA). The SUFA initiative originated with the provinces, which had been outraged by the unilateral federal announcement of the CHST in February 1995 (Chapter 8). In self-defence, the provincial governments banded together to devise "new ground rules to govern federal–provincial negotiations in the social policy arena."[74]

At the Annual Premiers' Conference in August 1995, the provincial governments agreed to establish the Ministerial Council on Social Policy Reform and Renewal. The council developed a set of proposals to "constrain the federal spending power [and] clarify the jurisdictions of each order of government."[75] In June 1996 the federal government agreed to work with the council to develop a national strategy to strengthen Canada's social union. The term "social union" is difficult to explicitly define. In this context, the term appears to refer to a nationwide system of social programs delivered by both levels of government, with primary program responsibility at the provincial level. In August 1997, as we have seen, the *Calgary Declaration* reaffirmed both provincial equality and Quebec's "unique character." In December 1997 the 11 First Ministers agreed to negotiate a Social Union Framework Agreement (SUFA). While it would not be entrenched in the *Constitution*, a SUFA would impose political pressure on the federal and provincial governments to cooperate and consult on future changes to social programs.

To secure Quebec's participation in the SUFA process, the other provinces agreed in 1998 that all provinces would have "the ability to opt out of any new or modified Canada-wide social program in areas of provincial/territorial jurisdiction with full compensation, provided that the province/territory carries on a program or initiative that addresses the priority areas of the Canada-wide program."[76] Since the 1960s, Quebec governments had insisted that they be given the chance to opt out of new national shared-cost programs, with full compensation from Ottawa for the benefits that they would have received had they agreed to the program. (As noted earlier, this demand played a key role in the constitutional bargaining of the 1980s and 1990s.)

The 1998 "Saskatoon Consensus" among the provinces and territories was translated into a formal SUFA proposal in January 1999. This "Victoria Proposal" declared that "Under the Constitution, provinces and territories are primarily responsible for social policy and the delivery of social programs."[77] It called for "full federal restoration of the funding cut from the Canada Health and Social Transfer"; full escalation of federal transfer payments to cover rising program costs; consent of a majority of provinces to "any new or modified Canada-wide program in areas of provincial jurisdiction"; "joint agreement of objectives and principles for new or modified Canada-wide programs"; and full compensation to any province that opted out of a new or modified program as long as it provided similar services under its own responsibility. The proposal also included mechanisms for resolving disputes between governments and for seeking "public input in developing priorities and objectives for social programs." No new federal shared-cost program would be introduced without the agreement of a majority of the provincial governments. There was no requirement that these governments represent a majority of the Canadian population; in principle, an agreement under this provision could exclude Ontario, British Columbia, Alberta, and (perhaps inevitably) Quebec. In political terms, however, this is surely a far-fetched scenario.[78] Finally, the Victoria Proposal recognized the close connection between the economic union and the social union; it contained explicit provisions to enhance social mobility, paralleling the AIT provisions on labour mobility.

On February 4, 1999, the federal government and all of the provinces except Quebec agreed to the final SUFA text.[79] The agreement differed from the Victoria Proposal in at least three key respects.[80] First, it contained an explicit declaration that "The use of the federal spending power under the Constitution has been essential to the development of Canada's social union," as the basis for both intergovernmental transfers and direct transfers to individuals. No such declaration was included in the provincial proposal. Second, the reference to provincial supremacy over social policy was deleted. Third, Ottawa refused to accept the opting-out provision in the Victoria Proposal. The SUFA simply states that "All provincial and territorial governments that meet or commit to meet the agreed Canada-wide objectives and agree to respect the accountability framework will receive their share of available funding." Without the opt-out provision, Quebec refused to sign the agreement.

The differences between the PT agreement and the final FPT version can be explained quite simply: when the federal government joined the SUFA process, it brought a large pot of money to the table. It used the promise of substantial increases to the CHST to win over nine of the premiers, persuading them to modify their opposition to the federal spending power in exchange for its more lavish employment.[81] So "what had begun in large part as a provincial and territorial initiative to bell the federal spending power ended up as a framework to facilitate federal government involvement in provincial programs."[82]

Reaction to the SUFA was mixed. Critics in Quebec condemned the other premiers for "selling out." Instead of keeping faith with Quebec, they jumped at Ottawa's promise of restored health-care funding.[83] Observers outside Quebec were more favourable, suggesting that "the provinces 'won' to the extent that Ottawa agreed to put into an intergovernmental agreement a set of decision rules that gives the provinces a formal if modest role in the exercise of [the federal spending] power that they had not previously had."[84]

The SUFA is only a political Accord, not an entrenched constitutional law. So while it might have ushered in "a new era of collaboration, mutual respect among orders of government and a more coherent and systematic approach to social policy-making,"[85] it could just as easily turn out to be a collection of hollow promises. Less than two weeks after the SUFA was signed, the 1999 federal budget introduced a new formula for calculating CHST transfers, which had not been crafted in consultation with the provinces. This unilateral federal announcement suggests that the agreement, despite its language about cooperation and joint decision-making, "offers no guarantee of stability or predictability in federal spending"[86]—a guarantee that had been one of the chief provincial goals in the SUFA process. The federal government has continued to make unilateral changes to transfers and policies, flouting the express terms of the agreement.

Unlike the AIT, the SUFA did not establish a dedicated intergovernmental secretariat to monitor implementation. Instead, "work on strengthening Canada's social union has been coordinated on two fronts—by the Provincial/Territorial Council on Social Policy Renewal and the Federal/Provincial/Territorial Council on Social Policy Renewal."[87] The Provincial/Territorial Council submitted an annual report to the Annual Premiers' Conference[88] on progress toward meeting SUFA goals. The 2000 and 2001 reports reflect considerable frustration with Ottawa, its refusal to recognize a lead role for the PT governments in the design of social policy, its reluctance to accept an effective dispute-resolution mechanism, and its insistence on altering transfer payments and creating new programs (e.g., the 2000 homelessness initiative) without proper consultation or advance notice.[89] All the council could do was to report on the problems and ask the premiers to make SUFA a central issue in their dealings with Ottawa.

Since 1999 the 10 participating governments have made modest progress on some policy fronts, including social mobility, child poverty, early childhood development, and disability.[90] However, the highest-profile social policy field—health care—seems relatively unaffected by SUFA. Ottawa and the 10 ROC provinces have signed two health Accords since 1999, neither of which contains any reference to the agreement.[91] One might well question the value of a supposedly binding agreement on social policy that seems to be irrelevant to the overriding social-policy issue in Canada. The SUFA is also invisible in other recent FPT agreements, such as the 2000 Accord on Early Childhood Development. All in all, the SUFA has not—despite its advance billing—transformed the process for making and implementing social policy in Canada. Nor has it had any significant effects on the content of policy.[92] Indeed, very few of the FPT agreements on social policy since 1999 contain any reference to the SUFA.

Harvey Lazar recently identified five "roadblocks" to the implementation of SUFA.[93] First, the federal and provincial governments came to the table in February 1999 with different objectives and visions; Ottawa managed to paper over the differences by promising larger transfers, but the diverging goals quickly re-emerged. Without a real shared understanding of the agreement and its purpose, it could not have any meaningful influence. Second, SUFA did nothing to resolve the underlying source of conflict: intergovernmental disputes over the vertical fiscal imbalance.[94] Third, as previously mentioned, the two levels of government cannot agree on the proper role of the two ministerial councils. Fourth, Ottawa refused to accede to provincial demands for an effective and binding dispute-resolution mechanism. When, in 2003, it finally accepted such a mechanism for health care, it did so only on the condition that the final decision be left to the federal Health minister. Fifth, there is no political constituency for the SUFA in the wider public. The 2003 review was supposed to be a model of the public consultation principle enshrined in the agreement; there was a call for groups and individuals to post contributions to a website, which was largely ignored. In the absence of public pressure on governments to fulfill their SUFA commitments, political will may be lacking.[95]

The 2003 review of the SUFA by the Federal/Provincial/Territorial Council was predictably anticlimactic. It accentuated the positive, focusing on the few success stories (e.g., the recent adoption of a dispute-resolution process for health care) and recommending that governments work together more collaboratively in the future.[96] The most notable feature of the review was the discussion of integrating Aboriginal organizations into the implementation process where appropriate. All in all, the low-key review process and the "rather lukewarm report" that resulted do not bode well for the future of the SUFA.[97]

CONCLUSION

The reforms and reform proposals discussed in this chapter, both constitutional and nonconstitutional, reflect the lack of consensus about the character of Canada's political community. Two strongly mobilized subcultures—Quebec nationalism and Western regionalism—have been joined by new, latent cleavages fostered by value change and the *Charter of Rights*. While these latter groups have not produced fully formed subcultures, they mobilized effectively around the perceived threat to the "citizens' constitution" from the Meech Lake and Charlottetown Accords. As the old territorial issues remained unresolved, the addition of new nonterritorial claims for constitutional recognition and the populist critique of executive federalism fatally complicated the process of megaconstitutional politics. The substitution of referenda for elite accommodation as the decisive decision-making device made it more difficult than ever to satisfy the rapidly multiplying demands for institutional reform.

At present, populism appears to be losing some of its political force. The new Conservative Party seems to lack the populist enthusiasm of its predecessors, the Reform Party and the Canadian Alliance. But the other pressures for change will persist. In times of crisis, they may escalate until Canada's political elites have no choice but to confront them. There is no guarantee, however, that a successful return to constitutional bargaining would have the desired effects. The *Constitution Act, 1982,* the only successful product of megaconstitutional politics to date, has had significant and partly unanticipated effects on our government and politics. We turn to the *Charter* in the next chapter.

GLOSSARY OF KEY TERMS

Amending formula: The formal process for changing a written constitution. The formula is usually included in the constitution itself. Amending a constitution is a complex and difficult process, requiring a broad consensus among the key players in the political system. Because the constitution sets out the rules of the political game, and it is intended to provide continuity and stability to the political system, the amending formula must protect the written constitution against changes that are purely temporary in nature, or that violate the core principles on which the political system is based (e.g., democracy and federalism).

Amendment: Any proposed or actual alteration in the wording of a written constitution. An amendment can insert one or more new provisions into the constitution; it can delete one or more existing provisions; or it can rewrite part of a constitution to keep it up to date with changing circumstances.

Economic union: The goal of creating a single national economy, without internal barriers to trade or mobility, transcending provincial jurisdictions. In Canada, this goal is manifested most prominently in the 1994 Agreement on Internal Trade (AIT).

Intrastate: See the Chapter 8, "Glossary of Key Terms."

Social union: The goal of creating a cohesive national network of social programs (e.g., health care), so that Canadians in every province and territory receive a similar package of services. The opposite of "checkerboard federalism," in which Canadians in one province receive fewer, lesser, or entirely different social programs from those available in a neighbouring province.

DISCUSSION QUESTIONS

1. Identify and briefly summarize *two* key elements in the 1980 constitutional proposal of Prime Minister Trudeau.
2. Name and briefly analyze *two* of Quebec's long-standing demands for reform of the Canadian *Constitution*. How, if at all, have these demands been met?
3. Why did the Meech Lake and Charlottetown Accords fail? In your opinion, would Canada be better off if either Accord had been ratified? Why or why not?
4. Can the competing constitutional (and nonconstitutional) agendas of Canada's major subcultures ever be reconciled? If so, how?
5. Are nonconstitutional reforms effective responses to megaconstitutional demands? Why or why not? Refer to at least one recent nonconstitutional initiative.

SUGGESTED READINGS

Books and Articles

Alain-G. Gagnon and Hugh Segal, eds., *The Canadian Social Union Without Quebec: Eight Critical Analyses* (Montreal: Institute for Research in Public Policy, 2000).

Sarah Fortin, Alain Noël, and France St-Hilaire, eds., *Forging the Canadian Social Union: SUFA and Beyond* (Montreal: Institute for Research on Public Policy, 2003).

James Ross Hurley, *Amending Canada's Constitution: History, Processes, Problems and Prospects* (Ottawa: Minister of Supply and Services Canada, 1996).

Harvey Lazar, "Non-Constitutional Renewal: Toward a New Equilibrium in the Federation," in Harvey Lazar, ed., *The State of the Federation 1997: Non-Constitutional Renewal* (Kingston, ON: Institute of Intergovernmental Relations, 1998).

Peter H. Russell, *Constitutional Odyssey: Can Canadians Become a Sovereign People?*, 2nd edition (Toronto: University of Toronto Press, 1993).

Robert A. Young, *The Struggle for Quebec: From Referendum to Referendum?* (Montreal and Kingston: McGill–Queen's University Press, 1999).

Websites

The most useful website for this chapter is maintained by the Canadian Intergovernmental Conference Secretariat (www.scics.gc.ca), which provides a full list of PT and FPT ministerial meetings and many of the countless gatherings of officials that have taken place since 1996. Go to the website, click on "Conference Information," and then select the month and year of a particular conference (e.g., the September 2004 FPT Health Care Summit). For the major meetings, you will often find links to official documents—the final communiqués as well as the working papers.

Another helpful source of information is the Intergovernmental Affairs page of the Privy Council Office website (www.pco-bcp.gc.ca). Click on "Intergovernmental Relations by Sector" to find a wealth of documents on the cooperation (and conflicts) among Canada's senior governments.

Finally, there are two outstanding sources of academic commentary on Canadian intergovernmental relations: the Institute for Research on Public Policy (www.irpp.org) and the Queen's University Institute of Intergovernmental Relations (www.iigr.ca). At the IRPP site, click "Publication Search" and select "Canadian federalism" or "Council of the Federation" from the pull-down menu of public policy subjects. Select "Research" from the menu at the top of the screen, and then "Browse Publications" or "Current Research" from the pull-down menu. The "Working Papers" page provides up-to-date analysis of trends in Canadian federalism and nonconstitutional renewal. The Queen's IIGR site also provides a wide range of information that is readily available.

▌ NOTES

1. James Ross Hurley, *Amending Canada's Constitution: History, Processes, Problems and Prospects* (Ottawa: Minister of Supply and Services Canada, 1996), 19–20.

2. There have been several amendments affecting the federal government, including changes to the representation formula used to allocate seats in the House of Commons and the creation of Nunavut as a separate territory. Amendments affecting only one province have also been successfully enacted, including changes to school boards in Quebec and Newfoundland and Labrador. However, these did not employ either the general amending formula or the unanimity rule.

3. Jennifer Smith, "Informal Constitutional Development: Change by Other Means," in Herman Bakvis and Grace Skogstad, eds., *Canadian Federalism: Performance, Effectiveness, and Legitimacy* (Toronto: Oxford University Press, 2002), 40.

4. Jennifer Smith, "The Constitutional Debate and Beyond," in François Rocher and Miriam Smith, eds., *New Trends in Canadian Federalism,* 2nd edition (Peterborough, ON: Broadview Press, 2003).

5. Roger Gibbins, "Shifting Sands: Exploring the Political Foundations of SUFA," in Sarah Fortin, Alain Noël, and France St-Hilaire, eds., *Forging the Canadian Social Union: SUFA and Beyond* (Montreal: Institute for Research on Public Policy, 2003).

6. Smith, "The Constitutional Debate and Beyond," 63.

7. Pierre Elliott Trudeau, "A Constitutional Declaration of Rights," in Pierre Elliott Trudeau, *Federalism and the French Canadians* (Toronto: Macmillan, 1968), 52–60.

8. Garth Stevenson, *Unfulfilled Union: Canadian Federalism and National Unity,* rev. edition (Toronto: Gage, 1982), 76–77.

9. Peter H. Russell, *Constitutional Odyssey: Can Canadians Become a Sovereign People?* 2nd edition (Toronto: University of Toronto Press, 1993), 109.

10. Roy Romanow, John Whyte, and Howard Leeson, *Canada Notwithstanding: The Making of the Constitution 1976–1982* (Toronto: Carswell/Methuen, 1984), 60–61

11. Alan C. Cairns, "Citizens (Outsiders) and Governments (Insiders) in Constitution-Making: The Case of Meech Lake," in Alan C. Cairns, *Disruptions: Constitutional Struggles, from the Charter to Meech Lake,* ed. Douglas E. Williams (Toronto: McClelland and Stewart, 1991), 110.

12. The text of the *Constitution Amendment Proclamation, 1983* and subsequent amendments to the *Constitution* can be found on the Nelson website at www.parametersofpower4e.nelson.com in the "Canadian Politics on the Web" section, under "The Constitution."

13. Romanow et al., 210–11.

14. Ibid., 130–31.

15. Ibid., 210–11.

16. Cairns, 133.

17. Resolution of the National Assembly, December 16, 1982. Reproduced in James Ross Hurley, *Amending Canada's Constitution: History, Processes, Problems and Prospects* (Ottawa: Minister of Supply and Services Canada, 1996), Appendix 15, 255.

18. The Meech Lake time line is adapted from Andrew Cohen, *A Deal Undone: The Making and Breaking of the Meech Lake Accord* (Vancouver: Douglas and McIntyre, 1991), 285–89; the Charlottetown Accord time line is adapted from Susan Delacourt, *United We Fall: The Crisis of Democracy in Canada* (Toronto: Viking, 1993).

19. *Shaping Canada's Future Together* (Ottawa: Minister of Supply and Services Canada, 1991).

20. Richard Simeon, "Meech Lake and Shifting Conceptions of Federalism," *Canadian Public Policy 14* (supp.) (1988), 10.

21. Cairns, "Citizens (Outsiders)," 135.

22. This is highly unlikely. With regard to gender equality, Quebec is probably the most progressive jurisdiction in the country.

23. Patrick J. Monahan, *Meech Lake: The Inside Story* (Toronto: University of Toronto Press, 1991), 144–45.

24. *Native Women's Association of Canada v. Canada* [1994] 3 S.C.R. 627.

25. Smith, "The Constitutional Debate and Beyond," 59.

26. Russell, *Constitutional Odyssey,* 226.

27. Michael Lusztig, "Constitutional Paralysis: Why Canadian Constitutional Initiatives Are Doomed to Fail," *Canadian Journal of Political Science,* XXVII:4 (December 1994), 747–71.

28. Ken S. Coates, *The Marshall Decision and Native Rights* (Montreal and Kingston: McGill–Queen's University Press, 2000), 78.

29. Harvey Lazar, "Non-Constitutional Renewal: Toward a New Equilibrium in the Federation," in Harvey Lazar, ed., *The State of the Federation 1997: Non-Constitutional Renewal* (Kingston, ON: Institute of Intergovernmental Relations, 1998).

30. Of course, the isolation of Quebec could be described as an instance of continuity rather than change, given the entrenchment of the *Constitution Act, 1982* without the province's consent.

31. Rodney Haddow, "Canadian Federalism and Active Labour Market Policy," in Rocher and Smith, eds.; Herman Bakvis, "Checkerboard Federalism? Labour Market Development Policy in Canada," in Bakvis and Skogstad, eds.

32. The *Constitutional Amendments Act* makes it all but impossible for the smallest provinces to veto a proposed amendment; decision-making under the SUFA is based on a majority of governments, so that no single government has a veto.

33. Gibbins, "Shifting Sands," 43.

34. Lazar, "Non-Constitutional Renewal," 26.

35. Even then, the courts are unlikely to accept challenges to their constitutionality. Law Professor Lorne Sossin suggested in 1998 that the CHST—specifically, the removal of the conditions under the CAP, which it replaced—might be open to a court challenge under the *Charter of Rights* (sections 7 and 15). Subsequently, the Supreme Court of Canada has rejected the claim that either section protects welfare recipients from the unilateral reduction of their benefits. See Sossin, "Salvaging the Welfare State? The Prospects for Judicial Review of the Canada Health and Social Transfer," *Dalhousie Law Journal,* 21:1 (Spring 1998); *Gosselin v. Quebec (Attorney General)* [2002] 4 S.C.R. 429.

36. As discussed in Chapter 8, CAP disappeared in 1995 (although it was technically rolled into the CHST).

37. *Reference Re Canada Assistance Plan (B.C.),* [1991] 2 S.C.R. 525

38. *Finlay v. Canada (Minister of Finance)* [1993] 1 S.C.R. 1080, head notes.

39. See Heather MacIvor, *Canadian Government and Politics in the Charter Era* (Toronto: Nelson Thomson, 2005), Chapter 7.

40. Johanne Poirier, "Intergovernmental Agreements in Canada: At the Crossroads Between Law and Politics," in J. Peter Meekison, Hamish Telford, and Harvey Lazar, eds., *Reconsidering the Institutions of Canadian Federalism* (Montreal and Kingston: Institute of Intergovernmental Relations/McGill–Queen's University Press, 2004), 435.

41. Smith, "Informal Constitutional Development," 49.

42. Gibbins, "Shifting Sands," 39.

43. Robert A. Young, *The Struggle for Quebec: From Referendum to Referendum?* (Montreal and Kingston: McGill–Queen's University Press, 1999), 18.

44. Young, 40–41.

45. Rhéal Séguin, "Landry stays as PQ leader—for now," *The Globe and Mail,* August 30, 2004 (accessed online at www.globeandmail.com); "Sovereigntists design new referendum rules," August 29, 2004 (accessed online at www.cbc.ca).

46. Alan C. Cairns, "The Legacy of the Referendum: Who Are We Now?," *Constitutional Forum 7,* nos. 2 and 3 (Winter and Spring 1996), 101.

47. Young, 95 and 175 (note 53).

48. *An Act Respecting Constitutional Amendments,* Royal Assent, February 2, 1996; formerly Bill C-110, 35th Parliament, 1st Session.

49. "Speech from the Throne to Open the Second Session of the Thirty-Fifth Parliament of Canada," February 27, 1996, 4–5; available online at www.pco-bcp.gc.ca.

50. Letter from Stéphane Dion to Lucien Bouchard, *Calgary Herald,* August 14, 1997.

51. Cairns, "The Legacy of the Referendum," 36.

52. Letter from Dion to Bouchard.

53. Young, 76.

54. House of Commons of Canada, 2nd Session, 36th Parliament, 48–49 Elizabeth II, 1999–2000, Bill C-20: *An Act to give effect to the requirement for clarity as set out in the opinion of the Supreme Court of Canada in the Quebec Secession Reference* (as adopted [March] 2000), section 1(3).

55. Ibid., section 3(2).

56. Bill C-20, section 1(4).

57. Québec, National Assembly, 2000, Bill 99: *An Act respecting the exercise of the fundamental rights and prerogatives of the Québec people and the Québec State,* section 1.

58. Joseph Facal, "Quebec Sovereignty and the Rule of Law," November 17, 1999; available on the Nelson website: www.parametersofpower4e.nelson.com. Click on "Quebec & National Unity" and then scroll down to "Quebec Sovereignty and the Rule of Law."

59. *Law Society of Upper Canada v. Skapinker* [1984] 1 S.C.R. 357; *Black v. Law Society of Alberta* [1989] 1 S.C.R. 591.

60. Mark R. MacDonald, "The Agreement on Internal Trade: Trade-offs for Economic Union and Federalism," in Bakvis and Skogstad, eds., 142.

61. On the creation of the AIT, see Robert H. Knox, "Economic Integration in Canada through the Agreement on Internal Trade," in Harvey Lazar, ed., *The State of the Federation 1997: Non-Constitutional Renewal* (Kingston, ON: Institute of Intergovernmental Relations, 1998), 139–43, and MacDonald, 140–41.

62. The text of the AIT, together with annual revisions, dispute-resolution panel reports, and other supporting documentation, is available at the Internal Trade Secretariat's website: www.intrasec.mb.ca.

63. Knox, 158–59.

64. Knox, 157–58.

65. Donald G. Lenihan with David Hume, "Governance in the Agreement on Internal Trade" (Ottawa: KTA Centre for Collaborative Government, 2004), 16.

66. MacDonald, 145.

67. MacDonald, 145–46.

68. MacDonald, 147.

69. Lenihan and Hume, 3.

70. Internal Trade Secretariat, "Status of Party-Specific Obligations," 2002–2003; available online at www.intrasec.mb.ca/index_he.htm.

71. Lenihan and Hume, 3.

72. Lenihan and Hume, 8.

73. MacDonald, 143.

74. Gagnon and Segal, "Introduction," 1.

75. Ibid., 2.

76. The "Saskatoon Consensus," reproduced in Gagnon and Segal, Appendix 1, 228.

77. The "Victoria Proposal," reproduced in Gagnon and Segal, Appendix 2, 231.

78. Linda A. White, "The Child Care Agenda and the Social Union," in Bakvis and Skogstad, eds., 114.

79. The full text of the SUFA is available online at www.socialunion.ca or at the website of the Canadian Intergovernmental Conference Secretariat: www.scics.gc.ca; click on "Conference Information," select "1999," and scroll down to "February."

80. "A Framework to Improve the Social Union for Canadians," reproduced in Gagnon and Segal, Appendix 3.

81. John Richards, "Backgrounder: The Paradox of the Social Union Framework Agreement" (Toronto: C.D. Howe Institute, March 2002), 4; available online at www.cdhowe.org.

82. Gibbins, "Shifting Sands," 33.

83. Alain-G. Gagnon, "Working in Partnership for Canadians," in Gagnon and Segal, 139.

84. Harvey Lazar, "The Social Union Framework Agreement and the Future of Fiscal Federalism," in Lazar, ed., Toward a New Mission Statement for Canadian Fiscal Federalism, 115.

85. Ibid., 100.

86. Noël, 24; see also Hobson and St-Hilaire, 177.

87. Provincial/Territorial Council on Social Policy Renewal, Progress Report to Premiers No. 5, August 10, 2000, 1; available online at www.scics.gc.ca.

88. Now the Council of the Federation; see Chapter 8.

89. Progress Report to Premiers No. 5, 5.

90. Michael J. Prince, "SUFA: Sea Change or Mere Ripple for Canadian Social Policy?," in Fortin, Noël, and St-Hilaire, eds.

91. Alain Noël, France St-Hilaire, and Sarah Fortin, "Learning from the SUFA Experience," in Fortin, Noël, and St-Hilaire, eds., 3. The two Accords mentioned are the 2000 First Ministers' Agreement on Health and the 2003 First Ministers' Accord on Health Care Renewal; both are available online at www.scics.gc.ca.

92. Harvey Lazar, "Managing Interdependencies in the Canadian Federation: Lessons from the Social Union Framework Agreement" (Kingston and Montreal: Institute for Intergovernmental Relations/Institute for Research on Public Policy, 2003), 2; available online at www.irpp.org.

93. Ibid., 3–4.

94. See Chapter 8 for a discussion of horizontal and vertical fiscal imbalances in the federation.

95. On a more positive note, interest groups have shown some interest in the SUFA; if they can find the resources to communicate effectively with the sponsoring governments, the future of the agreement could be less bleak than it presently appears. Susan D. Phillips, "SUFA and Citizen Engagement: Fake or Genuine Masterpiece?," in Fortin, Noël, and St-Hilaire, eds.

96. Federal/Provincial/Territorial Ministerial Council on Social Policy Renewal, *Three-Year Review: Social Union Framework Agreement (SUFA)*, June 2003; available online at www.canadiansocialresearch.net/socu.htm#sufareview.

97. Noël, St-Hilaire, and Fortin, 12.

10

CONSTITUTION III: THE *CANADIAN CHARTER OF RIGHTS AND FREEDOMS*

LEARNING OBJECTIVES

- *identify* and *explain* three key differences between the 1960 *Bill of Rights* and the 1982 *Charter of Rights and Freedoms;*
- *define* "first-order" and "second-order" *Charter* duties;
- *explain* the three-stage process of *Charter* application, and the relationship between section 1 and other *Charter* sections;
- *identify* and *analyze* two reasons why courts do not always make good public policy;
- *summarize* the legal debate over same-sex marriage;
- *identify* and *explain* the implications of the "war on terror" for *Charter* rights and freedoms.

INTRODUCTION

Canada's political institutions do not operate independently of each other. When one changes, for whatever reason, others must adapt to that change. The introduction of the *Charter,* which marked a significant change in the written *Constitution,* has had far-reaching effects on the courts, Parliament, and the policy-making process. However, these effects cannot be solely attributed to the *Charter* itself—which is, after all, only a piece of paper. They have been magnified by changes in the behaviour of other institutions and groups.[1] Canadian judges, especially in the appeal courts, modified their traditional attitude of **judicial deference** to Parliament and became more assertive under the *Charter.* In this respect, they were in accord with the general public; since World War II, Canada's political culture has been increasingly influenced by American conceptions of rights and freedoms. Appellate judges also gained almost complete freedom to decide which cases they would hear, which allowed them to devote as much time as possible to rights and freedoms. Interest groups added **public-interest litigation** to their toolkit for policy change. As policy-makers in the legislative and executive branches of government realized that their choices would face frequent challenges on *Charter* grounds, and that judges would often rule in favour of the **plaintiffs,** they began to incorporate the protected rights and freedoms into their own analyses and "outputs." After 20 years under the *Charter,* the courts, Parliament, or the executive cannot claim a monopoly over the interpretation and protection of rights and freedoms; each has its own distinct and important role to play.

Before the *Charter* took effect in 1982,[2] it was rare for Canadian policy-makers (including judges) to resolve controversial issues on the basis of rights. Today, there are few policy questions that do not touch on the *Charter* guarantees of rights and freedoms in some way:

- Under what circumstances can a doctor perform a legal abortion?[3]
- Can a terminally ill person seek a doctor's assistance to commit suicide?[4]
- Should public funds be spent on sign-language interpreters for deaf patients in hospitals?[5]
- Who is entitled to Canadian citizenship? How should the state treat Canadian residents who are not citizens?[6]
- Should state entitlements (such as pensions and parental benefits) be distributed without regard to marital status, sexual orientation, age, or gender?[7]
- Does a police officer have the right to search your home without a warrant, and, if so, under what conditions?[8]
- Can a police officer obtain your DNA without your consent?[9]
- Is a confession or plea bargain valid if you made it without consulting a lawyer?[10]
- What does "guilty beyond a reasonable doubt" mean in practice? Does it apply if you were drunk when you committed a crime?[11] Does it apply to a battered woman who killed her abuser?[12] Does it apply to a man who unsuccessfully tried to prevent his partner in crime from shooting a robbery victim, or who accidentally injected an overdose of cocaine into a woman's arm?[13]

Because these and other issues have been addressed in high-profile and controversial Supreme Court judgments, it is sometimes assumed that judges have taken too much power away from Parliament. Critics of the courts, in particular the Supreme Court of Canada, question the legitimacy of judicial policy-making. Should unelected judges have the power to overrule Parliament when the two institutions disagree? Has the Supreme Court been taken captive by "special interests" whose policy priorities conflict with those of most Canadians?

A closer look at the above cases reveals a more complicated relationship among the three branches of government:

- In the cases dealing with abortion, the distribution of state entitlements, and medical services for the hearing-impaired, the Supreme Court declared an existing policy unconstitutional—however, it left the details of any replacement policy to be determined by legislators or executives.

- After the rulings on warrantless searches, DNA, and intoxication, Parliament amended the *Criminal Code* to modify (or undo) the effects of the Supreme Court's decisions.
- The ruling on physician-assisted suicide upheld the existing law, and left any adjustments to be made by Parliament.

So it is wrong to suggest that the *Charter* transferred all policy-making power to unelected judges. While **judicial activism** should raise some concerns in a democratic political system—principally because judges lack the expertise to craft and enforce good public policy—the *Charter* does not spell the end of Canadian democracy. In this sense, the arguments of some *Charter* critics are exaggerated. For example, Manfredi argues that "judicial enforcement of rights in the name of liberal constitutionalism may destroy the most important right that citizens in liberal democracies possess, i.e., the right of self-government."[14] Mandel echoes this concern: "the laws that the judiciary apply are no longer our laws but their laws."[15]

Critics of "undemocratic" judicial power cite two reasons for its growth in the *Charter* era. First, the vague and general provisions of the *Charter* give judges carte blanche to rewrite and strike down laws; they "neither restrain nor guide the judges."[16] Second, the shift of policy-making power from legislatures to courts has created new centres of influence in Canadian politics: "national unity advocates, civil libertarians, equality-seekers, social engineers, and postmaterialists."[17] These "Court Party" groups, together with law professors, court clerks, and constitutional lawyers, allegedly work together to foist "the intensely held policy priorities of [left-wing] minorities"[18] on an unsuspecting majority.

These critiques of the *Charter* overstate its real impact on Canadian government and politics. Both rights-based **litigation** and judicial policy-making existed in Canada before 1982. It is certainly true that the *Charter* has inspired thousands of groups and individuals to seek a remedy in the courts for alleged violations of their rights and freedoms. However, it is equally true that the conditions for such lawsuits—a Supreme Court that controlled its own caseload, policy-oriented lawyers, and a rights-influenced political culture—were already in place before 1982, and that these heightened the impact of the *Charter*. Moreover, any group or individual who seeks to challenge the constitutionality of a law faces long odds of success. There are daunting procedural and financial barriers to litigation.[19] Once the case reaches the courts, the plaintiff must confront the vast resources and privileged status of the government that passed the law—or whose official allegedly breached the *Charter*—and now wishes to defend its actions.[20] The majority of *Charter* claims are dismissed by the courts,[21] a point overlooked by critics who focus selectively on controversial cases such as the 1988 *Morgentaler* ruling (Dossier 10.2).

If *Charter* critics focus on the undemocratic process of law-making by unelected judges, some of its defenders are more concerned with the substance of laws. Hiebert points out that under section 1 of the *Charter*, judges are required to evaluate laws in terms of their impact on "a free and democratic society." How public decisions are made—or who makes them—is less important in the long run than the content and impact of those decisions.[22] Laws that violate protected rights without justification have no place in a democratic society, even when they are made by elected officials. Hiebert also argues, along with other *Charter* advocates, that accusations of excessive judicial power are misplaced. When the Supreme Court strikes down an unconstitutional law, it is not arrogantly usurping the rightful place of Parliament; it is simply doing what the *Constitution* requires it to do (see the discussion of *Charter* remedies in "The Transformation of Judicial Review in the *Charter* Era" on page 499). When the Supreme Court defers to the legislative branch, upholding laws without stringent constitutional analysis, it fails in its duty to enforce the "supreme law of Canada."[23] In effect, if legislators were doing a better job of protecting *Charter* rights, judges would have less to occupy their time.

> *Where legislation that imposes limits on protected rights has not been the product of rigorous debate about alternative options, or where the policy has not been scrutinized by other organizations such as royal commissions or inquiries, judicial deference may be neither warranted nor appropriate.*[24]

It would be unwise to accept either side of the argument—pro-*Charter* or anti-*Charter*—uncritically. If the power of Supreme Court justices is absolute, and their contempt for the Parliament leads them to use it willy-nilly, why have they become increasingly deferential to legislators during the past decade? If the court has been captured by "special interests" and consistently flouts the will of the "silent majority," why is public support for the Supreme Court substantially higher than support for Parliament?[25] And if the justices are wise and impartial guardians of rights, as their defenders assume, then why are so many of their *Charter* decisions contradictory and fragmented?

In truth, the Supreme Court has not displaced the House of Commons. Judges are forced to confront moral issues—such as abortion and euthanasia—because legislators avoid them like the plague. When judges strike down laws or reinterpret them to conform to the *Charter*, they are not necessarily usurping the power of the legislature; rather, they are forcing legislators and the justice system to take rights seriously. Brian Slattery argues that the *Charter* imposes two types of duties on governing institutions: a "first-order" duty to ensure their own compliance with the guarantees of rights and freedoms, and a "second-order" duty to review the decisions of other institutions. The primary "first-order" duties lie with the executive branch that drafts laws; Parliament and the courts have a "second-order" duty to examine those laws. If MPs or judges find a contradiction between the law and a *Charter* guarantee, they are required to resolve the contradiction by amending or vetoing (**nullifying**) the offending provision(s).[26]

In some policy fields, notably criminal law, the Supreme Court and the House of Commons have engaged in a constructive "dialogue" about the practical difficulties of balancing individual rights against competing social values.[27] During the 1990s, the justices gradually moved away from the activism of the 1980s. Instead of imposing their own remedies for *Charter* violations, judges increasingly defer to Parliament to fix infringements of protected rights. This is not to imply that judicial activism is inherently bad; as we will see in "The Evolution of Rights in Canada" later in this chapter, neither the Canadian Parliament nor the deferential judiciary of the pre-*Charter* period paid sufficient attention to minority rights during times of "crisis."

The point is that, after a sometimes stressful period of adjustment, our political institutions have adapted to the presence of the *Charter* and a constructive balance among the three branches of government is being restored.

ENTRENCHED RIGHTS VERSUS PARLIAMENTARY SUPREMACY

Since 1867, and especially since the end of World War II, the influence of British political and legal traditions has diminished in Canada. Cairns identifies two primary reasons: "the prestige and status associated with connection to the United Kingdom eroded" as the British Empire faded into history, and the percentage of citizens with English and Scottish ancestry shrank as a result of changing immigration patterns.[28] As we have seen, the *Constitution Act, 1867* enshrined "a Constitution similar in Principle to that of the United Kingdom." Parliamentary supremacy is at the core of that inherited constitution. Under this model of the constitution, the legislative branch makes the law, subject to the financial control of the Crown, and the judicial branch is powerless to invalidate that law on substantive grounds. In other words, the courts have no discretion over the content of laws; they cannot declare a particular statute invalid because it treats a particular group unfairly or because the conditions under which it was passed are no longer in effect. If a statute is flawed in intent or in application, Parliament retains the sole authority to amend or revoke it.

The Canadian *Constitution* has always differed from the British *Constitution* in at least two primary respects: the balance between written and unwritten law, and the division of powers between the federal and provincial governments. Apart from a few key documents—such as the 1215 *Magna Carta* and the 1689 *Bill of Rights*—the British *Constitution* is essentially unwritten. It is based on conventions, not on entrenched written rules. Canada required the greater certainty of a written constitution, similar to that in the United States, mostly because of federalism. However, the *BNA Act* was virtually silent on the subject of rights. Judicial review of Canada's *Constitution* was essentially confined to the division of powers. Although the content of a particular law was clearly relevant to a division-of-powers case, it was relevant only insofar as it allowed the Supreme Court or the JCPC to determine whether the "pith and substance" of the statute fell within federal or provincial jurisdiction as defined in sections 91–95. A statute of the federal Parliament that "trenched on" provincial powers without justification was declared *ultra vires* (beyond the power of) the national government and struck down on that basis. Similarly, provincial laws that were found to be *ultra vires* were declared null and void.

Under the doctrine of parliamentary supremacy, the courts generally upheld any law that was enacted by the proper level of government. It was assumed that either Ottawa or the provinces could legislate on any matter as they saw fit, as long as they followed the proper procedures. In other words, the power to legislate was divided, but it was not restrained by any normative standard of right or morality. Finally, the courts almost always deferred to the legislative branch. Judges were loath to criticize the choices of legislators, even when those choices were clearly distasteful.

The American tradition of judicial review is very different from the British convention of parliamentary supremacy. It is founded on the assumption that the courts, and not the legislative branch, should provide the authoritative definition of law. As Britain's influence in Canadian society declined, it was replaced to a degree by the influence of American law and politics. People who watched American cop shows assumed that they could "plead the fifth" (i.e., invoke a constitutional right against self-incrimination); they also expected to be read their "*Miranda* rights" by a police officer. The absence of comparable rights in Canada eventually attracted public criticism.

The Evolution of Rights in Canada

Parliamentary supremacy means, among other things, that the legislative branch is the sole guardian of the rights and freedoms of citizens. The historical record shows that the unwritten rights embodied in British common law (e.g., the presumption of innocence or the civil rights of unpopular minorities) may be disregarded by parliamentarians in the grip of overwhelming public feeling. Canadians of Asian descent—not just naturalized immigrants, but citizens who were born in Canada—were barred from voting until 1947. In 1942, under the *War Measures Act,* the federal government arrested and interned thousands of Japanese Canadians whose only crime was their race. In the 1950s communists (actual or suspected) and Jehovah's Witnesses were persecuted by the Quebec government. Between the 1930s and the 1960s, hundreds of "mental defectives" were forcibly sterilized in Alberta. In 1970, after the kidnapping of British Trade Commissioner James Cross in Montreal, the Trudeau government suspended civil rights in the province of Quebec by imposing the *War Measures Act.* Hundreds of innocent Quebeckers were rounded up by the police and thrown into jail, without being charged with any offence or allowed to speak to lawyers.

Parliamentary supremacy, in other words, was no guarantee that rights and freedoms would always be protected against majority opinion or administrative expediency. Nor were the courts vigilant guardians of individual liberties. The JCPC upheld federal and provincial laws that violated human rights, as long as they were *intra vires.* In the 1903 *Tomey Homma* case, the JCPC upheld a British Columbia law that denied voting rights to persons of Asian descent. Because the law did not conflict with the federal power over "Naturalization of Aliens," it was *intra vires* the provincial government and therefore valid. The injustice of racial disqualification from the franchise "is not a topic which their Lordships are entitled to consider."[29] Similarly, the mistreatment of Japanese Canadians during and after World War II was accepted by the JCPC on the grounds that the *War Measures Act* overrode the provincial power over "Property and Civil Rights."[30]

The Supreme Court of Canada was slightly more willing to protect freedoms, particularly freedom of speech. In 1938, then-Chief Justice Sir Lyman Poore Duff argued that the *BNA Act*—specifically, the "Preamble" and the provision for a parliamentary system of government—contained an "implied bill of rights" inherited from Britain. The court struck down an Alberta censorship law, on the grounds that "free public discussion of public affairs . . . is the breath of life for parliamentary institutions." It established that any common-law right that was required to preserve "a Constitution similar in Principle to that of the United Kingdom" was worthy of judicial protection.[31] However, that precedent never commanded the support of a majority on the court.

After the abolition of Privy Council appeals in 1949, the Canadian Supreme Court became more vigorous in the protection of rights. It was particularly concerned about Quebec laws against religious and political minorities, including Jehovah's Witnesses and communists. Justice Ivan Rand, sometimes with the support of one or two colleagues, argued that such laws violated the "implied bill of rights" and should be nullified on that basis. Other justices preferred to use the division of powers to invalidate these laws; they argued the Quebec government could not usurp Ottawa's criminal-law power in order to persecute minorities. But because of parliamentary supremacy, most justices would not take the next step and "read in" protection for rights in the *BNA Act*. "The failure of the Supreme Court to establish clear, majority support for the jurisprudence of an implied bill of rights in the *BNA Act* was an important contributing factor in the movement to establish a formal bill of rights in Canada."[32] Ironically, the "implied bill of rights" has enjoyed a renaissance in the *Charter* era; the Supreme Court has repeatedly invoked the "Preamble" to the *Constitution Act, 1982* as the foundation of Canada's system of government.[33]

The establishment of the United Nations in 1948 gave further impetus to calls for an entrenched *Charter of Rights* in Canada. The UN *Charter* and the *Universal Declaration on Human Rights* influenced Canadian lawyers and academics and "provided domestic groups with a powerful rights rhetoric."[34] While the idea of entrenched rights still provoked unease, especially among those who feared the erosion of parliamentary supremacy, by the late 1950s "a Bill of Rights [had become] an almost essential attribute of contemporary statehood."[35]

DOSSIER 10.1 Excerpts from the 1960 *Bill of Rights*

1. It is hereby recognized and declared that in Canada there have existed and shall continue to exist without discrimination by reason of race, national origin, colour, religion or sex, the following human rights and fundamental freedoms, namely,

   (a) *the right of the individual to life, liberty, security of the person and enjoyment of property, and the right not to be deprived thereof except by due process of law;*

   (b) *the right of the individual to equality before the law and the protection of the law;*

   (c) *freedom of religion;*

   (d) *freedom of speech;*

   (e) *freedom of assembly and association; and*

   (f) *freedom of the press.*

2. Every law of Canada shall, unless it is expressly declared by an Act of the Parliament of Canada that it shall operate notwithstanding the Canadian Bill of Rights, be so construed and applied as not to abrogate, abridge or infringe or to authorize the abrogation, abridgment or infringement of any of the rights or freedoms herein

   (cont'd)

recognized and declared, and in particular, no law of Canada shall be construed or applied so as to

(a) authorize or effect the arbitrary detention, imprisonment or exile of any person;

(b) impose or authorize the imposition of cruel and unusual treatment or punishment;

(c) deprive a person who has been arrested or detained

  (i) of the right to be informed promptly of the reason for his arrest or detention,

  (ii) of the right to retain and instruct counsel without delay, or

  (iii) of the remedy by way of habeas corpus for the determination of the validity of his detention and for his release if the detention is not lawful;

(d) authorize a court, tribunal, commission, board or other authority to compel a person to give evidence if

he is denied counsel, protection against self-incrimination or other constitutional safeguards;

(e) deprive a person of the right to a fair hearing in accordance with the principles of fundamental justice for the determination of his rights and obligations;

(f) deprive a person charged with a criminal offence of the right to be presumed innocent until proved guilty according to law in a fair and public hearing by an independent and impartial tribunal, or of the right to reasonable bail without just cause; or

(g) deprive a person of the right to the assistance of an interpreter in any proceedings in which he is involved or in which he is a party or a witness, before a court, commission, board or other tribunal, if he does not understand or speak the language in which such proceedings are conducted.

Source: The Nelson website for this book: www.parametersofpower4e.nelson.com; click on "Canadian Politics on the Web," then "The Constitution," and then scroll down to "1960 Canadian Bill of Rights."

◼ The 1960 *Bill of Rights*

Partly in response to the rising interest in human rights, the federal government decided to codify existing common-law rights in statute law. An amendment to the *BNA Act,* which would have required provincial assent, was not in the cards; all of the provinces, except for Saskatchewan, were opposed to what they perceived as a direct attack on both parliamentary supremacy and provincial autonomy. Prime Minister Diefenbaker eventually adopted the Canadian *Bill of Rights* in 1960. Although its advocates hoped that it would provide effective protection for individual rights and freedoms, the Bill suffered from four serious limitations:

• The Bill was not entrenched in the *Constitution;* it was an ordinary federal statute. Therefore, it did not override other federal laws that violated its guarantees.

- The Bill did not apply to the provincial governments or to their areas of jurisdiction as defined by the *BNA Act*. Discriminatory provincial laws (e.g., in the fields of education, welfare, or health care) were not subject to the provisions of the Bill.
- The Bill contained no explicit judicial remedies for laws that conflicted with its provisions. At most, the Bill instructed courts in the proper interpretation of laws. Judges were required to interpret a statute in such a way that it did not conflict with the Bill. If they could not find a way to do this, there was no clear mandate to strike down the offending law or to impose another appropriate remedy for a person whose rights had been infringed.
- The language of the Bill—particularly the phrase "there have existed and shall continue to exist" in clause 1—implied that the protected rights were "frozen" at the moment when the Bill came into effect. It also suggested that the scope of each right was defined by the statutory and common-law limits in place in 1960. In other words, judges could not use the Bill to expand rights beyond the restrictions that had been imposed in previous decades, even where those restrictions were out of step with an evolving society.

Although the preamble promised to "ensure the protection of these rights and freedoms in Canada," the *Bill of Rights* had little impact on Canadian law. Apart from its own inherent weaknesses, its potential influence was greatly reduced by judicial reluctance to challenge parliamentary supremacy. Between 1960 and 1982, the justices invalidated only one law on the ground that it conflicted with the *Bill of Rights*. In the 1970 *Drybones* case, the Supreme Court struck down a section of the *Indian Act*. The **impugned** section made it illegal for an Indian to be intoxicated anywhere off-reserve. Justice Roland Almon Ritchie, writing for the majority, rejected the conservative approach to the Bill:

> *This proposition [i.e., that the impugned law was valid despite its violation of the Bill] appears to me to strike at the very foundations of the Bill of Rights and to convert it from its apparent character as a statutory declaration of the fundamental human rights and freedoms which it recognizes, into being little more than a rule for the construction of federal statutes . . .*[36]

Ritchie added that if a particular law could not conceivably be interpreted in such a way as to avoid violating the *Bill of Rights*, then it should be "declared inoperative" by the courts. In the case at hand, the *Indian Act* made intoxication an offence for one group of Canadians under circumstances that would be entirely legal for everyone else:

> *I think that s. 1(b) [of the Bill] means at least that no individual or group of individuals is to be treated more harshly than another under that law, and I am therefore of the opinion that an individual is denied equality before the law if it is made an offence punishable at law, on account of his race, for him to do something which his fellow Canadians are free to do without having committed any offence or having been made subject to any penalty.*[37]

The dissenting justices argued that the impugned law was valid, insofar as it was enacted under Parliament's authority to make special laws for Indians (section 91[24] of the *BNA Act*); even if the law were invalid, the *Bill of Rights* did not give judges the power to strike down legislation.

In all other *Bill of Rights* cases, the justices deferred to Parliament and refused to nullify laws on any of the enumerated grounds in the Bill. Whereas *Drybones* struck down a racist law, even though there was no evidence that it was being applied unfairly, the court reversed itself in subsequent cases and upheld racist or sexist laws on the grounds that they were administered equally.[38] Parliamentary supremacy was still a cardinal principle of the *Constitution,* and only Parliament could pass judgment on the substance of a law. The courts' reluctance to apply the *Bill of Rights* sparked demands for entrenched protection of rights and freedoms. Advocates of an entrenched *Charter* argued that if judges had a "supreme law" to work with, instead of an ordinary statute, they would take a more aggressive approach to violations of rights and freedoms. In this respect, at least, their hopes have been fulfilled.

Dossier 10.2 illustrates the major differences between pre- and post-*Charter* judicial review. After 1982, a majority of Supreme Court justices were willing to strike down laws that, in their view, infringed a protected right or freedom. Under the remedial sections of the *Charter,* they were authorized to take whatever steps were necessary to ensure that the legislative and executive branches respected the rights and freedoms of Canadians (for a detailed discussion of *Charter* remedies, see "The Transformation of Judicial Review in the *Charter* Era" on page 499). Although the rulings discussed in Dossier 10.2 applied to a federal law (the *Criminal Code*), the same remedies also apply to provincial laws (and to the administrative decisions of federal and provincial governments).

DOSSIER 10.2 The Transformation of Judicial Review: Pre-1982 and Post-1982

The *Charter's* impact on judicial review can best be understood by comparing the Supreme Court's approach to the same law before and after 1982. The two *Morgentaler* rulings serve the purpose well, because the justices themselves used the second ruling to clarify the *Charter's* impact on their interpretation of the abortion law. In 1975 the court upheld section 251 of the *Criminal Code,* which prohibited abortion. The only exceptions to the law were "therapeutic abortions": those performed in a hospital with the approval of a Therapeutic

Abortion Committee (TAC) made up of three doctors (not including the doctor who would perform the actual procedure).

In the mid-1970s, one-quarter of Canadian hospitals had fewer than four doctors on staff and were therefore unable to establish TACs. In larger hospitals, political pressure forced administrators either to forbid the creation of TACs or to disband existing committees. By 1982, only one in five Canadian hospitals had functioning TACs. Under the law, a TAC could authorize an abortion only if the continuation of the pregnancy "would or would be likely to endanger [the] life or health" of the woman. Some doctors interpreted the word "health" broadly, to include mental and emotional well-being, while others would not permit abortions except in medical emergencies. The procedural flaws in section 251 were serious: not only did access to abortion vary widely across the regions but also the bureaucracy and arbitrariness inherent in the committee system delayed abortion procedures—often by eight weeks or more. The result was a grave risk to the life and health of women seeking abortions.

Dr. Henry Morgentaler fought to change the law, largely through a one-man civil disobedience campaign. In 1973 he was charged with performing an illegal abortion in his Montreal clinic. The procedure violated section 251 because it did not take place in a hospital, and there was no TAC approval. He was acquitted by a jury, even though he was clearly in violation of the law; the Quebec Court of Appeal overturned the verdict and imposed a conviction. That decision was appealed to the Supreme Court in 1975.

The justices refused to consider Morgentaler's argument that the flawed TAC system violated the "due process" guarantee in the *Bill of Rights*. Chief Justice Bora Laskin did address the *Bill of Rights* arguments, but only for the purpose of debunking them. In the first place, he rejected Morgentaler's request for an American-style judicial review of the abortion law: "any interference by a court with the substantive content of legislation" would be "foreign to our constitutional traditions, to our constitutional law and to our conceptions of judicial review."[39] Canada, unlike the United States, did not have a "constitutionally entrenched Bill of Rights";[40] as a federal statute, the 1960 Bill did not give the courts the power to strike down other federal laws. Second, Laskin insisted that the courts could not second-guess Parliament, or usurp its power to make and amend laws:

I do not regard s. 1 (b) of the Canadian Bill of Rights as charging the courts with supervising the administrative efficiency of legislation or with evaluating the regional or national organization of its administration . . . Parliament has made a judgement which does not admit of any interference by the court . . . Any unevenness in the administration of the relieving provisions is for Parliament to correct and not for the courts to monitor as being a denial of equality before the law and the protection of the law.[41]

Morgentaler's conviction was upheld and he went to prison.

After his release, Morgentaler continued to challenge the abortion law. In 1984 he was arrested in Toronto; once again a jury acquitted him and an Appeals Court convicted him. In 1986 he returned to the Supreme Court, hoping that the entrenched *Charter* would embolden the justices to strike down the law. He argued that because the delays imposed by the TACs threatened "life" and "security of the person," the abortion law violated the rights guaranteed in section 7 of the *Charter*. The late Chief Justice Brian Dickson, who had participated in the 1975 ruling, made it clear from the outset that the court would treat the *Charter* very differently from the *Bill of Rights*:

[S]ince 1975, and the first Morgentaler decision, the Court has been given added responsibilities . . . Although no doubt it is

(cont'd)

still fair to say that courts are not the appropriate forum for articulating complex and controversial programmes of public policy, Canadian courts are now charged with the crucial obligation of ensuring that the legislative initiatives pursued by our Parliament and legislatures conform to the democratic values expressed in the Canadian Charter of Rights and Freedoms . . . It is in this latter sense that the current Morgentaler appeal differs from the one we heard a decade ago.[42]

Justice William Rogers McIntyre, the most conservative justice on the court, shared Dickson's view of the *Charter's* impact, even while warning against an overly broad interpretation of its provisions:

Before the adoption of the Charter, there was little question of the limits of judicial review of the criminal law. For all practical purposes it was limited to a determination of whether the impugned enactment dealt with a subject which could fall within the criminal law power in s. 91(27) of the Constitution Act, 1867 . . . The adoption of the Charter brought a significant change. The power of judicial review of legislation acquired greater scope but, in my view, that scope is not unlimited and should be carefully confined to that which is ordained by the Charter. I am well aware that there will be disagreement about what was ordained by the Charter and, of course, a measure of interpretation of the Charter will be required in order to give substance and reality to its provisions. But the courts must not, in the guise of interpretation, postulate rights and freedoms which do

not have a firm and a reasonably identifiable base in the Charter.[43]

Five of the seven justices on the panel voted to strike down the abortion law, although for varying reasons. The four male justices in the majority agreed with Morgentaler that the TACs violated section 7 of the *Charter*, because they threatened both the physical and psychological well-being of women seeking abortions. The law did not operate "in accordance with the principles of fundamental justice." Justice Bertha Wilson, in a separate opinion, found that the law violated the right to liberty, as well as the other rights in section 7: "the right to liberty contained in s. 7 guarantees to every individual a degree of personal autonomy over important decisions intimately affecting their private lives."[44] She also found that the law violated section 2(a) of the *Charter:* "I believe that the decision whether or not to terminate a pregnancy is essentially a moral decision, a matter of conscience."[45]

Finally, the court repudiated the previous *Morgentaler* ruling by assuming the power to judge the application of a law:

Although the mandate given to the courts under the Charter does not, generally speaking, enable the judiciary to provide remedies for administrative inefficiencies, when denial of a right as basic as security of the person is infringed by the procedure and administrative structures created by the law itself, the courts are empowered to act . . . If section 251 of the Criminal Code does indeed breach s. 7 of the Charter through its general effects, that can be sufficient to invalidate the legislation under s. 52.[46]

The 1960 *Bill of Rights* remains in force, despite the proclamation of the *Charter* in 1982. In a 1985 case concerning the rights of refugee claimants, half of the six Supreme Court justices relied on the Bill's guarantee of a fair hearing (clause 2[e]); the other three based their ruling on section 7 of the *Charter*.[47] The Bill has recently been used, with some success, in litigation touching on property rights; these are not enshrined in the *Charter*, but they are protected by clause 1(a) of the Bill. A class-action suit on behalf of mentally ill World War II veterans, whose pay and benefits were allegedly mismanaged by the federal government, succeeded in the Ontario courts. Unfortunately for the veterans, the Supreme Court of Canada unanimously overturned the earlier rulings. It held that in 1960, when the Bill took effect, the federal government had the power to take away the property of individuals; therefore, the Bill offered no relief to the veterans for the millions of dollars they had lost because of the government's mismanagement.[48] This revival of the "frozen rights" doctrine does not bode well for future attempts to use the Bill in order to fill gaps in the *Charter*'s protections.

The Evolution of *Charter* Guarantees

The draft *Charter* that Prime Minister Trudeau submitted for public debate in October 1980 was very different from the version that took effect in April 1982. (If necessary, refer back to the discussion of the 1980–82 constitutional round in "The *Constitution Act, 1982*" in Chapter 9.) A special joint committee of the House of Commons and Senate held public hearings on the federal package. For the most part, the witnesses demanded stronger entrenched protection for individual and group rights.[49] Some, including women, Aboriginal peoples, and people with disabilities, were successful; sections 15, 25, 28, and 35 were either added or reinforced during the committee process (see the text of the *Charter*, which starts on page 604 in the Appendix). Others, such as gays and lesbians and anti-abortion activists, failed to achieve constitutional recognition for their rights claims. The overall effect of the public hearings was to create strong public support for the *Charter* and its guaranteed rights and freedoms.

The evolution of two particular *Charter* sections merits some comment. Section 1, the "reasonable limitations" clause, had been watered down as part of Trudeau's strategy to win over the premiers. Because the Supreme Court sits at the top of Canada's judicial hierarchy, its interpretations of the *Charter* would bind both levels of government. Therefore, judicial review of the *Charter* would limit the discretion of provincial governments and legislatures. Not surprisingly, most of the provincial governments opposed any restrictions on their powers, and they refused to support the Trudeau *Charter* without the inclusion of a broad limitation clause. An early draft of that clause read as follows:

> *The Canadian Charter of Rights and Freedoms recognizes the following rights and freedoms subject only to such reasonable limits as are generally accepted in a free and democratic society with a parliamentary system of government.*[50]

Members of the Liberal Cabinet stand and applaud Prime Minister Pierre Trudeau in the House of Commons on November 5, 1981, after he signed an historic agreement with nine provinces that would lead to a new Canadian *Constitution*. (© CP/Andy Clark)

Several of the witnesses who appeared before the committee demanded that this clause be removed, arguing that it would allow governments to violate rights and freedoms at whim. Others wanted to clarify and strengthen the wording, eliminating the phrase "generally accepted" and inserting a reference to "law." Faced with a barrage of criticism, and now determined to proceed without provincial consent (recall the discussion of the "unilateral patriation" strategy in Chapter 9), the federal government amended the section "to narrow the scope of limits that could be applied to the rights and freedoms."[51] The final wording of section 1, which can be found in the Appendix on page 604, makes no reference to parliamentary government and requires any legal infringement of rights to be "demonstrably justified" by the state. The effect is to reduce judicial deference to Parliament and to place a heavy onus on the government that passed an impugned law to justify its impact on protected rights and freedoms.

Section 15 was also transformed during the public hearings. The original wording of the equality clause essentially reproduced the language of the *Bill of Rights:* it guaranteed "equality before the law and the equal protection of the law." Women's groups and others pointed out that the interpretation of those phrases by the

Supreme Court had been less than satisfactory, and demanded stronger guarantees. The first part of section 15 now protects equality under the law and "equal benefit of the law," to ensure that both the substance and the effects of legislation are taken into consideration by the courts. Finally, the federal government inserted a second provision into section 15, to address concerns that entrenched equality rights would prevent future affirmative action policies. All in all, the equality rights in today's *Charter* are a far cry from the original version tabled in October 1980. The impact of section 15 on Canadian law and politics has been significant and often surprising, as we will see in Dossier 10.3.

The Transformation of Judicial Review in the *Charter* Era

Many of the rights and freedoms protected by the *Charter* already existed in Canadian law, embedded in statutes and common-law precedents. In this sense, the *Charter* was not a radical break with our legal tradition; it simply entrenched long-standing rights and freedoms. The real innovation of the *Charter* lies in the explicit judicial powers of remedy and enforcement:

- Section 24(1) allows any individual or group whose *Charter* rights have been infringed to ask the courts for "such remedy as the court considers appropriate and just in the circumstances." For example, a person convicted of a criminal offence whose legal rights were violated by the police may be granted a new trial.
- Section 24(2) requires judges to exclude evidence obtained in violation of the rights guaranteed in sections 7–14. Without such evidence, criminal conviction "beyond a reasonable doubt" may be impossible.
- Section 52 gives the courts the power to strike down any law, federal or provincial, that is found to be inconsistent with the *Charter*, "to the extent of the inconsistency." In other words, a particular section of the *Criminal Code* may be struck down as an infringement on a *Charter* right, but the rest of the *Code* will remain in force.

The Supreme Court has broadened the range of available remedies through its interpretation of section 52. Instead of striking down a statute immediately, it can suspend the nullification for a specified period, to give the legislature a chance to amend the offending law before it expires. In addition, the court may provide guidelines to legislators for amending or reenacting the impugned law. For example, in 1991 the Supreme Court struck down the "rape shield" provision in the *Criminal Code*.[52] The purpose of the "rape shield" was to protect alleged victims of sexual assault from defence attorneys who sought to use their prior sexual history to destroy their credibility in the courtroom. The majority held that an absolute prohibition of evidence concerning prior sexual activity by the complainant violated the right of the accused to a fair trial (section 11[d] of the *Charter*). To fill the void created by the nullification, they set out rules for judges to use in determining the admissibility of such evidence.

In 1992 Parliament adopted a new "rape shield" law, which "essentially codifie[d] the decision in *Seaboyer*."[53] Bill C-49 contained a preamble that defined the objectives of the legislation—e.g., "encourag[ing] the reporting of incidents of sexual violence or abuse"—to prevent any future court from imposing its own interpretation of the law's purpose.[54] To an unusual degree, the legislative debate over Bill C-49 focused on the *Charter*. Justice Minister (later Prime Minister) Kim Campbell sought to balance the rights of women against those of criminal defendants, partly in anticipation of a future *Charter* challenge to the law. When the Supreme Court ruled on the constitutionality of the revised "rape shield" in 2000, it upheld the law on the ground that it did not violate the legal rights of the accused.[55] The "rape shield" case illustrates an often-overlooked feature of *Charter* politics: the aforementioned "dialogue" between courts and legislators, as opposed to the judicial supremacy alleged by *Charter* critics.[56]

If the court finds that a law violates the *Charter*, but it does not consider striking it down to be the appropriate remedy, it can effectively amend the law by either **"reading in"** or **"reading down"** the offending provision(s). "Reading in" *widens* the application of the law by adding one or more groups that were previously excluded from the wording of the provision.[57] The actual wording of the law does not change, but the Supreme Court's interpretation requires all lower courts and lawyers to treat the provision as though it had. If the Supreme Court "reads in" to an ordinary law, and the sponsoring legislature does not approve of the result, it has the power to amend the law in order to undo the court's work. For example, the 2001 *Sharpe* ruling from the Supreme Court "read in" two minor exemptions to the *Criminal Code* provisions banning child pornography. The federal government disapproved of the change, and introduced legislation to remove the new exemptions.[58]

Judges do not just "read in" to ordinary laws, however. For example, the Supreme Court has "read in" several groups that were not explicitly included in section 15(1) of the *Charter*: residents of Canada who are not legal citizens,[59] gays and lesbians,[60] and common-law spouses.[61] (See the discussion of "analogous grounds" in Dossier 10.3.) When courts alter the meaning of the *Charter* by "reading in," there is little that legislators or executives who disagree with the new interpretation can do. In theory, they can use the amending formula to undo the judges' decision, but such an amendment would require the unanimous consent of all 11 senior governments, which is all but impossible in practice.

When the courts "read down" a particular law, they reinterpret its meaning in such a way as to *narrow* its application. The purpose is to ensure that the law does not conflict with the *Charter*, either in general or in a particular case. According to the late Justice John Sopinka, "reading down" allows a court to protect guaranteed rights while respecting the authority of the legislature.[62] Note, however, that there are few restrictions on the Supreme Court's power to amend the *Constitution* through its remedial power. Critics of judicial power argue that in a democracy, the only legitimate way to alter the fundamental rules of the political system is to follow the formal amending process.

The Supreme Court of Canada issued its first major ruling on equality rights in 1989. One of the key principles in that ruling is that the list of prohibited grounds for discrimination is not exhaustive. Through the process of "reading in," section 15(1) can be expanded to cover personal characteristics "analogous" to those already enumerated.

The burden of proof for a new claim of "analogous grounds" rests with the party challenging the law. He must demonstrate unequal treatment arising from a genuine disability[63] or from "the stereotypical application of presumed group or personal characteristics."[64] Those characteristics must be directly relevant to the impugned law.[65] To trigger a judicial remedy under section 15(1), they must also be directly related to "the essential dignity and worth of the individual,"[66] and they must be either permanent or difficult to change. Analogous grounds accepted by the Supreme Court include sexual orientation,[67] marital status,[68] and parental status (i.e., adoptive versus biological parents).

Of all the analogous grounds read in to section 15(1), sexual orientation is by far the most controversial. The first unequivocal recognition that this section protects gays and lesbians from discrimination occurred in 1995, in the *Egan* case. Two men who had lived together in a committed relationship for decades had been denied pension benefits that would automatically have been provided to married or common-law heterosexual spouses. Although the appellants lost their case, they scored a major legal victory when a majority of the Supreme Court declared sexual orientation to be an "analogous ground." Once a personal

characteristic has been granted this recognition, it cannot be taken away in a subsequent ruling (see the discussion of *stare decisis* on page 517). On the same day as *Egan*, the court declared that it was unconstitutional to discriminate against heterosexual common-law couples by denying them benefits to which legally married couples were entitled.[69] The stage was set for the next battle: the designation of same-sex couples as "common-law."

That battle occurred in 1999, when the Supreme Court struck down an Ontario law that defined common-law "spouses" as two persons of the opposite sex.[70] This meant that two men or two women who cohabited as romantic partners for a specified period of time would be considered "common-law spouses," with all the attendant rights and responsibilities attaching to opposite-sex couples in the same situation. For many gays and lesbians, this was enough; the social and legal stigma of homosexuality was fading, and they saw no reason to go further. Others, however, wanted to challenge the last remaining barrier: the definition of legal marriage as an exclusively heterosexual institution.

Same-sex couples in several provinces launched *Charter* challenges by attempting to procure marriage licences; when they were rejected, they went to court. The first victories came in 2002, when trial courts in both Ontario and Quebec ruled that the heterosexual definition of marriage violated section 15 by discriminating on the basis of sexual orientation.[71] The federal government, which has jurisdiction over marriage and divorce, appealed both rulings. In the meantime, the BC Court of

(cont'd)

Appeal overturned a trial verdict and accepted the ruling of the Ontario and Quebec courts. It ordered that same-sex couples be permitted to marry, and suspended the effect of this order for two years to give Parliament a chance to amend the law. In June 2003 the Ontario Court of Appeal upheld the lower-court ruling in that province, as did the Quebec Court of Appeal in March 2004. The Ontario Court of Appeal ordered the province to issue marriage licences to same-sex couples immediately, prompting the BC Court of Appeal to lift its own suspension a few weeks later. Within hours of the Ontario appellate ruling, same-sex couples in the province flocked to registry offices to obtain marriage licences. In the following weeks and months, hundreds travelled from across Canada and other countries to get married in Ontario or British Columbia.[72] There was no guarantee that the marriages would receive legal recognition in other jurisdictions, but for many couples that had waited years for the chance to marry legally, the opportunity was too good to pass up.

The federal government decided not to appeal the Ontario and British Columbia rulings. Instead, in July 2003 it announced an amendment to the marriage law. The new law would define civil marriage as "the lawful union of two persons to the exclusion of all others." It would also exempt religious clergy and denominations from having to perform same-sex weddings if they objected to the new definition.[73] Before the law was submitted to a vote in Parliament, it was referred to the Supreme Court to test its constitutionality. Three questions were posed to the court: (1) which level of government had jurisdiction over the issue; (2) whether the law was consistent with the

equality rights in section 15; and (3) whether the proposed law violated the *Charter* guarantee of religious freedom (despite an explicit exemption for denominations that rejected same-sex marriage).[74] After Paul Martin became prime minister in late 2003, he referred a fourth question to the Court. The gist of the new question was whether a separate category of "civil unions" for same-sex couples—as distinct from full "marriage"—would violate section 15.[75]

The decision not to appeal the provincial rulings prompted considerable controversy. Opponents of same-sex marriage were predictably upset by what they perceived as an attack on their values and beliefs. Critics of judicial power argued that Parliament, not the Supreme Court, should have the final say on the issue. During the 2004 federal election campaign, both the Liberals and the new Conservative Party under Stephen Harper tried to use the issue to their own political advantage. Harper promised to withdraw the Supreme Court reference and allow Parliament to decide; he predicted (probably incorrectly) that if elected MPs refused to legalize same-sex marriage, the courts would respect that decision.[76] Harper also claimed that the *Charter* did not prohibit discrimination on the grounds of sexual orientation. This is inaccurate: while sexual orientation is not listed among the enumerated grounds, it is firmly established as an "analogous ground."

Paul Martin countered by accusing Harper of trying to weaken minority rights—a charge that gained some credibility when a videotaped interview with Conservative MP Randy White was leaked just before the election. In the interview, White said "To heck with the courts, eh?" and promised that a Conservative government would use the "notwithstanding clause" to overturn *Charter* rulings with which it disagreed.[77] After the Conservatives' disappointing election result, some party strategists blamed White and other indiscreet Conservative MPs for reinforcing Liberal charges of a "hidden agenda" and costing the party votes in Ontario.[78]

In December 2004, the Supreme Court issued its reference ruling on same-sex marriage. The nine justices, including two new justices, answered the first three questions unanimously: (1) the definition of marriage is a matter falling exclusively within federal jurisdiction, (2) the extension of civil marriage to same-sex couples does not violate the *Charter*—indeed, it "flows from" the equality rights in section 1, and (3) the provision in the law that exempted religious officials from performing same-sex marriages if this contravened their particular faiths was consistent with the guarantee of religious freedom.[79] However, the court refused to answer the fourth question that had been added by the Martin government. It ruled that the federal government had refused to appeal the earlier rulings from the provincial courts, deciding instead to accept the constitutionality of same-sex marriage and amend the law accordingly. Had it entertained doubts about the earlier rulings that altered the definition of marriage, the government should have appealed them. In addition, since June 2003, thousands of same-sex couples had relied in good faith on the government's acceptance of the earlier rulings and entered into legal marriages. For these reasons, the court gave no answer to the fourth question. It sent the issue of same-sex marriage back to Parliament.

Although the court did not issue a clear and explicit statement that the denial of marriage to same-sex couples violated the *Charter*, which might have made it easier for the prime minister to pass the legislation through a divided Parliament, it was clear to most observers that MPs had only two options: (1) to pass the Bill, as amended in response to the court ruling or (2) to invoke the "notwithstanding clause" in defence of "traditional marriage."[80] At the time of writing, the government had recently tabled the revised Bill in the Commons; although the final outcome of the debate over same-sex marriage was not yet known, it was safe to predict that the Bill would pass—if only because no one wanted to face the political consequences of invoking the "notwithstanding clause" and overriding *Charter* rights.

JUDICIAL POLITICS

Judicial Independence and the Separation of Law and Politics

Canadian judges are appointed, not elected. The members of the Supreme Court are chosen by the prime minister and the minister of Justice. Although there are no formal procedures for choosing justices, the normal practice is for the Justice minister to seek advice from the Department of Justice, the Canadian Bar Association, and the current chief justice (who can advise on particular gaps that need to be filled, e.g., corporate law).[81] The *Supreme Court Act* requires that three of the nine justices must be appointed from the civil bar of Quebec, to ensure that the court has the necessary expertise with the unique legal system of that province. By convention, three of the remaining justices come from Ontario, two from the Western provinces, and one from the Atlantic region. Most serve on provincial courts of appeal before their elevation to the Supreme Court of Canada, although a few active lawyers have been appointed in recent years (e.g., Justice Ian Binnie). Unlike their colleagues on the U.S. Supreme Court, Canada's justices are not subjected to legislative approval or rejection. Once appointed, all superior court judges enjoy security of tenure "during good behaviour" until the age of 75.

By the late 1990s, this appointment process was widely criticized. It was regarded by its critics as secretive and undemocratic, especially in an era when Supreme Court justices enjoyed considerable policy-making power under the *Charter*. In the spring of 2004 the House of Commons Standing Committee on Justice, Human Rights, Public Safety and Emergency Preparedness recommended reforms to the process.[82] Each of the four parties on the committee issued a separate report. They agreed that the pool of candidates should be chosen by an advisory committee of lawyers, judges, and laypeople, similar to the committees that already vet aspiring superior court and appellate judges in the provinces. They also agreed that Parliament should play some role in the nomination of justices, although they differed over the precise nature of that role. The Liberal majority called for the Justice minister to appear before the Justice Committee after the selection had been made, to explain why that particular person had been chosen. The Conservatives argued that the nominee should be required to appear in person, preferably before the final decision had been made, and that the Commons should have the power to veto proposed appointments. When the Justice Committee issued its report, shortly before the 2004 election, there were two unexpected Ontario vacancies on the court.[83] Nothing could be done until after the June 28 election, which left little time to implement the committee's recommendations.

As the Supreme Court's fall term approached, and with Parliament set to resume in October at the earliest, the Liberal minority government cobbled together an ad hoc response to the committee's call for more input. In late August 2004, Justice Minister Irwin Cotler announced the nomination of justices Louise Charron and Rosalie Silberman Abella. The following day, he appeared before an Interim Ad Hoc Committee on the Appointment of Supreme Court Judges to answer questions about the two nominees. The committee was made up of two Liberal MPs (one of whom was the chair), two Conservatives, one New Democrat, and one BQ MP; they were joined by a representative from the Law Society of Upper Canada, which speaks for the Ontario legal community, and one from the Canadian Judicial Council.[84]

The hearing degenerated into a predictable partisan battle: the Conservative and NDP members argued that the two nominees should have appeared in person, instead of being represented by the Justice minister. In the end, the committee raised no questions about the qualifications of the two candidates, preferring instead to argue about the process. Two days later the nominated justices were formally appointed, doubling the number of women on the Supreme Court to four.

In defending his decision not to require the nominees to appear before the MPs, Cotler invoked a key constitutional principle: the independence of the judiciary. As we saw in Chapter 1, the separation of the three branches of government is an essential condition for political liberty. While the legislative and executive branches of the Canadian government are closely linked (see Chapters 5 and 6), the judicial branch is expected to exercise its powers independently of the other two. Although the status of the courts vis-à-vis the legislature has been elevated by the *Charter*, the principle of judicial independence remains intact. In 1997, the Supreme Court identified the source of this principle:

> *Judicial independence is an unwritten norm, recognized and affirmed by the preamble to the Constitution Act, 1867. In fact, it is in that preamble, which serves as the grand entrance hall to the castle of the Constitution, that the true source of our commitment to this foundational principle is located.*[85]

The separation of powers (recall Dossier 1.1) implies more than the freedom of judges to interpret the law without interference from the legislative or executive branches. It also means that each of the three branches has its own unique sphere of activity, into which the others cannot legitimately intrude. Critics of the *Charter* argue that the courts, and the Supreme Court in particular, have assumed a policy-making role

DOSSIER 10.4 The Separation of Law and Politics[86]

One of the basic principles underlying the liberal democratic approach to government [is this]: There is a difference between politics and law.

There is a difference between making decisions according to how popular they are, how many people will support them, how organized the opposition might be or whether people are willing to pay for them—these are political calculations—and making decisions according to whether a particular result is rational, logical, consistent with past practice, appropriate in light of liberal democratic principles and morally defensible. These are legal determinations.

To insist that the courts must be independent of the political arms of government is to insist that law is and must be separate from politics. It is to believe that a decision can be *legally* correct even through it is *politically* insupportable.

Shielding the judiciary from inappropriate influences means, first and foremost, shielding it from other branches of government—because it is in these branches of government where political interests are most powerfully felt. Political power and interests are the lifeblood of a legislature, a Cabinet, a constituent assembly or a presidency. Their halls are filled with people who would love to be able to determine the outcome of legal disputes. Indeed, such people, especially if they represent a majority, would prefer that all disputes be political, rather than legal, because politics lets the powerful win. Only the law allows the weak to win against the strong . . .

(cont'd)

Recent changes in our *Constitution* and in the dynamics of society have made it more difficult for judges to maintain the appearance of impartiality. Until 1982 the role of judges in relation to legislation was to interpret the law. In addition, because we are a federation in which the power to pass legislation is divided between the federal government on the one hand and the provinces on the other, the courts were empowered to decide whether legislation was properly within the sphere of the branch of government that passed it.

In 1982 all that changed. With the adoption of a *Charter of Rights and Freedoms,* there are areas in which neither the federal Parliament nor the provinces can legislate. As well, all government action can be subjected to judicial scrutiny. These new powers have brought the court into the political arena. By way of example, our court struck down legislation in our *Criminal Code,* a federal statute, which prohibited abortion except under certain stringent terms; struck down federal legislation prohibiting all federal civil servants from engaging in partisan political activity; and passed upon the validity of a federal government order-in-council which authorized the testing of cruise missiles by the United States on Canadian soil.

This politicization of the courts has resulted in attacks on the courts from two fronts. Public-interest groups have become more vocal, waging long and loud campaigns seeking to influence the decision of a court or to influence the government to change a decision made by the court. Political figures both in power and opposition, spurred on by public clamour, indulge themselves in public criticism of judges and even demands for discipline . . .

The paradox created by the *Charter* is that it was adopted by means of a democratic process to protect the individual against an abuse of power by the majority, but many feel that it is undemocratic for unelected judges to overrule the majority. The majority does not like to be told it is wrong.

The unfortunate fact is that the *Charter* has turned the court into the messenger who is likely to get shot for bringing bad news. By enacting the *Charter,* the legislative branch of government enacted a permanent invitation to the judiciary to tell the majority that it is wrong—that it cannot do what it wants to do, or at least that it cannot do it in a way it wants to do it. If the majority is in a particularly surly mood, bringing this kind of bad news can be a singularly unpleasant business.

How does this relate to the topic of judicial independence? In a very direct way. The *Charter* is a law. It is the supreme law of the land. It is the duty of courts to apply the law. In order to apply the *Charter,* courts must be willing to declare laws enacted by elected representatives unconstitutional—to say, in effect, that the majority is breaking the law.

Now if the courts are subject to effective political pressure, whether that be through public criticism aimed at shaming judges into changing their rulings, or through the threat of disciplinary proceedings at the instigation of the executive branch, then the judicial system will be less capable of telling the majority that it is wrong. They will be less able to apply the *Charter* in an effective manner. And this means the end of the rule of law.

that should properly be left to the elected members of the House of Commons. Since 1982, judges have enjoyed greater influence in some of our most pressing social and political debates. But contrary to the claims of their critics, Supreme Court justices are uncomfortable with the exercise of political power. As they often point out, however, the *Charter* has left them little choice; they have been drawn into the policy-making process, whether their critics like it or not.[87] As former Chief Justice Antonio Lamer put it in 1985:

> *It ought not to be forgotten that the historic decision to entrench the Charter in our Constitution was taken not by the courts but by the elected representatives of the people of Canada. It was those representatives who extended the scope of constitutional adjudication and entrusted the courts with this new and onerous responsibility. Adjudication under the Charter must be approached free of any lingering doubts as to its legitimacy.*[88]

Judicial Procedures: Adjudication versus Policy-Making

Courts and court procedures were originally designed to **adjudicate** (i.e., definitively resolve) narrowly defined disputes. In principle, adjudicators do not make new law, nor do they strike down old law. They merely apply existing law to the facts of each individual case, without indulging in sweeping statements about the broader implications of their rulings.

The policy-making powers that courts are called upon to exercise in *Charter* cases are foreign to the adjudicative process, at least at the trial stage. As a case makes its way up the judicial hierarchy, from the lower courts to the superior courts and finally (though rarely) to the Supreme Court of Canada, the emphasis shifts from adjudication to policy-making. The facts of the case, which are the primary concern of the trial judge, yield to broader questions of law and policy.[89] This is because the ruling of the trial judge is only binding on the immediate parties to the case, whereas the rulings of appellate judges will apply to the entire province or country.

At all levels of the judicial hierarchy, the purpose of a trial—whether civil or criminal—is to provide an authoritative resolution to a dispute between two parties. In a criminal trial, the parties are the Crown (hence the title "Regina" [Latin for "Queen"] versus X [name(s) of the accused]). The issues are relatively narrow: Should the accused be found guilty or innocent? Should the accused go to jail, and, if so, for how long? In most civil cases, both parties are private actors (individuals or corporations). Which of two divorcing parents gets custody of the children, or is custody to be shared? Has there been a breach of contract between the seller and the buyer, and, if so, what is the remedy? These are the kinds of day-to-day conflicts that trial judges must decide. The focus is on the facts of the immediate situation: Was the gun fired in anger or with cool deliberation, or was it fired in self-defence? Once the facts are determined, the law must be applied to them; this may require the judge to interpret the law in a new way. At trial, however, such interpretive judicial law-making rarely exceeds what is required to resolve the immediate dispute.

CONSTITUTION III: THE CANADIAN CHARTER OF RIGHTS AND FREEDOMS

Supreme Court justices pose for an official photo at the Supreme Court (January 2000). Front row, L to R: Frank Iacobucci, Claire L'Heureux-Dubé, Chief Justice Beverley McLachlin, Charles Gonthier, and John Major. Back row, L to R: Louise Arbour, Michel Bastarache, Ian Binnie, and Louis LeBel. (© CP/Tom Hanson)

In a minority of cases, the key issue at trial is not the application of the law, but whether the law itself violates the *Constitution*. Because "no one can be convicted under an unconstitutional law," anyone accused of a crime can seek to have the law nullified (and the charges consequently dropped) under section 52 of the *Constitution Act, 1982*.[90] In these instances, the trial judge is required to assess the merits of the law on both legal and policy grounds. The policy considerations become particularly important if the judge finds that the law violates one or more *Charter* guarantees; the judge must then determine whether the violation is justified under section 1 (see the discussion of the *Oakes* test, page 510).

If one party is dissatisfied with the outcome of a trial, that person can appeal to a higher court. The party seeking to overturn the trial result is called the "appellant"; the other party is called the "respondent." For example, a person convicted of a crime who asks a higher court to overturn the conviction will be designated the appellant. However, if the trial judge found that the applicable section of the *Criminal Code* violated the *Charter* and struck it down, the federal government (embodied in the Crown) may seek a reversal at a higher court; in this instance, the Crown is the appellant.

Once the case moves on to appeal, the balance between adjudication and law-making shifts in favour of the latter. From an adjudicative perspective, appeal courts secure fairness for litigants. As we understand the adjudicative process today, we are entitled not only to our "day in court" but also to our day in a higher court that can "correct injustices or errors that may have occurred in the lower court."[91] These errors are generally of a legal nature, not a factual nature—e.g., whether the trial judge was correct in his or her assessment of the constitutionality of the law.

The judgment of an appellate court is binding on all lower courts within its jurisdiction.[92] Thus, the legal interpretations of the appeal court of any province become the law for the entire province. However, they are not legally binding outside the territory of that province. For example, the June 2003 *Halpern* ruling from the Ontario Court of Appeal made it legal for same-sex couples to marry in that province;[93] subsequent rulings from the appellate courts in British Columbia and Quebec opened the door to same-sex marriages in those provinces. Elsewhere in Canada, gay and lesbian couples were still prohibited from obtaining marriage licences. If they wished to wed, they had two options: to travel to one of the provinces where same-sex marriages were performed, or to wait for their own provincial courts (or the federal government) to change the law.

Although a provincial court of appeal has no legal jurisdiction outside the borders of the province, its rulings often influence other appellate courts when they deal with similar cases. In the above example, the court in *Halpern* refused to suspend the legality of same-sex marriage so that Parliament could amend the relevant laws. Instead, it declared that same-sex couples in Ontario could get married as soon as the ruling was issued. Shortly thereafter, as discussed in Dossier 10.3, the BC Court of Appeal amended its earlier ruling on the issue, in which it had suspended the remedy of permitting same-sex marriage for two years; it ordered the province to grant marriage licences to gay and lesbian couples immediately.[94] More generally, provincial appellate rulings are rarely appealed to the Supreme Court of Canada; when they are, the justices reject most applications for leave to appeal. In practical terms, therefore, the provincial courts of appeal often have the final word on legal and constitutional questions, and their influence can stretch well beyond their official jurisdictions.

The party that loses its case in a provincial court of appeal can try to appeal yet again, to the Supreme Court of Canada. As the highest court in the land, Supreme Court rulings are authoritative and binding on the entire country. (For this reason, most of the rulings discussed in this chapter come from the Supreme Court.) The judicial hierarchy does more than provide an avenue of appeal for disgruntled litigants in the immediate case; it also ensures that laws are applied consistently across Canada. Consequently, the facts of the immediate case are even less central at the Supreme Court than they are in the provincial appellate courts.

Since 1975, the Supreme Court has had the power to choose which appeals it will hear. The task of sorting through thousands of appellate petitions is left to three-judge panels, which rely heavily on the opinions of court clerks (recent law school graduates who spend a year working for particular justices). Appeals that raise important legal issues, particularly *Charter* issues, are the most likely to survive the winnowing process. The court's freedom to control its own docket clearly indicates that policy-making, not adjudication, is its primary function.

Whether or not one believes that judicial policy-making is inherently undemocratic, the more practical problem is the mismatch between policy-making and adjudication. The Supreme Court, like all adjudicative bodies, is made up of experts in law. They possess neither the expertise nor the institutional resources to evaluate public policy effectively, or to craft new policies to replace those that they have nullified on *Charter* grounds. For example, the rules of evidence in Canadian courts are designed to promote the resolution of specific cases. Trial judges normally exclude **extrinsic evidence:** materials that are not directly relevant to the case at bar (before the court). Until recently, appellate courts also refused to hear extrinsic evidence, either about the intent of legislators in drafting impugned laws or about the policy implications of the issues under consideration. The Supreme Court began to relax its ban on extrinsic evidence in the 1970s, though only in constitutional reference cases and only for the purpose of interpreting regular statutes.[95] The use of extrinsic evidence in constitutional interpretation dates back to the 1980 *Senate Reference,* in which the Supreme Court relied on the 1864 *Confederation Debates* to determine the intent of the Fathers of Confederation when they established the upper house.

In the *Charter* era, judges have relied heavily on one type of extrinsic evidence— social science data about the policy effects of impugned laws—while rejecting another: evidence of legislative intent. In other words, the courts are unable or unwilling to base their interpretations of the law—constitutional or otherwise—on the hopes and priorities of the people who wrote it. In the words of former Chief Justice Lamer, parliamentary speeches and committee testimony provide "inherently unreliable" evidence of legislative intent. This is particularly true of constitutional laws such as the *Charter,* which are drafted by "a multiplicity of individuals." Under these circumstances, "the intention of the legislative bodies which adopted the *Charter*" is impossible to determine with any accuracy.[96] We will return to this **"noninterpretivist"** approach to judicial review in "The 'Living Tree' Approach" on page 525.

Social science evidence plays a particularly important role at the second stage of the three-stage *Charter* analysis. As we will see in "The Three-Stage Approach" later in this chapter, the first stage requires a judge to determine whether an impugned law, or a particular act or omission by a public official, infringes a guaranteed right or freedom. If the answer is "yes," the judge moves on to the second stage: determining whether the infringement can be justified under section 1 of the *Charter*. Under the *Oakes* test for "reasonable limitations," he or she must answer four questions:[97]

1. Is the objective of the impugned law sufficiently "pressing and substantial" to justify infringing a protected right or freedom? In other words, does the problem that the law is designed to address outweigh the risk of violating rights or freedoms?
2. Assuming that the objective is indeed "pressing and substantial," is there a rational connection between the objective and the law itself? In effect, does the law actually address the problem identified in the first stage, or does it miss the target?

3. Does the law "minimally impair" the relevant right or freedom, or is there an alternative policy that would serve the same purpose with less impact on the *Charter*?
4. Are the effects of the law proportional to the objective? In its initial formulation, this question weighed the infringement of the *Charter* against the importance of the objective. A subsequent revision of the *Oakes* doctrine rephrased the standard as follows: "there must be a proportionality not only between the deleterious [harmful] effects of the measures which are responsible for limiting the rights or freedoms in question and the objective, but also between the deleterious and the salutary [beneficial] effects of the measures."[98]

These questions cannot be answered on the basis of traditional adjudicative facts—i.e., the facts of the specific case at bar.[99] The judge must rely on social science evidence about the seriousness of particular problems, the effects of the impugned law, and possible alternative policies.

At least three problems are raised by the Supreme Court's reliance on social science evidence. First, the justices cannot cross-examine the "expert witnesses" who write affidavits concerning extrinsic evidence; in most cases, they can only assume that the factual claims presented by the parties to the appeal are accurate.[100] In effect, the Supreme Court disregards the standards for expert testimony that it imposed on lower-court judges and trial juries. In *R. v. Mohan*, the justices expressed concern about the misleading effect of spurious or unsubstantiated "expert" testimony on impressionable jurors. They required trial judges or jurors to evaluate potential factual evidence "in light of its potential to distort the fact-finding process."[101] No such constraint applies to the Supreme Court's own deliberations. If they so wish, justices are free to fudge data, to ignore or downplay extrinsic evidence that conflicts with their own beliefs, and to base their findings on biased or incomplete research. (See the discussion of *R. v. Butler* in Dossier 10.6.)

Second, courts may make broad policy decisions based on insufficient or misinterpreted social science data, with potentially harmful results. Manfredi cites the 1990 ruling in *Askov v. the Queen*, in which the justices held that forcing defendants to wait for more than eight months for their trials violated section 11(b) of the *Charter*.[102] The decision was based, in part, on social science data about the impact of spending cuts on the operation of Crown prosecutors, data that did not support a fixed time limit for trials.[103] Tens of thousands of pending charges were dismissed[104] because of an apparent misreading of extrinsic evidence.

Third, judicial principles are inappropriate tools for evaluating legislative decisions. In effect, the courts have been granted the power to intervene in the policy-making process, without simultaneously acquiring the expertise to do it properly.

The complexity of policy development makes it difficult for those external to the process to know whether the policy scheme represents the best arrangement possible in terms of reconciling conflicting rights and values. The process of conceptualizing and drafting policy may have to address multiple objectives, and, when considering who will benefit or be affected, distinctions have to be made according to calculations that may not be based on objective principles of empirical certainties . . . In short, much of policy development is, of necessity, subject to discretionary judgement based on a combination of relevant expertise, comparative experience and informed best estimates.[105]

The justices themselves are aware of their limited policy-making skills, especially in the field of social policy.

Although courts are specialists in the protection of liberty and the interpretation of legislation and are, accordingly, well placed to subject criminal justice legislation to careful scrutiny—that is not so in the sphere of policy-making. Policy-making is a role properly assigned to elected parliamentarians who have the necessary institutional resources to enable them to compile and assess social science evidence, to mediate between competing social interests and to reach out and protect vulnerable groups. In according a greater degree of deference to social legislation than to ordinary criminal justice legislation, the courts recognize these important institutional differences.[106]

Notwithstanding this admission of incapacity, the Supreme Court's own interpretation of section 1 has opened the floodgates to extrinsic evidence in many areas of public policy. However, it has not changed the fact that judges and lawyers are not experts in public policy, nor are they trained to assess the credibility of social-science evidence. The difficulties arising from this change in evidentiary rules illustrates a basic problem of institutional adaptation: when an institution acquires new responsibilities for which its existing procedures are inadequate, it may not always discharge those responsibilities as well as we might wish.

The Supreme Court is deficient as a policy-making institution in one other respect: it does not have the power to implement and enforce its own rulings.[107] The practical effect of court decisions depends on the willingness of other government agencies—police, legislatures, public officials—to follow judge-made rules of conduct.[108] That willingness cannot be taken for granted. For example, the 1991 *Stinchcombe* ruling required Crown prosecutors to disclose all relevant evidence in a criminal trial to the defence in a timely manner.[109] Subsequent rulings, and anecdotal evidence from defence lawyers, reveal the resistance of some Crown prosecutors to their new responsibilities under *Stinchcombe.*[110]

Even when rulings are fully implemented by the responsible government actors, their impact on the daily lives of Canadians may still be less than the courts anticipated. A ruling that permits people to do something they were previously prohibited from doing (e.g., the 2002 *Sauvé* decision granting prisoners the right to vote) will have little practical effect unless the intended beneficiaries of the ruling actually choose to take the court up on its offer. So we should not assume that court rulings, including those based on the *Charter,* necessarily have a direct impact on the lives of Canadians.

THE IMPACT OF THE *CHARTER* ON CANADIAN POLITICS AND POLICY

The *Charter* has given new institutional expression to changing political values. In so doing, as we saw in Chapter 9, it has made the formal amendment of the *Constitution* extremely difficult. Previous sections of this chapter have identified a second consequence of the *Charter*: the changing relationship between the judiciary and the other two branches of government. This section discusses two additional changes to Canadian politics since the adoption of the *Charter*:

1. Legislators at both the federal and provincial levels must now take rights and freedoms into account in their policy deliberations.[111] To avoid passing laws that may be nullified on *Charter* grounds, legislators and ministers rely on legal advisers to assess the constitutionality of proposed legislation.[112] If those advisers identify a potentially unconstitutional element in the proposed legislation, the legislative and executive branches must either amend the draft law or risk the nullification of an entire policy. (See the earlier discussion of first-order and second-order *Charter* duties on page 488.) It should be noted that few laws or administrative decisions are ever subjected to a *Charter* challenge in the courts. This leaves the "*Charter*-proofing" conducted by the executive and legislative branches of government as the best guarantee of rights and freedoms in most instances.

2. The *Charter* has altered the relationship between the state and organized interests (see Chapter 7).[113] Pressure groups have two avenues of influence in the judicial process: they can directly challenge the constitutionality of a particular law through public-interest litigation, or they can apply for intervenor status in cases brought by other parties. Constitutional litigation is extremely expensive and beyond the means of most organizations and individuals. Although the payoff from a favourable ruling can be huge, the risk of losing in the courts diminishes the attractiveness of litigation for many groups.

   The intervenor strategy is less expensive, though still costly, but it carries its own disadvantages. In the first place, there is no guarantee that an application to intervene will be granted. The Supreme Court has complete discretion to accept or reject any would-be intervener, and it rarely explains its treatment of applicants. In a rare public ruling, the late Justice Sopinka identified two criteria: (1) whether the applicant has a demonstrated interest in the outcome of the case, and (2) whether the applicant can demonstrate "an expertise which can shed fresh light or provide new information on the matter."[114] Second, a successful application to intervene does not automatically ensure a meaningful influence on the outcome of the case. Some interventions have been remarkably successful, at least from the viewpoint of the intervenors themselves. The *Butler* case (Dossier 10.6) is a good example: the court's ruling was likely influenced by the intervention of LEAF, the Women's Legal Education and Action Fund. Others, probably the vast majority, have either been ignored altogether or reflected in dissenting opinions that have little effect on the law.

The overall point is that the *Charter*'s impact on Canadian politics and policy-making, while significant, should not be overstated. As the following section explains, the *Charter* leaves many areas of government and policy unaffected.

The Scope and Application of the *Charter*

Section 32 of the *Constitution Act, 1982* states that the *Charter* applies to both levels of government "in respect of all matters" within their respective jurisdictions. In the early years of *Charter* jurisprudence, the Supreme Court had to determine exactly what those words meant. Did the *Charter* apply to private litigation? Did it apply to universities, hospitals, and other quasi-public agencies? Did it give the courts the power to review Orders in Council and other executive decrees, or was its effect restricted to the acts of legislators? Finally, was the court itself bound by the *Charter*?

The justices were divided. Some of their opinions narrowed the application of the *Charter*, while others expanded it. In the 1985 *Operation Dismantle* case, Justice Wilson rejected the argument that certain "political questions"—specifically, the Crown's prerogative over foreign affairs and defence policy—fell outside the purview of the courts. She held that any executive decree that violates a *Charter* right is subject to judicial review and remedy, in the same manner as a law emanating from Parliament or a provincial legislature.[115] The following year, Justice McIntyre ruled in *Dolphin Delivery* that "the *Charter* applies to the legislative, executive and administrative branches of government . . . whether or not their action is invoked in public or private litigation."[116] However, the *Charter* does not apply to purely private disputes in which no government action is involved. The state "owes a constitutional duty" to its citizens, which private individuals do not owe to one another.[117] In the process of narrowing the *Charter*'s application, however, Justice McIntyre exempted court rulings—including those of the Supreme Court—from *Charter* scrutiny:

> *I cannot equate for the purposes of Charter application the order of a court with an element of governmental action. This is not to say that the courts are not bound by the Charter. The courts are, of course, bound by the Charter as they are bound by all law. It is their duty to apply the law, but in doing so they act as neutral arbiters, not as contending parties involved in a dispute. To regard a court order as an element of governmental intervention necessary to invoke the Charter would, it seems to me, widen the scope of Charter application to virtually all private litigation.[118]*

Intentionally or otherwise, *Dolphin Delivery* not only placed judges above the reach of the law but also "implied that legislatures are incapable of unbiased constitutional interpretation."[119] At the same time, it insulated private economic relations—between employers and employees, for example—from *Charter* remedies. The exclusion of the private sector from the scope of protected rights was strongly condemned by left-wing critics of the court, who had hoped that courts would use the new *Constitution* to advance social and economic justice.

In the 1990 *McKinney* case,[120] Justice Gérard La Forest ruled that the *Charter* did not apply to the mandatory retirement policies in force at most universities. A university is a private corporation (albeit one incorporated by provincial statute) that receives public money to carry out a public purpose. Because universities lie outside the apparatus of government, their collective agreements with their employees are beyond the scope of *Charter* review. Had the mandatory retirement policies at issue in *McKinney* been subject to *Charter* review, they would have been found to be unconstitutional on the grounds of age discrimination (section 15[1]). The court subsequently ruled, however, that discriminatory employment policies based on statute law, as opposed to private contracts, are subject to *Charter* remedies. While "private activity" is not open to judicial review, "laws that regulate private activity" are fair game.[121] Therefore, private corporations are subject to *Charter* scrutiny in the performance of their "delegated public functions," but not in the conduct of their internal private operations.

More recently, the court has ruled that semi-public agencies such as hospitals and universities may be held liable for exercising their statutory authority in a way that violates the *Charter*. In *Eldridge*, the court ruled that hospitals must provide sign-language interpreters for deaf patients. The British Columbia *Hospital Insurance Act* was held to be constitutional, because it did not prevent the provision of interpreters, but the failure of particular hospitals to assist hearing-impaired patients violated section 15(1) of the *Charter*.

> *Legislatures may not enact laws that infringe the Charter and they cannot authorize or empower another person or entity to do so. Even though a legislature may give authority to a body that is not subject to the Charter, the Charter applies to all the activities of government whether or not they may be otherwise characterized as "private" and it may apply to nongovernmental entities in respect of certain inherently governmental actions. Governments, just as they are not permitted to escape Charter scrutiny by entering into commercial contracts or other "private" arrangements, should not be allowed to evade their constitutional responsibilities by delegating the implementation of their policies and programs to private entities.*[122]

Where a particular law is constitutional but its application by a private agency is not, the remedy lies in section 24(1) of the *Charter*. In the *Eldridge* case, the court ordered the provincial government to administer its health-care system "in a manner consistent with the requirements of section 15(1)," without specifying how it should do so.

Finally, the court has held that the *Charter* guarantees certain rights to Canadian citizens and noncitizens alike. In *Singh*, Justice Wilson argued that the word "everyone" in section 7 "includes every human being who is physically present in Canada and by virtue of such presence amenable to Canadian law."[123] At the same time, she argued that deporting someone who could face persecution in his native country violated his right to "security of the person." The *Singh* doctrine has two implications. First, landed immigrants and refugee claimants are entitled to "due process" in their dealings with Canadian officials. Immediately after the *Singh* decision was issued, the immigration and refugee system was overwhelmed with appeals on the ground of insufficient due

A protester listens to speeches at a protest for land rights outside the Supreme Court of Canada (June 21, 2001). Protesters laid hundreds of blankets on the front lawn, representing land and security. (© CP/Tom Hanson)

process. Second, the Canadian government may not expose any person on its soil to the threat of a punishment that exceeds that imposed by Canadian law. In other words, a noncitizen who has been accused or convicted of a crime may not be extradited to a country that uses the death penalty, unless the minister of Justice has first received a written assurance that the individual will not be executed.

KEY PRINCIPLES OF *CHARTER* INTERPRETATION

Since 1982, the Supreme Court has developed several principles to guide *Charter* interpretation—both by lower courts and by policymakers in the executive and legislative branches. As we saw in Chapter 8, the written *Constitution* cannot be understood simply by reading the text. One must also consider the ways in which that text has been interpreted and applied by the courts—the common law (case law) of constitutional jurisprudence. This is particularly true for the *Charter*, given the broad language in which its provisions are phrased and the huge volume of *Charter* rulings since 1984. We will discuss five key principles in this section:

1. *stare decisis* (Latin for "the decision stands");
2. the purposive approach;
3. the contextual approach;
4. the three-stage approach; and
5. the "living tree" approach.

Stare Decisis: The Binding Power of Precedent

In theory, each court is bound by precedents—relevant rulings handed down by earlier judges. The Supreme Court of Canada, like all courts, is expected to follow its own precedents where these exist. In addition, all lower courts are restricted in their interpretation of the law by doctrines established by higher courts. The rule of *stare decisis* has two principal advantages. First, it imposes a degree of consistency and predictability on what might otherwise become a chaotic and contradictory mass of jurisprudence. Policy-makers and lower-court judges need guidelines to follow when they apply existing laws or make new ones. Second, *stare decisis* encourages higher courts to make principled decisions. Instead of following their own personal preferences, judges are expected to develop the law within the parameters set by precedent.

In practice, the *stare decisis* rule is more flexible than one might expect. Although their interpretive freedom is restricted by existing precedents, judges are free to decide which precedents apply to a particular case and how, if at all, established legal principles may be modified to suit changing social needs. A judge who disagrees with a Supreme Court precedent can "distinguish" it from the case at bar, by ruling that the facts of the two cases are sufficiently different to preclude the application of the earlier ruling. At the Supreme Court itself, the justices have demonstrated considerable ingenuity in evading their own prior decisions without formally overturning them (which they very rarely do). For example, the court unanimously ruled in 2001 that the minister of Justice could not extradite a murder suspect to a jurisdiction that practised capital punishment without first securing a written assurance that the suspect, if convicted, would not be executed. This was a clear reversal of a 1991 ruling, in which seven justices held that the risk of capital punishment should not be a factor in extradition proceedings.[124] The court refused to acknowledge the reversal in the second ruling; it simply stated that the factors to be weighed by the minister remained the same, but the balance among them had shifted over the preceding decade.

The Purposive Approach

Before it can determine whether a particular law or administrative Act violates a particular *Charter* guarantee, a court must identify the purpose of that guarantee— "the nature of the interests [that the relevant *Charter* provision] is meant to protect."[125] This interpretive rule was explained by the late Chief Justice Dickson in one of the first *Charter* cases before the Court, the 1985 *Big M Drug Mart* case:

In my view this analysis is to be undertaken, and the purpose of the right or freedom in question is to be sought by reference to the character and the larger objects of the Charter itself, to the language chosen to articulate the specific right or freedom, to the historical origins of the concepts enshrined, and where applicable, to the meaning and purpose of the other specific rights and freedoms with which it is associated within the text of the Charter. The interpretation should be . . . a generous rather than a legalistic one, aimed at fulfilling the purpose of the guarantee and securing for individuals the full benefit of the Charter's protection. At the same time it is important not to overshoot the actual purpose of the right or freedom in question, but to recall that the Charter was not enacted in a vacuum, and must therefore . . . be placed in its proper linguistic, philosophic and historical contexts.[126]

Dossier 10.5 explains how the determination of purpose works, focusing on the "right to vote" in section 3 of the *Charter*.

The Contextual Approach

Once a court has determined the purpose of a particular *Charter* guarantee, it must specify the precise application of that purpose to the facts of the case at bar. Instead of interpreting *Charter* guarantees abstractly, in a factual vacuum, the court is required to interpret them in relation to the specific dispute that it is called upon to resolve. Former Justice Bertha Wilson, the author of the contextual approach, argued that "a right or freedom may have different meanings in different contexts. Security of the person, for example, might mean one thing when addressed to the issue of over-crowding in prisons and something quite different when addressed to the issue of noxious fumes from industrial smoke-stacks."[127] She also pointed out that the task of balancing rights against competing social values, which is required under section 1 of the *Charter,* can be performed more effectively when both are defined with specific reference to the dispute at bar.

The contextual approach has been particularly important in cases involving freedom of expression (section 2[b]). The Supreme Court distinguishes among various types of expressive content, based on their perceived value to individuals and to Canadian society as a whole. "Core" content includes political speech, artistic self-expression, and the search for scientific truth. Expressive activity that falls into the "core" category may not be restricted by the state without an extremely good reason; in other words, laws that infringe "core" expression will be subject to a strict standard of justification under section 1. On the other end of the spectrum, "peripheral" content—e.g., hate speech and child pornography—merits little *Charter* protection, and legal restrictions on it are relatively easy to justify. Commercial advertising falls somewhere in between, depending on its intent: manipulative tobacco ads that portray smoking as a fun or "cool" activity enjoy less protection from the *Charter* than ads that provide useful information to consumers.

Section 3 of the *Charter* guarantees to every Canadian citizen the right to vote in federal and provincial elections, and the right to run for public office. The Supreme Court has ruled that the right to vote protects two distinct interests. First, it guarantees "effective representation" in government to every citizen. "Representation comprehends the idea of having a voice in the deliberations of government as well as the idea of the right to bring one's grievances and concerns to the attention of one's government representative."[128] "Effective representation" also implies "relative parity of voting power" among citizens. This means that the population in one constituency may not grossly exceed the population in another, although some variation in constituency size may be justified for geographic or other reasons. Where the variance is too great, the voting rights of citizens in large constituencies are diluted relative to those in less-populated ridings. In other words, a ballot cast in a constituency with 250 000 voters has less impact on the election of an MP than a ballot cast in a constituency with 100 000 voters.

The second interest protected by the right to vote is "the right to play a meaningful role in the selection of elected representatives."[129] The content of that "meaningful role" was spelled out in the 2003 *Figueroa* ruling, which struck down the law requiring political parties to run at least 50 candidates in a general election to qualify for state benefits (see the discussion of party registration in Chapter 3). At a minimum, each citizen must have the opportunity to vote and, if desired, to seek election to a federal or provincial legislature. She must be able to choose among a wide range of competing political parties or candidates, so that her own political views are reflected in public debate and, perhaps, in government. Any law that erects barriers to free and fair competition among political parties and candidates restricts the range of political options and makes it more difficult for some citizens to play a "meaningful role" in elections.

Whereas the first "purpose" of section 3 emphasizes the outcome of an election, the second focuses on the electoral process. The identification of two distinct purposes for a single *Charter* guarantee caused some legal confusion. The trial judge who heard the *Figueroa* case ruled that the party-registration law violated section 3, and struck down or modified several sections of the *Canada Elections Act*. She followed the "meaningful role" interpretation of the guarantee. The federal government appealed parts of her ruling to the Ontario Court of Appeal, which relied on the "effective representation" purpose; it overturned most of the trial ruling and restored the impugned sections of the Act. The Supreme Court of Canada finally resolved the issue when it declared that the true purpose of section 3, in relation to electoral participation, was the "meaningful role." Consequently, it restored much of the original ruling of the trial judge. The fluctuating and uncertain status of Canada's election law might have been avoided if the Supreme Court had identified a single purpose for section 3 in the first place.

The Three-Stage Approach

The Supreme Court has established a three-stage process for determining the constitutionality of laws that are alleged to violate the *Charter,* and determining appropriate remedies for those that are found to be unconstitutional:

- In the first stage, the court determines whether the impugned law infringes a *Charter* right or freedom. The person or group alleging the infringement must prove beyond a reasonable doubt that the impugned law violates the *Charter.* The Supreme Court has consistently held that *Charter* guarantees must receive a "large and liberal" interpretation at this first stage of analysis. This principle makes it more likely that an impugned law will be found to infringe a particular right or freedom. In consequence, judges often move on to the second stage of analysis: whether the sponsoring government can justify the infringement under section 1.

- In the second stage, the burden of proof shifts to the government that passed the impugned law. It must prove, on a balance of probabilities, that the law constitutes "a reasonable limit" on the infringed *Charter* right and that this limit is "demonstrably justifiable in a free and democratic society." (Note that the onus for the state is less burdensome than the onus required in the first stage of the test—establishing that a right or freedom has been violated.) If the court finds that the law meets the four criteria of the *Oakes* test (see page 510), it is declared to be constitutional and the court will uphold it. Laws that do not appear to serve "pressing and substantial" social interests, or whose effects on the right in question are considered serious enough to outweigh their stated objectives, will trigger some kind of judicial remedy.

- In the third stage, the court must determine the appropriate remedy for the party or parties whose rights have been infringed by the impugned law. As we have seen, the court can strike down the law "to the extent of the inconsistency" with the *Charter;* it can suspend the law, to give legislators time to bring it into conformity with the *Constitution;* it can order the government in question to apply the law according to the *Constitution;* it can "read down" the offending law to exclude the unconstitutional application; or it can "read in" a group that was previously excluded from the benefit of the law. In a criminal appeal, the appropriate remedy may be purely individual: the court may grant a new trial to the accused, with or without the exclusion of improperly obtained evidence.

From the very beginning of *Charter* jurisprudence, the Supreme Court has held that individual guarantees must be interpreted broadly at the first stage of analysis. Any limits on the protected rights and freedoms should be imposed at the section 1 stage, when they are balanced against competing social interests. However, this principle is not always applied consistently. The court has interpreted narrowly some *Charter* guarantees, notably freedom of association (section 2[d]) and equality rights (section 15[1]). Until recently, a majority of the justices held that the guarantee of associative freedom did not protect specifically collective activities; it permitted the exercise of individual rights and freedoms only in concert with others. Nor did section 2(d) afford any protection to labour unions: there was no *Charter* basis for a right to strike, or even to bargain collectively on behalf of the union membership.

More recently, the court has repudiated this narrow approach to associative freedom (although it has not yet recognized a constitutionally protected right to strike).[130] In a similar vein, the court has decreed that the guarantee of equality rights does not prevent the state from *distinguishing* between different groups of people (e.g., by requiring separate bathroom and locker facilities for men and women). It prevents the adoption only of laws that *discriminate* against a specific group (e.g., a law that prohibits qualified women from working as police officers).

As we saw earlier, the wording of section 1 changed significantly during the debate over the draft *Charter*. Its purpose, however, remained constant: to limit the application of the enumerated rights and freedoms and to balance *Charter* guarantees against competing social interests. In practice, no right or freedom can be exercised without restraint. For example, freedom of speech is a prerequisite for a healthy democracy. The liberty to express unpopular opinions must be protected against the annoyance of the majority. But hate propaganda against scapegoated minorities undermines the social tolerance on which democracy depends and threatens the safety of the targeted groups. Where do we draw the line between protected and unprotected speech?

The inclusion of an explicit limitation clause has had a marked influence on *Charter* interpretation. Whereas American courts have "read down" the provisions in the *Bill of Rights* to create internal limits on each protected right, Canadian courts have interpreted *Charter* rights broadly and then turned to section 1 to determine reasonable limits.[131] Dossier 10.6 describes a fairly typical application of the *Oakes* test, which ended at the second stage with a finding that the impugned law was constitutional under section 1.

In the early days of *Charter* jurisprudence, lawyers were uncertain about how to use section 1 in their constitutional arguments. In its first major rulings on the *Charter*, the Supreme Court made it clear that it could not evaluate section 1 claims without substantial evidence.[132] In effect, the court told lawyers that section 1 was not clear enough to apply in the absence of extrinsic social science evidence. The first major ruling on section 1 was *R. v. Oakes* (1986), a criminal appeal challenging the constitutionality of the federal *Narcotics Act*. Writing for the majority, the late Chief Justice Dickson offered a sweeping definition of the phrase "free and democratic society":

> *Inclusion of these words as the final standard of justification for limits on rights and freedoms refers the Court to the very purpose for which the Charter was originally entrenched in the Constitution: Canadian society is to be free and democratic. The Court must be guided by the values and principles essential to a free and democratic society which I believe embody, to name but a few, respect for the inherent dignity of the human person, commitment to social justice and equality, accommodation of a wide variety of beliefs, respect for cultural and group identity, and faith in social and political institutions which enhance the participation of individuals and groups in society.[133]*

Despite the breadth of the judicial discretion that this statement implies, the court's application of section 1 has narrowed over the years—which makes it easier for sponsoring governments to justify laws that infringe protected rights and freedoms.[134] In general, the court has lightened the burden of proof on the state. It usually defers to legislators' claims of "a pressing and substantial objective," "rational connection," "minimal impairment," and "salutary effects," especially in the field of social policy.[135] As long as the state can argue that the legislators who enacted the law made a "reasonable judgment," even in the absence of hard evidence, the court will generally accept that argument as valid.

However, the court has been more willing to challenge the use of state power against criminal suspects and defendants. In part, the court's aggressive approach to legal rights reflects its acknowledgment that its expertise about the legal process itself is greater than its capacity to make policy in social areas. The justices acknowledge that social policy—which may involve "striking a balance between the claims of competing groups" on the basis of social science evidence—is more effectively made by legislators than by courts. The criminal justice system, in contrast, does not require such delicate policy choices:

> In [criminal] cases, rather than mediating between different groups, the government is best characterized as the singular antagonist of the individual whose right has been infringed. For example, in justifying an infringement of legal rights enshrined in ss. 7 to 14 of the Charter, the state, on behalf of the whole community, typically will assert its responsibility for prosecuting crime whereas the individual will assert the paramountcy of principles of fundamental justice. There might not be any further competing claims among different groups. In such circumstances, and indeed whenever the government's purpose relates to maintaining the authority and impartiality of the judicial system, the courts can assess with some certainty whether the "least drastic means" for achieving the purpose have been chosen, especially given their accumulated experience in dealing with such questions . . . [136]

Whereas critics of the court argue that the justices have gone too far in protecting the rights of the accused,[137] its defenders applaud the justices for bringing the law up to date: "Many *Charter* decisions can be seen as a response to legislative inertia and statutory obsolescence."[138] If legislators are slow to reform the *Criminal Code*, whether because of neglect or from a desire to avoid controversy, the courts can hardly be faulted for stepping in.

The "large and liberal" approach to interpreting the *Charter* has sometimes been criticized for encouraging the judges to be too "activist"—i.e., too willing to strike down or amend laws passed by elected legislators. This argument overlooks the fact that the "large and liberal" court of the mid-1980s has evolved into a "cautious and conservative" court.[139] The court's change in attitude may be attributed, in part, to turnover in its membership.[140] Different judges interpret the law in different ways,[141] so we should not be surprised to find that personnel changes shift the balance of power between majorities and minorities.

In 1987 the Winnipeg police raided an "adult video" store and seized the entire inventory. The store's owner, Donald Butler, was charged with selling obscene materials as defined under section 163 of the *Criminal Code* and convicted on eight counts. He appealed his conviction, on the ground that the law violated the *Charter*. Any person charged with or convicted of a crime may appeal on the ground that the law that defines that crime is unconstitutional. In this case, Butler argued that the law prohibiting the sale of obscene materials constituted an unreasonable limit on the freedom of expression guaranteed in section 2(b) of the *Charter*.

In 1992 the Supreme Court unanimously dismissed Butler's appeal.[142] In the first stage of the analysis, the court addressed the question of whether section 163 of the *Code* infringes freedom of expression. To convict under section 163, the Crown must prove that the materials in question fit the following definition of "obscenity": "any publication a dominant characteristic of which is the undue exploitation of sex, or of sex and any one or more of the following subjects, namely, crime, horror, cruelty and violence, shall be deemed to be obscene." Since the law was enacted in 1959, two common-law tests for its application had been developed by the courts. The first is the "community standards" test, which defines the "undue exploitation of sex" with reference to social mores and the intended audience. The second is the "degradation or dehumanization" test, according to which any material that portrays human beings (usually women or children) in a

position of "subordination, servile submission or humiliation" will fail the community standards test even in the absence of violence. According to the justices, "It would be reasonable to conclude that there is an appreciable risk of harm to society in the portrayal of such material." This harm allegedly results from the "moral desensitization" produced in some viewers of sexually degrading material.

Although the court conceded that the social science evidence of a causal connection between degrading pornography and harmful behaviour—e.g., sexual assault—was shaky at best, they got around this problem by asserting that "the public has concluded that exposure to material which degrades the human dimensions of life to a subhuman or merely physical dimension and thereby contributes to a process of moral desensitization must be harmful in some way."

The justices concluded, in the words of Justice Sopinka, that "both the purpose and effect of s. 163 are specifically to restrict the communication of certain types of materials based on their content . . . there is no doubt that s. 163 seeks to prohibit certain types of expressive activity and thereby infringes s. 2(b) of the *Charter*." Having completed the first stage of the analysis, the court moved on to the second stage: the application of the *Oakes* test to determine whether the impugned law could be upheld under section 1 of the *Charter*. The justices determined that section 163 was intended to achieve a "pressing and substantial" social objective, namely "the avoidance of harm resulting from antisocial attitudinal changes

(cont'd)

that exposure to obscene material causes." Even in the absence of conclusive extrinsic proof that obscene materials promote sexual crimes, the justices decided that degrading portrayals of female sexuality undermine "true equality between male and female persons." Further, the protection afforded by section 2(b) of the *Charter* varies with the type of expression under consideration. Political speech is a key element of a "free and democratic society"; commercial advertising and pornography are not. Therefore, section 163 met the first criterion of the *Oakes* test: the restriction of obscenity was declared to be a "pressing and substantial" objective, which could outweigh the need to protect this particular form of expression.

The justices also found that section 163 met the "rational connection" test, even though they could not point to conclusive proof that the unrestricted distribution of obscene materials causes harm to society. Sopinka wrote: "While a direct link between obscenity and harm to society may be difficult, if not impossible, to establish, it is reasonable to presume that exposure to images bears a causal relationship to changes in attitudes and beliefs." In this instance, the court deferred to the legislative branch: "Parliament was entitled to have a 'reasoned apprehension of harm' resulting from the desensitization of individuals exposed to materials which depict violence, cruelty, and dehumanization in sexual relations."[143] The problem with this reasoning is that

the Parliament that enacted section 163 had no such apprehension, as the justices themselves admitted in their earlier discussion of changing approaches to obscenity. When section 163 was enacted in 1959, its purpose was to protect "public decency." The claim that obscene materials promote sexual crime did not enter the policy debate until the 1970s. This part of the *Butler* ruling may be interpreted as a case of judicial sleight of hand in the service of policy preferences.

Because section 163 provides an "artistic merit" defence, and because it is not intended to restrict the distribution of harmless erotica, the court concluded that it meets the "minimal impairment" test. Finally, the justices ruled that the effects of section 163 on freedom of expression did not outweigh its alleged objective: "to enhance respect for all members of society, and nonviolence and equality in their relations with each other." All the elements of the *Oakes* test were met, and section 163 was upheld as a reasonable and justifiable limitation on freedom of expression. As a result, the court did not proceed to the third stage of inquiry; no remedy was required.

The *Butler* ruling shows that "judicial creativity" need not be based on the remedial powers in the *Constitution Act, 1982*. By redefining the legislative intent of the obscenity law as the promotion of gender equality, the justices indulged in "considerable policy innovation in the very course of upholding a statute."[144]

The most important reason for the revival of judicial deference is probably the nature of judicial review itself. When judges are presented with a new constitutional document, they must create an entirely new set of doctrines and principles for its interpretation. Once those doctrines have taken shape, the impetus for judicial activism weakens, and the court becomes more deferential to the legislature.[145] It is also likely that the Supreme Court struck down more laws in the first decade after the *Charter* came into effect because it was confronted with a backlog of pre-*Charter* legislation. After nearly two decades, legislative drafters have become more careful to avoid remedial action by the courts. In effect, the "large and liberal" approach of the early years forced the other branches of government to take their first-order *Charter* duties more seriously than they might otherwise have done;[146] consequently, fewer laws require "fixing" to conform to the *Charter* (as interpreted by the courts).

It is also likely that the justices have been chastened by public criticism of their more controversial forays into policy-making and have tried to keep their heads down in recent years. They also seem to have become more acutely aware of their limitations as policy-makers. In response, they have become more cautious in the use of their remedial powers: instead of striking down laws immediately, the Supreme Court is increasingly likely to suspend the nullification of a law in order to allow the sponsoring legislature to fix problems as it sees fit.

The "Living Tree" Approach

The fifth general principle is that the *Charter* is a "living tree" that must be allowed to grow and develop in ways that its drafters could not foresee. The phrase first appeared in Canadian jurisprudence in the 1929 "Persons Case" (Dossier 8.1). As a principle of judicial review, it originally meant that a constitution must be interpreted in a flexible manner that permits its application to unforeseen circumstances, without the necessity of formal amendment (which, as discussed in Chapter 8, is deliberately difficult to accomplish). In the very first major *Charter* case at the Supreme Court, the late Justice Willard Estey observed that "The *Charter* is designed and adopted to guide and serve the Canadian community for a long time. Narrow and technical interpretation, if not modulated by a sense of the unknowns of the future, can stunt the growth of the law and hence the community it serves."[147]

As we noted earlier, the court has refused to be bound by the evidence of the framers' intent when it interprets the *Charter*. This attitude arises, in part, from the court's adherence to the "living tree" principle. As former Chief Justice Lamer put it, an over-emphasis on the views of those who wrote the *Charter* risks "freezing" the meaning of its guarantees as they were understood in 1982. The "frozen rights" in the 1960 Bill have no place in the interpretation of the supreme law of Canada. "If the newly planted 'living tree' which is the *Charter* is to have the possibility of growth and adjustment over time, care must be taken to ensure that historical materials . . . do not stunt its growth."[148]

According to Morton and Knopff, Lamer and his colleagues have distorted the "living tree" metaphor beyond recognition. They "want more than the flexibility of applying existing rights to new facts; they want the freedom to create new rights and then apply them to old facts."[149] In effect, the justices have grafted new branches onto a tree that was originally planted by legislators and thus transformed the tree in a way that the framers of the *Constitution* never intended.

The debate over the "living tree" metaphor illustrates a central controversy over judicial review: Should judges adopt an **"interpretivist"** or a "noninterpretivist" approach to constitutional provisions? Interpretivists believe that "constitutional law should be firmly anchored in the text of the *Constitution* itself."[150] Judges must respect the original intent of the framers, insofar as that intent can be determined and applied to unforeseen circumstances. The noninterpretivist approach treats the written *Constitution* as a starting point for policy-making, in which the preferences of today's judges can legitimately outweigh the choices of the framers. Interpretivist judges defer to the legislative branch and regard themselves as equally bound by the *Constitution.* Noninterpretivist judges give themselves wide latitude to reinterpret rights and overrule legislators, without taking the original intent of either the impugned law or the *Constitution* into account. According to Morton and Knopff,

> *One cannot escape the conclusion that the Supreme Court has adopted an entirely unprincipled approach to the question of original intent, subordinating it to the question of desired policy result. If the judges can find evidence of original intent that supports their policy predilections, they will embrace it; if original intent would obstruct the desired policy, they ignore or reject it. Far from being a constraint on judicial discretion, original intent has itself become a matter of judicial discretion.*[151]

This critique is inaccurate, inasmuch as it implies that judges are free to impose their own policy preferences without constraint. In reality, there are at least three constraints on judicial policy-making. First, appellate courts are collegial institutions. An individual judge has no power unless she can command the support of a majority of her colleagues. In rare cases, a lone dissenting judge can exert a long-term influence on the development of the law; over time, the consensus of a court can shift away from the previous majority opinion to embrace a new interpretation of the *Constitution.*[152] But in general, a maverick judge who refuses to compromise his or her policy preferences risks isolation and impotence. Second, as noted earlier, judges are restrained (at least to a degree) by the principle of *stare decisis.* They cannot just make up the law as they go along.

Third and finally, judges are not solely responsible for the interpretation and enforcement of the *Charter.* If they choose, policy-makers in the legislative and executive branches can modify or even reject the choices enshrined in court rulings. As noted above, the Supreme Court has generally favoured the due-process rights of criminal suspects over the investigative discretion of the police, where the two conflict. On the other hand, recent federal governments have been pressured by Opposition MPs (especially those in the Reform/Alliance Party, now the Conservatives) and victims' rights groups to crack down on crime. In several instances, Parliament has amended the *Criminal Code* to undo the effect of court rulings that it perceived as unduly favourable toward alleged criminals.[153] At least one of these amendments was subsequently upheld by the Supreme Court on the ground that "Courts do not hold a monopoly on the protection and promotion of rights and freedoms; Parliament also plays a role in this regard and is often able to act as a significant ally for vulnerable groups."[154] Even without recourse to the unpopular "notwithstanding clause" (section 33), which allows a legislature to override certain rights and freedoms for a five-year period, the other two branches of government are not helpless in the face of court rulings on the *Charter*. To suggest otherwise is to present a distorted picture of the relationship among Canada's political institutions.

CONCLUSION

The impact of the *Charter* on Canadian politics and policy-making, while significant, should not be overstated. Nor should it be viewed simply as a product of the *Charter* itself. Changes to the Supreme Court—its ability to control its own docket, and the appointment of more activist justices—ensured that the *Charter* would have a greater effect on public policy than it would otherwise have had. So did the willingness of interest groups to seek policy change through the courts, and the creation of support networks for public-interest litigation. All of these developments, which were evident before 1982, made important contributions to the *Charter's* impact on Canadian government and politics.

Perhaps most important, judicial attitudes toward their own role—in particular, the willingness of judges to challenge the other two branches of government—determine the *Charter's* practical effect on the lives of Canadians. When judges defer to legislators or executives, their policy-making power shrinks; when *Charter* rights and freedoms yield to other priorities, their influence wanes. This relationship between judicial attitudes and *Charter* enforcement has become increasingly apparent since 9/11. In the wake of the terrorist attacks in the United States, heightened national security concerns partially eclipsed *Charter* rights and freedoms. A month after the attacks, the federal government introduced Bill C-36 into Parliament. The Bill, which is now the *Anti-Terrorism Act* (*ATA*), contained numerous amendments to the *Criminal Code*, the *Official Secrets Act*, and other federal legislation. Among other things, the *ATA* makes it a criminal offence to participate in a terrorist organization (whether or not the accused individual knows of any planned terrorist activity); permits a police officer to arrest a person whom he or she suspects of planning to commit a terrorist act; provides for secret investigative hearings at which any individual may be compelled to testify, whether or not a terrorist act has taken place; and defines terrorism as any criminal offence committed "in whole or in part for a political, religious or ideological purpose, objective or cause."[155] The *ATA* appears to infringe several of the protected rights and freedoms in the *Charter*, especially the legal rights in sections 7–13 and the fundamental freedoms in section 2.[156]

Despite these apparent infringements, the Supreme Court of Canada upheld parts of the *ATA* in June 2004.[157] The justices had previously signalled their willingness to accept anti-terrorism laws as "reasonable limitations" on the *Charter* in the *Suresh* case, which was decided shortly after the attacks on Washington and New York.[158] When national security concerns become paramount, courts usually defer to the executive branch, which is ultimately responsible for protecting life and property within a particular state.[159] In a British case concerning the deportation of an alleged

Islamic terrorist, issued a month after 9/11, Lord Leonard Hoffmann of the U.K. House of Lords made this explicit:

> [T]he recent events in New York and Washington . . . are a reminder that in matters of national security, the cost of failure can be high. This seems to me to underline the need for the judicial arm of government to respect the decisions of ministers of the Crown on the question of whether support for terrorist activities in a foreign country constitutes a threat to national security . . . the executive has access to special information and expertise in these matters.[160]

As in previous "crises," the judicial branch of government seems willing to allow greater discretion and powers to the police and executive. Such sweeping discretion is not always compatible with the rule of law and the enforcement of human rights. Before 9/11, few Canadians would have believed that deliberate violations of rights and freedoms, like those committed against Japanese Canadians in World War II or the mass arrests without charge in the "October crisis" of 1970,[161] could happen again. The 1988 *Emergencies Act,* which replaced the old *War Measures Act,* was carefully crafted to conform to the requirements of the *Charter.* It explicitly referred to "those fundamental rights that are not to be limited or abridged even in a national emergency," limited the exercise of emergency powers to strict time periods, and forbade "the detention, imprisonment or internment of Canadian citizens or permanent residents as defined in the *Immigration Act* on the basis of race, national or ethnic origin, colour, religion, sex, age or mental or physical disability."[162] There are no such protections in the *ATA*. Muslim and Arab Canadians have complained that the police are using their powers under the *ATA* to harass and "profile" them; to date, none of these allegations have been proven in a court of law.

The apparent willingness of the federal government to water down *Charter* rights in the name of national security, justified or otherwise, reveals the influence of external forces on our domestic political institutions. The motivation behind the *ATA* was twofold: (1) to comply with Canada's international obligations under United Nations Conventions on terrorism,[163] and (2) to reassure the U.S. government that Canada was not a "safe haven" for terrorists, as a means to keep the border between the two countries open for trade.[164] These goals seem to be shared by all three branches of government: in January 2002 the Supreme Court upheld the deportation of an Iranian citizen suspected of terrorism, further reassuring nervous American officials.[165] The decision marked a substantial modification, if not an outright reversal, of previous court rulings on the treatment of refugee claimants.[166]

In general, it is fair to say that the *Charter* has expanded the policy influence of the judicial branch—although that influence is limited, as previously discussed, by the deficiencies of courts as policy-making institutions. Since the early "activist" period of the *Charter,* judges have increasingly acknowledged that they lack the expertise to design and implement effective policies. In consequence, they properly defer to the executive and the legislature in most instances.

The appropriateness of their post-9/11 deference in the name of national security may be a different story. It is by no means clear that efforts to prevent terrorism are made more effective by permitting police to arrest without warrant, to "profile" particular groups, or to distinguish between ordinary crimes and those committed "for a political, religious or ideological purpose." As the Supreme Court itself noted in the immediate aftermath of 9/11, "liberty, the rule of law, and the principles of fundamental justice" are the fundamental principles of our constitutional and political order. "In the end, it would be a Pyrrhic victory if terrorism were defeated at the cost of sacrificing our commitment to those values."[167]

GLOSSARY OF KEY TERMS

Adjudication: The process by which the courts resolve disputes.

Extrinsic evidence: Facts placed before a court that do not arise directly from the case at bar. Two types of extrinsic evidence are discussed in this chapter: social science evidence relating to the policy impact of a particular law (used to weigh infringed rights against competing social purposes under section 1 of the *Charter*), and evidence of legislative intent in the drafting of the impugned law.

Impugned: When a court is asked to rule on the constitutionality of a particular law, that legal provision is said to be "impugned." In a *Charter* case, one or more parties before the court seeks to prove that the law is unconstitutional, on the grounds that it conflicts with a *Charter* right or freedom. The challenged law, or the specific sections of the law on which the appeal turns, are impugned by the plaintiff. The term applies whether or not the court agrees that the law is unconstitutional.

Interpretivist judicial review: The reliance by judges on evidence of legislative intent, as a guide to interpreting constitutional principles. In other words, the judges try to determine what the framers of the *Constitution* were trying to accomplish when they drafted the relevant provisions and follow that intent in applying those provisions to the facts of a particular case.

Judicial activism: Activist judges use their policy-making power to overturn or effectively rewrite ordinary statutes and constitutional texts. Activist judges are less likely to defer to the legislative or executive branches of government and more likely to put their own stamp on the law through judicial review.

Judicial deference: Also called "judicial conservatism." An institutional norm among appeal court judges that restrains them in their legal interpretations. Judges defer to Parliament, upholding most or all of the laws passed by the legislative branch and taking a narrow (**interpretivist**) approach to constitutional law.

Litigation: Seeking the resolution of a dispute in the courts. Examples include constitutional challenges, private lawsuits, and criminal appeals.

Noninterpretivist judicial review: Noninterpretivist judges do not perceive themselves as bound by the intentions of the framers when they interpret and apply the *Constitution*. They go beyond the original intent of each provision, expanding or contracting its meaning to cover circumstances that could not be foreseen at the time of adoption.

Nullification: When a court finds an impugned law to be unconstitutional, it can declare that law to be null and void (section 52 of the *Constitution Act, 1982*). This power to nullify laws is also referred to as "striking down."

Plaintiff: In the context of this chapter, an individual or group that challenges the constitutionality of a particular law or administrative act under the *Charter*. The plaintiff must demonstrate that his *Charter* rights or freedoms, or those of the represented group, have been infringed. If the plaintiff succeeds in proving that an impugned law infringes the *Charter*, the court proceeds to consider whether that law should be upheld as a "reasonable limit" under section 1. In the case of an administrative act—e.g., a police investigation or an adverse ruling on a refugee claim—there is no section 1 analysis; a proven *Charter* infringement will usually trigger a remedy from the court.

Public-interest litigation: The effort to change laws and other government policies through the courts. In the *Charter* context, this involves a legal challenge to the constitutionality of a particular law or program, or a claim that a specific government official violated the rights or freedoms of the plaintiff.

"Reading down": When a court finds that an impugned law violates the *Charter* under a certain set of circumstances, it can set out a narrow interpretation of that law that prevents such a violation in the future. The application of the law is restricted, but it is not struck down altogether.

"Reading in": When a court finds that a particular group has been unfairly excluded from constitutional protection, it can use the remedial power under section 52 to "read in" that group. In effect, the court rewrites the *Charter*—usually section 15—to broaden the rights guaranteed therein. The actual wording of the *Constitution* does not change, but lawyers and judges know that they are bound to interpret its provisions as though they had been formally amended.

DISCUSSION QUESTIONS

1. What is the significance of section 1 of the *Charter*? How does it affect the ways in which the courts approach judicial review?

2. Identify and briefly explain the various remedies available to the courts under the *Constitution Act, 1982*. How have those remedies affected the making of public policy in Canada?

3. Is it acceptable for nine unelected judges to nullify laws made by elected legislators? Why or why not?

4. Are judges competent to make and enforce public policy? Why or why not?

5. In your own words, explain three of the five principles of *Charter* interpretation that were discussed in this chapter.

SUGGESTED READINGS

Books and Articles

W.A. Bogart, *Courts and Country: The Limits of Litigation and the Social and Political Life of Canada* (Toronto: Oxford University Press, 1994).

Ronald J. Daniels, Patrick Macklem, and Kent Roach, eds., *The Security of Freedom: Essays on Canada's Anti-Terrorism Bill* (Toronto: University of Toronto Press, 2002).

Charles R. Epp, *The Rights Revolution: Lawyers, Activists, and Supreme Courts in Comparative Perspective* (Chicago: University of Chicago Press, 1998).

Janet L. Hiebert, *Charter Conflicts: What Is Parliament's Role?* (Montreal and Kingston: McGill–Queen's University Press, 2002).

Janet L. Hiebert, *Limiting Rights: The Dilemma of Judicial Review* (Montreal and Kingston: McGill–Queen's University Press, 1996).

Paul Howe and Peter H. Russell, eds., *Judicial Power and Canadian Democracy* (Montreal and Kingston: McGill–Queen's University Press/Institute for Research on Public Policy, 2001).

James B. Kelly, "Bureaucratic Activism and the Charter of Rights and Freedoms: The Department of Justice and its entry into the centre of government," *Canadian Public Administration,* 42:4 (Winter 1999).

James B. Kelly, "The Charter of Rights and Freedoms and the Rebalancing of Liberal Constitutionalism in Canada, 1982–1997," *Osgoode Hall Law Journal,* volume 37 (Fall 1999).

Heather MacIvor, *Canadian Government and Politics in the Charter Era* (Toronto: Nelson Thomson, 2005).

Christopher P. Manfredi, *Judicial Power and the Charter: Canada and the Paradox of Liberal Constitutionalism,* 2nd edition (Toronto: Oxford University Press, 2001).

F.L. Morton and Rainer Knopff, *The Charter Revolution and the Court Party* (Peterborough, ON: Broadview Press, 2000).

Kent Roach, *September 11: Consequences for Canada* (Montreal and Kingston: McGill–Queen's University Press, 2003).

Kent Roach, *The Supreme Court on Trial: Judicial Activism or Democratic Dialogue?* (Toronto: Irwin Law, 2001).

Peter H. Russell, *Constitutional Odyssey: Can Canadians Become a Sovereign People?* 2nd edition (Toronto: University of Toronto Press, 1993).

Peter H. Russell, Rainer Knopff, and Ted Morton, eds., *Leading Constitutional Decisions: Federalism and the Charter* (Ottawa: Carleton University Press, 1989).

F. Leslie Seidle, ed., *Equity and Community: The Charter, Interest Advocacy and Representation* (Montreal: Institute for Research on Public Policy, 1993).

Robert J. Sharpe, Katherine E. Swinton, and Kent Roach, *The Charter of Rights and Freedoms,* 2nd edition (Toronto: Irwin Law, 2002).

Brian Slattery, "A Theory of the Charter," *Osgoode Hall Law Journal,* volume 25 (1987), 701.

Websites

All of the *Charter* rulings by the Supreme Court of Canada are available online at the LexUM website (www.lexum.umontreal.ca; click on "Supreme Court of Canada"), which offers a searchable database of rulings issued back to 1985 and the ability to download these rulings in WordPerfect. An option is to go to the Supreme Court of Canada website (www.scc-csc.gc.ca) and click on "Judgments" at the top of the screen. Follow the links to LexUM.

Another source of Supreme Court rulings is the Canadian Legal Information Institute website (www.canlii.org); under "Canada," click on "Supreme Court of Canada." The CanLII site also offers a useful digest of *Charter* rulings by a senior official at the federal Department of Justice (under "Canada," in the "Commentary" section, click on "Decisions Digest") and a searchable database of federal and provincial laws and court rulings.

NOTES

1. See Charles R. Epp, "Do Bills of Rights Matter? The Canadian Charter of Rights and Freedoms," *American Political Science Review,* 90:4 (December 1996); Charles R. Epp, *The Rights Revolution: Lawyers, Activists, and Supreme Courts in Comparative Perspective* (Chicago: University of Chicago Press, 1998), Chapter One.

2. The *Charter* was proclaimed into law on April 17, 1982. However, the implementation of section 15 (equality rights) was delayed for three years to allow governments to bring their laws into conformity with its provisions.

3. *R. v. Morgentaler* [1988] 1 S.C.R. 30.

4. *Rodriguez v. British Columbia (Attorney General)* [1993] 3 S.C.R. 519.

5. *Eldridge v. British Columbia (Attorney General)* [1997] 3 S.C.R. 624.

6. *Singh v. Minister of Employment and Immigration* [1985] 1 S.C.R. 177; *Andrews v. Law Society of British Columbia* [1989] 1 S.C.R. 143; *Benner v. Canada (Secretary of State)* [1997] 1 S.C.R. 358.

7. *Vriend v. Alberta* [1998] 1 S.C.R. 493; *McKinney v. University of Guelph* [1990] 3 S.C.R. 229; *Egan v. Canada* [1995] 2 S.C.R. 513; *Law v. Canada (Minister of Employment and*

Immigration) [1999] 1 S.C.R. 497; *Schachter v. Canada* [1992] 2 S.C.R. 679; *Thibaudeau v. Canada* [1995] 2 S.C.R. 627.

8. *R. v. Feeney* [1997] 2 S.C.R. 13.

9. *R. v. Stillman* [1997] 1 S.C.R. 607.

10. *R. v. Manninen* [1987] 1 S.C.R. 1233; *R. v. Burlingham* [1995] 2 S.C.R. 206.

11. *R. v. Daviault* [1994] 3 S.C.R. 63.

12. *R. v. Lavallee* [1990] 1 S.C.R. 852; *R. v. Malott* [1998] 1 S.C.R. 123.

13. *R. v. Vaillancourt* [1987] 2 S.C.R. 636; *R. v. Creighton* [1993] 3 S.C.R. 3.

14. Christopher P. Manfredi, *Judicial Power and the Charter: Canada and the Paradox of Liberal Constitutionalism,* 2nd edition (Toronto: Oxford University Press, 2001), 22.

15. Michael Mandel, *The Charter of Rights and the Legalization of Politics in Canada,* rev. edition (Toronto: Thomson, 1994), 43.

16. Ibid., 43.

17. F. L. Morton and Rainer Knopff, *The Charter Revolution and the Court Party* (Peterborough, ON: Broadview Press, 2000), 31.

18. Ibid., 166. In reality, right-wing groups and corporations use the *Charter* at least as often as the "Court Party" groups identified by Morton and Knopff, with considerable success. See, for example, *Lavigne v. Ontario Public Service Employees Union* [1991] 2 S.C.R. 211, an anti-union challenge funded by the right-wing National Citizens' Coalition (NCC), and the NCC's own challenges to the *Canada Elections Act: Somerville v. Canada (Attorney General)* (1996), 136 D.L.R. (4th) 205 and *Harper v. Attorney General for Canada* [2000]. Note, however, that the NCC eventually lost the Harper case—a challenge to the laws restricting interest-group advertising during election campaigns—in a May 2004 ruling from the Supreme Court of Canada. See *Harper v. Canada (Attorney General)* [2004] 1 S.C.R. 827.

19. Kent Roach, "The Role of Litigation and the Charter in Interest Advocacy," in F. Leslie Seidle, ed., *Equity and Community: The Charter, Interest Advocacy and Representation* (Montreal: Institute for Research on Public Policy, 1993), 173–74.

20. Ibid., 174–75.

21. A survey of *Charter* rulings from 1984 to 1997 found that roughly one-third of plaintiffs succeeded at the Supreme Court. James B. Kelly, "The Charter of Rights and Freedoms and the Rebalancing of Liberal Constitutionalism in Canada, 1982–1997," *Osgoode Hall Law Journal,* volume 37 (Fall 1999), Table 2, 641.

22. Janet L. Hiebert, *Limiting Rights: The Dilemma of Judicial Review* (Montreal and Kingston: McGill–Queen's University Press, 1996), 118.

23. David Beatty, *Constitutional Law in Theory and Practice* (Toronto: University of Toronto Press, 1995), 91 and 95.

24. Hiebert, *Limiting Rights,* 125.

25. Between 1987 and 2000, national surveys have found that roughly twice as many Canadians trust the courts to have "the final say" on laws that conflict with the *Charter,* compared to those who prefer Parliament to have the last word. See Paul Howe and David Northrup, *Strengthening Canadian Democracy: The Views of Canadians* (Montreal: Institute for Research on Public Policy, July 2000), Table 24, 42; available online at www.irpp.org. A 2003 survey for the Centre for Research and Information on Canada found a decline in the percentage of court supporters, but the overall figures were consistent with the trend since 1987. See www.cric.ca/pdf/cric_poll/portraits/portraits_2003/portraits03_same_sex_marriage_eng.pdf.

26. Brian Slattery, "A Theory of the Charter," *Osgoode Hall Law Journal*, volume 25 (1987).

27. See Kent Roach, *The Supreme Court on Trial: Judicial Activism or Democratic Dialogue?* (Toronto: Irwin Law, 2001); Janet L. Hiebert, *Charter Conflicts: What Is Parliament's Role?* (Montreal and Kingston: McGill–Queen's University Press, 2002).

28. Alan C. Cairns, *Charter versus Federalism: The Dilemmas of Constitutional Reform* (Montreal and Kingston: McGill–Queen's University Press, 1992), 17–18.

29. *Attorney General for British Columbia v. Tomey Homma*, JCPC 1903, in Richard A. Olmsted, ed., *Decisions of the Judicial Committee of the Privy Council*, volume 1 (Ottawa: Queen's Printer, 1954), 484.

30. *Co-operative Committee on Japanese Canadians v. Attorney General for Canada*, JCPC 1947, in Olmsted, volume 3, 472–73.

31. *Reference re Alberta Statutes*, S.C.R. 1938, in Peter H. Russell, Rainer Knopff, and Ted Morton, eds., *Leading Constitutional Decisions: Federalism and the Charter* (Ottawa: Carleton University Press, 1989), 293–98.

32. Russell, Knopff, and Morton, "Comment on *Switzman v. Elbling*," in *Leading Constitutional Decisions*, 318.

33. *Ontario (Attorney General) v. OPSEU* [1987] 2 S.C.R. 2; *New Brunswick Broadcasting Co. v. Nova Scotia (Speaker of the House of Assembly)* [1993] 1 S.C.R. 319; *Reference re Remuneration of Judges of the Provincial Court (P.E.I.)* [1997] 3 S.C.R. 3; *Reference re Secession of Quebec* [1998] 2 S.C.R. 217.

34. Cairns, 29.

35. Ibid.

36. *R. v. Drybones* [1970] S.C.R. 282.

37. Ibid.

38. *Attorney General of Canada v. Lavell; Isaac v. Bedard* [1974] S.C.R. 1349.

39. *Morgentaler v. the Queen*, S.C.R. 1976, 632.

40. Ibid., 633.

41. Ibid., 636.

42. *R. v. Morgentaler*, S.C.R. 1988, paragraph 3.

43. Ibid., paragraph 185.

44. Ibid., paragraph 237.

45. Ibid., paragraph 246.

46. Ibid., paragraphs 31 and 32.

47. *Singh v. Minister of Employment and Immigration* [1985] 1 S.C.R. 177.

48. *Authorson v. Canada (Attorney General)* [2003] 2 S.C.R. 40.

49. Peter H. Russell, *Constitutional Odyssey: Can Canadians Become a Sovereign People?* 2nd edition (Toronto: University of Toronto Press, 1993), 114.

50. Reproduced in Hiebert, *Limiting Rights*, 21.

51. Hiebert, *Limiting Rights*, 24.

52. *R. v. Seaboyer; R. v. Gayme* [1991] 2 S.C.R. 577.

53. *R. v. Darrach*, S.C.R. 2000, paragraph 1.

54. Janet Hiebert, "Debating Policy: The Effects of Rights Talk," in F. Leslie Seidle, ed., *Equity and Community: The Charter, Interest Advocacy and Representation* (Montreal: Institute for Research on Public Policy, 1993), 51.

55. *R. v. Darrach,* S.C.R. 2000.

56. Peter W. Hogg and Allison A. Bushell, "The Charter Dialogue Between Courts and Legislatures (Or Perhaps The Charter of Rights Isn't Such a Bad Thing After All)," *Osgoode Hall Law Journal,* volume 35 (Spring 1997), 75. See also Hiebert, *Charter Conflicts,* Chapter 5, and Kent Roach, *Due Process and Victims' Rights: The New Law and Politics of Criminal Justice* (Toronto: University of Toronto Press, 1999), Chapter 5. For critiques of the "dialogue" metaphor, see Christopher P. Manfredi and James B. Kelly, "Six Degrees of Dialogue: A Response to Hogg and Bushell," *Osgoode Hall Law Journal,* volume 37, (Fall 1999), 513, and F.L. Morton, "Dialogue or Monologue?" in Paul Howe and Peter H. Russell, eds., *Judicial Power and Canadian Democracy* (Montreal and Kingston: McGill–Queen's University Press/Institute for Research on Public Policy, 2001).

57. *Schachter v. Canada* [1992] 2 S.C.R. 679.

58. See *R. v. Sharpe* [2001] 1 S.C.R. 45. The new law, Bill C-12, died on the Order Paper when Parliament was dissolved for the 2004 federal election.

59. *Andrews v. Law Society of British Columbia* [1989] 1 S.C.R. 143; *Benner v. Canada (Secretary of State)* [1997] 1 S.C.R. 358.

60. *Egan v. Canada* [1995] 2 S.C.R. 513; *Vriend v. Alberta* [1998] 1 S.C.R. 493; *M. v. H.* [1999] 2 S.C.R. 3.

61. *Miron v. Trudel* [1995] 2 S.C.R. 418.

62. *Osborne v. Canada (Treasury Board)* [1991] 2 S.C.R. 69.

63. *Eaton v. Brant County Board of Education* [1997] 1 S.C.R. 241, paragraph 67.

64. *Miron v. Trudel* [1995] 2 S.C.R. 418, paragraph 131.

65. *Eldridge v. British Columbia (Attorney General),* paragraph 56.

66. *Miron v. Trudel,* paragraph 151.

67. *Egan v. Canada* [1995] 2 S.C.R. 513, paragraph 5.

68. *Miron v. Trudel,* paragraph 156.

69. *Miron v. Trudel* [1995] 2 S.C.R. 418.

70. *M. v. H.* [1999] 2 S.C.R. 3.

71. *Halpern v. Canada (Attorney General)* [2002] O.J. No. 2714 (2002) 215 D.L.R. (4th) 223; *Hendricks v. Québec (Attorney General)* [2002] J.Q. No. 3816.

72. Kathleen A. Lahey and Kevin Alderson, *Same-Sex Marriage: The Personal and the Political* (Toronto: Insomniac Press, 2004), 91–92.

73. The text of the July 2003 draft law was accessed online at the Department of Justice website: www.canada.justice.gc.ca.

74. Department of Justice website: www.canada.justice.gc.ca.

75. The Justice department claimed that the new question would address public concerns that the government had prejudged the issue in its original reference questions, and that it would "allow individuals and groups who disagree with the Government's approach to put their case before the Supreme Court." The revised reference, which was filed on January 28, 2004, was accessed at www.canada.justice.gc.ca/en/news.

76. Brian Laghi, "Top court wouldn't block same-sex law, Harper says," *The Globe and Mail,* June 3, 2004; accessed at www.globeandmail.com.

77. Rod Mickleburgh and Mark Hume, "White harsh critic of justice, immigration systems," *The Globe and Mail,* June 26, 2004 (accessed at www.globeandmail.com); Canadian Press,

"We'd use notwithstanding clause: Tory MP," *Toronto Star,* June 25, 2004 (accessed at www.thestar.com).

78. Robert Benzie, "Tories pin blame on fear, rogue candidates," *Toronto Star,* June 30, 2004 (accessed at www.thestar.com).

79. *Reference re Same-Sex Marriage* [2004] S.C.C. 79.

80. Jeffrey Simpson, "Stephen Harper just doesn't get it," *The Globe and Mail,* December 15, 2004; Peter Hogg, "So, where do we go from here?," *The Globe and Mail,* December 15, 2004.

81. Justice Minister Irwin Cotler, testimony before the House of Commons Standing Committee on Justice, Human Rights, Public Safety and Emergency Preparedness, March 30, 2004.

82. Canada, House of Commons Standing Committee on Justice, Human Rights, Public Safety and Emergency Preparedness, *Improving the Supreme Court of Canada Appointments Process* (Ottawa: House of Commons, May 2004).

83. In early 2004, Justice Louise Arbour was appointed to lead the United Nations Human Rights Commission. Shortly thereafter, Justice Frank Iacobucci announced his early retirement from the court. Both represented Ontario on the court.

84. Kim Lunman and Brian Laghi, "Commons panel to accept judges," *The Globe and Mail,* August 26, 2004 (accessed at www.globeandmail.com); Tonda MacCharles and Mary Gordon, "MPs to vet top judge picks," *Toronto Star,* August 24, 2004 (accessed at www.thestar.com).

85. *Reference re Remuneration of Judges of the Provincial Court (P.E.I.)* [1997] 3 S.C.R. 3, paragraph 109.

86. From a speech given by the late Justice John Sopinka of the Supreme Court of Canada. Reprinted from *The Globe and Mail,* November 28, 1997.

87. See, for example, former Justice Bertha Wilson's article "We Didn't Volunteer," in Howe and Russell, eds., 73–79.

88. *Re B.C. Motor Vehicle Act* [1985] 2 S.C.R. 486, paragraph 16.

89. Indeed, appellate judges try to avoid readjudicating the facts of the case, unless "the trial judge has made a 'palpable and overriding error.'" See *Housen v. Nikolaisen* [2002] 2 S.C.R. 235.

90. *R. v. Big M Drug Mart Ltd.* [1985] 1 S.C.R. 295.

91. Peter H. Russell, *The Judiciary in Canada: The Third Branch of Government* (Toronto: McGraw-Hill Ryerson, 1987), 289.

92. Peter McCormick and Ian Greene, *Judges and Judging* (Toronto: James Lorimer, 1990), 9.

93. *Halpern v. Canada (Attorney General),* Ontario Court of Appeal, June 10, 2003; accessed at www.canlii.org.

94. *Barbeau v. British Columbia,* British Columbia Court of Appeal, July 8, 2003; accessed at www.canlii.org.

95. *Re B.C. Motor Vehicle Act,* paragraphs 38–42.

96. Ibid., paragraphs 50–52.

97. *R. v. Oakes* [1986] 1 S.C.R. 103, paragraphs 69 and 70.

98. *Dagenais v. Canadian Broadcasting Corp.* [1994] 3 S.C.R. 835, paragraph 95.

99. Manfredi, *Judicial Power and the Charter,* 157.

100. There is a partial exception: the *Rules of the Supreme Court of Canada* permit a lawyer appointed by the court to conduct a cross-examination of an expert witness on the

written evidence that he or she has submitted on behalf of one of the parties. The cross-examination does not take place before the justices; instead, a transcript must be provided within a specified time.

101. *R. v. Mohan* [1994] 2 S.C.R. 9.

102. *R. v. Askov* [1990] 2 S.C.R. 1199.

103. Manfredi, *Judicial Power and the Charter,* 159–60.

104. More than 60 000 charges were dropped, although the actual number of cases was considerably smaller because many accused faced multiple charges. Most of the stayed charges were relatively minor. Some 90 percent of the criminal charges pending in Ontario when *Askov* was released were unaffected by the stays, and proceeded normally through the justice system. Kent Roach, *Due Process and Victims' Rights,* 92.

105. Hiebert, "Debating Policy," 55.

106. *RJR-MacDonald Inc. v. Canada (Attorney General)* [1995] 3 S.C.R. 199, paragraph 68.

107. In a 2003 case involving minority-language education rights, the court narrowly upheld a Nova Scotia ruling in which the trial judge ordered provincial officials to report back to him about the progress of implementing his remedial orders. This might indicate a more aggressive attitude on the part of judges toward the enforcement of *Charter* rulings. See *Doucet-Boudreau v. Nova Scotia (Minister of Education)* [2003] 3 S.C.R. 3.

108. See Bradley C. Canon and Charles A. Johnson, *Judicial Policies: Implementation and Impact,* 2nd edition (Washington: CQ Press, 1999); Gerald N. Rosenberg, *The Hollow Hope: Can Courts Bring About Social Change?* (Chicago: University of Chicago Press, 1991); and W.A. Bogart, *Courts and Country: The Limits of Litigation and the Social and Political Life of Canada* (Toronto: Oxford University Press, 1994).

109. *R. v. Stinchcombe* [1991] 3 S.C.R. 326.

110. In *R. v. O'Connor* [1995] 4 S.C.R. 411, the Supreme Court stayed sexual abuse charges against a former Catholic bishop because the Crown had refused to disclose evidence in a timely manner. See also Gerald Owen, "Disclosure after *Stinchcombe,*" in Anthony A. Peacock, ed., *Rethinking the Constitution: Perspectives on Canadian Constitutional Reform, Interpretation, and Theory* (Toronto: Oxford University Press, 1996).

111. Hiebert, *Limiting Rights,* 122–23.

112. For an excellent description of "Charter-proofing" by the Human Rights Law Section in the federal Department of Justice, see James B. Kelly, "Bureaucratic Activism and the Charter of Rights and Freedoms: The Department of Justice and its entry into the centre of government," *Canadian Public Administration,* 42:4 (Winter 1999). See also Hiebert, *Charter Conflicts,* 7–13.

113. See Christopher P. Manfredi, "Constitutional Rights and Interest Advocacy: Litigating Educational Reform in Canada and the United States"; Leslie A. Pal, "Advocacy Organizations and Legislative Politics: The Effect of the Charter of Rights and Freedoms on Interest Lobbying of Federal Legislation, 1989–91"; and Kent Roach, "The Role of Litigation and the Charter in Interest Advocacy," all in Seidle, ed., *Equity and Community.*

114. *Reference re Workers' Compensation Act, 1983 (Nfld.)* (Application to intervene), [1989] 2 S.C.R. 335.

115. *Operation Dismantle v. The Queen* [1985] 1 S.C.R. 441, paragraph 64.

116. *RWDSU v. Dolphin Delivery Ltd.* [1986] 2 S.C.R. 573, paragraph 34.

117. Ibid., paragraph 39.

118. Ibid., paragraph 36.

119. Manfredi, *Judicial Power and the Charter,* 46.

120. *McKinney v. University of Guelph* [1990] 3 S.C.R. 229.

121. *Vriend v. Alberta* [1998] 1 S.C.R. 493, paragraph 66.

122. *Eldridge v. British Columbia (Attorney General)* [1997] 3 S.C.R. 624.

123. *Singh v. Minister of Employment and Immigration* [1985] 1 S.C.R. 177, paragraph 35.

124. *Kindler v. Canada (Minister of Justice)* [1991] 2 S.C.R. 779; *United States v. Burns* [2001] 1 S.C.R. 283.

125. *Hunter v. Southam Inc.* [1984] 2 S.C.R.

126. *R. v. Big M Drug Mart Ltd.,* paragraph 117.

127. *Edmonton Journal v. Alberta (Attorney General)* [1989] 2 S.C.R. 1326, paragraph 52.

128. *Reference re Prov. Electoral Boundaries (Sask.)* [1991] 2 S.C.R. 158, paragraph 49.

129. *Haig v. Canada; Haig v. Canada (Chief Electoral Officer)* [1993] 2 S.C.R. 995, paragraph 61.

130. *Reference Re Public Service Employee Relations Act (Alta.)* [1987] 1 S.C.R. 313; *Dunmore v. Ontario* [2001] 3 S.C.R. 1016.

131. Hiebert, *Limiting Rights,* 6.

132. *Law Society of Upper Canada v. Skapinker* [1984] 1 S.C.R.; *Hunter v. Southam Inc.* [1984] 2 S.C.R.

133. *R. v. Oakes,* paragraph 64.

134. Leon Trakman, William Cole-Hamilton, and Sean Gatien, "*R. v. Oakes* 1986–1997: Back To the Drawing Board," *Osgoode Hall Law Journal,* volume 36 (Spring 1998), 83.

135. David Beatty, *Constitutional Law in Theory and Practice* (Toronto: University of Toronto Press, 1995), 82–83.

136. *Irwin Toy Ltd. v. Quebec (Attorney General)* [1989] 1 S.C.R. 927.

137. Morton and Knopff, 14.

138. Roach, "The Role of Litigation and the Charter in Interest Advocacy," 179.

139. Beatty, 82.

140. Ibid., 75.

141. Andrew Heard, "The Charter in the Supreme Court of Canada: The Importance of Which Judges Hear an Appeal," *Canadian Journal of Political Science,* XXIV:2 (June 1991), 289–307.

142. *R. v. Butler* [1992] 1 S.C.R. 452.

143. Ibid.

144. Morton and Knopff, 20.

145. Beatty, 11–12.

146. Kelly, "Bureaucratic Activism and the Charter of Rights and Freedoms."

147. *Law Society of Upper Canada v. Skapinker* [1984] 1 S.C.R. 358. See also *Hunter v. Southam Inc.*

148. *Re B.C. Motor Vehicle Act,* paragraph 53.

149. Morton and Knopff, 46.

150. Manfredi, *Judicial Power and the Charter,* 27.

151. Morton and Knopff, 49.

152. Former Justice Claire L'Heureux-Dubé, nicknamed "The Great Dissenter" for her frequent disagreements with her colleagues, managed over several years to shift the focus of

equality-rights jurisprudence from tangible harms to human dignity. The late Chief Justice Brian Dickson dissented from the majority judgment in the 1987 *Alberta Labour Reference,* arguing that section 2(d) of the *Charter* protected the collective activities of labour unions; his dissenting judgment was later adopted by a majority of the court in the 2002 *Dunmore* ruling.

153. As mentioned earlier, the Supreme Court ruled in the 1994 *Daviault* case that extreme intoxication could be used as a legal defence to a charge of sexual assault. After a public outcry from women's groups and the media, the federal government quickly amended the *Criminal Code* to rule out such a defence. See Heather MacIvor, *Canadian Politics and Government in the Charter Era* (Toronto: Nelson, 2005), Chapter 4; see also Roach, *Due Process and Victims' Rights,* Chapter 5.

154. *R. v. Mills* [1999] 3 S.C.R. 668, paragraph 58.

155. *Anti-Terrorism Act,* S.C. 2001, c. 41, sections 83.18, 83.3, 83.28, and 83.01(b)(i)(A).

156. See Ronald J. Daniels, Patrick Macklem, and Kent Roach, eds., *The Security of Freedom: Essays on Canada's Anti-Terrorism Bill* (Toronto: University of Toronto Press, 2002), and Kent Roach, *September 11: Consequences for Canada* (Montreal and Kingston: McGill–Queen's University Press, 2003), Chapters 2–4.

157. *Application under s. 83.28 of the Criminal Code (Re)* [2004] S.C.C. 42; *Vancouver Sun (Re)* [2004] S.C.C. 43.

158. *Suresh v. Canada (Minister of Citizenship and Immigration)* [2002] 1 S.C.R. 3.

159. See David Dyzenhaus, "The Permanence of the Temporary: Can Emergency Powers be Normalized?"; Oren Gross, "Cutting Down Trees: Law-Making Under the Shadow of Great Calamities"; and David Schneiderman, "Terrorism and the Risk Society," all in Daniels, Macklem, and Roach, eds.

160. *Secretary of State for the Home Department v. Rehman* [2001] 3 W.L.R. 877, paragraph 62. This passage was cited with approval in the *Suresh* ruling from the Supreme Court of Canada, at paragraph 33.

161. In Montreal in October 1970, a small group of radical separatists, the Front de Libération du Québec (FLQ), first kidnapped British Trade Commissioner James Cross and, five days later, provincial Labour Minister Pierre Laporte. The Quebec government asked Prime Minister Trudeau to invoke the *War Measures Act,* which gave police and soldiers the power to arrest and detain potential suspects without charge. The Act remained in force for several weeks, during which time hundreds of innocent people were rounded up and thrown into jail. Only five were ever convicted of a criminal offence relating to the crisis. Most of the FLQ members involved were given safe passage to Cuba in return for releasing the trade commissioner, although a few served relatively short jail sentences after returning to Canada. Shortly after the Act was imposed, Laporte was murdered by his kidnappers. See Denis Smith, *Bleeding Hearts . . . Bleeding Country* (Edmonton: Hurtig, 1971), and Walter Surma Tarnopolsky, *The Canadian Bill of Rights,* 2nd rev. edition (Toronto: McClelland and Stewart, 1975).

162. *Emergencies Act,* 1988, c. 29.

163. Richard Mosley, assistant deputy minister of Justice, remarks to the Security of Freedom Conference, University of Toronto, November 10, 2001; printed in Daniels, Macklem, and Roach, eds., 436–37.

164. Stephen Clarkson, "The View From the Attic: Toward a Gated Continental Community?," in Peter Andreas and Thomas J. Biersteker, eds., *The Rebordering of North America: Integration and Exclusion in a New Security Context* (New York: Routledge, 2003), 80.

165. Clarkson, 82. The case is *Ahani v. Canada (M.C.I.)* [2002] 1 S.C.R. 72.

166. In *Singh v. Minister of Employment and Immigration* [1985] 1 S.C.R. 177, the majority ruled that section 7 of the *Charter* required the federal government to follow accepted norms of due process in assessing refugee claims. Those norms do not appear to have been followed in either the *Ahani* case or the *Suresh* case, both of which dealt with suspected terrorists. The latter was awarded a new hearing, because he made a convincing case that he would be tortured if he was deported to his native Sri Lanka; Ahani failed to make such a case, and lost his appeal against deportation. It appears that alleged terrorists are not entitled to the procedural rights mandated in the *Singh* ruling, unless they can prove a genuine risk of torture.

167. *Suresh,* paragraph 4.

ASSEMBLING THE PUZZLE PIECES

████████ LEARNING OBJECTIVES

- *review* how Canada's political institutions operate;
- *analyze* possible future political trends;
- *determine* how *you* can play a role in Canada's political future.

INTRODUCTION

In the preceding chapters, we have examined each of Canada's major political institutions, discussing their formal and informal rules, the incentives that they set for ambitious politicians, and some possible reforms. This final chapter assembles the pieces of the puzzle, explaining briefly how these institutions work together, and demonstrating that a change in one can affect some or all of the others.

In the first chapter, we defined a political institution as an organization that makes and enforces rules and decisions for a given population. In Chapter 8, we noted that the *Constitution* assigns different tasks to each of our major institutions. At the national level, the permanent executive proposes amendments to the rules; these must be approved by the political executive (Cabinet) before being submitted to the House of Commons and Senate for enactment into law. When Parliament passes a Bill, it authorizes the executive branch to make detailed decisions about its implementation. These decisions are embodied in delegated legislation (regulations). Laws and regulations are enforced by certain elements of the permanent executive (e.g., the police). Where necessary, they are interpreted and applied by courts. If the content of a law, or the manner of its enforcement, violates the *Constitution*—the division of powers in sections 91–95, or the rights and freedoms guaranteed in the *Charter*—the courts can impose a remedy. In the process, judges create or amend common-law rules that will guide decision-makers and legislators in the future.

Parliament and the executive branch are not the only institutions involved in rule-making. Pressure groups seek to influence the substance of laws, both directly (through lobbying and litigation) and indirectly through the news media. Within Parliament and the political executive, decisions are affected by partisan and electoral considerations.

The leaders of the governing party impose strict discipline on their MPs to ensure that they vote for the laws sponsored by the Cabinet, and to secure the government as a whole against the threat of a defeat in the Commons.

On the Opposition side, party leaders and their caucuses try to embarrass the government by revealing flaws in its legislative program and its management of the nation's business. They hope to take advantage of these flaws (real or alleged) when the next election comes around. In the process, they create exciting political drama for the news media to cover; they can also damage the relationship between the political and permanent executives, which makes it more difficult for the federal government to work effectively. Over time, they may contribute to public disenchantment with the institutions of representative government and fuel demands for reform.

The rule-makers in Ottawa are constrained by the *Constitution*. They must either respect the division of powers between the federal and provincial governments or negotiate intergovernmental agreements to achieve their goals. Canada's federal system, like most of the other institutions discussed in this book, has experienced few formal changes since 1867. In practical terms, however, it operates very differently from the way it was originally designed. The "watertight compartments" and fiscal arrangements that seemed appropriate at Confederation have long since been overtaken by economic and political forces.

The partisan and electoral considerations that operate at the national level are equally significant in provincial capitals. While premiers and prime ministers compete against their immediate rivals, they are sometimes pitted against each other in the contest for political advantage. That contest complicates the day-to-day management of the federation, and sometimes provokes heated clashes over constitutional issues. However, all of the First Ministers reap at least one benefit from their participation in the peak institutions of federalism: the creation and implementation of intergovernmental agreements strengthens the power of the political executive in relation to the legislature. Consequently, executive federalism makes the executive branch as a whole less accountable to the electorate.

From the preceding discussion, we may conclude that the process by which rules are made, enforced, and interpreted is not entirely consistent with the political attitudes of many Canadians. The executive branch generally operates behind closed doors, even in the relatively high-profile arena of intergovernmental relations. This privacy ensures the confidentiality and mutual trust that executive decision-making demands; but it leaves Cabinet ministers and their officials vulnerable to accusations of excessive secrecy and a lack of accountability. The House of Commons and Senate are more open to the public, although this is not always a good thing: the more Canadians see of their elected and appointed legislators at work, the less impressed they seem to be. A degree of party discipline, adversarialism, and executive dominance are built into our parliamentary institutions, but their excesses in the federal Parliament have reduced Canadians' trust in the legislative branch. For their part, courts conduct much of their business in the open. Unfortunately, the norms and the language of the legal process are far removed from the everyday experience of most people. Even the *Charter*, which enjoys the support of a majority of Canadians, is applied and interpreted in ways that provoke bafflement and occasional outrage.

All three branches of government are subject to criticism from pressure groups, Opposition parties, and journalists, who play to their various constituencies (members, voters, readers, media owners) by attacking the institutions that govern us. The fact that most of the people who work in our political system do their jobs well is drowned out in the clamour of complaint. Small wonder that fewer and fewer Canadians choose to engage in the political process by joining political parties, or even casting ballots.

CALLS FOR REFORM

As we have seen throughout these pages, the ills afflicting our political system—both real and imagined—have prompted calls for reform. Some of the proposed changes would require constitutional amendment, which seems unlikely given the difficulty of megaconstitutional politics in Canada. Others can be, and have been, achieved via nonconstitutional renewal. Some of these informal changes to the process of government evolved unintentionally, as short-term solutions that persisted long after an immediate problem was resolved. Examples include fiscal federalism and the Cabinet committee system. Others, like party discipline, flowed from the incentives created by particular institutional arrangements (in this case, the exercise of executive power by the party with the most seats in the Commons). A few of these ad hoc practices have acquired the status of constitutional conventions (e.g., the requirement of substantial provincial consent to formal amendments); others have been enshrined in law (transfer payments to the provinces).

In the future, we will likely see further reforms to our political institutions. Some will be deliberate and carefully engineered; others will arise in response to short-term political conditions. As these words were written, a minority government in Ottawa was considering the issue of electoral reform. This was a concession to the Opposition parties, who understand the unfairness of the single-member plurality system all too well. The Opposition members on parliamentary committees were flexing their political muscles, seeking to influence the substance of policy and secure permanent changes to the process of governing. They demanded that treaties between the federal government and other nation–states be subjected to ratification by the Commons. This proposal might help to address the "democratic deficit" created by internationalization, but it flies in the face of the separation of powers, under which the executive has the sole responsibility for relations with foreign governments.

If we are to fashion deliberate reforms to our political institutions, we should be guided by three principles. First, reformers must agree on exactly what they are trying to accomplish. In other words, they must decide what they want the reformed institutions to do. Do we want a Triple-E Senate to give the smaller provinces a bigger voice in the national legislative process, or to put a brake on the power of the Cabinet? In either case, we should reconsider the proposal to elect senators. Elections inevitably involve political parties. Party discipline interferes with regional representation. If the same party controlled both houses of Parliament, the political executive would be just as dominant in the Senate as the Commons; if an Opposition party held a majority in the upper house, the legislative process could be stalemated by unproductive clashes between the two chambers.

Second, any change to a particular institution will have repercussions for other institutions. Therefore, would-be reformers should consider the impact of their proposals on the entire political system. Would the introduction of a more proportional electoral system increase the number of parties in Parliament? If so, what are the implications for the legislative process? If the abolition of the single-member plurality system meant the end of single-party majority governments, how would this affect the political executive?

Third, reformers cannot design an institution in the abstract; they must take into account the incentives that it would impose on the human beings whose professional roles are scripted by that institution. As we saw in Dossier 1.4, a well-crafted institution channels individual ambition into constructive activities. When Canada's political parties abandoned leadership conventions in favour of "one member, one vote" methods for choosing their leaders, they may inadvertently have encouraged aspirants to weaken party organizations. We might well wish to reform our current institutions in order to weaken or eliminate harmful incentives that presently exist; the behavioural norms of party discipline and adversarialism in the House of Commons are good examples.

But whatever we decide to do, we must be careful to avoid changes that could tempt the ambitious to engage in self-seeking behaviour contrary to the public good. As we saw in Dossier 2.4, some items on the populist agenda (especially initiatives and recall) have had unintended negative consequences in the United States. At present, the populist wave seems to be ebbing in Canada, but it is likely to rise again in the future. If it does, we should take a cautious approach to any democratic reform that could undermine the integrity of our rule-making processes.

INFLUENCING CANADA'S FUTURE

Whether or not Canadians can agree on specific institutional reforms, our politics and government will continue to function reasonably well. The flexibility provided by our constitutional conventions, and the deep reservoir of general support for the political system (Chapter 2), will allow our institutions to continue to adapt—however slowly and perhaps reluctantly—to the challenges of the twenty-first century. The form that our institutions take, and how well they serve the citizens of Canada, depends on us as much as it does on our political leaders. As John Stuart Mill argued more than a century ago, the surest safeguard of good government is a well-informed population prepared to preserve its political institutions, even while it demands improvements to keep pace with its own "moral and intellectual" evolution.

Instead of turning away from politics, Canadians should consider getting involved. They should learn as much as they can about our political institutions, rather than accepting the biased critiques of journalists, political parties, and pressure groups at face value. Canada's political institutions are not perfect, and they cannot be made perfect. But whatever their failings, they are far superior to their equivalents in much of the world. They must not be taken for granted or unfairly abused. Democracy imposes duties on citizens as well as on those who govern them. If we do not take our duties seriously, we cannot complain if we perceive our politicians as unaccountable and out of touch. The bottom line is this: countries get the political system that they deserve. If you think that Canadians deserve better, it's up to you to provide it.

APPENDIX

The Constitution Acts
1867 to 1982

THE CONSTITUTION ACT, 1867

30 & 31 Victoria, c. 3. (U.K.)
(Consolidated with amendments)

An Act for the Union of Canada, Nova Scotia, and New Brunswick, and the Government thereof; and for Purposes connected therewith

(29th March 1867.)

WHEREAS the Provinces of Canada, Nova Scotia, and New Brunswick have expressed their Desire to be federally united into One Dominion under the Crown of the United Kingdom of Great Britain and Ireland, with a Constitution similar in Principle to that of the United Kingdom:

And whereas such a Union would conduce to the Welfare of the Provinces and promote the Interests of the British Empire:

And whereas on the Establishment of the Union by Authority of Parliament it is expedient, not only that the Constitution of the Legislative Authority in the Dominion be provided for, but also that the Nature of the Executive Government therein be declared:

And whereas it is expedient that Provision be made for the eventual Admission into the Union of other Parts of British North America:[1]

---

(1) The enacting clause was repealed by the *Statute Law Revision Act, 1893*, 56-57 Vict., c. 14 (U.K.). It read as follows:

Be it therefore enacted and declared by the Queen's most Excellent Majesty, by and with the Advice and Consent of the Lords Spiritual and Temporal, and Commons, in this present Parliament assembled, and by the Authority of the same, as follows:

I. PRELIMINARY

Short title

1. This Act may be cited as the *Constitution Act, 1867.*[2]

2. Repealed[3]

II. UNION

Declaration of Union

3. It shall be lawful for the Queen, by and with the Advice of Her Majesty's Most Honourable Privy Council, to declare by Proclamation that, on and after a Day therein appointed, not being more than Six Months after the passing of this Act, the Provinces of Canada, Nova Scotia, and New Brunswick shall form and be One Dominion under the Name of Canada; and on and after that Day those Three Provinces shall form and be One Dominion under that Name accordingly.[4]

Construction of subsequent Provisions of Act

4. Unless it is otherwise expressed or implied, the Name Canada shall be taken to mean Canada as constituted under this Act.[5]

Four Provinces

5. Canada shall be divided into Four Provinces, named Ontario, Quebec, Nova Scotia, and New Brunswick.[6]

---

(2) As enacted by the *Constitution Act, 1982,* which came into force on April 17, 1982. The section, as originally enacted, read as follows:

> **1.** This Act may be cited as The British North America Act, 1867.

(3) Section 2, repealed by the *Statute Law Revision Act, 1893,* 56-57 Vict., c. 14 (U.K.), read as follows:

> **2.** The Provisions of this Act referring to Her Majesty the Queen extend also to the Heirs and Successors of Her Majesty, Kings and Queens of the United Kingdom of Great Britain and Ireland.

(4) The first day of July, 1867, was fixed by proclamation dated May 22, 1867.

(5) Partially repealed by the *Statute Law Revision Act, 1893,* 56-57 Vict., c. 14 (U.K.). As originally enacted the section read as follows:

> **4.** The subsequent Provisions of this Act shall, unless it is otherwise expressed or implied, commence and have effect on and after the Union, that is to say, on and after the Day appointed for the Union taking effect in the Queen's Proclamation; and in the same Provisions, unless it is otherwise expressed or implied, the Name Canada shall be taken to mean Canada as constituted under this Act.

(6) Canada now consists of ten provinces (Ontario, Quebec, Nova Scotia, New Brunswick, Manitoba, British Columbia, Prince Edward Island, Alberta, Saskatchewan and Newfoundland) and two territories (the Yukon Territory and the Northwest Territories).

The first territories added to the Union were Rupert's Land and the North-Western Territory, (subsequently designated the Northwest Territories), which were admitted pursuant to section 146 of the *Constitution Act, 1867* and the *Rupert's Land Act, 1868,* 31-32 Vict., c. 105 (U.K.), by the *Rupert's Land and North-Western Territory Order* of June 23, 1870, effective July 15, 1870. Prior to the admission of those territories the Parliament of Canada enacted *An Act for the temporary Government of Rupert's Land and the North-Western Territory when united with Canada* (32-33 Vict., c. 3), and the *Manitoba Act, 1870,* (33 Vict., c.3), which provided for the formation of the Province of Manitoba.

British Columbia was admitted into the Union pursuant to section 146 of the *Constitution Act, 1867,* by the *British Columbia Terms of Union,* being Order in Council of May 16, 1871, effective July 20, 1871.

Prince Edward Island was admitted pursuant to section 146 of the *Constitution Act, 1867,* by the *Prince Edward Island Terms of Union,* being Order in Council of June 26, 1873, effective July 1, 1873.

On June 29, 1871, the United Kingdom Parliament enacted the *Constitution Act, 1871* (34-35 Vict., c. 28) authorizing the creation of additional provinces out of territories not included in any province. Pursuant to this statute, the Parliament of Canada enacted the *Alberta Act,* (July 20, 1905, 4-5 Edw. VII c. 3) and the *Saskatchewan Act,* (July 20, 1905, 4-5 Edw. VII, c. 42), providing for the creation of the provinces of Alberta and Saskatchewan, respectively. Both these Acts came into force on Sept. 1, 1905.

6. The Parts of the Province of Canada (as it exists at the passing of this Act) which formerly constituted respectively the Provinces of Upper Canada and Lower Canada shall be deemed to be severed, and shall form Two separate Provinces. The Part which formerly constituted the Province of Upper Canada shall constitute the Province of Ontario; and the Part which formerly constituted the Province of Lower Canada shall constitute the Province of Quebec.

Provinces of Ontario and Quebec

7. The Provinces of Nova Scotia and New Brunswick shall have the same Limits as at the passing of this Act.

Provinces of Nova Scotia and New Brunswick

8. In the general Census of the Population of Canada which is hereby required to be taken in the Year One thousand eight hundred and seventy-one, and in every Tenth Year thereafter, the respective Populations of the Four Provinces shall be distinguished.

Decennial Census

III. EXECUTIVE POWER

9. The Executive Government and Authority of and over Canada is hereby declared to continue and be vested in the Queen.

Declaration of Executive Power in the Queen

10. The Provisions of this Act referring to the Governor General extend and apply to the Governor General for the Time being of Canada, or other the Chief Executive Officer or Administrator for the Time being carrying on the Government of Canada on behalf and in the Name of the Queen, by whatever Title he is designated.

Application of Provisions referring to Governor General

11. There shall be a Council to aid and advise in the Government of Canada, to be styled the Queen's Privy Council for Canada; and the Persons who are to be Members of that Council shall be from Time to Time chosen and summoned by the Governor General and sworn in as Privy Councillors, and Members thereof may be from Time to Time removed by the Governor General.

Constitution of Privy Council for Canada

Meanwhile, all remaining British possessions and territories in North America and the islands adjacent thereto, except the colony of Newfoundland and its dependencies, were admitted into the Canadian Confederation by the *Adjacent Territories Order*, dated July 31, 1880.

The Parliament of Canada added portions of the Northwest Territories to the adjoining provinces in 1912 by *The Ontario Boundaries Extension Act*, S.C. 1912, 2 Geo. V, c. 40, *The Quebec Boundaries Extension Act*, 1912, 2 Geo V, c. 45 and *The Manitoba Boundaries Extension Act, 1912*, 2 Geo. V, c. 32, and further additions were made to Manitoba by *The Manitoba Boundaries Extension Act, 1930*, 20-21 Geo. V, c. 28.

The Yukon Territory was created out of the Northwest Territories in 1898 by *The Yukon Territory Act*, 61 Vict., c. 6, (Canada).

Newfoundland was added on March 31, 1949, by the *Newfoundland Act*, (U.K.), 12-13 Geo. VI, c. 22, which ratified the Terms of Union of Newfoundland with Canada.

All Powers under Acts to be exercised by Governor General with Advice of Privy Council, or alone

12. All Powers, Authorities, and Functions which under any Act of the Parliament of Great Britain, or of the Parliament of the United Kingdom of Great Britain and Ireland, or of the Legislature of Upper Canada, Lower Canada, Canada, Nova Scotia, or New Brunswick, are at the Union vested in or exerciseable by the respective Governors or Lieutenant Governors of those Provinces, with the Advice, or with the Advice and Consent, of the respective Executive Councils thereof, or in conjunction with those Councils, or with any Number of Members thereof, or by those Governors or Lieutenant Governors individually, shall, as far as the same continue in existence and capable of being exercised after the Union in relation to the Government of Canada, be vested in and exerciseable by the Governor General, with the Advice or the Advice and Consent of or in conjunction with the Queen's Privy Council for Canada, or any Members thereof, or by the Governor General individually, as the Case requires, subject nevertheless (except with respect to such as exist under Acts of the Parliament of Great Britain or the Parliament of the United Kingdom of Great Britain and Ireland) to be abolished or altered by the Parliament of Canada.[7]

Application of Provisions referring to Governor General in Council

13. The Provisions of this Act referring to the Governor General in Council shall be construed as referring to the Governor General acting by and with the Advice of the Queen's Privy Council for Canada.

Power to Her Majesty to authorize Governor General to appoint Deputies

14. It shall be lawful for the Queen, if Her Majesty thinks fit, to authorize the Governor General from Time to Time to appoint any Person or any Persons jointly or severally to be his Deputy or Deputies within any Part or Parts of Canada, and in that Capacity to exercise during the Pleasure of the Governor General such of the Powers, Authorities, and Functions of the Governor General as the Governor General deems it necessary or expedient to assign to him or them, subject to any Limitations or Directions expressed or given by the Queen; but the Appointment of such a Deputy or Deputies shall not affect the Exercise by the Governor General himself of any Power, Authority, or Function.

Command of Armed Forces to continue to be vested in the Queen

15. The Command-in-Chief of the Land and Naval Militia, and of all Naval and Military Forces, of and in Canada, is hereby declared to continue and be vested in the Queen.

Seat of Government of Canada

16. Until the Queen otherwise directs, the Seat of Government of Canada shall be Ottawa.

---

(7) See the note to section 129, *infra*.

IV. LEGISLATIVE POWER

17. There shall be One Parliament for Canada, consisting of the Queen, an Upper House styled the Senate, and the House of Commons.

Constitution of Parliament of Canada

18. The privileges, immunities, and powers to be held, enjoyed, and exercised by the Senate and by the House of Commons, and by the members thereof respectively, shall be such as are from time to time defined by Act of the Parliament of Canada, but so that any Act of the Parliament of Canada defining such privileges, immunities, and powers shall not confer any privileges, immunities, or powers exceeding those at the passing of such Act held, enjoyed, and exercised by the Commons House of Parliament of the United Kingdom of Great Britain and Ireland, and by the members thereof.[8]

Privileges, etc., of Houses

19. The Parliament of Canada shall be called together not later than Six Months after the Union.[9]

First Session of the Parliament of Canada

20. Repealed.[10]

The Senate

21. The Senate shall, subject to the Provisions of this Act, consist of One Hundred and five Members, who shall be styled Senators.[11]

Number of Senators

22. In relation to the Constitution of the Senate Canada shall be deemed to consist of *Four* Divisions: ——

Representation of Provinces in Senate

---

(8) Repealed and re-enacted by the *Parliament of Canada Act*, 1875, 38-39 Vict., c. 38 (U.K.). The original section read as follows:

> **18.** The Privileges, Immunities, and Powers to be held, enjoyed, and exercised by the Senate and by the House of Commons and by the Members thereof respectively shall be such as are from Time to Time defined by Act of the Parliament of Canada, but so that the same shall never exceed those at the passing of this Act held, enjoyed, and exercised by the Commons House of Parliament of the United Kingdom of Great Britain and Ireland and by the Members thereof.

(9) Spent. The first session of the first Parliament began on November 6, 1867.

(10) Section 20, repealed by the *Constitution Act, 1982*, read as follows:

> **20.** There shall be a Session of the Parliament of Canada once at least in every Year, so that Twelve Months shall not intervene between the last Sitting of the Parliament in one Session and its first sitting in the next Session.

Section 20 has been replaced by section 5 of the *Constitution Act, 1982*, which provides that there shall be a sitting of Parliament at least once every twelve months.

(11) As amended by the *Constitution Act, 1915*, 5-6 Geo. V, c. 45 (U.K.) and modified by the *Newfoundland Act*, 12-13 Geo. VI, c. 22 (U.K.), and the *Constitution Act (No. 2), 1975*, S.C. 1974-75-76, c. 53, and the *Constitution Act, 1999 (Nunavut)*, S.C. 1998, c. 15, Part 2.

1. Ontario;

2. Quebec;

3. The Maritime Provinces, Nova Scotia and New Brunswick, and Prince Edward Island;

4. The Western Provinces of Manitoba, British Columbia, Saskatchewan, and Alberta;

which Four Divisions shall (subject to the Provisions of this Act) be equally represented in the Senate as follows: Ontario by twenty-four senators; Quebec by twenty-four senators; the Maritime Provinces and Prince Edward Island by twenty-four senators, ten thereof representing Nova Scotia, ten thereof representing New Brunswick, and four thereof representing Prince Edward Island; the Western Provinces by twenty four senators, six thereof representing Manitoba, six thereof representing British Columbia, six thereof representing Saskatchewan, and six thereof representing Alberta; Newfoundland shall be entitled to be represented in the Senate by six members; the Yukon Territory and the Northwest Territories shall be entitled to be represented in the Senate by one member each.

In the Case of Quebec each of the Twenty-four Senators representing that Province shall be appointed for One of the Twenty-four Electoral Divisions of Lower Canada specified in Schedule A. to Chapter One of the Consolidated Statutes of Canada.[12]

The original section read as follows:

> **21.** The Senate shall, subject to the Provisions of this Act, consist of Seventy-two Members, who shall be styled Senators.

The *Manitoba Act, 1870,* added two for Manitoba; the *British Columbia Terms of Union* added three; upon admission of Prince Edward Island four more were provided by section 147 of the *Constitution Act, 1867;* the *Alberta Act* and the *Saskatchewan Act* each added four. The Senate was reconstituted at 96 by the *Constitution Act, 1915.* Six more Senators were added upon union with Newfoundland, and one Senator each was added for the Yukon Territory and the Northwest Territories by the *Constitution Act (No. 2), 1975.* One Senator was added for Nunavut by the *Constitution Act 1999 (Nunavut).*

(12) As Amended by the *Constitution Act, 1915,* 5-6 Geo. V, c. 45 (U.K.), the *Newfoundland Act,* 12-13 Geo. VI, c. 22 (U.K.), and the *Constitution Act (No. 2), 1975,* S.C. 1974-75-76, c. 53. The original section read as follows:

> **22.** In relation to the Constitution of the Senate, Canada shall be deemed to consist of Three Divisions:
>
> 1. Ontario;
>
> 2. Quebec;
>
> 3. The Maritime Provinces, Nova Soctia and New Brunswick;

23. The Qualifications of a Senator shall be as follows:

(1) He shall be of the full age of Thirty Years:

(2) He shall be either a natural-born Subject of the Queen, or a Subject of the Queen naturalized by an Act of the Parliament of Great Britain, or of the Parliament of the United Kingdom of Great Britain and Ireland, or of the Legislature of One of the Provinces of Upper Canada, Lower Canada, Canada, Nova Scotia, or New Brunswick, before the Union, or of the Parliament of Canada after the Union:

(3) He shall be legally or equitably seised as of Freehold for his own Use and Benefit of Lands or Tenements held in Free and Common Socage, or seised or possessed for his own Use and Benefit of Lands or Tenements held in Franc-alleu or in Roture, within the Province for which he is appointed, of the Value of Four thousand Dollars, over and above all Rents, Dues, Debts, Charges, Mortgages, and Incumbrances due or payable out of or charged on or affecting the same:

(4) His Real and Personal Property shall be together worth Four thousand Dollars over and above his Debts and Liabilities:

(5) He shall be resident in the Province for which he is appointed:

(6) In the case of Quebec he shall have his Real Property Qualification in the Electoral Division for which he is appointed, or shall be resident in that Division.[13]

24. The Governor General shall from Time to Time, in the Queen's Name, by Instrument under the Great Seal of Canada, summon qualified Persons to the Senate; and, subject to the Provisions of this Act, every person so summoned shall become and be a Member of the Senate and a Senator.

Qualifications of Senator

Summons of Senator

---

which Three Divisions shall (subject to the Provisions of this Act) be equally represented in the Senate as follows: Ontario by Twenty-four Senators; Quebec by Twenty-four Senators; and the Maritime Provinces by Twenty-four Senators, Twelve thereof representing Nova Scotia, and Twelve thereof representing New Brunswick.

In the case of Quebec each of the Twenty-four Senators representing that Province shall be appointed for One of the Twenty-four Electoral Divisions of Lower Canada specified in Schedule A. to Chapter One of the Consolidated Statutes of Canada.

(13) Section 44 of the *Constitution Act, 1999 (Nunavut)*, S.C. 1998, c. 15, Part 2, provided that, for the purposes of that Part (which added one Senator for Nunavut), the word "Province" in section 23 of the *Constitution Act, 1867*, has the same meaning as is assigned to the word "province" by section 35 of the *Interpretation Act*, R.S.C. 1985, c. I-21, which provides that the term "province" means "a province of Canada, and includes the Yukon Territory, the Northwest Territories and Nunavut."

Section 2 of the *Constitution Act (No. 2), 1975*, S.C. 1974-75-76, c. 53 provided that for the purposes of that Act (which added one Senator each for the Yukon Territory and the Northwest Territories) the term "Province" in section 23 of the *Constitution Act, 1867*, has the same meaning as is assigned to the term "province" by section 28 of the *Interpretation Act*, R.S.C. 1970, c. I-23, which provides that the term "province" means "a province of Canada, and includes the Yukon Territory and the Northwest Territories."

25. Repealed.[14]

Addition of Senators in certain cases

26. If at any Time on the Recommendation of the Governor General the Queen thinks fit to direct that Four or Eight Members be added to the Senate, the Governor General may by Summons to Four or Eight qualified Persons (as the Case may be), representing equally the Four Divisions of Canada, add to the Senate accordingly.[15]

Reduction of Senate to normal Number

27. In case of such Addition being at any Time made, the Governor General shall not summon any Person to the Senate, except on a further like Direction by the Queen on the like Recommendation, to represent one of the Four Divisions until such Division is represented by Twenty-Four Senators and no more.[16]

Maximum Number of Senators

28. The Number of Senators shall not at any Time exceed One Hundred and thirteen.[17]

Tenure of Place in Senate

29. (1) Subject to subsection (2), a Senator shall, subject to the provisions of this Act, hold his place in the Senate for life.

Retirement upon attaining age of seventy-five years

(2) A Senator who is summoned to the Senate after the coming into force of this subsection shall, subject to this Act, hold his place in the Senate until he attains the age of seventy-five years.[18]

---

(14) Repealed by the *Statute Law Revision Act, 1893,* 56-57 Vict., c. 14 (U.K.). The section read as follows:

> **25.** Such persons shall be first summoned to the Senate as the Queen by Warrant under Her Majesty's Royal Sign Manual thinks fits to approve, and their Names shall be inserted in the Queen's Proclamation of Union.

(15) As amended by the *Constitution Act, 1915,* 5-6 Geo. V, c. 45 (U.K.). The original section read as follows:

> **26.** If at any time on the Recommendation of the Governor General the Queen thinks fit to direct that Three or Six Members be added to the Senate, the Governor General may by Summons to Three or Six qualified Persons (as the Case may be), representing equally the Three Divisions of Canada, add to the Senate accordingly.

(16) As amended by the *Constitution Act, 1915,* 5-6 Geo. V, c. 45 (U.K.). The original section read as follows:

> **27.** In case of such Addition being at any Time made the Governor General shall not summon any Person to the Senate except on a further like Direction by the Queen on the like Recommendation, until each of the Three Divisions of Canada is represented by Twenty-four Senators and no more.

(17) As amended by the *Constitution Act, 1915,* 5-6 Geo. V, c. 45 (U.K.), and the *Constitution Act (No. 2), 1975,* S.C. 1974-75-76, c. 53, and the *Constitution Act 1999 (Nunavut),* S.C. 1998, c. 15, Part 2. The original section read as follows:

> **28.** The Number of Senators shall not at any Time exceed Seventy-eight.

(18) As enacted by the *Constitution Act, 1965,* S.C., 1965, c. 4, which came into force on June 1, 1965. The original section read as follows:

> **29.** A Senator shall , subject to the Provisions of this Act, hold his Place in the Senate for Life.

30. A Senator may by Writing under his Hand addressed to the Governor General resign his Place in the Senate, and thereupon the same shall be vacant.

31. The Place of a Senator shall become vacant in any of the following Cases:

(1) If for Two consecutive Sessions of the Parliament he fails to give his Attendance in the Senate:

(2) If he takes an Oath or makes a Declaration or Acknowledgment of Allegiance, Obedience, or Adherence to a Foreign Power, or does an Act whereby he becomes a Subject or Citizen, or entitled to the Rights or Privileges of a Subject or Citizen, of a Foreign Power:

(3) If he is adjudged Bankrupt or Insolvent, or applies for the Benefit of any Law relating to Insolvent Debtors, or becomes a public Defaulter:

(4) If he is attainted of Treason or convicted of Felony or of any infamous Crime:

(5) If he ceases to be qualified in respect of Property or of Residence; provided, that a Senator shall not be deemed to have ceased to be qualified in respect of Residence by reason only of his residing at the Seat of the Government of Canada while holding an Office under that Government requiring his Presence there.

32. When a Vacancy happens in the Senate by Resignation, Death, or otherwise, the Governor General shall by Summons to a fit and qualified Person fill the Vacancy.

33. If any Question arises respecting the Qualification of a Senator or a Vacancy in the Senate the same shall be heard and determined by the Senate.

34. The Governor General may from Time to Time, by Instrument under the Great Seal of Canada, appoint a Senator to be Speaker of the Senate, and may remove him and appoint another in his Stead.[19]

---

(19) Provision for exercising the functions of Speaker during his absence is made by Part II of the *Parliament of Canada Act*, R.S.C. 1985, c. P-1 (formerly the *Speaker of the Senate Act*, R.S.C. 1970, c. S-14). Doubts as to the power of Parliament to enact the *Speaker of the Senate Act* were removed by the *Canadian Speaker (Appointment of Deputy) Act, 1895*, 2nd Sess., 59 Vict., c. 3 (U.K.), which was repealed by the *Constitution Act, 1982*.

35. Until the Parliament of Canada otherwise provides, the Presence of at least Fifteen Senators, including the Speaker, shall be necessary to constitute a Meeting of the Senate for the Exercise of its Powers.

36. Questions arising in the Senate shall be decided by a Majority of Voices, and the Speaker shall in all Cases have a Vote, and when the Voices are equal the Decision shall be deemed to be in the Negative.

The House of Commons

37. The House of Commons shall, subject to the Provisions of this Act, consist of two hundred and ninety-five members of whom ninety-nine shall be elected for Ontario, seventy-five for Quebec, eleven for Nova Scotia, ten for New Brunswick, fourteen for Manitoba, thirty-two for British Columbia, four for Prince Edward Island, twenty-six for Alberta, fourteen for Saskatchewan, seven for Newfoundland, one for the Yukon Territory and two for the Northwest Territories.[20]

38. The Governor General shall from Time to Time, in the Queen's Name, by Instrument under the Great Seal of Canada, summon and call together the House of Commons.

39. A Senator shall not be capable of being elected or of sitting or voting as a Member of the House of Commons.

40. Until the Parliament of Canada otherwise provides, Ontario, Quebec, Nova Scotia, and New Brunswick shall, for the Purposes of the Election of Members to serve in the House of Commons, be divided into Electoral districts as follows:

1. — ONTARIO

Ontario shall be divided into the Counties, Ridings of Counties, Cities, Parts of Cities, and Towns enumerated in the First Schedule to this Act, each whereof shall be an Electoral District, each such District as numbered in that Schedule being entitled to return One Member.

---

(20) The figures given here result from the application of Section 51, as enacted by the *Constitution Act, 1985 (Representation)*, S.C., 1986, c. 8, Part 1, and readjusted pursuant to the *Electoral Boundaries Readjustment Act*, R.S.C., 1985, c. E-3. The original section (which was altered from time to time as the result of the addition of new provinces and changes in population) read as follows:

37. The House of Commons shall, subject to the Provisions of this Act, consist of one hundred and eighty-one members, of whom Eighty-two shall be elected for Ontario, Sixty-five for Quebec, Nineteen for Nova Scotia, and Fifteen for New Brunswick.

2. — QUEBEC

Quebec shall be divided into Sixty-five Electoral Districts, composed of the Sixty-five Electoral Divisions into which Lower Canada is at the passing of this Act divided under Chapter Two of the Consolidated Statutes of Canada, Chapter Seventy-five of the Consolidated Statutes for Lower Canada, and the Act of the Province of Canada of the Twenty-third Year of the Queen, Chapter One, or any other Act amending the same in force at the Union, so that each such Electoral Division shall be for the Purposes of this Act an Electoral District entitled to return One Member.

3. — NOVA SCOTIA

Each of the Eighteen Counties of Nova Scotia shall be an Electoral District. The County of Halifax shall be entitled to return Two Members, and each of the other Counties One Member.

4. — NEW BRUNSWICK

Each of the Fourteen Counties into which New Brunswick is divided, including the City and County of St. John, shall be an Electoral District. The City of St. John shall also be a separate Electoral District. Each of those Fifteen Electoral Districts shall be entitled to return One Member.[21]

41. Until the Parliament of Canada otherwise provides, all Laws in force in the several Provinces at the Union relative to the following Matters or any of them, namely, — the Qualifications and Disqualifications of Persons to be elected or to sit or vote as Members of the House of Assembly or Legislative Assembly in the several Provinces, the Voters at Elections of such Members, the Oaths to be taken by Voters, the Returning Officers, their Powers and Duties, the Proceedings at Elections, the Periods during which Elections may be continued, the Trial of controverted Elections, and Proceedings incident thereto, the vacating of Seats of Members, and the Execution of new Writs in case of Seats vacated otherwise than by Dissolution, — shall respectively apply to Elections of Members to serve in the House of Commons for the same several Provinces.

Continuance of existing Election Laws until Parliament of Canada otherwise provides

---

(21) Spent. The electoral districts are now established by Proclamations issued from time to time under the *Electoral Boundaries Readjustment Act*, R.S.C. 1985, c. E-3, as amended for particular districts by Acts of Parliament, for which see the most recent Table of Public Statutes and Responsible Ministers.

Provided that, until the Parliament of Canada otherwise provides, at any Election for a Member of the House of Commons for the District of Algoma, in addition to Persons qualified by the Law of the Province of Canada to vote, every Male British Subject, aged Twenty-one Years or upwards, being a Householder, shall have a Vote.[22]

42. Repealed.[23]

43. Repealed.[24]

As to Election of Speaker of House of Commons

44. The House of Commons on its first assembling after a General Election shall proceed with all practicable Speed to elect One of its Members to be Speaker.

As to filling up Vacancy in Office of Speaker

45. In case of a Vacancy happening in the Office of Speaker by Death, Resignation, or otherwise, the House of Commons shall with all practicable Speed proceed to elect another of its Members to be Speaker.

Speaker to preside

46. The Speaker shall preside at all Meetings of the House of Commons.

Provision in case of Absence of Speaker

47. Until the Parliament of Canada otherwise provides, in case of the Absence for any Reason of the Speaker from the Chair of the House of Commons for a Period of Forty-eight consecutive Hours, the House may elect another of its Members to act as Speaker, and the Member so elected shall during the Continuance of such Absence of the Speaker have and execute all the Powers, Privileges, and Duties of Speaker.[25]

---

(22) Spent. Elections are now provided for by the *Canada Elections Act*, R.S.C. 1985, c. E-2; controverted elections by the *Dominion Controverted Elections Act*, R.S.C. 1985, c. C-39; qualifications and disqualifications of members by the *Parliament of Canada Act*, R.S.C. 1985, c. P-1. The right of citizens to vote and hold office is provided for in section 3 of the *Constitution Act, 1982*.

(23) Repealed by the *Statute Law Revision Act, 1893*, 56-57 Vict., c. 14 (U.K.). The section read as follows:

> **42.** For the First Election of Members to serve in the House of Commons the Governor General shall cause Writs to be issued by such Person, in such Form, and addressed to such Returning Officers as he thinks fit.
>
> The Person issuing Writs under this Section shall have the like Powers as are possessed at the Union by the Officers charged with the issuing of Writs for the Election of Members to serve in the respective House of Assembly or Legislative Assembly of the Province of Canada, Nova Scotia, or New Brunswick; and the Returning Officers to whom Writs are directed under this Section shall have the like Powers as are possessed at the Union by the Officers charged with the returning of Writs for the Election of Members to serve in the same respective House of Assembly or Legislative Assembly.

(24) Repealed by the *Statute Law Revision Act, 1893*, 56-57 Vict. c. 14 (U.K.). The section read as follows:

> **43.** In case a Vacancy in the Representation in the House of Commons of any Electoral District happens before the Meeting of the Parliament, or after the Meeting of the Parliament before Provision is made by the Parliament in this Behalf, the Provisions of the last foregoing Section of this Act shall extend and apply to the issuing and returning of a Writ in respect of such Vacant District.

(25) Provision for exercising the functions of Speaker during his absence is now made by Part III of the *Parliament of Canada Act*, R.S.C. 1985, c. P-1.

48. The Presence of at least Twenty Members of the House of Commons shall be necessary to constitute a Meeting of the House for the Exercise of its Powers, and for that Purpose the Speaker shall be reckoned as a Member.

Quorum of House of Commons

49. Questions arising in the House of Commons shall be decided by a Majority of Voices other than that of the Speaker, and when the Voices are equal, but not otherwise, the Speaker shall have a Vote.

Voting in House of Commons

50. Every House of Commons shall continue for Five Years from the Day of the Return of the Writs for choosing the House (subject to be sooner dissolved by the Governor General), and no longer.[26]

Duration of House of Commons

51. (1) The number of members of the House of Commons and the representation of the provinces therein shall, on the coming into force of this subsection and thereafter on the completion of each decennial census, be readjusted by such authority, in such manner, and from such time as the Parliament of Canada from time to time provides, subject and according to the following rules:

Readjustment of representation in Commons

1. There shall be assigned to each of the provinces a number of members equal to the number obtained by dividing the total population of the provinces by two hundred and seventy-nine and by dividing the population of each province by the quotient so obtained, counting any remainder in excess of 0.50 as one after the said process of division.

Rules

2. If the total number of members that would be assigned to a province by the application of rule 1 is less than the total number assigned to that province on the date of coming into force of this subsection, there shall be added to the number of members so assigned such number of members as will result in the province having the same number of members as were assigned on that date.[27]

---

(26) The term of the twelfth Parliament was extended by the *British North America Act, 1916*, 6-7 Geo. V. c. 19 (U.K.), which Act was repealed by the *Statute Law Revision Act, 1927*, 17-18 Geo. V, c. 42 (U.K.). See also subsection 4(1) of the *Constitution Act, 1982*, which provides that no House of Commons shall continue for longer than five years from the date fixed for the return of the writs at a general election of its members, and subsection 4(2) thereof, which provides for continuation of the House of Commons in special circumstances.

(27) As enacted by the *Constitution Act, 1985 (Representation)*, S.C. 1986, c. 8, Part I, which came into force on March 6, 1986 (See SI86-49). The section, as originally enacted, read as follows:

51. On the Completion of the Census in the Year One Thousand eight hundred and seventy-one, and of each subsequent decennial Census, the Representation of the Four Provinces shall be readjusted by such Authority, in such Manner, and from such Time, as the Parliament of Canada from Time to Time provides, subject and according to the following Rules:

(1) Quebec shall have the fixed Number of Sixty-five Members:

(2) There shall be assigned to each of the other Provinces such a Number of Members as will bear the same Proportion to the Number of its Population (ascertained at such Census) as the Number Sixty-five bears to the Number of the Population of Quebec (so ascertained):

(3) In the Computation of the Number of Members for a Province a fractional Part not exceeding One Half of the whole Number requisite for entitling the Province to a Member shall be disregarded; but a fractional Part exceeding One Half of that Number shall be equivalent to the whole Number:

(4) On any such Re-adjustment the Number of Members for a Province shall not be reduced unless the Proportion which the Number of the Population of the Province bore to the Number of the aggregate Population of Canada at the then last preceding Re-adjustment of the Number of Members for the Province is ascertained at the then latest Census to be diminished by One Twentieth Part or upwards:

(5) Such Re-adjustment shall not take effect until the Termination of the then existing Parliament.

The section was amended by the *Statute Law Revision Act, 1893,* 56-57 Vict., c. 14 (U.K.) by repealing the words from "of the census" to "seventy-one and" and the word "subsequent".

By the *British North America Act, 1943,* 6-7 Geo. VI., c. 30 (U.K.), which Act was repealed by the *Constitution Act, 1982,* redistribution of seats following the 1941 census was postponed until the first session of Parliament after the war. The section was re-enacted by the *British North America Act, 1946,* 9-10 Geo. VI., c. 63 (U.K.), which Act was also repealed by the *Constitution Act, 1982,* to read as follows:

51. (1) The number of members of the House of Commons shall be two hundred and fifty-five and the representation of the provinces therein shall forthwith upon the coming into force of this section and thereafter on the completion of each decennial census be readjusted by such authority, in such manner, and from such time as the Parliament of Canada from time to time provides, subject and according to the following rules:

(1) Subject as hereinafter provided, there shall be assigned to each of the provinces a number of members computed by dividing the total population of the provinces by two hundred and fifty-four and by dividing the population of each province by the quotient so obtained, disregarding, except as hereinafter in this section provided, the remainder, if any, after the said process of division.

(2) If the total number of members assigned to all the provinces pursuant to rule one is less than two hundred and fifty-four, additional members shall be assigned to the provinces (one to a province) having remainders in the computation under rule one commencing with the province having the largest remainder and continuing with the other provinces in the order of the magnitude of their respective remainders until the total number of members assigned is two hundred and fifty-four.

(3) Notwithstanding anything in this section, if upon completion of a computation under rules one and two, the number of members to be assigned to a province is less than the number of senators representing the said province, rules one and two shall cease to apply in respect of the said province, and there shall be assigned to the said province a number of members equal to the said number of senators.

(4) In the event that rules one and two cease to apply in respect of a province then, for the purpose of computing the number of members to be assigned to the provinces in respect of which rules one and two continue to apply, the total population of the provinces shall be reduced by the number of the population of the province in respect of which rules one and two have ceased to apply and the number two hundred and fifty-four shall be reduced by the number of members assigned to such province pursuant to rule three.

(5) Such readjustment shall not take effect until the termination of the then existing Parliament.

(2) The Yukon Territory as constituted by Chapter forty-one of the Statutes of Canada, 1901, together with any Part of Canada not comprised within a province which may from time to time be included therein by the Parliament of Canada for the purposes of representation in Parliament, shall be entitled to one member.

The section was re-enacted by the *British North America Act, 1952,* S.C. 1952, c. 15, which Act was also repealed by the *Constitution Act, 1982,* as follows:

51. (1) Subject as hereinafter provided, the number of members of the House of Commons shall be two hundred and sixty-three and the representation of the provinces therein shall forthwith upon the coming into force of this section and thereafter on the completion of each decennial census be readjusted by such authority, in such manner, and from such time as the Parliament of Canada from time to time provides, subject and according to the following rules:

1. There shall be assigned to each of the provinces a number of members computed by dividing the total population of the provinces by two hundred and sixty-one and by dividing the population of each province by the quotient so obtained, disregarding, except as hereinafter in this section provided, the remainder, if any, after the said process of division.

2. If the total number of members assigned to all the provinces pursuant to rule one is less than two hundred and sixty-one, additional members shall be assigned to the provinces (one to a province) having remainders in the computation under rule one commencing with the province having the largest remainder and continuing with the other provinces in the order of the magnitude of their respective remainders until the total number of members assigned is two hundred and sixty-one.

3. Notwithstanding anything in this section, if upon completion of a computation under rules one and two the number of members to be assigned to a province is less than the number of senators representing the said province, rules one and two shall cease to apply in respect of the said province, and there shall be assigned to the said province a number of members equal to the said number of senators.

4. In the event that rules one and two cease to apply in respect of a province then, for the purposes of computing the number of members to be assigned to the provinces in respect of which rules one and two continue to apply, the total population of the provinces shall be reduced by the number of the population of the province in respect of which rules one and two have ceased to apply and the number two hundred and sixty-one shall be reduced by the number of members assigned to such province pursuant to rule three.

5. On any such readjustment the number of members for any province shall not be reduced by more than fifteen per cent below the representation to which such province was entitled under rules one to four of the subsection at the last preceding readjustment of the representation of that province, and there shall be no reduction in the representation of any province as a result of which that province would have a smaller number of members than any other province that according to the results of the then last decennial census did not have a larger population; but for the purposes of any subsequent readjustment of representation under this section any increase in the number of members of the House of Commons resulting from the application of this rule shall not be included in the divisor mentioned in rules one to four of this subsection.

6. Such readjustment shall not take effect until the termination of the then existing Parliament.

(2) The Yukon Territory as constituted by chapter forty-one of the statutes of Canada, 1901, shall be entitled to one member, and such other part of Canada not comprised within a province as may from time to time be defined by the Parliament of Canada shall be entitled to one member.

Subsection 51(1) was re-enacted by *Constitution Act, 1974,* S.C. 1974-75-76, c. 13 to read as follows:

51. (1) The number of members of the House of Commons and the representation of the provinces therein shall upon the coming into force of this subsection and thereafter on the completion of each decennial census be readjusted by such authority, in such manner, and from such time as the Parliament of Canada from time to time provides, subject and according to the following Rules:

1. There shall be assigned to Quebec seventy-five members in the readjustment following the completion of the decennial census taken in the year 1971, and thereafter four additional members in each subsequent readjustment.

2. Subject to Rules 5(2) and (3), there shall be assigned to a large province a number of members equal to the number obtained by dividing the population of the large province by the electoral quotient of Quebec.

3. Subject to Rules 5(2) and (3), there shall be assigned to a small province a number of members equal to the number obtained by dividing

(*a*) the sum of the populations, determined according to the results of the penultimate decennial census, of the provinces (other than Quebec) having populations of less than one and a half million, determined according to the results of that census, by the sum of the numbers of members assigned to those provinces in the readjustment following the completion of that census; and

(*b*) the population of the small province by the quotient obtained under paragraph (*a*).

4. Subject to Rules 5(1) (*a*), (2) and (3) there shall be assigned to an intermediate province a number of members equal to the number obtained

(*a*) by dividing the sum of the populations of the provinces (other than Quebec) having populations of less than one and a half million by the sum of the number of members assigned to those provinces under any of Rules 3,5 (1) (b), (2) and (3);

(*b*) by dividing the population of the intermediate province by the quotient obtained under paragraph (*a*); and

(*c*) by adding to the number of members assigned to the intermediate province in the readjustment following the completion of the penultimate decennial census one-half of the difference resulting from the subtraction of that number from the quotient obtained under paragraph (*b*).

5. (1) On any readjustment,

(*a*) if no province (other than Quebec) has a population of less than one and a half million, Rule 4 shall not be applied and, subject to Rules 5(2) and (3), there shall be assigned to an intermediate province a number of members equal to the number obtained by dividing

(i) the sum of the populations, determined according to the results of the penultimate decennial census, of the provinces, (other than Quebec) having populations of not less than one and a half million and not more than two and a half million, determined according to the results of that census, by the sum of the numbers of members assigned to those provinces in the readjustment following the completion of that census, and

(ii) the population of the intermediate province by the quotient obtained under subparagraph (i);

(*b*) if a province (other than Quebec) having a population of

(i) less than one and a half million, or

(ii) not less than one and a half million and not more than two and a half million

does not have a population greater than its population determined according to the results of the penultimate decennial census, it shall, subject to Rules 5 (2) and (3), be assigned the number of members assigned to it in the readjustment following the completion of that census.

(2) On any readjustment,

(*a*) if, under any of Rules 2 to 5 (1), the number of members to be assigned to a province (in this paragraph referred to as " the first province") is smaller than the number of members to be assigned to any other province not having a population greater than that of the first province, those Rules shall not be applied to the first province and it shall be assigned a number of members equal to the largest number of members to be assigned to any other province not having a population greater than that of the first province;

(*b*) if, under any of Rules 2 to 5 (1)(*a*), the number of members to be assigned to a province is smaller than the number of members assigned to it in the readjustment following the completion of the penultimate decennial census, those Rules shall not be applied to it and it shall be assigned the latter number of members;

(*c*) if both paragraphs (*a*) and (*b*) apply to a province, it shall be assigned a number of members equal to the greater of the numbers produced under those paragraphs.

(3) On any readjustment,

(*a*) if the electoral quotient of a province (in this paragraph referred to as "the first province") obtained by dividing its population by the number of members to be assigned to it under any of Rules 2 to 5 (2) is greater than the electoral quotient of Quebec, those Rules shall not be applied to the first province and it shall be assigned a number of members equal to the number obtained by dividing its population by the electoral quotient of Quebec;

(*b*) if, as a result of the application of Rule 6 (2) (*a*), the number of members assigned to a province under paragraph (*a*) equals the number of members to be assigned to it under any of Rules 2 to 5 (2), it shall be assigned that number of members and paragraph (*a*) shall cease to apply to that province.

(2) The Yukon Territory as bounded and described in the schedule to chapter Y-2 of the Revised Statutes of Canada, 1985, shall be entitled to one member, and the Northwest Territories as bounded and described in section 2 of the chapter N-27 of the Revised Statutes of Canada, 1985, as amended by section 77 of chapter 28 of the Statutes of Canada, 1993, shall be entitled to one member, and Nunavut as bounded and described in section 3 of chapter 28 of the Statutes of Canada, 1993, shall be entitled to one member.[28]

Yukon Territory, Northwest Territories, and Nunavut

51A. Notwithstanding anything in this Act a province shall always be entitled to a number of members in the House of Commons not less than the number of senators representing such province.[29]

Constitution of House of Commons

52. The Number of Members of the House of Commons may be from Time to Time increased by the Parliament of Canada, provided the proportionate Representation of the Provinces prescribed by this Act is not thereby disturbed.

Increase of Number of House of Commons

---

6. (1) In these Rules,

"electoral quotient" means, in respect of a province, the quotient obtained by dividing its population, determined according to the results of the then most recent decennial census, by the number of members to be assigned to it under any of Rules 1 to 5 (3) in the readjustment following the completion of that census;

"intermediate province" means a province (other than Quebec) having a population greater than its population determined according to the results of the penultimate decennial census but not more than two and a half million and not less than one and a half million;

"large province" means a province (other than Quebec) having a population greater than two and a half million;

"penultimate decennial census" means the decennial census that preceded the then most recent decennial census;

"population" means, except where otherwise specified, the population determined according to the results of the then most recent decennial census;

"small province" means a province (other than Quebec) having a population greater than its population determined according to the results of the penultimate decennial census and less than one and half million.

(2) For the purposes of these Rules,

(*a*) if any fraction less than one remains upon completion of the final calculation that produces the number of members to be assigned to a province, that number of members shall equal the number so produced disregarding the fraction;

(*b*) if more than one readjustment follows the completion of a decennial census, the most recent of those readjustments shall, upon taking effect, be deemed to be the only readjustment following the completion of that census;

(*c*) a readjustment shall not take effect until the termination of the then existing Parliament.

(28) As enacted by the *Constitution Act, 1999 (Nunavut)*, S.C. 1998, c. 15, Part 2. Subsection 51(2) was previously amended by the *Constitution Act (No. 1), 1975*, S.C. 1974-75-76, c. 28, and read as follows:

(2) The Yukon Territory as bounded as described in the schedule to chapter Y-2 of the Revised Statutes of Canada, 1970, shall be entitled to one member, and the Northwest Territories as bounded and described in section 2 of chapter N-22 of the Revised Statutes of Canada, 1970, shall be entitled to two members.

(29) As enacted by the *Constitution Act, 1915*, 5-6 Geo. V, c. 45 (U.K.).

Appropriation and Tax Bills

53. Bills for appropriating any Part of the Public Revenue, or for imposing any Tax or Impost, shall originate in the House of Commons.

Recommendation of Money Votes

54. It shall not be lawful for the House of Commons to adopt or pass any Vote, Resolution, Address, or Bill for the Appropriation of any Part of the Public Revenue, or of any Tax or Impost, to any Purpose that has not been first recommended to that House by Message of the Governor General in the Session in which such Vote, Resolution, Address, or Bill is proposed.

Royal Assent to Bills, etc.

55. Where a Bill passed by the Houses of the Parliament is presented to the Governor General for the Queen's Assent, he shall declare, according to his Discretion, but subject to the Provisions of this Act and to Her Majesty's Instructions, either that he assents thereto in the Queen's Name, or that he withholds the Queen's Assent, or that he reserves the Bill for the Signification of the Queen's Pleasure.

Disallowance by Order in Council of Act assented to by Governor General

56. Where the Governor General assents to a Bill in the Queen's Name, he shall by the first convenient Opportunity send an authentic Copy of the Act to One of Her Majesty's Principal Secretaries of State, and if the Queen in Council within Two Years after Receipt thereof by the Secretary of State thinks fit to disallow the Act, such Disallowance (with a Certificate of the Secretary of State of the Day on which the Act was received by him) being signified by the Governor General, by Speech or Message to each of the Houses of the Parliament or by Proclamation, shall annul the Act from and after the Day of such Signification.

Signification of Queen's Pleasure on Bill reserved

57. A Bill reserved for the Signification of the Queen's Pleasure shall not have any Force unless and until, within Two Years from the Day on which it was presented to the Governor General for the Queen's Assent, the Governor General signifies, by Speech or Message to each of the Houses of the Parliament or by Proclamation, that it has received the Assent of the Queen in Council.

An Entry of every such Speech, Message, or Proclamation shall be made in the Journal of each House, and a Duplicate thereof duly attested shall be delivered to the proper Officer to be kept among the Records of Canada.

V. PROVINCIAL CONSTITUTIONS

Executive Power

58. For each Province there shall be an Officer, styled the Lieutenant Governor, appointed by the Governor General in Council by Instrument under the Great Seal of Canada.

Appointment of Lieutenant Governors of Provinces

59. A Lieutenant Governor shall hold Office during the Pleasure of the Governor General; but any Lieutenant Governor appointed after the Commencement of the First Session of the Parliament of Canada shall not be removable within Five Years from his Appointment, except for Cause assigned, which shall be communicated to him in Writing within One Month after the Order for his Removal is made, and shall be communicated by Message to the Senate and to the House of Commons within One Week thereafter if the Parliament is then sitting, and if not then within One Week after the Commencement of the next Session of the Parliament.

Tenure of Office of Lieutenant Governor

60. The Salaries of the Lieutenant Governors shall be fixed and provided by the Parliament of Canada.[30]

Salaries of Lieutenant Governors

61. Every Lieutenant Governor shall, before assuming the Duties of his Office, make and subscribe before the Governor General or some Person authorized by him Oaths of Allegiance and Office similar to those taken by the Governor General.

Oaths, etc., of Lieutenant Governor

62. The Provisions of this Act referring to the Lieutenant Governor extend and apply to the Lieutenant Governor for the Time being of each Province, or other the Chief Executive Officer or Administrator for the Time being carrying on the Government of the Province, by whatever Title he is designated.

Application of Provisions referring to Lieutenant Governor

63. The Executive Council of Ontario and of Quebec shall be composed of such Persons as the Lieutenant Governor from Time to Time thinks fit, and in the first instance of the following Officers, namely, — the Attorney General, the Secretary and Registrar of the Province, the Treasurer of the Province, the Commissioner of Crown Lands, and the Commissioner of Agriculture and Public Works, with in Quebec the Speaker of the Legislative Council and the Solicitor General.[31]

Appointment of Executive Officers for Ontario and Quebec

---

(30) Provided for by the *Salaries Act*, R.S.C. 1990, c. E. 25, , c. S-3.

(31) Now provided for in Ontario by the *Executive Council Act*, R.S.C. 1990, c. E.25, and in Quebec by the *Executive Power Act*, R.S.Q. 1977, c. E-18.

Executive Government of Nova Scotia and New Brunswick

64. The Constitution of the Executive Authority in each of the Provinces of Nova Scotia and New Brunswick shall, subject to the Provisions of this Act, continue as it exists at the Union until altered under the Authority of this Act.[32]

Powers to be exercised by Lieutenant Governor of Ontario or Quebec with Advice, or alone

65. All Powers, Authorities, and Functions which under any Act of the Parliament of Great Britain, or of the Parliament of the United Kingdom of Great Britain and Ireland, or of the Legislature of Upper Canada, Lower Canada, or Canada, were or are before or at the Union vested in or exerciseable by the respective Governors or Lieutenant Governors of those Provinces, with the Advice or with the Advise and Consent of the respective Executive Councils thereof, or in conjunction with those Councils, or with any Number of Members thereof, or by those Governors or Lieutenant Governors individually, shall, as far as the same are capable of being exercised after the Union in relation to the Government of Ontario and Quebec respectively, be vested in and shall or may be exercised by the Lieutenant Governor of Ontario and Quebec respectively, with the Advice or the Advice and Consent of or in conjunction with the respective Executive Councils, or any Members thereof, or by the Lieutenant Governor individually, as the Case requires, subject nevertheless (except with respect to such as exist under Acts of the Parliament of Great Britain, or of the Parliament of the United Kingdom of Great Britain and Ireland,) to be abolished or altered by the respective Legislatures of Ontario and Quebec.[33]

Application of Provisions referring to Lieutenant Governor in Council

66. The Provisions of this Act referring to the Lieutenant Governor in Council shall be construed as referring to the Lieutenant Governor of the Province acting by and with the Advice of the Executive Council thereof.

Administration in Absence, etc., of Lieutenant Governor

67. The Governor General in Council may from Time to Time appoint an Administrator to execute the Office and Functions of Lieutenant Governor during his Absence, Illness, or other Inability.

Seats of Provincial Governments

68. Unless and until the Executive Government of any Province otherwise directs with respect to that Province, the Seats of Government of the Provinces shall be as follows, namely, — of Ontario, the City of Toronto; of Quebec, the City of Quebec; of Nova Scotia, the City of Halifax; and of New Brunswick, the City of Fredericton.

---

(32) A similar provision was included in each of the instruments admitting British Columbia, Prince Edward Island, and Newfoundland. The Executive Authorities for Manitoba, Alberta and Saskatchewan were established by the statutes creating those provinces. See the notes to section 5, *supra*.

(33) See the notes to section 129, *infra*.

Legislative Power

1. — ONTARIO

69. There shall be a Legislature for Ontario consisting of the Lieutenant Governor and of One House, styled the Legislative Assembly of Ontario.

Legislature for Ontario

70. The Legislative Assembly of Ontario shall be composed of Eighty-two Members, to be elected to represent the Eighty-two Electoral Districts set forth in the First Schedule to this Act.[34]

Electoral districts

2. — QUEBEC

71. There shall be a Legislature for Quebec consisting of the Lieutenant Governor and of Two Houses, styled the Legislative Council of Quebec and the Legislative Assembly of Quebec.[35]

Legislature for Quebec

72. The Legislative Council of Quebec shall be composed of Twenty-four Members, to be appointed by the Lieutenant Governor, in the Queen's Name, by Instrument under the Great Seat of Quebec, one being appointed to represent each of the Twenty-four Electoral Divisions of Lower Canada in this Act referred to, and each holding Office for the Term of his Life, unless the Legislature of Quebec otherwise provides under the Provisions of this Act.

Constitution of Legislative Council

73. The Qualifications of the Legislative Councillors of Quebec shall be the same as those of the Senators for Quebec.

Qualification of Legislative Councillors

74. The Place of a Legislative Councillor of Quebec shall become vacant in the Cases, *mutatis mutandis,* in which the Place of Senator becomes vacant.

Resignation, Disqualification, etc.

75. When a Vacancy happens in the Legislative Council of Quebec by Resignation, Death, or otherwise, the Lieutenant Governor, in the Queen's Name, by Instrument under the Great Seal of Quebec, shall appoint a fit and qualified Person to fill the Vacancy.

Vacancies

---

(34) Spent. Now covered by the *Representation Act,* R.S.O. 1990, c. R.26.

(35) The Act respecting the Legislative Council of Quebec, S.Q. 1968, c.9, provided that the Legislature for Quebec shall consist of the Lieutenant Governor and the National Assembly of Quebec, and repealed the provisions of the *Legislature Act,* R.S.Q. 1964, c. 6, relating to the Legislative Council of Quebec. Now covered by the *Legislative Act,* R.S.Q. 1977, c. L-1. Sections 72 to 79 following are therefore completely spent.

Questions as to Vacancies, etc.

76. If any Question arises respecting the Qualification of a Legislative Councillor of Quebec, or a Vacancy in the Legislative Council of Quebec, the same shall be heard and determined by the Legislative Council.

Speaker of Legislative Council

77. The Lieutenant Governor may from Time to Time, by Instrument under the Great Seal of Quebec, appoint a Member of the Legislative Council of Quebec to be Speaker thereof, and may remove him and appoint another in his Stead.

Quorum of Legislative Council

78. Until the Legislature of Quebec otherwise provides, the Presence of at least Ten Members of the Legislative Council, including the Speaker, shall be necessary to constitute a Meeting for the Exercise of its Powers.

Voting in Legislative Council

79. Questions arising in the Legislative Council of Quebec shall be decided by a Majority of Voices, and the Speaker shall in all Cases have a Vote, and when the Voices are equal the Decision shall be deemed to be in the Negative.

Constitution of Legislative Assembly of Quebec

80. The Legislative Assembly of Quebec shall be composed of Sixty-five Members, to be elected to represent the Sixty-five Electoral Divisions or Districts of Lower Canada in this Act referred to, subject to Alteration thereof by the Legislature of Quebec: Provided that it shall not be lawful to present to the Lieutenant Governor of Quebec for Assent any Bill for altering the Limits of any of the Electoral Divisions or Districts mentioned in the Second Schedule to this Act, unless the Second and Third Readings of such Bill have been passed in the Legislative Assembly with the Concurrence of the Majority of the Members representing all those Electoral Divisions or Districts, and the Assent shall not be given to such Bill unless an Address has been presented by the Legislative Assembly to the Lieutenant Governor stating that it has been so passed.[36]

3. — ONTARIO AND QUEBEC

81. Repealed.[37]

---

(36) The Act respecting electoral districts, S.Q. 1970, c. 7, s. 1, provides that this section no longer has effect.

(37) Repealed by the *Statute Law Revision Act, 1893*, 56-57 Vict. c. 14 (U.K.). The section read as follows:

> **81.** The Legislatures of Ontario and Quebec respectively shall be called together not later than Six Months after the Union.

82. The Lieutenant Governor of Ontario and of Quebec shall from Time to Time, in the Queen's Name, by Instrument under the Great Seal of the Province, summon and call together the Legislative Assembly of the Province.

Summoning of Legislative Assemblies

83. Until the Legislature of Ontario or of Quebec otherwise provides, a Person accepting or holding in Ontario or in Quebec any Office, Commission, or Employment, permanent or temporary, at the Nomination of the Lieutenant Governor, to which an annual Salary, or any Fee, Allowance, Emolument, or Profit of any Kind or Amount whatever from the Province is attached, shall not be eligible as a Member of the Legislative Assembly of the respective Province, nor shall he sit or vote as such; but nothing in this Section shall make ineligible any Person being a Member of the Executive Council of the respective Province, or holding any of the following Offices, that is to say, the Offices of Attorney General, Secretary and Registrar of the Province, Treasurer of the Province, Commissioner of Crown Lands, and Commissioner of Agriculture and Public Works, and in Quebec Solicitor General, or shall disqualify him to sit or vote in the House for which he is elected, provided he is elected while holding such Office.[38]

Restriction on election of Holders of offices

84. Until the legislatures of Ontario and Quebec respectively otherwise provide, all Laws which at the Union are in force in those Provinces respectively, relative to the following Matters, or any of them, namely, — the Qualifications and Disqualifications of Persons to be elected or to sit or vote as Members of the Assembly of Canada, the Qualifications or Disqualifications of Voters, the Oaths to be taken by Voters, the Returning Officers, their Powers and Duties, the Proceedings at Elections, the Periods during which such Elections may be continued, and the Trial of controverted Elections and the Proceedings incident thereto, the vacating of the Seats of Members and the issuing and execution of new Writs in case of Seats vacated otherwise than by Dissolution, — shall respectively apply to Elections of Members to serve in the respective Legislative Assemblies of Ontario and Quebec.

Continuance of existing Election Laws

---

(38) Probably spent. The subject-matter of this section is now covered in Ontario by the *Legislative Assembly Act*, R.S.O. 1990, c. L.10, and in Quebec by the *National Assembly Act*, R.S.Q. c. A-23.1.

Provided that, until the Legislature of Ontario otherwise provides, at any Election for a Member of the Legislative Assembly of Ontario for the District of Algoma, in addition to Persons qualified by the Law of the Province of Canada to vote, every Male British Subject, aged Twenty-one Years or upwards, being a Householder, shall have a Vote.[39]

Duration of Legislative Assemblies

85. Every Legislative Assembly of Ontario and every Legislative Assembly of Quebec shall continue for Four Years from the Day of the Return of the Writs for choosing the same (subject nevertheless to either the Legislative Assembly of Ontario or the Legislative Assembly of Quebec being sooner dissolved by the Lieutenant Governor of the Province), and no longer.[40]

Yearly Session of Legislature

86. There shall be a Session of the Legislature of Ontario and of that of Quebec once at least in every Year, so that Twelve Months shall not intervene between the last Sitting of the Legislature in each Province in one Session and its first Sitting in the next Session.[41]

Speaker, Quorum, etc.

87. The following Provisions of this Act respecting the House of Commons of Canada shall extend and apply to the Legislative Assemblies of Ontario and Quebec, that is to say, — the Provisions relating to the Election of a Speaker originally and on Vacancies, the Duties of the Speaker, the Absence of the Speaker, the Quorum, and the Mode of voting, as if those Provisions were here re-enacted and made applicable in Terms to each such Legislative Assembly.

4. — NOVA SCOTIA AND NEW BRUNSWICK

Constitutions of Legislatures of Nova Scotia and New Brunswick

88. The Constitution of the Legislature of each of the Provinces of Nova Scotia and New Brunswick shall, subject to the Provisions of this Act, continue as it exists at the Union until altered under the Authority of this Act.[42]

---

(39) Probably spent. The subject-matter of this section is now covered in Ontario by the *Election Act*, R.S.O. 1990, c. E.6, and the *Legislative Assembly Act*, R.S.O. 1990, c. L.10, in Quebec by the *Elections Act*, R.S.Q. c. E-3.3 and the *National Assembly Act*, R.S.Q. c. A-23.1.

(40) The maximum duration of the Legislative Assemblies of Ontario and Quebec has been changed to five years. See the *Legislative Assembly Act*, R.S.O. 1990, c. L.10, and the *National Assembly Act*, R.S.Q. c. A-23.1, respectively. See also section 4 of the *Constitution Act, 1982*, which provides a maximum duration for a legislative assembly of five years but also authorizes continuation in special circumstances.

(41) See also section 5 of the *Constitution Act, 1982*, which provides that there shall be a sitting of each legislature at least once every twelve months.

(42) See next page.

5. — ONTARIO, QUEBEC, AND NOVA SCOTIA

89. Repealed.[43]

6. — THE FOUR PROVINCES

90. The following Provisions of this Act respecting the Parliament of Canada, namely, — the Provisions relating to Appropriation and Tax Bills, the Recommendation of Money Votes, the Assent to Bills, the Disallowance of Acts, and the Signification of Pleasure on Bills reserved, — shall extend and apply to the Legislatures of the several Provinces as if those Provisions were here re-enacted and made applicable in Terms to the respective Provinces and the Legislatures thereof, with the Substitution of the Lieutenant Governor of the Province for the Governor General, of the Governor General for the Queen and for a Secretary of State, of One Year for Two Years, and of the Province for Canada.

Application to Legislatures of Provisions respecting Money Votes, etc.

---

(42) Partially repealed by the *Statute Law Revision Act, 1893*, 56-57 Vict., c. 14 (U.K.), which deleted the following concluding words of the original enactment:

> and the House of Assembly of New Brunswick existing at the passing of this Act shall, unless sooner dissolved, continue for the Period for which it was elected.

A similar provision was included in each of the instruments admitting British Columbia, Prince Edward Island and Newfoundland. The Legislatures of Manitoba, Alberta and Saskatchewan were established by the statutes creating those provinces. See the footnotes to section 5, *supra*.

See also sections 3 to 5 of the *Constitution Act, 1982*, which prescribe democratic rights applicable to all provinces, and subitem 2(2) of the Schedule to that Act, which sets out the repeal of section 20 of the *Manitoba Act, 1870*. Section 20 of the *Manitoba Act, 1870*, has been replaced by section 5 of the *Constitution Act, 1982*.

Section 20 reads as follows:

> **20.** There shall be a Session of the Legislature once at least in every year, so that twelve months shall not intervene between the last sitting of the Legislature in one Session and its first sitting in the next Session.

(43) Repealed by the *Statute Law Revision Act, 1893*, 56-57 Vict. c. 14 (U.K.). The section read as follows:

> **5.** — Ontario, Quebec, and Nova Scotia.

> **89.** Each of the Lieutenant Governors of Ontario, Quebec and Nova Scotia shall cause Writs to be issued for the First Election of Members of the Legislative Assembly thereof in such Form and by such Person as he thinks fit, and at such Time and addressed to such Returning Officer as the Governor General directs, and so that the First Election of Member of Assembly for any Electoral District or any Subdivision thereof shall be held at the same Time and at the same Places as the Election for a Member to serve in the House of Commons of Canada for that Electoral District.

VI. DISTRIBUTION OF LEGISLATIVE POWERS

Powers of the Parliament

Legislative Authority
of Parliament of
Canada

91. It shall be lawful for the Queen, by and with the Advice and Consent of the Senate and House of Commons, to make Laws for the Peace, Order, and good Government of Canada, in relation to all Matters not coming within the Classes of Subjects by this Act assigned exclusively to the Legislatures of the Provinces; and for greater Certainty, but not so as to restrict the Generality of the foregoing Terms of this Section, it is hereby declared that (notwithstanding anything in this Act) the exclusive Legislative Authority of the Parliament of Canada extends to all Matters coming within the Classes of Subjects next hereinafter enumerated; that is to say,—

1. Repealed.[44]

1A. The Public Debt and Property.[45]

2. The Regulation of Trade and Commerce.

2A. Unemployment insurance.[46]

3. The raising of Money by any Mode or System of Taxation.

4. The borrowing of Money on the Public Credit.

5. Postal Service.

6. The Census and Statistics.

7. Militia, Military and Naval Service, and Defence.

---

(44) Class I was added by the *British North America (No. 2) Act, 1949,* 13 Geo. VI, c. 81 (U.K.). That Act and class I were repealed by the *Constitution Act, 1982.* The matters referred to in class I are provided for in subsection 4 (2) and Part V of the *Constitution Act, 1982.* As enacted, class I read as follows:

1. The amendment from time to time of the Constitution of Canada, except as regards matters coming within the classes of subjects by this Act assigned exclusively to the Legislatures of the provinces, or as regards rights or privileges by this or any other Constitutional Act granted or secured to the Legislature or the Government of a province, or to any class of persons with respect to schools or as regards the use of the English or the French language or as regards the requirements that there shall be a session of the Parliament of Canada at least once each year, and that no House of Commons shall continue for more than five years from the day of the return of the Writs for choosing the House: provided, however, that a House of Commons may in time of real or apprehended war, invasion or insurrection be continued by the Parliament of Canada if such continuation is not opposed by the votes of more than one-third of the members of such House.

(45) Re-numbered by the *British North America (No. 2) Act, 1949.*

(46) Added by the *Constitution Act, 1940,* 3-4 Geo. VI, c. 36 (U.K.).

8. The fixing of and providing for the Salaries and Allowances of Civil and other Officers of the Government of Canada.

9. Beacons, Buoys, Lighthouses, and Sable Island.

10. Navigation and Shipping.

11. Quarantine and the Establishment and Maintenance of Marine Hospitals.

12. Sea Coast and Inland Fisheries.

13. Ferries between a Province and any British or Foreign Country or between Two Provinces.

14. Currency and Coinage.

15. Banking, Incorporation of Banks, and the Issue of Paper Money.

16. Savings Banks.

17. Weights and Measures.

18. Bills of Exchange and Promissory Notes.

19. Interest.

20. Legal Tender.

21. Bankruptcy and Insolvency.

22. Patents of Invention and Discovery.

23. Copyrights.

24. Indians, and Lands reserved for Indians.

25. Naturalization and Aliens.

26. Marriage and Divorce.

27. The Criminal Law, except the Constitution of Courts of Criminal Jurisdiction, but including the Procedure in Criminal Matters.

28. The Establishment, Maintenance, and Management of Penitentiaries.

29. Such Classes of Subjects as are expressly excepted in the Enumeration of the Classes of Subjects by this Act assigned exclusively to the Legislatures of the Provinces.

And any Matter coming within any of the Classes of Subjects enumerated in this Section shall not be deemed to come within the Class of Matters of a local or private Nature comprised in the Enumeration of the Classes of Subjects by this Act assigned exclusively to the Legislatures of the Provinces.[47]

---

(47) Legislative authority has been conferred on Parliament by other Acts as follows:

1. The *Constitution Act, 1871,* 34-35 Vict., c. 28 (U.K.).

> **2.** The Parliament of Canada may from time to time establish new Provinces in any territories forming for the time being part of the Dominion of Canada, but not included in any Province thereof, and may, at the time of such establishment, make provision for the constitution and administration of any such Province, and for the passing of laws for the peace, order, and good government of such Province, and for its representation in the said Parliament.

> **3.** The Parliament of Canada may from time to time, with the consent of the Legislature of any province of the said Dominion, increase, diminish, or otherwise alter the limits of such Province, upon such terms and conditions as may be agreed to by the said Legislature, and may, with the like consent, make provision respecting the effect and operation of any such increase or diminution or alteration of territory in relation to any Province affected thereby.

> **4.** The Parliament of Canada may from time to time make provision for the administration, peace, order, and good government of any territory not for the time being included in any Province.

> **5.** The following Acts passed by the said Parliament of Canada, and intituled respectively —"An Act for the temporary government of Rupert's Land and the North Western Territory when united with Canada"; and "An Act to amend and continue the Act thirty-two and thirty-three Victoria, chapter three, and to establish and provide for the government of "the Province of Manitoba", shall be and be deemed to have been valid and effectual for all purposes whatsoever from the date at which they respectively received the assent, in the Queen's name, of the Governor General of the said Dominion of Canada.

> **6.** Except as provided by the third section of this Act, it shall not be competent for the Parliament of Canada to alter the provisions of the last-mentioned Act of the said Parliament in so far as it relates to the Province of Manitoba, or of any other Act hereafter establishing new Provinces in the said Dominion, subject always to the right of the Legislature of the Province of Manitoba to alter from time to time the provisions of any law respecting the qualification of electors and members of the Legislative Assembly, and to make laws respecting elections in the said province.

The *Rupert's Land Act, 1868,* 31-32 Vict., c. 105 (U.K.) (repealed by the *Statute Law Revision Act, 1893,* 56-57 Vict., c. 14 (U.K.)) had previously conferred similar authority in relation to Rupert's Land and the North Western Territory upon admission of those areas.

2. The *Constitution Act, 1886,* 49-50 Vict., c. 35, (U.K.).

> **1.** The Parliament of Canada may from time to time make provision for the representation in the Senate and House of Commons of Canada, or in either of them, of any territories which for the time being form part of the Dominion of Canada, but are not included in any province thereof.

3. The *Statute of Westminster, 1931,* 22 Geo. V, c.4 (U.K.).

> **3.** It is hereby declared and enacted that the Parliament of a Dominion has full power to make laws having extra-territorial operation.

4. Under section 44 of the *Constitution Act, 1982,* Parliament has exclusive authority to amend the Constitution of Canada in relation to the executive government of Canada or the Senate and House of Commons. Sections 38, 41, 42, and 43 of that Act authorize the Senate and House of Commons to give their approval to certain other constitutional amendments by resolution.

Exclusive Powers of Provincial Legislatures

92. In each Province the Legislature may exclusively make Laws in relation to Matters coming within the Classes of Subjects next hereinafter enumerated; that is to say, —

Subjects of exclusive Provincial Legislation

1. Repealed.[48]

2. Direct Taxation within the Province in order to the raising of a Revenue for Provincial Purposes.

3. The borrowing of Money on the sole Credit of the Province.

4. The Establishment and Tenure of Provincial Offices and the Appointment and Payment of Provincial Officers.

5. The Management and Sale of the Public Lands belonging to the Province and of the Timber and Wood thereon.

6. The Establishment, Maintenance, and Management of Public and Reformatory Prisons in and for the Province.

7. The Establishment, Maintenance, and Management of Hospitals, Asylums, Charities, and Eleemosynary Institutions in and for the Province, other than Marine Hospitals.

8. Municipal Institutions in the Province.

9. Shop, Saloon, Tavern, Auctioneer, and other Licences in order to the raising of a Revenue for Provincial, Local, or Municipal Purposes.

---

(48) Class I was repealed by the *Constitution Act, 1982*. As enacted, it read as follows:

> 1. The Amendment from Time to Time, notwithstanding anything in this Act, of the Constitution of the Province, except as regards the Office of Lieutenant Governor.

Section 45 of the *Constitution Act, 1982* now authorizes legislatures to make laws amending the constitution of the province. Sections 38, 41, 42, and 43 of that Act authorize legislative assemblies to give their approval by resolution to certain other amendments to the Constitution of Canada.

10. Local Works and Undertakings other than such as are of the following Classes:—

(a) Lines of Steam or other Ships, Railways, Canals, Telegraphs, and other Works and Undertakings connecting the Province with any other or others of the Provinces, or extending beyond the Limits of the Province:

(b) Lines of Steam Ships between the Province and any British or Foreign Country:

(c) Such Works as, although wholly situate within the Province, are before or after their Execution declared by the Parliament of Canada to be for the general Advantage of Canada or for the Advantage of Two or more of the Provinces.

11. The Incorporation of Companies with Provincial Objects.

12. The Solemnization of Marriage in the Province.

13. Property and Civil Rights in the Province.

14. The Administration of Justice in the Province, including the Constitution, Maintenance, and Organization of Provincial Courts, both of Civil and of Criminal Jurisdiction, and including Procedure in Civil Matters in those Courts.

15. The Imposition of Punishment by Fine, Penalty, or Imprisonment for enforcing any Law of the Province made in relation to any Matter coming within any of the Classes of Subjects enumerated in this Section.

16. Generally all Matters of a merely local or private Nature in the Province.

Non-Renewable Natural Resources, Forestry Resources and Electrical Energy

Laws respecting non-renewable natural resources, forestry resources and electrical energy

92A. (1) In each province, the legislature may exclusively make laws in relation to

(*a*) exploration for non-renewable natural resources in the province;

(*b*) development, conservation and management of non-renewable natural resources and forestry resources in the province, including laws in relation to the rate of primary production therefrom; and

(*c*) development, conservation and management of sites and facilities in the province for the generation and production of electrical energy.

(2) In each province, the legislature may make laws in relation to the export from the province to another part of Canada of the primary production from non-renewable natural resources and forestry resources in the province and the production from facilities in the province for the generation of electrical energy, but such laws may not authorize or provide for discrimination in prices or in supplies exported to another part of Canada. Export from provinces of resources

(3) Nothing in subsection (2) derogates from the authority of Parliament to enact laws in relation to the matters referred to in that subsection and, where such a law of Parliament and a law of a province conflict, the law of Parliament prevails to the extent of the conflict. Authority of Parliament

(4) In each province, the legislature may make laws in relation to the raising of money by any mode or system of taxation in respect of Taxation of resources

(*a*) non-renewable natural resources and forestry resources in the province and the primary production therefrom, and

(*b*) sites and facilities in the province for the generation of electrical energy and the production therefrom,

whether or not such production is exported in whole or in part from the province, but such laws may not authorize or provide for taxation that differentiates between production exported to another part of Canada and production not exported from the province.

(5) The expression "primary production" has the meaning assigned by the Sixth Schedule. "Primary production"

(6) Nothing in subsections (1) to (5) derogates from any powers or rights that a legislature or government of a province had immediately before the coming into force of this section.[49] Existing powers or rights

---

(49) Added by the *Constitution Act, 1982.*

Education

Legislation respecting Education

93. In and for each Province the Legislature may exclusively make Laws in relation to Education, subject and according to the following Provisions:—

(1) Nothing in any such Law shall prejudicially affect any Right or Privilege with respect to Denominational Schools which any Class of Persons have by Law in the Province at the Union:

(2) All the Powers, Privileges, and Duties at the Union by Law conferred and imposed in Upper Canada on the Separate Schools and School Trustees of the Queen's Roman Catholic Subjects shall be and the same are hereby extended to the Dissentient Schools of the Queen's Protestant and Roman Catholic Subjects in Quebec:

(3) Where in any Province a system of separate or Dissentient Schools exists by Law at the Union or is thereafter established by the Legislature of the Province, an Appeal shall lie to the Governor General in Council from any Act or Decision of any Provincial Authority affecting any Right or Privilege of the Protestant or Roman Catholic Minority of the Queen's Subjects in relation to Education:

(4) In case any such Provincial Law as from Time to Time seems to the Governor General in Council requisite for the due Execution of the Provisions of this Section is not made, or in case any Decision of the Governor General in Council on any appeal under this Section is not duly executed by the proper Provincial Authority in that Behalf, then and in every such Case, and as far only as the Circumstances of each Case require, the Parliament of Canada may make remedial Laws for the due Execution of the Provisions of this Section and of any Decision of the Governor General in Council under this Section.[50]

---

(50) An alternative was provided for Manitoba by section 22 of the *Manitoba Act, 1870,* 33 Vict., c.3 (Canada), (confirmed by the *Constitution Act, 1871*), which reads as follows:

22. In and for the Province, the said Legislature may exclusively make Laws in relation to Education, subject and according to the following provisions:

(1) Nothing in any such Law shall prejudicially affect any right or privilege with respect to Denominational Schools which any class of persons have by Law or practice in the Province at the Union:

(2) An appeal shall lie to the Governor General in Council from any Act or decision of the Legislature of the Province, or of any Provincial Authority, affecting any right or privilege, of the Protestant or Roman Catholic minority of the Queen's subjects in relation to Education:

(3) In case any such Provincial Law, as from time to time seems to the Governor General in Council requisite for the due execution of the provisions of this section, is not made, or in case any decision of the Governor General in Council on any appeal under this section is not duly executed by the proper Provincial Authority in that behalf, then, and in every such case, and as far only as the circumstances of each case require, the Parliament of Canada may make remedial Laws for the due execution of the provisions of this section, and of any decision of the Governor General in Council under this section.

An alternative was provided for Alberta by section 17 of the *Alberta Act,* 4-5 Edw. VII, c. 3, 1905 (Canada), which reads as follows:

17. Section 93 of the *Constitution Act, 1867,* shall apply to the said province, with the substitution for paragraph (1) of the said section 93 of the following paragraph:

(1) Nothing in any such law shall prejudicially affect any right or privilege with respect to separate schools which any class of persons have at the date of the passing of this Act, under the terms of chapters 29 and 30 of the Ordinances of the Northwest Territories, passed in the year 1901, or with respect to religious instruction in any public or separate school as provided for in the said ordinances.

2. In the appropriation by the Legislature or distribution by the Government of the province of any moneys for the support of schools organized and carried on in accordance with the said chapter 29 or any Act passed in amendment thereof, or in substitution therefor, there shall be no discrimination against schools of any class described in the said chapter 29.

3. Where the expression "by law" is employed in paragraph 3 of the said section 93, it shall be held to mean the law as set out in the said chapters 29 and 30, and where the expression "at the Union" is employed, in the said paragraph 3, it shall be held to mean the date at which this Act comes into force.

An alternative was provided for Saskatchewan by section 17 of the *Saskatchewan Act,* 4-5 Edw. VII, c. 42, 1905 (Canada), which reads as follows:

17. Section 93 of the *Constitution Act, 1867,* shall apply to the said province, with the substitution for paragraph (1) of the said section 93, of the following paragraph:

(1) Nothing in any such law shall prejudicially affect any right or privilege with respect to separate schools which any class of persons have at the date of the passing of this Act, under the terms chapters 29 and 30 of the Ordinances of the Northwest Territories, passed in the year 1901, or with respect to religious instruction in any public or separate school as provided for in the said ordinances.

2. In the appropriation by the Legislature or distribution by the Government of the province of any moneys for the support of schools organized and carried on in accordance with the said chapter 29, or any Act passed in amendment thereof or in substitution therefor, there shall be no discrimination against schools of any class described in the said chapter 29.

3. Where the expression "by law" is employed in paragraph (3) of the said section 93, it shall be held to mean the law as set out in the said chapters 29 and 30; and where the expression "at the Union" is employed in the said paragraph (3), it shall be held to mean the date at which this Act comes into force.

An alternative was provided for Newfoundland by Term 17 of the Terms of Union of Newfoundland with Canada (confirmed by the *Newfoundland Act,* 12-13 Geo. VI, C. 22 (U.K)). Term 17 of the Terms of Union of Newfoundland with Canada set out in the Schedule to the *Newfoundland Act,* which was amended by the *Constitution Amendment, 1998 (Newfoundland Act),* (see SI/98-25) and now reads as follows:

17. (1) In lieu of section ninety-three of the *Constitution Act, 1867,* the following term shall apply in respect of the Province of Newfoundland.

(2) In and for the Province of Newfoundland, the Legislature shall have exclusive authority to make laws in relation to education, but shall provide for courses in religion that are not specific to a religious denomination.

Quebec

93A. Paragraphs (1) to (4) of section 93 do not apply to Quebec.[50.1]

Uniformity of Laws in Ontario, Nova Scotia, and New Brunswick

Legislation for
Uniformity of Laws
in Three Provinces

94. Notwithstanding anything in this Act, the Parliament of Canada may make Provision for the Uniformity of all or any of the Laws relative to Property and Civil Rights in Ontario, Nova Scotia, and New Brunswick, and of the Procedure of all or any of the Courts in those Three Provinces, and from and after the passing of any Act in that Behalf the Power of the Parliament of Canada to make Laws in relation to any Matter comprised in any such Act shall, notwithstanding anything in this Act, be unrestricted; but any Act of the Parliament of Canada making Provision for such Uniformity shall not have effect in any Province unless and until it is adopted and enacted as Law by the Legislature thereof.

Old Age Pensions

Legislation
respecting old age
pensions and sup-
plementary benefits

94A. The Parliament of Canada may make laws in relation to old age pensions and supplementary benefits, including survivors' and disability benefits irrespective of age, but no such law shall affect the operation of any law present or future of a provincial legislature in relation to any such matter.[51]

---

(3) Religious observances shall be permitted in a school where requested by parents.

[Publisher's note: The history of amendments to Term 17 of the Terms of Union of Newfoundland with Canada can be found on the Department of Justice Web site at <http://lois.justice.gc.ca/en/const/endnts_e.html>.]

See also sections 23, 29, and 59 of the *Constitution Act, 1982.* Section 23 provides for new minority language educational rights and section 59 permits a delay in respect of the coming into force in Quebec of one aspect of those rights. Section 29 provides that nothing in the *Canadian Charter of Rights and Freedoms* abrogates or derogates from any rights or privileges guaranteed by or under the Constitution of Canada in respect of denominational, separate or dissentient schools.

(50.1) Added by the *Constitution Amendment, 1997 (Quebec).* See SI/97-141.

(51) Added by the *Constitution Act, 1964,* 12-13 Eliz. II, c. 73 (U.K.). As originally enacted by the *British North America Act, 1951,* 14-15 Geo. VI, c. 32 (U.K.), which was repealed by the *Constitution Act, 1982,* section 94A read as follows:

> **94A.** It is hereby declared that the Parliament of Canada may from time to time make laws in relation to old age pensions in Canada, but no law made by the Parliament of Canada in relation to old age pensions shall affect the operation of any law present or future of a Provincial Legislature in relation to old age pensions.

95. In each Province the Legislature may make Laws in relation to Agriculture in the Province, and to Immigration into the Province; and it is hereby declared that the Parliament of Canada may from Time to Time make Laws in relation to Agriculture in all or any of the Provinces, and to Immigration into all or any of the Provinces; and any Law of the Legislature of a Province relative to Agriculture or to Immigration shall have effect in and for the Province as long and as far only as it is not repugnant to any Act of the Parliament of Canada.

Concurrent Powers of Legislation respecting Agriculture, etc.

VII. JUDICATURE

96. The Governor General shall appoint the Judges of the Superior, District, and County Courts in each Province, except those of the Courts of Probate in Nova Scotia and New Brunswick.

Appointment of Judges

97. Until the Laws relative to Property and Civil Rights in Ontario, Nova Scotia, and New Brunswick, and the Procedure of the Courts in those Provinces, are made uniform, the Judges of the Courts of those Provinces appointed by the Governor General shall be selected from the respective Bars of those Provinces.

Selection of Judges in Ontario, etc.

98. The Judges of the Courts of Quebec shall be selected from the Bar of that Province.

Selection of Judges in Quebec

99. (1) Subject to subsection two of this section, the Judges of the Superior Courts shall hold office during good behaviour, but shall be removable by the Governor General on Address of the Senate and House of Commons.

Tenure of office of Judges

(2) A Judge of a Superior Court, whether appointed before or after the coming into force of this section, shall cease to hold office upon attaining the age of seventy-five years, or upon the coming into force of this section if at that time he has already attained that age.[52]

Termination at age 75

---

(52) Repealed and re-enacted by the *Constitution Act, 1960,* 9 Eliz. II, c. 2 (U.K.), which came into force on March 1, 1961. The original section read as follows:

99. The Judges of the Superior Courts shall hold Office during good Behaviour, but shall be removable by the Governor General on Address of the Senate and House of Commons.

100. The Salaries, Allowances, and Pensions of the Judges of the Superior, District, and County Courts (except the Courts of Probate in Nova Scotia and New Brunswick), and of the Admiralty Courts in Cases where the Judges thereof are for the Time being paid by Salary, shall be fixed and provided by the Parliament of Canada.[53]

General Court of
Appeal, etc.

101. The Parliament of Canada may, notwithstanding anything in this Act, from Time to Time provide for the Constitution, Maintenance, and Organization of a General Court of Appeal for Canada, and for the Establishment of any additional Courts for the better Administration of the Laws of Canada.[54]

VIII. REVENUES; DEBTS; ASSETS; TAXATION

Creation of
Consolidated
Revenue Fund

102. All Duties and Revenues over which the respective Legislatures of Canada, Nova Scotia, and New Brunswick before and at the Union had and have Power of Appropriation, except such Portions thereof as are by this Act reserved to the respective Legislatures of the Provinces, or are raised by them in accordance with the special Powers conferred on them by this Act, shall form One Consolidated Revenue Fund, to be appropriated for the Public Service of Canada in the Manner and subject to the Charges in this Act provided.

Expenses of
Collection, etc.

103. The Consolidated Revenue Fund of Canada shall be permanently charged with the Costs, Charges, and Expenses incident to the Collection, Management, and Receipt thereof, and the same shall form the First Charge thereon, subject to be reviewed and audited in such Manner as shall be ordered by the Governor General in Council until the Parliament otherwise provides.

Interest of
Provincial Public
Debts

104. The annual Interest of the Public Debts of the several Provinces of Canada, Nova Scotia, and New Brunswick at the Union shall form the Second Charge on the Consolidated Revenue Fund of Canada.

Salary of Governor
General

105. Unless altered by the Parliament of Canada, the Salary of the Governor General shall be Ten thousand Pounds Sterling Money of the United Kingdom of Great Britain and Ireland, payable out of the Consolidated Revenue Fund of Canada, and the same shall form the Third Charge thereon.[55]

---

(53) Now provided for in the *Judges Act*, R.S.C. 1985, c. J-1.

(54) See the *Supreme Court Act*, R.S.C. 1985, c. S-26, the *Federal Court Act*, R.S.C. 1985, c. F-7 and the *Tax Court of Canada Act*, R.S.C. 1985, c. T-2.

(55) Now covered by the *Governor General's Act*, R.S.C. 1985, c. G-9.

106. Subject to the several Payments by this Act charged on the Consolidated Revenue Fund of Canada, the same shall be appropriated by the Parliament of Canada for the Public Service.

Appropriation from Time to Time

107. All Stocks, Cash, Banker's Balances, and Securities for Money belonging to each Province at the Time of the Union, except as in this Act mentioned, shall be the Property of Canada, and shall be taken in Reduction of the Amount of the respective Debts of the Provinces at the Union.

Transfer of Stocks, etc.

108. The Public Works and Property of each Province, enumerated in the Third Schedule to this Act, shall be the Property of Canada.

Transfer of Property in Schedule

109. All Lands, Mines, Minerals, and Royalties belonging to the Several Provinces of Canada, Nova Scotia, and New Brunswick at the Union, and all Sums then due or payable for such Lands, Mines, Minerals, or Royalties, shall belong to the several Provinces of Ontario, Quebec, Nova Scotia, and New Brunswick in which the same are situate or arise, subject to any Trusts existing in respect thereof, and to any Interest other than that of the Province in the same.[56]

Property in Lands, Mines, etc.

110. All Assets connected with such Portions of the Public Debt of each Province as are assumed by that Province shall belong to that Province.

Assets connected with Provincial Debts

111. Canada shall be liable for the Debts and Liabilities of each Province existing at the Union.

Canada to be liable for Provincial Debts

112. Ontario and Quebec conjointly shall be liable to Canada for the Amount (if any) by which the Debt of the Province of Canada exceeds at the Union Sixty-two million five hundred thousand Dollars, and shall be charged with Interest at the Rate of Five per Centum per Annum thereon.

Debts of Ontario and Quebec

113. The Assets enumerated in the Fourth Schedule to this Act belonging at the Union to the Province of Canada shall be the property of Ontario and Quebec conjointly.

Assets of Ontario and Quebec

---

(56) Manitoba, Alberta and Saskatchewan were placed in the same position as the original provinces by the *Constitution Act, 1930,* 20-21 Geo. V, c. 26 (U.K.).

These matters were dealt with in respect of British Columbia by the *British Columbia Terms of Union* and also in part by the *Constitution Act, 1930.*

Newfoundland was also placed in the same position by the *Newfoundland Act,* 12-13 Geo. VI, c. 22 (U.K.).

With respect to Prince Edward Island, see the Schedule to the *Prince Edward Island Terms of Union.*

Debt of Nova Scotia

114. Nova Scotia shall be liable to Canada for the Amount (if any) by which its Public Debt exceeds at the Union Eight million Dollars, and shall be charged with Interest at the Rate of Five per Centum per Annum thereon.[57]

Debt of New Brunswick

115. New Brunswick shall be liable to Canada for the Amount (if any) by which its Public Debt exceeds at the Union Seven million Dollars, and shall be charged with Interest at the Rate of Five per Centum per Annum thereon.

Payment of interest to Nova Scotia and New Brunswick

116. In case the Public Debts of Nova Scotia and New Brunswick do not at the Union amount to Eight million and Seven million Dollars respectively, they shall respectively receive by half-yearly Payments in advance from the Government of Canada Interest at Five per Centum per Annum on the Difference between the actual Amounts of their respective Debts and such stipulated Amounts.

Provincial Public Property

117. The several Provinces shall retain all their respective Public Property not otherwise disposed of in this Act, subject to the Right of Canada to assume any Lands or Public Property required for Fortifications or for the Defence of the Country.

118. Repealed.[58]

---

(57) The obligations imposed by this section, sections 115 and 116, and similar obligations under the instruments creating or admitting other provinces, have been carried into legislation of the Parliament of Canada and are now to be found in the *Provincial Subsidies Act,* R.S.C. 1985, c. P-26.

(58) Repealed by the *Statute Law Revision Act, 1950,* 14 Geo. VI, c. 6 (U.K.). As originally enacted the section read as follows:

118. The following Sums shall be paid yearly by Canada to the several Provinces for the Support of their Governments and Legislatures:

Dollars.

Ontario..Eighty thousand.

Quebec ....Seventy thousand.

Nova Scotia...Sixty thousand.

New Brunswick...Fifty thousand.

Two hundred and sixty thousand;

and an annual Grant in aid of each Province shall be made, equal to Eighty cents per Head of the Population as ascertained by the Census of One thousand eight hundred and sixty-one, and in the case of Nova Scotia and New Brunswick, by each subsequent Decennial Census until the Population of each of those two Provinces amounts to Four hundred thousand Souls, at which Rate such Grant shall thereafter remain. Such Grants shall be in full Settlement of all future Demands on Canada, and shall be paid half-yearly in advance to each Province; but the Government of Canada shall deduct from such Grants, as against any Province, all Sums chargeable as Interest on the Public Debt of that Province in excess of the several Amounts stipulated in this Act.

The section was made obsolete by the *Constitution Act, 1907,* 7 Edw. VII , c. 11 (U.K.) which provided:

1. (1) The following grants shall be made yearly by Canada to every province, which at the commencement of this Act is a province of the Dominion, for its local purposes and the support of its Government and Legislature: —

(a) A fixed grant —

where the population of the province is under one hundred and fifty thousand, of one hundred thousand dollars;

where the population of the province is one hundred and fifty thousand, but does not exceed two hundred thousand, of one hundred and fifty thousand dollars;

where the population of the province is two hundred thousand, but does not exceed four hundred thousand, of one hundred and eighty thousand dollars;

where the population of the province is four hundred thousand, but does not exceed eight hundred thousand, of one hundred and ninety thousand dollars;

where the population of the province is eight hundred thousand, but does no exceed one million five hundred thousand, of two hundred and twenty thousand dollars;

where the population of the province exceeds one million five hundred thousand, of two hundred and forty thousand dollars; and

(b) Subject to the special provisions of this Act as to the provinces of British Columbia and Prince Edward Island, a grant at the rate of eighty cents per head of the population of the province up to the number of two million five hundred thousand, and at the rate of sixty cents per head of so much of the population as exceeds that number.

(2) An additional grant of one hundred thousand dollars shall be made yearly to the province of British Columbia for a period of ten years from the commencement of this Act.

(3) The population of a province shall be ascertained from time to time in the case of the provinces of Manitoba, Saskatchewan, and Alberta respectively by the last quinquennial census or statutory estimate of population made under the Acts establishing those provinces or any other Act of the Parliament of Canada making provision for the purpose, and in the case of any other province by the last decennial census for the time being.

(4) The grants payable under this Act shall be paid half-yearly in advance to each province.

(5) The grants payable under this Act shall be substituted for the grants or subsidies (in this Act referred to as existing grants) payable for the like purposes at the commencement of this Act to the several provinces of the Dominion under the provisions of section one hundred and eighteen of the *Constitution Act, 1867*, or of any Order in Council establishing a province, or of any Act of the Parliament of Canada containing directions for the payment of any such grant or subsidy, and those provisions shall cease to have effect.

(6) The Government of Canada shall have the same power of deducting sums charged against a province on account of the interest on public debt in the case of the grant payable under this Act to the province as they have in the case of the existing grant.

(7) Nothing in this Act shall affect the obligation of the Government of Canada to pay to any province any grant which is payable to that province, other than the existing grant for which the grant under this Act is substituted.

(8) In the case of the provinces of British Columbia and Prince Edward Island, the amount paid on account of the grant payable per head of the population to the provinces under this Act shall not at any time be less than the amount of the corresponding grant payable at the commencement of this Act, and if it is found on any decennial census that the population of the province has decreased since the last decennial census, the amount paid on account of the grant shall not be decreased below the amount then payable, notwithstanding the decrease of the population.

Further Grant to
New Brunswick

119. New Brunswick shall receive by half-yearly Payments in advance from Canada for the Period of Ten Years from the Union an additional Allowance of Sixty-three thousand Dollars per Annum; but as long as the Public Debt of that Province remains under Seven million Dollars, a Deduction equal to the Interest at Five per Centum per Annum on such Deficiency shall be made from that Allowance of Sixty three thousand Dollars.[59]

Form of Payments

120. All Payments to be made under this Act, or in discharge of Liabilities created under any Act of the Provinces of Canada, Nova Scotia, and New Brunswick respectively, and assumed by Canada, shall, until the Parliament of Canada otherwise directs, be made in such Form and Manner as may from Time to Time be ordered by the Governor General in Council.

Canadian
Manufactures, etc.

121. All Articles of the Growth, Produce, or Manufacture of any one of the Provinces shall, from and after the Union, be admitted free into each of the other Provinces.

Continuance of
Customs and Excise
Laws

122. The Customs and Excise Laws of each Province shall, subject to the Provisions of this Act, continue in force until altered by the Parliament of Canada.[60]

Exportation and
Importation as
between Two
Provinces

123. Where Customs Duties are, at the Union, leviable on any Goods, Wares, or Merchandises in any Two Provinces, those Goods, Wares, and Merchandises may, from and after the Union, be imported from one of those Provinces into the other of them on Proof of Payment of the Customs Duty leviable thereon in the Province of Exportation, and on Payment of such further Amount (if any) of Customs Duty as is leviable thereon in the Province of Importation.[61]

See the *Provincial Subsidies Act*, R.S.C. 1985, c. P-26 and the *Federal-Provincial Fiscal Arrangements and Federal Post-Secondary Education and Health Contributions Act*, R.S.C. 1985, c. F-8.

See also Part III of the *Constitution Act, 1982*, which sets out commitments by Parliament and the provincial legislatures respecting equal opportunities, economic development and the provision of essential public services and a commitment by Parliament and the government of Canada to the principle of making equalization payments.

(59) Spent.

(60) Spent. Now covered by the *Customs Act*, R.S.C. 1985, c. 1 (2nd Supp.), the *Customs Tariff*, R.S.C. 1985, c. 41 (3rd Supp.), the *Excise Act*, R.S.C. 1985, c. E-14 and the *Excise Tax Act*, R.S.C. 1985, c. E-15.

(61) Spent.

124. Nothing in this Act shall affect the Right of New Brunswick to levy the Lumber Dues provided in Chapter Fifteen of Title Three of the Revised Statutes of New Brunswick, or in any Act amending that Act before or after the Union, and not increasing the Amount of such Dues; but the Lumber of any of the Provinces other than New Brunswick shall not be subject to such Dues.[62]

125. No Lands or Property belonging to Canada or any Province shall be liable to Taxation.

126. Such Portions of the Duties and Revenues over which the respective Legislatures of Canada, Nova Scotia, and New Brunswick had before the Union Power of Appropriation as are by this Act reserved to the respective Governments or Legislatures of the Provinces, and all Duties and Revenues raised by them in accordance with the special Powers conferred upon them by this Act, shall in each Province form One Consolidated Revenue Fund to be appropriated for the Public Service of the Province.

IX. MISCELLANEOUS PROVISIONS

General

127. Repealed.[63]

---

(62) These dues were repealed in 1873 by 36 Vict., c. 16 (N.B). And see *An Act respecting the Export Duties imposed on Lumber,* etc. (1873) 36 Vict., c. 41 (Canada), and section 2 of the *Provincial Subsidies Act,* R.S.C. 1985, c. P-26.

(63) Repealed by the *Statute Law Revision Act, 1893,* 56-57 Vict., c. 14 (U.K.). The section read as follows:

127. If any Person being at the passing of this Act a Member of the Legislative Council of Canada, Nova Scotia, or New Brunswick, to whom a Place in the Senate is offered, does not within Thirty Days thereafter, by Writing under his Hand addressed to the Governor General of the Province of Canada or to the Lieutenant Governor of Nova Scotia or New Brunswick (as the Case may be), accept the same, he shall be deemed to have declined the same; and any Person who, being at the passing of this Act a Member of the Legislative Council of Nova Scotia or New Brunswick, accepts a Place in the Senate shall thereby vacate his Seat in such Legislative Council.

Oath of Allegiance, etc.

128. Every Member of the Senate or House of Commons of Canada shall before taking his Seat therein take and subscribe before the Governor General or some Person authorized by him, and every Member of a Legislative Council or Legislative Assembly of any Province shall before taking his Seat therein take and subscribe before the Lieutenant Governor of the Province or some Person authorized by him, the Oath of Allegiance contained in the Fifth Schedule to this Act; and every Member of the Senate of Canada and every Member of the Legislative Council of Quebec shall also, before taking his Seat therein, take and subscribe before the Governor General, or some Person authorized by him, the Declaration of Qualification contained in the same Schedule.

Continuance of existing Laws, Courts, Officers, etc.

129. Except as otherwise provided by this Act, all Laws in force in Canada, Nova Scotia or New Brunswick at the Union, and all Courts of Civil and Criminal Jurisdiction, and all legal Commissions, Powers, and Authorities, and all Officers, Judicial, Administrative, and Ministerial, existing therein at the Union, shall continue in Ontario, Quebec, Nova Scotia, and New Brunswick respectively, as if the Union had not been made; subject nevertheless (except with respect to such as are enacted by or exist under Acts of the Parliament of Great Britain or of the Parliament of the United Kingdom of Great Britain and Ireland), to be repealed, abolished, or altered by the Parliament of Canada, or by the Legislature of the respective Province, according to the Authority of the Parliament or of that Legislature under this Act.[64]

Transfer of Officers to Canada

130. Until the Parliament of Canada otherwise provides, all Officers of the several Provinces having Duties to discharge in relation to Matters other than those coming within the Classes of Subjects by this Act assigned exclusively to the Legislatures of the Provinces shall be Officers of Canada, and shall continue to discharge the Duties of their respective Offices under the same Liabilities, Responsibilities, and Penalties as if the Union had not been made.[65]

Appointment of new Officers

131. Until the Parliament of Canada otherwise provides, the Governor General in Council may from Time to Time appoint such Officers as the Governor General in Council deems necessary or proper for the effectual Execution of this Act.

---

(64) The restriction against altering or repealing laws enacted by or existing under statutes of the United Kingdom was removed by the *Statute of Westminster, 1931*, 22 Geo. V. c. 4 (U.K.) except in respect of certain constitutional documents. Comprehensive procedures for amending enactments forming part of the Constitution of Canada were provided by Part V of the *Constitution Act, 1982*, (U.K.) 1982, c. 11.

(65) Spent.

132. The Parliament and Government of Canada shall have all Powers necessary or proper for performing the Obligations of Canada or of any Province thereof, as Part of the British Empire, towards Foreign Countries, arising under Treaties between the Empire and such Foreign Countries.

Treaty Obligations

133. Either the English or the French Language may be used by any Person in the Debates of the Houses of the Parliament of Canada and of the Houses of the Legislature of Quebec; and both those Languages shall be used in the respective Records and Journals of those Houses; and either of those Languages may be used by any Person or in any Pleading or Process in or issuing from any Court of Canada established under this Act, and in or from all or any of the Courts of Quebec.

Use of English and French Languages

The Acts of the Parliament of Canada and of the Legislature of Quebec shall be printed and published in both those Languages.[66]

Ontario and Quebec

134. Until the Legislature of Ontario or of Quebec otherwise provides, the Lieutenant Governors of Ontario and Quebec may each appoint under the Great Seal of the Province the following Officers, to hold Office during Pleasure, that is to say, — the Attorney General, the Secretary and Registrar of the Province, the Treasurer of the Province, the Commissioner of Crown Lands, and the Commissioner of Agriculture and Public Works, and in the Case of Quebec the Solicitor General, and may, by Order of the Lieutenant Governor in Council, from Time to Time prescribe the Duties of

Appointment of Executive Officers for Ontario and Quebec

---

(66) A similar provision was enacted for Manitoba by section 23 of the *Manitoba Act, 1870*, 33 Vict., c. 3 (Canada), (confirmed by the *Constitution Act, 1871*). Section 23 read as follows:

23. Either the English or the French language may be used by any person in the debates of the Houses of the Legislature, and both these languages shall be used in the respective Records and Journals of those Houses; and either of those languages may be used by any person, or in any Pleading or Process, in or issuing from any Court of Canada established under the British North America Act, 1867, or in or from all or any of the Courts of the Province. The Acts of the Legislature shall be printed and published in both those languages.

Sections 17 to 19 of the *Constitution Act, 1982*, restate the language rights set out in section 133 in respect of Parliament and the courts established under the *Constitution Act, 1867*, and also guarantees those rights in respect of the legislature of New Brunswick and the courts of that province.

Section 16 and sections 20, 21 and 23 of the *Constitution Act, 1982* recognize additional language rights in respect of the English and French languages. Section 22 preserves language rights and privileges of languages other than English and French.

those Officers, and of the several Departments over which they shall preside or to which they shall belong, and of the Officers and Clerks thereof, and may also appoint other and additional Officers to hold Office during Pleasure, and may from Time to Time prescribe the Duties of those Officers, and of the several Departments over which they shall preside or to which they shall belong, and of the Officers and Clerks thereof.[67]

Powers, Duties, etc. of Executive Officers

135. Until the Legislature of Ontario or Quebec otherwise provides, all Rights, Powers, Duties, Functions, Responsibilities, or Authorities at the passing of this Act vested in or imposed on the Attorney General, Solicitor General, Secretary and Registrar of the Province of Canada, Minister of Finance, Commissioner of Crown Lands, Commissioner of Public Works, and Minister of Agriculture and Receiver General, by any Law, Statute, or Ordinance of Upper Canada, Lower Canada, or Canada, and not repugnant to this Act, shall be vested in or imposed on any Officer to be appointed by the Lieutenant Governor for the Discharge of the same or any of them; and the Commissioner of Agriculture and Public Works shall perform the Duties and Functions of the Office of Minister of Agriculture at the passing of this Act imposed by the Law of the Province of Canada, as well as those of the Commissioner of Public Works.[68]

Great Seals

136. Until altered by the Lieutenant Governor in Council, the Great Seals of Ontario and Quebec respectively shall be the same, or of the same Design, as those used in the Provinces of Upper Canada and Lower Canada respectively before their Union as the Province of Canada.

Construction of temporary Acts

137. The words "and from thence to the End of the then next ensuing Session of the Legislature," or Words to the same Effect, used in any temporary Act of the Province of Canada not expired before the Union, shall be construed to extend and apply to the next Session of the Parliament of Canada if the Subject Matter of the Act is within the Powers of the same as defined by this Act, or to the next Sessions of the Legislatures of Ontario and Quebec respectively if the Subject Matter of the Act is within the Powers of the same as defined by this Act.

---

(67) Spent. Now covered in Ontario by the *Executive Council Act*, R.S.O. 1990, c. E.25 and in Quebec by the *Executive Power Act*, R.S.Q. 1977, c. E-18.

(68) Probably spent.

138. From and after the Union the Use of the Words "Upper Canada" instead of "Ontario," or "Lower Canada" instead of "Quebec," in any Deed, Writ, Process, Pleading, Document, Matter, or Thing shall not invalidate the same.

As to Errors in Names

139. Any Proclamation under the Great Seal of the Province of Canada issued before the Union to take effect at a Time which is subsequent to the Union, whether relating to that Province, or to Upper Canada, or to Lower Canada, and the several Matters and Things therein proclaimed, shall be and continue of like Force and Effect as if the Union had not been made.[69]

As to issue of Proclamations before Union, to commence after Union

140. Any Proclamation which is authorized by any Act of the Legislature of the Province of Canada to be issued under the Great Seal of the Province of Canada, whether relating to that Province, or to Upper Canada, or to Lower Canada, and which is not issued before the Union, may be issued by the Lieutenant Governor of Ontario or of Quebec, as its Subject Matter requires, under the Great Seal thereof; and from and after the Issue of such Proclamation the same and the several Matters and Things therein proclaimed shall be and continue of the like Force and Effect in Ontario or Quebec as if the Union had not been made.[70]

As to issue of Proclamations after Union

141. The Penitentiary of the Province of Canada shall, until the Parliament of Canada otherwise provides, be and continue the Penitentiary of Ontario and of Quebec.[71]

Penitentiary

142. The Division and Adjustment of the Debts, Credits, Liabilities, Properties, and Assets of Upper Canada and Lower Canada shall be referred to the Arbitrament of Three Arbitrators, One chosen by the Government of Ontario, One by the Government of Quebec, and One by the Government of Canada; and the Selection of the Arbitrators shall not be made until the Parliament of Canada and the Legislatures of Ontario and Quebec have met; and the Arbitrator chosen by the Government of Canada shall not be a Resident either in Ontario or in Quebec.[72]

Arbitration respecting Debts, etc.

---

(69) Probably spent.

(70) Probably spent.

(71) Spent. Penitentiaries are now provided for by the *Corrections and Conditional Release Act*, S.C. 1992, c. 20.

(72) Spent. See pages (xi) and (xii) of the Public Accounts, 1902-1903.

Division of Records

143. The Governor General in Council may from Time to Time order that such and so many of the Records, Books, and Documents of the Province of Canada as he thinks fit shall be appropriated and delivered either to Ontario or to Quebec, and the same shall thenceforth be the Property of that Province; and any Copy thereof or Extract therefrom, duly certified by the Officer having charge of the Original thereof, shall be admitted as Evidence.[73]

Constitution of Townships in Quebec

144. The Lieutenant Governor of Quebec may from Time to Time, by Proclamation under the Great Seal of the Province, to take effect from a Day to be appointed therein, constitute Townships in those Parts of the Province of Quebec in which Townships are not then already constituted, and fix the Metes and Bounds thereof.

X. INTERCOLONIAL RAILWAY

145. Repealed.[74]

XI. ADMISSION OF OTHER COLONIES

Power to admit Newfoundland, etc., into the Union

146. It shall be lawful for the Queen, by and with the Advice of Her Majesty's Most Honourable Privy Council, on Addresses from the Houses of the Parliament of Canada, and from the Houses of the respective Legislatures of the Colonies or Provinces of Newfoundland, Prince Edward Island, and British Columbia, to admit those Colonies or Provinces, or any of them, into the Union, and on Address from the Houses of the Parliament of Canada to admit Rupert's Land and the North-western Territory, or either of them, into the Union, on such Terms and Conditions in each Case as are in the Addresses expressed and as the Queen thinks fit to approve, subject to the Provisions of this Act; and the Provisions of any Order in Council in that Behalf shall have effect as if they had been enacted by the Parliament of the United Kingdom of Great Britain and Ireland.[75]

---

(73) Probably spent. Two orders were made under this section on January 24, 1868.

(74) Repealed by the *Statute Law Revision Act, 1893*, 56-57 Vict., c. 14 (U.K.). The section read as follows:

X. Intercolonial Railway

145. Inasmuch as the Provinces of Canada, Nova Scotia, and New Brunswick have joined in a Declaration that the Construction of the Intercolonial Railway is essential to the Consolidation of the Union of British North America, and to the Assent thereto of Nova Scotia and New Brunswick, and have consequently agreed that Provision should be made for its immediate Construction by the Government of Canada; Therefore, in order to give effect to that Agreement, it shall be the Duty of the Government and Parliament of Canada to provide for the Commencement, within Six Months after the Union, of a Railway connecting the River St. Lawrence with the City of Halifax in Nova Scotia, and for the Construction thereof without Intermission, and the Completion thereof with all practicable Speed.

(75) All territories mentioned in this section are now part of Canada. See the notes to section 5, *supra*.

147. In case of the Admission of Newfoundland and Prince Edward Island, or either of them, each shall be entitled to a Representation in the Senate of Canada of Four Members, and (notwithstanding anything in this Act) in case of the Admission of Newfoundland the normal Number of Senators shall be Seventy-six and their maximum Number shall be Eighty-two; but Prince Edward Island when admitted shall be deemed to be comprised in the third of the Three Divisions into which Canada is, in relation to the Constitution of the Senate, divided by this Act, and accordingly, after the Admission of Prince Edward Island, whether Newfoundland is admitted or not, the Representation of Nova Scotia and New Brunswick in the Senate shall, as Vacancies occur, be reduced from Twelve to Ten Members respectively, and the Representation of each of those Provinces shall not be increased at any Time beyond Ten, except under the Provisions of this Act for the Appointment of Three or Six additional Senators under the Direction of the Queen.[76]

---

(76) Spent. See the notes to sections 21, 22, 26, 27 and 28, *supra*.

SCHEDULES

THE FIRST SCHEDULE[77]

Electoral Districts of Ontario

A.

EXISTING ELECTORAL DIVISIONS

COUNTIES

1. Prescott.
2. Glengarry.
3. Stormont.
4. Dundas.
5. Russell.
6. Carleton.
7. Prince Edward.
8. Halton.
9. Essex.

RIDINGS OF COUNTIES

10. North Riding of Lanark.
11. South Riding of Lanark.
12. North Riding of Leeds and North Riding of Grenville.
13. South Riding of Leeds.
14. South Riding of Grenville.
15. East Riding of Northumberland.
16. West Riding of Northumberland (excepting therefrom the Township of South Monaghan).
17. East Riding of Durham.
18. West Riding of Durham.
19. North Riding of Ontario.
20. South Riding of Ontario.
21. East Riding of York.
22. West Riding of York.
23. North Riding of York.
24. North Riding of Wentworth.
25. South Riding of Wentworth.
26. East Riding of Elgin.

---

(77) Spent. *Representation Act*, R.S.O. 1990, c. R.26.

27. West Riding of Elgin.
28. North Riding of Waterloo.
29. South Riding of Waterloo.
30. North Riding of Brant.
31. South Riding of Brant.
32. North Riding of Oxford.
33. South Riding of Oxford.
34. East Riding of Middlesex.

CITIES, PARTS OF CITIES, AND TOWNS

35. West Toronto.
36. East Toronto.
37. Hamilton.
38. Ottawa.
39. Kingston.
40. London.
41. Town of Brockville, with the Township of Elizabethtown thereto attached.
42. Town of Niagara, with the Township of Niagara thereto attached.
43. Town of Cornwall, with the Township of Cornwall thereto attached.

B.

NEW ELECTORAL DIVISIONS

44. The Provisional Judicial District of ALGOMA.

The County of BRUCE, divided into Two Ridings, to be called respectively the North and South Ridings:

45. The North Riding of Bruce to consist of the Townships of Bury, Lindsay, Eastnor, Albermarle, Amable, Arran, Bruce, Elderslie, and Saugeen, and the Village of Southampton.

46. The South Riding of Bruce to consist of the Townships of Kincardine (including the Village of Kincardine), Greenock, Brant, Huron, Kinloss, Culross, and Carrick.

The County of HURON, divided into Two Ridings, to be called respectively the North and South Ridings:

47. The North Riding to consist of the Townships of Ashfield, Wawanosh, Turnberry, Howick, Morris, Grey, Colborne, Hullett, including the Village of Clinton, and McKillop.

48. The South Riding to consist of the Town of Goderich and the Townships of Goderich, Tuckersmith, Stanley, Hay, Usborne, and Stephen.

The County of MIDDLESEX divided into three Ridings, to be called respectively the North, West, and East Ridings:

49. The North Riding to consist of the Townships of McGillivary and Biddulph (taken from the County of Huron), and Williams East, Williams West, Adelaide, and Lobo.

50. The West Riding to consist of the Townships of Delaware, Carradoc, Metcalfe, Mosa and Ekfrid, and the Village of Strathroy.

[The East Riding to consist of the Townships now embraced therein, and be bounded as it is at present.]

51. The County of LAMBTON to consist of Townships of Bosanquet, Warwick, Plympton, Sarnia, Moore, Enniskillen, and Brooke, and the Town of Sarnia.

52. The County of KENT to consist of the Townships of Chatham, Dover, East Tilbury, Romney, Raleigh, and Harwich, and the Town of Chatham.

53. The County of BOTHWELL to consist of the Townships of Sombra, Dawn, and Euphemia (taken from the County of Lambton), and the Townships of Zone, Camden with the Gore thereof, Orford, and Howard (taken from the County of Kent).

The County of GREY divided into Two Ridings to be called respectively the South and North Ridings:

54. The South Riding to consist of the Townships of Bentinck, Glenelg, Artemesia, Osprey, Normanby, Egremont, Proton, and Melancthon.

55. The North Riding to consist of the Townships of Collingwood, Euphrasia, Holland, Saint-Vincent, Sydenham, Sullivan, Derby, and Keppel, Sarawak and Brooke, and the Town of Owen Sound.

The County of PERTH divided into Two Ridings, to be called respectively the South and North Ridings:

56. The North Riding to consist of the Townships of Wallace, Elma, Logan, Ellice, Mornington, and North Easthope, and the Town of Stratford.

57. The South Riding to consist of the Townships of Blanchard, Downie, South Easthope, Fullarton, Hibbert, and the Villages of Mitchell and Ste. Marys.

The County of WELLINGTON divided into Three Ridings to be called respectively North, South and Centre Ridings:

58. The North Riding to consist of the Townships of Amaranth, Arthur, Luther, Minto, Maryborough, Peel, and the Village of Mount Forest.

59. The Centre Riding to consist of the Townships of Garafraxa, Erin, Eramosa, Nichol, and Pilkington, and the Villages of Fergus and Elora.

60. The South Riding to consist of the Town of Guelph, and the Townships of Guelph and Puslinch.

The County of NORFOLK, divided into Two Ridings, to be called respectively the South and North Ridings:

61. The South Riding to consist of the Townships of Charlotteville, Houghton, Walsingham, and Woodhouse, and with the Gore thereof.

62. The North Riding to consist of the Townships of Middleton, Townsend, and Windham, and the Town of Simcoe.

63. The County of HALDIMAND to consist of the Townships of Oneida, Seneca, Cayuga North, Cayuga South, Raynham, Walpole, and Dunn.

64. The County of MONCK to consist of the Townships of Canborough and Moulton, and Sherbrooke, and the Village of Dunnville (taken from the County of Haldimand), the Townships of Caister and Gainsborough (taken from the County of Lincoln), and the Townships of Pelham and Wainfleet (taken from the County of Welland).

65. The County of LINCOLN to consist of the Townships of Clinton, Grantham, Grimsby, and Louth, and the Town of St. Catharines.

66. The County of WELLAND to consist of the Townships of Bertie, Crowland, Humberstone, Stamford, Thorold, and Willoughby, and the Villages of Chippewa, Clifton, Fort Erie, Thorold, and Welland.

67. The County of PEEL to consist of the Townships of Chinguacousy, Toronto, and the Gore of Toronto, and the Villages of Brampton and Streetsville.

68. The County of CARDWELL to consist of the Townships of Albion and Caledon (taken from the County of Peel), and the Townships of Adjala and Mono (taken from the County of Simcoe).

The County of SIMCOE, divided into Two Ridings, to be called respectively the South and North Ridings:

69. The South Riding to consist of the Townships of West Gwillimbury, Tecumseth, Innisfil, Essa, Tosorontio, Mulmur, and the Village of Bradford.

70. The North Riding to consist of the Townships of Sunnidale, Vespra, Flos, Oro, Medonte, Orillia and Matchedash, Tiny and Tay, Balaklava and Robinson, and the Towns of Barrie and Collingwood.

The County of VICTORIA, divided into Two Ridings, to be called respectively the South and North Ridings:

71. The South Riding to consist of the Townships of Ops, Mariposa, Emily, Verulam, and the Town of Lindsay.

72. The North Riding to consist of the Townships of Anson, Bexley, Carden, Dalton, Digby, Eldon, Fenelon, Hindon, Laxton, Lutterworth, Macaulay and Draper, Sommerville, and Morrison, Muskoka, Monck and Watt (taken from the County of Simcoe), and any other surveyed Townships lying to the North of the said North Riding.

The County of PETERBOROUGH, divided into Two Ridings, to be called respectively the West and East Ridings:

73. The West Riding to consist of the Townships of South Monaghan (taken from the County of Northumberland),

North Monaghan, Smith, and Ennismore, and the Town of Peterborough.

74. The East Riding to consist of the Townships of Asphodel, Belmont and Methuen, Douro, Dummer, Galway, Harvey, Minden, Stanhope and Dysart, Otonabee, and Snowden, and the Village of Ashburnham, and any other surveyed Townships lying to the North of the said East Riding.

The County of HASTINGS, divided into Three Ridings, to be called respectively the West, East, and North Ridings:

75. The West Riding to consist of the Town of Belleville, the Township of Sydney, and the Village of Trenton.

76. The East Riding to consist of the Townships of Thurlow, Tyendinaga, and Hungerford.

77. The North Riding to consist of the Townships of Rawdon, Huntingdon, Madoc, Elzevir, Tudor, Marmora, and Lake, and the Village of Stirling, and any other surveyed Townships lying to the North of the said North Riding.

78. The County of LENNOX to consist of the Townships of Richmond, Adolphustown, North Fredericksburg, South Fredericksburg, Ernest Town, and Amherst Island, and the Village of Napanee.

79. The County of ADDINGTON to consist of the Townships of Camden, Portland, Sheffield, Hinchinbrooke, Kaladar, Kennebec, Olden, Oso, Anglesea, Barrie, Clarendon, Palmerston, Effingham, Abinger, Miller, Canonto, Denbigh, Loughborough, and Bedford.

80. The County of FRONTENAC to consist of the Townships of Kingston, Wolfe Island, Pittsburg and Howe Island, and Storrington.

The County of RENFREW, divided into Two Ridings, to be called respectively the South and North Ridings:

81. The South Riding to consist of the Townships of McNab, Bagot, Blithfield, Brougham, Horton, Admaston, Grattan, Matawatchan, Griffith, Lyndoch, Raglan, Radcliffe, Brudenell, Sebastopol, and the Villages of Arnprior and Renfrew.

82. The North Riding to consist of the Townships of Ross, Bromley, Westmeath, Stafford, Pembroke, Wilberforce, Alice, Petawawa, Buchanan, South Algona, North Algona, Fraser, McKay, Wylie, Rolph, Head, Maria, Clara, Haggerty, Sherwood, Burns, and Richards, and any other surveyed Townships lying North-westerly of the said North Riding.

————————

Every Town and incorporated Village existing at the Union, not especially mentioned in this Schedule, is to be taken as Part of the County or Riding within which it is locally situate.

————————
————————

THE SECOND SCHEDULE

————————

Electoral Districts of Quebec specially fixed

COUNTIES OF —

Pontiac.	Missisquoi.	Compton.
Ottawa.	Brome.	Wolfe and
Argenteuil.	Shefford.	Richmond.
Huntingdon.	Stanstead.	Megantic.
	Town of Sherbrooke.	

————————
————————

THE THIRD SCHEDULE

————————

Provincial Publics Works and Property to be the Property of Canada

1. Canals, with Lands and Water Power connected therewith.
2. Public Harbours.
3. Lighthouses and Piers, and Sable Island.
4. Steamboats, Dredges, and public Vessels.
5. Rivers and Lake Improvements.

6. Railways and Railway Stocks, Mortgages, and other Debts due by Railway Companies.

7. Military Roads.

8. Custom Houses, Post Offices, and all other Public Buildings, except such as the Government of Canada appropriate for the Use of the Provincial Legislatures and Governments

9. Property transferred by the Imperial Government, and known as Ordnance Property.

10. Armouries, Drill Sheds, Military Clothing, and Munitions of War, and Lands set apart for general Public Purposes.

THE FOURTH SCHEDULE

Assets to be the Property of Ontario and Quebec conjointly

Upper Canada Building Fund.
Lunatic Asylums.
Normal School.
Court Houses in ⎫
Aylmer. ⎪
Montreal. ⎬ Lower Canada.
Kamouraska. ⎭
Law Society, Upper Canada.
Montreal Turnpike Trust.
University Permanent Fund.
Royal Institution.
Consolidated Municipal Loan Fund, Upper Canada.
Consolidated Municipal Loan Fund, Lower Canada.
Agricultural Society, Upper Canada.
Lower Canada Legislative Grant.
Quebec Fire Loan.
Temiscouata Advance Account.
Quebec Turnpike Trust.
Education — East.
Building and Jury Fund, Lower Canada.
Municipalities Fund.
Lower Canada Superior Education Income Fund.

THE FIFTH SCHEDULE

OATH OF ALLEGIANCE

I *A.B.* do swear, That I will be faithful and bear true Allegiance to Her Majesty Queen Victoria.

Note. — The Name of the King or Queen of the United Kingdom of Great Britain and Ireland for the Time being is to be substituted from Time to Time, with proper Terms of Reference thereto.

DECLARATION OF QUALIFICATION

I *A.B.* do declare and testify, That I am by Law duly qualified to be appointed a Member of the Senate of Canada [*or as the Case may be*], and that I am legally or equitably seised as of Freehold for my own Use and Benefit of Lands of Tenements held in Free and Common Socage [*or* seised or possessed for my own Use and Benefit of Lands or Tenements held in Franc-alleu or in Roture (*as the Case may be*),] in the Province of Nova Scotia [*or as the Case may be*] of the Value of Four thousand Dollars over and above all Rents, Dues, Debts, Mortgages, Charges, and Incumbrances due or payable out of or charged on or affecting the same, and that I have not collusively or colourably obtained a Title to or become possessed of the said Lands and Tenements or any Part thereof for the Purpose of enabling me to become a Member of the Senate of Canada [*or as the Case may be*], and that my Real and Personal Property are together worth Four thousand Dollars over and above my Debts and Liabilities.

THE SIXTH SCHEDULE[78]

Primary Production from Non-Renewable Natural Resources and Forestry Resources

1. For the purposes of Section 92A of this Act,

---

(78) As enacted by the *Constitution Act, 1982.*

(*a*) production from a non-renewable natural resource is primary production therefrom if

(i) it is in the form in which it exists upon its recovery or severance from its natural state, or

(ii) it is a product resulting from processing or refining the resource, and is not a manufactured product or a product resulting from refining crude oil, refining upgraded heavy crude oil, refining gases or liquids derived from coal or refining a synthetic equivalent of crude oil; and

(*b*) production from a forestry resource is primary production therefrom if it consists of sawlogs, poles, lumber, wood chips, sawdust or any other primary wood product, or wood pulp, and is not a product manufactured from wood.

SCHEDULE B

CONSTITUTION ACT, 1982[79]

PART I

CANADIAN CHARTER OF RIGHTS AND FREEDOMS

Whereas Canada is founded upon principles that recognize the supremacy of God and the rule of law:

Guarantee of Rights and Freedoms

Rights and freedoms in Canada

1. The *Canadian Charter of Rights and Freedoms* guarantees the rights and freedoms set out in it subject only to such reasonable limits prescribed by law as can be demonstrably justified in a free and democratic society.

Fundamental Freedoms

Fundamental freedoms

2. Everyone has the following fundamental freedoms:

(*a*) freedom of conscience and religion;
(*b*) freedom of thought, belief, opinion and expression, including freedom of the press and other media of communication;

---

(79) Enacted as Schedule B to the *Canada Act 1982,* (U.K.) 1982, c. 11, which came into force on April 17, 1982. *The Canada Act 1982,* other than Schedules A and B thereto, reads as follows:

An Act to give effect to a request by the Senate and House of Commons of Canada

Whereas Canada has requested and consented to the enactment of an Act of the Parliament of the United Kingdom to give effect to the provisions hereinafter set forth and the Senate and the House of Commons of Canada in Parliament assembled have submitted an address to Her Majesty requesting that Her Majesty may graciously be pleased to cause a Bill to be laid before the Parliament of the United Kingdom for that purpose.

Be it therefore enacted by the Queen's Most Excellent Majesty, by and with the advice and consent of the Lords Spiritual and Temporal, and Commons, in this present Parliament assembled, and by the authority of the same, as follows:

1. The *Constitution Act, 1982* set out in Schedule B to this Act is hereby enacted for and shall have the force of law in Canada and shall come into force as provided in that Act.

2. No Act of Parliament of the United Kingdom passed after the *Constitution Act, 1982* comes into force shall extend to Canada as part of its law.

3. So far as it is not contained in Schedule B, the French version of this Act is set out in Schedule A to this Act and has the same authority in Canada as the English version thereof.

4. This Act may be cited as the *Canada Act 1982.*

(*c*) freedom of peaceful assembly; and

(*d*) freedom of association.

Democratic Rights

3. Every citizen of Canada has the right to vote in an election of members of the House of Commons or of a legislative assembly and to be qualified for membership therein.

Democratic rights of citizens

4. (1) No House of Commons and no legislative assembly shall continue for longer than five years from the date fixed for the return of the writs of a general election of its members.[80]

Maximum duration of legislative bodies

(2) In time of real or apprehended war, invasion or insurrection, a House of Commons may be continued by Parliament and a legislative assembly may be continued by the legislature beyond five years if such continuation is not opposed by the votes of more than one-third of the members of the House of Commons or the legislative assembly, as the case may be.[81]

Continuation in special circumstances

5. There shall be a sitting of Parliament and of each legislature at least once every twelve months.[82]

Annual sitting of legislative bodies

Mobility Rights

6. (1) Every citizen of Canada has the right to enter, remain in and leave Canada.

Mobility of citizens

(2) Every citizen of Canada and every person who has the status of a permanent resident of Canada has the right

Rights to move and gain livelihood

(*a*) to move to and take up residence in any province; and

(*b*) to pursue the gaining of a livelihood in any province.

(3) The rights specified in subsection (2) are subject to

Limitation

(*a*) any laws or practices of general application in force in a province other than those that discriminate among persons primarily on the basis of province of present or previous residence; and

---

(80) See section 50 and the footnotes to sections 85 and 88 of the *Constitution Act, 1867.*

(81) Replaces part of Class 1 of section 91 of the *Constitution Act, 1867,* which was repealed as set out in subitem 1(3) of the Schedule to this Act.

(82) See the footnotes to sections 20, 86 and 88 of the *Constitution Act, 1867.*

(*b*) any laws providing for reasonable residency require-ments as a qualification for the receipt of publicly pro-vided social services.

Affirmative action programs

(4) Subsections (2) and (3) do not preclude any law, program or activity that has as its object the amelioration in a province of con-ditions of individuals in that province who are socially or economi-cally disadvantaged if the rate of employment in that province is below the rate of employment in Canada.

Legal Rights

Life, liberty and security of person

7. Everyone has the right to life, liberty and security of the person and the right not to be deprived thereof except in accor-dance with the principles of fundamental justice.

Search or seizure

8. Everyone has the right to be secure against unreasonable search or seizure.

Detention or imprisonment

9. Everyone has the right not to be arbitrarily detained or imprisoned.

Arrest or detention

10. Everyone has the right on arrest or detention

(*a*) to be informed promptly of the reasons therefor;

(*b*) to retain and instruct counsel without delay and to be informed of that right; and

(*c*) to have the validity of the detention determined by way of *habeas corpus* and to be released if the detention is not lawful.

Proceedings in criminal and penal matters

11. Any person charged with an offence has the right

(*a*) to be informed without unreasonable delay of the specific offence;

(*b*) to be tried within a reasonable time;

(*c*) not to be compelled to be a witness in proceedings against that person in respect of the offence;

(*d*) to be presumed innocent until proven guilty according to law in a fair and public hearing by an independent and impartial tribunal;

(*e*) not to be denied reasonable bail without just cause;

(*f*) except in the case of an offence under military law tried before a military tribunal, to the benefit of trial by jury where the maximum punishment for the offence is imprisonment for five years or a more severe punishment;

(*g*) not to be found guilty on account of any act or omission unless, at the time of the act or omission, it constituted an offence under Canadian or international law or was criminal according to the general principles of law recognized by the community of nations;

(*h*) if finally acquitted of the offence, not to be tried for it again and, if finally found guilty and punished for the offence, not to be tried or punished for it again; and

(*i*) if found guilty of the offence and if the punishment for the offence has been varied between the time of commission and the time of sentencing, to the benefit of the lesser punishment.

12. Everyone has the right not to be subjected to any cruel and unusual treatment or punishment.

Treatment or punishment

13. A witness who testifies in any proceedings has the right not to have any incriminating evidence so given used to incriminate that witness in any other proceedings, except in a prosecution for perjury or for the giving of contradictory evidence.

Self-crimination

14. A party or witness in any proceedings who does not understand or speak the language in which the proceedings are conducted or who is deaf has the right to the assistance of an interpreter.

Interpreter

Equality Rights

15. (1) Every individual is equal before and under the law and has the right to the equal protection and equal benefit of the law without discrimination and, in particular, without discrimination based on race, national or ethnic origin, colour, religion, sex, age or mental or physical disability.

Equality before and under law and equal protection and benefit of law

Affirmative action programs

(2) Subsection (1) does not preclude any law, program or activity that has as its object the amelioration of conditions of disadvantaged individuals or groups including those that are disadvantaged because of race, national or ethnic origin, colour, religion, sex, age or mental or physical disability.[83]

Official Languages of Canada

Official languages of Canada

16. (1) English and French are the official languages of Canada and have equality of status and equal rights and privileges as to their use in all institutions of the Parliament and government of Canada.

Official languages of New Brunswick

(2) English and French are the official languages of New Brunswick and have equality of status and equal rights and privileges as to their use in all institutions of the legislature and government of New Brunswick.

Advancement of status and use

(3) Nothing in this Charter limits the authority of Parliament or a legislature to advance the equality of status or use of English and French.

English and French linguistic communities in New Brunswick

16.1. (1) The English linguistic community and the French linguistic community in New Brunswick have equality of status and equal rights and privileges, including the right to distinct educational institutions and such distinct cultural institutions as are necessary for the preservation and promotion of those communities.

Role of the legislature and government of New Brunswick

(2) The role of the legislature and government of New Brunswick to preserve and promote the status, rights and privileges referred to in subsection (1) is affirmed.[83.1]

Proceedings of Parliament

17. (1) Everyone has the right to use English or French in any debates and other proceedings of Parliament.[84]

Proceedings of New Brunswick legislature

(2) Everyone has the right to use English or French in any debates and other proceedings of the legislature of New Brunswick.[85]

---

(83) Subsection 32(2) provides that section 15 shall not have effect until three years after section 32 comes into force.

Section 32 came into force on April 17, 1982; therefore, section 15 had effect on April 17, 1985.

(83.1) Section 16.1 was added by the *Constitution Amendment, 1993 (New Brunswick)*. See SI/93-54.

(84) See section 133 of the *Constitution Act, 1867,* and the footnote thereto.

(85) *Id.*

18. (1) The statutes, records and journals of Parliament shall be printed and published in English and French and both language versions are equally authoritative.[86]

(2) The statutes, records and journals of the legislature of New Brunswick shall be printed and published in English and French and both language versions are equally authoritative.[87]

19. (1) Either English or French may be used by any person in, or in any pleading in or process issuing from, any court established by Parliament.[88]

(2) Either English or French may be used by any person in, or in any pleading in or process issuing from, any court of New Brunswick.[89]

20. (1) Any member of the public in Canada has the right to communicate with, and to receive available services from, any head or central office of an institution of the Parliament or government of Canada in English or French, and has the same right with respect to any other office of any such institution where

    (*a*) there is a significant demand for communications with and services from that office in such language; or

    (*b*) due to the nature of the office, it is reasonable that communications with and services from that office be available in both English and French.

(2) Any member of the public in New Brunswick has the right to communicate with, and to receive available services from, any office of an institution of the legislature or government of New Brunswick in English or French.

21. Nothing in sections 16 to 20 abrogates or derogates from any right, privilege or obligation with respect to the English and French languages, or either of them, that exists or is continued by virtue of any other provision of the Constitution of Canada.[90]

---

(86) *Id.*

(87) *Id.*

(88) *Id.*

(89) *Id.*

(90) See, for example, section 133 of the *Constitution Act, 1867,* and the reference to the *Manitoba Act, 1870,* in the footnote thereto.

Rights and privileges preserved

22. Nothing in sections 16 to 20 abrogates or derogates from any legal or customary right or privilege acquired or enjoyed either before or after the coming into force of this Charter with respect to any language that is not English or French.

Minority Language Educational Rights

Language of instruction

23. (1) Citizens of Canada

(*a*) whose first language learned and still understood is that of the English or French linguistic minority population of the province in which they reside, or

(*b*) who have received their primary school instruction in Canada in English or French and reside in a province where the language in which they received that instruction is the language of the English or French linguistic minority population of the province,

have the right to have their children receive primary and secondary school instruction in that language in that province.[91]

Continuity of language instruction

(2) Citizens of Canada of whom any child has received or is receiving primary or secondary school instruction in English or French in Canada, have the right to have all their children receive primary and secondary school instruction in the same language.

Application where numbers warrant

(3) The right of citizens of Canada under subsections (1) and (2) to have their children receive primary and secondary school instruction in the language of the English or French linguistic minority population of a province

(*a*) applies wherever in the province the number of children of citizens who have such a right is sufficient to warrant the provision to them out of public funds of minority language instruction; and

(*b*) includes, where the number of those children so warrants, the right to have them receive that instruction in minority language educational facilities provided out of public funds.

---

(91) Paragraph 23(1)(*a*) is not in force in respect of Quebec. See section 59 *infra*.

Enforcement

24. (1) Anyone whose rights or freedoms, as guaranteed by this Charter, have been infringed or denied may apply to a court of competent jurisdiction to obtain such remedy as the court considers appropriate and just in the circumstances.

Enforcement of guaranteed rights and freedoms

(2) Where, in proceedings under subsection (1), a court concludes that evidence was obtained in a manner that infringed or denied any rights or freedoms guaranteed by this Charter, the evidence shall be excluded if it is established that, having regard to all the circumstances, the admission of it in the proceedings would bring the administration of justice into disrepute.

Exclusion of evidence bringing administration of justice into disrepute

General

25. The guarantee in this Charter of certain rights and freedoms shall not be construed so as to abrogate or derogate from any aboriginal, treaty or other rights or freedoms that pertain to the aboriginal peoples of Canada including

Aboriginal rights and freedoms not affected by Charter

(*a*) any rights or freedoms that have been recognized by the Royal Proclamation of October 7, 1763; and

(*b*) any rights or freedoms that now exist by way of land claims agreements or may be so acquired.[92]

26. The guarantee in this Charter of certain rights and freedoms shall not be construed as denying the existence of any other rights or freedoms that exist in Canada.

Other rights and freedoms not affected by Charter

27. This Charter shall be interpreted in a manner consistent with the preservation and enhancement of the multicultural heritage of Canadians.

Multicultural heritage

28. Notwithstanding anything in this Charter, the rights and freedoms referred to in it are guaranteed equally to male and female persons.

Rights guaranteed equally to both sexes

29. Nothing in this Charter abrogates or derogates from any rights or privileges guaranteed by or under the Constitution of Canada in respect of denominational, separate or dissentient schools.[93]

Rights respecting certain schools preserved

---

(92) Paragraph 25(*b*) was repealed and re-enacted by the *Constitution Amendment Proclamation, 1983. See* SI/84-102.

Paragraph 25(*b*) as originally enacted read as follows:

"(*b*) any rights or freedoms that may be acquired by the aboriginal peoples of Canada by way of land claims settlement."

(93) See section 93 of the *Constitution Act, 1867,* and the footnote thereto.

Application to territories and territorial authorities

30. A reference in this Charter to a Province or to the legislative assembly or legislature of a province shall be deemed to include a reference to the Yukon Territory and the Northwest Territories, or to the appropriate legislative authority thereof, as the case may be.

Legislative powers not extended

31. Nothing in this Charter extends the legislative powers of any body or authority.

Application of Charter

Application of Charter

32. (1) This Charter applies

> (*a*) to the Parliament and government of Canada in respect of all matters within the authority of Parliament including all matters relating to the Yukon Territory and Northwest Territories; and

> (*b*) to the legislature and government of each province in respect of all matters within the authority of the legislature of each province.

Exception

(2) Notwithstanding subsection (1), section 15 shall not have effect until three years after this section comes into force.

Exception where express declaration

33. (1) Parliament or the legislature of a province may expressly declare in an Act of Parliament or of the legislature, as the case may be, that the Act or a provision thereof shall operate notwithstanding a provision included in section 2 or sections 7 to 15 of this Charter.

Operation of exception

(2) An Act or a provision of an Act in respect of which a declaration made under this section is in effect shall have such operation as it would have but for the provision of this Charter referred to in the declaration.

Five year limitation

(3) A declaration made under subsection (1) shall cease to have effect five years after it comes into force or on such earlier date as may be specified in the declaration.

Re-enactment

(4) Parliament or the legislature of a province may re-enact a declaration made under subsection (1).

Five year limitation

(5) Subsection (3) applies in respect of a re-enactment made under subsection (4).

Citation

Citation

34. This Part may be cited as the *Canadian Charter of Rights and Freedoms.*

PART II

RIGHTS OF THE ABORIGINAL PEOPLES OF CANADA

35. (1) The existing aboriginal and treaty rights of the aboriginal peoples of Canada are hereby recognized and affirmed.

Recognition of existing aboriginal and treaty rights

(2) In this Act, "aboriginal peoples of Canada" includes the Indian, Inuit and Métis peoples of Canada.

Definition of "aboriginal peoples of Canada"

(3) For greater certainty, in subsection (1) "treaty rights" includes rights that now exist by way of land claims agreements or may be so acquired.

Land claims agreements

(4) Notwithstanding any other provision of this Act, the aboriginal and treaty rights referred to in subsection (1) are guaranteed equally to male and female persons.[94]

Aboriginal and treaty rights are guaranteed equally to both sexes

35.1 The government of Canada and the provincial governments are committed to the principle that, before any amendment is made to Class 24 of section 91 of the *"Constitution Act, 1867"*, to section 25 of this Act or to this Part,

Commitment to participation in constitutional conference.

(*a*) a constitutional conference that includes in its agenda an item relating to the proposed amendment, composed of the Prime Minister of Canada and the first ministers of the provinces, will be convened by the Prime Minister of Canada; and

(*b*) the Prime Minister of Canada will invite representatives of the aboriginal peoples of Canada to participate in the discussions on that item.[95]

---

(94) Subsections 35(3) and (4) were added by the *Constitution Amendment Proclamation, 1983. See* SI/84-102.

(95) Section 35.1 was added by the *Constitution Amendment Proclamation, 1983. See* SI/84-102.

THE CONSTITUTION ACTS, 1867 TO 1982

PART III

EQUALIZATION AND REGIONAL DISPARITIES

Commitment to
promote equal
opportunities

36. (1) Without altering the legislative authority of Parliament or of the provincial legislatures, or the rights of any of them with respect to the exercise of their legislative authority, Parliament and the legislatures, together with the government of Canada and the provincial governments, are committed to

(*a*) promoting equal opportunities for the well-being of Canadians;

(*b*) furthering economic development to reduce disparity in opportunities; and

(*c*) providing essential public services of reasonable quality to all Canadians.

Commitment
respecting public
services

(2) Parliament and the government of Canada are committed to the principle of making equalization payments to ensure that provincial governments have sufficient revenues to provide reasonably comparable levels of public services at reasonably comparable levels of taxation.[96]

PART IV

CONSTITUTIONAL CONFERENCE

37.[97]

---

(96) See the footnotes to sections 114 and 118 of the *Constitution Act, 1867.*

(97) Section 54 provided for the repeal of Part IV one year after Part VII came into force. Part VII came into force on April 17, 1982 thereby repealing Part IV on April 17, 1983.

Part IV, as originally enacted, read as follows:

37.1 (1) A constitutional conference composed of the Prime Minister of Canada and the first ministers of the provinces shall be convened by the Prime Minister of Canada within one year after this Part comes into force.

(2) The conference convened under subsection (1) shall have included in its agenda an item respecting constitutional matters that directly affect the aboriginal peoples of Canada, including the identification and definition of the rights of those peoples to be included in the Constituion of Canada, and the Prime Minister of Canada shall invite representatives of those peoples to participate in the discussions on that item.

(3) The Prime Minister of Canada shall invite elected representatives of the governments of the Yukon Territory and the Northwest Territories to participate in the discussions on any item on the agenda of the conference convened under subsection (1) that, in the opinion of the Prime Minister, directly affects the Yukon Territory and the Northwest Territories.

PART IV.1

CONSTITUTIONAL CONFERENCES

37.1.[98]

PART V

PROCEDURE FOR AMENDING CONSTITUTION OF CANADA[99]

38. (1) An amendment to the Constitution of Canada may be made by proclamation issued by the Governor General under the Great Seal of Canada where so authorized by

General procedure for amending Constitution of Canada

---

(98) Part IV.1, which was added by the *Constitution Amendment Proclamation, 1983* (see SI/84-102), was repealed on April 18, 1987 by section 54.1.

Part IV.1, as originally enacted, read as follows:

37.1 (1) In addition to the conference convened in March 1983, at least two constitutional conferences composed of the Prime Minister of Canada and the first ministers of the provinces shall be convened by the Prime Minister of Canada, the first within three years after April 17, 1982 and the second within five years after that date.

(2) Each conference convened under subsection (1) shall have included in its agenda constitutional matters that directly affect the aboriginal peoples of Canada, and the Prime Minister of Canada shall invite representatives of those peoples to participate in the discussions on those matters.

(3) The Prime Minister of Canada shall invite elected representatives of the governments of the Yukon Territory and the Northwest Territories to participate in the discussions on any item on the agenda of a conference convened under subsection (1) that, in the opinion of the Prime Minister, directly affects the Yukon Territory and the Northwest Territories.

(4) Nothing in this section shall be construed so as to derogate from subsection 35(1).

(99) Prior to the enactment of Part V certain provisions of the Constitution of Canada and the provincial constitutions could be amended pursuant to the *Constitution Act, 1867*. See the footnotes to section 91, Class 1 and section 92, Class 1 thereof, *supra*. Other amendments to the Constitution could only be made by enactment of the Parliament of the United Kingdom.

(*a*) resolutions of the Senate and House of Commons; and

(*b*) resolutions of the legislative assemblies of at least two-thirds of the provinces that have, in the aggregate, according to the then latest general census, at least fifty per cent of the population of all the provinces.

Majority of members

(2) An amendment made under subsection (1) that derogates from the legislative powers, the proprietary rights or any other rights or privileges of the legislature or government of a province shall require a resolution supported by a majority of the members of each of the Senate, the House of Commons and the legislative assemblies required under subsection (1).

Expression of dissent

(3) An amendment referred to in subsection (2) shall not have effect in a province the legislative assembly of which has expressed its dissent thereto by resolution supported by a majority of its members prior to the issue of the proclamation to which the amendment relates unless that legislative assembly, subsequently, by resolution supported by a majority of its members, revokes its dissent and authorizes the amendment.

Revocation of dissent

(4) A resolution of dissent made for the purposes of subsection (3) may be revoked at any time before or after the issue of the proclamation to which it relates.

Restriction on proclamation

39. (1) A proclamation shall not be issued under subsection 38 (1) before the expiration of one year from the adoption of the resolution initiating the amendment procedure thereunder, unless the legislative assembly of each province has previously adopted a resolution of assent of dissent.

Idem

(2) A proclamation shall not be issued under subsection 38 (1) after the expiration of three years from the adoption of the resolution initiating the amendment procedure thereunder.

Compensation

40. Where an amendment is made under subsection 38(1) that transfers provincial legislative powers relating to education or other cultural matters from provincial legislatures to Parliament, Canada shall provide reasonable compensation to any province to which the amendment does not apply.

Amendment by unanimous consent

41. An amendment to the Constitution of Canada in relation to the following matters may be made by proclamation issued by the Governor General under the Great Seal of Canada only where authorized by resolutions of the Senate and House of Commons and of the legislative assembly of each province:

(*a*) the office of the Queen, the Governor General and the Lieutenant Governor of a province;

(*b*) the right of a province to a number of members in the House of Commons not less than the number of Senators by which the province is entitled to be represented at the time this Part comes into force;

(*c*) subject to section 43, the use of the English or the French language;

(*d*) the composition of the Supreme Court of Canada; and

(*e*) an amendment to this Part.

42. (1) An amendment to the Constitution of Canada in relation to the following matters may be made only in accordance with subsection 38(1): Amendment by general procedure

(*a*) the principle of proportionate representation of the provinces in the House of Commons prescribed by the Constitution of Canada;

(*b*) the powers of the Senate and the method of selecting Senators;

(*c*) the number of members by which a province is entitled to be represented in the Senate and the residence qualifications of Senators;

(*d*) subject to paragraph 41(*d*), the Supreme Court of Canada;

(*e*) the extension of existing provinces into the territories; and

(*f*) notwithstanding any other law or practice, the establishment of new provinces.

(2) Subsections 38(2) to (4) do not apply in respect of amendments in relation to matters referred to in subsection (1). Exception

43. An amendment to the Constitution of Canada in relation to any provision that applies to one or more, but not all, provinces, including Amendment of provisions relating to some but not all provinces

(*a*) any alteration to boundaries between provinces, and

(*b*) any amendment to any provision that relates to the use of the English or the French language within a province, may be made by proclamation issued by the Governor General under the Great Seal of Canada only where so authorized by resolutions of the Senate and House of Commons and of the legislative assembly of each province to which the amendment applies.

Amendments by Parliament

44. Subject to sections 41 and 42, Parliament may exclusively make laws amending the Constitution of Canada in relation to the executive government of Canada or the Senate and House of Commons.

Amendments by provincial legislatures

45. Subject to section 41, the legislature of each province may exclusively make laws amending the constitution of the province.

Initiation of amendment procedures

46. (1) The procedures for amendment under sections 38, 41, 42 and 43 may be initiated either by the Senate or the House of Commons or by the legislative assembly of a province.

Revocation of authorization

(2) A resolution of assent made for the purposes of this Part may be revoked at any time before the issue of a proclamation authorized by it.

Amendments without Senate resolution

47. (1) An amendment to the Constitution of Canada made by proclamation under section 38, 41, 42 or 43 may be made without a resolution of the Senate authorizing the issue of the proclamation if, within one hundred and eighty days after the adoption by the House of Commons of a resolution authorizing its issue, the Senate has not adopted such a resolution and if, at any time after the expiration of that period, the House of Commons again adopts the resolution.

Computation of period

(2) Any period when Parliament is prorogued or dissolved shall not be counted in computing the one hundred and eighty day period referred to in subsection (1).

Advice to issue proclamation

48. The Queen's Privy Council for Canada shall advise the Governor General to issue a proclamation under this Part forthwith on the adoption of the resolutions required for an amendment made by proclamation under this Part.

Constitutional conference

49. A constitutional conference composed of the Prime Minister of Canada and the first ministers of the provinces shall be convened by the Prime Minister of Canada within fifteen years after this Part comes into force to review the provisions of this Part.

PART VI

AMENDMENT TO THE CONSTITUTION ACT, 1867

50.[100]

51.[101]

PART VII

GENERAL

52. (1) The Constitution of Canada is the supreme law of Canada, and any law that is inconsistent with the provisions of the Constitution is, to the extent of the inconsistency, of no force or effect.

Primacy of Constitution of Canada

(2) The Constitution of Canada includes

Constitution of Canada

    (*a*) the *Canada Act 1982,* including this Act;

    (*b*) the Acts and orders referred to in the schedule; and

    (*c*) any amendment to any Act or order referred to in paragraph (*a*) or (*b*).

(3) Amendments to the Constitution of Canada shall be made only in accordance with the authority contained in the Constitution of Canada.

Amendments to Constitution of Canada

53. (1) The enactments referred to in Column I of the schedule are hereby repealed or amended to the extent indicated in Column II thereof and, unless repealed, shall continue as law in Canada under the names set out in Column III thereof.

Repeals and new names

(2) Every enactment, except the *Canada Act 1982,* that refers to an enactment referred to in the schedule by the name in Column I thereof is hereby amended by substituting for that name the corresponding name in Column III thereof, and any British North America Act not referred to in the schedule may be cited as the *Constitution Act* followed by the year and number, if any, of its enactment.

Consequential amendments

---

(100) The amendment is set out in the Consolidation of the *Constitution Act, 1867,* as section 92A thereof.

(101) The amendment is set out in the Consolidation of the *Constitution Act, 1867,* as the Sixth Schedule thereof.

54. Part IV is repealed on the day that is one year after this Part comes into force and this section may be repealed and this Act renumbered, consequentially upon the repeal of Part IV and this section, by proclamation issued by the Governor General under the Great Seal of Canada.[102]

54.1.[103]

55. A French version of the portions of the Constitution of Canada referred to in the schedule shall be prepared by the Minister of Justice of Canada as expeditiously as possible and, when any portion thereof sufficient to warrant action being taken has been so prepared, it shall be put forward for enactment by proclamation issued by the Governor General under the Great Seal of Canada pursuant to the procedure then applicable to an amendment of the same provisions of the Constitution of Canada.

56. Where any portion of the Constitution of Canada has been or is enacted in English and French or where a French version of any portion of the Constitution is enacted pursuant to section 55, the English and French versions of that portion of the Constitution are equally authoritative.

57. The English and French versions of this Act are equally authoritative.

58. Subject to section 59, this Act shall come into force on a day to be fixed by proclamation issued by the Queen or the Governor General under the Great Seal of Canada.[104]

59. (1) Paragraph 23(1)(a) shall come into force in respect of Quebec on a day to be fixed by proclamation issued by the Queen or the Governor General under the Great Seal of Canada.

---

(102) Part VII came into force on April 17, 1982. *See* SI/82-97.

(103) Section 54.1, which was added by the *Constitution Amendment Proclamation, 1983* (see SI/84-102), provided for the repeal of Part IV.1 and section 54.1 on April 18, 1987.

Section 54.1, as originally enacted, read as follows:

"**54.1** Part IV.1 and this section are repealed on April 18, 1987."

(104) The Act, with the exception of paragraph 23(1)(a) in respect of Quebec, came into force on April 17, 1982 by proclamation issued by the Queen. *See* SI/82-97.

(2) A proclamation under subsection (1) shall be issued only where authorized by the legislative assembly or government of Quebec.[105]

Authorization of Quebec

(3) This section may be repealed on the day paragraph 23(1)(*a*) comes into force in respect of Quebec and this Act amended and renumbered, consequentially upon the repeal of this section, by proclamation issued by the Queen or the Governor General under the Great Seal of Canada.

Repeal of this section

60. This Act may be cited as the *Constitution Act, 1982,* and the Constitution Acts 1867 to 1975 (No. 2) and this Act may be cited together as the *Constitution Acts, 1867 to 1982.*

Short title and citations

61. A reference to the *"Constitution Acts, 1867 to 1982"* shall be deemed to include a reference to the *"Constitution Amendment Proclamation, 1983."* [106]

References

---

(105) No proclamation has been issued under section 59.

(106) Section 61 was added by the *Constitution Amendment Proclamation, 1983. See* SI/84-102.

See also section 3 of the *Constitution Act, 1985 (Representation),* S.C. 1986, c. 8, Part I and the *Constitution Amendment, 1987 (Newfoundland Act)* SI/88-11.

INDEX

Orchard, David, 95, 112–114
Ordinal systems of voting, 156, 158
Organization of American States
    (OAS), 61
Orientations, 30

Pacific Scandal (1873), 121
Paramountcy, 388
Parizeau, Jacques, 460, 463, 465
Parliament of Canada. *See also*
    Cabinet; House of Commons;
    Prime Minister; Senate
        component institutions, 213
        diminishing independence
            from executive, 213
        functions, 202
        reform. *See* Reform of national
            parliament
        relationship to interest
            groups, 340
Parliamentary secretaries, 283
Parliamentary supremacy, 444, 447,
    489, 490, 493, 517–518
        history and evolution of British
            system, 213–218
        vs. entrenched rights, 489–503
Parti Action Democratique, 463
Parti Quebecois (PQ), 49–50, 411,
    459–461, 463
Parties. *See* Political parties
Partisanship, 175–180
Party discipline, 7, 15, 120, 204, 217,
    226–227
        effect on party caucuses,
            205–207
        public discontent with, 226, 252
        within Commons committees,
            248, 252
Party identification, 175–180
Party leaders
    history, 121
    increased importance, 126, 127
    selection, 93
    voters, and, 126, 183–185
Party system, 103–116
    electoral system, and, 166–167
    future, 128
    history in Canada, 117–129
    mobilization of voters, 106–110
    social cleavages, and, 106
Patriation of the Constitution, 439
    patriation reference, 383,
        384–385, 443, 468
Patriation reference, 361
Patronage, 41, 83, 84, 121, 122
Patronage politics, 117
Peace, order and good government
    (POGG) power, 393–394
Pearson, Lester, 442

Peckford, Brian, 456
Permanent executive, 4, 6, 269–270,
    275, 299–309
        accountability to Parliament,
            303, 305–306, 312, 316–317
        central agencies, 270, 275,
            299–302
        contracting out service delivery,
            312, 316
        downsizing the public
            service, 306
        federal public service, 304–306
        finance department, 301–302
        interest groups, and, 337–338
        line departments, 270, 303
        news media, and, 360–361
        policy-making, and, 271,
            309–311
        Prime Minister's Office (PMO),
            285, 300–301
        Privy Council Office (PCO),
            299–300
        Public Service Commission
            (PSC), 302
        regulations, 307–309
        representative democracy,
            and, 275
        services and programs, 306
        Treasury Board Secretariat
            (TBS), 302
Personal parties, 117
"Persons case," 381–382
Pettigrew, Pierre, 290
Pictorial representation, 219
Picture given of executive branch,
    360–361
        private ownership, 351–352
        relationship with Opposition,
            224, 359
        television, 356
Pink-collar ghetto, 36
Pith and substance, 489
Plaintiffs, 486
Platform, 82
Plebiscitary democracy, 75
Pluralism, 341
Policy capacity, 334, 342
Policy community, 334, 338
Policy-making, 309–311, 507–512
Policy networks, 334, 336–337, 338
Political actors, 31, 48
Political community, 31, 46, 47
Political culture, 29, 30–32, 106
    demography, 43–45
    economics, 45
    geography, 43
    history, 37–43
    ideology, 34–37
Political entrepreneurs, 107

Political executive, 4, 5–6, 269,
    280–298
        policy making, and, 309–311
Political Financing Act, 148
Political institutions
    challenges, 4
    defined, 4
    ideologies, and, 36
    influence on political
        behaviour, 12–19, 144
    interaction with society, 1–5
    judiciary, 6, 8
    legislature and executive, 5–8
    legitimacy, 2
    liberal approach, 6
    political and nonpolitical, 2–3
    political parties, and, 114
    proposals for reform of. *See*
        Reform of national
        parliament
    public disappointment with,
        4, 47, 54
    underlying principles, 11–12
Political orientations, three
    categories, 31
Political parties
    brokerage or cadre parties, 77
    constituency organizations,
        76, 77, 80
    conventions, 78–79
    definitions, 76–78
    extraparliamentary
        organizations, 73, 124
    federalism, and, 74
    functions, 90
    funding, 96–103, 127
    incentives, 74, 75
    leadership. *See* Party leaders
    missionary or ideological
        parties, 77
    organizational structures,
        74, 78–82
    party identification, Canada
        and U.S., 175–180
    party membership, 83, 116
    party networks, 85–90
    party system. *See* Party system
    platforms, 77
    pressure groups, and, 348
    referenda, 78
    regional bases, 75, 127–128, 129
    registration, 97, 103–104,
        127, 128
    relationship with the
        state, 73–75
    selection of candidates, 90
    selection of leaders, 93
    smaller parties, 127, 128
    subcultures, and, 109, 110, 112

Wells, Clyde, 18, 452, 456
West Nile virus, 421
Western Canada
    alienation, 16–17, 167
    discontent with the federal
        system, 400–401
    prefers intrastate
        federalism, 401
    western populism, 33, 121, 126
Western populists, 33

Westminster-style parliamentary
    government, 6–8, 213, 214,
    377, 388
    history in Britain, 214–217
Wheare, K.C., 387
Women
    delegates to political
        conventions, 80
    disputes over Meech Lake
        accord, 340

national parliaments, in, 75,
    160–162, 221
"Persons case," 381–382
Woodsworth, J.S., 123
World Trade Organization
    (WTO), 19–20, 271,
    309, 417
World Values Survey, 60

Youth, in political parties, 80, 82